ECONOMICS TODAY
Principles and Applications

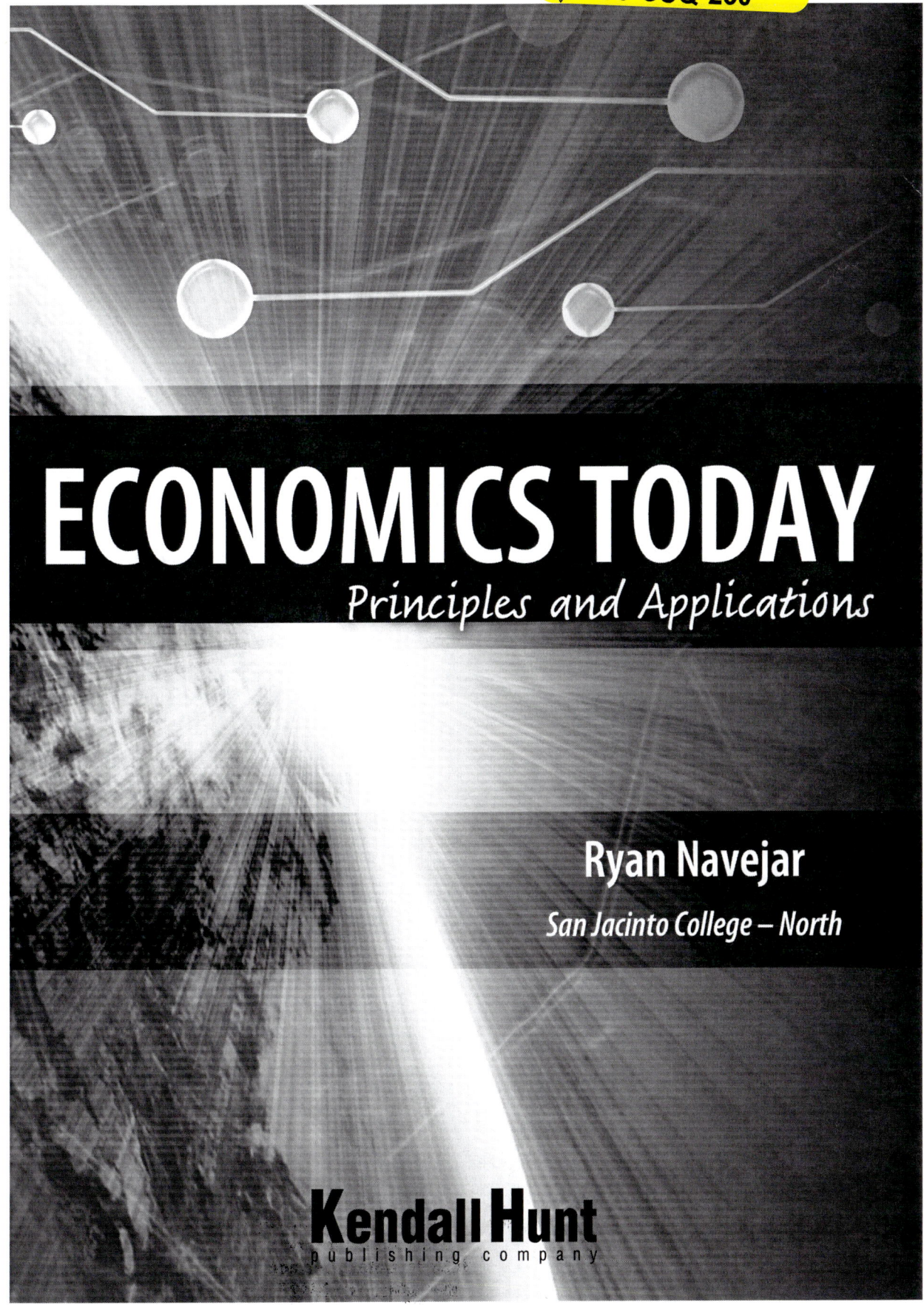

Ryan Navejar

San Jacinto College – North

Kendall Hunt
publishing company

Cover images © Shutterstock, Inc.

Kendall Hunt
publishing company

www.kendallhunt.com
Send all inquiries to:
4050 Westmark Drive
Dubuque, IA 52004-1840

Copyright © 2011 by Kendall Hunt Publishing Company

ISBN 978-0-7575-7741-3

All rights reserved. No part of this publication may be reproduced, stored in a retrieval system, or transmitted, in any form or by any means, electronic, mechanical, photocopying, recording, or otherwise, without the prior written permission of the copyright owner.

Printed in the United States of America
10 9 8 7 6 5 4 3 2 1

Contents

Chapter 1 The Economic Way of Thinking — 1

What Is Economics?
The Fundamental Questions
Production Possibilities
Economics as a Science

Chapter 2 The Market System — 15

Characteristics of the Market System
How America Answers the Fundamental Questions
The Invisible Hand
The Role of the Government

Chapter 3 Market Interactions — 29

The Circular Flow
Demand
Supply
Equilibrium
Changes in Equilibrium

Chapter 4 The Public Sector — 49

The Government's Role
Fixing Market Failures
Public Finance

Chapter 5 Measuring the Economy — 73

Gross Domestic Product
Calculating GDP
Relationship between Output and Income

Chapter 6 Unemployment — 87
- Measuring Unemployment
- Types of Unemployment
- Cost of Unemployment

Chapter 7 Inflation — 101
- What Is Inflation?
- Measuring Inflation
- Cost of Inflation

Chapter 8 Economic Growth and Business Cycles — 117
- Economic Growth
- Achieving Faster Growth
- The Business Cycle
- Modeling the Economy
- Aggregate Supply and Aggregate Demand

Chapter 9 Aggregate Demand and Fiscal Policy — 143
- Macro Failures
- Macro Equilibrium
- Consumption
- The Consumption Function
- Investment
- Government Purchases and Net Exports

Chapter 10 Government Deficits and Debt — 161
- Effect of Fiscal Policy on the Government Budget
- Economic Effect of Deficits
- Economic Effects of Surpluses
- The Accumulation of Debt
- Who Owns the Debt?
- Burden of the Debt
- External Debt

Chapter 11 Money, Banking, and the Federal Reserve 177

What Is Money?
The Money Supply
Deposit Creation
A Many Bank World
The Federal Reserve
Tools of Monetary Policy

Chapter 12 Monetary Policy 195

The Money Market
Interest Rates and Spending
Policy Constraints
Monetarist Perspective

Chapter 13 Review of Economic Foundations 219

Decision Making
United States Economy
Supply and Demand
The Role of the Government

Chapter 14 Consumer Demand 239

Determinants of Demand
The Demand Curve
Price Elasticity
Price Elasticity and Total Revenue
Other Elasticities
Choosing Among Products

Chapter 15 Costs of Production 257

The Production Function
Marginal Productivity
Resource Costs
Dollar Costs
Economic vs. Accounting Costs
Long-Run Costs
Economies of Scale

Chapter 16 Producer Theory: The Competitive Firm — 277

- The Profit Motive
- Economic vs. Accounting Profits
- Market Structure
- The Production Decision
- The Profit-Maximizing Rule
- The Shutdown Decision
- The Investment Decision

Chapter 17 Perfect Competition — 305

- Determinants of Supply
- The Market Supply Curve
- Mobile Phone Market
- The Competitive Process

Chapter 18 Monopoly — 323

- Market Power
- Market Power at Work
- Comparison with Competition
- Pros and Cons of Market Power

Chapter 19 Oligopoly — 339

- Market Structure
- Oligopoly Behavior
- The Kinked Demand Curve
- Game Theory
- Comparison to Competition
- Coordination Problems

Chapter 20 Monopolistic Competition — 353

- Structure
- Behavior
- Outcome

Chapter 11 Money, Banking, and the Federal Reserve — 177

- What Is Money?
- The Money Supply
- Deposit Creation
- A Many Bank World
- The Federal Reserve
- Tools of Monetary Policy

Chapter 12 Monetary Policy — 195

- The Money Market
- Interest Rates and Spending
- Policy Constraints
- Monetarist Perspective

Chapter 13 Review of Economic Foundations — 219

- Decision Making
- United States Economy
- Supply and Demand
- The Role of the Government

Chapter 14 Consumer Demand — 239

- Determinants of Demand
- The Demand Curve
- Price Elasticity
- Price Elasticity and Total Revenue
- Other Elasticities
- Choosing Among Products

Chapter 15 Costs of Production — 257

- The Production Function
- Marginal Productivity
- Resource Costs
- Dollar Costs
- Economic vs. Accounting Costs
- Long-Run Costs
- Economies of Scale

Chapter 16 — Producer Theory: The Competitive Firm — 277

- The Profit Motive
- Economic vs. Accounting Profits
- Market Structure
- The Production Decision
- The Profit-Maximizing Rule
- The Shutdown Decision
- The Investment Decision

Chapter 17 — Perfect Competition — 305

- Determinants of Supply
- The Market Supply Curve
- Mobile Phone Market
- The Competitive Process

Chapter 18 — Monopoly — 323

- Market Power
- Market Power at Work
- Comparison with Competition
- Pros and Cons of Market Power

Chapter 19 — Oligopoly — 339

- Market Structure
- Oligopoly Behavior
- The Kinked Demand Curve
- Game Theory
- Comparison to Competition
- Coordination Problems

Chapter 20 — Monopolistic Competition — 353

- Structure
- Behavior
- Outcome

Chapter 21 Government Regulation — 373

Antitrust vs. Regulation
Natural Monopoly
Regulatory Options
Costs of Regulation
Deregulation in Practice

Chapter 22 Labor Markets — 387

Labor Supply
Market Supply
Labor Demand
Firm's Decision
Equilibrium
Choosing Among Inputs

Chapter 23 Financial Markets — 405

The Role of Financial Markets
Present Value of Future Profits
The Stock Market
The Bond Market

Chapter 24 International Trade — 421

The United States and World Trade
Specialization and Comparative Advantage
The Foreign Exchange Market
Arguments Against Free Trade
Government and Trade
Trade Agreements and Free Trade Zones
Global Competition

Unit Review Answers — 445

Chapter 1

The Economic Way of Thinking

I. WHAT IS ECONOMICS?

We are the Economy

While on the surface it may seem like economics is only important to stock brokers, bankers, and other people in finance-related industries, economics permeates each and every one of our lives and will continue to do so for the foreseeable future. Whether you realize it or not, you have been using economics your entire life to make decisions. Even if only for a split second, you weigh the pros and cons of each and every decision before making a choice. We must make a distinction here between economics and the economy. Economics is a way of thinking about how and why people make choices and a science that explores how they can make better ones. The economy is the result of all those choices.

The economy is not a place, a thing, or a person. The economy is made up of all the decisions about production, consumption, savings, and investments that we make as individuals. Economic production in the US, for example, is simply the sum total of the production of all the companies and producers in the country. The total consumption for the economy of California is the sum total bought by all of the consumers in California, and so on. The statistics that are so often reported in the news are meant to represent this idea of aggregation. While these total figures do not affect anyone in particular, they do represent the sum total of our individual actions. By aggregating the

Gross Domestic Product (US, 2008)	$14.26 Trillion
Gross Domestic Product (World, 2008)	$61.07 Trillion
Unemployment Rate (US, Nov. 2009)	10.00%
Inflation (US, Nov. 2009)	−0.20%
Personal Consumption (US)	$10.14 Trillion
Savings Rate (US, 3rd Q 2009)	4.50%

Sources: CIA World Factbook, Bureau of Labor Statistics, Bureau of Economic Analysis

Figure 1.1 • **Common Economic Figures**

decisions we all make, we can see how the economy as a whole is doing, which is the first step to improving it. Figure 1.1 shows some of the important statistics that define the United States economy. These numbers may mean little to you now, but soon they will speak volumes about the current health and future performance of the economy.

Scarcity and Choice

Economics would not exist if we did not have to make choices. If we could have whatever we wanted whenever we wanted it, there would be no need to make the tough choices in life. Unfortunately, humans have unlimited wants and must attempt to satiate them through the proper allocation of limited resources. This is what it means to live under the condition of scarcity. Since we can't have everything we want, we must decide what to purchase and what to forgo. Economics is the study of how to do so. Economics, then, is the study of how economic agents—be they households, businesses, or governments—make choices about how best to satisfy their unlimited wants with limited resources.

What we mean by resources here is not just oil, minerals, and other materials that come out of the ground, but all the factors of production: land, labor, capital (physical capital and human capital), and entrepreneurship. Wants are a little more obvious, they are those things we would buy if had unlimited income. We will contrast this with the concept of demand in Chapter 3.

Scarcity does not mean a shortage of something. A shortage is a specific condition in a market that can be corrected by a price change. Scarcity always exists since goods and resources cannot be had for a zero price. Scarcity is not only a problem for people with little money or resources. Even Bill Gates has to decide how to use his limited time and money. He cannot give infinite amounts of money to all of his business and charitable endeavors or spend more than 24 hours in day on any combination of activities. No amount of money can buy away scarcity.

Opportunity Costs

Since resources are scarce there is indeed no such thing as a free lunch, as the saying goes. Everything produced and purchased in the economy has a price, but that price is more than just monetary. Every time you choose to spend your time, money, or resources on one activity, you are implicitly choosing to not spend those resources on some other activity. The value of the next best alternative that could have been produced using the resources consumed by a choice is called the opportunity cost of that choice, since the opportunity to pursue that alternative activity has been lost.

The opportunity cost is the true cost of any decision. For example, suppose you chose to go to class from 8AM–9:30AM. What is the cost of that decision? You might be tempted to say no to the tuition and books required for the class. These, however, are sunk costs. Regardless of whether you go to class or not, you will never get the money you paid in tuition or books back (assuming we are past the refund date). As a result, sunk costs are irrelevant to the decision. So then, what is the true cost of attending class? It is simply the value of the time that you spend in class. Time, a resource, could be spent in a variety of ways—you could sleep in, chat with friends, do work for another class, or even go to work. It is important to note the opportunity cost of a choice is only the value of the *best* foregone alternative. You can only do one thing with a given amount of time, resources, or money so it does not make any sense to add up the value of every alternative since you could only do one thing at a time.

While opportunity costs drive most decisions, they are still not fully understood by people without a working knowledge of economics. In fact, Article 1.1 describes how retailers can increase their sales of lower- and medium-priced items by educating consumers about the opportunity cost of buying high-priced luxury items.

Rationality

Another key component of economics is the assumption that people do not make choices randomly or without thinking. Instead, economists propose that people behave in a way that maximizes their utility subject to their limited income. Utility here doesn't mean electricity or water, but happiness or satisfaction. The idea that economic agents act rationally does not mean that people are walking calculators that never make mistakes. All the rationality assumption means is that people make decisions based on some sort of analysis and choose the option that will benefit them the most.

You make rational decisions based on your own self-interest every day. For example, when you signed up for this class you had no idea who I was; you signed up for this class because it was the best option you had to further your own goals. Yet, the more people that sign up for my class, the better off I am, so without knowing it you helped me.

This is how capitalism works; people usually have to satisfy somebody else's wants in order to pursue their own self-interest. People who seem like they are "giving money away"—philanthropists who donate to charity, parents who send their children to the best schools they can afford, and businesses that forgo sales today in order to invest in new technology—are all actually behaving rationally based on their desires.

If people avoid decisions that leave them worse off, and by extension pursue decisions that leave them better off, it is safe to assume that people respond to incentives. People make choices either to attain rewards or avoid punishments. For example, as the gap between what people earn with a high school degree and what they can earn with a college degree grows, enrollment in college increases since the incentives related to education choice are changing. Incentives are the signals the market gives to help people make decisions.

Article 1.1:
Taking Advantage of Rationality

Opportunity Cost: Why Buy a Mercedes... When You Can Get All This?
By Sarah Boesveld

Dec. 8, 2009

You're in the local big-box electronics store, standing before a wall of flat-screen TVs. Dazed by the glowing scenes of *A Charlie Brown Christmas* and those fake-fireplace flames, your eyes dart between an $800 40-incher and a $1,000 46-incher until a store clerk saunters over and plants the seed of possibility.

"If you go with the $800 one," he tells you, "think of all the DVDs you could buy with the $200 you'll have left."

You rush to the cash and snap up the 40-inch TV. *Voilà!* You're the unwitting participant in a cunning salesman's trick: highlighting opportunity cost to close a deal.

It's a tool retailers use to land a sale rather than see a customer turn on her heel without buying anything. And it's one store clerks might be trying a little more frequently this season as shoppers try to stretch their dollars, experts say.

Most shoppers don't consider the other ways they could spend money without a few well-placed cues, a new study from the Yale School of Management has found.

If a customer shows interest in two items, a salesperson can likely land a sale on the cheaper model by making her think about all the other Christmas gifts she'll be able to buy with the savings, says lead study author Shane Frederick, an associate professor of marketing at the Yale School of Management.

"I don't know that people very often think spontaneously, 'Here are the other five things I can buy for this price.'"

Politicians and activists also raise the spectre of opportunity cost—think U.S. President Dwight Eisenhower's iconic costs-of-war speech from 1953, referenced by President Barack Obama last week as he tried to rally support for sending more troops to Afghanistan.

Questions:
1. According to the article, what is a person truly giving up when they purchase a $1,000 TV instead of an $800 one?
2. Why do you think people do not think about opportunity costs until someone mentions it directly?
3. How can a president use opportunity cost to help gain support for sending more troops into battle? What costs will the country face if additional troops are not sent?

From *Globe and Mail*, December 7, 2009 by Sarah Boesveld. Copyright © 2009 by CTVglobalmedia Publishing Group Ltd. Reprinted by permission.

On the Margin

People make rational economic decisions based on marginal analysis. This means that they analyze the effect of small changes in behavior on their utility. The reason for this is that most decisions focus on a small change from the normal routine, or "status quo." Should I buy two quarts of milk this week or just one? Should a company increase or decrease its advertising budget? Should the government lower taxes or keep them the same? In each of these cases there is a marginal benefit and a marginal cost associated with the proposed change.

The marginal cost of any choice is what you have to give up (in terms of opportunity cost) in order to obtain one more unit of something (study for one more hour, go to school for one more year, or buy one more pack of gum). Marginal also means additional, so the marginal cost is only the cost of adding one more unit, not the total cost.

It is important to note, though, that almost every activity experiences increasing marginal costs. That means, the more you do something, the more it costs each time. This may not make sense at first since no matter how many slices of pizza you eat, for example, the menu price never changes. But if you think of the opportunity cost of eating too much pizza as a queasy feeling in your stomach and an expanding waistline, you can see that eating two slices a week may not be so bad, but for each slice you eat your health suffers more and more.

The benefit from a choice to obtain one more unit of something is called the marginal benefit. In dollar terms, the marginal benefit is equal to the amount of money someone would have to give you for you to give up one more unit of a good. Just like marginal cost, the marginal benefit of an activity changes as you increase its frequency. The first trip on a roller coaster may be exhilarating, but if you've been riding roller coasters all day you may not be willing to stand in line again. The more you have of something, the less willing you are to give up anything to get more of it; that is, the marginal benefit falls as the amount of the good you have increases.

Microeconomics vs. Macroeconomics

At the most basic level economics is split into two broad areas of analysis: microeconomics and macroeconomics. Microeconomics studies the behavior of individual economic agents such as households, firms (businesses), and the market for one product. Microeconomists want to understand how economic agents respond to changes in the economic environment. The effect of a change in price of one good on the demand for another, or the effect of a change in the tax assessed on a single product, would both fall under the purview of microeconomics.

Macroeconomics, on the other hand, focuses on the behavior of the economy of an entire nation or large region (such as the European Union). A recession would be a macroeconomic issue since it refers to a general downturn in economic growth for the entire country. Inflation would be another, since it is based on changes in the nationwide average price level. In general, macroeconomics studies the level and behavior of aggregates, or sum totals, such as the national unemployment rate, total production, and total spending.

The line between these two areas is starting to blur, however, as economists begin to move away from aggregation and realize aggregates are really the sum of many microeconomic decisions. Also, some ideas in economics cannot be put entirely into one category. Unemployment is generally thought of as a macro measure, but it can be studied at the individual, firm, or market level as well. Figure 1.2 illustrates that many macroeconomic topics are simply larger-scale views of microeconomic issues.

Microeconomic Concepts	Macroeconomic Concepts
• Price of a Product	• Average Price Level and Inflation
• Hiring Decision of a Firm	• National Unemployment Rate
• Company's Stock Price	• Dow Jones Industrial Average
• Buying Habits of a Household	• Total Consumption Spending
• Number of Hours Worked by an Individual	• Aggregate Labor Hours

Figure 1.2 • **Microeconomics vs. Macroeconomics**
Many important numbers in macroeconomics are simply the sum of millions of individual microeconomic decisions.

II. THE FUNDAMENTAL QUESTIONS

What to Produce?

Societies create and participate in economic systems that answer the big economic questions, also called the fundamental questions of economics. Since an economy's primary function is to turn limited resources into goods and services that people desire, an economic system needs to determine what to produce. Money or resources by themselves do not make people happy; people need goods and services to satisfy their wants. The kinds of products and services available in a society change over time, according to the preferences, income, and productive capability of the society.

For example, between 1998 and 2000 Tiger electronics created millions of Furby dolls a year, yet now hardly any are made. Why? Did they become exceedingly expensive to make? Did the government tell them to stop making them? No—people just stopped buying them. In the United States and other capitalist countries, the 'what to produce' question is answered by consumer choice. This is not the only possibility, however. In Communist countries, for example, a group of political leaders decide the types and amounts of goods that will be produced.

How to Produce?

Once society has chosen what to produce, they must face how they will produce these goods and services. The same good can be produced in many different ways and society needs to have an economic system that decides whether a process that uses more manual labor or one that uses more capital is better for society. Cars, homes, and just about every other consumer good used to be produced by hand. Now, almost every large-scale production process is automated. Did people forget how to make things by hand? Did some committee mandate this? No—automation is cheaper and in a competitive economic world, cheaper wins.

For Whom to Produce?

While some problems arise when determining what to produce and how to produce, the most passionate arguments against modern economics revolve around deciding who gets the production of society. Almost everyone agrees that we should produce what people want to buy in the most efficient way possible, but when it comes to deciding for whom to produce many people tend to argue for equity over efficiency. Efficiency refers to trying to make the economic pie (total output) as big as possible, while equity means everyone has a relatively equal slice. Most economists agree there is some trade-off between equity and efficiency; every time you try to split up the pie more equally, you make it a little smaller.

III. PRODUCTION POSSIBILITIES

Factors of Production

Improving the economy requires finding the optimal allocation of its scarce resources: land, labor, capital, and entrepreneurship. With so many possible uses for our resources, how do we know which activity is best? Luckily, the market helps us with this problem. If resources are not being put to the most profitable use, someone will buy them and put them to better use.

Land. The first and most obvious resource, or factor of production, is land. In economics land includes all natural resources or "gifts of nature," such as oil, water, mined materials, trees, and land used for farming. The factor payment associated with land is called rent.

Labor. Labor consists of the physical and mental effort exerted by workers of all types. This factor is usually measured in hours or man-hours and is paid wages.

Capital. Capital goods are those that aid in the production of other goods and services like factories, tools, and machinery. Businesses pay interest to those that lend them capital. Be sure to note the difference between the capital we are talking about here, physical capital, and the financial capital you hear about on the news. Financial capital is not counted as a factor of production since it is just the money used to buy factors of production.

Entrepreneurship. Entrepreneurship was recently added as a factor of production. Entrepreneurs need to be involved in the productive process because they combine the other factors of production in strategic ways and bear the risk if the product fails. Entrepreneurs earn profits for their services.

Trade-offs

Just as individuals face opportunity costs when choosing between alternative uses of their time, society faces costs when choosing where and how to employ its scarce resources. The production possibilities model illustrates all of the possible combinations of two alternatives a society can choose from, assuming full employment and given that technology and the amounts of resources do not change.

One simple way of looking at the production possibilities of an economy is through a production possibilities table. The production possibilities table illustrates that society must give up some of one of the alternatives to get more of the other—there is always a trade-off. Take a look at the table in figure 1.3. What do you notice about the trade-off as you produce more tanks? The table tells us that as you produce more tanks the amount of trucks you have to give up in order to get the same amount of tanks rises.

Tanks	Trucks
0	60
5	57
10	52
15	45
20	37
25	28
30	16
35	0

Figure 1.3 • **Production Possibilities Table**
You only have to give up three trucks to produce the first five tanks. The next five tanks cost five trucks. As you produce more tanks, you are taking away resources that are better at truck production, so the price of tanks in terms of the number of trucks given up rises.

The downside to this table is that you can only get so many alternatives onto a single table. In contrast, we can see all of the alternatives available to the society with a production possibilities curve. The production possibilities curve is the first of many graphs we will be using in this course. As you can see in figure 1.4, the production possibilities curve uses a line on a graph (the production possibilities frontier, or PPF) to separate the possible combinations from the impossible ones.

Increasing Opportunity Costs

One special characteristic you may notice about the PPF is that it is not a straight line; in fact, it bows away from the origin. The reason for this is the law of increasing opportunity costs. At the society level, the opportunity cost related to the production of a certain good increases as the production of that good increases. As you can see the from the PPF in figure 1.4, the amount of trucks you have to give up in order to get one more tank increases as the amount of tanks increases. In economics terms, the relative price—the price of tanks in terms of trucks—increases as you go from left to right.

The economic rationale is much simpler. Imagine you start off producing only trucks. If you decided you wanted some tanks, you need to pull resources away from producing trucks. What resources would you start with? You would pull away the resources that are the most effective at producing tanks first. As a result, you would not have to pull very many resources away in order to get quite a bit of tanks. But as you produce more and more tanks (moving down the PPF) you are going to pull resources that are not as good as producing tanks into production. The resources used to produce the two goods are not interchangeable; some are better at producing one or the other. The rubber used to produce the truck tires, for example, is probably not very useful when trying to build a tank track. The law of increasing opportunity costs becomes especially important when trading off between two very different goods—like health care and military spending, for example.

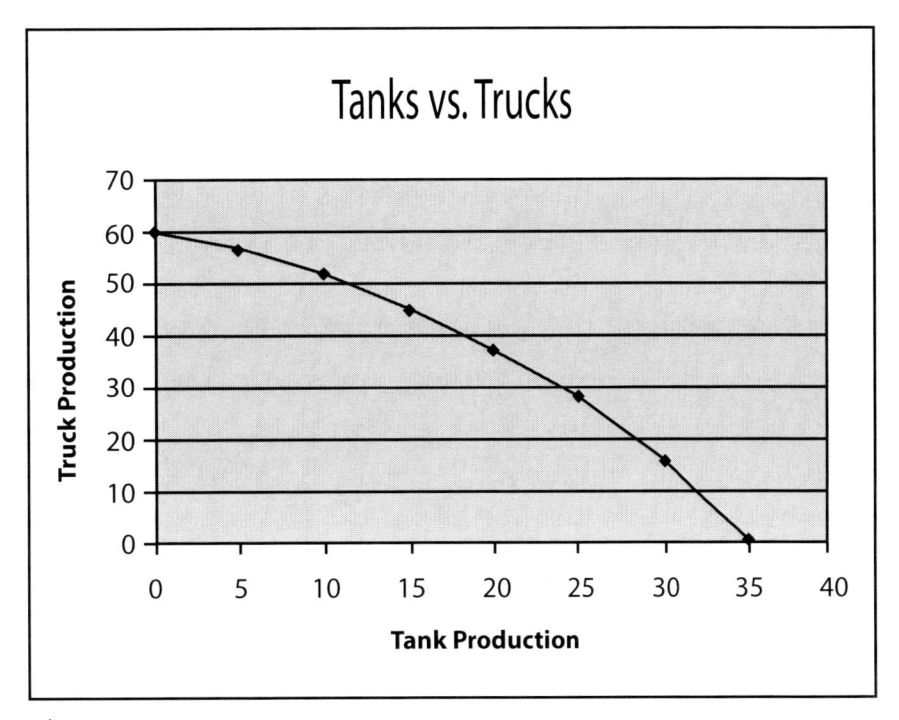

Figure 1.4 • Production Possibilities Curve
Like most production possibilities curves, Figure 1.4 bows away from the origin due to the law of increasing opportunity costs. The more different two products are, the greater this bowing will be.

Efficiency and Inefficiency

Technically, any point along the production possibilities frontier is productively efficient since you cannot increase the production of one good without giving up some of the other. If there are many points at which a society can produce at full employment, how do they choose one? Just like individuals, societies weigh marginal cost and marginal benefit. Societies continue an economic activity (like trading off trucks for tanks) as long as marginal benefit exceeds marginal cost. In other words, optimal allocation of resources is at the point where marginal benefit equals marginal cost.

What is certain, however, is that every point on the PPF is more efficient than any point inside the curve. While the production possibilities curve shows the output combinations that can be attained if all resources are used efficiently, we know that this is not always the case. Bureaucracy, laziness, and other inefficiencies lead to output not being maximized. A point inside the production possibilities curve illustrates this type of inefficient production.

As figure 1.5 demonstrates, having a point inside the curve means that you can produce more of one of the goods without giving up any of the other. This is the definition of inefficiency; you do not have to obtain more resources to produce more, just use the ones you have smarter or better. Another way to achieve inefficient allocation (a point inside the PPF) is through higher than usual unemployment. During economic downturns, like the Great Depression, or even the recession of 2007-2009, the economy may not be performing at full employment. Remember that full employment was one of the

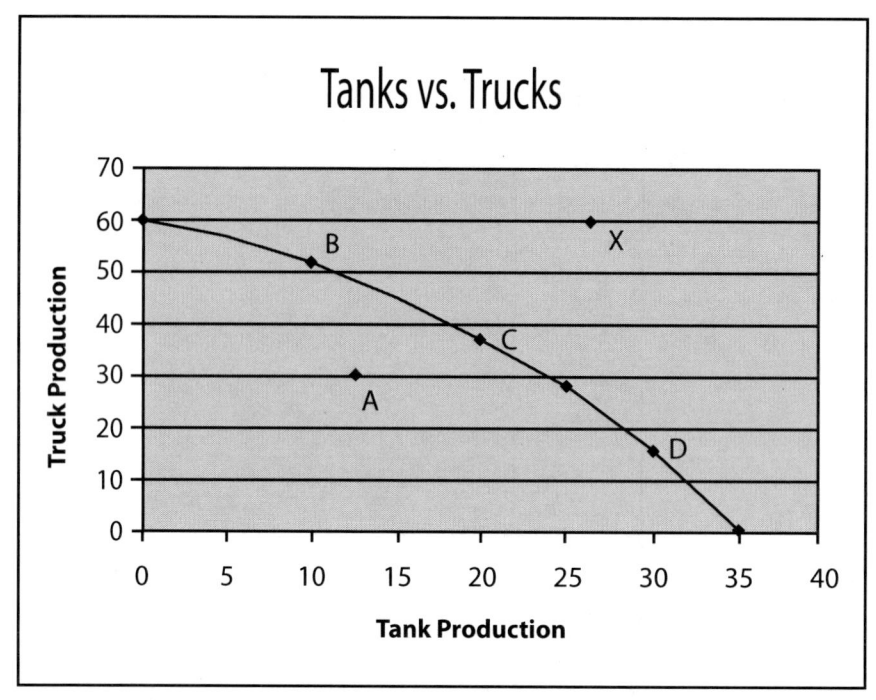

Figure 1.5 • **Efficient, Inefficient, and Unattainable Combinations**
In this production possibilities model, the government trades off tank production for truck production. If it wants to produce more military goods, it must produce fewer consumer goods. On this PPC, points B, C, and D are all productively efficient, but point A is inefficient. Point X is impossible to reach given current levels of resources or technology. What might the government do to reach Point X?

assumptions that the production possibilities model was based on. If we relax this assumption, we see that the optimal choice allocation may lie within the PPF, not on it.

Economic Growth

Another way to shake the model up is to relax the assumption of fixed resources. Labor quantity (population), as well as quality, is improving over time; and new resource deposits and extraction techniques are constantly being discovered, so assuming fixed resources for any lengthy period of time is not very realistic. Such resource growth makes it possible for society to produce more of one or possibly both goods at each alternative, causing the PPF to shift to the right.

In a more realistic setting, technology is not fixed either. New production techniques and the proliferation of computer and telecommunications technology will continue to improve productive processes. By reducing costs and speeding up production, technology also leads to a rightward shift in productive capacity. Figure 1.6, for example, illustrates the result of improvements in the technology used to produce tanks.

A country does not have to wait for economic growth to kick in to live beyond its PPF. Through specialization and trade, a country can go beyond the limits of PPF by trading with another country. This is why the US is the highest volume trading nation on Earth; we want to exceed our PPF now, not in a few years. We will talk more about comparative advantage and mutual gains from trade later.

Effect of Growth

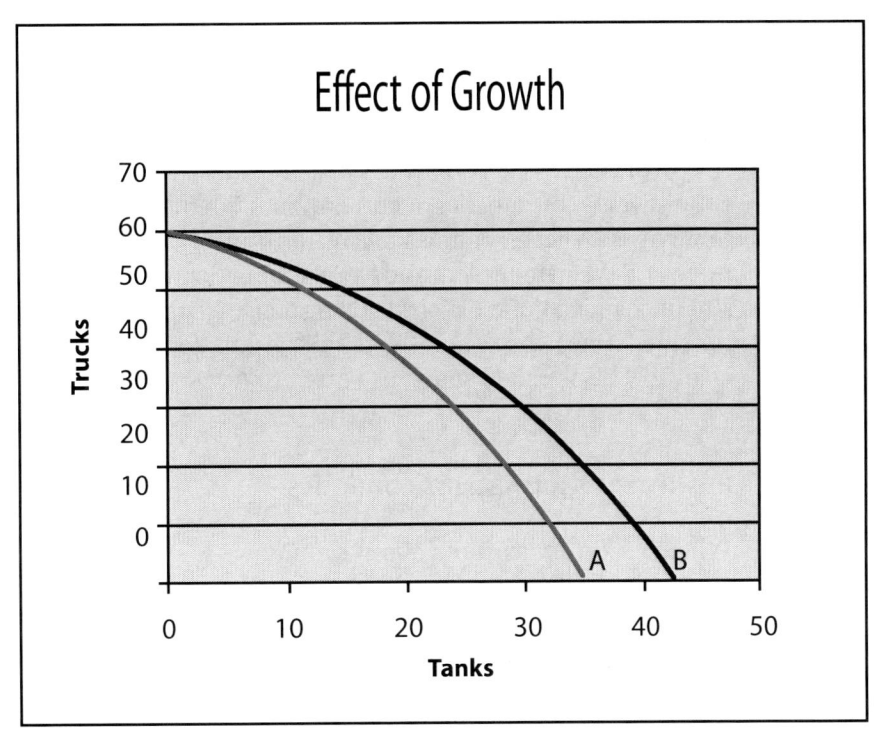

Figure 1.6 • Economic Growth
If a technological improvement made it possible to produce tanks using fewer resources, then we would be able produce more tanks given our current level of resources. The shift of the *x*-intercept of the PPF from thirty-five to forty-two illustrates this improvement. Further, each truck given up produces more tanks since more tanks can be produced within any given amount of resources.

IV. ECONOMICS AS A SCIENCE

Models

Economics is a science, and as a science it tries to determine the underlying link between two events. Since economists cannot readily perform lab experiments like the other "hard sciences," it must rely on predictions made by economic models. An economic model cannot incorporate every detail of the real world, just as a chemist or physicist cannot account for the position of every molecule or particle. However, models can still provide salient results. Models are necessary simplifications of the highly complex "real world" which still accurately predict and explain the behavior of economic agents using empirical data (evidence). Models often make generalizations—not treating everybody as if they are the same, but focusing on the behavior or reaction of a typical or average agent.

The *ceteris paribus* assumption is an idea that allows for much of the simplification in economic models. *Ceteris paribus* is a Latin phrase meaning "all other things being equal" or "everything else stays the same" and it lets the reader know that the economist is only focusing on the effect of changes in a very specific subset of variables. For example, an economist might want to know the affect of a change in the price of Ray's hamburgers on the sales at Martin's Burger Barn. However, when a company raises its prices, it may affect many different aspects of the economy. The *ceteris paribus* assumption lets the reader know to treat all variables other than the price of Ray's hamburgers as constant when determining the change in sales of Martin's hamburgers predicted by the model.

With the *ceteris paribus* assumption in place, economists look for correlations between events. In statistics, a correlation is a tendency for one variable to move when another does (whether in the same or the opposite direction). If two variables (such as the price of Ray's hamburgers and the sales of Martin's hamburgers) are correlated, it is possible a change in one may be causing a change in the other. Economists must be careful, however, since there may be a third factor causing one or both of the variables to change. This is called spurious correlation.

Positive vs. Normative Economics

Whether you are learning about economics for the first time or you are a seasoned veteran policymaker, it is important to distinguish between positive and normative economics. Positive economic statements can be proven to be true or false. A rise in gas prices will lower the demand for large trucks is a positive statement. Normative economics, on the other hand, deals with what ought to be or what should be. Normative statements are value judgments and should be handled very carefully. Trying to pass off a judgment or opinion as economic fact can be dangerous since, by its very nature, it cannot be proven or disproven.

Economists are not policy makers. We do not, on the whole, decide what the country or its citizens should or should not do. What we can do is tell the government or citizens how to reach their economic goals once they have decided on what they are. For example, an economist cannot say whether the unemployment rate is too high or too low, this is a value judgment. What he can tell you is how you can go about lowering the unemployment rate, if that is in fact your goal. While economics is a science in some respects, we do not have the luxury of doing laboratory experiments to test our theories. While we do understand many aspects of the economy and we can predict how changes in them will affect the big picture, predicting the changes before they occur still eludes economists to a large extent.

CHAPTER 1 SUMMARY

- **Economics** is the study of how people make choices and the results of those choices.
- People have to make choices because of **scarcity**. Since there are limited resources we search for ways to put those resources to their most productive uses.
- Every choice imposes an **opportunity cost**.
- People are **rational**. They do not make the correct decision every time, but they will never purposely make a decision that makes them worse off.
- People created **economic systems** to help them make production decisions.
- The **production possibilities curve** illustrates the possible and impossible production combinations a society can choose between two goods.
- Economists use **models** to understand the effect that one variable has on another.
- Economists use the *ceteris paribus* assumption to simplify the relationship between two variables.

CHAPTER 1 Exercises

Name _____

1) Scarcity
   A) is not a problem for the wealthy.
   B) can be fixed by raising the price of the scarce item.
   C) is unavoidable since humans have limited resources and unlimited wants.
   D) only applies to nonrenewable resources.

   1) _____

2) If you have a choice between skateboarding, going to the movies, and doing your homework what is the opportunity cost of deciding to do your homework?
   A) skateboarding
   B) going to the movies
   C) skateboarding and going to the movies
   D) the highest valued alternative

   2) _____

3) What is the marginal cost of sleeping?
   A) the value of one additional hour of sleep
   B) zero, sleeping is free
   C) the value of what you could have been doing instead of sleeping
   D) the average hourly value of what you could have been doing instead of sleeping

   3) _____

4) Which of the following is a macroeconomic issue?
   A) one firm's decision about how many workers to hire
   B) the national unemployment rate
   C) one individual's decision about whether or not to work overtime
   D) one firm's decision about how much to advertise

   4) _____

5) Which of the following is not a factor of production?
   A) money   C) capital
   B) entrepreneurship   D) labor

   5) _____

6) Answer the following question based on figure 1.3 in the text. What is the opportunity cost of producing the first five tanks? What about the last five?
   A) 60; 0   C) 3; 16
   B) 3; 0   D) 60; 16

   6) _____

7) Which of the following is NOT a way for a country to produce on a point beyond its production possibilities frontier?
   A) produce more efficiently   C) discover new technologies
   B) obtain more resources   D) open up trade

   7) _____

8) *Ceteris Paribus* means
   A) only one moves.   C) uncertain.
   B) all other things being equal. D) jump around.

   8) _____

13

9) Why do people not support efficiency over equity when it comes to answering the "for whom to produce" question?

_____
_____
_____
_____

10) Write one positive statement and one normative statement relating to economics.

_____
_____
_____
_____

Chapter 2

The Market System

I. CHARACTERISTICS OF THE MARKET SYSTEM

In order to answer the fundamental questions of economics—what, how, and for whom to produce—societies must choose an economic system. An economic system is a set of institutions, rules, and mechanisms that coordinate a society's attempt to maximize social welfare. The primary economic systems, communism and capitalism, differ in who owns the factors of production and in how they encourage and organize economic activity.

The market system allows for private ownership of resources and relies on prices and markets (places where buyers and sellers come together) to direct economic activity. Prices in the market create incentives that move resources to their most productive use and inspire entrepreneurs to invent new products and production techniques. Instead of being forced to follow government edicts, agents in the market system follow their own self-interest. Economic decision-making is dispersed among all of the agents in the economy rather than being concentrated in the hands of a central planning authority.

No large economy operates under pure capitalism. This extreme form of capitalism has very little government intervention and can lead to many people "falling through the cracks." Most successful economies, including the United States, employ a modified market system with significant government intervention. The government in this type of system does redistribute resources to a degree, providing goods and services that would otherwise not be produced as well as improving social welfare, but is not the main coordinating force of the economy.

Private Property

Capitalism gets its name from the fact that individuals, not the government, own the productive resources (including capital) in the economy. Private ownership combined with legal contracts and the ability to leave property in a will helps sustain the institution of private property. Private property spurs investment and innovation since no one would spend money developing a product if they knew the government could come in and take over it whenever they wanted.

Property rights also include intellectual property rights like copyrights and trademarks. Property rights led to the development of titles and deeds that have made buying, selling, and trading goods much easier. In some countries without strong property rights people have to spend lots of time and resources protecting their property, decreasing economic efficiency. Developing countries such as Venezuela in particular suffer from government expropriation, or seizure, of private property. This is not just a problem for big businesses, as small family farms are being taken for government use as well.

Freedom of Choice

The dispersion of economic choices in the market system implies that agents are allowed freedom of enterprise and freedom of choice. Freedom of enterprise means that businesses have the right to obtain and use resources to produce any product for any market. Freedom of choice allows capital owners to use and divest property as they see fit. It also applies to consumers using their money to buy any goods and services they want and workers being free to choose their line of work. Of course, some choices are considered illegal, so there are limits to these freedoms.

Choices in the market economy are motivated by self-interest. Each particular agent has a different goal in the economy. Businesses want to maximize profits, property owners want to extract the highest rents possible, workers want to find the job with the greatest combination of wage and nonwage benefits, and consumers want to maximize their utility based on their preferences and income. The pursuit of self-interest ensures that each individual will put his or her own resources to their most productive use.

Competition

Since buyers and sellers are free to decide what markets they choose to enter based on the profit motive, the market system encourages competition. Competition requires a minimum of two buyers and sellers in a single product or resource market, and buyers and sellers are free to enter and leave the market. Competition ensures that no one buyer or seller can dictate prices. If a seller offers a price that is higher than the market will bear, someone will undercut that price.

People in favor of communism or socialism usually claim that capitalism "abuses" and takes advantage of workers, but the competition and diffusion of power embedded in the market system actually protects workers. Any employer paying unfair wages or treating workers poorly will lose workers to other businesses. Communism offers no such protection since businesses do not have to compete with each other for customers.

Price System

Economic decisions in a capitalist economy are determined by the interaction between buyers and sellers in a market. A market is an institution or mechanism that brings buyers and sellers together. The New York Stock Exchange is the quintessential example, but a mall, a farmer's market, or the trunk of someone's car are all examples of markets. Even though it is based on millions of people pursuing their own self-interest, the economy does not fall into chaos because prices and markets coordinate economic decision-making. Those who do not heed the signals of the market are penalized and those who do are rewarded through profits. There is not a big rush to enter the cotton swab and thumbtack markets because these products are relatively cheap and have low profit margins. However, new companies enter the electronics and financial services markets every day, since rising prices indicate that consumers want more of these products. It is through the mechanism of markets that economies decide how to answer the three fundamental questions of economics.

The primary problem in any communist economy lies in coordinating production. Instead of relying on the market to decide what and how much to produce, command economies leave the decision to a central planning authority. This board must predict exactly how much of each type of good or service the entire society will need during the production period. This is too much to ask of anyone. Shortages and bottlenecks were and are common in command economies. As societies and economies grow, these production decisions become even more difficult, leading the planning boards to rely on a small variety of products and direct, inefficient production methods.

Technological Advancement

The fact that innovators can corner the market and reap all the benefits of their invention or discovery encourages the improvement of technology in a market economy. Technological advances are brought about by investment in capital goods and the larger a country's capital stock, the faster its economic growth. The profit motive encourages technological innovation since a producer can benefit at the expense of his competitors by introducing a new product or discovering a new, more efficient production method. The protection of intellectual property rights promised by the market system and government interventions like the patent system, means that the innovator alone would accrue the gains of his invention.

The rapid spread of new technology through an industry or an entire economy is known as creative destruction. The typewriter industry suffered greatly at the hands of home computer and word processor companies, but the switch has unquestionably led to greater productivity. This dynamic aspect of capitalism is one of its most controversial elements. Capitalism also encourages the acquisition of capital goods since the most efficient forms of production are often the least direct; that is, they require intermediate goods. If a business wants to be competitive it must use capital goods and produce efficiently.

Specialization

Most consumers produce virtually none of the goods and services they use on a daily basis. This can happen because of specialization. Specialization occurs when individuals focus on small, well-defined activities and trade with other specialists. This results in an increase in efficiency over a system that requires everyone to do everything for himself.

When firms employ human and other resources in specialized ways, it is known as division of labor. Henry Ford may be famous for using the assembly line and division of labor, but one of the earliest examples comes from Adam Smith's *Wealth of Nations* published in 1776. Smith asserted that ten workers with little real skill could produce 40,000 pins a day in a factory while they could only produce about twenty if they worked alone. This is the power of specialization. Specialization allows people to take advantage of differences in ability. Specialization also increases efficiency because specialists become more skilled in their activity over time—in a process called learning-by-doing—and less time is wasted switching jobs and tools.

There is even room for specialization and gains from trade among regions of the same country. This is evidenced in the fact that Nebraska and other Plains states ship wheat and grains to the east in exchange for manufactured goods. Specialization in each region's particular comparative advantage provides greater economic efficiency for all. This specialization and trade also occurs on the international level.

Trade and Comparative Advantage

Specialization gives rise to trade. Since the US is not a closed economy, it can produce more of some goods (exports) and fewer of others (imports) than it would if it was forced to be self-sufficient in all areas of production. The question is then: Why does the US choose to move resources away from automobiles and clothing (products it imports) and toward aircrafts and wheat (things it exports)? Are there economic benefits from these decisions? The answer, of course, is yes. Specializing and trading allow for both parties to gain and produce beyond their production possibilities curves. People have figured out over time that it does not make sense to make at home what you can buy at a lower cost. The shoemaker does not bake his own bread and the baker does not try to make his own shoes; people specialize and trade. Smith asserted that the same is true for economies as a whole.

Specialization occurs because people incur different costs from the same activities; that is, they experience different opportunity costs. Someone who can perform a task at a lower opportunity cost than someone else is said to have a comparative advantage in that activity. Someone who can produce more than someone else in the same amount of time in every activity they perform is said to have an absolute advantage in production. But since we do not have an unlimited amount of time or resources, we face an opportunity cost every time we perform an economic activity. As a result, absolute advantage is irrelevant when determining the benefits of specialization and trade; what matters is comparative advantage.

For example, let's assume an economy can produce either corn or wheat. If the US can produce more of either than Mexico, then the US is said to have an absolute advantage in the production of both. This does not mean there can be no mutually beneficial gains from trade, however. Since the US is more productive in both types of goods, it faces substantial opportunity costs when it reallocates resources from one type of production to another. Each trading partner can produce one good at a lower opportunity cost than the other partner so they can both gain by producing that one good and trading with each other.

To be more specific, imagine the US can produce 160 tons of wheat or eighty tons of corn per day. In other words, if the US wants to produce eighty tons of corn, it must give up 160 tons of wheat. The opportunity cost of eighty tons of corn is 160 tons of wheat.

What is the opportunity cost of one ton of corn? It would be two tons of wheat (160 divided by eighty). Similarly, the opportunity cost of one ton of wheat is one half of a ton of corn (eighty divided by 160).

Mexico has different resources than the US and can produce corn and wheat at different rates. Using all of its resources, Mexico can either produce 120 tons of wheat or forty tons of corn per day. Therefore, the opportunity cost of producing 120 tons of wheat is forty tons of corn. Mexico must give up three tons of wheat for every one ton of corn it produces. On the other hand, the opportunity cost of one ton of wheat is only one third of a ton of corn.

Absolute Advantage and Comparative Advantage. In one day, the US can produce more corn than Mexico or more wheat than Mexico; it has an absolute advantage in production. It can produce more of each product in the same amount of time. But since they cannot do both activities at the same time, it is better to focus on one activity and let your partner focus on the other. But what activity do you focus on? Remember the definition of comparative advantage: being able to produce something at a lower opportunity cost than your trading partner. The US's comparative advantage is in corn production, because it only has to give up two tons of wheat to produce one ton of corn whereas Mexico would have to give up three tons to get that much. If the US has a comparative advantage in corn production, Mexico must have a comparative advantage in wheat production. Indeed, this is the case. Mexico only has to give up .333 tons of corn to produce a ton of wheat while the US has to give up .5 tons of corn.

Terms of Trade. Since each partner has a comparative advantage, there will be mutually beneficial gains from trade if they specialize and trade with each other. Let's assume that before they thought about trading each country split its resources so it would produce some of each good as illustrated in figure 2.1. Based on their opportunity costs, one possible combination would have the US producing sixty tons of corn and forty tons of wheat and Mexico producing twenty tons of corn and sixty tons of wheat for a total of eighty tons of corn and 100 tons of wheat.

Once they decide to trade, the countries need to find a term of trade, a price of corn in terms of wheat (or wheat in terms of corn) that they both find acceptable. Any term of trade in between their respective opportunity costs will be acceptable. For example, the US's opportunity cost is two tons of wheat per ton of corn and Mexico's is three tons of wheat per ton of corn. The US will accept any trade that gets them more than two tons of wheat per ton of corn and Mexico will accept any trade in which they can get a ton of corn for less than three tons of wheat. Let's assume they agree on 2.5 tons of wheat per ton of corn (or 2/5 of a ton of corn per ton of wheat).

United States					
Corn Production	0	20	40	60	80
Wheat Production	160	120	80	40	0

Mexico					
Corn Production	0	10	20	30	40
Wheat Production	120	90	60	30	0

Figure 2.1 • Production Possibilities for US and Mexico
In this fictional scenario the United States can produce more wheat and more corn than Mexico, but both countries will gain from specialization and trade.

Gains from Trade. The US will focus all of its production on corn and produce eighty tons. It will trade twenty tons to Mexico for fifty tons of wheat. The US has increased its wheat production by ten tons without losing any corn. Mexico now has twenty tons of corn and seventy tons of wheat, a combination that was unattainable before trade. Just as important as the increase in each country is the increase in world production. These countries used to produce a combined 100 tons of wheat and eighty tons of corn. By specializing and trading, their citizens can now enjoy twenty more tons of wheat without losing any corn production. It seems like we have performed economic magic here; we have achieved greater world output with the same amount of world resources. Free market economies engage in trade because the increased efficiency it provides allows the trading partners to overcome their domestic production constraints and consume beyond their production possibilities.

Limited Government

While the interactions between buyers and sellers determine most of the allocations in a market economy, sometimes market failures occur. Market failures occur when a good or service is overproduced, underproduced, or not produced at all because it would not be profitable for any one producer to do so. Would it be practical for a private company to provide the country with national defense, space exploration, or environmental protection? Probably not. In a market economy, the government's primary role is to fix these market failures by creating the proper incentives or just producing the good itself. We will discuss the role of the US government in the economy in more detail later in this chapter.

II. HOW AMERICA ANSWERS THE FUNDAMENTAL QUESTIONS

What to Produce?

In a capitalist economy, incentives are set in such a way that goods and services that are produced at a profit will continue to be produced, while those that do not sell well will not be produced. An industry in which total revenue exceeds total costs for producers will attract investment of resources as well as new firms, causing the industry to expand. Industries in which total costs exceed total revenue will contract as a result of resources and firms fleeing the industry.

When talking about what a country produces, we usually break production down into various categories or sectors. The percentage of production coming from each sector is known as a country's output mix. This output mix constantly changes over time. For example, the percentages of production coming from the farming and manufacturing sectors have fallen over time while the production coming from the health care and service sectors have risen.

One of the biggest changes to the output mix of the US economy has been the fall in the production of tangible goods and the rise of the service sector. You have no doubt heard the United States referred to as a service-oriented economy and that we don't make anything anymore. This transition is not necessarily a bad thing and certainly not unique to the US. This transition is consistent with development patterns we have seen throughout the world. The pattern of development is the idea that most countries start with most of their resources going toward producing food in the agriculture sector. As technologies advance, some people are able to move off the farm and engage in manufacturing. As technologies streamline manufacturing, incomes rise and people start demanding more services.

How to Produce?

In capitalist countries, the how to produce question is answered by the forces of competition. In fact, to achieve profitability in a competitive market, firms must produce at the minimum cost level given current technology and resource prices. Since different resources have different costs, firms must find the least costly mix of inputs. Changes in technology, the mix of resources needed to produce the amount of output, or resource prices can change the cost minimizing combination.

The reason the US produces so much more than most other countries in the world is not because we have more resources, but rather that our resources are much more productive. Labor, in particular, is much more productive in the US than in other countries. Labor is much more productive in advanced economies than it is in developing countries in general; it takes less man-hours to do the same amount of work. The reason for this is that the average worker in a developed country has much more human capital than that of developing countries. Not only is the population of advanced countries more educated and afforded better opportunities for training, they are generally healthier and better fed than workers in developing countries, and that helps them work harder and smarter.

But the major disparity that differentiates developed countries from developing countries is the level of capital available in each country. Remember businesses use capital because the most efficient method of producing something is often the least direct. For example, if you want to get a delivery across town you could walk it over item by item until you were done, or you could use a truck. Often, businesses in developing countries do not have access to capital like delivery trucks and have to make do with human or animal power, reducing the amount of business that can be done.

For Whom to Produce?

In the capitalist system, those who are willing and able to pay will receive the goods and services produced by society. Willingness comes from a consumer's preference ordering, and ability to pay comes from the consumer's income as well as the price of the good they want to purchase. A person's share of society's output is a function of two market values: the value of the property and human resources supplied to the market by the consumer, and the price of the goods that consumer wants to buy. At a given price level, a doctor can buy more goods and services than a janitor.

When households supply resources for economic activity they receive income. Although capitalism is sometimes thought of as a system that abuses and exploits workers, the vast majority, over 70 percent, of all income in society is paid to labor in the form of wages. This does not even include income paid to proprietors like small-business owners, farmers, and doctors and lawyers with their own practice, even though the money made, at least in part, comes from their labor.

You have no doubt heard that the distribution of income in the US economy is relatively unequal. In fact, the richest 20 percent of households in the US receive about 50 percent of the income in a given year. In addition, the personal distribution of income in the United States has become more and more unequal in recent years. Certainly, the rich are getting richer, but it is not necessarily the case that the poor are getting poorer. What is going on instead is that the income of people in the middle and lower parts of the income distribution is not growing as fast as that of the richest people. One of the prime reasons for this change is that the real wage at the middle and lower parts of the income distribution has been stagnant for the last thirty-five years. In other words, people who are not at the top of the income distribution have about the same buying power as people in similar occupations had in 1975. This stagnation can partially be explained by an increase in the labor force, particularly among women and minorities. New entrants into the work force tend to go into middle and low paying jobs, thus creating more competition and keeping the real wage from rising.

III. THE INVISIBLE HAND

Adam Smith and *The Wealth of Nations*

In the 1776 treatise which became the basis of classical economics and laid out the framework of the market system, *The Wealth of Nations*, Adam Smith noted that although economic agents are primarily motivated by their own self-interest, the market will force them to satisfy society's interests as well. Smith named this seemingly magical force exerted by the market system the "invisible hand." Remember that a competitive market forces firms to use cost minimizing input combinations or face failure. This efficient use of resources benefits society by freeing up the maximum amount of resources for other uses. Since each individual is maximizing his own incomes and profits, consumers and producers inadvertently maximize the output and income of society.

Self-Interest vs. Social Interest

As we saw in Chapter 1, people make economic decisions that make them better off; we want the job that will pay us the most money, we want to buy what we want at the lowest possible price, and when we sell things we want to get the highest possible price. In other words, people usually aren't worried about what is best for society at large when they make economic decisions. Why then, does our system not resolve into chaos? Why, when there are so many people with so many different preferences and incomes, can we create a system where people, for the most part, can buy what they want at reasonable prices?

Economists believe that when people are free to pursue their own self-interest, they actually pursue the best interest of society as well. Even the greediest businessman has to produce goods and services that people want in order to make money. Whether he cares about his customers or not he must follow their desires and wants closely if he wants to get rich.

Efficiency

Neither Adam Smith nor the modern economists that he influenced believed that free markets offer a perfect solution to the world's economic problems. No matter how we organize economic activity, scarcity still exists and we will have to make choices that leave some people unhappy. What free markets can do is offer a solution that provides both productive and allocative efficiency.

Productive efficiency means all resources are fully employed and we are producing as much as we possibly can. The competitive nature of the market system guarantees productive efficiency because if resources are not fully employed there are profits that can be made by putting them to a more productive use. An economy that is productively efficient is producing on its production possibilities frontier.

Allocative efficiency means that the economy is producing at the exact point on the production possibilities curve that society values the most. The price system guarantees allocative efficiency since prices signal to businesses which products consumers want more of and which they want less of. While the market system does not claim to make everyone happy, what it can promise is that no other economic system gets as much total utility out of society's limited resources.

IV. THE ROLE OF THE GOVERNMENT

Providing the Legal Framework

Although the market system is noted for its limited government involvement, the government still has a role to play in the United States economy. The government is also known as the public sector, since its intention is to focus on society's interests rather than any private interests. The primary role of government in the economy is to provide a legal framework. The government sets the rules of the game, encouraging policies that help the economy like ensuring property rights and competition, enforcing contracts, and punishing those who violate the rules.

The US government also sets up institutions that facilitate exchange and improve the allocation of resources. The government prints currency for use as a medium of exchange and increases the volume exchange by enforcing contracts and property rights. Of course, this leads to the question: How much should the government intervene in the economy? Just like any decision in the economy, the answer is based on marginal benefit and marginal cost. The government should increase regulation until the marginal benefit of regulation equals its marginal cost.

Protecting Consumers

The government also uses its authority to protect consumers from exploitation by businesses. Advocating for consumers can be helpful in getting a politician reelected, but most likely at the cost of shrinking the economic pie. Governments protect consumers by prosecuting companies that engage in anti-competitive practices and violate antitrust laws. These companies try to use monopoly power to extract additional profits out of consumers. Recent action against AT&T, Microsoft, and Intel show that the United States is serious about preventing monopolies.

The government further protects consumers by setting up consumer advocacy groups like the Better Business Bureau to enforce contracts and truth in advertising. One of the most visible ways the government intervenes on behalf of consumers is by fighting what it sees as "price gouging." In the aftermath of Hurricane Ike, for example, the government cracked down on gas stations charging what they saw as unreasonably high prices. But who decides when prices are too high? By not allowing prices to rise, the government created shortages and some people that really needed gasoline could not find any. In attempting to protect consumers, the government created even more problems for them.

Protecting Labor

The government also enacts policies to protect labor from being "exploited" by employers. Examples of such policies are child labor laws and the minimum wage. While it feels good to pass a law banning "exploitative" practices, the government must consider the true cost of these policies. For example, while child sweatshop labor is a horrible thing and in a better world it wouldn't exist, one must think about the alternative before condemning it. Children take these jobs because the alternative, either starving or getting involved in crime, gangs, or the sex trade, is so much worse. Should the government really be in the business of limiting the options of society's most vulnerable citizens? Most agree they should, but the answer is not so clear. Some argue that greater globalization and free trade are better ways to improve the lives of child workers than policies that prohibit child labor outright.

Fixing Market Failures

Another important role for the government is the solving of market failures. Market failures occur when the market either allocates a non-optimal amount of resources to the production of a good or service, or fails to produce the good at all. A misallocation of resources results from the costs or benefits of a product spilling over to a third party (not the buyer or the seller) and a lack of strong property rights.

I have mentioned before that the price system results in the efficient use of resources, but this assumes that all the benefits and costs of production are reflected in the supply and demand curves. For certain goods the benefits or costs may not be fully internalized by the buyer or seller. An externality exists when some the costs or benefits spill over to someone other than the immediate buyer or seller. They are called externalities because some party external to the market in question accrues some of the cost or benefits.

By dumping waste directly into a river untreated, for example, a firm forces an outside party to pay some of the cost of production. As a result the output of this product becomes too high and the price too low; the negative externality results in an overallocation of resources and leads to a market failure. It takes government intervention to fix a market failure. In the case of a negative externality the government needs to correct the overallocation by promoting policies that force producers to internalize the cost of production. We will continue the discussion of the correction of market failures in Chapter 4.

CHAPTER 2 SUMMARY

- The **market system** encourages each economic agent to pursue his or her own self-interest.

- There will always be mutually beneficial gains from trade because each trading partner will have a **comparative advantage** in only one of the goods being traded.
- Classical economics asserts that in pursuing their own self-interests, agents in a market system will, as if guided by an **invisible hand**, unknowingly maximize social welfare.
- No one can say for sure whether the market system is better than any other economic system, but there is no doubt that is the most **efficient.**
- The government's primary role in the economy is to fix **market failures**, areas in the economy where the invisible hand has failed to produce the socially optimal outcome.

CHAPTER 2 Exercises

Name _____

1) Which of the following is **not** a characteristic of the market system?
   A) government sets the prices   C) competition
   B) private property   D) specialization

   1) _____

2) If the United States can produce more cars and more computers per hour than India, then the US
   A) has a comparative advantage in both products.
   B) has an absolute advantage in both products.
   C) has nothing to gain by trading with India.
   D) will gain from trade, but India will not.

   2) _____

3) How is the 'what to produce' question answered in the United States?
   A) the government decides what is to be produced
   B) goods they sell profitably are produced while goods that do not sell are discontinued
   C) firms sell what they believe people need
   D) consumer groups decide what is to be produced

   3) _____

4) Why would an increase in the amount of women and minorities in the labor force drive keep the average real wage from rising?
   A) it should have no impact
   B) firms feel they can exploit these groups of workers
   C) these groups do not work as hard as other groups
   D) more competition to get middle- and low-income jobs drives the wage down

   4) _____

5) What process did Adam Smith propose to achieve maximum social happiness?
   A) government control of all resources   C) the invisible hand
   B) heavy taxation and redistribution   D) Communism

   5) _____

6) What type of efficiency does the market system guarantee?
   A) productive efficiency   C) distributive efficiency
   B) allocative efficiency   D) both A and B

   6) _____

7) Which of the following is NOT a role of the government in the market system?
   A) allocating output
   B) promoting competition
   C) protecting labor
   D) fixing market failures

   7) _____

8) A market failure occurs when
   A) no one wants to buy a particular product.
   B) sellers charge too much for a particular product.
   C) price information is not available.
   D) too many or not enough resources are allocated to a particular market.

   8) _____

27

9) Why is competition so important to the functioning of the market system? What would happen if every market had only one buyer or one seller?

_____
_____
_____
_____

10) How does the economy keep working despite the fact that everyone is only looking out for only his or her own self-interest?

_____
_____
_____
_____

Chapter 3

Market Interactions

I. THE CIRCULAR FLOW

Benefits from Trade

In capitalist countries, the market organizes economic activity. That is, no one has to tell people what to buy and sell; they simply buy what they want and sell what people want to buy. The market system works because everyone wants to get the most out of their limited resources. Since people do not have unlimited income, they will only purchase goods which they deem the most valuable. Likewise, businesses want to make the most profits possible so they will allocate resources to the products that people want to buy the most. Markets also exist because it is more efficient to specialize in one type of production than to try to make everything yourself. Specialization requires trade with others to get the most of the goods and services we use in our daily lives.

The Two Markets

A dynamic economy like that of the United States entails a repeated flow of goods and services between households and businesses. Economists illustrate this flow in the circular flow model. In a free market economy like the United States, households own all of the factors of production (land, labor, capital, and entrepreneurship). Households provide these resources to firms so that firms can produce goods and services. Households,

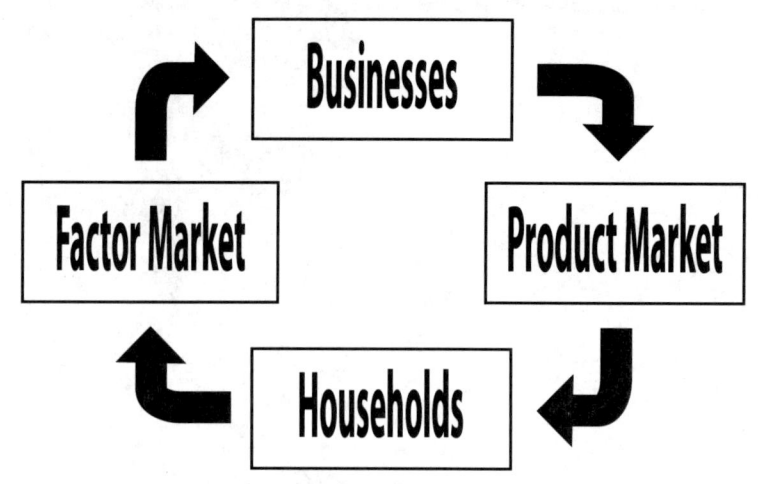

Figure 3.1 • **The Circular Flow Model**
This figure illustrates the flow of real goods and services in the economy. Money flows in the opposite direction.

in turn, buy these goods and services, completing the circle. An example of this circular relationship between households and businesses can be seen in figure 3.1.

Households and businesses interact in two equally important markets: the factor market and the product or goods market. Resources like labor, land, and capital are bought and sold in the factor market. Households own the resources in a market economy and sell these resources to businesses that wish to produce goods for sale in the product market. The incomes returned to households have special names depending on what resource is being purchased (wages for labor, interest for capital, rent for land, and profit for entrepreneurship). The product market is the market we are most familiar with. Producers take the resources they have purchased in the resource market and combine them into products that consumers are willing to buy. Consumers buy these products with the income they earned in the resource market. Money earned by businesses in the product market is called revenue.

Real Flows and Money Flows

The circular flow model, then, actually consists of two circles, or flows, running in opposite directions. First, firms receive factors of production and use them to produce goods and services that they sell to households. Since these flows consist of actual products of value, they are called real flows. Our economy uses money to finance and facilitate the transfers that take place in the resource and goods markets; hence, money flows move counter to real flows. Firms pay households for their resources (in the form of wages, rent, interest, and profit) and households pay firms for the goods and services they consume.

II. DEMAND

The Law of Demand

In economics, demand refers to the specific amounts of a particular good or service that individuals or groups of people are willing to buy at different prices. The Law of De-

Price (P)	Quantity Demanded (Q$_d$)
5	10
10	8
15	6
20	4
30	2
35	0

Figure 3.2 • Demand Schedule for Video Games
As the price of video games rise, the consumer chooses to buy fewer video games.

mand states that when the price of a good goes down, people will want to buy more of it. When the price goes up, people will want to buy less of it. This of course means that price and quantity demanded are inversely related, as they move in opposite directions. The statements in the Law of Demand should all technically include "all other things being equal" since the law operates under the *ceteris paribus* assumption. When we are using the Law of Demand to predict consumer behavior we leave income and all other prices fixed. The Law of Demand may seem like an abstract mathematical theorem, but it can easily be applied to real life. Since any good gives us satisfaction, we will buy more of it if the price falls and all other prices remain the same. As housing prices fall, for example, people should buy more houses, assuming all other prices and consumer income stay the same.

The first step in determining the demand for product is constructing a demand schedule, a table containing the quantity demanded of a certain product by a certain individual or market at various prices. It is also important to note a specific and consistent time dimension for the demand schedule. In addition to the time dimension and *ceteris paribus* assumptions, we also add the assumption that we are referring to constant-quality units. It is obvious fast food hamburgers and hamburgers from a steakhouse are not the same. As a result, it may seem silly to talk about someone's demand for hamburgers without knowing where the hamburgers came from. Instead of making separate demand curves for every type of hamburger, we only have to worry about one demand curve if we convert every different type into a single reference value. It may take three or four McDonald's burgers to equal one constant-quality unit while it may take only one from the steakhouse, for example.

Figure 3.2, for example, describes an individual's quantity demanded of video games as the price changes. The demand schedule clearly illustrates the inverse relationship between price and quantity predicted by the Law of Demand. Much like with the production possibilities table of figure 1.3 in Chapter 1, the demand schedule can only show a limited number of data points. Translating the demand schedule into a demand curve can give much more information about the buyer's purchasing plan. The demand curve contains the points of the demand schedule and connects them in space. For whatever reason, economists decided to put price on the *y*-axis and quantity demanded on the *x*-axis, which runs contrary to our ideas about independent and dependent variables. Figure 3.3 shows that the demand curve is downward sloping, supporting the inverse relationship predicted by the law of demand.

Market Demand

We have so far discussed the demand schedule and curve for an individual. While this analysis is useful for microeconomics, in macroeconomics we are going to need to analyze the demand of all consumers in the market for a given good or service. The equilibrium (market-clearing) price and the quantity of a good or service, which are so critical for the functioning of the market system, are determined by its market demand. Market demand, in turn, is determined by summing the quantity demanded of each individual at each price. Simply summing the demands of each individual buyer in a market is infeasible in practice, so we usually depend on national aggregates given by industry leaders or, rarely, national surveys of consumption. Figure 3.4 shows how this aggregation would work for an extremely small video game market with only three consumers.

Determinants of Demand

A shift in demand refers to the situation where the quantity demanded at every price increases or decreases at the same time. These shifts occur due to the relaxing of one or more of the *ceteris paribus* conditions, the factors that are held constant when drawing a demand curve. Figure 3.5 illustrates the effect of an increase in demand: Every point on the original demand curve shifts to the right, creating an entirely new demand curve. A decrease in demand would cause every point to shift to the left.

Income. There are many factors that can shift the demand curve. The most obvious factor that shifts the demand curve is consumer income; losing one's job or winning the

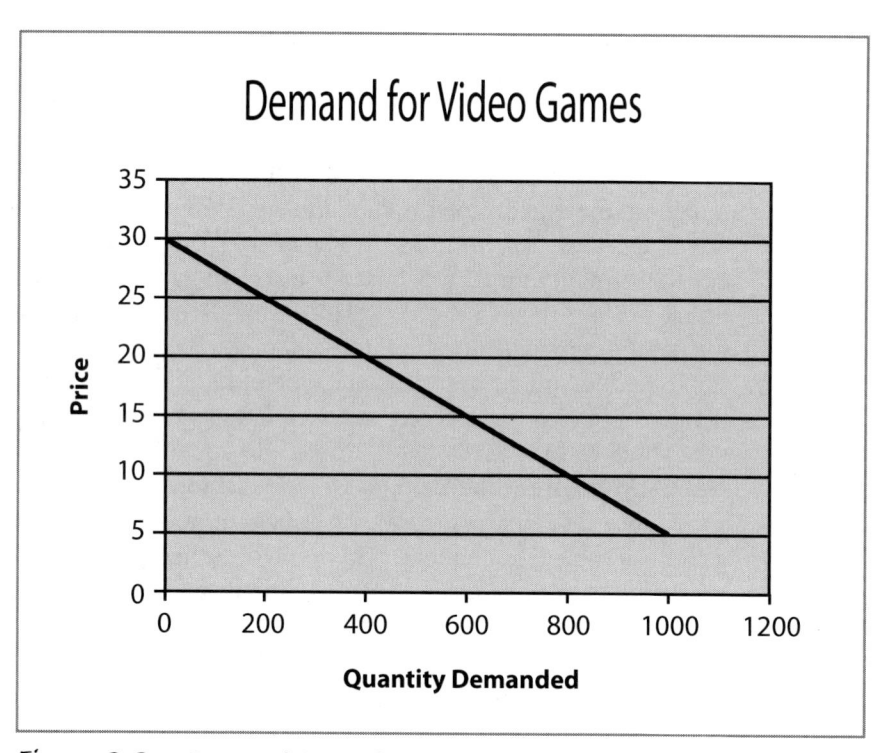

Figure 3.3 • **Demand Curve for Video Games**
Demand curves are downward sloping because the Law of Demand states that people will buy less of a product the higher the price goes.

lottery would certainly have an effect on how much we buy of a particular good. For most goods, an increase in income will lead to an increase in demand at every price, shifting the demand curve to the right. These goods are known as normal goods.

However, some goods work in the opposite fashion. People purchase fewer of these informal goods as their income rises. Lower quality foods such as beans and hamburger meat sometimes behave as inferior goods. The term inferior here contains no value judgments; it only conveys the way the demand curves shift with changes in income. In fact, some people enjoy products like secondhand clothes, canned meat, and bus travel and would buy more of these goods when their income rises, treating them like normal goods. As a result, no definite list of inferior goods exists; it is a purely individual distinction. However, when talking about market demand, an inferior good is one that is treated as inferior by most people.

Tastes and Preferences. Fashions, fads, and trends can shift demand curves. When consumer tastes turn in favor of a particular good or service the demand curve for that product shifts to the right. When the trend dies out, the demand curve shifts to the left. The demand for certain products also change with the season. Christmas trees fly off the lot in November and December, but cannot be sold at any price in July. The demand curve for this product is very sensitive to consumer tastes.

Prices of Related Goods. The price of related goods is an important factor to hold constant when drawing a demand curve, since related goods have interdependent demands. What would happen to the demand for generic drugs if the price of name brand drugs were to rise? It would increase or shift to the right. This occurs because name

Mark's Demand	
Price	Q_d
5	10
10	8
15	6
20	4
25	2
30	0

+

Jim's Demand	
Price	Q_d
5	5
10	4
15	3
20	2
25	1
30	0

+

Tina's Demand	
Price	Q_d
5	15
10	12
15	9
20	6
25	3
30	1

=

Market Demand	
Price	Q_d
5	30
10	24
15	18
20	12
25	6
30	1

Figure 3.4 • Adding Up Market Demand

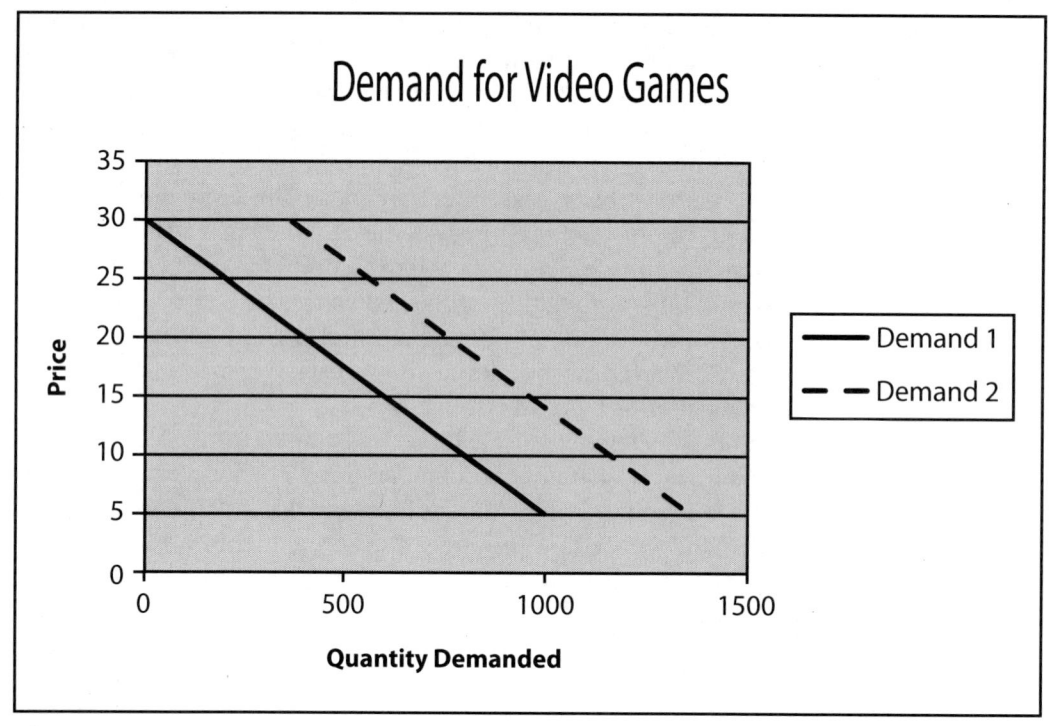

Figure 3.5 • **Shift in Demand**
When the demand for a product increases, the consumers in the market want to buy more at each price, causing the curve to shift to the right. A change in price will only move you from one point on the existing demand curve to another point on that same curve.

brand drugs and generic drugs are substitutes, goods that satisfy the same basic want. A change in the price of one good will cause the demands of its substitutes to move in the same direction. This does not mean no one will buy name brand drugs anymore, but some people will be convinced to switch.

Substitutes are not the only types of related goods; goods can also be complements. Complementary goods are goods that tend to be or need to be consumed together. What would happen to the demand of peanut butter if the price of jelly were to rise? Some people who were buying peanut butter only to pair it with jelly will now find the combination too expensive and cease buying either product. As a result, demand for peanut butter would decrease, or shift to the left. A change in the price of a good causes the demand of its complements to shift in the opposite direction.

Expectations. Expectations can affect demand curves in many ways. In economics, perception is reality, so the way consumers view the future can be just as important in determining demand as current conditions are. If consumers were to believe that the price of a certain good was going to rise or that it would be completely unavailable in the future, they would want to stock up on that good now, causing demand to increase. If consumers anticipated a future rise in incomes, they would have the power to spend more money today, again causing demand to shift to the right.

Number of Buyers. Holding income constant, an increase in the number of buyers in a market will increase demand in that market. Recall from figure 3.4 that market is simply the sum of every individual demand. What would happen if we added another consumer to the market in figure 3.4? As long as he or she will demand at least one video game, adding another buyer will certainly increase the amount of video games demanded at each price.

Changes in Demand vs. Changes in Quantity Demanded

It is crucial that you recognize the distinction between a change in demand and a change in quantity demanded. A change in quantity demanded is simply a movement along a single demand curve. It is a result of a change in price of the good in question while all of the *ceteris paribus* conditions are still in place. It is movement from one point on the existing curve to another. A change in demand, however, represents a shift of the entire demand curve. It requires that one of the *ceteris paribus* conditions change; a change in price cannot change demand, only quantity demanded. A movement from one curve to another illustrates a change in demand.

III. SUPPLY

The Law of Supply

Now that we have looked at demand curves, it is only natural that we look at the supply side of the economy. If people demand all types of goods and services at positive prices, there must be firms selling these products in the market. The supply of a good is the amount that a firm or market is willing to offer for sale at various prices in a given period of time. The Law of Supply states that greater quantities of a good will generally be supplied at higher prices than at lower prices, all other things being equal. This law suggests a direct relationship between price and quantity supplied.

The market offers us many examples of firms increasing quantity supplied when prices increase. On a theoretical level, a firm incurs greater costs as it increases production (increasing marginal cost) and will only accept these rising costs if it receives a higher price for all of its output. A supply schedule can be constructed in much the same way as we constructed a demand schedule. It consists of a table with different price-quantity combinations chosen by the firm. We can also convert the supply schedule into a curve as we did with the demand schedule; this is what we call a supply curve. Notice it is upward sloping in accordance with the Law of Supply, as shown in figure 3.6. Just as with the demand curve, we are focusing on constant-quality units on the *x*-axis.

Market Supply

The market supply is determined by summing the quantity supplied by each firm at each price. These totals are plotted and connected to form the market supply curve. This market supply curve obeys the Law of Supply just like the individual supply curves do.

Determinants of Supply

While a change in price moves the market from one point on the supply curve to another, any factor other than price that changes the willingness of firms to supply a good will shift the supply curve to the left or right. Just as with demand, an increase in supply is illustrated by a shift of the curve to the right and a shift to the left represents a

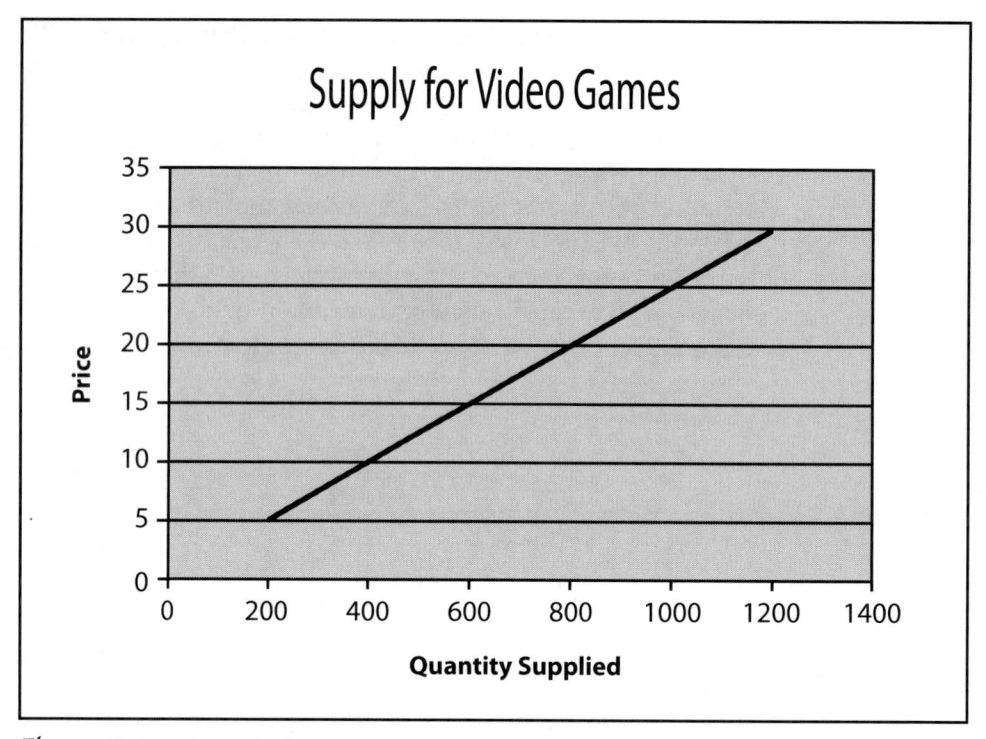

Figure 3.6 • Supply Curve

The supply curve is upward-sloping since businesses earn more profits at higher prices, assuming everything else stays the same.

decrease in supply. In general, any factor that reduces the cost of production will increase profits and convince firms to supply more at the market price, shifting the market supply to the right. Figure 3.7 illustrates the effect of a decrease in supply: every point on the original supply curve shifts to the left, creating an entirely new supply curve. An increase in supply would cause every point to shift to the right.

Price of Inputs. All firms need inputs—raw materials, workers, and equipment—to produce their goods. An increase in the cost of inputs causes the cost of production to rise and will lead firms to produce less at every price. The opposite will occur if input prices fall. This is similar to the idea of complements in our discussion of determinants of demand. Since your inputs and output are used together, like complementary goods, the price of one affects the other.

Technology and Productivity. Increases in technology can lead to falling production costs. New production techniques find more efficient methods of putting resources together and allow for more production at every price, shifting supply to the right. Natural disasters on the other hand can wipe out capital and decrease productivity. The tsunamis, hurricanes, and fires that constantly threaten human life also increase the cost of production and cause supply to shift to the left.

Price of Related Goods. Just like there are substitute and complement goods in demand, there are substitutes and complements in production. A substitute in production is something a firm can make instead of what it is currently making at very little or no additional cost. Cars might be a substitute in production for trucks, for example. What happens when the market price of trucks rises? Firms want to put more resources toward building trucks and less toward building cars. In general, when the price of a good changes the supply of its substitutes in production change in the opposite direction.

Supply for Video Games

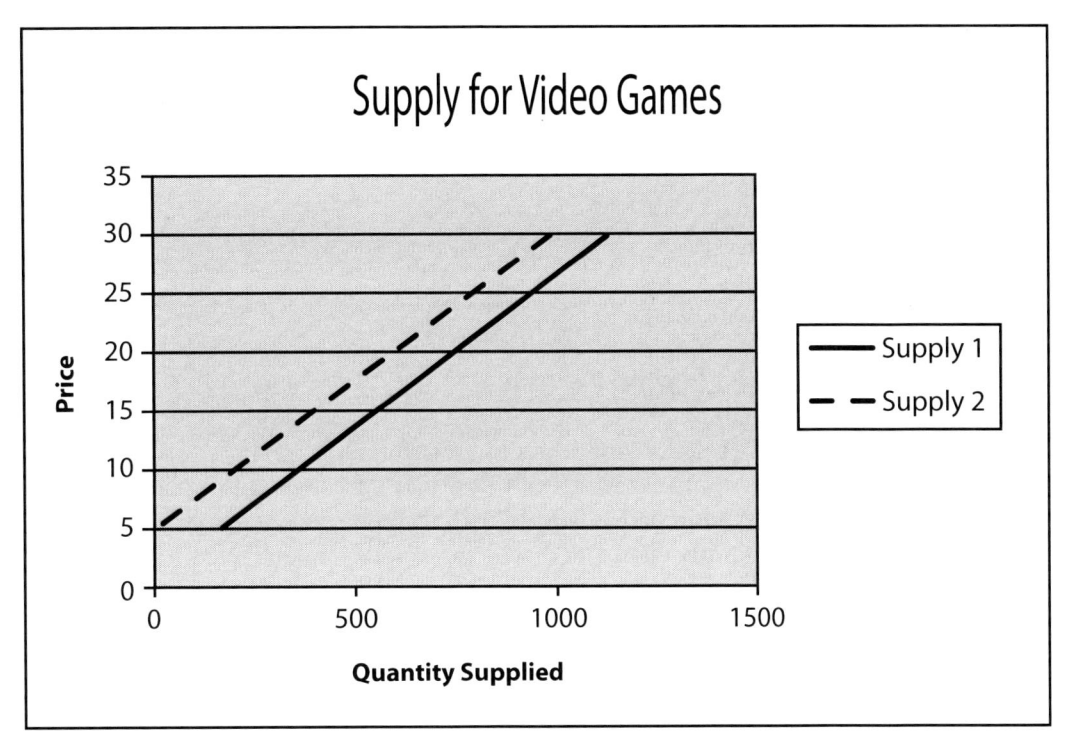

Figure 3.7 • Shift in Supply
If something occurred in the economy that increased the cost of production, businesses would want to produce less of the product at every price, causing the supply curve to shift back to the left.

Likewise, there are complements in production—goods that tend to be produced together. Beef and leather are complements in production. When beef prices rise, firms want more resources in cattle production to reap the large profits in the beef market. Doing so necessarily increases the supply of leather since there are more cows around, lowering the price of a major input for leather manufacturers. When the price of a good changes, the supply of its complements in production change in the same direction. Notice the difference between how supply responds to changes in the price of related goods and how demand responds to the same.

Expectations. Firm expectations can affect the market just like consumer expectations do. If firms anticipate a future rise in prices, they may hold back a portion of their output today, causing supply to shift to the left. If firms anticipate a fall in prices in the future, they will try to unload their output today causing supply to increase. Firms also respond to disasters such as hurricanes and oil spills by limiting supply so more of the product will be available in the aftermath.

Number of Sellers. The number of firms in a market can cause the market supply to change since the market supply is simply the sum of all individual supply schedules. An increase in the total number of sellers will cause market supply to rise.

Changes in Supply vs. Changes in Quantity Supplied

Just as with demand curves, it is important to stress that there is a clear distinction between supply and quantity supplied and it works the same way. A change in quantity supplied refers to a movement from one point on a supply curve to another point on that same supply curve. It is the result of a price change of the good in question when all of the *ceteris paribus* assumptions hold. A change in supply, however, refers to a shift from one supply curve to another. It occurs as a result of a relaxation of one or more of the *ceteris paribus* assumptions.

IV. EQUILIBRIUM

Market-Clearing Price

At most prices, combining the market supply schedule and the market demand schedule for a product will result in either excess quantity demanded (a shortage) or excess quantity supplied (a surplus). At one particular price, however, the quantity supplied and quantity demanded will be exactly equal. Since there is no excess quantity demanded or quantity supplied, the market is said to clear; every seller who is willing can sell as much as he wants at this price and every buyer who is willing can buy as much as he wants at this price. Hence, this special price is called the market-clearing price. We also call the market-clearing price an equilibrium price since it will not change unless the *ceteris paribus* conditions change. Any movement away from this point will be temporary, as market forces will force the market back into equilibrium; the equilibrium is stable. Producers and consumers can mutually do no better than the equilibrium point. Figure 3.8 shows that we can identify the market-clearing price as the point where the supply and demand curves intersect.

Surpluses and Shortages

Any price below the market-clearing price results in a shortage. Shortages occur because the quantity demanded exceeds the quantity supplied at any price below the equilibrium price, as shown in figure 3.9. At below-equilibrium, buyers demand more than firms are willing to sell. Luckily, market forces can help us adjust toward the equilibrium. Since quantity demanded exceeds quantity supplied, consumers will compete for the scarce output by bidding up the price, causing a movement up the demand curve. Firms will see this increase in price and increase production, causing a movement up the supply curve. These forces will continue to act until equilibrium is reached.

Any price above the market-clearing price results in a surplus. As figure 3.10 illustrates, surpluses occur because the quantity supplied exceeds the quantity demanded at any price above the equilibrium price; sellers offer more than consumers are willing to purchase in the market at this price. In this situation, the market signals to firms to cut production and reduce prices. As prices fall, consumers are willing to buy more and move down along the demand curve. Again the economy will stabilize when the two parties meet at the equilibrium point.

Price Ceilings

Supply and demand coordinate the actions of buyers and sellers and lead to establishment of equilibrium. Even if equilibrium is not reached right away, market forces will

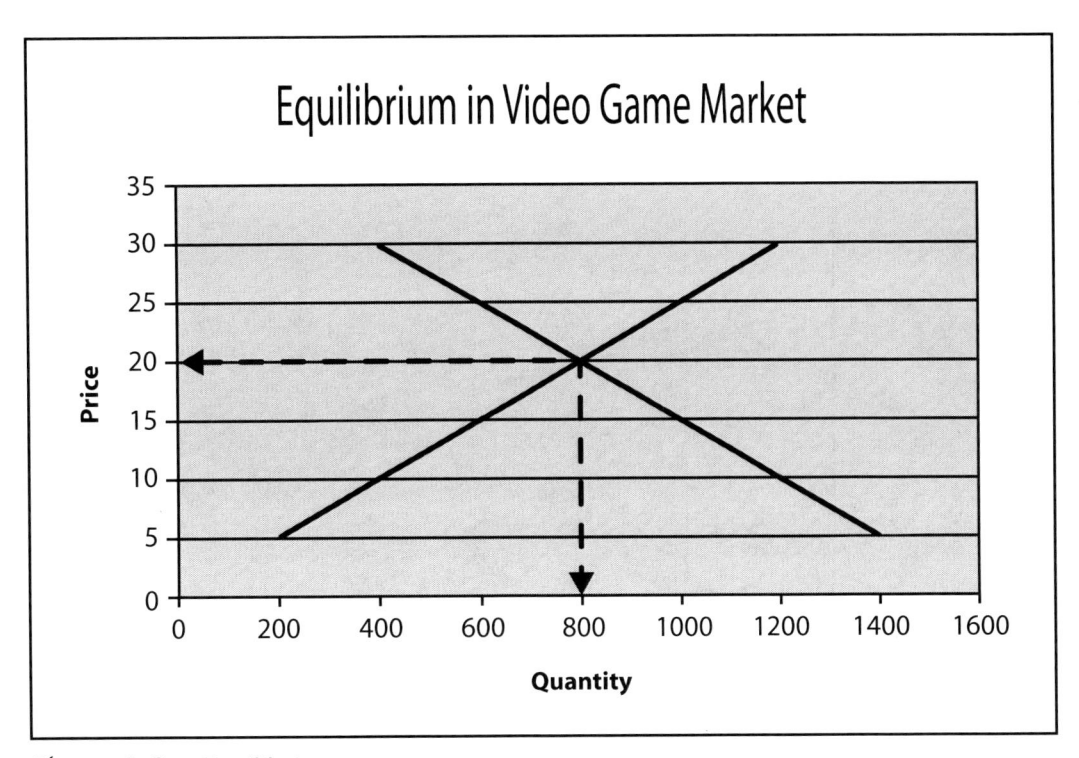

Figure 3.8 • Equilibrium
The supply and demand curves cross at one and only point. At a price of $20, consumers want to purchase 800 units and producers want to sell 800 units. The market clears at this price.

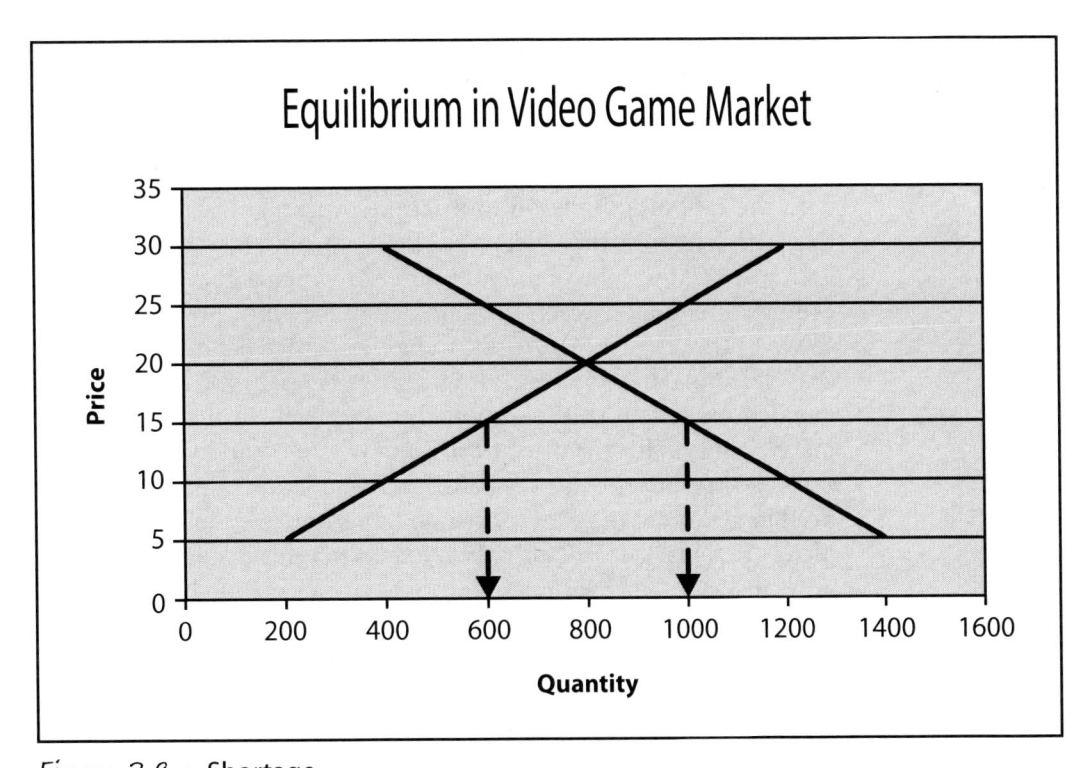

Figure 3.9 • Shortage
If a price of $15 was imposed on the market consumers would want to buy 1000 units, but producers would only want to sell 600. A shortage of 400 units would occur and consumers would bid up the price, pushing the market back toward equilibrium.

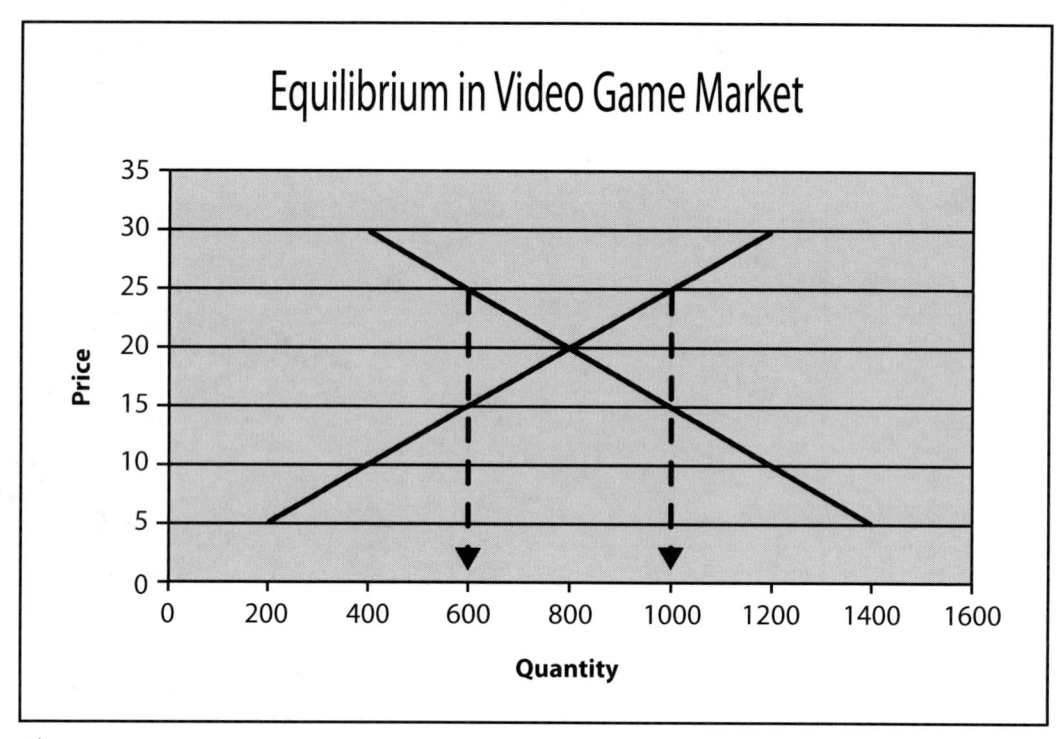

Figure 3.10 • Surplus

If a price of $25 was imposed on the market, producers would want to sell 1000 units but consumers would only want to buy 600 units. A surplus of 400 units would exist. Market forces would push the market back toward equilibrium.

move the market back toward the market-clearing price in time. This coordination is called the rationing function prices since it ensures that everyone willing to buy a particular good or service can do so at equilibrium price and everyone willing to sell can do so at equilibrium price. Any intervention by the government in price making interferes with the rationing function of prices. Governments can impose different mechanisms that interfere with the price system: price ceilings and price floors. We will first deal with price ceilings, the maximum price at which a good can be legally exchanged. Price ceilings only matter when they are below the equilibrium price so we will restrict ourselves to this case. As figure 3.9 shows, any price below the equilibrium will lead to excess demand, therefore imposing a price ceiling will lead to a shortage (quantity demanded exceeds quantity supplied). The problem lies in the fact that a price ceiling makes it illegal for the price to rise and put the market back into equilibrium.

Take the aftermath of a natural disaster for example. Utilities are out and people need to get out of the affected region but gasoline supplies are running low. Under completely free markets, the price would rise to put the market back into equilibrium. Suppose, instead, the government imposed a price ceiling below this new equilibrium price because they see this as price gouging. The result is an ongoing shortage that must be resolved by long lines or some other rationing mechanism less efficient than the price system. Numerous state and local governments have imposed price ceilings to help citizens still dealing with the recession of 2007–2009. But are the benefits of these price controls worth the costs?

Price ceilings may also create black markets where people who are willing to pay a price higher than the government-imposed price get priority at the expense of those who follow the rules. For example, people can receive more than their allotment of gasoline if they are willing to give the attendant a little money under the table. Black markets also exist for illegal goods, such as illicit drugs and human organs, since illegal goods are effectively just goods with a price ceiling of zero.

Price Floors

Price supports in agriculture are examples of price floors, minimum prices at which goods and services can be purchased. Price supports in agriculture are the remnants of policies created during the Great Depression to ensure that the entire agricultural sector did not stop producing all at once. Under the system of price support, the government ensures farmers the price of a good well never fall below the support level. Obviously, this is only relevant if the support level is above the market price. Unlike price ceilings, which created a shortage, price floors create a surplus; quantity supplied exceeds quantity demanded. Governments cannot force people to buy the goods at the higher price, so they must purchase the difference. They then sell the surplus to other countries (at the lower world price) or give it away as a goodwill gesture. During the Great Depression, the government actually burned surplus crops to maintain support-level prices.

Another prime example of a price floor is the minimum wage. The minimum wage creates a higher than market price in the market for unskilled labor. While it certainly benefits those who get paid the higher wage, we know that a price floor creates a surplus, and a surplus in the labor market means there are not enough jobs to go around. Article 3.1 asserts that due to the excess supply it creates in the labor market, a higher minimum wage may actually hurt the people it is supposed to help.

Article 3.1
Price Floors

The Case against a Higher Minimum Wage

The voices clamoring for a minimum wage hike are getting ever louder. Proponents argue that the current wage level does not provide an adequate incentive for work. Also, they argue that an increase in the minimum wage will have only a very minor impact on jobs. These arguments are not grounded in fact. The impact of raising the minimum wage has been studied since its inception. All credible research has come to the same conclusion: raising the minimum wage hurts the poor. It takes away jobs, keeps people on welfare, and encourages high-school students to drop out. Policy makers should be clear on the consequence of higher minimum wages.

Jobs and the Minimum Wage

Economists have studied the job-destroying features of a higher minimum wage. Estimates of the job losses of raising the minimum wage from $4.25 to $5.15 have ranged from 625,000 to 100,000 lost jobs. It is important to recognize that the jobs lost are mainly entry-level jobs. By destroying entry-level jobs, a higher minimum wage harms the lifetime earnings prospects of low-skilled workers.

Proponents have been able to muddle the debate by pointing to a study done by two Princeton economists, David Card and Alan Krueger. These economists claimed to find

Continued.

that raising the minimum wage does not lower employment. In one paper, they succeeded in casting doubt on 200 years of economic research and theory. Economists took their challenge seriously and attempted to recreate their results. It could not be done. Economists who attempted to replicate their work demonstrated conclusively that raising the minimum wage destroys jobs.

Minimum wage workers are not parents struggling to feed their children. Rather, they are high school or college students living at home. The level of the minimum wage is irrelevant for most people in poverty. Only 9.2 percent of poor people of working age have full-time jobs.

Side Effects of Raising the Minimum Wage

It has been well documented that the minimum wage destroys jobs, particularly the jobs of low-skilled, young workers. However, there are other equally pernicious side effects of higher minimum wages. Higher minimum wages make it more difficult for people to leave welfare and induce high-school students to drop out.

Conclusion

The campaign to raise the minimum wage will have little positive impact on the lives of poor people. Rather, it is a political measure that plays to a misunderstanding of the impact of higher minimum wages. The future of the American economy depends on a correct understanding of the causes of prosperity. For too long, attempts to relieve poverty have been misguided. To lift people out of poverty, we need a system that maximizes opportunities for economic well-being of low-skilled workers. Raising the minimum wage is a wrong-headed solution that will deprive young, poor Americans of an opportunity to improve their economic situation.

Reed Garfield
Senior Economist

Questions:
1. What type of equilibrium problem does a minimum wage cause in the labor market?
2. According to the article, why does the argument that a higher minimum wage is needed so working class people can support themselves not really make sense?
3. What are some other ways to increase the earnings of working class people?

From the Joint Economic Commission Report, May 1996.

V. CHANGES IN EQUILIBRIUM

Shift in Demand

We know that changes in the *ceteris paribus* conditions will shift supply and demand, but what effect will this have on equilibrium? Suppose that the supply of a good or service remains constant. A shift in the demand for that good to the right (and we know there are many different potential causes for that shift) will result in the intersection of the curves to have higher values for both price and quantity. As figure 3.11 shows, there is no ambiguity here; a rise in demand will lead to higher equilibrium price and quantity. The opposite is true for a decrease in demand.

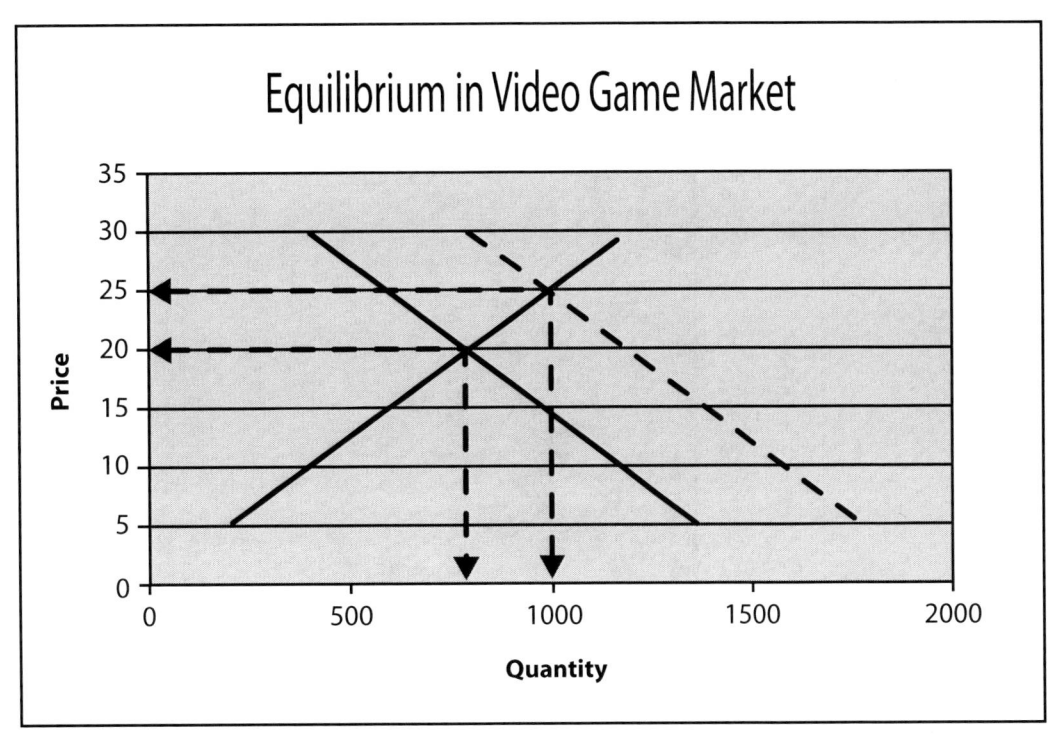

Figure 3.11 • **Shift in Equilibrium—A Change in Demand**
If demand for the product rises, the demand curve shifts to the right changing the point of intersection. As a result, the equilibrium quantity and the price both rise.

Shift in Supply

A similar graphical exercise can be done to analyze the effect of a change in supply given demand remains constant. An increase in supply will cause the supply curve to shift to the right. As figure 3.12 shows, the resulting equilibrium will have a higher quantity, but a lower equilibrium price, than the one you started with. The opposite is true for a decrease in supply.

Complex Cases

Unfortunately there some more complex cases we need to consider. What if both supply and demand change at the same time? It isn't out of the question; they have completely different *ceteris paribus* conditions. First, let's talk about shifting in the same direction.

Increase in Supply and Demand. If both supply and demand increase, surely equilibrium quantity will increase; we know this from our analysis of single curve shifts. An increase in supply and an increase in demand both result in an increase in equilibrium quantity. These shifts, though, force price in opposing directions and the resulting effect is ambiguous.

Decrease in Supply and Demand. The next case has both curves shifting to the left, indicating a decrease in both supply and demand. We can clearly state that equilibrium quantity will decrease, but what about price? Again, it is indeterminate. You may notice a pattern developing here: If both curves move together, equilibrium quantity moves in the same direction, but the effect on price is ambiguous. In fact, it is possible that

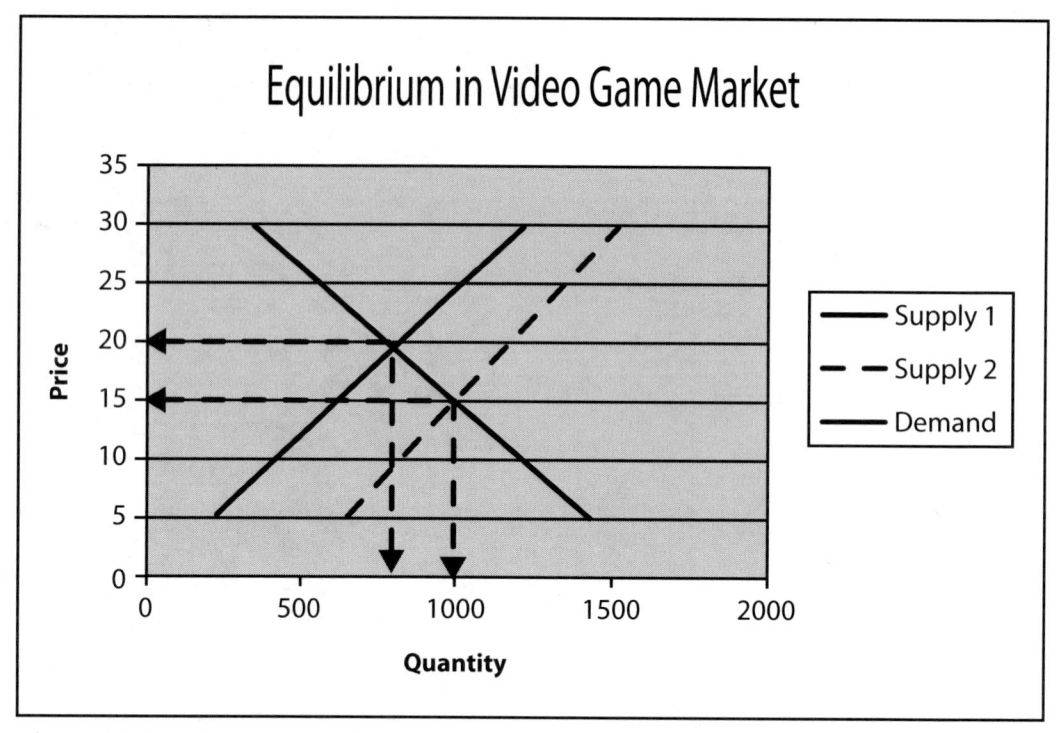

Figure 3.12 • **Shift in Equilibrium—A Change in Supply**
The market equilibrium will also shift if the supply curve shifts. If the supply of video games increased, for example, the equilibrium quantity would rise, but the equilibrium price would fall.

change in demand and change in supply exactly cancel out, leaving price unchanged and changing only quantity.

Increase in Supply, Decrease in Demand. Suppose supply increased while demand decreased. What would that look like? Supply would shift to the right and demand would shift to the left. Now what happens to equilibrium? Both an increase in supply and a decrease in demand lower price, so it is clear that this simultaneous movement will lead to a lower equilibrium price. However, these movements disagree about the effect on quantity (an increase in supply decreases quantity and a decrease in demand decreases quantity). As a result, we say the effect on quantity is ambiguous or indeterminate.

Decrease in Supply, Increase in Demand. Finally, let's try a decrease in supply and a simultaneous increase in demand. Again, we check the section on single curve shifts. Both of these movements result in an increase in equilibrium price, so we know that this simultaneous shift will result in a higher equilibrium price. The effect on quantity is again ambiguous, though. Here is our second pattern: when the two curves shift in opposite directions, equilibrium price moves with demand, but the effect on quantity is ambiguous.

CHAPTER 3 SUMMARY

- Businesses and households interact with each other in the **factor market** and the **product market**. Households are the sellers in the factor market and businesses are the sellers in the product market.

- The **Law of Demand** states that as the price of a good rises, people will want to buy less of it.
- A change in price can only change **quantity demanded**; it cannot change demand. Only a change in one of the **determinants of demand** can shift the demand curve.
- The **Law of Supply** states that as the price of a good rises, businesses will want to sell more of it.
- A change in price can only change **quantity supplied**; it cannot change supply. Only a change in one of the **determinants of supply** can shift the supply curve.
- A market is at **equilibrium** at the price where quantity supplied and quantity demanded are exactly equal.
- At any price other than the equilibrium price, there will be **excess supply** or **excess demand**.
- A shift in either the supply or demand curve will result in a new equilibrium.

CHAPTER 3

Exercises

Name _____

1) Which of the following correctly describes the circular flow model?
   A) households are buyers in product and factor markets
   B) businesses are buyers in product and factor markets
   C) household are buyers in product market, but sellers in factor market
   D) businesses are buyers in product market, but sellers in factor market

   1) _____

2) Law of Demand states that as the price of a product rises
   A) demand falls.
   B) quantity demanded falls.
   C) demand rises.
   D) quantity demanded rises.

   2) _____

3) Which of the following is NOT a determinant of demand?
   A) price of inputs
   B) income
   C) expectations
   D) price of a related good

   3) _____

4) What would happen to the demand curve for jelly if the price of peanut butter doubled?
   A) shift to the left
   B) nothing
   C) shift downward
   D) shift to the right

   4) _____

5) What would happen to the demand curve for gasoline if everyone expected his or her income to fall in the near future?
   A) shift to the left
   B) nothing
   C) shift upward
   D) shift to the right

   5) _____

6) What do all the shifters of supply have in common?
   A) They always shift the supply curve to the right
   B) They all cause changes in cost of production
   C) They all cause demand to fall
   D) They always shift the supply curve to the left

   6) _____

7) Suppose a farmer could grow corn or wheat on his land. What would happen to the supply curve for corn if the market price of wheat doubled?
   A) shift to the left
   B) shift to the right
   C) nothing
   D) shift upward

   7) _____

8) Why is the equilibrium price also called the market-clearing price?
   A) because no exchanges are made at this price
   B) because it is the highest price at which people will buy any of the good
   C) because it is the lowest price allowed by the government
   D) because it is the only price where quantity demanded and quantity supplied are equal

   8) _____

9) When a good selling for higher than its market price, what kind of problem occurs?
   A) scarcity
   B) market failure
   C) surplus
   D) shortage

   9) _____

47

10) What happens to equilibrium price and quantity when supply increases and demand remains unchanged?   10) _____
   A) price rises; quantity falls
   B) price and quantity both rise
   C) price and quantity both fall
   D) price falls, quantity rises

11) Answer the question given the demand and supply schedules.

Price	Quantity demanded (bushels of wheat)	Price	Quantity supplied (bushels of wheat)
$4.20	125,000	$4.20	230,000
4.00	150,000	4.00	220,000
3.80	175,000	3.80	210,000
3.60	200,000	3.60	200,000
3.40	225,000	3.40	190,000
3.20	250,000	3.20	180,000
3.00	275,000	3.00	170,000

If the federal government decided to support the price of wheat at $4.00 per bushel (price floor), would there be a surplus or shortage? How much it would be?

_____
_____
_____
_____

12) Why does the demand for some products rise when income falls? What is special about these products?

_____
_____
_____
_____

13) Why does a minimum wage above the equilibrium wage cause unemployment?

_____
_____
_____
_____

14) Draw what would happen to equilibrium if both supply and demand shifted to the right at the same time. What happens to equilibrium quantity and price?

Chapter 4

The Public Sector

I. THE GOVERNMENT'S ROLE

Legal Structure

The government is also known as the public sector, since its intention is to focus on society's interests rather than on private interests. As we discussed in Chapter 2, one of the most important roles of the government is to set the rules of the game, encouraging policies that help the economy like ensuring property rights and competition, enforcing contracts, and punishing those who violate the rules.

Government also sets up institutions that facilitate exchange and improve the allocation of resources. The government prints currency for use as a medium of exchange and increases the volume exchange by enforcing contracts and property rights. Of course, this leads to the question: How much should the government intervene in the economy? Just like any decision in the economy, the answer is based on marginal benefit and marginal cost. The government should increase regulation until the marginal benefit of regulation equals its marginal cost.

Promoting Competition

Competition ensures that no one in an economy can unilaterally set prices; it regulates the system. Without competition, producers would have no incentive to listen to the demands of consumers and respond to the signals of the market. Therefore, it is imperative that the government encourages competition. When a single seller dominates an industry, we say that seller has a monopoly. In a monopoly, the producer controls the price by controlling the supply of the entire market. A monopolist will maximize his profits by charging a price higher than the one that would have occurred under competition. Governments attempt to fight monopolies using regulation and antitrust legislation. Some industries, such as telephone and energy utilities, lend themselves to being "natural monopolies": only one firm can achieve lowest cost production. The United States allows monopolies like these to exist, but regulates them strictly. Recently the United States has acted swiftly against alleged monopoly practices by computer chip producer Intel. The government sued Intel for the damages it caused its competitors as detailed in Article 4.1.

Article 4.1:
Maintaining Competition

U.S. Sues Intel Alleging Market Abuses
FTC Action Against Chip Giant Comes Same Day That Microsoft Resolves Its Longtime Antitrust Problems in Europe

By Don Clark and Thomas Catan

December 16, 2009

One U.S. technology giant was attacked by its own government, while another resolved major antitrust troubles of its own in Europe.

The U.S. Federal Trade Commission Wednesday sued Intel Corp. seeking to stop what it claimed was a decade of illegal sales tactics that hobbled competitors in the semiconductor market, adding to prior accusations against the company. Intel denied the charges and called the case "misguided."

The complaint in Washington came the same day the regulators in Brussels agreed to abandon their decade-long antitrust battle against Microsoft Corp. in exchange for a commitment from the software giant to distribute competing Web browsers alongside its own products.

FTC officials say Intel not only used improper tactics against Advanced Micro Devices Inc.—its longtime competitor in microprocessors—but add allegations that Intel improperly quashed competition from Nvidia Corp. in graphics processing units, or GPUs. Those chips control three-dimensional images in computer games as well as display video on computers, and are increasingly seen an alternative to microprocessors.

The Obama administration has vowed to vigorously enforce federal antitrust laws against dominant companies after eight years in which the Bush administration largely put the issue on the back burner. Arguing market forces can best maintain competition, the Department of Justice under President Bush didn't file any cases accusing a single, dominant firm of abusing its market position.

Significantly, much of the FTC case against Intel isn't based on the Sherman Antitrust Act—the longtime foundation for most such actions—but Section 5 of the FTC act. The FTC rule is broader than conventional antitrust laws and prohibits unfair tactics and deceptive acts. Its use is part of a wider effort by the FTC, the Justice Department and Democrats in Congress to bolster antitrust powers.

As in prior complaints filed in Europe, Japan, South Korea and by New York state, the FTC alleged that Intel used rebates or threats of retaliation to deter computer makers such as Hewlett-Packard Co., Dell Inc. and International Business Machines Corp. from using AMD microprocessors.

The complaint also alleges Intel improperly bundled sales of microprocessors with its chip sets and made it hard for rivals to connect to its newer products, hurting Nvidia. The FTC also said Intel secretly redesigned programs called compilers to hurt the performance of software running on non-Intel chips.

Questions:
1. Why is the government cracking down on Intel's business practices? What does it hope to gain?
2. Why did the previous administration not do anything when it was clear that Intel had been engaging in anti-competitive practices for years?
3. Why is it significant that the government's case is based on the FTC act and not the Sherman Antitrust Act?

Reprinted by permission of *Wall Street Journal*, Copyright © 2009 Dow Jones & Company, Inc. All Rights Reserved Worldwide. License number 2560980075175.

Redistributing Income

The income in any market economy will not be divided equally among all citizens. Most modern governments have found it worthwhile to redistribute income; that is, to take income from some people and give it to others. This redistribution can be performed by a variety of different programs and policies. The most visible form of redistribution of income comes in the form of transfer payments. Transfer payments are simple cash payments the government makes to people they deem worthy of assistance. Welfare checks and unemployment insurance payments are examples of transfer payments.

A different method of redistributing income involves the government intervening in markets, in particular the determination of market prices. We have already talked about two of these interventions: agricultural subsidies and the minimum wage. The government imposes price floors in these markets to transfer income from buyers to sellers. Another common form of redistribution comes from the tax system itself. The personal income tax system in the United States is progressive; the higher the income, the greater the percentage of your income you must pay in taxes. This effectively decreases after-tax income inequality. Again, all of these policies sound noble and worthwhile, but keep in mind they are not costless. Any policies that redistributes income from richer people to poorer people distort the incentives to work, save, and invest, resulting in a reduction in output and future growth. If you want the economic pie to have more equal slices you face the tradeoff of making the pie smaller.

Ensuring Economic Stability

The government wants to balance spending and production so that resources will always be fully employed. When spending and production are not balanced, unemployment or inflation can result. One of the government's primary economic tasks is keeping these two forces under control. When private spending falls (as it is does during a recession) the government may attempt to increase public spending so that total spending in the economy (public plus private) is high enough to achieve full employment. Think of all the stimulus projects and bailout programs the government added to its budget during the most recent recession in order to fight unemployment. The central bank of the United States, the Federal Reserve, also tries to increase employment by lowering interest rates and encouraging spending. When spending exceeds the productive capacity, prices tend to rise all at once, a situation called inflation. The government can curtail inflation by reducing its own spending and increasing taxes to discourage private spending. The central bank can also discourage spending (encourage savings) by raising interest rates.

II. FIXING MARKET FAILURES

An important role for the government is the solving of market failures. Market failures occur when the market either allocates a non-optimal amount of resources to the production of a good or service or fails to produce the good at all. A misallocation of resources results from externalities and failure to produce results in the creation of public goods. I have mentioned before that the price system results in the efficient use of resources, but this assumes that all the benefits and costs of production are reflected in the supply and demand curves. For certain goods, though, the benefits or costs may spill over to someone other than the buyer or the seller.

Public Goods

Nearly every good produced for sale in the competitive market are private goods. Private goods have two defining characteristics: rivalry and excludability. Rivalry means that consuming a product keeps someone else from consuming that same product. A good is excludable if you can keep people who did not pay for it from receiving any of its benefits. There are certain goods, however, that are nonrival and nonexcludable. These goods are called public goods since everyone in society can benefit from them without reducing anyone else's benefit (nonrival) and it is practically impossible to keep anyone from benefiting from the good (nonexcludable). Examples of public goods include national defense, streetlights, and a clean environment.

The fact that it is impossible to keep anyone from enjoying the benefits of public good means that even someone who does not pay for it will benefit from it. This is known as the free-rider problem. If people can benefit from the good without paying for it, it will be unprofitable for any private company to provide it; as soon as you sell it to one person, everyone else can enjoy it for free. As a result many beneficial goods will not be produced at all unless the government intervenes. Since the market will not allocate sufficient resources even to worthwhile public goods, the government uses the political system to do so. The government discerns which projects are worthwhile based on the candidates and projects people vote for. They then finance these projects through the collection of tax revenue. As we will see later in this chapter, the political system is nowhere near as efficient an allocation mechanism as the price system.

Merit and Demerit Goods

The government aims to allocate more resources to merit goods and fewer to demerit goods. A merit good is a subjective designation given to a good that the current political process has deemed especially desirable for society. The government funds the production and distribution either by providing them itself or by subsidizing suppliers in the market. We already know the government chooses to produce some goods that would never be provided by the private market because of the free-rider problem. This, however, is a very limited list of goods. Most goods produced or subsidized by the government are also produced by private businesses, but not at a high enough level to satisfy the social need according to the government.

Since these goods could have been profitably produced in the market (though underproduced in the eyes of the government) they are not technically public goods. However, since they are financed and produced by the government, just as public goods are, they are sometimes called quasi-public goods. Examples include museums, sports arenas, and opera houses. The government also discourages the productions of some types of goods and would prefer that fewer resources be allocated to their production. Such goods are called demerit goods. Demerit goods are often heavily taxed or even expressly prohibited by the government altogether. Some examples include alcohol, cigarettes, and illicit drugs.

Externalities

Merit and demerit goods usually produce some sort of externality. An externality exists when some of the costs or benefits of consuming or producing a good spill over to someone other the immediate buyer or seller. They are called externalities because some party external to the market in question accrues some of the cost or benefits. Key to the existence of externalities is the lack of clearly assigned property rights. If you are next to someone on a bus and he is smoking but you would rather he did not, who has the rights? Do you have the right to smoke-free air or does he have the right to smoke wherever he wants? The property rights are not clearly defined. The same thing happens on a larger scale when a factory pollutes the air or water of the town it inhabits. Does the firm have a right to produce its good at the lowest possible cost or do the people have a right to a clean environment? The lack of property rights makes compensating the offended party impossible and an externality results.

Negative Externalities. A negative externality exists when costs are inflicted on some party outside the market. This creates a problem because the true cost of the product is not reflected in its market price. Environmental pollution is a prime example of a negative externality. Chemical factories can reduce costs by dumping waste untreated directly into a river, but other people pay the price for this pollution and get no benefit. By dumping waste directly into a river untreated, a firm reduces its cost of production and its supply curve shifts to the right. By forcing an outside party to pay some of the cost of production, the output of this product comes too high and the price too low; the negative externality results in an overallocation of resources and leads to a market failure.

Negative externalities can also exist on the demand side. Suppose you live in an apartment with thin walls and your neighbor is listening to music so loud that it interferes with your ability to work, watch television, or sleep. The neighbor's consumption of music imposes a spillover cost on you. Clearly, the neighbor is consuming more than the social optimum amount of loud music. His demand curve for loud music is solely based on his private costs and benefits. If he could somehow feel the total social cost of his consumption—private plus spillover costs—his demand curve would shift back and we would be at the socially optimal equilibrium as shown in figure 4.1.

Fixing a Negative Externality. Since property rights are not defined, it takes government intervention to fix a market failure. In the case of a negative externality the government needs to correct the overallocation of resources to a market where the seller does not pay the full cost of production or the full cost of consumption. The government achieves this by promoting policies that force producers and consumers to internalize the cost of production. The first policy the government can use relies on the fact that taxes effectively increase the per-unit cost of production or consumption. The government levies a tax on a product roughly equal to the estimated amount of negative externality produced by the good. Therefore, the firm reduces production to the optimal level and resources are no longer overallocated to this market. Proposed taxes on sugary drinks and snack foods, for example, might not only improve state and federal budgets but can also improve health and reduce negative health outcomes. The second policy the government can pursue is one of legislation and regulation. The government can create laws that require potential polluters to pay for and install technology that reduces or eliminates waste. Any firm that refuses to internalize the full cost of production faces legal action. This policy increases the cost of production and reduces supply. These laws can also be applied to consumers of products with negative externalities, such as ordinances that prohibit smoking in public buildings.

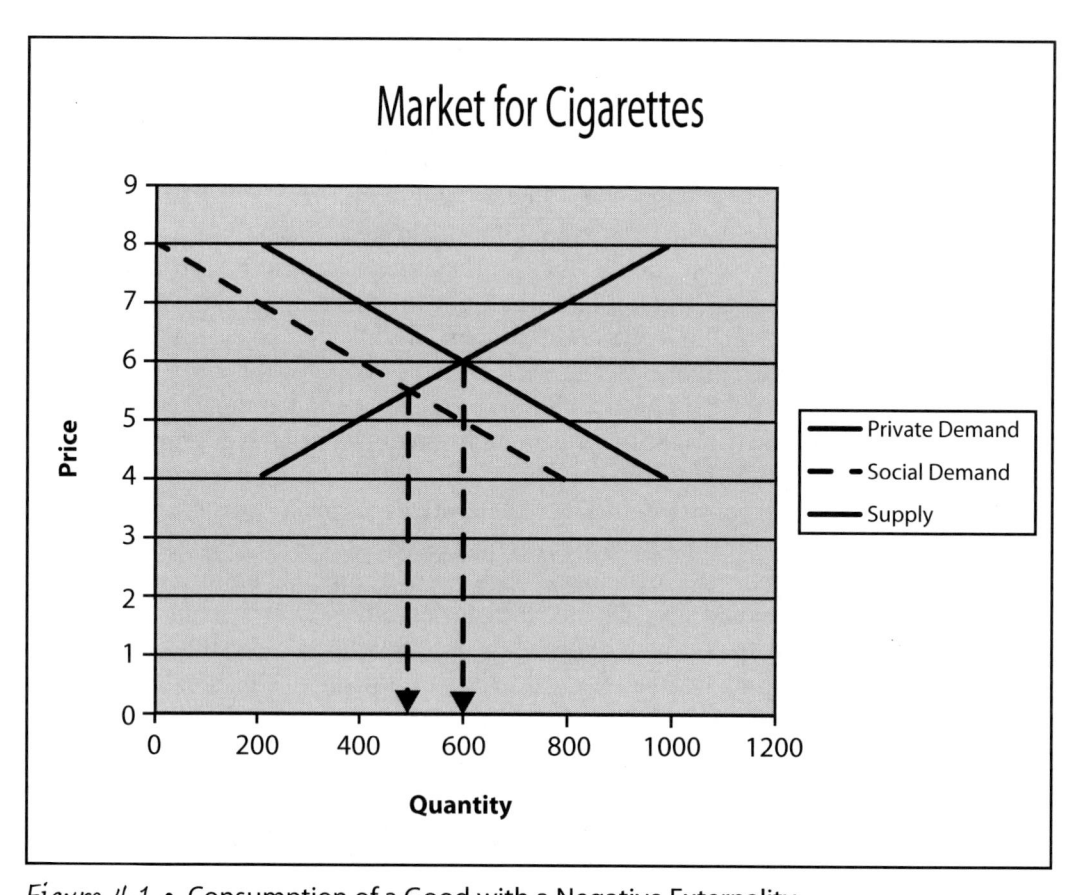

Figure 4.1 • Consumption of a Good with a Negative Externality
If the market for a product with a negative externality is left unregulated, the market will overproduce the good. Social welfare is not being maximized since the consumer is not internalizing all of the costs related to the good.

Positive Externalities. Positive externalities occur when the benefits of a good or service are not all received by the buyer. Sometimes the benefits of a good or service spills over to other people in the community. Examples of goods with positive externalities are immunizations and education. When people are immunized they of course receive direct benefits, but the community benefits as well by having one more individual immune to that particular disease.

Education provides direct benefits to the buyer in terms of higher future incomes. Education also leads to a more productive workforce and less resources being spent on welfare and crime prevention. These additional benefits are accrued to the society at large, not the buyer himself. Since the buyer does not receive all of the benefits of the good, the demand curve for a good with a positive externality will lie to the left of the optimal location as illustrated in figure 4.2. As a result, there is underallocation of resources to these goods and another market failure occurs.

Fixing a Positive Externality. To correct a positive externality, a government must pursue policies that allow buyers to internalize the full benefits of the good or service in question. The government may just choose to completely finance or independently operate the industry experiencing the externality. This allows the government to control the amount of the good produced instead of relying on market forces.

An alternative policy involves subsidizing consumers that buy the good. The United States subsidizes higher education by providing low-interest loans to qualifying students. These loans encourage more resources to be allocated to purchasing higher

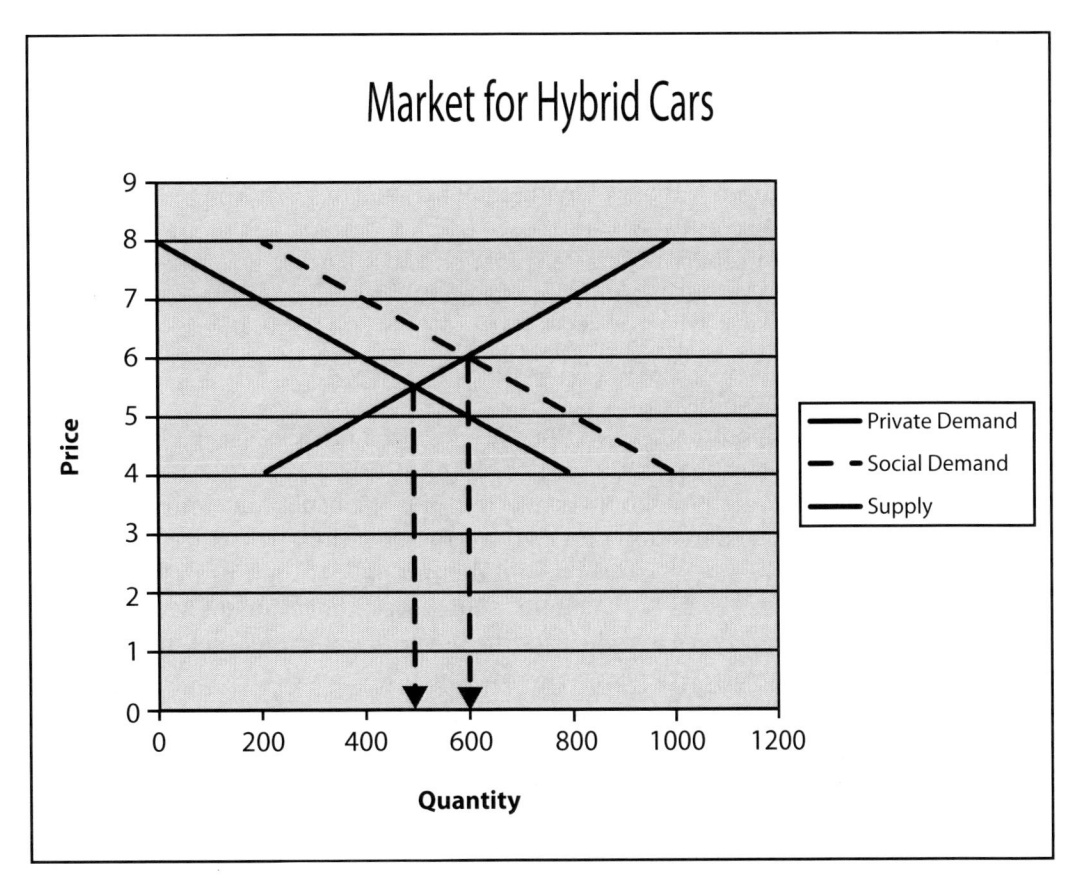

Figure 4.2 • **Consumption of a Good with a Positive Externality**
In the market for a good with a positive externality, consumers do not receive all of the benefits of consuming the good. Without regulation, the good is underproduced relative to the socially-desired equilibrium.

education and bring the demand closer to the optimal level. A similar policy involves subsidizing the producers of goods with positive externalities. Since there are usually more buyers than sellers in a market, this policy tends to be simpler for the government to pursue. Some subsidization policies include state funded schools, hospitals, and immunization programs. All of these programs increase the supply of these underallocated goods and bring the output closer to the optimal level. The government can also increase the allocation of resources to certain activities by passing laws that require people to undertake these actions. Examples include mandatory immunizations for school-age children and compulsory education at the primary and secondary level. These laws will certainly encourage the consumption of these services.

Government Failure

While most people agree that some government intervention is necessary because of the possibility of market failure, how much is enough? Communist countries believe that the government should control every aspect of the economy while most countries take a more laissez-faire approach. We know that excessive government intervention in markets distorts incentives and slow growth. So how do we know when enough government intervention is enough, and how do we communicate this to the government?

Government failure occurs when government intervention takes us farther away from the socially optimal mix of goods and services. Government intervention may cost so many resources that we may actually move inside the production possibilities curve, representing inefficiency. Even when the government uses resources efficiently, it may lead to producing a mix of goods and services that is farther from the optimal mix than the market allocation was and that does not making things better either. If the optimal allocation in figure 4.3 was C, for example, government action might move the economy from D to E, reducing total utility. The government should only act if the benefit of doing so outweighs the cost.

Perceptions of Waste. Most citizens distrust government intervention because they presume the government wastes much of its resources. Unlike a private business, the government does not have to produce efficiently to stay alive, so people assume it does not. If the government is wasting resources, any government intervention will lead to an allocation inside the PPC.

Opportunity Cost. Even if the government is acting efficiently, there is still the question of opportunity cost to deal with. Is a particular act of government intervention worth it? It will only be worth it if it the benefit outweighs the opportunity cost. Every good and service provided by the government (police officers, teachers, and so on) takes away resources for production by private business. This lost production by the private sector is the opportunity cost of government production. We can agree on the general types of industries the government should get involved in, but how much they get involved depends on how much it costs (in terms of lost private sector production for them to do so). As a result, there is no single answer for whether a government has grown too large. All that matters is whether the goods and services produced by the government are valued more highly than the other production we give up in order to produce those government goods. So the government may be too involved in road construction, but not involved enough in the education industry, for example.

Cost-Benefit Analysis. We know it is difficult to say whether the government in general is too involved with the market or not. What we can say, however, is if we want the government to be more or less involved in a particular industry. If the benefit of in-

Production Possibilities Curve

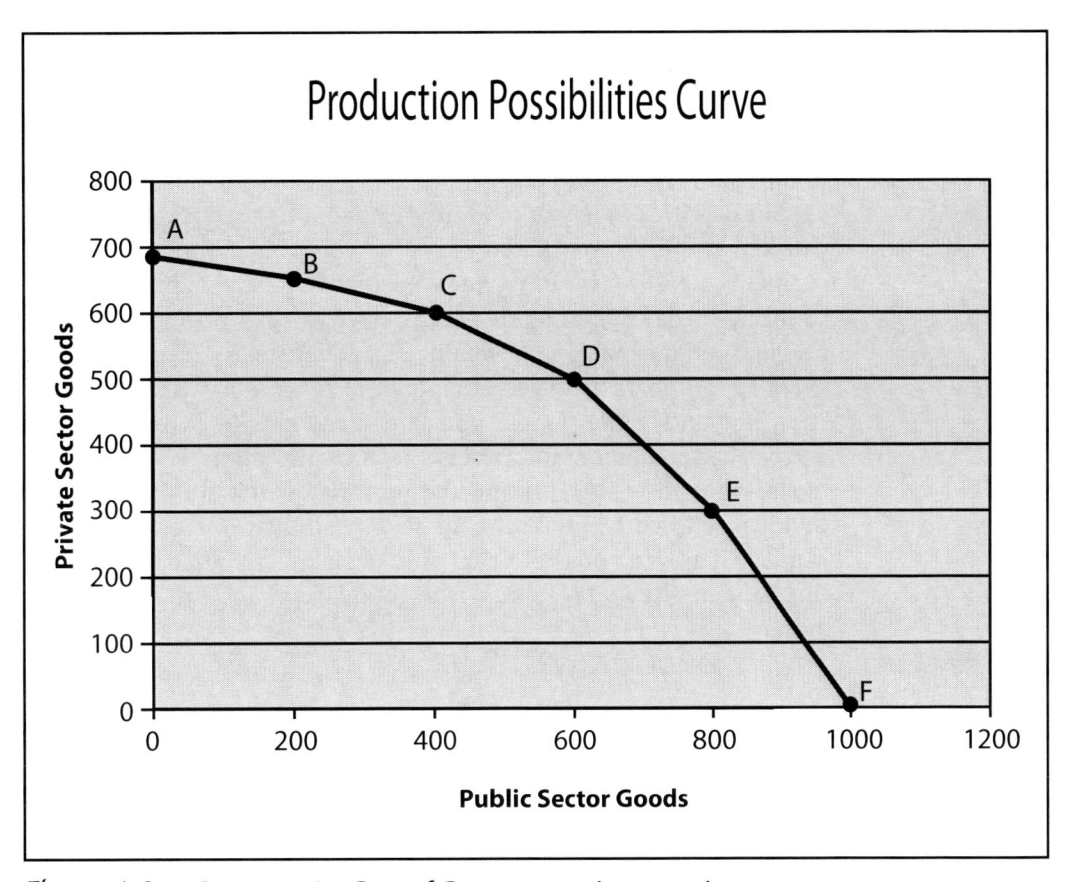

Figure 4.3 • Opportunity Cost of Government Intervention
Every time the government uses resources to enforce regulations, subsidize the production of a merit good, or provide a public good, it takes resources that could have been used to produce private sector goods.

creased government involvement in a particular economic activity exceeds the opportunity cost of that increase, then we should increase government involvement in that industry. If not, we should decrease it.

While cost-benefit analysis can help us determine whether or not increased government intervention is worth it, the problem becomes: How do we calculate the benefit of increased government intervention? How do we calculate the value of increased military spending, more police protection, or more teachers? It is not exactly straightforward. We can easily calculate the cost of a government project; it is the market value of the private sector goods that are given up to provide more resources to the government. On the other hand, most publicly provided goods and services do not have a reliable market value because they either create externalities or a free-rider problem. Therefore, the value of individual units of these goods must be estimated. As a result, cost-benefit analysis can only take us so far in determining the optimal amount of government involvement.

Ballot Box Economics. In reality, the political process, not cost-benefit analysis, makes decisions about the level of government involvement in different industries. In this sense, the value or price of a public good or service is how many votes it commands. High prices signal business to allocate more resources to that good, and lots of votes signal politicians to allocate resources to a particular public good or service.

School and city bond elections are examples of times when the government asks the public directly if they should increase government spending or not. More often than not, these bonds pass. Unfortunately, bonds only represent a small *frac*tion of government spending. In most cases, the link between votes and government spending decisions is much less direct.

While citizens have the ability to kick out politicians who spend recklessly, they can only do this at particular election cycles. We choose the general direction of government spending by our choice of representatives, but we have very little control over day-to-day spending decisions. As a result, voting is a pretty poor substitute for the market mechanism. Even if the government directly asked the public about every spending decision, the democratic process may result in a suboptimal solution. If 51 percent of the people voted in favor of a new highway and 49 percent voted against it, the democratic process tells us the highway would be built. The majority would be made better off and the minority worse off, but by how much? If each individual who voted yes will benefit only slightly and each who voted no will be devastated, it is very possible that this decision may decrease total utility. The market mechanism allows us to view the intensity of individual demands while the voting system does not.

III. PUBLIC FINANCE

Government Revenue: Taxation

It is clear that we pay for government spending in the form of taxes, but we have seen that what is not as clear is the opportunity cost of government spending. Every resource spent on goods and services for the public sectors means less output for the private sector. We do not directly hand over these resources to the government, but by transferring income to the government (taxes) we transfer the ability to buy these resources. Ultimately, the goal of taxation is to transfer the ownership of some resources to the government.

Income Taxes. The most well known tax in the United States is the personal income tax. Governments receive taxes from a variety of tax bases; each taxed at a specific tax rate. As far as the personal income tax is concerned, for example, all income after certain deductions and exemptions are removed is taxable. The tax base would then be the sum of every individual's taxable income. The tax rate is simply the proportion of the tax base that must be paid to the government. Figure 4.4 gives the tax rate schedules for both single and married tax filers in 2009.

The tax brackets so often referred to when discussing personal income tax actually refer to marginal tax rates, not the percentage of one's income due to the government (average tax rate). Indeed, if a person is in the 28 percent tax bracket this does not mean he owes the government 28 percent of his taxable income. What it means he owes the government 28 percent of every dollar he earns within the 28 percent bracket. Average tax rate is defined as total taxes due divided by total taxable income. While marginal tax rate changes are not continuous (there are large jumps at certain income levels), average tax rates increase with every dollar earned; this is what it means to have a progressive tax. In a progressive tax system, the marginal rate increases in set intervals as the income increases. For instance, you may pay 5 percent on your first $10,000, 10 percent on the next, and 15 percent on the third $10,000 you earn.

This tax accounts for just over 40 percent of federal tax receipts. There exists much controversy about the redistributive nature of the personal income tax system. Some people believe a flat (or proportional) tax where everyone pays the same percentage of their income in tax would be fairer. While a progressive tax system should redistribute income in theory, about 85 percent of taxpaying residents pay roughly the same percentage of their income in taxes so there is not much redistribution going on, except at the extreme ends of the tax schedules.

Capital Gains Taxes. Capital gains, the difference between what you paid for an asset and what you sold it for, are taxed separately from other forms of income. Unfortunately for asset holders, the government taxes nominal capital gains, not real capital gains. For example, if you bought a piece of land in 1950 and sold it today, you would probably sell it for more than you paid for it. But how much of that increase is from actual appreciation of the asset and how much is due to inflation, a general rise in prices over time? The government adjusts the tax brackets of the personal income tax system for inflation every year, but makes no attempt to adjust taxable capital gains for inflation. Such a policy discourages investments in general, and in particular discourages investors from holding long-term assets, reducing future growth.

The Corporate Income Tax. People who hold stock in companies must pay taxes on income received in the form of dividends or gains from selling their stock. However, corporate profits are already taxed before they are ever shared with stockholders or reinvested back into the company by the corporate income tax. Congress has tried to reduce the effect of this double taxation by lowering the tax rate on dividend income below that of other forms of income. While corporations are legal persons, it is people who end up paying for the corporate income tax. There are many theories explaining who the bears the incidence of this tax. It is possible that it is paid for by consumers in the form of higher prices, stockholders by receiving lower dividends, or by employees who must work harder for lower wages. Regardless, the nature of corporations allows them to shift the burden of tax to others.

Taxable Income		Marginal Tax Rate
Single	Married	
$0 – $8,350	$0 – $16,700	10%
$8,350 – $33,950	$16,700 – $67,900	15%
$33,950 – $82,250	$67,900 – $137,050	25%
$82,250 – $171,550	$137,050 – $208,850	28%
$171,550 – $372,950	$208,850 – $372,950	33%
$372,950 and up	$372,950 and up	35%

Source: IRS 2009 Tax Table

Figure 4.4 • **Tax Schedules**
The federal income tax is a progressive tax since the marginal tax rate rises as income rises. An individual only pays the marginal tax rate on the income earned in that bracket.

Payroll Taxes. Payroll taxes come in a close second to income taxes when it comes to providing money for the government. Payroll tax receipts mainly come in the form of contributions to the social security program and Medicare. Contributions to these programs are ostensibly split fifty-fifty between employee and employer, but at least part of the employer's contribution comes from lower wages. Contributions to the unemployment insurance system are also taken from one's pay. Many states include a tax above the federal level to support its unemployment insurance system. An increasing workforce and extensions of the social security program have made payroll taxes an increasingly important component of federal finance.

Excise Taxes. Excise taxes are taxes on the purchase of a certain subset of goods. Gasoline, alcohol, and cigarettes are all covered by federal excise taxes. While the federal government clearly has no problem levying taxes on the purchase of individual products, there is currently no federal sales tax.

State and Local Government Revenues. States, on the other hand, get nearly half of their revenue from sales and excise taxes. Nearly every state has a sales tax with notable exceptions being Oregon, New Hampshire, and Alaska. Most states also have personal income taxes in addition to the federal income tax; notable exceptions here include Florida and Texas. Income tax receipts account for about one third of state revenues. Payments from the federal government also make a large part of state revenues and many states would run significant budget deficits without federal grants. In fact, much of the gigantic federal budget deficit can be attributed to states overspending and asking for federal grants. Even smaller than states are local governments like counties, municipalities, and school districts. Local governments receive nearly three fourths of their revenue from property taxes; most of the rest comes from sales taxes.

Growth of the Government

Federal Growth. Prior to the 1930s, there was very little government intervention in the economy. The federal government offered a few public services like national defense, the court system, and the postal service, but for the most part allowed the market to decide how to coordinate economic activity. The Great Depression changed everything. The government expanded its limited workplace protections and spawned massive social welfare and public works projects. In the second half of the twentieth century, the government became increasingly involved with stabilizing the business cycle and safeguarding public health, as well as the environment, from unchecked economic growth. The result of this government growth can be seen in figure 4.5. Over the past one hundred years, federal spending has increased in real terms from $650 million to about $4 trillion per year.

State and Local Growth. State and local government spending took a very different pattern from federal spending. Prior to the Great Depression, almost all government spending came at the state and local level. It was thought that local governments knew how best to spend the tax revenues of their populations. The coming of World War II required more federal organization and caused a precipitous drop in local government spending. In the 1960s state and local government purchases overtook federal purchases again, and continued to rise. Today, state and local governments still spend more on output and resources than the federal government, including employing more than five times as many workers.

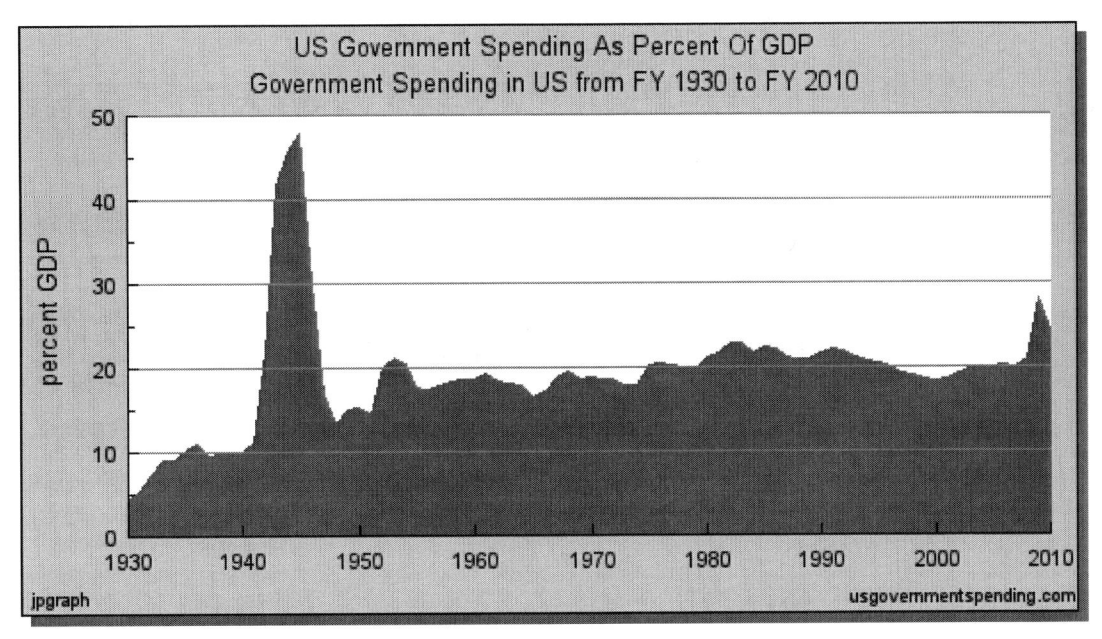

Figure 4.5 • Opportunity Cost of Government Intervention

Government Spending

Direct Expenditures. As mentioned before, the percentage of output accounted for by the government changes over time. During World War II, government purchases accounted for 40 percent of total output, but this share declined after the war ended. It declined further after the conclusion of the Korean War and has stayed relatively constant since then. How do we reconcile this decline in the share of GDP taken up by the government with our understanding that the government has in fact grown steadily throughout the past century? Even though the absolute size of government purchases is growing, the private sector (consumption, investment, and net exports) is growing even faster. As a result, the government's share of the total falls.

Income Transfers. The second reason we do not see government dwarfing the other sectors of the economy is that GDP or output only counts government spending which goes to the purchase of goods and services. Much of the money spent by the government is just handed to people without any goods or services received in exchange. We call this transaction a transfer payment. If we were to include transfer payments as a part of government purchases, its relative size would be much larger and its growth much more startling. In fact, most of the growth in government spending since World War II has come in the form of transfer payments, not the purchase of goods and services.

Types of Expenditures. The federal government and local governments clearly spend their money on different things. As illustrated in the pie chart in figure 4.6, most federal spending goes to four items: health care, national defense, transfer payments (mostly in the form of social security), and interest on the national debt. At the more local levels, education takes up a larger *frac*tion of spending (although most of this money comes from the federal government). States focus their educational spending on colleges and universities, while local governments (including school boards) focus on elementary

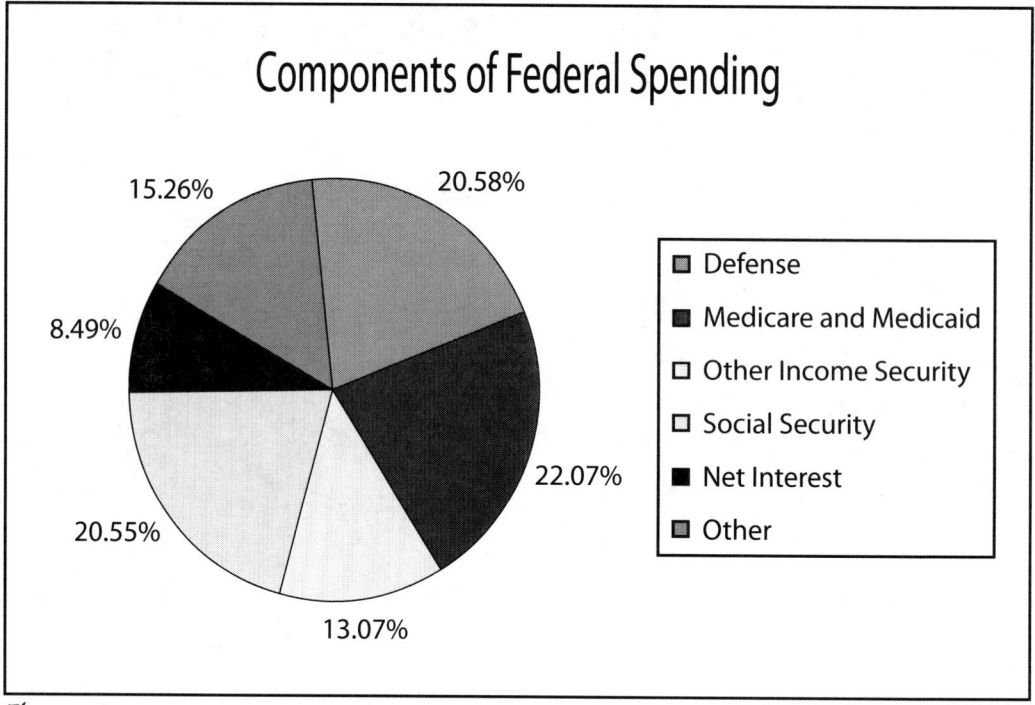

Figure 4.6 • Components of Federal Spending 2008
The vast majority of federal spending goes toward only four components: national defense, health care, income security, and interest on the national debt.
Source: Congressional Budget Office Historical Budget Data

and secondary education. At the state level, welfare and the prison systems are taking up a larger share of spending over time, while smaller local governments are increasing spending on sewage and sanitation.

CHAPTER 4 SUMMARY

- The government attempts to keep the economy running smoothly by **providing the legal structure, promoting competition, redistributing income,** and **ensuring economic stability.**
- A **public good** would never be sold by a private company because of the free-rider problem. If the government wants the people to have this good, it will have to provide it itself.
- A good with a **negative externality** is overproduced since the buyers and/or sellers do not realize the true costs of the good.
- A good with a **positive externality** is underproduced since the buyers and/or sellers do not feel all of the benefits of the good.
- **Government failure** occurs when the cost of government action exceeds the benefit of the action.
- The government receives its revenue through **taxation.**
- Most government **expenditures** go to four items: income security, defense, health care, and interest on the national debt.

CHAPTER 4 Exercises

Name _____

1) Which of the following is NOT a way the United States government redistributes income?
   A) transfers to qualifying individuals
   B) national lotteries
   C) progressive tax system
   D) intervening in particular markets

1) _____

2) What are two characteristics all public goods have in common?
   A) rivalry and excludability
   B) nonrivalry and excludability
   C) rivalry and nonexcludability
   D) nonrivalry and nonexcludability

2) _____

3) Why does the market fail with products that have externalities?
   A) some of the costs or benefits spill over to a third party
   B) nobody wants to buy these products
   C) nobody wants to sell these products
   D) the government takes over their production

3) _____

4) Which of the following is an example of a product with a negative externality in consumption?
   A) books
   B) coffee
   C) loud music
   D) shoes

4) _____

5) Which of the following is NOT a way the government can increase the consumption of a good with a positive externality?
   A) require it by law
   B) subsidize the consumer
   C) subsidize the producer
   D) A, B, & C are all legitimate ways of increasing consumption

5) _____

6) What is the opportunity cost of increased government activity?
   A) higher taxes
   B) private sector goods that could been produced with resources used by government
   C) higher national debt
   D) higher unemployment

6) _____

7) In 2009, workers in the United States paid a social security tax equal to 6.2 percent of all wages earned until a cap of $106,800 was reached. After that, the tax rate was 0 percent. What kind of tax is the social security tax?
   A) regressive
   B) progressive
   C) flat
   D) proportional

7) _____

63

8) Which of the following is NOT a major expenditure component of the federal government?
   A) national defense
   B) health care
   C) interest on the national debt
   D) space exploration

8) _____

9) Why does a tax on a product that has a negative externality help get the market closer to the social optimum? How does the tax change the behavior of the consumer or producer?

10) When is more government involvement in a particular market justified?

Article Review 1

Name _____

Choose any one of the articles from Chapters 1–4. Use the space provided below to summarize the article. Then, answer the questions at the end of the article on the back of this page.

1.

2.

3.

Unit 1 Review

Name _____

Use this review to prepare for Exam 1. You can view the answers in the "unit review answers" section in the back of the text, but try to complete it on your own first.

1) If you have a choice between studying, going to the mall, and sleeping what is the opportunity cost of deciding to study?
   A) the value of going to the mall
   B) the value of sleeping
   C) the value of going to the mall and sleeping
   D) there is not enough information to answer the question

   1) _____

2) Which of the following is a microeconomic issue?
   A) the national unemployment rate
   B) one firm's decision about how to spend on advertising
   C) inflation
   D) the national savings rate

   2) _____

3) Which of the following is NOT an example of capital?
   A) stocks   C) tools
   B) machinery   D) factories

   3) _____

4) Which of the following is NOT a reason why a country might produce inside its production possibilities frontier?
   A) bureaucracy (red tape)   C) laziness
   B) it is producing efficiently D) unemployment

   4) _____

5) Which of the following is a characteristic of the market system?
   A) the government decides what is to be produced
   B) buyers and sellers determine prices in markets
   C) there are no prices
   D) goods are distributed according to need

   5) _____

6) How is the 'how to produce' question answered in the United States?
   A) the government tells businesses how to produce
   B) unions tell businesses how to produce
   C) businesses produce using the fewest resources possible
   D) businesses produce in the that provides the most jobs for Americans

   6) _____

7) What process did Adam Smith propose to achieve maximum social happiness?
   A) government control of all resources
   B) heavy taxation and redistribution
   C) Communism
   D) the invisible hand

   7) _____

8) Which of the following is a role of the government in the market system?
   A) determining prices   C) fixing market failures
   B) allocating output   D) all of the above

   8) _____

9) Government failure occurs when
   A) the cost of government action exceeds the benefit.
   B) government action has any cost.
   C) the government does not act when it should.
   D) government action gets society closer to allocative efficiency.

10) Law of Demand states that as the price of a product falls
    A) quantity demanded rises.
    B) quantity demanded falls.
    C) demand rises.
    D) demand falls.

11) Which of the following is a determinant of demand?
    A) expectations
    B) technology
    C) price of inputs
    D) none of the above

12) What would happen to the demand curve for gasoline if everyone expected the price of gasoline to rise in the near future?
    A) nothing
    B) shift to the left
    C) shift upward
    D) shift to the right

13) Suppose a farmer could grow corn or wheat on his land. What would happen to the supply curve for corn if the market price of wheat fell dramatically?
    A) shift to the left
    B) nothing
    C) shift downward
    D) shift to the right

14) When the government imposes a price ceiling, what kind of problem occurs?
    A) market failure
    B) surplus
    C) shortage
    D) scarcity

15) What happens to equilibrium price and quantity when demand increases and supply remains unchanged?
    A) price and quantity both fall
    B) price falls, quantity rises
    C) price and quantity both rise
    D) price rises; quantity falls

16) What are two characteristics all public goods have in common?
    A) rivalry and excludability
    B) nonrivalry and nonexcludability
    C) nonrivalry and excludability
    D) rivalry and nonexcludability

17) Why does the market fail with products that have externalities?
    A) nobody wants to buy these products
    B) the government takes over their production
    C) nobody wants to sell these products
    D) some of the costs or benefits spillover to a third party

18) Which of the following is an example of product with a positive externality in consumption?
    A) cheese
    B) education
    C) shoes
    D) loud music

19) What is the opportunity cost of increased government activity?
    A) higher unemployment
    B) lost private sector goods that could been produced with resources used by government
    C) higher taxes
    D) higher national debt

Name _____

20) In 2009, one worker in the country of Xanthia paid $10,000 in taxes on his salary of $200,000. Another paid $5,000 on his salary of $100,000. What type of income tax does Xanthia employ?
A) fair
B) progressive
C) regressive
D) proportional

20) _____

21) What does it mean for a country to pursue efficiency? What about equity?

22) Why is the system of private property so important for the functioning of a market economy? What would happen if someone could just take your property away at any time?

23) Answer the question given the demand and supply schedules.

Price	Quantity demanded (bushels of wheat)	Price	Quantity supplied (bushels of wheat)
$4.20	125,000	$4.20	230,000
4.00	150,000	4.00	220,000
3.80	175,000	3.80	210,000
3.60	200,000	3.60	200,000
3.40	225,000	3.40	190,000
3.20	250,000	3.20	180,000
3.00	275,000	3.00	170,000

If the Federal government decided to support the price of wheat at $4.20 per bushel (price floor), would there be a surplus or shortage? How much it would be?

24) Draw what would happen to equilibrium if both supply and demand shifted to the left at the same time. What happens to equilibrium quantity and price?

25) When is more government involvement in a particular market justified?

Exam 1 Formula Sheet

Name _____

Chapter 2

Opportunity Cost:
Must give up X units of good 1 to get Y units of good 2, then
Opportunity Cost of 1 unit of good 1 = Y/X units of good 2
Opportunity Cost of 1 unit of good 2 = X/Y units of good 2

Chapter 3

Size of Surplus = $Q_s - Q_d$
Size of Shortage = $Q_d - Q_s$

Effect of change in demand on equilibrium:
Increase in Demand — Increase in Equilibrium Quantity, Increase in Equilibrium Price
Decreae in Demand — Decrease in Equiligrium Quantity, Decrease in Equilibrium Price

Effect of change in supply on equilibrium:
Increase in Supply — Increase in Equilibrium Quantity, Decrease in Equilibrium Price
Decreae in Supply — Decrease in Equiligrium Quantity, Increase in Equilibrium Price

Chapter 4

$$Average\ Tax\ Rate = \frac{Total\ Taxes\ Paid}{Taxable\ Income}$$

Chapter 5

Measuring the Economy

I. GROSS DOMESTIC PRODUCT

GDP Defined

Fundamental to the understanding of fluctuations of our economy is the need to have some number or statistic to tell us about the state of the economy as a whole. Economists use these numbers, called national income accounts, to test the effectiveness of different economic policies. The most commonly used and reported national income statistic is the gross domestic product, or GDP. The GDP is the total value of a nation's annual output produced by factors of production located within the country's borders. GDP uses dollar value to compare production from year to year.

It may not be immediately clear whether a country was more productive in a year when it produced three hundred cars and two hundred computers or in another year when it produced two hundred cars and three hundred computers. Once you attach dollar values to the different types of production, however, the answer reveals itself. If cars are worth $10,000 each and computers are worth $2,000 then the country produced $6,400,000 worth of output in the first year and $4,600,000 worth in the second year; total output or GDP was higher in the first year.

We exclude the sale of intermediate goods from the calculation of GDP since the final sale price already includes the value of these goods. The same good can be a final good or an intermediate good depending on how it is used. A tire purchased by Ford to put on a new truck is an intermediate good since the value of the tire will be included in the market price of the truck. A replacement tire purchased by a consumer is a final good since that will be its final use. In addition, GDP only includes the value of goods and services sold in the market. As we will discuss in more detail later, goods and services produced in the home or in the underground economy do not count toward the GDP. Both cars produced by an American-owned factory in Detroit and those produced by a Japanese company in Ohio count toward GDP since the production is occurring within US borders. The production of a Nike plant in Korea, however, counts towards Korea's GDP not the US's.

The GDP is a flow statistic; it represents the increase in total production from one year to the next just like a person's salary represents the additional income they received that year. Contrast this notion with a stock statistic like total wealth, which has been accumulated and saved over several years. GDP is not the total wealth of a nation, but its output per year. Economists sometimes use quarterly GDP, the GDP for a three-month period, to study more short-term fluctuations. A recession, for example, is defined as a drop in GDP for two consecutive quarters.

Exclusions from GDP

Calculation of the GDP explicitly excludes intermediate goods (goods entirely used up in the production of a final good) in order to avoid double counting. For example, wheat used to make bread is not sold on the market but instead is used up to make bread that is a final good. This leads us to a discussion of value added. Each stage of production leads to value being added to a product (like oil going from its raw state to refined gasoline). Each member of the production chain must compensate each previous member for his value added; meaning the steps prior to retail sale would be double counted if we did not exclude them from the calculation of the GDP.

Some transactions in the economy do not involve the transaction of goods or services and these transactions should not be included in GDP because they have nothing to do with the generation of final goods. Financial transactions make up the bulk of these so-called nonproduction transactions. One type of financial transaction we have already discussed consists of government transfer payments. We know that transfer payments are the form of government spending that produce no output, so it should not be surprising that it needs to be excluded from GDP calculation. Similar to government transfer payments are private transfer payments, monetary gifts from one individual to another. The reason both government and private transfers need to be excluded from GDP is that the money would be double counted once the recipient of the transfer spent the money on some final good. Another type of financial transaction is a stock market transaction. The buying and selling of stock is simply a paper transaction and does not involve payment for any current production. If you hire a stockbroker to buy and sell stock for you, then his salary would be part of GDP but the stocks he bought would not.

Secondhand sales do not involve the transaction of current production and as such are not include in GDP. If you sold your car to someone else, this transaction would not be included in GDP regardless of whether you bought the car ten years ago or ten minutes ago; it would only count when you bought it from the dealer. The same principle applies to real estate. New homes count toward GDP, but the resales of existing homes do not.

Limitations of GDP

Household production. To be sure, GDP is a useful and broad measure of economic health but economists that use it must recognize its limitations. One limitation of GDP is the exclusion of nonmarket activities. Since GDP only attempts to calculate the market value of all final goods and services, activities like cleaning your own house or mowing your own lawn do not count.

Underground economy. Another area of limitation is the exclusion of underground, or unreported, economic activity. The underground economy consists both of legal activities that remain hidden from the IRS and illicit activities like prostitution, gambling, and the drug trade. The extent of these activities is by its very nature impossible to calculate and is not included in GDP. The size (as a percentage of GDP) of the underground economy differs from country to country, but it is estimated that underground transactions in the US totaled $1 trillion in 2005 alone. It is not just criminals that are forced into the underground economy; many hard-working people are forced into underground forms of financial activity due to strict regulations and high fees.

Quality improvements. A $150 calculator purchased today has much greater capability than a similarly priced calculator purchased forty years ago once you adjust for inflation, but GDP does not reflect the benefits this quality improvement creates since it is only a quantitative measure. According to GDP, a $150 calculator is always the same regardless of quality. GDP further understates social welfare by ignoring the utility of leisure time. Reductions in both the workweek and the shortening of the work year through paid vacations and holidays have certainly increased overall well-being in recent years, but national income accounting cannot account for increases in this "psychic income."

Noneconomic measures of well-being. GDP cannot account for harm done to social welfare by the inevitable damage done to the environment by increased production. Any complete measure of well-being must include a factor for environmental health, but GDP does not, resulting in an overstating of the standard of living. You cannot put a price tag on human life so any measure of standard of living that does not take health or life expectancy into account will not be fully accurate. While GDP and life expectancy generally move in the same direction there is nothing that says they have to. The United States, for example, has a much higher infant mortality rate than countries with similar GDPs. GDP and even per capita GDP (GDP divided by population) make no attempt to quantify the affect that political oppression or social injustice has on standard of living. If two countries have the same per capita GDP but one has a powerful dictator that keeps all the wealth to himself and the other has equally distributed wealth, where would you rather live?

International Comparisons

Since GDP is a monetary measure, each country measures GDP in its own local currency. In order to make comparisons, then, we need to convert foreign GDPs into a single reference currency, usually dollars. The simplest and most direct way to achieve this is by using the exchange rate between the dollar and the foreign currency. Using exchange rates as the only tool to convert GDP from foreign currency to US currency directly may not be accurate since some products (like most services) must be purchased in the local market. In a country with a low wage level, these services may cost much less than they do in the United States, leading to a higher purchasing power than the exchange rate would indicate. While it may be impossible to imagine anyone living on the equivalent of $3,000 or $4,000 a year, when you account for the fact that many goods and services in that country are much cheaper than they are in the United States, it is clear that the true purchasing power of that income is much higher than it would be here. As a result, economists use both per capita GDP based on exchange rates and GDP based on purchasing power parity (adjusting exchange rates for differences in cost of living) to compare output and economic performance across countries. Not surprising, the United States ranks number one among all countries in GDP.

Since GDP measures only the total output of a country, it is a pretty poor measure of standard of living. As figure 5.1 shows, most of the countries with the highest GDPs have relatively large populations; it is easy to produce more when you have more resources. The size of the pie is only one part of understanding the material well-being of a country's citizens; we also need to know how many slices that pie is getting cut into. In other words, we need to account for population differences. Per capita GDP does this. As you can see in figure 5.2, many of the nations with the highest per capita GDPs

Ranking	Country	Real GDP (in billions)
1	United States	$14,440
2	China	$7,992
3	Japan	$4,340
4	India	$3,304
5	Germany	$2,925
6	Russia	$2,271
7	United Kingdom	$2,236
8	France	$2,133
9	Brazil	$1,998
10	Italy	$1,827

Source: CIA World Factbook (2008)

Figure 5.1 • GDP Rankings
Since GDP measures total output, most of the countries with the highest GDPs have very large populations.

Ranking	Country	GDP per capita
1	Liechtenstein	$118,000
2	Qatar	$111,000
3	Luxembourg	$81,200
4	Bermuda	$69,900
5	Norway	$59,500
6	Kuwait	$57,500
7	Jersey	$57,000
8	Singapore	$51,600
9	Brunei	$51,300
10	United States	$47,500

Source: CIA World Factbook (2008)

Figure 5.2 • GDP per capita Rankings
Since GDP per capita is a function of output and population, many of the nations on the top of the GDP per capita list are small dependencies and microstates.

have small populations. Per capita GDP takes total GDP and divides it by population. This gives us the size of the average slice of the pie if we were to split it equally. Of course, income distribution is not equal and per capita GDP tells us very little about how GDP is split up. Still, it is useful in comparing the relative standards of living in other countries. Due to the problem of distribution and the exclusion of many aspects of well-being from per capita GDP, you may be tempted to discard it altogether. The fact is, virtually every other measure of well-being—life expectancy, literacy rate, infant mortality, and access to education (to name a few)—is correlated with per capita GDP. While per capita GDP itself does not tell you how the people are doing, countries with high per capita GDPs tend to have a higher standard of living.

II. CALCULATING GDP

The circular flow model we examined in Chapter 3 helps explains why production (what GDP measures) and income (what we use to determine standard of living) are essentially the same the same thing. In the circular flow, households buy the goods and services businesses produce in the goods market. The value of these goods (GDP) is the total amount of money households spend on them. Therefore, GDP and total expenditure are equivalent.

Consumption

Expenditure can be split into four areas: consumption (purchases by households), investment (purchases by businesses), government purchases, and net exports. Not surprisingly, a major portion of national spending comes from household consumption. In national accounting this spending is called personal consumption expenditures. These expenditures, identified by the letter C in accounting formulas, include all the dollars spent by households on durable goods, nondurablegoods, and services. Figure 5.3 shows that services have become an increasingly important part of personal consumption over time.

Investment

The second component of GDP is gross private investment. This component includes expenditures on physical capital like machinery and tools, all construction, and changes in inventory. When it comes to GDP, investment includes all construction both commercial and residential. It makes sense that commercial construction would be included since it is usually rented or leased, but why include housing when it is usually viewed as consumption? The fact is that even if you own your home it could be rented out to bring in income, so it counts as investment. Inventory is the stock of goods businesses keep in the warehouse; think of it as "unconsumed" output.

To an economist, any output that is not consumed counts as a capital investment and is included in gross private investment. Clearly inventories can decrease or increase depending on the outlook of the market and the individual choices of firms. An increase in inventories in a given year means there was output produced by businesses that was not purchased and consumed. Unless you add this inventory increase to GDP,

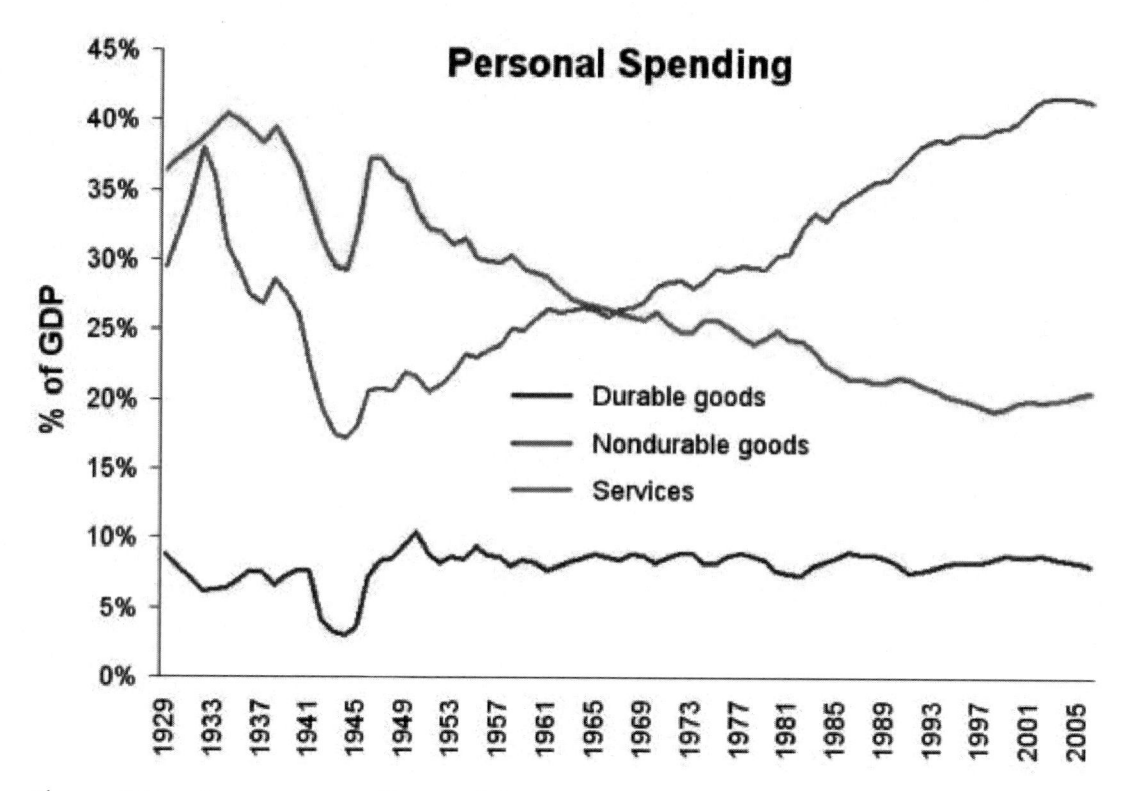

Figure 5.3 • **Components of Personal Consumption**
While durable good spending has been fairly consistent since the end of World War II, a major shift has occurred in the consumption patterns of Americans regarding nondurable goods and services.

the measure will underestimate the total value of output that year. The opposite is true for an inventory decrease. If inventories decrease, this means that some output produced in a previous year has been sold and consumed this year. Unless you subtract this decrease in inventories, or negative investment, from GDP the measure will overestimate total output for the year.

Government Purchases

The third component of GDP is government expenditures and includes government spending both on consumption and investment goods. Government expenditures include all spending on final goods (like computers and tanks), as well as all spending on resources (land, labor, and capital). It does not include government transfers since these payments create no output. The letter G denotes government expenditures in national income accounting.

Net Exports

Since we do not live in a closed economy, international transactions make up a significant portion of annual expenditure. Consumers in other countries purchase some of

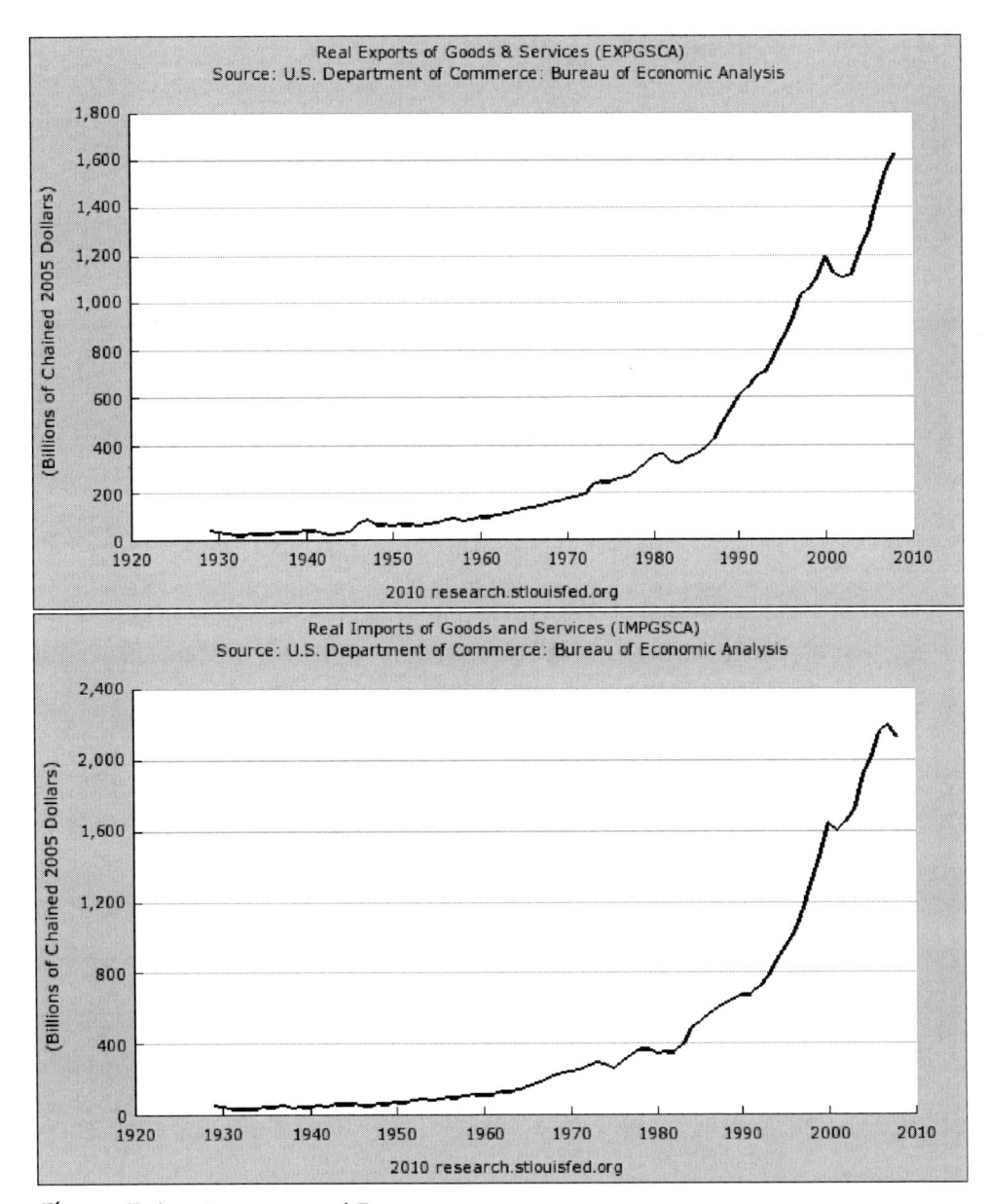

Figure 5.4 • Imports and Exports
Trade in the United States exploded in the late 1970s and early 1980s. The United States is the largest importer and exporter in the world.

the output produced by the US (exports) and these expenditures must be accounted for in order to accurately measure output. Likewise, some the spending that we included in the consumption and investment items was actually on goods produced in other countries (imports) and we need subtract this value so as to not overstate national output. In other words, we need to add net exports, the value of total exports minus total imports, to GDP. Figure 5.4 illustrates how the total amount of money spent on imports and exports (adjusted for price changes) has risen sharply in the United States since the 1970s. Since the imports exceed exports in the United States, its net exports are negative.

Putting it All Together

Putting all the components together, we accurately measure the production of a nation based on the money spent on these different types of expenditures. In 2009, the GDP of the US based in this approach was about fourteen trillion dollars.

$$GDP = C + I + G + X_n$$

Real GDP vs. Nominal GDP

We know that GDP is denominated in dollars in order to turn all the different types of production into a single value that we can compare year to year and across countries. But using a nominal value creates a problem when trying to compare GDP from year to year. What happens when inflation (a general increase in prices) or deflation (a general decline in prices) changes the value of money itself?

For instance, without adjusting for this problem there is no way to tell whether a country that went from a GDP of $100 billion to a GDP of $105 billion experienced a 5 percent increase in output and no inflation, a 5 percent increase in prices and no increase in output, or some combination in between. Since it is the quantity of output and not the price that affects the standard of living in a society, we need some way to separate these two effects. The solution then is to turn nominal GDP (the actual dollar value of production in a given year) into real GDP (the dollar value of production if prices were the same as they were in some reference year) by deflating GDP when prices rise and inflating it when prices fall.

$$Nominal\ GDP = Current\ Output \times Current\ Prices$$
$$Real\ GDP = Current\ Output \times Base\ Year\ Prices$$

Calculating real GDP requires separating expenditure data into two parts: quantity and price. Figure 5.5 contains such data for a fictional country. Remember GDP equals total expenditure on consumption, investment, government expenditures, and net exports in a year. For simplicity, figure 5.5 assumes exports equal imports so that net exports equal zero. In the first year the country sold ten DVDs, three hammers, and one cell phone for a government worker. The DVDs cost $20 each, the hammers cost $30, and the phone cost $60. What is the nominal GDP of the country?

$$(10 \times \$20) + (3 \times \$30) + (1 \times \$60) = \$350$$

What is the real GDP of the country using this year's prices as the base? It's exactly the same since the base year prices and the current prices are the same.

Now let's calculate the GDP for a year that isn't the base year. In the current year the country sold four DVDs, two hammers, and six cell phones. Between the base year and the current year, the prices of DVDs have not changed but the prices of hammers and cell phones have doubled from $30 and $60 to $60 and $120. Now what is the nominal GDP? Again, you multiply the quantity by the current price and add.

$$(4 \times \$20) + (2 \times \$60) + (6 \times \$120) = \$920$$

Clearly, nominal GDP has increased greatly between the base year and the current year, but how much of this increase is due to the increase in prices? This is exactly what

Base Year				
Product	GDP Component	Output	Price	Value
DVD	Consumption	10	$20	$200
Hammer	Investment	3	$30	$ 90
Cell Phone	Government	1	$60	$ 60
Nominal GDP				$350

Current Year				
Product	GDP Component	Output	Price	Value
DVD	Consumption	4	$20	$ 80
Hammer	Investment	2	$60	$120
Cell Phone	Government	6	$120	$720
Nominal GDP				$920

Real GDP in Current Year				
Product	GDP Component	Output	Price	Value
DVD	Consumption	4	$20	$ 80
Hammer	Investment	2	~~$60~~ $30	$ 60
Cell Phone	Government	6	~~$120~~ $60	$360
Nominal GDP				$500

Figure 5.5 • Real GDP Example
The real GDP in the base year is the same as the nominal GDP. To determine the real GDP in any other year simply replace the current price with the price from the base year for each product.

real GDP helps us discover. To find the real GDP in the current year you multiply the current quantities by the base year prices.

$$Real\ GDP = (4 \times \$20) + (2 \times \$30) + (6 \times \$60) = \$500$$

As you can see, real GDP increased, but not nearly as much as nominal GDP did.

By comparing the real GDP for different periods (years or quarters) we can determine the GDP growth rate. To calculate any growth rate or percentage change you subtract the old value of the figure from the current value, divide it by the old value and multiply by one hundered.

$$\frac{(New\ Value - Old\ Value)}{Old\ Value} \times 100 = Percentage\ Change$$

In our example, for instance, the GDP growth rate from the base year and the current year was:

$$\frac{(500 - 350)}{350} \times 100 = 42.86\%.$$

III. RELATIONSHIP BETWEEN OUTPUT AND INCOME

Instead of adding up all of the things we spend money on, we can calculate GDP by measuring how much money each of the different factors of production earns. Based on our discussion of the circular flow model, we know the economy consists of two equal and opposite flows, an income flow and an output flow. Income flows into households in the form of rents, wages, interest, and profits; and payment for output flows into businesses in the form of consumption. GDP, then, can either be described as the total value of output produced by society, or the total income earned from this production. Measuring the total income received by resource suppliers from the sale of this output is referred to as the income approach to GDP. Every dollar spent on production is received by someone as income. Therefore, income must equal expenditure and, by extension, GDP.

While GDP is useful for understanding the overall size and performance of the economy, what we really want to know is how much income the people have to make consumption decisions with. Finding this number requires making several adjustments to the GDP figure.

Net Domestic Product

The investment component of GDP includes the word gross to indicate that it encompasses all investment goods and makes no attempt to separate goods meant to replace old and used up capital and those that are adding to the overall stock of capital in the economy. Net investment, on the other hand, only counts this new investment by subtracting depreciation (the amount of capital that has become obsolete this year) from gross investment.

$$Net\ Investment = Gross\ Investment - Depreciation$$

Some of our output, then, is being used to replace this worn out capital and is not available for sale. We call GDP minus this depreciation allowance net domestic product, or NDP. The key difference between GDP and NDP is that GDP includes gross investment and NDP only includes net investment. Gross investment includes all investment goods while net investment only counts new investment meant to add to the capital stock. The capital stock, and our production possibilities, will only grow if net investment is positive.

National Income

Next, we need to adjust for the difference between net domestic product and national income. National income includes all income earned by Americans whether they supplied these resources for production here or abroad. NDP only counts output produced within the borders of the US and should not include income earned from the use of American resources abroad, but should include income earned from the use of foreign assets used for production here. The difference between income earned by US resources abroad and income earned by foreign resources in the US is called net foreign factor income. Since the US resources earned more abroad than foreign assets earned here, the US has a negative net foreign factor income. Adding this item to net national product gives us net national product, the total amount of income earned by US factors of production. The only step remaining in turning net national product into national income is the addition of the statistical discrepancy, a small mathematical adjustment that results from the differences in calculating total expenditure and total income.

Personal Income

Recently economists added a new item to national income that encompassed sales taxes, excise taxes, business property taxes, license fees, and import taxes. These indirect business taxes are part of the national income because they increased the price of goods (and therefore national expenditure on the same output), but are not part of personal income because they do not increase the amount of wages, rent, interest, or profits earned by anyone. In addition, all of the income received by corporations counts toward national income, but the corporation's shareholders do not receive some of that income. Some corporate profits have to be returned to the government in the form of taxes and some are kept by the firm for reinvestment. As a result, both corporate taxes and retained earnings are subtracted from national income to get personal income. Like corporate taxes and retained earnings, social security tax contributions represent income that is earned by individuals, but not received by them. This number, too, must be subtracted from national income to get personal income.

On the other hand there are a few numbers that need to be added to national income to get personal income. These numbers represent types of income that are received by individuals, but not earned by them. The majority of these types of income are a variety of transfers from the government: social security checks, unemployment insurance, and welfare checks.

Disposable Income

We have finally come to personal income, the amount of income actually received by individuals in a given year. However, people are not free to use all of this income, as some of it must be given to the government in the form of personal taxes. Subtracting total personal taxes from personal income leaves disposable income, the amount of money citizens have available to spend. Disposable income is about 70 percent of GDP; the rest has either been retained by businesses as a depreciation allowance or for reinvestment in the corporation, or taken by the government in the form of taxes. People can only do two things with disposable income, consume or save. By definition, any disposable income not spent on consumption is considered savings; it does not matter if was used to buy stocks, put in a bank, or stuffed in a mattress. Figure 5.6 details the various additions and subtractions that turn GDP into disposable income.

Gross Domestic Product (all numbers in billions $)	14242.1
Plus: Income receipts from the rest of the world	590.6
Less: Income payments to the rest of the world	469.1
Equals: **Gross National Product**	14363.7
Less: Depreciation	−1850.7
Equals: **Net National Product**	12512.9
Less: Statistical discrepancy	−163.2
Equals: **National Income**	12349.7
Less: Retained Earnings	−1358.9
Taxes on production and imports less subsidies	955.4
Contributions for government social insurance, domestic	974
Net interest and miscellaneous payments on assets	759.7
Business current transfer payments (net)	124.8
Current surplus of government enterprises	−6.3
Wage accruals less disbursements	0
Plus: Personal income receipts on assets	1763.1
Personal current transfer receipts	2137.5
Equals: **Personal Income**	12083.9
Less: Personal Income Taxes	811
Equals: **Disposable Income**	11272.9

Source: Bureau of Labor Statistics

Figure 5.6 • From GDP to Disposable Income (3rd Quarter 2009)
About 75 percent of GDP is returned to citizens in the form of disposable income. The rest gets taken by businesses for reinvesting or the government in the form of taxes.

CHAPTER 5 SUMMARY

- The most commonly used figure for measuring the economy is the **gross domestic product**.
- Intermediate goods, secondhand sales, and financial transactions are **excluded from GDP** because they do not represent new production.
- GDP consists of four expenditure components: **personal consumption, private investment, government purchases**, and **net exports**.
- **Nominal GDP** over time can be misleading since it can change as a result of price changes or output changes. Price changes have no effect on **real GDP**.
- **Net Domestic Product (NDP)** equals GDP minus depreciation.
- **National Income (NI)** equals NDP minus net foreign factor income and the statistical discrepancy.
- **Personal Income (PI)** equals NI minus retained earnings and business taxes plus personal transfers.
- **Disposable Income (DI)** equals PI minus personal income taxes.

CHAPTER 5 Exercises

Name _____

1) Which of the following would count toward US GDP?
    A) McDonald's Happy Meal sold in France
    B) chocolate imported from Germany
    C) wool purchased by a suit maker in California
    D) Toyota car made at a factory in Kentucky

1) _____

2) Which of the following would be counted toward GDP?
    A) babysitting your cousins
    B) buying stock in a company
    C) buying a new home
    D) buying a previously owned home

2) _____

3) Which of the following correctly identifies the four expenditure components of GDP?
    A) consumption, investment, government purchases, net exports
    B) durable goods, nondurable goods, services. savings
    C) consumption, saving, government spending, exports
    D) land, labor, capital, entrepreneurship

3) _____

4) Which of the following correctly identifies the treatment of exports and imports in GDP?
    A) subtract value of exports and imports
    B) add value of exports and imports
    C) add value of exports and subtract value of imports
    D) add value of imports and subtract value of exports

4) _____

5) If the nominal GDP in 2009 is $10 billion and the GDP deflator is 160, what is the real GDP?
    A) $16 billion
    B) $625 million
    C) $6.25 billion
    D) $1.6 trillion

5) _____

6) If the real GDP is $12 trillion in 2007 and $13 trillion in 2008, what was the growth rate between 2007 and 2008?
    A) 8.3%
    B) .083%
    C) 1%
    D) 100%

6) _____

7) What is the difference between gross domestic product and net domestic product?
    A) net domestic product includes value produced by US factors of production in other countries
    B) gross domestic product includes spending on replacing depreciated capital
    C) net domestic product includes only spending on durable goods
    D) gross domestic product includes government spending on transfer payments

7) _____

8) What is the difference between personal income and disposable income? 8) _____
   A) PI = DI + unemployment benefits
   B) PI = DI + social security benefits
   C) PI = DI - social security taxes
   D) PI = DI - personal income taxes

9) Describe the limitations that make GDP an imperfect measure of standard of living.

10) Is nominal GDP or real GDP a better measure of standard of living across time? Why?

Chapter 6

Unemployment

I. MEASURING UNEMPLOYMENT

The Labor Force

Another important measure for the health of the economy is the unemployment rate. If people are not working then we are not employing all of our resources and therefore are not producing efficiently. The unemployment rate is not the same as the percentage of the population that does not have a job. Certain segments of the population like children, retired people, and students are not looking for jobs so counting them as unemployed would overstate how far we are from efficient production.

The Bureau of Labor Statistics conducts a survey called the Current Population Survey to measure the labor force and unemployment. The CPS splits the population into several groups to determine the unemployment rate. First, everyone over sixteen and not in the military, in jail, or in a mental institution is classified as part of the working-age population. Even if they wanted to, it would be nearly impossible for someone in one of these groups to get a job so they aren't considered part of unemployment. Next, the working-age population is split between those in the labor force and those outside the labor force. People outside the labor force do not have a job, but aren't looking for one. This group mainly consists of full-time students, retired people, and homemakers.

Everyone in the labor force is either employed or unemployed. To count as employed, a person must have either worked at least one hour as a paid worker or fifteen hours as an unpaid family worker in the past week, or be temporarily absent from a steady job. Anyone in the labor force who does not meet these criteria counts as unemployed. It is not enough to not have a job; you need to also be available for work (be part of the working-age population), and have made an effort to find a job in the previous four weeks or be waiting to be recalled from a previous job (be part of the labor force).

The Labor Force Participation Rate

Another factor we can define when discussing the labor force is the labor force participation rate, or LFPR. The LFPR is defined as the proportion of the non-institutionalized (not in jail or a mental hospital) population that has a job or is looking for one. The present labor force participation is about 66 percent.

$$Labor\ Force\ Participation\ Rate = \frac{Labor\ Force}{Working\ Age\ Population}$$

Labor force participation has increased greatly over the past fifty years, primarily because of the increased presence of women in the labor force. About 75 percent of men and 60 percent of women currently participate in the work force compared to 83 percent and 35 percent in 1950.

The Unemployment Rate

Once you know the level of unemployment (the number of unemployed people), calculating the unemployment rate is a simple proposition. The unemployment rate is simply the percentage of the labor force that is unemployed. To calculate it, you divide the number of unemployed people by the labor force and multiply by one hundred.

$$Unemployment\ Rate = \frac{Number\ of\ Unemployed\ People}{Labor\ Force} \times 100$$

The unemployment rate as of November 2010 was 9.8 percent in the United States which is fairly high, but not alarmingly so. Figure 6.1 summarizes some of the important employment figures from the United States in 2008.

The unemployment rate continually fluctuates but has remained between 4 and 10 percent since World War II. Not surprisingly, the unemployment rate reached its peak during the Great Depression when approximately one-fourth of the labor force was without work. The recession of 2007–2009 drove the economy to double-digit unemployment for the first time since the early 1980s.

Discouraged Workers

One controversial element of determining the unemployment rate involves how to treat so-called discouraged workers. Discouraged workers are those that are physically able to work, but have stopped looking for a job because they do not believe there is any

		Amount	Percentage of Total
1	Population of United States	303,824,000	100%
2	Under 16 or Institutionalized	70,036,000	23.05%
3	Working-Age Population	1 − 2 = 233,788,000	76.95%
4	Out of Labor Force	79,501,000	26.17%
5	Labor Force	5 − 4 = 154,287,000	50.78%
6	Employed	145,362,000	47.84%
7	Unemployed	8,924,000	2.94%

Labor Force Participation Rate	5/3	65.99%
Unemployment Rate	7/5	5.78%

Source: Bureau of Labor Statistics

Figure 6.1 • **Employment Breakdown 2008**
At any one time, only about half of the total population, or two-thirds of the adult civilian population, is employed or looking for work.

work available for them. Economists and policymakers often disagree on whether to count these people as unemployed or not because it is unclear whether or not they are truly available for production.

Part-Time Workers

Notice that our definition of employment made no distinction between full-time workers and part-time workers; as long as you worked one hour for pay, you count as employed. Some people work part-time for economic reasons (the company cannot afford to hire them full-time) and some work part-time for noneconomic reasons (they are not available to work full-time). To the extent that people who are part-time workers for economic reasons are counted exactly the same as full-time workers, the unemployment rate may be understating the slack in the labor market. These people want to work full-time, but the company won't let them; they are underemployed or involuntary part-time workers. Voluntary part-time workers work part-time because they want to, so they do not create the same problem. On the other hand, people that work sixty to seventy hours per week only count as much as a worker that works thirty-five hours a week and this helps cancel out the problem created by involuntary part-time workers.

Historical Trends

Unemployment Rate Trends. The average US unemployment rate between 1967 and 2007 was 5.9 percent. From about 1993 to 2008, the unemployment rate was almost always below this level; it seemed like prosperity was here to stay. As we know, however, unemployment rose steadily following the stock market crash in late 2008. The unemployment rate moves in the opposite direction of the business cycle. During expansions, businesses want to increase production so they hire more workers and unemployment falls. During recessions, sales fall and businesses cut payroll to reduce costs and are slow to hire new workers. Unemployment rises as a result.

Participation Rate Trends. Over the same forty-year period from 1967 to 2007, the labor force participation rate has increased from 60 percent to 67 percent; more people are getting involved in production. While participation ebbs and flows slightly with the business cycle, the primary reason for this upward trend is the increased labor force participation of women and minorities since the passage of the Civil Rights Act. The labor force participation rate of women has skyrocketed from 40 percent to 60 percent since 1967, more than compensating for the slight decline in male labor force participation over this same period. As figure 6.2 illustrates, labor force participation has increased for women of nearly every age group. A variety of political and economic changes altered the incentives to work for women in such a way that the marginal benefit now exceeded the marginal cost.

Part-Time Worker Trends. The trend for part-time workers shows this type of employment is remarkably consistent throughout the period between 1967 and 2007. You might think that part-time employment increases during recessions as businesses want to save money and households want a second or third source of income, but the evidence does not bear this out. On the other hand, the number of people working as involuntary part-time workers (they would rather be working full-time) does increase sharply during recessions. Since the total number of part-time workers is constant, it must be the case that the number of voluntary workers decreases during recessions. Many of these workers decide to make the jump to full-time workers as recessions hit.

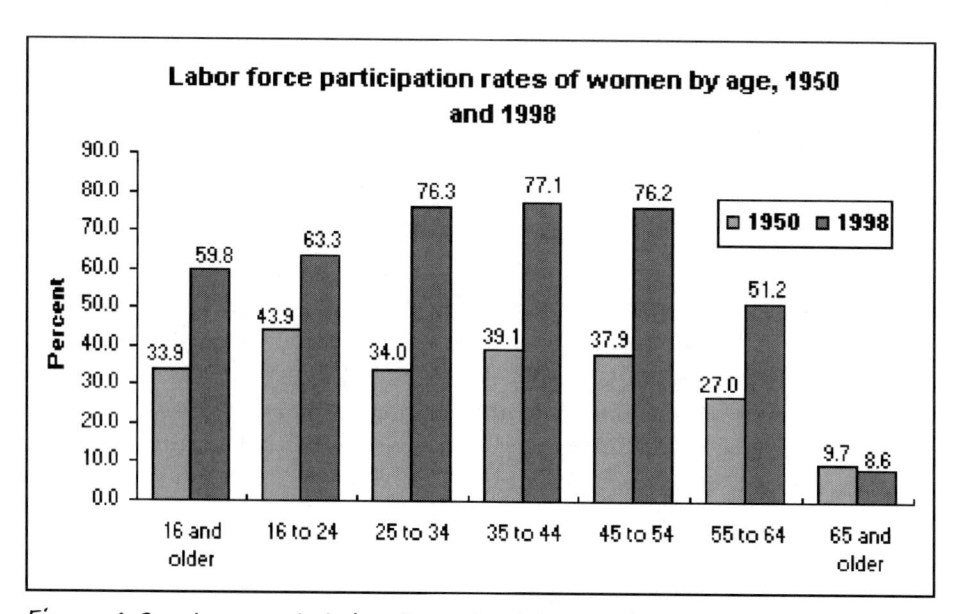

Figure 6.2 • Increase in Labor Force Participation by Women
Due to a decline in opportunity costs (i.e., less social stigma, easier access to child care services) the labor force participation of women increased drastically over the second half of the twentieth century.
Source: The Bureau of Labor Statistics

II. TYPES OF UNEMPLOYMENT

Sources of Unemployment

Job Losers. Since unemployment is so narrowly defined, we can pinpoint the few ways people move into the unemployment pool. Job losers are people who are laid off or fired from a job; they are forced to leave involuntarily. Job losses happen for a variety of reasons from economic downturns to outsourcing. A job loser can choose to look for a new job or leave the labor force. If he decides to look for another job, he joins the ranks of the unemployed.

Job Leavers. Job leavers voluntarily leave a job. Most job leavers either have a better job lined up or leave the labor force. In either case they will not be unemployed for very long. If they choose to leave their job without a new one lined up, they will count as unemployed until they find a new one.

Entrants and Reentrants. An entrant is someone who has never been in the labor force and is looking for his first job. Entrants are generally individuals coming out of school. A reentrant is someone who is returning to the labor force after being out for some time. These could be homemakers, retirees, or discouraged workers deciding to look for a job once more. Unlike job loser and job leavers, entrants and reentrants move from being out of the labor force to being unemployed, increasing the unemployment rate and the labor force participation rate.

Duration of Unemployment. The duration of unemployment can be just as important as the unemployment rate to the health of the economy. If the average duration of unemployment increases then the unemployment rate will rise since job acquisitions are slowing down. As figure 6.3 illustrates, recessions tend to create spikes in the duration

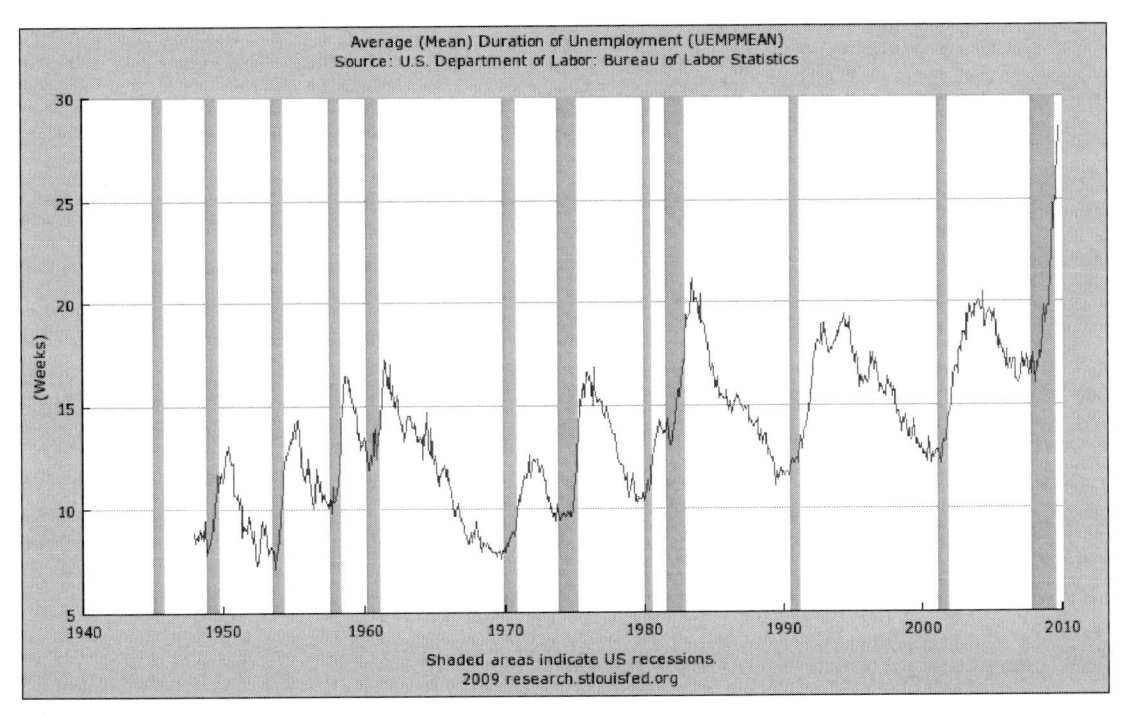

Figure 6.3 • Duration of Unemployment
The duration of unemployment spikes during and immediately after recessions. Since businesses are wary about adding new workers to the payroll until they are sure the recession is over, the flow of people from the pool of the unemployed to the pool of the employed slows down.

of unemployment. In fact, it is actually the increase in the duration of unemployment, a slowdown in hiring, which leads the unemployment rate to rise during an economic recession. There is a great deal of variance in the duration of unemployment since one third of all unemployment spells end within a month and another third end within two months. In other words, the majority of unemployment spells are less than two months, but those who are unemployed for longer than two months accumulate the majority of total weeks of unemployment.

Types of Unemployment

Frictional. Every year, 50 million of the over 150 million people in the labor force change jobs or start a new job for one reason or another. The continuous flow of workers in and out of jobs is called frictional unemployment. Just like microscopic holes and crevices cause friction along surfaces, imperfect information and job-seeking costs cause friction in the labor market. The only way to reduce or eliminate frictional unemployment would be to force people to remain in their current job or out of the labor force until they had a new job lined up. This is not exactly feasible or efficient. Since we allow people to change jobs freely, there will always be frictional unemployment.

Structural. Sometimes the structure of a particular market changes around a worker and he finds that his skills no longer fit that particular line of work. If this person becomes unemployed it is an example of structural unemployment. Structural unemployment can also refer to a loss of jobs as the result of changes in the labor market itself. For instance, government policies have encouraged companies to rely more heavily upon temporary workers and private consultants and less on salaried employees, resulting in some structural unemployment. As workers age, they may also find that their skills are no longer sufficient to compete in the modern labor market. Article 6.1 gives an example of an agency that works toward teaching older workers new skills to reduce the rate of structural unemployment.

As with frictional unemployment, reduces or eliminating structural unemployment may not actual be in the country's best interest. Since structural unemployment happens as a direct result of economic growth, they only way to be rid of it for good would be to require that businesses never change the way they produce their products. Any new advancement in technology that threatened the jobs of current workers would have to be prohibited, causing all economic growth to grind to a halt.

Cyclical. Unlike structural unemployment, cyclical unemployment occurs as a result of economy-wide fluctuations, not a personal skills mismatch. Economic downturns like recessions and depressions often lead to the cutting of payroll and a slowdown in hiring. Attempts to lessen the intensity of business cycle fluctuations often focus on the reduction of cyclical unemployment as a primary goal. Cyclical unemployment can occur even during periods of moderate expansion. As long as the economy is not growing fast enough to create enough jobs to keep up with the growing labor force, cyclical unemployment will arise.

Seasonal. Some jobs are only available at certain times of the year: ski resort worker, farm worker, mall Santa Claus, and the like. When these workers are out of a job it is referred to as seasonal unemployment. The seasons can have a large and misleading impact on unemployment figures so these statistics are usually "seasonally adjusted"; that is, they only count unemployment that can be attributed to friction, changes in market structure, or the business cycle.

Article 6.1:
Reducing Structural Unemployment

Older Adults Learn New Skills, Gain Experience in Jobs Program
By Don Norfleet

The Fulton Sun Dec 29, 2009

Frances Keel of Guthrie knows first-hand how a nonprofit organization known as Experience Works helps older adults get back into the work force.

The current economic downturn has hit older workers especially hard. The nationwide unemployment rate is hovering at about 10 percent. But for older adults over age 55 the jobless rate has soared to 54 percent with more than 2 million seniors unemployed in November.

Keel is learning to be a receptionist and how to operate office machines, including a copier and a computer. "I still haven't mastered a computer but I am learning," Keel says.

"I can't say enough good things about the Experience Works program. It's wonderful for older people. Only a week after I contacted them I was in training and then I was working part-time. I am looking for full-time employment as a receptionist," Keel says.

Experience Works pays older workers over age 55 a minimum wage. Because of fund limitations, most of them work no more than 18 hours a week. They are placed with nonprofit or government agencies that participate in the program. The agencies receive what is essentially a free worker for participating in the Experience Works program.

Many older workers lack training for modern jobs and some have been out of the workforce for a few years. They have no recent work experience on their resume. This makes it difficult for them to be hired.

Experience Works was created to help with both problems. It provides training to help older workers develop current skills and it offers a part-time job to give the workers recent work experience and a reference to help them get a job on their own, perhaps even one paying more than the minimum wage.

Questions:
1. Why do seniors have such a high unemployment rate? Remember that retired persons do not count toward the unemployment rate.
2. How does the Experience Works program attempt to reduce structural unemployment?
3. What would you rather see the government do to help senior citizens—reduce the minimum age to receive social security benefits, increase funding to programs like Experience Works, or nothing at all? Why?

From *Fulton Sun*, December 29, 2009 by Don Norfleet. Copyright © 2009 by Fulton Sun. Reprinted by permission.

Demographics of Unemployment

Increases in unemployment do not affect all sectors of the labor market to the same degree; the burden of unemployment is not shared equally. For example, while the overall unemployment rate increased less than two percentage points from 1999 to 2002, some demographics were hit much harder than others. Low-skilled workers bear relatively more of the burden of unemployment. Low-skilled workers often find themselves as structural unemployed as the labor market changes and businesses are much more likely to fire low-skilled workers in bad times since they did not invest much in their training. Likewise, less educated workers are often the lowest on the totem pole and are the first let go during recessions.

Teenagers are less mobile and less skilled than their older counterparts and as a result have a much higher rate of unemployment. While age has an impact on unemployment rate, gender has very little; women and men usually have nearly identical unemployment rates. The gap between male and female unemployment, though, began to widen for a variety of reasons during the recession of the late 2000s. African-Americans and Hispanics have higher unemployment rates than Whites. Part of this gap comes from differences in education and skills, but it is almost certain that some of it results from discrimination.

III. COST OF UNEMPLOYMENT

Natural Rate of Unemployment

The ideal situation for the economy is of course full employment. Full employment does not mean everyone has a job; we have already discussed some people who remain outside the labor force. Further, an unemployment rate of zero is not possible either, since labor markets are not perfectly flexible; job seeking is not free, there are transaction costs on both the employer and employee sides. There will always be some level of frictional unemployment as people move from job to job, industry to industry, and market to market. The goal, then, is to find some equilibrium level of employment that takes this friction into account.

Economists refer to this equilibrium as the natural rate of unemployment, the unemployment rate that will prevail once workers adjust to any changes in the macroeconomy. By definition then, the natural rate of unemployment will only include structural and frictional unemployment since there is no cyclical unemployment once firms and workers have adjusted to the new state of the labor market. This also means that each point in the business cycle has its own natural rate of unemployment (higher during recession, lower during booms). This fact has led to a difficulty in quantifying the natural rate of unemployment. During the 1980s, economists consistently estimated it to be around 6.5 percent. When the unemployment fell to 4 percent in 2000 and stayed there, economists were forced to reconsider and lowered their estimate to 5 percent. Whatever the true natural rate of unemployment, it is clear that during recessions the actual unemployment rate exceeds the natural rate. What are the macroeconomic costs of such a rise in the unemployment rate?

Okun's Law

Every claim we made about production possibilities in Chapter 1 assumed full employment of all resources. Therefore, unemployment results in us producing inside the production possibilities curve and forgoing some possible output, as shown in figure 6.4. The difference between what we could be producing and what we actually are producing is called the GDP gap. Whenever unemployment is above the natural rate, actual GDP falls short of potential GDP and the GDP gap is negative. Potential GDP is the GDP that we could have had if unemployment was at the natural rate.

$$GDP\ Gap = Potential\ GDP - Actual\ GDP$$

The formula shows that the higher the unemployment rate, the lower the actual GDP and the greater the GDP gap. Economist Arthur Okun was the first to note the relationship between unemployment and the GDP gap. He theorized that for every one percentage point the actual unemployment rate is over the natural rate, a two percentage point negative GDP gap occurs, a theory that came to be known as Okun's Law.

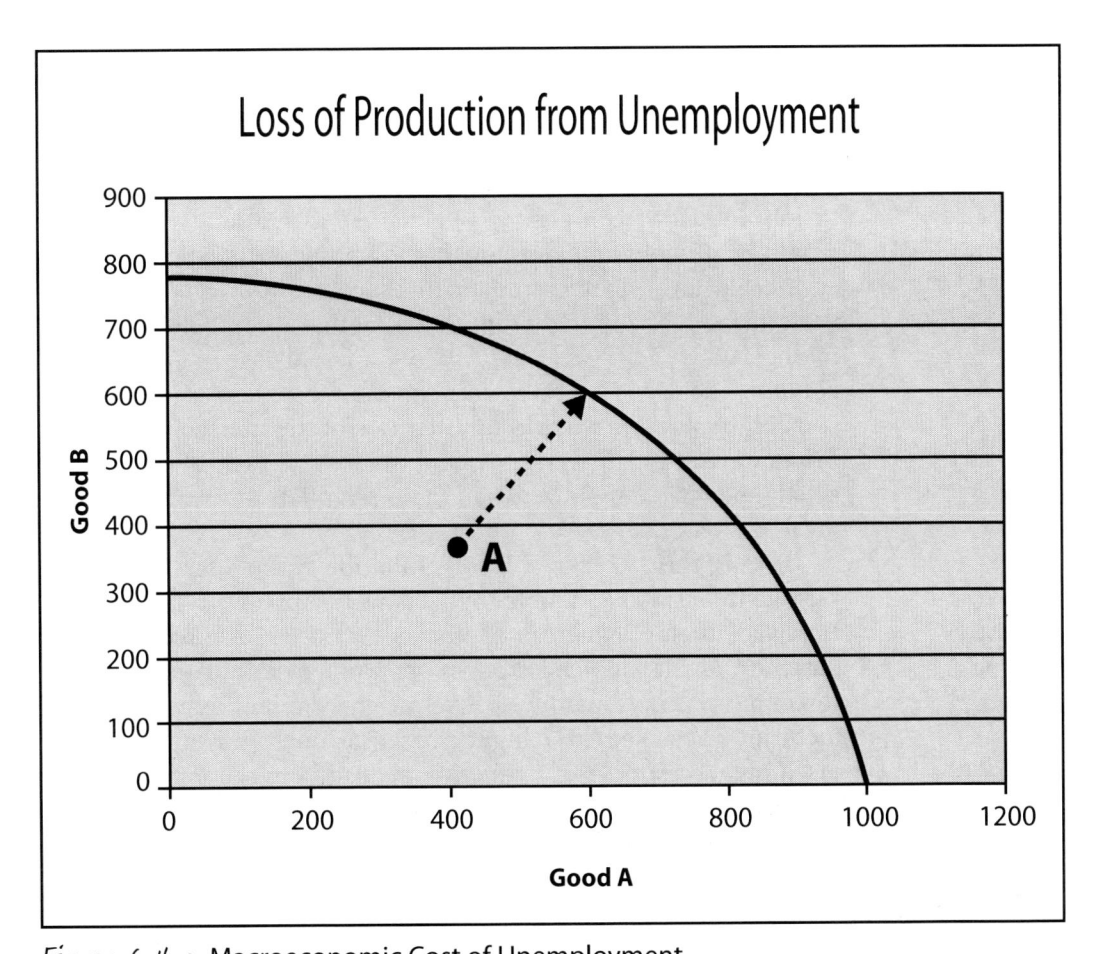

Figure 6.4 • **Macroeconomic Cost of Unemployment**
When unemployment is above the natural rate, the country is producing within its production possibilities curve, missing out on potential output.

Social Costs

Lost Income. The effects of unemployment on the economy are clear, but the effects on individuals are just as significant. Obviously, losing one's job will primarily result in a loss of income. Without a regular source of income, workers must begin to siphon from their savings, deteriorating any wealth they may have saved up.

Lost Confidence. Once those savings are gone, people then turn to family and friends for assistance, creating feelings of inadequacy and self-doubt. Even for people for whom having a job is not financially necessary, not being able to land a job when you are trying hard to find one can be devastating on one's psyche.

Social Stress. There are other non-financial effects of unemployment. Studies show that higher rates of unemployment lead to higher crime rates, more divorces, and interruptions in medical treatment and education. The stress imposed by prolonged unemployment can begin to rip a society apart if not brought under control. Studies show that many of the individuals who had lost their jobs during the recession of the late 2000s have experienced a loss of self-worth and security, in addition to their loss of income.

Health Effects. During economic downturns, closely tied to rising unemployment rates, suicide rates skyrocket and life expectancy shrinks. Not only do people forego medical treatment because of financial reasons, the stress of being unemployed itself causes health to deteriorate.

Government's Goal

There will always be some level of frictional unemployment as people move from job to job, industry to industry, and market to market. A goal of zero unemployment would be a dangerous one for the government to set. Instead, they need to find an acceptable level of unemployment that does not sacrifice other areas of economic performance. The first attempt to define this acceptable level of unemployment came in the 1960s. The Council of Economic Advisors surmised that full employment could be identified by price changes. As we get closer to full employment of our resources, businesses will bid up the price of the increasingly scarce resources, causing prices to rise. The full employment, or natural rate, of unemployment was originally set at 4 percent. Any lower than that and inflation would start to rise to unacceptable levels.

During the 1970s and 1980s, inflation rose to record levels even though unemployment was above double digits as well. Apparently the connection between inflation and unemployment was not as strong as originally believed. Changes in the structure of the labor market—more women, minorities, and teenagers in the labor force; more people willing to live on government assistance; and the loss of manufacturing jobs—led to a higher baseline unemployment rate. The government revised the natural rate of unemployment to between 6 and 7 percent. Welfare reform, increased college enrollment, and a leveling off of women entering the workforce decreased the unemployment rate in the 1990s. Although the Bush and Clinton administrations declared the natural rate of unemployment to be between 5 and 6 percent, the actual rate stayed below 5 percent throughout the 1990s without any effect on inflation. Economists are now considering whether today's high unemployment rates are only temporary or represent a "new normal" for the natural rate of unemployment.

CHAPTER 6 SUMMARY

- The **unemployment rate** shows what percentage of the **labor force**, not the total population, is out of work and actively looking for a job.
- The unemployment rate does include **discouraged workers** or involuntary part-time workers.
- People can show up in the unemployment pool for three reasons: they **lost a job**, they voluntary **left a job**, or they **entered** or **reentered** the labor force.
- There are four types of unemployment: **frictional, structural, cyclical,** and **seasonal**. Frictional and seasonal unemployment are generally temporary while structural and cyclical unemployment could last for months or even years.
- An unemployment rate of zero is impossible without destroying the freedom of movement that makes our economy work.
- **Okun's Law** states that for every one percentage point the unemployment rises, GDP falls by two percentage points.

CHAPTER 6 Exercises

Name _____

1) Which of the following groups is included in the labor force?
   A) full-time students
   B) military personnel
   C) employed persons
   D) retirees

   1) _____

2) Which of the following is the correct formula for the unemployment rate?
   A) (number unemployed/population) × 100
   B) (number unemployed/labor force) × 100
   C) (number unemployed/working age population) × 100
   D) (number unemployed/number employed) × 100

   2) _____

3) Which of the following the following is NOT a way a person can join the unemployed pool?
   A) enter labor force for the first time
   B) lose a job
   C) leave a job
   D) A, B, & C are all ways to become unemployed

   3) _____

4) What type of unemployment occurs when a firm decides to outsource customer service jobs?
   A) structural
   B) frictional
   C) cyclical
   D) seasonal

   4) _____

5) What type of unemployment occurs when firms cease hiring during a recession?
   A) structural
   B) frictional
   C) cyclical
   D) seasonal

   5) _____

6) What is the macroeconomic cost of unemployment?
   A) social stress
   B) inflation
   C) national production falls inside the production possibilities curve
   D) increased national debt

   6) _____

7) The natural rate of unemployment only includes which two types of unemployment?
   A) structural and seasonal
   B) structural and cyclical
   C) frictional and cyclical
   D) frictional and structural

   7) _____

8) What is the tradeoff of government policies to reduce unemployment?
   A) none, reducing unemployment is always a good thing
   B) increased inflation
   C) increased social stress
   D) reduced labor force participation rate

   8) _____

9) Why is an unemployment rate of zero impossible?

_____

_____

_____

_____

10) Why might increasing unemployment benefits increase the duration of unemployment? What impact would this increase have on the economy?

_____

_____

_____

_____

Chapter 7

Inflation

I. WHAT IS INFLATION?

Average Price Level

During World War II a new car was less than $700, the average house cost less than $3,000, and a half-gallon of milk cost 25 cents and was delivered straight to your door. I think it goes without saying that these things, and indeed everything, costs a lot more today then they did back then. In fact, the general price level in the United States has increased twelve-fold since 1940 as evidenced by figure 7.1. Prior to 1940, on the other hand, the average price level had changed very little since the founding of the nation. This general upward movement in the average level of prices is called inflation. The opposite of inflation is deflation, a general downward movement in prices. Notice that these phenomena refer to average prices meaning that some prices can fall even during periods of inflation. For instance, prices of electronics (TVs and DVD players) tend to fall over time even through periods of inflation.

We can easily measure how much the price of one good has gone up over time: just subtract the old price from the current price. Now you can say how much the price of the good has gone up by expressing the new price as a multiple of the old price. For example, if a pack of gum cost one dollar last year and costs $1.50 today then we say the price has gone up 50 percent or it costs 1.5 times what it cost last year. Another way to express the price change involves using an index number. An index number takes how

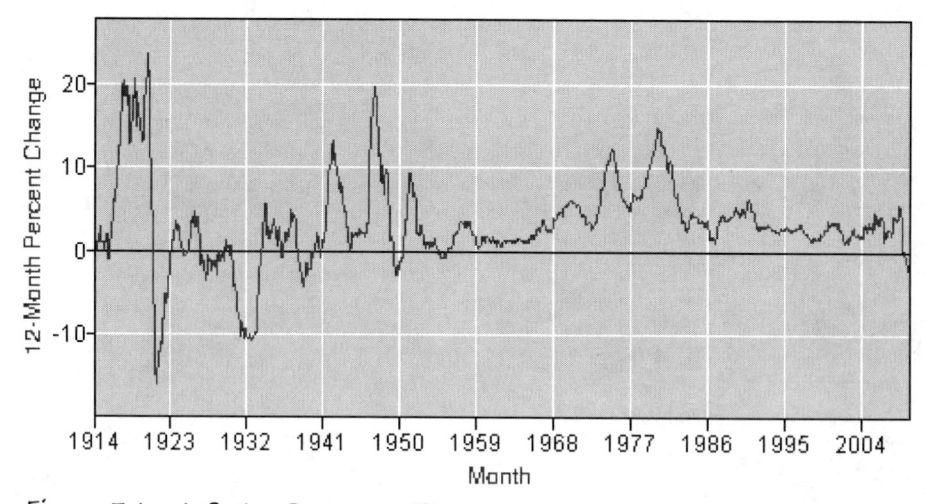

Figure 7.1 • Inflation Rates over Time
There has not been a single year of deflation since 1954. As a result, the average price level and the cost of living continue to rise.
Source: Bureau of Labor Statistics

much higher the current price is over the original price (1.5 times in the gum example) and multiples it by one hundred to get rid of the decimal points. Index numbers are the conventional tool for measuring inflation. This is all very easy for one good, but measuring inflation requires measuring changes in the prices of a large number of goods, some of which are changing faster and in different directions than others. Economists solve this problem by comparing the price of a single bundle of goods, a so-called market basket, over time.

One can then obtain the price index by dividing the current price of the basket by the original (or base year) price of the basket and multiplying by one hundred. We will return to our investigation of using index numbers to determine inflation later in this chapter.

Purchasing Power

The reason people fear inflation and the government works so hard to fight it is that an increase in inflation reduces the purchasing power of the dollar. As prices of goods rise, a dollar buys fewer goods. Therefore, the other reason we need to have an accurate measure of inflation is so that we can convert nominal values (values in today's dollars) into real values (values in constant dollars). This brings us again to the discussion of real versus nominal values that we started in Chapter 5. If your parents give you a $100 bill and you keep it for a year, the nominal value of it is still $100; this is also called its face value. If there was inflation during the year, however, the real value of the $100—the amount of goods you can buy with it—has fallen. For instance, if there was 3 percent inflation during the year (average price level rises by 3 percent) then you will need $103 to buy the same amount of goods that could be purchased for $100 last year.

Types of Inflation

Demand-Pull. The most common cause of inflation is an excess of total spending over the economy's productive capacity. When the economy is producing at full employment, it cannot increase production so it must raise prices to allocate scarce goods. In a case like this, too many dollars are chasing too few goods causing a situation called demand-pull inflation.

Cost-Push. While less common, it is also possible for inflation to arise from the supply side of the economy. At some points in history, notably the oil crisis of the 1970s, the prices of inputs have increased suddenly and unexpectedly and with them per-unit production costs. Per-unit production cost is the total amount it costs to make one unit of output. When per-unit production costs rise, firms demand more compensation for each unit of output it sells; in other words, prices rise. This is called cost-push inflation; increasing costs are pushing the price level up.

Do not make the mistake, however, that demand-pull inflation and cost-push inflation are mutually exclusive. For instance, an increase in total spending may result in prices increasing in resource markets, which in turn will cause per-unit production costs to rise. If you focus on the wrong part of the chain, you may get the cause of inflation wrong and enact useless or harmful policies.

II. MEASURING INFLATION

The CPI

The US uses many different price indices to measure inflation and each has its own strengths and weaknesses. The Consumer Price Index (CPI) is the most widely reported price index in use today. Its sole focus is price changes on goods and services purchased by the typical consumer. Both economists and media outlets rely on the CPI as a measure of inflation since it is updated and published on a monthly basis. The CPI measures the average price paid by consumers purchasing a predetermined fixed basket of goods and services. By comparing the price index from one period to the next, we can measure the rate at which the cost of living is going up. Just like with real GDP, we need to establish a base year to use the CPI or any price index. In the United States, the base year is actually the three-year average price index from 1982 to 1984. We define the CPI in this base period to be one hundred for ease of calculation; if the CPI in some period is two hundred, we know the price level increased 100 percent (or doubled) since the base period.

The Market Basket. To calculate the price of a fixed basket purchased by the average consumer, we must first determine what exactly is in the basket. The Bureau of Labor Statistics (BLS) assigns a weight to different types of goods and services based on what percentage of household income is spent on that type of good or service. Figure 7.2 gives the actual weights of the components of the market basket. Then the weight is multiplied by the price of the individual goods and services in each type according to how often they are purchased by consumers. While the BLS conducts an on-going survey, the Consumer Expenditure Survey, to determine what goods and services people actually buy, the market basket for the base year (1982–1984) has not changed for over twenty years. The single biggest component of the market basket is housing (rent and mortgage payments), followed by transportation, and food. Together, these categories account for about 75 percent of the cost of living. Each category can be broken down into smaller subunits for greater study. Bear in mind, these percentages represent an average for all households and the spending for each individual household can be very different.

Components of CPI Market Basket

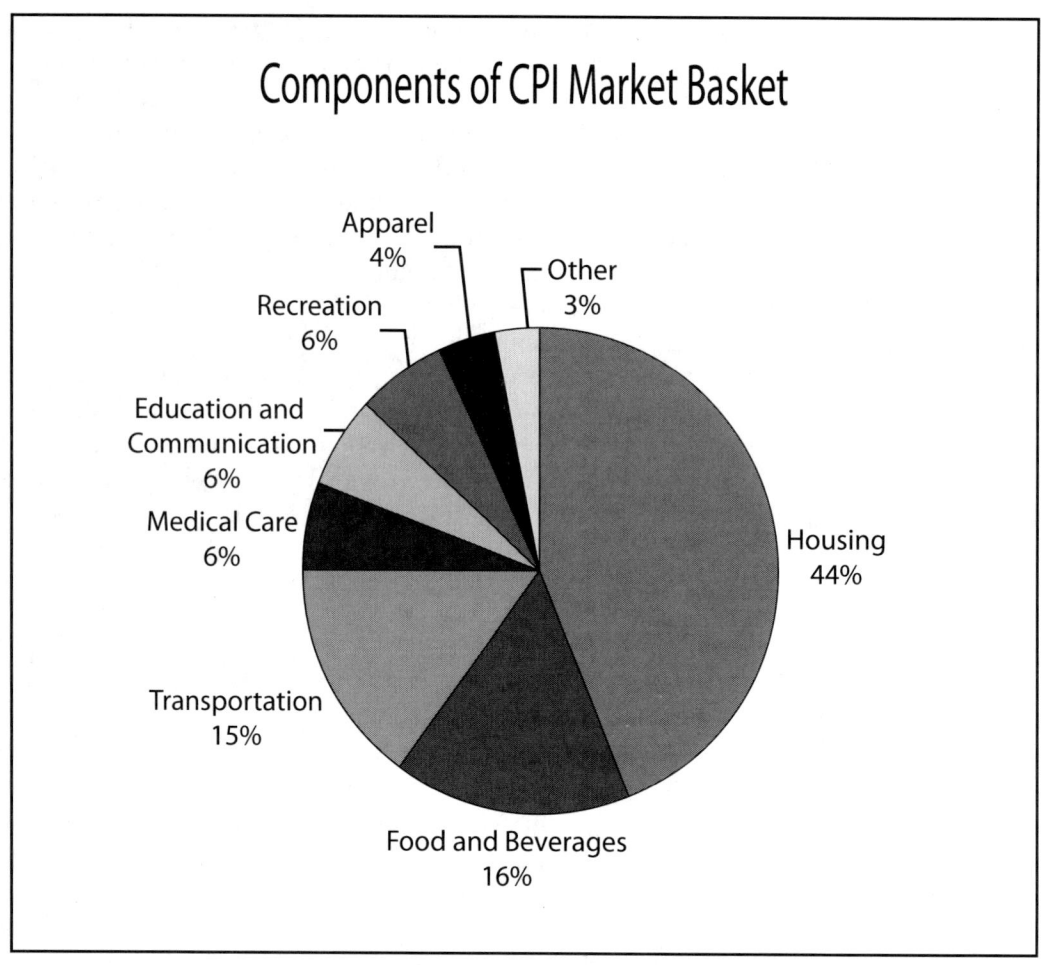

- Housing 44%
- Food and Beverages 16%
- Transportation 15%
- Medical Care 6%
- Education and Communication 6%
- Recreation 6%
- Apparel 4%
- Other 3%

Figure 7.2 • **The CPI Market Basket**
The Bureau of Labor Statistics estimates changes in the cost of living by attaching weights to different types of consumption. Changes in items consumers spend a large portion of their annual budgets on cause big changes in the CPI.
Source: Bureau of Labor Statistics

Computing the CPI. With the items of the market basket and their prices in hand, the BLS can go about the business of calculating the CPI. The CPI, like any price index, measures the change in prices from the base year to the current year. Doing so requires a three-step process: calculate the cost of the market basket in the base year, calculate the cost of the market basket in the current year, divide cost in current year by cost in base year and multiply by one hundred.

$$CPI = \frac{Cost\ of\ Market\ Basket\ in\ Current\ Year}{Cost\ of\ Market\ Basket\ in\ Base\ Year} \times 100$$

For example, imagine the market basket contained only pizza and haircuts. In the base year (2000) we define the market basket to consist of ten pizzas and five haircuts based on consumer spending habits. We discover that pizzas cost $10 each and haircuts cost $20 each. Therefore, the cost of the basket in the base year is $200. In the current pe-

Base Year		
Item	Amount in Market Basket	Price
Pizza	10	$10
Haircut	5	$20

Cost of Market Basket	$200

Current Year		
Item	Amount in Market Basket	Price
Pizza	10	$20
Haricut	5	$25

Cost of Market Basket	$325
CPI ([Current Cost of Basket/ Cost of Basket in Base Year] × 100)	162.5

Figure 7.3 • Calculating the CPI
Since the CPI is a fixed-basket index, the composition of the market basket does not change from the base year, only the prices.

riod (2008), the prices have increased to $20 per pizza and $25 per haircut. What does the market basket cost in this period? Well, since the CPI uses a fixed basket, the amounts of each good should not change, only the price. Multiply current prices by the quantities determined in the base year: $325.

Now we can use these figures to calculate the CPI in each year. The CPI in the base year is simple since the base year and the current year are one in the same in this case. As a result, the CPI in the base year is always one hundred. Calculating the CPI in 2008 is only slightly less trivial; just take the cost of the market basket in 2008 and divide by the cost in the base year, then multiply by one hundred.

$$CPI \text{ in } 2008 = \frac{\$325}{\$200} \times 100 = 162.5$$

Aside from the number of items in the market basket, these are essentially the same calculations BLS economists use to find the CPI in the real world.

The Inflation Rate. Calculating the CPI is crucial since it allows economists to measure the rate of inflation. The government defines inflation as the percentage increase, or growth rate, of the CPI over a given period. Just as with the real GDP, the growth rate of the CPI is calculated by subtracting the previous value from the current value, dividing by the old value, and multiplying by one hundred.

$$\text{Inflation Rate} = \frac{\text{New CPI} - \text{Old CPI}}{\text{Old CPI}} \times 100$$

Suppose the current CPI is 150 and it used to be 125. If you want to know the rate of inflation between these two periods simply apply the percentage change formula:

$$\text{Inflation Rate} = \frac{150 - 125}{125} \times 100 = 20\%$$

This example represents an inflation rate much higher than that of the United States, which tends to fall between 2 and 5 percent per year. Some countries experiencing hyperinflation see inflation rates well above one million percent a month.

Bias in the CPI

New Goods. The base period for the CPI is 1982–1984. Think of how many different goods and services the average consumer buys today that were luxuries or not even available twenty-five years ago. Likewise, consider the many goods that were essential to the 1980s consumers but are rarely on the shelves today. The CPI cannot perfectly measure the cost of living because the market basket was fixed so long ago. The calculators of the CPI attempt to adjust for this by making the items in the basket broader (for example, listing the price of a portable music player instead of the price of a cassette player). Still, most economists agree that the new good bias leads to the CPI being higher than it should be through not taking into account the improved quality of new goods.

Quality Improvements. Even goods that have remained in the basket for the past twenty-five years have changed in quality. Cars, for example, are safer and more powerful today than their older counterparts were. How much of the increase in price is due to inflation and how much is due to increased quality? CPI calculators do what they can to make the distinction, but it is likely that the quality change bias also leads to the CPI being overstated.

Substitution. Another problem with the CPI market basket being fixed is that it cannot adjust when consumers substitute away from a more expensive product. Assume that the 1982–1984 basket contained a large amount of oranges because there was a good crop in those years and oranges were relatively cheap. If a freeze hits and orange prices rise, consumers will not stubbornly purchase the same amount of oranges just because they did so in 1984; they will buy apples or some other fruit instead. Not adjusting the basket for this substitution leads one to believe the cost of living has increased more than it actual has.

Outlet. Just like consumers choose low-priced substitutes when individual prices rise, they choose to shop at discount stores or outlets when they face general price increases or income drops. Outlet substitution helps explain why stores like Wal-Mart do so well during recessions. CPI calculators claim that the lower prices at outlet stores come from lower quality and therefore require no adjustment, but studies have shown this is not the case; the price reduction at outlet stores cannot be fully explained by quality reductions. While discount store products may be of slightly lower quality, the lower price more than makes up for this. By not adjusting for outlet substitution, the CPI again overstates cost of living.

Consequences of the Bias. These several biases add up to make a very big difference. A government commission found that the CPI overstates true inflation by about 1.1 percentage points. That is, if the CPI grows 5 percent in a year, the actual inflation is probably closer to 3.9 percent. What difference does this bias really make? Why do we care what the level of inflation really is? The CPI needs to be as accurate as possible because it is used to provide cost-of-living adjustments to both private contracts and government payments.

Many private labor contracts, particularly long-term contracts for union workers, have cost-of-living adjustments to ensure that the wage keeps up with inflation. By tying their wages to the CPI, workers ensure that the amount of goods they can buy with their pay stays the same. But since the CPI overstates inflation, tying cost-of-living adjustments to it causes workers to gain at their employer's expense. A similar issue occurs with government outlays that are tied to the CPI.

Government payments like social security, food stamps, welfare, and retirement benefits for government workers move along the CPI to make sure the recipients do not lose purchasing power because prices rise. Since the CPI is biased upward, however, payments rise faster than the true cost-of-living. As a result, the government may be paying more than it needs to offset the cost of inflation. A more accurate measure of inflation could save the government, and taxpayers, billions of dollars a year.

Alternative Measures

Producer Price Indices. There are numerous producer price indices, including ones for food products, intermediate goods, and finished goods. These indices focus on firms rather than consumers. Despite this, both the CPI and the PPI tend to follow the same patterns in the long run. In the short run, however, the PPI moves first since price changes affect producers first, then are passed on to consumers.

GDP Deflator. The gross domestic product, (GDP) deflator is the broadest price index since it works off the gross domestic product, or total national output. As we will explore later in this chapter, the GDP deflator is used to turn, or deflate, nominal GDP into real GDP. The GDP deflator is not a fixed quantity index since it is based on actual consumer expenditures not just a basket constructed by economists. The GDP deflator is not a perfect measure of inflation either, however, since calculating requires using estimates based on the CPI. As a result, the GDP deflator is subject to the same biases as the CPI. In addition, since the GDP deflator includes many types of goods and services not regularly purchased by consumers, it does not serve as good measure of cost-of-living.

PCE Index. The Personal Consumption Expenditure (PCE) index uses annual surveys on consumption to update its basket every year. The Federal Reserve uses this index as its measure of inflation because it believes its updated basket provides a more accurate picture of consumer purchasing power and cost of living. The government, however, continues to use the CPI to adjust social security benefits and the personal income tax brackets. The PCE deflator overcomes the biases of the CPI by using current expenditures instead of being limited by a fixed basket. Unlike the GDP deflator, however, the PCE deflator can be used as a cost-of-living measure since it only focuses on consumption expenditures. Indeed, both the GDP deflator and the PCE deflator report lower levels of inflation than the CPI.

III. COST OF INFLATION

Resource Cost

Protecting Against Inflation. Lenders can easily raise nominal interest rates to combat anticipated inflation. They can also use instruments like adjustable-rate mortgages that automatically move with other interest rates in the economy. Workers with cost of living adjustments (COLAs) in their contracts get automatic raises when the price level rises. These adjustments and preparations all cost time and resources. Inflation also raises the cost of holding cash. Any money that you have on hand or in a non-interest-bearing account like a checking account loses purchasing power during times of inflation. Increasing the cost of holding cash decreases economic activity.

Menu Costs. If inflation is anticipated (as it is for the most part in the United States), its primary cost comes in the resources used by firms and individuals to protect against future inflation. Individuals and firms have to spend time and resources working out contracts with stipulations for different inflation scenarios. The cost imposed by changing one's behavior to protect against inflation is generally called shoe leather costs, in reference to the result of running back and forth from the bank to cash one's paycheck before it loses purchasing power. Inflation also imposes menu costs on firms; if the price level rises, firms must literally change their price listings and this takes time and money. The higher the rate of inflation, the more often these changes must be done.

Redistribution

Unlike unemployment, the primary impact of inflation or deflation is not a general decline in economic activity or GDP, but an unexpected redistribution of income and wealth from one group to another. Some people are hurt by inflation while other groups benefit. Which group you fall into will depend on what type of products you buy and what type of assets you own.

Income Effects. Remember that not all prices rise during inflation. People who spend a larger portion of their income on goods that go up in price the most will be hurt the most by inflation. This is little comfort to college students who saw tuition and textbooks rise in price more than almost any other product over the past two decades.

Regardless of what they spend their money on, inflation is going to hurt people on a fixed income. Even though the check they receive every month has the exact same amount, their quality of life will fall because the amount they can buy with that amount of money will fall when average prices rise. Banks also rely on fixed payments for a major portion of their income. Loans have interest payments that are set months and sometimes years in advance. These payments are usually nominal in nature; there is no attempt to adjust for inflation. Therefore, when inflation occurs, the money the bank receives is not worth as much as the money it lent out and their real income falls.

Not everyone loses in this game, however. If lenders lose from inflation, clearly debtors gain. If you borrow $5,000 from the bank in one year and inflation occurs at a rate of 10 percent, the money you pay them back is only worth $4,500 (plus interest) so you come out ahead. Likewise, businesses that sell products that go up in price faster than average prices will see their incomes go up faster than average prices. As a result, their real incomes rise. Every transaction has two sides, and just as the purchasers of fast-rising products suffer during inflation, the sellers of these products win.

Since inflation affects different groups of people differently, inflation redistributes real income (purchasing power) from one group to another. People that buy products that go up in price faster than the average price level, people whose nominal incomes are fixed or related to products whose prices are rising slowly, and people that hold assets that are declining in real value see their real incomes fall as a result of inflation. On the other hand, people who spend a large portion of their income on products that are going down in price relative to the average price level, have incomes tied to the price of products that are going up in price quickly, or those who hold assets that are growing in real value see their real income rise as a result of inflation.

Effect on Lending. Creditors (or lenders) are perhaps those hit hardest by unexpected inflation. If a bank loans you $1,000 and prices increase unexpectedly over the life of the loan, then the money you pay back is worth less than the money you borrowed. As a result, banks insert an inflationary premium in the interest rates they lend at. The interest rates advertised on TV and the Internet are called nominal interest rates; they are the sum of the real interest rate (the percentage the bank expects its real income to increase as a result of the loan) earned by the lender and the inflationary premium.

Nominal Interest Rate = Real Interest Rate + Inflationary Premium

If there is unanticipated inflation, then the lender will not receive as high a real interest rate as he predicted.

Just as creditors are hurt by unanticipated inflation, borrowers benefit from it. The money that they pay back is not worth as much as the money they borrowed in terms of purchasing power. It should be no surprise, then, that the biggest debtor in the world, the United States government, also benefits from inflation by paying back its debts with cheaper dollars. It should be noted that many economists advise against allowing an entity that benefits from inflation controlling the money supply.

Social Stress. Inflation is basically a tax, taking money from one group and giving it to another. This redistribution can make people angry if they are the ones on the losing end. Indeed, one of the real costs of inflation is the social tension it causes. When prices change radically and seemingly for no reason, the explicit and implicit contracts that our economy is based on begin to come into question. Radical, unanticipated inflation has been known to make people's life savings worthless as occurred in Germany following World War I and Russia after the fall of Communism. This loss of wealth creates the same stresses and tensions as we discussed for unemployment in the previous chapter.

Even people who are not hurt very much by inflation (their real incomes stay relatively constant) still feel damaged by it. People feel cheated when their rising incomes do not translate to a higher standard of living. They see rising prices as the culprit. When people complain that tuition used to be $50 or they remember when they could go to a movie for 25 cents, they fail to realize if prices had stayed that low, so would wages and their purchasing power will still be the same. We call this feeling of suffering from inflation even though real income stayed the same, the money illusion. According to Article 7.1, the money illusion is so strong that the money affects the brain in much the same way as illicit drugs.

Macro Effects

Uncertainty. Beyond the personal redistributions and tensions caused by inflation, there also serious macroeconomic consequences to consider. The primary concern is one of uncertainty. The money-based economy requires some assurance that the value of the dollar will be constant, or at least predictable, in the future. Making long-term economic decisions becomes almost impossible if you do not know what your decisions will end up costing you in the future. Deciding whether or not to attend a four-year college depends partly on what you think tuition will be four years from now. If inflation is stable, you can accurately predict the price and make a good decision. When inflation is large and wildly unpredictable, people may choose not to enter college even though it may turn out they could have afforded it.

Article 7.1:
The Power of the Money Illusion

Why Spending Money is Like a Drug
Parts of the brain are stimulated by higher salaries, even when prices rise and purchasing power drops
By Steve Connor

March 24, 2009

Money works like a drug on the human brain–and even just the thought of earning a higher salary gives us a physical buzz, a study has found.

Scientists have discovered that thinking about cash stimulates the reward centres involved in pleasure and the higher the salary—even if it is just imagined—the greater the pleasure generated in the brain.

This may be no great surprise, but the most intriguing aspect of the research is that the findings hold true even if what we want to buy costs more, for example in times of high inflation, and our actual spending power drops.

The results of the study suggest that the human brain is innately susceptible to the illusion of wealth that money can bring. This is known in economics as "money illusion"—when people get fixated on the nominal value of money, rather than on its actual purchasing power. Some economists have proposed that people behave irrationally when it comes to wages by being happier with higher salary increases in times of high inflation than they are with lower salary rises in times of low inflation.

It has now emerged that more money really does seem to generate the feelings of reward in the brain that are also involved in irrational or addictive behaviour, even if the purchasing power of higher salaries is reduced by high inflation.

"Intuitively, money illusion implies that an increase in income is valued positively, even when prices go up by the same amount, leaving real purchasing power unchanged," [Professor Armin Falk, of the University of Bonn] said.

"Economists have traditionally been sceptical about the notion of money illusion, but recent behavioural evidence has challenged this view," added Professor Falk, whose study is published in the journal Proceedings of the National Academy of Sciences.

"This result means that reward activation generally increases with income, but was significantly higher in situations where nominal incomes and prices were both 50 per cent higher, which supports the hypothesis that activity in the ventromedial prefrontal cortex is subject to money illusion," Professor Falk said.

Questions:
1. What was the result of the experiment described in the article?
2. Why is it strange for someone to be happy about earning a 50 percent larger salary if all prices have risen 50 percent? What has happened to this person's standard of living?
3. What kind of social problems can occur if standard of living does not rise as fast as nominal income (the size of one's paycheck)?

From *The Independent*, March 24, 2009 by Steve Connor. Copyright © 2009. Reprinted by permission of The Independent.

Not knowing future prices can also prevent growth in production. When a company is deciding whether or not to build a new factory, they are engaging in a long-term planning process where the actual factory may not be built for several years. If the price of construction materials and workers is markedly higher years later, it might turn out that the firm might not be able to finish the project. This possibility means that investment slows during heavy inflation.

Speculation. Taken to the extreme, it may become possible that investing in production itself is not profitable at all. High inflation might lead to a transformation of the economy from one based on production to one based on speculation. Since people who hold assets that rise in value faster than the price level win during inflation, entrepreneurs might turn their attention from producing products people want, to trying to guess which assets will rise in real value (speculation). Eventually goods become so scarce relative to currency that the currency itself becomes worthless; it took a barrel full of marks to buy a loaf of bread in 1920s Germany, for example. When people would rather hold and trade goods than currency, hyperinflation has occurred and the currency has lost its value as a form of money.

Deflation. Deflation, a decline in the average price level, will create the same harm as inflation, just for a different group of people. People who gained from inflation will be hurt by deflation, and vice versa. On the macro side, businesses would rather lend money than borrow for investment because the money paid back at the end of the loan will be worth more than when it was borrowed. People become distressed at their shrinking paychecks, even though their purchasing power may not be declining at all.

Nominal vs. Real Values

Nominal GDP vs. Real GDP. We have already talked about why it is important to use real GDP instead of nominal GDP to compare the size of an economy over time. Real GDP factors out the affect of price changes on GDP and focuses on quantity changes, the only part of GDP that affects standard of living. In Chapter 5 we discovered how to calculate real GDP directly (multiplying today's quantities by the base year price), but here we will discuss how to convert nominal GDP into real GDP. Imagine you knew the nominal GDP for a year, but not the real GDP (perhaps you don't know the prices for the base year so you cannot calculate real GDP directly). You could implicitly calculate the real GDP using a ratio of the price levels for the base year and the current year called the GDP deflator. The real GDP for a year is equal to the nominal GDP for that year divided by the GDP deflator year multiplied by one hundred.

$$Real\ GDP = \frac{Nominal\ GDP}{GDP\ Deflator} \times 100$$

Here we can see where the GDP deflator gets its name: It deflates nominal GDP so that it only reflects change in quantities, not prices.

Nominal Wage vs. Real Wage. The wage rate is another important macroeconomic variable in need of a real value. Since wages rise with prices, looking at a graph of nominal wage rates might give us the idea that the standard of living for workers is steadily rising in our country. But in actuality, it is not how much you get paid that determines your lifestyle; it is how much you can buy with your pay. If prices have risen faster than wages, workers might be worse off than in previous years. The real wage rate tells us how many goods and services workers can buy with an hour of work. Calculating the real wage rate is very similar to that of real GDP:

$$\text{Real Wage Rate} = \frac{\text{Nominal Wage Rate}}{\text{CPI}} \times 100$$

Dividing by the CPI deflates the nominal wage rate to reflect the actual increase in standard of living. Interestingly, the real wage rate of the average American worker has changed very little since the late 1970s, something that concerns many observers. If the real wage rate stagnates, people may not want to work. In actuality, the labor force participation rate during this time has increased greatly. In fact, increased labor force participation may actually be keeping the real wage rate from rising. In addition, the increase in two-income families means that the real wage rate of the average household has increased quite significantly.

Nominal Interest Rate vs. Real Interest Rate. The existence of inflation leads to a scenario where the interest rate advertised by a bank or lending institution does not represent the true transfer of purchasing power between lender and borrower. In the face of inflation, the money the lender pays back is not worth as much as the money he borrowed. If you borrow $100 from a bank for a year at 5 percent interest, you owe them $105. If there is inflation, however, this $105 cannot buy what $105 could buy a year ago, so the bank did not increase its purchasing power by 5 percent. This is the difference between the nominal interest rate and the real interest rate: The nominal interest rate describes how much money you have to pay back and the real interest rate describes how much purchasing power is actually transferred.

While the real GDP and real wage rate were calculated by dividing the respective nominal value by a price index and then multiplying by one hundred, the real interest rate is calculated a little differently.

$$\text{Real Interest Rate} = \text{Nominal Interest Rate} - \text{Inflation Rate}$$

The real interest rate equals the nominal interest rate minus the rate of inflation. We have seen that banks try to protect themselves from inflation by charging a nominal interest rate equal to the real interest rate it wishes to earn plus the level of inflation they believe will prevail—the inflationary premium discussed earlier. After the fact, the real interest rate is calculated by subtracting the actual level of inflation (measured by the CPI) from the nominal interest rate. There have been times in recent history when banks underestimated inflation and charged a nominal interest rate lower than the rate of inflation, resulting in a situation where the real interest rate was negative; and purchasing power was actually transferred to borrowers. However, since the CPI likely overstated inflation, this situation may be slightly exaggerated.

Government's Goal

According to the Full Employment and Balanced Growth Act of 1978, the government's goal is to maintain mild inflation—around 3 percent—not zero inflation. One of the primary reasons Congress chose mild inflation over zero inflation as a goal is that reducing inflation comes with a trade-off: rising unemployment. The contractionary policies that keep prices from rising also restrain spending and business activity. Economists are not in full agreement on whether mild inflation (less than 3 percent) is good for the economy. Even at these low levels, some argue, there are undeniable time and resource costs of inflation. Proponents of mild inflation argue that it is better to enact policies that encourage too much spending and employment and result in mild inflation, than those that encourage too little spending in order to maintain zero inflation.

CHAPTER 7 SUMMARY

- **Inflation** is an increase in the average price level or the cost of living.
- When the average price level rises, the **purchasing power** of any sum of money falls.
- The primary tool for measuring inflation is the **Consumer Price Index (CPI)**.
- The CPI is a **fixed-basket index**, which creates some measurement problems when the buying patterns of consumers change.
- If inflation is fully anticipated, the main economic problem it causes is **redistribution** and the **resource cost** of protecting against inflation.
- Inflation is the reason we need to distinguish between **real values** and **nominal values**.
- The government does not pursue a zero inflation policy because **every effort to reduce inflation slows down economic activity and raises unemployment.**

CHAPTER 7

Exercises

Name _____

1) Inflation
   A) increases the purchasing power of an amount of money.
   B) decreases the purchasing power of an amount of money.
   C) has no effect on purchasing power.
   D) the effect depends on whether the inflation is anticipated or not.

   1) _____

2) If the government printed $100 trillion and sent it out to every citizen, what type of inflation would occur?
   A) demand-pull inflation
   B) cost-push inflation
   C) deflation
   D) no price level change

   2) _____

3) What is the CPI in the base year?
   A) 1
   B) 0
   C) 100
   D) not enough information

   3) _____

4) If the CPI is 225, how much has the price risen since the base year?
   A) 225%
   B) 25%
   C) 125%
   D) 200%

   4) _____

5) What is the inflation rate between 2000 and 2009 if the CPI was 172.2 in 2000 and 214.5 in 2009?
   A) 42.3%
   B) 114.5%
   C) .25%
   D) 24.6%

   5) _____

6) Which of the following is NOT a bias present in the CPI?
   A) time bias
   B) substitution bias
   C) new good bias
   D) outlet substitution bias

   6) _____

7) Who gains the most from inflation?
   A) lenders
   B) people who sell goods that have risen in price faster than inflation
   C) people who buy goods that have risen in price faster than inflation
   D) people who live on fixed incomes

   7) _____

8) If your paycheck rises from $2,000 a month to $2,100 month and inflation is at 5 percent, how has your real wage changed?
   A) real wage has risen
   B) real wage has fallen
   C) no impact on real wage
   D) not enough information

   8) _____

9) Why do borrowers win and lenders lose when unexpected inflation occurs?

10) Why did the government choose 3 percent as its inflation goal instead of 0 percent? What is the opportunity cost of pursuing a zero inflation rate policy?

Chapter 8

Economic Growth and Business Cycles

I. ECONOMIC GROWTH

Measuring Growth

A good measure of economic growth should illustrate the idea that when growth occurs, a country's citizens become better off, at least in a material sense. The figure that we generally use to measure material well-being is per capita real GDP. Then, we can define economic growth as the rate of change of per capita real GDP from one year to the next. While per capita GDP is more useful for comparing the purchasing power and standards of living for people in different countries, real GDP itself is still important for measuring the overall economic power and political clout of a country. However, real GDP growth can be misleading if a country's population is growing even faster over the same period. Figure 8.1 gives the per capita real GDP growth rates of several countries.

Growth is one of the most widely publicized goals of macroeconomic policy. Every political candidate promises greater economic growth. The reason for this emphasis is that growth results in higher real wages and standards of living for citizens. In addition, socioeconomic problems become easier to deal with because the pie we have to share becomes larger. A growing economy can undertake more social programs and other new projects without sacrificing existing levels of consumption and investment.

Country	Real GDP Growth Rate (2008)
China	9.00%
Iraq	7.80%
India	7.40%
Russia	5.60%
Switzerland	1.80%
Mexico	1.30%
United Kingdom	0.70%
United States	0.40%
Japan	−0.70%
Zimbabwe	−14.40%

Source: CIA World Factbook

Figure 8.1 • **Growth Rates of Selected Countries**
Economic growth rates vary widely throughout the world. Less developed countries tend to have higher growth rates due to the catch-up effect.

Sustained Growth

Most countries have economic growth rates that are within two or three percentage points of each other, and that might lead you to believe that every country grows at about the same rate. How much difference can there be between a 3 percent growth rate and a 4 percent growth rate? True, a difference of one percentage point may not matter from one year to the next, but it matters a great when it comes to long-term growth.

Let's imagine three economies with an identical $1 trillion real GDP but three different growth rates: 3 percent, 4 percent, and 5 percent. After one year the economies still have basically the same output—$1.03 trillion, $1.04 trillion, and $1.05 trillion—but let's see what happens after fifty years. Country One would have a real GDP of $4.38 trillion, Country Two would have nearly twice that at $7.11 trillion, and Country Three would have nearly three times that at $11.5 trillion. This is the power of compounding. Another way to grasp how growth rates affect the size of the economy is by the rule of 70. The rule of 70 allows us to approximate how many years it will take an economy to double in size (in terms of real GDP) if it maintains its current growth rate.

$$Number\ of\ Years\ to\ Double\ in\ Size = \frac{70}{Growth\ Rate}$$

The rule of 70 also works for other statistics like price level (how long it takes prices to double) and savings (how long it will take the money in your savings account to double).

Sources of Growth

If you consider land to be a fixed resource (we can't produce any more natural resources) then growth can only come from four sources: growth of capital (both human and physical), growth of labor (greater labor force participation or larger population), and the growth in the productivity of capital or labor. An increase in the rate of growth for any of these items will lead to an increase in economic growth and greater material well-being.

We know that saving more leads to a faster build up of physical capital, but does the growth of capital and technology lead to greater productivity and higher levels of output? These increases will result in higher levels of output only if they lead to more aggregate hours of work or if they make labor more productive.

Labor. The amount of total hours of work employed by all businesses in a country increases over time. This increase comes primarily from an increase in the labor force through population growth (average hours per worker is actually falling in the United States). Older theories of economic growth believed population growth was the only sustainable way to increase output. Indeed, a larger population will increase aggregate hours and raise real GDP for a given level of labor productivity. However, if population growth is the only source of growth, GDP per person will not rise; the growth in output will be exactly equal to the growth in population. Only by increasing the productivity of labor can real GDP per person, and the standard of living, rise.

Each year, workers become better at their jobs through training as well as basic repetition. This allows them to produce more output with the same amount of inputs. Dividing real GDP by the number of workers gives us labor productivity (output per worker) for the economy as a whole.

$$Labor\ Productivity = \frac{Total\ Output}{Number\ of\ Workers}$$

Greater labor productivity occurs when workers are healthier and better trained, have better and more productive capital to work with, are better managed and organized, and are put to work in the most efficient industries.

Capital. Increases in productivity do not just happen magically, but are the result of investment in capital goods and future production. As a result, economies that forego consumption today are rewarded with high economic growth and greater consumption in the future. The great majority of economic growth that has occurred in history has occurred since the Industrial Revolution, when capital per worker increased. This implies that higher savings rates on a national level result in higher rates of growth and eventually higher standards of living. The US has been able to get away with ridiculously low saving rates since other countries want to invest in our capital stock for us.

Human Capital. Human capital is the stock of skills, training, and knowledge people earn while forgoing work in favor of school or training. Society also invests in human capital in the form of libraries and state-funded teachers. Different levels of investment in human capital go a long way towards explaining the divergent living standards of countries throughout the world. In fact, economists contend that one of the best policies developing countries can pursue to increase growth is investing in secondary education. Increases in human capital can also lead to increases in technological innovation since a more educated workforce is more likely to make new discoveries. Education is only one part of human capital accumulation; job training is important as well. In a process called learning-by-doing, a workforce becomes better and more productive the more it produces something. Therefore, over time you get more out of your workforce even if education and physical capital do not increase.

New Discoveries. Growth in technology is a driving force for productivity increases. The increase in computing power over recent years has allowed for faster and more precise production and will continue to improve in the coming years. Technology does not grow on trees, but is a factor of production that responds to incentives. If there are ample rewards available to someone who invents or implements new technology, technological advancements are sure to come.

Much technological advancement comes from research and development departments at private firms. National spending on R&D can increase the economic growth rate. The goal of these divisions is to develop new products and procedures that can increase the profitability of the firm so the amount firms are willing to spend on it depends on how much they will be rewarded for any discovery. But as Article 8.1 explains, the benefits of a new technology may stretch far beyond the firm that introduced it. Technological advancement requires the destruction of old, obsolete, and less efficient industries, companies, and jobs in favor of new ones. While this creative destruction is painful and often unpopular, it will benefit society in the long run. Governments in developing countries tend to protect existing industries and companies even more than those in developed countries do, preventing creative destruction and limiting economic growth.

Article 8.1:
The Value of New Discoveries

LED Industry Could Spark New Growth in the Treasure Valley
A cluster of startups hopes to capitalize on the efficiency and low cost of light-emitting diode technology.

By Rocky Barker

May 18, 2009

Boise startup lights way to 'smart grid'

A Boise company's solar-powered streetlight doesn't just save electricity by tapping the sun to run its lamp—it one day may feed power back to the grid at times of peak demand.

The Inovus Solar SmartPole—created and marketed from a small office in Downtown Boise—demonstrates the promise of "smart grid" technology, which could revolutionize electric power in the United States.

And the young outfit behind it represents what some local business leaders say could help define Boise's future: A cluster of high-tech energy companies that could tap into the nation's "green" revolution and attract the kind of creative professionals that Micron and Hewlett-Packard have brought here for years.

Name a major Boise company that already has invested millions in the future of a new technology that is expected to revolutionize the way we light the world.

If you thought Micron Technology, you're wrong. It's J. R. Simplot Co.

Simplot helped a former Micron executive form light-emitting diode manufacturer SemiLEDs Corp. in 2005. The company, headquartered in Boise, has a fabrication plant in Taiwan rolling out some of the leading lighting technology in the world. The World Economic Forum recognized SemiLEDs as a 2009 Technology Pioneer whose products may allow low-energy LEDs to replace today's incandescent and compact fluorescent bulbs.

"The world needs low-cost lighting," said Trung Doan, SemiLEDs' CEO, who lives in Taiwan. "That's why we started SemiLEDs and that's the reason Simplot supports us."

Doan's dream to quickly convert the world to LED lighting comes as Congress is seeking a dramatic new energy policy promoting efficiency and non-carbon fuel alternatives to combat climate change. LEDs use one-seventh the power and last years longer than current bulbs.

Twenty-two percent of all electricity use in the United States is devoted to lighting, according to the U.S. Department of Energy. Switching to the semiconducting technology could save $280 billion by 2028.

And the LED market is growing at a rate of 30 to 40 percent a year, Doan said.

Then it will join a cadre of start-ups that is banking on the potential of the lighting revolution. In addition to SemiLEDs, Boise's Inovus Solar and AeroLEDs already are manufacturing LED products. Inovus uses LEDs in its solar-powered street poles and retrofits outdoor lighting with LEDs.

Micron's move into the manufacture of high-brightness semiconductor diodes could help the shrinking company diversify. Micron is laying off 2,000 people by August as it ends computer-chip manufacturing on its Boise campus.

"I welcome and applaud Micron for getting into the LED business," Calvin said. "But if they're coming out from ground zero, it's going to be tough."

Still, the opportunity for large and small companies to get in on the same kind of growth that powered the computer industry in the 1990s is there, he said.

"This is the beginning of the moment," Calvin said.

Question:
1. What product is SemiLEDs trying to replace? What effect will this have on companies that produce this product?
2. What positive effects might LED technology have on costs and the economy as a whole once businesses and homes are converted to the new technology?
3. What types of new businesses have already sprung up to take advantage of LED technology? What effect is LED technology having on the overall amount of investment?

© McClatchy-Tribune Information Services. All Rights Reserved. Reprinted with permission.

Progress Paradox

One unfortunate drawback to this definition of economic growth is that it still does not address the problem of distribution. Is it better for a country to have slow growth that is shared equally by all of its citizens or to have rapid growth that increases income inequality? If you relied solely on the growth rate of per capita real GDP, you would have to unequivocally say the bigger the growth rate the better. Basing economic growth solely on growth in per capita real GDP also fails to capture the effect leisure has on well-being. If a country's real GDP did not change from one year to the next, you would conclude that there was no growth and therefore well-being did not change. It may be possible, however, that there was reduction in the workweek that increased leisure without decreasing production. Such a change would clearly make workers better off but it would not show up as economic growth.

Some social scientists believe that basing economic growth on real GDP growth ignores the psychological costs of growth. Increasing productive capacity has changed the definition of what is a necessity and led to a collective malaise or disappointment as we try to keep up with some abstract standard. Economist Gregg Easterbrook calls this idea that we feel poorer even though we are getting richer the Progress Paradox. If the goal of a society is to make its citizens as happy as possible, per capita real GDP may be an inadequate measure.

II. ACHIEVING FASTER GROWTH

Preconditions for Growth

Economic Freedom. Since growth depends on firms wanting to achieve greater profits, it is certainly necessary to allow firms the freedom to use their resources in whatever way they see fit. A country that allows for and protects private property will have faster growth than a country with many restrictions and barriers to trade. What incentive does a company have to spend millions on research and development if the government can seize its results at any time? Economic freedom involves not only shielding businesses from corruption, needless bureaucracy and regulations, and crippling taxes, but also creating a court system that enforces contracts and defends intellectual property rights.

Property Rights. It is difficult to maintain and grow wealth in a country that does not actively enforce property rights. Socialist countries like Cuba do not allow much private property and as such have little economic growth. Developed countries rarely have arbitrary expropriation of private property. There is little incentive to work or save if the government can take away the fruits of your labor at any time.

Markets. Economic freedom also includes the existence and freedom of markets. A government that constantly interferes in markets where buyers and sellers interact dampens the motive for companies to innovate. The existence of markets, property rights, and economic freedom allowed people to start specializing in the industries they were best at and increased productivity. While these preconditions made growth possible, growth will only continue if people pursue activities that increase labor productivity (investing in physical capital, expanding human capital, and discovering new technologies).

Policies to Encourage Growth

Proper Incentives. In order for people to choose to allocate resources to the accumulation of human and physical capital, they must see some payoff in the future. In other words, the economy must create incentives for people to save, invest, and create new technologies. Countries that seize private property or bail out failing industries do not promote incentives to grow.

Encourage Saving. Savings finance investment in physical capital so, all other things being equal, the higher the savings rate the faster the growth rate. The governments of advanced economies have tax incentives to encourage saving and investment. Economists agree that a more direct way to encourage savings would be to eliminate income taxes and replace them with consumption or sales taxes so that all savings would be exempt from taxes.

Education. A highly educated population is a more productive one and leads to higher levels of economic growth. Having more educated people in the population also makes it more likely someone will develop a significant innovation that increases economic growth.

Research and Development. Since inventors have a very limited window in which they can profit from their discovery, there is an underallocation of resources to research and development. Therefore the government has programs such as the National Science Foundation to fund some of the most promising research projects. The government also has its own research labs for the military and NASA, for example.

International Trade. Similarly, economic growth can be accelerated by limiting protection of domestic industries and encouraging free trade. We saw in Chapter 2, that free trade will allow both trading partners to reach points beyond their production possibilities curves. Increased free trade opens up larger markets for producers, increasing the incentive for innovation, and reduces prices to consumers, increasing the real wage. Again, developing countries tend to protect domestic industries, partially because of historical tensions with the industrialized world.

III. THE BUSINESS CYCLE

Phases

While the long-run trend of the economy has been one of consistent growth, in the short run the economy can be up or down. The fluctuation of macroeconomic variables from year to year is called the business cycle. In periods of expansion, unemployment and inflation are low and national economic activity speeds up. During contractions the opposite occurs. As seen in figure 8.2, the point at which an expansion ends and a contraction begins is called a peak and the end of a contraction is called a trough. Despite being called cycles, there is nothing regular or predictable about business cycles; expansions and contractions vary in length and intensity. In spite of their up and down

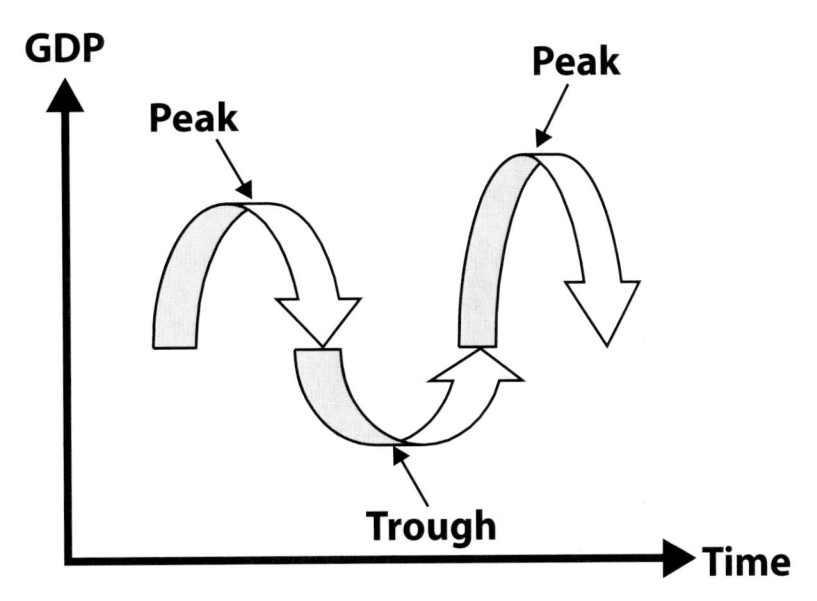

Figure 8.2 • **Phases of the Business Cycle**
Business activity rises and falls over time. The cycles do not have a predictable length or timing.

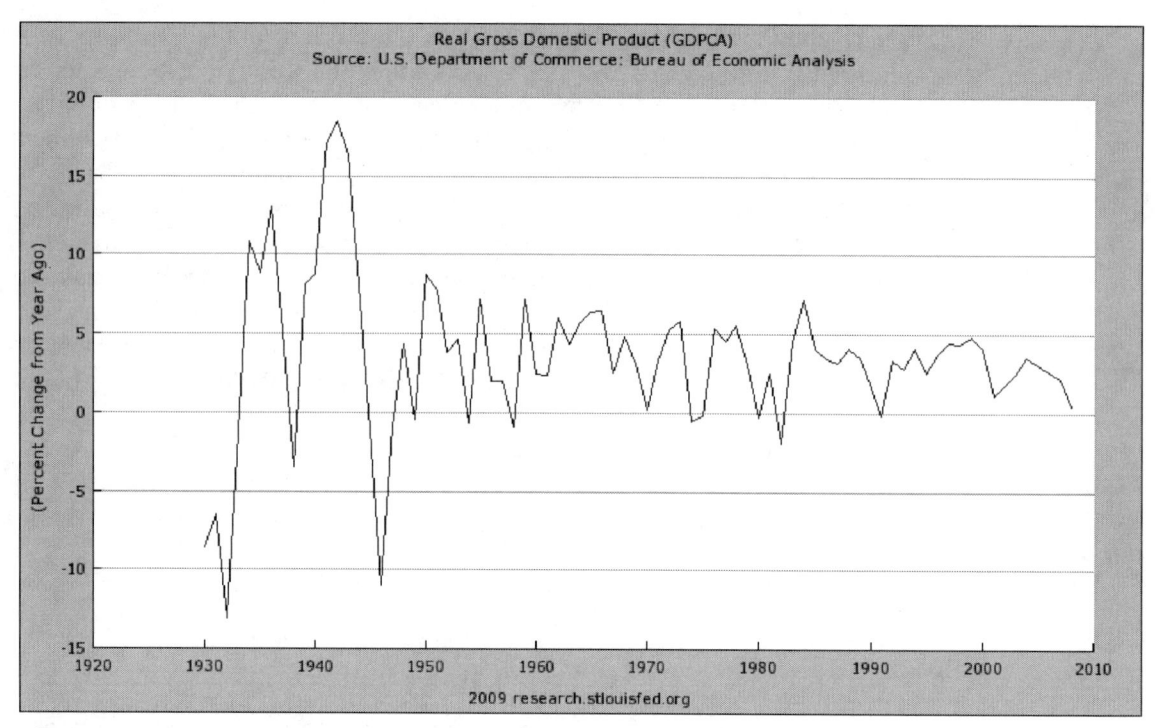

Figure 8.3 • US Real GDP Changes
Although the United States economy grew steadily throughout the twentieth century, the rate of growth was not constant. The economy constantly experiences periods of rapid expansion and downturns.

nature, business cycles follow an overall upward trend with the current peak typically being higher than the previous one.

History

We measure the business cycle by changes in the total output (GDP). During expansionary periods business activity speeds up, unemployment falls, and total output rises rapidly. During economic downturns business activity slows down, unemployment rises, and total output decreases or at least rises at a slow pace. GDP in the United States has grown steadily at an average of about 3 percent a year since the Great Depression; in other words, the average American can now consume about thirteen times what he could in 1929. Looking more closely at figure 8.3, however, we see that growth has not been constant or steady at all. Instead, short-run business activity looks more like a roller coaster. The growth of the United States has been anything but smooth. Just because the average growth of the United States has been about 3 percent does not mean the economy grew at exactly this rate every year. In some years the economy grew at a slower pace. In fact, sometimes the economy has contracted, that is, ended up with a lower GDP than the year before.

Classical Theory. Understanding the business cycle has never come easy to economists and different schools of thought on the matter have developed. The Classical School grew out of the work of Adam Smith in the late eighteenth century and David Ricardo early in the nineteenth century. Proponents of the Classical School believed strongly in the invisible hand, the idea that when left alone markets will move resources to their most effective use and maximize the standard of living for society. Sure there would be short-term periods of adjustment, but after these adjustments everybody who wanted a job could find one and everything that was produced would be sold. There could be no contracted depression because eventually price and wages would fall low enough that everything would be purchased and everyone would get hired. Classical economists held a wait and see approach to the financial panics that plagued the United States in the late nineteenth and early twentieth century.

The Great Depression. Classical economists could no longer ignore the business cycle when the Great Depression hit. GDP decreased every year from 1929 to 1933, dropping further and further from pre-Depression levels. In total, the economy contracted about 30 percent from its pre-Depression level of GDP. Economies around the world ground to a halt as businesses found little incentive to invest in new production. The economy seemed to turn things around in 1933 and GDP grew for the next four years. But even after the end of that growth cycle, GDP was still lower than when the Depression started. Then the bottom fell out again; the economy contracted during 1938 and 1939 as well. The US had experienced a Lost Decade; GDP was lower when the decade was over than it was when it started.

The Great Depression led to a backlash against the Classical School. How can free markets be the answer if they allow such an economic downturn to happen? Socialism, with state ownership of property and central planning, was seen as a pleasant alternative at the time. People demanded a more active government that intervened when the economy went sour.

Keynesian Theory. The Keynesian School grew out of the desire for a government that actively intervened in the economy. Keynesians believe that the economy is inherently unstable and that some central force needs to be continuously coaxing and pushing it in the right direction to achieve high levels of production and employment. The Keynesian School grew out of the ideas of British economist John Maynard Keynes and his reflections on the causes of, and possible solutions to, the Great Depression. Keynes believed that the Great Depression, indeed any recession, happened because private spending (consumption expenditure plus investment expenditure) fell. In order to keep this decrease in private spending from derailing business, the government needs to increase public spending and pick up the slack. Many believed the Keynesian policies of FDR's New Deal ended the Depression in the US, and by the 1950s Keynesian economics was the mainstream.

Post-World War II. We will never know how or if the Great Depression would have ended if not for World War II. The demand of wartime production combined with the enlistment of millions of working-age men in the military vastly increased business activity and reduced unemployment. GDP grew at an unheard of rate of 19 percent in 1942 and the economy was back on track. Following the war, the economy seemed to be back on a more reasonable path of alternating expansion and contraction periods. These periods of contraction, called recessions, are what we are most concerned with. There have been twelve recessions since the end of World War II, the most significant being the one right after the war as businesses and individuals attempted to adjust to the new peacetime economy.

Two recessions, one in 1980 and another beginning in July 1981 mark the early 1980s. When another recession occurs during or immediately following the recovery from a previous recession we call it a W-shaped recession because of its appearance on the graph of GDP growth rate. Since the second recession started mid-year after the recovery from another recession, GDP actually went up during 1981, but at a slower rate than average. Following the second recession in the 1980s, the US enjoyed a considerable period of growth and prosperity.

The 1990s began just as poorly as the 1980s did. Although the early 1990s recession only lasted eight months, a slow recovery continued to drag down the unemployment rate and much of the gains of the 1980s were lost. The rest of the 1990s, however, proved to be quite prosperous. By 2000, unemployment had fallen below 4 percent, one of the lowest rates ever. The popping of the dot-com bubble and the September 11 terrorist attacks led to another brief recession in 2001. GDP growth eventually accelerated and unemployment fell while investment reached new heights. A combination of poor financial regulation, overextension of credit, and a housing market collapse led to the most recent recession in our history, which officially ended in October 2009.

IV. MODELING THE ECONOMY

Outcomes

The historical record seems to show that each decade has at least one bust cycle. But the historical record can't tell us why this happens or if we can do anything to prevent it. Keynesian economists believed that government intervention could solve business cycles while Classical economists believed trying to intervene would only make thinks worse.

To understand how to approach business cycles, we need to know why they happen and what elements of the market can correct or exacerbate the situation. We want to amplify the self-correcting elements and dampen the elements that make things worse. The macroeconomy is basically a technology or a function; you put in some inputs and you get out some macroeconomic outcomes. These outcomes include all of the macro measures we have been studying—GDP (total output), unemployment, inflation—as well as the growth rate and other measures like the value of the dollar, the government budget deficit, and our trade balance. Our score on each of these measures determines our level of overall economic performance.

Determinants

The levels of outcomes all depend on various factors or determinants of economic activity. These determinants can be placed into three broad categories: internal market forces, external shocks, and government policy. Internal market forces like demand, investment, and population growth go a long way in explaining macro outcomes but they are constantly being manipulated and altered by external shocks like wars and natural disasters or policy decisions related to taxes, the money supply, and trade restrictions. A Keynesian economist would advocate employing the create policies to manipulate the internal market forces into producing desirable macroeconomic outcomes.

Stability?

The crucial question here is the need for government policy at all. Classical economists believed that the market could adequately adjust to both internal and external shocks and saw no need for government intervention. Keynes believed that without the government, the economy would eventually derail in a Depression-like disaster. Even today, the argument over the effectiveness of government intervention in the market continues. Many economists still believe that the market can self-stabilize and any government stabilization policy is a waste of money at best. We will return to the debate between the Keynesian and Classical schools in Chapter 9.

V. AGGREGATE SUPPLY AND AGGREGATE DEMAND

Aggregate Demand

But how do these determinants become macro outcomes? Since all of the macro outcomes depend on some form of market transaction that seems like a good place to start. In order to alter macro outcomes, these determinants must alter supply or demand at the national level in some way. Aggregate demand is like the market demand for all products put together. Just as demand illustrates how much of a product the market wants to buy at various prices, aggregate demand describes the total spending all buyers in the country want to make at different possible price levels. As figure 8.4 illustrates, the aggregate demand curve shows that as the price level in the economy rises, people are willing to spend less and less; as a result, real output (GDP) demanded in the economy falls. This can be thought of as the law of aggregate demand.

Just like the demand curve for any single product, the aggregate demand curve slopes downward. The reasoning for this inverse relationship is not the same as it was for the demand curve for a single product, however. The law of demand for a single

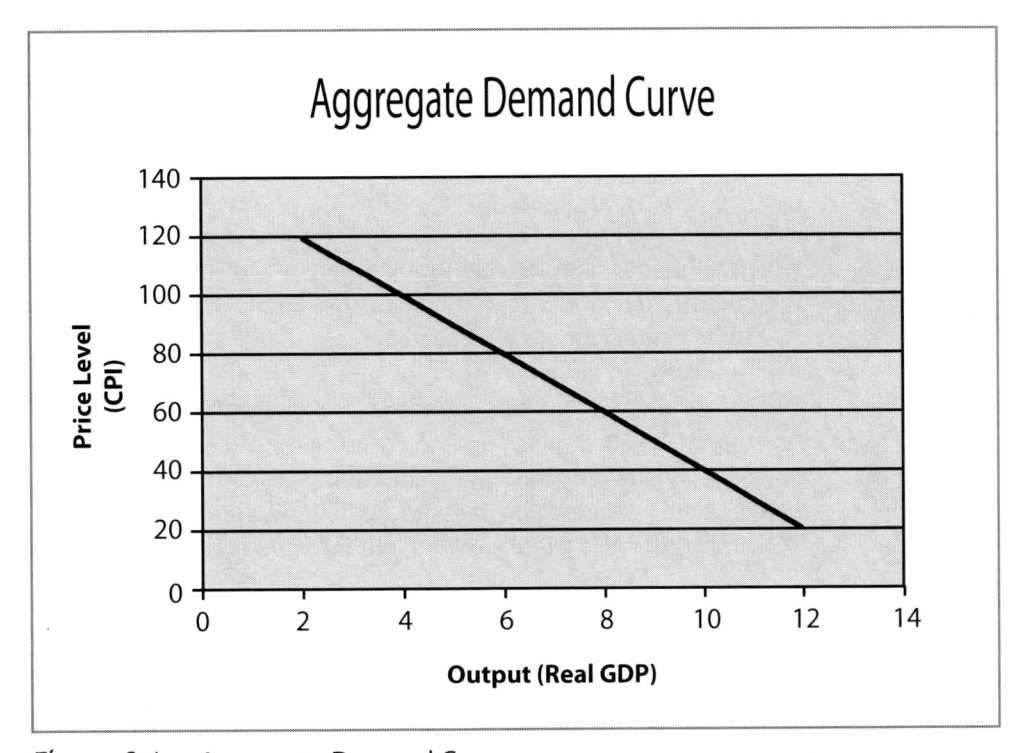

Figure 8.4 • Aggregate Demand Curve
The aggregate demand curve is downward-sloping just like the market demand curve, but not for the same reasons.

product holds because of the income and substitution effects; as the price of a good rises, people can afford less of the product (income effect) and people will choose to put more money towards relatively less expensive goods (substitution effect).

These explanations do not extend to the aggregate demand curve, though. For instance, since the aggregate demand curve refers to the overall price level, not the price of one product, no product is becoming relatively less expensive as you move down the curve. As such, there is no substitution effect. Likewise, a movement down (to the right) of the aggregate demand curve results from a decrease in the overall price level, not a decrease of the price of any one product. When the overall price level decreases, products become cheaper, but incomes fall because the people are receiving a lower price for the products they produce. Therefore, a decrease in the overall price level does not necessarily produce an income effect. Why, then, is the aggregate demand curve downward sloping?

Real Balances Effect. A change in the price level has three specific effects that change the quantity of aggregate demand. The first effect is called the real-balances effect. This effect rests on the idea that a rise in the overall price level reduces the purchasing power of the public's accumulated savings; inflation hurts savers. As a result, the country is technically poorer and spending will fall. People need to use money to replace their eroding savings accounts before they buy things they want today.

Interest Rate Effect. The second reason behind the inverse relationship between the price level and aggregate demand is the interest-rate effect. An increase in the price level means more money is needed for the everyday transactions people and businesses need to make. In other words, when the price level increases the demand for money rises. We know that, everything else being equal, when the demand for something rises, its equilibrium price rises; since the price of money is the interest rate, this means the interest rate rises. A rise in the interest rate reduces consumption spending, especially on things that are bought on credit like cars and houses. When the interest rate rises, it is more difficult for businesses to find investment opportunities with an expected rate of return high enough to be profitable, so the quantity of investment spending falls. Higher interest rates even cause the stock market to slump.

Foreign Purchases Effect. The final reason the aggregate demand curve slopes downward is the foreign purchases effect. When the price level in the United States rises quickly relative to that in other countries, American consumers find that foreign goods are relatively cheaper, causing imports to rise. At the same time, foreign consumers see American goods as relatively more expensive, resulting in a drop in exports. As result the quantity demanded of net exports fall and GDP decreases.

Shifts in the Aggregate Demand Curve. Just like the demand curve for a product, we need to distinguish between a movement along the curve and a shift of the entire curve. When nothing else in the economy changes, a change in the overall price level will change the level of spending and thus the output of the economy. A movement along a single aggregate demand curve illustrates this change. However, a change in one of the determinants of aggregate demand, which we will discuss in greater detail in Chapter 9, will shift the entire aggregate demand curve to the left or right.

Aggregate Supply

If the aggregate demand curve shows the different levels of real output people demand at different possible price levels, it should be no surprise that the aggregate supply curve would illustrate the different levels of real output supplied by the entire economy at different possible price levels. Where this curve differs from the single product sup-

Long-Run Aggregate Supply Curve

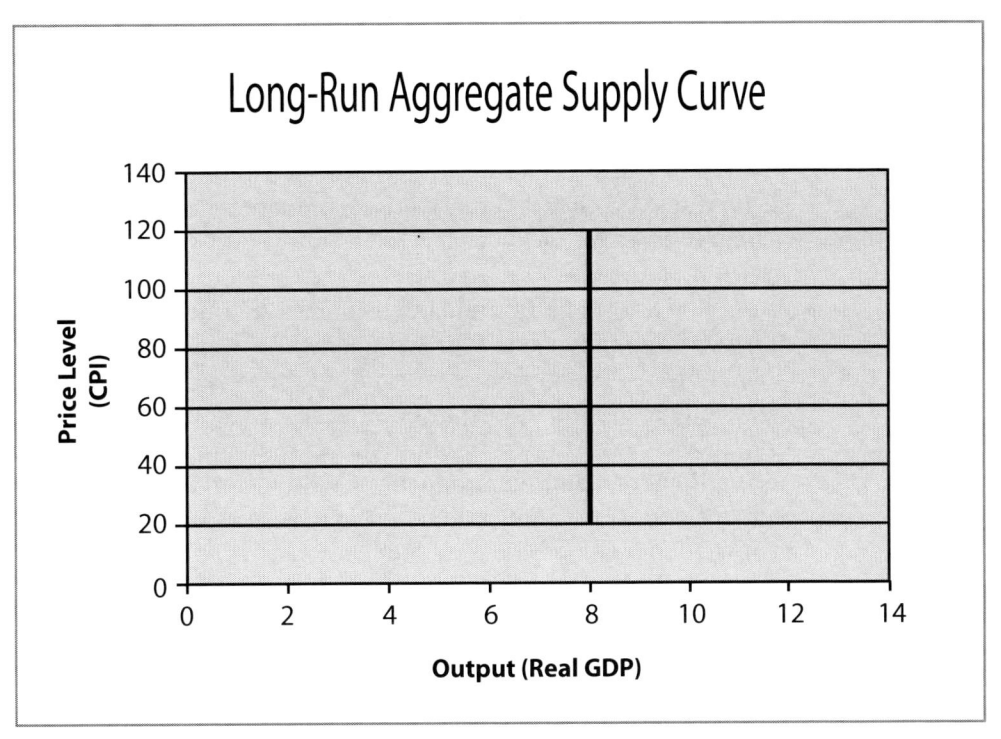

Figure 8.5 • Aggregate Supply Curve in the Long-Run
In the long-run, any increase in product prices will lead to increases in input prices, leaving profits unchanged. Without any change in profits, businesses have no incentive to increase production as price level rises.

ply curve we studied in Chapter 3 is that responses to price level changes by the production side of the economy differ depending on whether we are interested in the short run or the long run. There no set time period (a month, a year, two years) we can define as separating the short run from the long run. Instead, the long run is considered any time period long enough for wages (and all other resource prices) to adjust to price changes and the short run is any time period in which wages do not have time to adjust price changes.

Long-run. Unlike any curve we have seen so far, figure 8.5 shows that the long-run aggregate supply curve is completely vertical at the full-employment level of output. No matter what the price level is, the economy will always produce the full-employment level of output in the long run (the time period long enough for resource prices to adjust to price changes). In other words, long-run aggregate supply is perfectly inelastic, or unresponsive to price changes.

Why does this occur? Why don't businesses want to supply more at higher prices and less at lower prices like they did in Chapter 3? The answer lies in the difference between the price level of the entire economy and the price of one product. If the price level in the economy increases then the nominal price that any one producer receives for his goods increases. But since we are talking about the long run, the price of each of the inputs this producer uses in production has increased at the same rate; workers, suppliers, and landlords all demand higher pay since prices are rising. As a result, the real profit he receives per unit of output does not change at all and so he has no incentive to increase quantity supplied. If every producer in the economy faces the same situation, aggregate output supplied will not change.

Short-run. In real life, though, wages and other resource prices do not immediately adjust to price level changes. If the price level rises, but input prices do not, firms will see an increase in real profit if they ramp up production. This increase in real profit encourages firms to produce more at higher price levels in the short run. As a result, the short-run aggregate supply curve is upward sloping just like the supply curve for a single product. Another difference arises, though, when you notice that the aggregate supply curve is flatter at lower levels of output and steeper at higher levels of output as shown in figure 8.6.

At low levels of output, many resources are idle or under-utilized. As result, adding one new machine or one new worker to a business can produce a great deal of additional output. At higher levels of output, however, adding one new resource does not create much additional output because most resources are already employed. In addition, in the short run we are limited to certain amounts of fixed capital—like factories and equipment—and the production facility would just get too crowded at some point. In other words, per-unit production costs rise as output rises, and this reduces the incentive to increase production. Since the macroeconomic policy deals with solutions to short-run problems, we will focus our attention on the short-run aggregate supply curve.

Curve Shifts. The price level and quantity of aggregate output supplied are directly related (in the short run) so any increase in the price level will move you along the short-run aggregate supply, all else being equal. Sometimes, however, factors in the economy change which affect the level of aggregate supply at every possible level. Such factors, called aggregate supply shifters, can shift the entire aggregate supply curve to the left or right. A shift of the aggregate supply curve to the right indicates that firms are

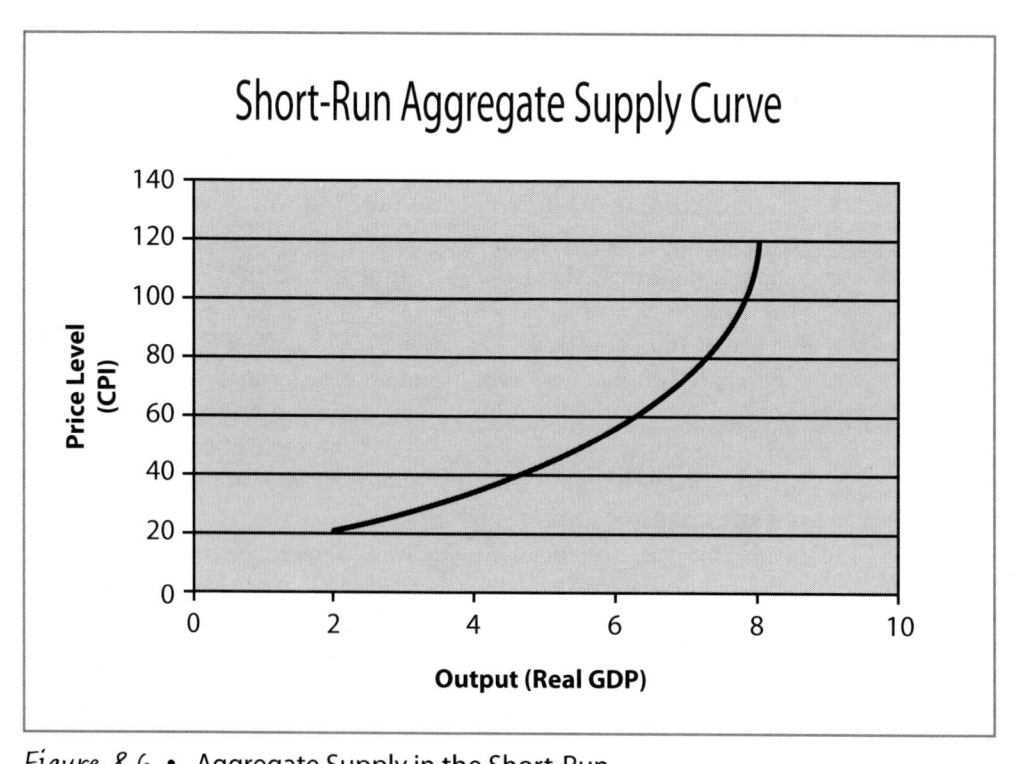

Figure 8.6 • **Aggregate Supply in the Short-Run**
In the short-run, businesses can take advantage of the profit effect resulting in the aggregate supply curve being upward-sloping. There is a limit to how much they can increase production in the short-run, however, causing the curve to be steeper at higher levels of output.

willing to produce more aggregate output at a given price level, usually because of a reduction in per-unit production costs. A leftward shift indicates just the opposite.

Equilibrium

Okay, now for the fun the part. Just like we did in Chapter 3, we are going to put supply and demand together and notice something quite interesting. The point that the economy will gravitate to in the short run, macroeconomic equilibrium, is indicated by the intersection of the aggregate demand curve and the aggregate supply curve. Only at the price level of this intersection are aggregate output demanded and aggregate output supplied exactly equal, as figure 8.7 illustrates. This price level is called the equilibrium price level and the real output at this point is called the equilibrium real output.

At any price level below the equilibrium level, output demanded will exceed output supplied and buyers will compete over the scarce supply and bid up the price level throughout the economy. This increase in the level will encourage producers to increase their amount of output supplied and buyers to reduce their quantity of output demanded until equilibrium is achieved. At any price above the equilibrium level output supplied will exceed output demanded, and businesses will lower prices and cut back production to encourage more people to buy their products.

As was the case in Chapter 3, a shift in either or both of the curves will cause the equilibrium price and quantity to change. Now that we see the basics of equilibrium determination in the AD-AS Model, in the next chapter we will focus on how the government uses shifts in the curves to change the equilibrium.

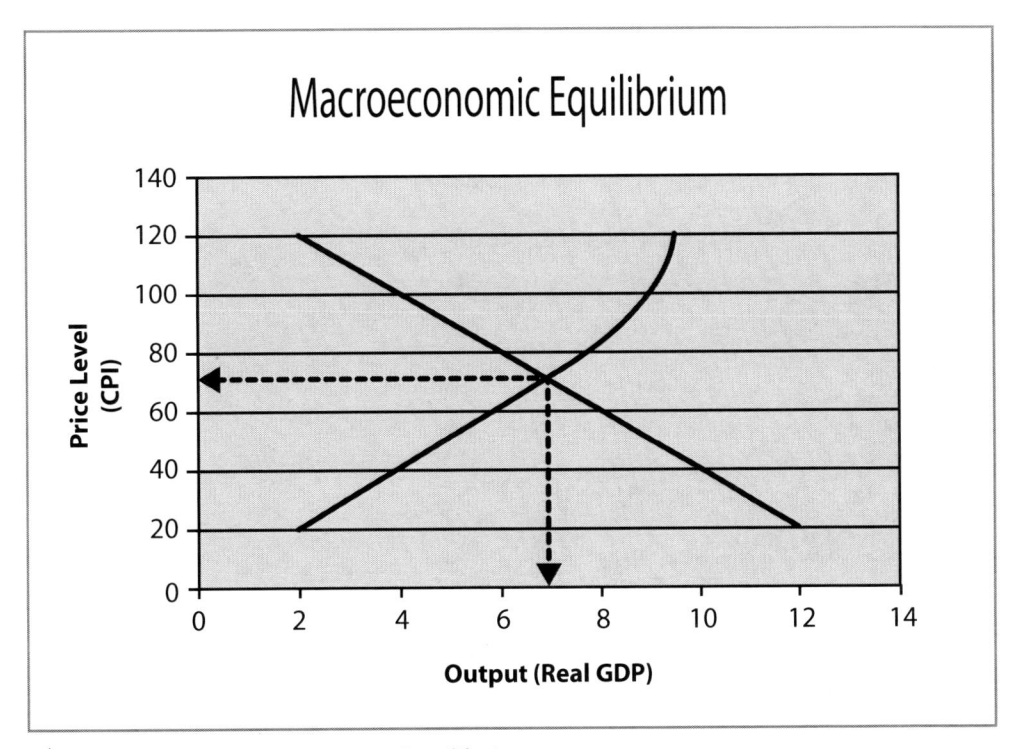

Figure 8.7 • Macroeconomic Equilibrium
The aggregate demand and short-run aggregate supply curves intersect at one and only one point. At this macroeconomic equilibrium, all of the output produced by all of the businesses in the economy is sold.

CHAPTER 8 SUMMARY

- Economic growth rates are measured using the change in **real GDP per capita** over time.
- The **Rule of 70** states that if a country grows consistently at rate X, it will double in size in $\frac{70}{X}$ years.
- Most of the growth in the United States results from increases in **productivity**.
- Increasing **economic freedom** speeds up economic growth.
- The **business cycles** that cause economic activity to rise and fall are not predictable, cyclical, or consistent.
- **Keynesian economics** asserts that the market economy is **inherently unstable** and needs government intervention to keep it on track. **Classical economists** believe that the market will **self-adjust** if you leave it alone.
- Business cycles because of changes in **aggregate demand** and **aggregate supply**.
- The aggregate demand curve is downward-sloping because of the **real balances effect**, the **interest rate effect**, and the **foreign purchases effect**.
- The aggregate supply curve is **vertical in the long-run** because once input prices catch up to product prices, there is increased profits to be gained from increasing output.

CHAPTER 8 Exercises

Name _____

1) Which figure is commonly used to measure economic growth?
   A) unemployment rate
   B) real GDP
   C) real GDP per capita
   D) nominal GDP

1) _____

2) If country is growing at a rate of 2% per year, how long will it take for that country's GDP to double?
   A) 35 years
   B) 50 years
   C) 100 years
   D) not enough information

2) _____

3) Which of the following is NOT a source of economic growth?
   A) growth in labor productivity
   B) human capital
   C) new discoveries
   D) reduced international trade

3) _____

4) Classical economists believe that the economy will bounce back from a recession
   A) after a period self-adjustment.
   B) only after government intervention.
   C) once businesses control all economic decisions.
   D) none of the above, classical economists do not believe in recessions.

4) _____

5) Keynesian economists promote government intervention because
   A) the market is inherently unstable.
   B) sometimes private spending falls below what is necessary to maintain full employment.
   C) the market needs constant coaxing to maintain the natural rate of unemployment.
   D) all of the above

5) _____

6) Which of the following is NOT a reason why the aggregate demand curve slopes downward?
   A) real balances effect
   B) income effect
   C) interest rate effect
   D) foreign purchases effect

6) _____

7) What is the shape of the long-run aggregate supply curve?
   A) horizontal
   B) vertical
   C) upward-sloping
   D) downward-sloping

7) _____

8) What is true at the equilibrium price level?
   A) the economy is at full employment
   B) there is 0% inflation
   C) aggregate output supplied equals aggregate output demanded
   D) GDP is maximized

8) _____

9) If you were the president of a developing country, what are some of the policies you would promote to accelerate economic growth?

_____
_____
_____
_____

10) Explain why the long-run aggregate supply curve is vertical, but the short-run aggregate supply curve is upward sloping.

_____
_____
_____
_____

Article Review 2

Name _____

Choose any one of the articles from Chapters 5–8. Use the space provided below to summarize the article. Then, answer the questions at the end of the article on the back of this page.

1.

2.

3.

Unit 2 Review

Name _____

Use this review to prepare for Exam 2. You can view the answers in the "unit review answers" section in the back of the text, but try to complete it on your own first.

1) Which of the following would be counted toward GDP?
   A) babysitting your cousins
   B) buying stock in a company
   C) buying a previously owned home
   D) buying a new home

   1) _____

2) Which of the following correctly identifies the treatment of exports and imports in GDP?
   A) subtract value of exports and imports
   B) add value of imports and subtract value of exports
   C) add value of exports and imports
   D) add value of exports and subtract value of imports

   2) _____

3) If the nominal GDP in 2009 is $14 billion and the GDP deflator is 150, what is the real GDP?
   A) $14 billion
   B) $9.3 billion
   C) $1.4 billion
   D) $6.25 billion

   3) _____

4) If the real GDP is $10 trillion in 2007 and $11 trillion in 2008, what was the growth rate between 2007 and 2008?
   A) 10%
   B) 100%
   C) 1%
   D) .1%

   4) _____

5) What is the difference between net domestic product and national income?
   A) NI = NDP − personal income taxes
   B) NI = NDP − depreciation
   C) NI = NDP + net foreign factor income
   D) NI = NDP + net foreign factor income − statistical discrepancy

   5) _____

6) Which of the following groups is NOT included in the labor force?
   A) employed persons
   B) retirees
   C) unemployed persons
   D) people who were temporarily laid off

   6) _____

7) What type of unemployment occurs when a person goes on several job interviews before picking the job they like the best?
   A) frictional
   B) cyclical
   C) structural
   D) seasonal

   7) _____

8) What type of unemployment occurs when firms let people go after the holiday buying season?
   A) frictional
   B) cyclical
   C) structural
   D) seasonal

   8) _____

9) The natural rate of unemployment only includes which two types of unemployment?
   A) structural and cyclical
   B) frictional and cyclical
   C) structural an seasonal
   D) frictional and structural

9) _____

10) What is the tradeoff of government policies to reduce unemployment?
    A) reduced labor force participation rate
    B) increased social stress
    C) none, reducing unemployment is always a good thing
    D) increased inflation

10) _____

11) If oil prices tripled, what type of inflation would occur, considering oil is an important input for many different products?
    A) deflation
    B) demand-pull inflation
    C) no price level change
    D) cost-push inflation

11) _____

12) If the CPI is 175, how much has the price level risen since the base year?
    A) 25%
    B) 75%
    C) 175%
    D) 1.75%

12) _____

13) What is the inflation rate between 1990 and 2009 if the CPI was 136 in 1990 and 214.5 in 2009?
    A) .58%
    B) 57.7%
    C) 114.5%
    D) 78.5%

13) _____

14) Who loses the most from inflation?
    A) people who buy goods that have risen in price slower than inflation
    B) people who sell goods that have risen in price faster than inflation
    C) people who live on fixed incomes
    D) borrowers

14) _____

15) If your paycheck rises from $2,000 a month to $2,100 month and inflation is at 8%, how has your real wage changed?
    A) real wage has fallen
    B) no impact on real wage
    C) not enough information
    D) real wage has risen

15) _____

16) If country is growing at a rate of 3% per year, how long will it take for that country's GDP to double?
    A) 35 years
    B) 33 years
    C) 23 years
    D) not enough information

16) _____

17) Which of the following is a source of economic growth?
    A) human capital
    B) bailing out dying industries
    C) increased government regulation of business
    D) reduced international trade

17) _____

18) Keynesian economists promote government intervention because
    A) the market needs constant coaxing to maintain the natural rate of unemployment.
    B) the market is inherently unstable.
    C) sometimes private spending falls below what is necessary to maintain full employment.
    D) all of the above

18) _____

Name _____

19) Which of the following is a reason why the aggregate demand curve slopes downward?
    A) income effect
    B) interest rate effect
    C) substitution effect
    D) law of demand

19) _____

20) Why is long-run aggregate supply curve vertical?
    A) prices do not rise in the long-run
    B) businesses cannot see price increases
    C) consumers are unwilling to buy more if prices rise
    D) because there is no additional profits if prices and costs both rise

20) _____

21) Is nominal GDP or real GDP a better measure of standard of living across time? Why?

22) Why is an unemployment rate of zero impossible?

23) Why did the government choose 3% as its inflation goal instead of 0%? What is the opportunity cost of pursuing a zero inflation rate policy?

24) If you were the president of a developing country, what are some of the policies you would promote to accelerate economic growth?

25) What are some of the main differences between Keynesian economic theory and Classical economic theory?

139

Exam 2 Formula Sheet

Name _____

Chapter 5

$$GDP\ per\ capita = \frac{GDP}{Popluation}$$

$$GDP = C + I + G + X_n$$

Nominal GDP = Current Output × Current Prices

Real GDP = Current Output × Base Year Prices

$$\frac{(New\ Value - Old\ Value)}{Old\ Value} \times 100 = Percentage\ Change$$

Net Investment = Gross Investment − Depreciation

Chapter 6

$$Labor\ Force\ Participation\ Rate = \frac{Labor\ Force}{Working\ Age\ Population}$$

$$Unemployment\ Rate = \frac{Number\ of\ Unemployed\ People}{Labor\ Force} \times 100$$

GDP Gap = Potential GDP − Actual GDP

Chapter 7

$$CPI = \frac{Cost\ of\ Market\ Basket\ in\ Current\ Year}{Cost\ of\ Market\ Basket\ in\ Base\ Year} \times 100$$

$$Inflation\ Rate = \frac{New\ CPI - Old\ CPI}{Old\ CPI} \times 100$$

Nominal Interest Rate = Real Interest Rate + Inflationary Premium

$$Real\ GDP = \frac{Nominal\ GDP}{GDP\ Deflator} \times 100$$

$$Real\ Wage\ Rate = \frac{Nominal\ Wage\ Rate}{CPI} \times 100$$

Chapter 8

Rule of 70:

$$\text{Number of Years to Double in Size} = \frac{70}{\text{Growth Rate}}$$

$$\text{Labor Productivity} = \frac{\text{Total Output}}{\text{Number of Workers}}$$

Aggregate Demand and Fiscal Policy

I. MACRO FAILURES

While the intersection of the aggregate demand and aggregate supply curves indicate that the amount of total output people want to buy is equal to the total amount of output businesses want to produce, there is in nothing stating that this output level is efficient or desirable. In fact, it is entirely possible that the equilibrium level of output is far below the full-employment level of output. If the economy tends toward a point below the full-employment level of output, people will compete over this relatively scarce output causing the equilibrium price to be higher than the desired level (demand-pull inflation). A low-output, high-price equilibrium would certainly be undesirable.

Even if the aggregate demand and aggregate supply curves do intersect at the perfect spot, giving us full-employment level output, there is nothing guaranteeing they will stay there. The aggregate demand and aggregate supply curves can and do shift for a variety of reasons, meaning any optimal equilibrium will probably be short-lived.

The perfect macro outcome would be if aggregate demand and aggregate supply intersected exactly at the full-employment output level. At this point the government would be meeting both its employment and price stability goals. Keynes advocated government intervention because he believed the possibility of the market reaching or maintaining this outcome without any intervention was microscopic. The aggregate demand curve alone is the result of independent decisions by millions of consumers, thousands of businesses, and hundreds of government entities. What reason is there to believe that these independent decisions will add up to the single perfect outcome? The more likely scenario is that there will be too little or too much aggregate demand and we will end up at the wrong equilibrium.

Recession: Too Little Aggregate Demand

Each of these scenarios has its drawbacks. Too little aggregate demand occurs when the amount of output demanded at the price level associated with full-employment output is lower than the amount of output supplied at that price level. In other words, the aggregate demand curve is to the left of where it would need to be to achieve the perfect outcome.

Since businesses would be producing way more output than people would want to buy if they operated at full-employment in this scenario, they will slow down the hiring process and increase firing to reduce the costs of production. A new equilibrium would occur at a lower price level and lower output level than at the perfect outcome as indicated by the intersection of AS and AD_1 in figure 9.1; in short, a recession.

Keynes referred to the distance between the full-employment level of output and equilibrium output, when there is insufficient demand, as the recessionary gap. When aggregate demand falls, people are not willing to purchase the full-employment level of

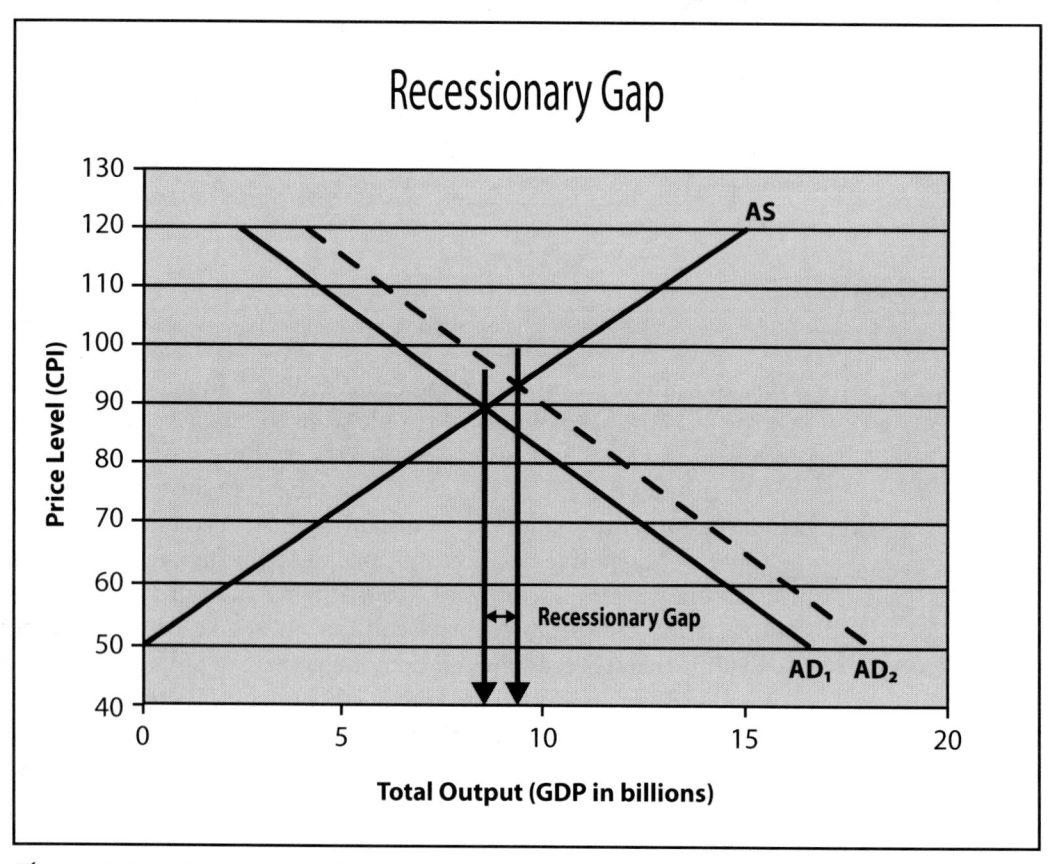

Figure 9.1 • Recessionary Gap
When the aggregate supply and aggregate demand curves intersect at a point below full-employment, the gap between the equilibrium output level and the full-employment level is called the recessionary gap. In order to close the recessionary gap, Keynesian policy suggests shifting the aggregate demand curve up from AD_1 to AD_2.

output at the prevailing price level. The market will settle at a new equilibrium at a lower output level, resulting in at least some cyclical unemployment.

Inflation: Too Much Aggregate Demand

Since he developed his policies during the Great Depression, Keynes focused on the problems that occur when aggregate demand is insufficient (below the full-employment level). On the other hand, it is certainly also possible that aggregate demand could exceed businesses' ability to supply goods and services, creating an entirely different set of problems.

If the aggregate demand curve shifted to the right from the perfect outcome, then the level of output demanded at the prevailing price level will exceed the output supplied. To achieve equilibrium, producers will work overtime and strain capacity to meet demand. This strain will raise prices as well as output as shown by the intersection of AS and AD_1 in figure 9.2. The distance between the full-employment level of output and the output when there is excessive demand is called the inflationary gap because of its tendency to induce demand-pull inflation. Keynes realized that an equilibrium output level above or below the full-employment level would be problematic.

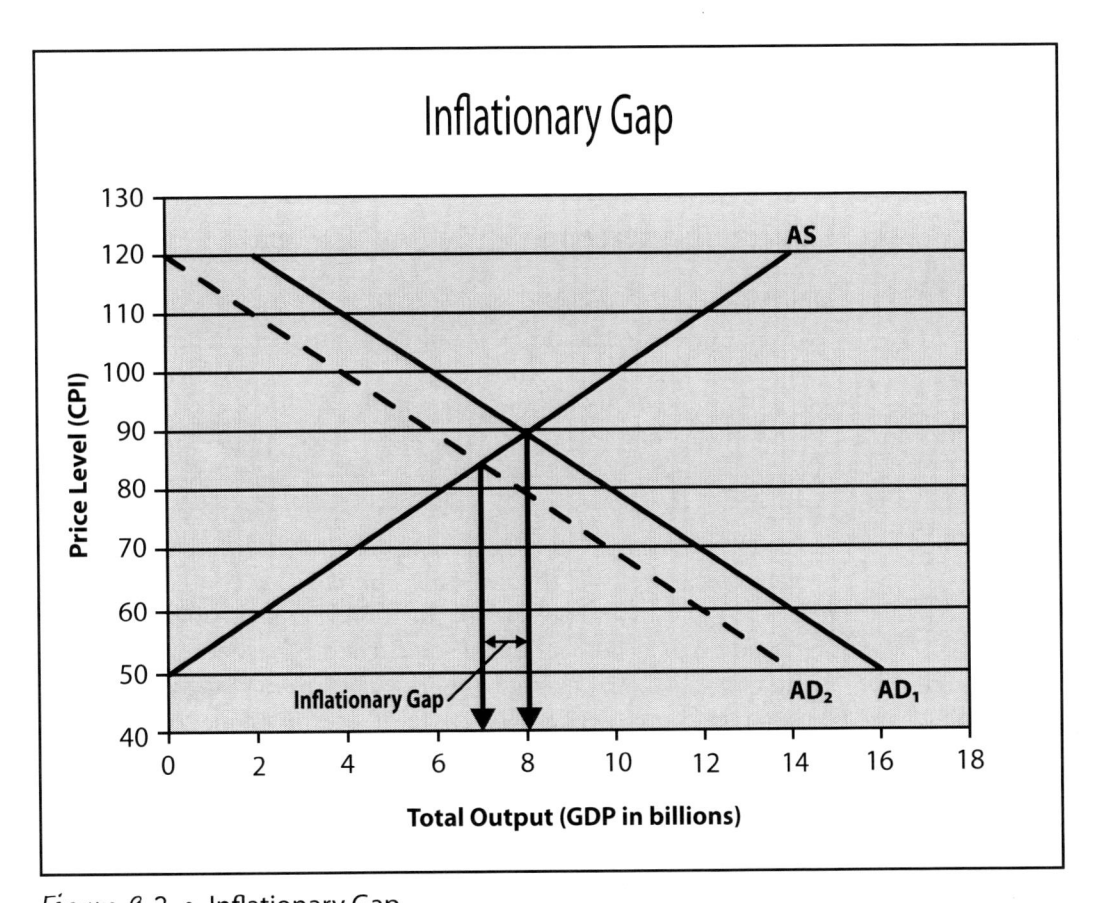

Figure 9.2 • Inflationary Gap
When the aggregate supply and aggregate demand curves intersect at a point above full-employment, the gap between the equilibrium output level and the full-employment level is called the inflationary gap. In order to close the inflationary gap, Keynesian policy suggests shifting the aggregate demand curve back from AD_1 to AD_2.

Keynesian Solutions

All of these factors seem to suggest that short-run economic stability is merely a pipe dream. Further, even if we were to succeed, that success would most likely be short-lived since the curves will inevitably shift again. Classical economists had no such worries, but Keynesian economists use these arguments to suggest the necessity of government intervention.

In fact, the AD-AS model does little to settle the controversy. As mentioned before, both groups believe that aggregate demand and aggregate supply are responsible for business cycle changes. In addition, both believe that one can achieve any outcome by manipulating the shapes and shifts of these curves. The difference lies in whether one can achieve the perfect outcome and how to do so.

Most demand-side economists and policymakers fall into the Keynesian camp, which argues that recessions happen because of declines in private spending on consumption and investment. This deficiency causes aggregate demand to shift back and creates a new equilibrium with a much lower level of output than is preferable. As a result, inadequate spending leads to persistent unemployment.

It is no coincidence that Keynes developed his theory during the Great Depression, the time in history with the biggest deficiency in private spending. Keynes argued that the only way to improve the economy was a massive increase in government spending to make up for the lack of private spending. This increase would shift aggregate demand to the right and equilibrium output levels closer to full employment. The United States government unknowingly tested Keynes's policy with its rapid increase in government spending during World War II. The Great Depression ended and Keynesian economics became the dominant force in economic policymaking.

Classical Theory: Long-Run Self-Adjustment

Many economists find the arguments about short-run fluctuations meaningless, and believe that what we should be trying to improve is the long-run trend of economic performance. Classical economists, for example, believe that the market is self-adjusting and will return to the full-employment level after some time.

Another group of demand-side economists, the monetarists, offer a middle road between Keynesian and Classical economics. Though they agree with Keynesians about the causes of short-run fluctuations, monetary economists believe that in the long run the aggregate supply curve is vertical. That is, it does not matter how you shift the aggregate demand curve, there is only one possible equilibrium level of output. We will return to theories and policies of the monetarists in Chapter 12.

According to both monetary and classical economists, shifting the aggregate demand curve will only change the price level in the long run, not the output level. Since the aggregate supply curve is vertical it does not depend on prices at all, only on institutional factors like technology, tax policy, and the labor force. The profit effect that encouraged greater levels of output at higher price levels and caused the short-run aggregate supply curve to be upward sloping disappears as costs catch up to prices in the long run.

The vertical aggregate supply curve helps explain the Classical economists' assertion that the economy is self-adjusting. Even if some factor causes aggregate demand to shift to the left causing unemployment and recession in the short-run, eventually businesses and factor owners (workers, landlords, etc.) will lower prices so they can sell their excess inventory. Thus there will be a new equilibrium at a lower price level, but the same natural rate of output will be sold as before.

However, to a classical economist, the question is not whether or not macro failures will occur; in a dynamic economy, of course there will bumps in the road. The true question is whether these failures will persist or whether the market will self-adjust. It is true that a lack of aggregate demand will result in short-run unemployment, but it should also result in a drop in the price level. Eventually, people increase their spending as businesses drop prices, and businesses will increase their investment as they see customers start to buy more. The result will be a return to production at the full-employment level of output at a new price level.

II. MACRO EQUILIBRIUM

When interacting in the market, consumers and producers realize there is only one price level where the output demanded and the output supplied are the same. The economy will gravitate toward this macroeconomic equilibrium over time. As we have seen above, this equilibrium may or may not be desirable to the government. If it isn't, how can they attempt to improve upon it? According to Keynesian theory, we need to shift the aggregate demand curve to the right if we are facing a recession and to the left if we are facing inflation. In order to make these adjustments, we need to know the factors that compose the aggregate demand curve.

Components of Aggregate Demand

The four components of aggregate demand are the same four components of GDP we saw in Chapter 5. All of the spending in the economy flows toward consumption, investment, government purchases, and net exports. A shift in aggregate demand, then, would entail changing the amount that is spent on one or more these components at the current price level. How does a change in one these components affect the aggregate demand curve? Let's start with the biggest single component of GDP, consumption, and find out.

III. CONSUMPTION

Disposable Income and Consumption

It is a generally accepted macroeconomic rule that when a person's income rises so does their consumption. The exact relationship between income and consumption can tell us something about the relationship between income and saving, since saving is defined as disposable income not spent on consumption.

Plotting disposable income against consumption on a graph, as in figure 9.3, we see that consumption usually lies below a 45-degree line on which consumption equals disposable income at every point. This makes sense since in most years some of disposable

Consumption Function

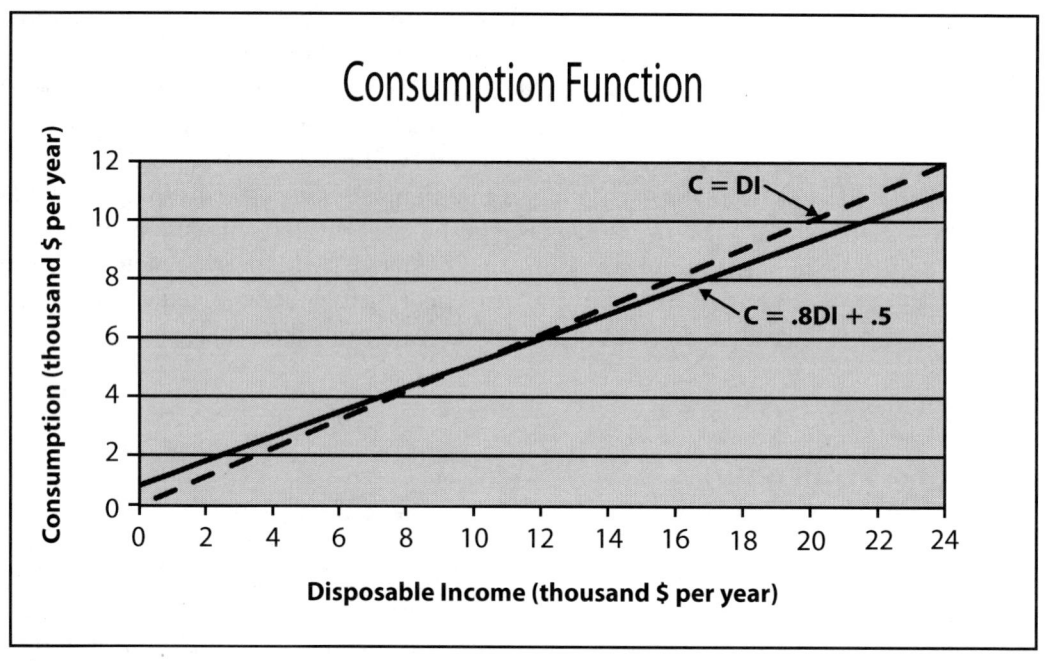

Figure 9.3 • **Consumption Function**
Comparing the consumption function to a 45-degree line allows us to measure savings at the same time. The level of savings is the vertical distance between the 45-degree line and the consumption at any income level.

income goes to saving instead of consumption. In years when consumption lies above the 45-degree line, however, savings is negative. The vertical distance between the consumption line and the 45-degree line increases as disposable income increases, implying a direct relationship between saving and disposable income.

Consumption and Saving

A consumption schedule is a table showing the total amount of consumption that would prevail in a society at different levels of disposable income. A consumption schedule like figure 9.4 illustrates the direct relationships between income and consumption and income and saving; they will both move in the same direction. As income increases households consume more, and households will consume a greater fraction of their income at lower levels of income.

By definition, savings equals disposable income less consumption, so we can develop a savings schedule without any additional data. We simply subtract consumption from disposable income and compare the difference to disposable income. Since households consume a smaller proportion of their income as it increases, there is a direct relationship between income and saving.

For very low levels of disposable income, it is possible that people will have to borrow just to pay for the necessities of life; thus, they will have negative savings. This dissaving is illustrated by a consumption schedule above the 45-degree line; consumption is greater than disposable income, savings is negative.

When the consumption schedule intersects the 45-degree line, consumption is exactly equal to disposable income and savings is zero. This is called the break-even level of income; wealth will be no larger or smaller. Our consumption schedule shows that

Disposable Income	− Consumption	= Savings
$0	$0.5	−$0.5
$1	$1.3	−$0.3
$2	$2.1	−$0.1
$3	$2.9	$0.1
$4	$3.7	$0.3
$5	$4.5	$0.5
$6	$5.3	$0.7
$7	$6.1	$0.9
$8	$6.9	$1.1
$9	$7.7	$1.3
$10	$8.5	$1.5
$11	$9.3	$1.7
$12	$10.1	$1.9

Figure 9.4 • Consumption Schedule (in thousands)

the break-even level will be somewhere between $2 and $3 billion in disposable income. At any income level higher than the break-even level, savings will be positive and can be measured either by the vertical distance between the consumption schedule and the 45-degree line, or directly from the savings schedule.

We might be able to learn more about the relationship between income and consumption and income and saving by developing additional statistics. The first statistics we will discuss are the average propensity to consume (APC) and average propensity to save (APS).

At any point in the consumption or saving schedule dividing consumption or saving by the income at that point will give you the respective average propensity; that is, the proportion of income spent on that activity.

$$APC = \frac{Total\ Consumption}{Total\ Disposable\ Income} \quad APS = \frac{Total\ Savings}{Total\ Disposable\ Income}$$

Since the gap between disposable income and consumption gets bigger as income rises, APC falls and APS rises as income increases. By definition, APC + APS must equal one since disposable income is either spent on consumption or saved.

MPC

While it is important to know how much of their income households spend on consumption, what is of greater importance to a policymaker is how much of each additional dollar a household will spend on consumption. For example, if the government were planning a tax refund to increase spending, they would need to know what fraction of the refund households were going to spend on consumption.

The proportion of any additional or extra income spent on consumption is the marginal propensity to consume. For instance, if a family received a $600 tax refund and spent $540 additional dollars on consumption as a result, then its MPC is .90 or 90 percent. Therefore, MPC can be calculated as the change in consumption divided by the change in income.

$$MPC = \frac{Change\ in\ Consumption}{Change\ in\ Income}$$

MPS

Likewise, the proportion of any additional income that is saved is called the marginal propensity to save, and can be calculated as the change in savings divided by the change in income.

$$MPS = \frac{Change\ in\ Savings}{Change\ in\ Income}$$

However, since each additional dollar must be either consumed or saved, MPC + MPS must equal one. Therefore, MPS can be found by subtracting MPC from one.

$$MPC = 1 - MPS$$

IV. THE CONSUMPTION FUNCTION

Autonomous Consumption

Wealth Effect. While the amount of disposable income plays a crucial role in determining consumption and savings, other economic variables can shift the consumption and savings schedules just like the determinants of supply and demand shifted those curves. In particular, changes that impact the level of consumption at any income level will change the y-intercept of the consumption function, also called the level of autonomous consumption–the amount people would consume if they had no income.

Households save to accumulate wealth, the total amount of real and financial assets in their portfolio. If households already have high levels of wealth, they spend less of their income on savings (saving schedule shifts downward) and spend more of their income on consumption (consumption schedule shifts upward) in what is known as the wealth effect. Upswings in the stock market, for example, convince consumers that their collective wealth has increased, leading to increases in consumption.

Expectations. Price and income expectations can also affect the consumption and saving schedules. If consumers believe prices will rise in the future, they will purchase more goods today, causing the consumption schedule to shift upward and the saving schedule downward. Expectations of a recession (lower income) will cause households to save more today, causing the opposite effect.

Availability of Credit. Increased borrowing by households as whole, as we have seen in the United States over the last twenty years or so, increases the money available for consumption at each level of disposable income; in other words, the consumption schedule shifts upward. Decreasing the level of household debt in the country would cause the opposite effect.

Taxes. When using disposable income as the *x*-axis of the consumption function, taxes are viewed as a change in income, but when using GDP as the *x*-axis, taxes are viewed as a schedule shifter. In particular, changes in taxes shift the consumption and savings schedules in the same direction since increased taxes are financed partly at the expense of consumption and partly at the expense of saving. Likewise, any decrease in taxes will increase saving and consumption at every possible level of GDP.

Income-Dependent Consumption

While some consumption is independent of income, income plays a huge role as well. The rate at which disposable income is turned into consumption is summarized by the MPC, which also happens to be the slope of the consumption function. Because of this relationship, the consumption function informs us not only about how consumers have spent their money, but also how they will spend future income. The MPC tells us how consumption (and by extension aggregate demand) will change when income changes.

Aggregate Consumption

The relationship described in the consumption function works just as well for the country as it does for the individual; you just have to change the scale. Just as individuals save more as their incomes rise, a country with higher disposable income will save more than a poorer country, *ceteris paribus*.

Shifts in the consumption function reveal changes in the amount spent on consumption at various income levels. Changes in autonomous consumption will change the *y*-intercept and move the curve up and down, while changes in MPC will make the curve flatter or steeper. Autonomous consumption, the *y*-intercept, will change when expectations, wealth, credit, or taxes change. Shocks to consumer confidence like stock market crashes or natural disasters will reduce expectations about future income and shift the consumption function down, for example.

Aggregate Demand Shifters

Since consumption is a determinant of aggregate demand, shifts in the consumption function will be reflected in the aggregate demand curve. Remember that the aggregate demand curve depicts the level of output demanded at various price levels with income held constant. If the amount of consumption at a given income level falls (the consumption function shifts down) the amount of output demanded at any given price level will fall, too. A downward shift of the consumption function implies a leftward shift of the aggregate demand curve.

As a result we know that the factors that shift the consumption function—expectations, wealth, credit, and taxes—also shift the aggregate demand curve. A rise in consumer income will cause a movement along the consumption function and also raise the level of aggregate demand if the price level remains constant.

Aggregate Demand Shifts and the Business Cycle

Keynesians believe that changes in aggregate demand cause business cycles. Recessions occur when aggregate demand falls off and expansions occur when aggregate demand

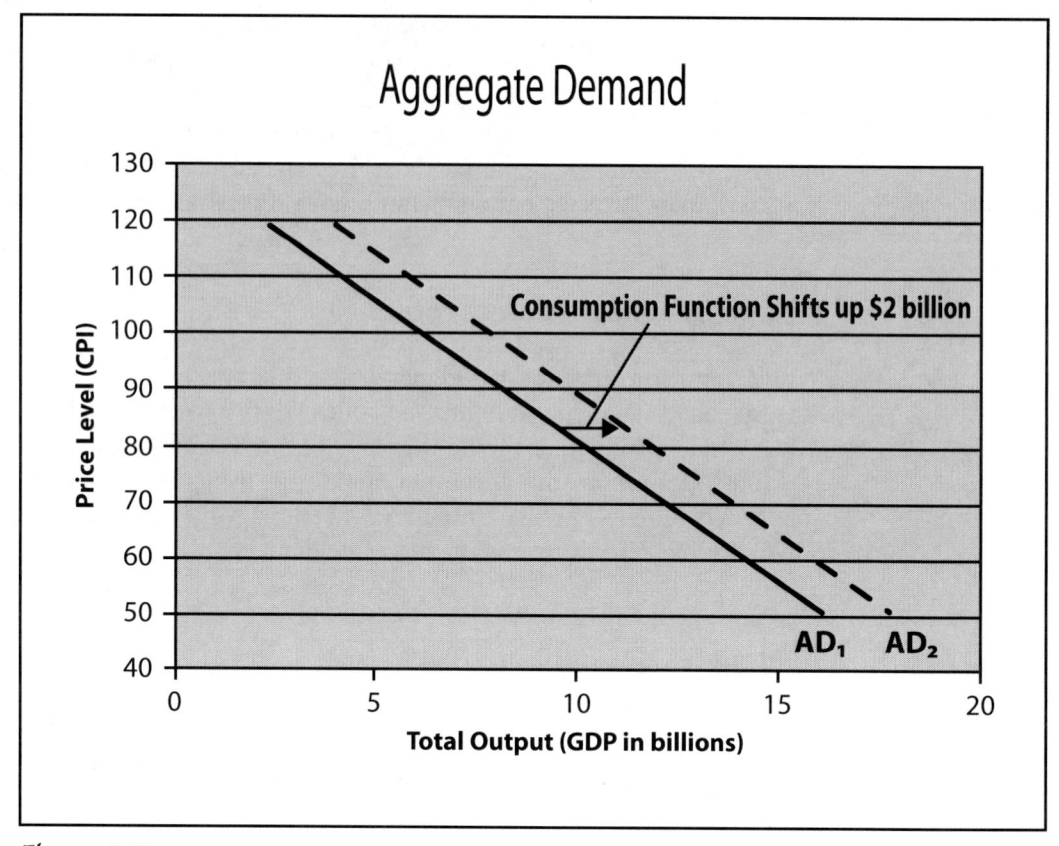

Figure 9.5 • Aggregate Demand Shift
Since aggregate demand consists of spending on the four types of production, an increase in spending on any of those components will cause the aggregate demand curve to shift to the right.

increases. As we have seen, these aggregate demand shifts may be the result of consumer responses to changes in income or to other factors like wealth, credit, taxes, or expectations.

But if we are looking for an explanation to the swings that characterize the modern economy, we may need to look elsewhere. The consumption and saving schedules are usually fairly stable unless there is a radical change in tax policy. Households set their consumption and saving schedules to meet long-term goals like saving for retirement, so short-term fluctuations do not influence them much. In addition, the shifters often work in opposing directions (increased wealth and decreased household debt, for example) and therefore tend to cancel each other out. Investment, on the other hand, tends to be much more volatile.

V. INVESTMENT

Determinants of Investment

Expected Rate of Return. Another important relationship in macroeconomics is the one between real interest rate and investment. Investment (the purchase of new factories, machines, and equipment to expand production) is an important factor in determining aggregate demand and the real interest rate has a large impact on the level of investment.

Investment, like any other economic decision, requires marginal cost-benefit analysis. The marginal cost of investment is the real interest rate firms must pay the people they are borrowing from, and the marginal benefit is the expected rate of return of the investment (how much money the firm thinks it will make by adding a new factory, machine, etc.).

Imagine a furniture-making company is deciding whether to invest in a new sanding machine that will cost $1,000 and lasts for exactly one year. Since the firm would only add this machine if it increased revenues, let's say that the firm expects the machine to add $1,100 worth of new sales (once you subtract operating costs). Then, the expected net profit added by this machine would be $100.

The deciding factor on whether or not this investment is profitable is the expected rate of return.

$$Expected\ Rate\ of\ Return = \frac{Expected\ Net\ Profit}{Cost\ of\ Investment} \times 100$$

Dividing this net profit by the cost of the machine gives us the expected rate of return on the investment, 10 percent. That is, each dollar invested on the machine returns $1.10 after using the machine for a year. Remember, this is only expected return; nothing guarantees the firm that they will get increased business just because they buy a new piece of equipment.

Real Interest Rate. Most businesses do not have enough money sitting around to invest in new equipment. Instead, businesses borrow money from financial institutions to purchase new capital. When borrowing, a firm must not only pay for the cost of the machine, but also pay interest to the creditor.

Refer back to the furniture store example above. Let's assume the firm borrowed the $1,000 it needed to buy the machine at 7 percent interest, it would need to pay back $1,070 to the bank after on year. Since this is still less than the expected net revenue $1,100, purchasing the machine remains a profitable decision.

In general, if the expected rate of return (10 percent in our example) exceeds the interest rate (7 percent in our example), the investment should be undertaken. In contrast, if the interest rate exceeds the expected rate of return, the investment will be unprofitable and the firm should not do it. Therefore, in order to be efficient the firm should invest until the expected rate of return equals the interest rate.

In fact, this principle applies even if the firm is not borrowing to finance its investment; that is, if it is financing investment through retained earnings. If the prevailing interest rate exceeds the expected rate of return of an investment, the firm would be better off loaning the money it would have spent on the investment to someone else and just earning the high interest rate.

It is crucial to note that what matters when analyzing whether an investment is profitable is the real interest rate (the amount the borrower's real income will fall after paying back the loan) not the nominal interest rate. For example, if an investment has an expected real rate of return of 10 percent and the prevailing nominal interest rate is 15 percent, it may seem like the project is unprofitable. However, if there is 10 percent inflation in the economy, the money the firm would be paying back would be worth 10 percent less than the money it borrowed; that is, the real interest rate is only 5 percent. Comparing this 5 percent real interest rate to the 10 percent expected rate of real return, it becomes clear that the project is in fact profitable.

Investment Demand Curve

Now that we know that businesses base their decision of whether or not to invest based on whether the expected rate of return exceeds the real interest rate, we can develop an investment demand curve for the entire economy.

The investment demand will look a lot like the market demand curve we studied in Chapter 3 except the *x*-axis will be dollars of investment demanded (instead of quantity demanded) and the *y*-axis will be the real interest rate (the price of investing). As figure 9.6 illustrates, the investment demand curve is downward sloping because at lower interest rates it is easier to find an investment project with an expected return that exceeds that interest rate.

Investment Demand Shifters

Technology. While the real interest rate certainly influences the level of investment, other factors can convince businesses to invest more or less even if the interest rate remains unchanged. Technological innovations stimulate investment because they reduce production costs and/or increase product quality. These effects make any investment more profitable. Major innovations like the building of the transcontinental railroad or the development of the Internet led to rapid increases in investment in related fields. Governments, therefore, can increase investment spending by encouraging technological innovation.

Altered Expectations. All investment decisions are based on the expected rate of return which itself depends on future projections of market size, costs, revenues, and

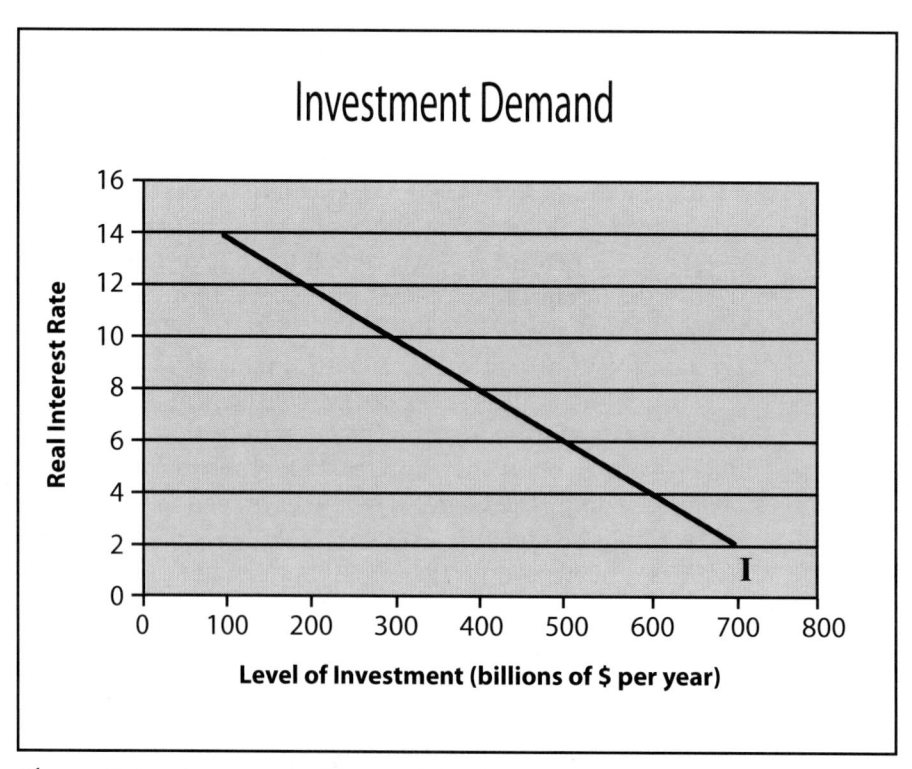

Figure 9.6 • Investment Demand Curve
As the real interest rate rises, businesses find it harder to justify borrowing money to finance new projects and investment slows down.

profits. These expectations can also change due to tax policy, technology changes, or the level of capitalization. If firms become more optimistic in their expectations for the future, the investment demand curve will shift to the right. The opposite is true if they become more pessimistic.

AD Shifts. Just as with consumption, investment is a component of aggregate demand. As a result, anything that reduces the level of investment—a higher interest rate, lower expectations in business, slow growth in technology—will reduce the level of output demanded at the prevailing price level, shifting the aggregate demand curve to the left.

Instability

Durability. While the consumption and saving schedules are relatively stable regardless of changes in the schedule shifters, historical data shows that investment demand is quite volatile. In fact, investment demand changes drastically in response to even mild changes in the overall economy.

Households like to keep consumption smooth; they like to have at least the same amount of food, clothes, and medical care this year that they did last year. A business, on the other hand, can wait until the economy gets better before they buy a new factory. As a result, investment tends to be much less smooth: High amounts of investment occurring during good times and almost none occurring in slimping times.

Irregularity of Innovation. Technological innovations do not occur on any schedule and instead occur at irregular intervals, causing business cycle fluctuations. Since technological change plays such a large role in determining investment demand the irregularity of innovation affects investment even more than it does the economy at large.

Variability of Expectations. Expectations play a large role in determining investment demand and can sometimes swing wildly in response to even modest changes in economic and political conditions. One key area that defines variability of expectations is the stock market. Businesses use the stock market as a crucial indicator of future business activity but, as we have seen, the stock market's daily swings often magnify feelings of optimism or pessimism.

VI. GOVERNMENT PURCHASES AND NET EXPORTS

Together, consumption and investment compose about 80 percent of total output. As a result, most policies to adjust aggregate demand are going to focus on those two components. Changes in government spending and net exports, though, can also cause shifts in the aggregate demand curve. What are the determinants of these final two components?

Government Spending

While government spending on income transfers grows and contracts with changes in the administration, federal government purchases of goods and services stand at about $2 billion per year and grows at a rate fairly consistent with GDP growth; that is, the share of GDP taken up by government purchases has been constant for some time now.

This spending is not immune to business cycles, however. Two-thirds of all government spending comes at the state and local levels, and unlike the federal government they cannot just finance spending through borrowing; the payment for the spending must come from tax receipts.

Since tax receipts fall during recessions, so must government demand for goods and services. This helps explain why state spending on education and other programs had to be reined in during the most recent recession.

Federal government spending, on the other hand, does not depend solely on tax receipts. The federal government can, and often does, borrow and spend more in a year than it raised in tax money. This puts the federal government in the unique position to increase aggregate demand when the market says it should be falling—saving the economy as advocated by Keynes.

Unfortunately, the government still has to borrow from somewhere to finance its increase in spending. Their increased demand for loans will increase the interest rate, reducing the level of private investment and consumption spending, and further depressing aggregate demand. Likewise, the increased borrowing will eventually have to be funded by increased taxes, which reduce consumption and investment. We will look more closely at the consequences of government borrowing in the following chapter.

Net Exports

Since exports are viewed as a positive from the point of view of GDP, any factor that increases exports relative to imports increases GDP and shifts the aggregate demand curve to the right. That is, any factor other than a change in the national price level; the price level can only cause a movement along the aggregate demand curve (the foreign purchases effect from Chapter 8), not a shift of the whole curve. Surprisingly, though, there are some factors unrelated to the price level that can cause net exports to change.

A rise in incomes in foreign countries will increase the demand for all normal goods. Some of those goods are movies, cars, and clothing produced in the United States. All else equal, a rise in income in foreign countries increases net exports and shifts the aggregate demand curve to the right. A decrease in foreign incomes will reduce net exports and shift the aggregate demand curve to the left.

A change in the exchange rate (the price of foreign currencies in terms of the dollar) will clearly have an impact on the demand for American exports. Suppose the dollar depreciates relative to the Euro; that is, it now takes more dollars to buy any amount of Euros. As a result, any product denominated in euros becomes more expensive to US consumers: imports fall. At the same time, a single Euro can buy more dollars so any product priced in dollars becomes cheaper to European consumers: exports rise. With exports rising and imports falling, net exports increase and the aggregate demand curve shifts to the right.

The Aggregate Demand Curve

Now that we know the four components of aggregate demand, we have a better understanding of how the aggregate demand curve is constructed. At any price level, the amount of output demanded will be the sum of output demanded from each of the four categories. Therefore, an increase in the amount of spending on any of the components at the given price level will push the aggregate demand curve to the right. Government

Aggregate Demand

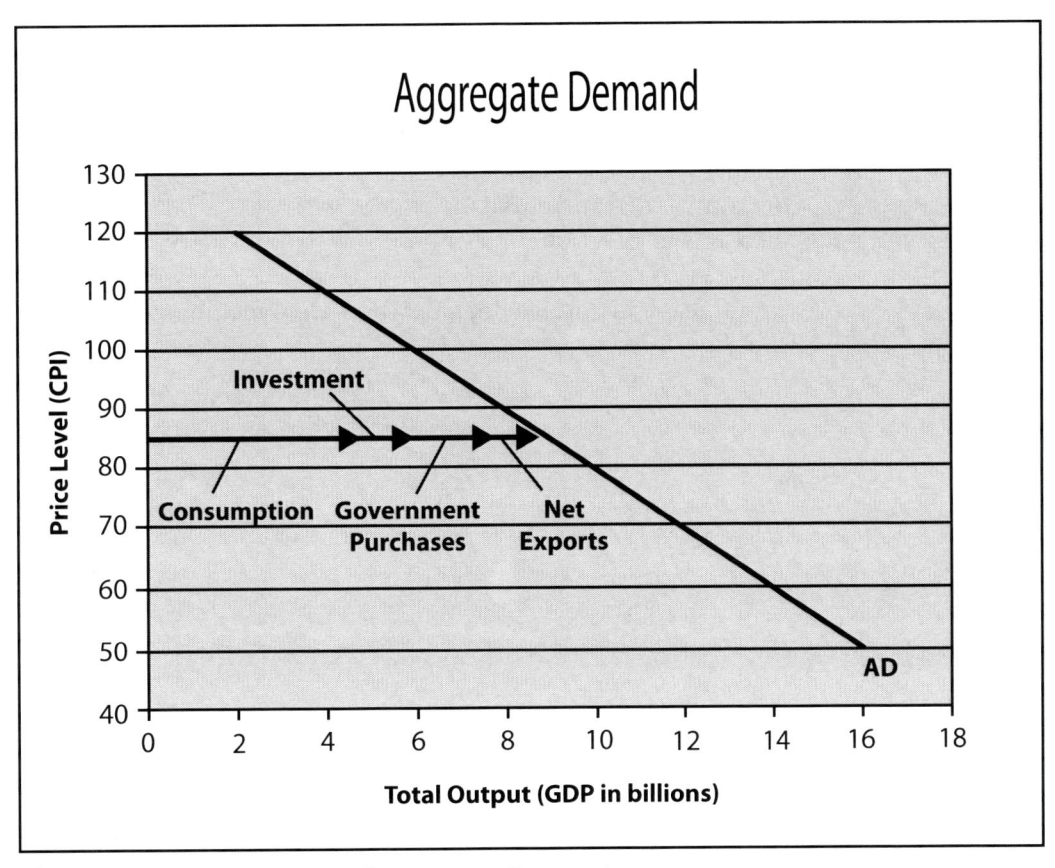

Figure 9.7 • Components of Aggregate Demand
Aggregate demand represents the sum of spending on the four types of production by all of the citizens of a nation.

policies aimed at stimulating the economy during a recession will focus on increasing spending on these components to close the recessionary gap.

CHAPTER 9 SUMMARY

- A **macro failure** occurs when there is too much aggregate demand or too little aggregate demand.
- When aggregate demand falls short of aggregate supply at the full-employment price level, a **recessionary gap** occurs.
- An **inflationary gap** occurs when aggregate demand exceeds aggregate supply at the full-employment price level.
- Increasing any of the four components of aggregate demand—consumption, investment, government purchases, or net exports—**will shift the aggregate demand curve to the right.**
- The **consumption function** shows the relationship between disposable income, savings, and consumption as income rises.
- The slope of the consumption function is the **marginal propensity to consume.**

- The consumption function consists of two parts: **autonomous consumption** and **income-dependent consumption**.
- The investment demand curve shows that the **amount that businesses want to invest decreases as the interest rate rises.**
- Changes in **technology, expectations, and the business environment** will shift the investment demand curve.
- Increases in government spending may cause a decrease in consumption and investment spending.
- An **increase in foreign incomes** or **a depreciation of the dollar** will increase net exports.

CHAPTER 9 Exercises

Name _____

1) A recessionary gap implies that
   A) aggregate demand exceeds aggregate supply at the full-employment price level.
   B) aggregate demand is less than aggregate supply at the full-employment price level.
   C) unemployment is at its natural rate.
   D) the country is producing right at its production productions curve.

1) _____

2) Keynes was concerned that at macroeconomic equilibrium the economy would experience
   A) full employment and price stability.
   B) full employment but not price stability.
   C) price stability but not full employment.
   D) neither full employment nor price stability.

2) _____

3) The marginal propensity to consume can be found by dividing
   A) total consumption by total saving.
   B) total consumption by the population.
   C) the change in total consumption by the change in disposable income.
   D) the change in disposable income by the change in consumption.

3) _____

4) If the MPC is 0.85 and the APC is 0.9, then the MPS equals:
   A) .1   C) 0.15
   B) 0.05   D) 1.75

4) _____

5) The consumption function implies that
   A) disposable income inversely influences savings.
   B) consumption directly influences disposable income.
   C) autonomous consumption changes when people have low incomes.
   D) consumption increases as disposable income increases.

5) _____

6) Suppose the consumption function is $C = \$200 + 0.8YD$. If disposable income is $400, consumption is:
   A) $520   C) $400
   B) $200   D) $560

6) _____

7) Which of the following causes a shift of investment demand curve?
   A) The interest rate rises.
   B) Business become more optimistic about future profits.
   C) The interest rate falls.
   D) None of the above

7) _____

159

8) Which of the following would NOT cause the AD curve to shift to the right? 8) _____
   A) The dollar depreciates relative foreign currencies.
   B) Technological innovations increase investment spending.
   C) An increase in taxes decreases disposable income.
   D) The government increases social program spending.

9) What is the marginal propensity to consume and marginal propensity to save of a consumer whose income went up $1,000 and increased his consumption from $150 to $900?

10) Why might an increase in government spending actually decrease aggregate demand?

Chapter 10

Government Deficits and Debt

I. EFFECT OF FISCAL POLICY ON THE GOVERNMENT BUDGET

Budget Surpluses and Deficits

The Keynesian policies discussed in Chapters 8 and 9 advocated using fiscal policy (changes in government spending to influence aggregate demand) to adjust macro outcomes. When aggregate demand is too low Keynesians advocate increasing federal spending, and when aggregate demand is too high they recommend restraining government spending to rein in inflation.

Each of these policies has an effect on the government budget deficit—the difference between government spending and government revenue for the year. Increased government spending, during recessions in particular, has the tendency to swell the budget deficit. Expansionary fiscal policy typically involves reducing taxes and increasing spending at the same time tax receipts are falling naturally due to the business cycle. As a result the government will be spending more than it is bringing in.

Whenever government spending exceeds tax revenues for the year, the government is running a deficit. As shown in figure 10.1, history shows us that the government usually runs a deficit. The only prolonged period of consistent surpluses (more tax revenues than spending) in recent history came in the late 1990s.

Keynes would not necessarily see these deficits as a bad thing. The government may need to spend more to fight off the effects of decreased private spending. According to

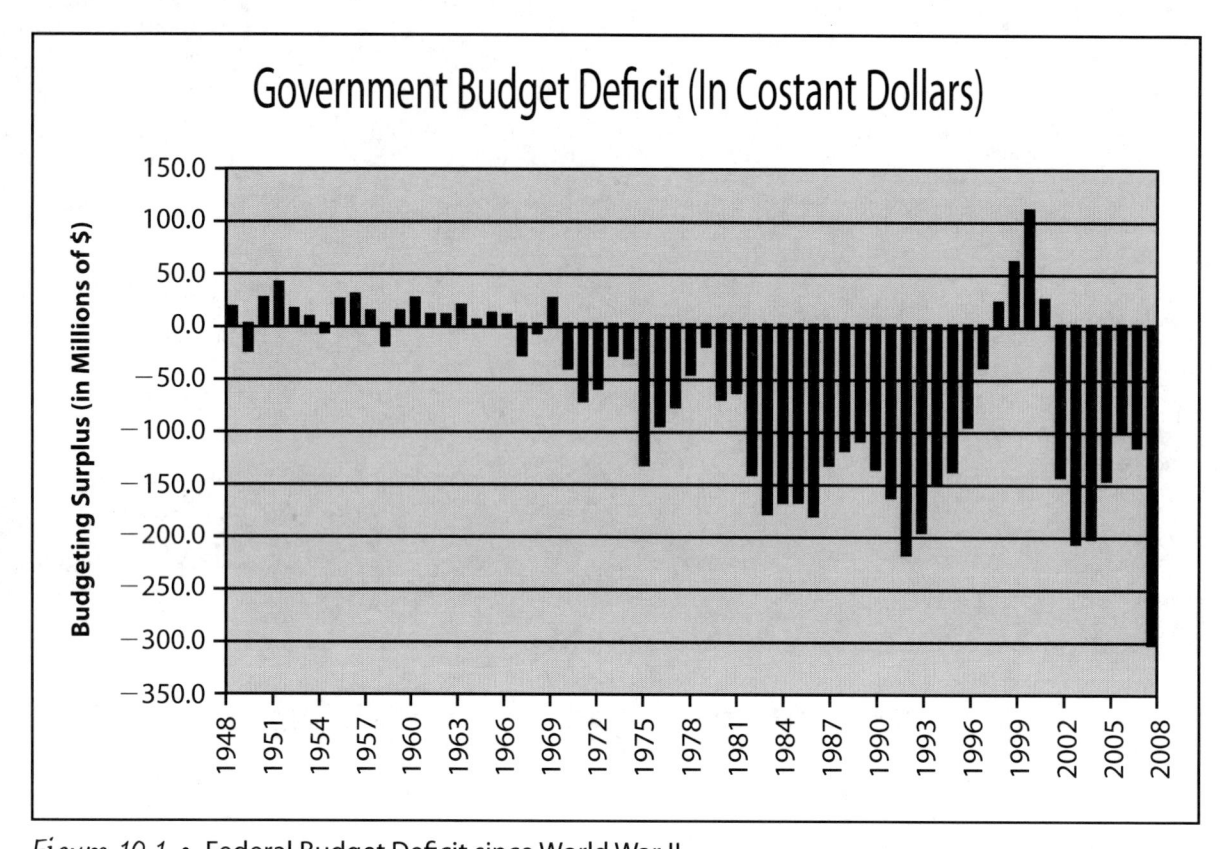

Figure 10.1 • Federal Budget Deficit since World War II
The government budget deficit has risen as the government has taken on more economic responsibilities.

Keynes, the goal of fiscal policy should be to keep the real economy at the full-employment equilibrium, not balancing the budget. Most governments, in fact, seem to have to no problem running government deficits.

Discretionary vs. Automatic Spending

It makes sense for deficits to occur when the government issues a tax cut or passes a large stimulus package, but why are we consistently running deficits even when there are no obvious fiscal policy changes? The truth is, the president and Congress have little direct control over the spending in any particular year. Much of it, around 80 percent, was already promised to certain people and programs in decisions in previous years. Congress can only adjust the remaining 20 percent, called discretionary spending. Congress does have some power to increase or decrease federal spending to engage in Keynesian policy, just not as much as it would seem at first glance.

Automatic Stabilizers. Even though many spending programs funded by the federal government are set up well in advance, the exact amounts they pay out are not. Still, Congress does not decide how much they pay out; these amounts are adjusted automatically as economic conditions change. Unemployment insurance benefits and welfare payments increase during recessions and decrease during periods of expansion, for example.

Such spending programs are called automatic stabilizers because they enact whatever Keynesian policy is called for (increase spending during recession, decrease when private spending rises) without Congress having to make any action. Taxes are another automatic stabilizer. When incomes rise people have to pay more taxes, shifting the aggregate demand curve to the left and preventing demand-pull inflation. During recessions, on the other hand, incomes fall and so do tax obligations, leaving more money for spending.

Cyclical Deficits. Since most of government deficit spending comes from automatic stabilizers, one could make the case that the business cycle has just as much if not more impact on the budget deficit as fiscal policy does. When GDP growth slows down, more people qualify for government assistance programs, increasing spending. At the same time, tax revenues fall due to falling sales and incomes. The result is a tendency toward deficit spending during recessions.

On the other hand, an increase in the growth rate would mean less unemployment and less people qualifying for government assistance. At the same time those workers are now paying more in to social security and the businesses they work for are paying more in business taxes. The result is a tendency for the deficit to shrink.

In the end, it becomes clear that deficits do not shrink or swell solely because of irresponsible actions by Congress or the president. Sometimes, economic conditions cause automatic stabilizers to kick in and change the level of the deficit regardless of the current administration's policies.

For example, although both President Reagan and President Bush promised to balance the budget without raising taxes, recessions early in their terms caused deficit spending. President Clinton on the other hand spent freely, but falling unemployment during his presidency led to the largest surplus we have ever seen.

Structural Deficits. To isolate the effect of Keynesian policy on the deficit, we need to separate the effect of cyclical changes (through the effect of automatic stabilizers) from the effect of policy action. The change in the deficit caused by automatic stabilizers is called the cyclical deficit; Congress has little control over this part of the deficit.

Congress has a great amount of control on the structural deficit; the part of the deficit caused by new fiscal policy. Changes in discretionary spending affect the structural deficit: more discretionary spending increases the structural deficit while less decreases it. For example, one might perceive the drop in the budget surplus from 2001 to 2002 as an increase in discretionary spending. In actuality, nearly the entire drop in surplus came from automatic stabilizers that increased spending and decreased tax revenues as the economy suffered from both the September 11th attacks and the collapse of many dot-com companies.

Separating deficits into their cyclical and structural components also gives a new way to look at the Great Depression. The large budget deficits may give us the impression that the government was spending like crazy to fix the Depression, but most of that deficit spending came from cyclical disturbances, not policy action. Discretionary spending was actually tightened throughout most of the era as macro stability took a back seat to a balanced budget.

II. ECONOMIC EFFECT OF DEFICITS

Crowding Out

Whether deficits occur because of automatic stabilizers or new policy action, the fact remains that these deficits have consequences for the economy. Deficit spending must be financed from borrowing, and increased borrowing by the government means there are less funds to be borrowed by consumers and businesses to finance consumption and investment. In Article 10.1, the director of the Congressional Budget Office voices his concerns over how proposed stimulus legislation may result in crowding out and a slowing of economic growth.

The extent of the crowding-out problem, as we saw during the Great Depression, depends heavily upon how national resources are employed. During the Depression, many resources lay idle—we were producing inside of our production possibilities curve—so taking them to increase government spending added public sector production without taking away much private sector production.

If the government tried to increase deficit spending in a period where resources are more utilized—when we are at or near the production possibilities curve—we would

Article 10.1:
Macroeconomic Effects of the Senate Stimulus Legislation

In a letter sent today to Senators Grassley and Gregg, CBO analyzed the macroeconomic effects of an initial Senate version of the stimulus legislation . . .

Most of the budgetary effects of the Senate legislation would occur over the next few years. Even if the fiscal stimulus persisted, however, the short-run effects on output that operate by increasing demand for goods and services would eventually fade away. In the long run, the economy produces close to its potential output on average, and that potential level is determined by the stock of productive capital, the supply of labor, and productivity. Short-run stimulative policies can affect long-run output by influencing those three factors, although such effects would generally be smaller than the short-run impact of those policies on demand.

In contrast to its positive near-term macroeconomic effects, the Senate legislation would reduce output slightly in the long run, CBO estimates, as would other similar proposals. The principal channel for this effect is that the legislation would result in an increase in government debt. To the extent that people hold their wealth in the form of government bonds rather than in a form that can be used to finance private investment, the increased government debt would tend to "crowd out" private investment—thus reducing the stock of private capital and the long-term potential output of the economy.

The negative effect of crowding out could be offset somewhat by a positive long-term effect on the economy of some provsions [sic]—such as funding for infrastructure spending, education programs, and investment incentives, which might increase economic output in the long run. CBO estimated that such provisions account for roughly one-quarter of the legislation's budgetary cost. Including the effects of both crowding out of private investment (which would reduce output in the long run) and possibly productive government investment (which could increase output), CBO estimates that by 2019 the Senate legislation would reduce GDP by 0.1 percent to 0.3 percent on net.

by Douglas Elmendorf

Questions:
1. According to the author, what will the long-run impact of stimulus legislation be?
2. How does government spending crowd out private investment?
3. How could government spending encourage long-term growth?

From the Congressional Budget Office Director's Blog.

have to give up quite a bit of private sector goods as a trade off. In other words, the crowding out effect is greater the closer the economy is to full employment.

Opportunity Cost

The existence of the crowding out effect does not mean that deficit spending is always bad, it simply reminds us that there is a trade off to the increased amount of public sector goods purchased through deficit spending; namely, the amount of private sector output that is crowded out. If this public sector output is more highly valued, if its marginal benefit exceeds the marginal cost, than the deficit spending is justified.

President Clinton, for example, justified his shrinking of the budget surplus by arguing that increased spending on education, health care, and transportation infrastructure represented an investment that would increase long-term growth. President Bush, on the other hand, advocated tax cuts since his policymakers believed the opportunity cost of increased government spending was too high.

Interest-Rate Movements

The crowding out effect occurs as a result of increased interest rates. Increased government borrowing shifts the investment demand curve to the right, creating a shortage in the market for loanable funds, as figure 10.2 illustrates. This shortage puts a strain on

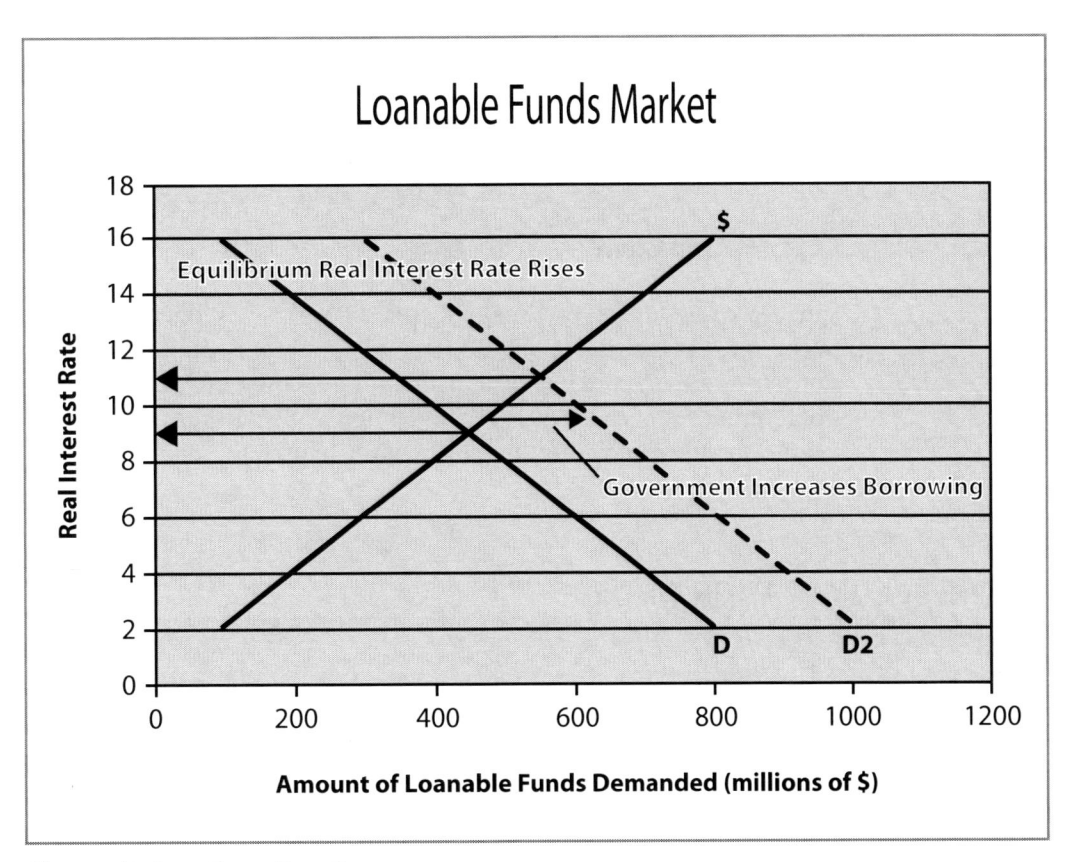

Figure 10.2 • **Crowding Out**
As the government increases deficit spending, it must borrow funds from the same sources that fund private investment. The increased competition in the loan market causes the equilibrium interest rate to rise.

lenders to find funds, forcing them to charge a higher interest rate. As a result, businesses find it harder to finance investments and consumers find large purchases like houses, cars, and appliances even more expensive. This interest rate response is larger the closer the economy is to full employment since there would be much more slack in the loanable funds market during a recession.

III. ECONOMIC EFFECTS OF SURPLUSES

Crowding In

While deficits are clearly the bigger issue both in terms of frequency and effect on the economy, budget surpluses also have macroeconomic effects. When the government brings in more money than it spends, it must do something with that money. The amount is too large to put in any bank or invest in any company without affecting the private control of industry, so what can the government do with the money?

The government essentially has four choices of how to spend a surplus: buy more goods and services, cut taxes, increase transfers, or pay off some of the national debt. The first three options eliminate the surplus by turning it into goods. The first option increases the amount of public sector goods while the other two expand private sector production.

The final option refers to paying back individuals that are holding government bonds. This has a similar, but less direct, impact on private spending. The tendency of surpluses to increase consumption and investment spending is called crowding in. Even people and businesses that do not hold government bonds will benefit from lower interest rates as a result of crowding in.

Cyclical Sensitivity

Just as with deficits, the final effect of a surplus will depend on the cyclical state of the economy. As we saw in the 2001 recession, a crowding in of government surplus will not translate to a big increase in spending if consumers and business are holding off on big purchases because of low expectations. We will return to the effect of low expectations on attempted stimulus policies in Chapter 12.

IV. THE ACCUMULATION OF DEBT

Debt Creation

Every year that ends in a deficit adds to the national debt and every year that ends in surplus takes away from it. Since the government runs a deficit almost every year, it is no surprise that the United States has stacked up a sizable national debt—nearly $14 trillion by the end of 2010. Our country has been racking up this debt since its founding, but the rate of its growth has certainly picked up in recent times.

Deficit spending, and the debt it creates, is financed through the issue of government bonds, which are promissory notes or IOUs from the federal government. A treasury bond represents a promise to pay the bondholder a certain amount of money, plus interest, at the date of maturity. The national debt is therefore the total face value of the outstanding bonds added together. The national debt rises when more bonds are issued than are paid back.

Historical Debt Levels

1776–1900. While the US had a much better grip on balancing the budget in previous years, it still had its share of deficits and debt. As soon as the Revolutionary War was over, the government already owed $8 million to France and $250,000 to Spain. The US was able to quickly repay its debt in the early part of the country's history until the War of 1812 sent debt soaring.

By 1835, though, the US had paid that debt back and experienced the last debt-free period in the country's history. With no debt to pay off, the country was faced with the question of how to spend the surplus. The Mexican-American and Civil Wars, however, ended any illusion that the US could remain debt-free.

Pre-Depression. The turn of the century brought the Spanish-American War and its deficits, but all previous debts were dwarfed by those racked up during World War I. The first total war increased the debt from 3 percent of national income to 41 percent in just the two years of US involvement. The prosperity of the 1920s, on the other hand, led to consistent surpluses and a decline in the national debt.

World War II. Drops in tax revenue and increases in transfer payments caused the debt to rise during the Depression even as structural deficits shrank. The most explosive jump in the debt in American history, though, occurred during World War II as illustrated by figure 10.3. The government purposely limited consumption through a system of rationing in order to force people to save their money in the form of treasury bonds to finance deficit spending. By the end of the war the debt was 125 percent of GDP, the highest rate ever.

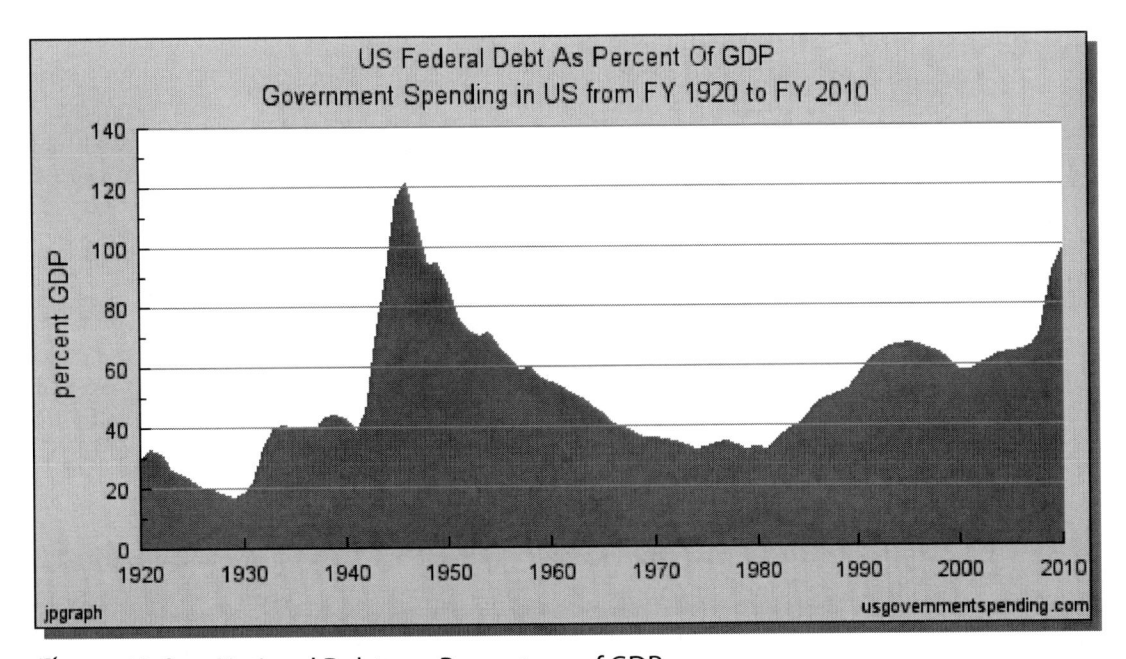

Figure 10.3 • **National Debt as a Percentage of GDP**
While the national debt has never been higher in numerical terms, there have been periods in history when the debt was larger relative to the size of the economy.

1980s. The United States accumulated huge debt during the 1980s despite the longest-lasting period of peace in the twentieth century. A combination of recession, tax cuts, and increase in Cold War military spending caused both the cyclical and structural deficits to rise consistently during this decade. Despite being the hallmark of fiscal restraint, President Reagan saw the structural deficit increase by a multiple of four during his first term.

1990s. Although the fall of the Soviet Union allowed for military to cut back a bit, the savings and loans collapse and recession of 1990–1991 meant the debt continued to rise through the early part of the 1990s. The recovery from the recession and the raising of taxes during the Clinton administration led to the few surpluses that characterized the late 1990s.

Twenty-First Century. In terms of pure dollars, President Bush increased the national debt more than any other president in history up to that time. Tax cuts, defense spending, and financial bailouts caused the debt to rise from $5 trillion to $10 trillion in just eight years. In other words, the federal government accumulated as much debt in those eight years as it had in the previous 225 years of the country's history. President Obama has continued the accumulation of debt through more bailouts and fiscal stimulus programs.

V. WHO OWNS THE DEBT?

Liabilities = Assets

While this rapid accumulation of debt may seem like a dangerous turn of events, to understand the cost of the debt we need to know who has to pay it and who it gets paid to. The idea that our government owes somebody nearly $14 trillion is certainly a frightening proposition, but we need to remember that every dollar that the government owes also a represents a dollar of wealth for somebody.

Government bondholders hold an asset, a claim for repayment in the future. They can even sell that claim for money today in a bond market if they do not want to wait. No money or wealth is lost when the government borrows money; someone just converts some of his wealth into government bonds. But the fact that government bonds represent assets for some people does little to alleviate the fear that the government may someday be bankrupted by its high debt.

Ownership of Government Debt

The fear of bankruptcy becomes a little less acute when you realize that over 50 percent of all government bonds, and therefore all government debt, is held by federal agencies. Clearly these agencies have little interest in bankrupting the United States government. State and local governments buy government bonds with their budget surpluses and hold about 7 percent of government debt.

The Federal Reserve, for example, owns about 10 percent of all government debt. It uses treasury bonds to conduct monetary policy and control interest rates. The Social Security Administration owns more government debt than any other entity (about 20 percent). It keeps most surplus funds (the excess of payroll tax receipts over retiree benefits) in the form of treasury bonds.

Ownership of US Debt

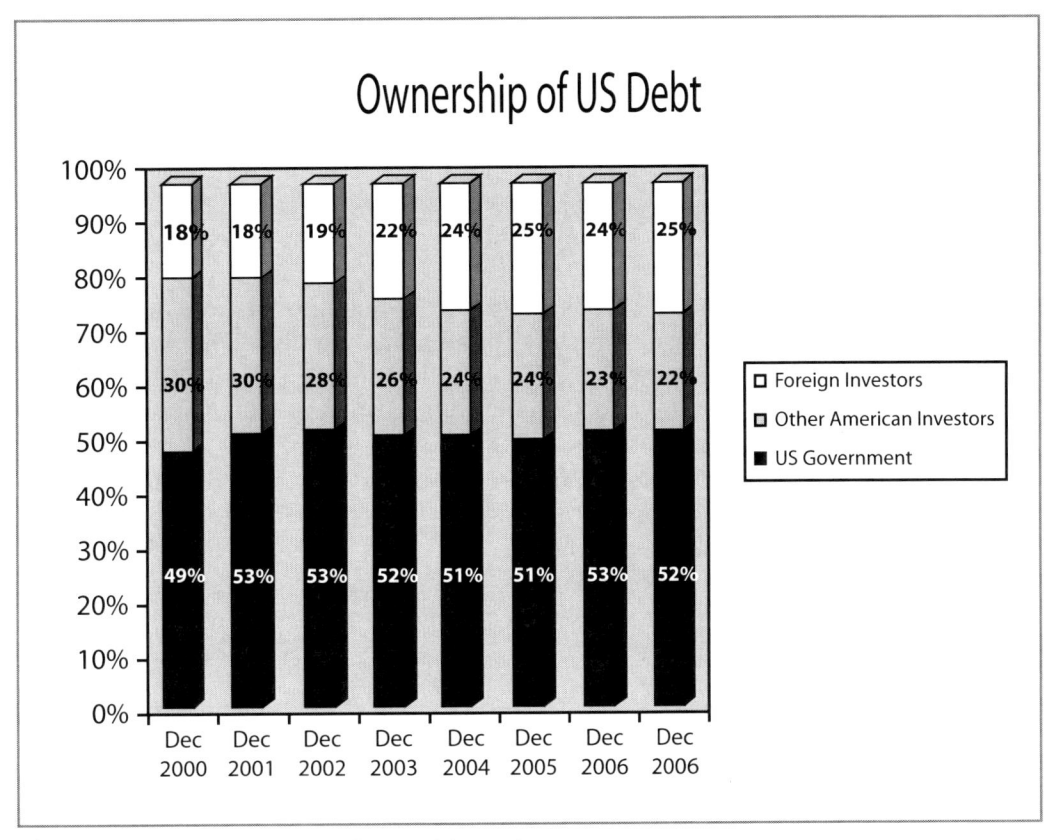

Date	US Government	Other American Investors	Foreign Investors
Dec 2000	49%	30%	18%
Dec 2001	53%	30%	18%
Dec 2002	53%	28%	19%
Dec 2003	52%	26%	22%
Dec 2004	51%	24%	24%
Dec 2005	51%	24%	25%
Dec 2006	53%	23%	24%
Dec 2006	52%	22%	25%

Figure 10.4 • Ownership of US Public Debt
The share of the national debt held by foreign investors has risen in recent years, but other US government agencies still hold more of the public debt than other group.

The private sector owns only about 14 percent of government debt. Banks, mutual funds, and insurance companies hold most of these bonds and people buy them indirectly when they invest in these companies' securities. Very little of the government debt is actually held directly by individual households.

Altogether, domestic agents, whether they are public or private, own about 75 percent of US government debt. Figure 10.4 shows that in the average year, about 25 percent of government debt is held by foreigners and is referred to as external debt. Foreign businesses, governments, and consumers happily snatch up US bonds because of their relative security, relatively high interest, and the acceptability of dollar-denominated assets in the world economy.

VI. BURDEN OF THE DEBT

Refinancing

The fact that most of the national debt is owned domestically may quell fears about the prospect of bankruptcy, but the sheer size of the debt remains daunting to many Americans, especially those who do not own any of the debt. People want to know what kind of damage all of this debt is doing to the economy. In other words, what is the burden of the debt and on whom does it fall?

The size of debt does not collapse or even drag down the economy much because of the government's seemingly infinite capacity to refinance it. That is, whenever some bondholder is due repayment, the government will just borrow from someone else to pay them; much like someone using a cash advance on one credit card to pay the balance on other. Assuming the government could keep this behavior up, the debt could continue to grow ad infinitum. Some people worry that this sounds like a pyramid scheme in which larger and larger amounts of investments are needed to keep the scheme going. Eventually, the amount of funds required to pay off old debts and finance new spending will exceed all of the money in the world and the scheme will collapse; such an amount is astronomical and assumes the debt will continue to rise at the current pace instead of returning to a pace more consistent with historical norms.

A second problem arises from the apparent violation of the economic principle "there ain't no such thing as a free lunch." If the government can keep using new borrowed funds to pay off old debts, what is the cost of racking up huge debts? Is it costless? These two important questions can be answered by looking at how the government pays back or services its debt, and at the real (rather than monetary) cost of government spending.

Debt Service

As we saw in Chapter 4, the government spends about 10 percent of its yearly budget paying interest on the national debt; if you had a credit card with a $14 trillion balance, you would have a pretty big finance charge, too. Clearly then, debt has an effect on the government's spending habits. The higher the debt, the higher the interest payment and therefore the less money the government has to spend on other activities.

Since the government loses purchasing power through debt service, who gains and what effect does that transfer have on the economy as a whole? Since most debt is held domestically, interest payments on the debt are simply transfers of income from taxpayers to bondholders. In any case, total income remains unchanged by these transfers and aggregate demand changes very little, if at all.

Other than the redistribution of income, interest payments on the debt cause almost no opportunity cost. The resources used in collecting taxes and paying the bondholders associated with the transfer are miniscule compared to the amount of money changing hands. The number of resources used for production remains the same, it is only who gets to buy and control them that has changed.

Opportunity Cost

Even though racking up debt and servicing that debt causes little change to the total amount of resources, we cannot conclude that debt accumulation is truly costless. Debt accumulation implies an increase in government spending—there is no other reason for the government to borrow—and we know that results in more public-sector goods and less private-sector goods.

For example, when President Clinton ate into the budget surplus to finance spending on health care, education, and transportation infrastructure he also reduced the resources available for production in the private sector. If he had raised the money for his programs through taxation instead of borrowing, the effect on the real economy (a decrease in the amount of resources available) would have been the same. The idea that the opportunity cost (lost private sector production) of any government action remains the same, regardless of the method of finance, is called Ricardian Equivalence.

Real Trade-offs. The debt creates no greater additional burden on the taxpayer or the economy than any other transfer does. The real cost of the debt is not in lost resources or total output, but in reorganization of the mix of output toward more of the goods the government wants. As mentioned before, increased government borrowing and spending crowds out private spending by individuals and businesses.

The massive bailouts of private companies by the government in the past few years have indeed been unpopular, but if they were financed through increased taxation rather than increased borrowing, they would have caused a riot. While taxation is a blatantly obvious transfer of purchasing power to the government, increasing the government debt is subtler but has the same effect.

Regardless of the method of financing, the fact remains that fewer resources will be available for private sector production when the government purchases more resources for its activities. Therein lies the true cost of the government debt: The larger the debt, the more the public sector will expand relative to the private sector.

The size of this cost, the crowding effect, depends both on where the economy is on the production possibilities curve and on how consumers and businesses respond to the government activity. Also important to note is that the cost of the debt—the lost resources for private sector production—occurs not when the debt is repaid but when the action is taken. The private sector loses some of its productive capacity when the government buys more tanks or planes or the military, not when the debt is paid.

Many pundits and television talking heads decry the national debt as an unfair burden we are passing on to future generations, but this is an inaccurate portrayal of how government borrowing works. Once the government project is done, the resources are once again available for private sector production. The cost or burden of government debt cannot be passed on to future generations since the cost—the lost private sector production—must be faced in the present by giving up private sector goods that could have been produced had the government not used borrowed funds to finance its projects.

On the contrary, future generations will be able to enjoy the additional public sector goods we produce today without having to give up anything to produce them. Of course, if the government continues to rack up deficits and accumulate debt in their time, future generations will have costs to bear, but those will be completely separate from the choices made by the government today.

Economic Growth. Of particular concern to future generations, however, is the effect that crowding out has on the rate of economic growth. All other things being equal, less investment today means slower economic growth and fewer jobs in the future. In other words, the larger the debt, the slower our production possibilities curve will shift outward. This slowdown will limit the production choices of future generations.

While debt and deficit spending will no doubt crowd out private investment, the net effect of this increased government spending on economic growth is not necessarily negative. If the goods purchased through deficit spending—education, infrastructure, and health care—benefit future growth more than the foregone private sector spending would have, then future generations may be better off. The argument over deficit spending versus balancing the budget really comes down to arguing over the optimal mix of public versus private sector goods, not how those public goods are financed.

Repayment. But what about when the bill comes? All this talk about incurring the cost of the debt today is nice, but won't our children eventually have to pay off this huge debt we are amassing? Of course they will, but remember who receives the payments.

For the most part it is other US citizens and government agencies. Future payments on the debt do not represent a loss of wealth, but a transfer of income from taxpayers to bondholders in the future.

VII. EXTERNAL DEBT

No Crowding Out

Since we must face the opportunity cost of the debt today, it becomes difficult to pass that burden on to future generations. This is only the case, however, if the debt comes from internal sources. Borrowing from foreign citizens, businesses, and governments, on the other hand, could end up taking resources away from the private sector in the future instead of the present.

Borrowing funds from other countries means we can increase government spending without taking away resources needed for private sector production; there is no crowding out. Without the crowding out effect, there is no opportunity cost. As a result we can move to a point beyond the production possibilities curve; we can have more public sector goods without giving up any private sector production.

If foreign investors are willing to accept government bonds in exchange for goods and services, we have achieved the proverbial free lunch. In other words, purchases financed through external debt impose no resource cost since no goods are given up in exchange for the additional output financed by the foreign funds.

Repayment

In reality, though, no investor is willing to hold on to bonds indefinitely. Eventually, they will sell the bonds in order to buy goods and services. The external debt is paid by sending output to the lending country at some point in the future, reducing the output available for future generations of American citizens. In other words, external debt allows the current generation to shift the burden of the debt on to future generations, a tempting opportunity indeed.

CHAPTER 10 SUMMARY

- The **government budget deficit** is the difference between government revenue and government expenditures.
- Congress only controls about 20 percent of government spending, a fraction known as **discretionary spending.**
- The portions of government spending not controlled by Congress are called **automatic stabilizers** since they increase during recessions and decrease during expansions.
- Increases in automatic stabilizers cause **cyclical deficits**, increases in discretionary spending cause **structural deficits.**

- Increases in government borrowing **crowd-out** private borrowing by increasing the equilibrium interest rate.
- The sum total of the government's borrowing throughout history created the **national debt**.
- 50 percent of the national debt is owned by **US government agencies, 75 percent is owned by Americans.**
- As long as the debt is owed to domestic lenders, the primary burden of the debt is the **private sector production sacrificed** by transferring purchasing power to the government and is paid by the current generation.
- Future generations may be hurt by government borrowing if the crowding-out effect **discourages private saving and investment.**
- **External debt** has a much greater capacity to pass a burden on to future generations since the current generation does not have to sacrifice anything.

CHAPTER 10 Exercises

Name _____

1) Much of each year's federal budget is considered "uncontrollable" because
   A) it must be spent for purchasing goods and services.
   B) most of the current government expenditures are the result of decisions made in previous years.
   C) it is determined by someone other than Congress.
   D) government spending is so large that it is literally out of control.

1) _____

2) The government is pursuing a stimulus policy if, regardless of the budget balance (surplus or deficit), it
   A) increases its spending and increases taxes.
   B) reduces its spending and reduces taxes.
   C) increases its spending and reduces taxes.
   D) reduces its spending and increases taxes.

2) _____

3) Which of the following is NOT an automatic stabilizer?
   A) Income taxes
   B) Unemployment benefits
   C) Welfare payments
   D) National security spending

3) _____

4) The concept of crowding out refers to the idea that
   A) increased government borrowing will make private borrowing more expensive.
   B) increased borrowing from foreign countries will increase the current opportunity cost of borrowing.
   C) the Federal Reserve will refuse to lend if the government borrows too much.
   D) state and local governments cannot borrow when the federal government borrows too much.

4) _____

5) The national debt
   A) imposes an unfair burden on future generations.
   B) is paid off at the end of each fiscal year.
   C) is the dollar amount of outstanding treasury bonds.
   D) is wholly a modern problem.

5) _____

6) The period in history when the United States had the highest national debt relative to the size of the economy is/was
   A) today.
   B) during the 1980s.
   C) during the Depression.
   D) during WWII.

6) _____

7) Deficit financing tends to change the mix of output in the direction of more
   A) private-sector goods.
   B) foreign goods.
   C) business-sector goods.
   D) government goods.

7) _____

8) The primary burden of the internal portion of the debt is incurred 8) _____
   A) by future generations.
   B) when the government uses the borrowed funds.
   C) approximately one year after the debt is incurred.
   D) when the debt is refinanced.

9) How do rising interest rates cause crowding out?
   _____
   _____
   _____
   _____

10) Why is borrowing from foreign sources worse than borrowing from internal sources for the debt burden we leave future generations?
    _____
    _____
    _____
    _____

Chapter 11

Money, Banking, and the Federal Reserve

I. WHAT IS MONEY?

Commodity or Token

Many different standards for what constitutes money have existed throughout history. For most of economic history some commodity (a physical product that has value beyond its use as money) had functioned as money. While some interesting commodity monies such as salt, feathers, and red woodpecker caps proliferate through history, the most common forms of commodity money were and remain gold and silver. While the commodity money system had its advantages, the modern economy requires a much more flexible money system.

Today, most people accept paper money, coins, and checks in exchange for goods and services. Why are we willing to accept essentially worthless pieces of paper in exchange for our hard work? What backs money? Nothing but faith. The modern economy works on a fiduciary or fiat monetary system. There is no longer a law requiring that currency be convertible to a fixed amount of gold, silver, or any commodity, yet it is still useful as money because of its acceptability and predictability of value.

Acceptability

Since everyone knows that currency and checking account balances (in the form of checks and debit cards) are widely accepted as a method of payment for goods and services, people accept them as payment for labor and other resources. It takes prolonged periods of hyperinflation for people to eschew currency in favor of bartering, illustrating the power and convenience of paper currency as a form of money.

Even though paper money like the dollar loses some of it purchasing power during periods of inflation, it can still maintain its predictability of value if the inflation is anticipated. Just because you expect any dollar you receive today will be worth 3 percent less in a year (you expect 3 percent inflation), that does not mean you will refuse to accept dollars as payment. You may, however, attempt to make contracts that compensate you for this expected decline in purchasing power.

Means of Payment

To be considered money, a commodity or token needs to be accepted as a means of payment for goods and services. If someone uses a loan or credit card to pay for something, the debt has not been settled until he pays off the loan or credit card. As such, loans and credit cards are not money, but the money used to pay the debt is.

The United States government designates paper dollars and coins as legal tender, meaning they are always a valid and legal means of paying both public and private debts. This imbues currency with the power of the government: As long as the government remains strong and unchallenged, so will the acceptability of the dollar. The government also adds legitimacy to checkable deposits by insuring bank deposits up to $250,000 through the Federal Deposit Insurance Corporation (FDIC) and similar agencies.

Functions of Money

Medium of Exchange. Money serves many functions in the economy, but its primary function is as a medium of exchange. Since every seller accepts money as payment for its goods, we do not have to worry about the double coincidence of wants the way people did when the barter system was used.

The double coincidence of wants is a scenario where trades only occur if the buyer has something the seller wants and the seller has something the buyer wants. This was the hallmark of the barter system, the traditional mode of exchange before money existed. In order to get what they wanted, people had to go through a complex series of exchanges or hold many different types of goods that sellers might want as payment. Money clearly facilitates exchange by letting people know that they only need one item to get all the different goods they could possibly want. More money will translate into more goods.

Unit of Account. Money also serves as a way to compare the value of different goods, companies, and accounts. Businesses know how they are doing based on their profit in dollars, economists know the size of the economy based on the GDP in dollars, and households know what they can and cannot afford based on their dollar incomes. It also serves to quickly compare the relative worth of two goods or services. Before money, people needed to know the relative price of the goods they possessed in terms of every good the might want to buy, but now knowing the dollar price tells you everything you need to know.

Store of Value. Finally, money can be used to transfer purchasing power into the future. If you chose not to spend all of your money at once, you can save some for purchases in the future and it will not fall in nominal value (though it may fall in real value due to inflation). Imagine instead you were a farmer in a world without money. You must consume or trade your crop right away or it will spoil; money does not spoil.

II. THE MONEY SUPPLY

Measuring the Money Supply

The supply of money and the rate at which it changes are important factors that affect crucial macroeconomic variables likes inflation, interest rates, and real GDP. The problem is that economists have yet to decide on a single definition and measure of money. The two methods of measuring money are the transactions approach, which uses money's function as a medium of exchange to measure it, and the liquidity approach, which uses money's function as a store of value to measure it.

M1

Currency. If we use the transactions approach to measuring the money supply, then we are focusing on types of money that can be directly used to purchase goods and services: currency (cash), transaction deposits (checking account balances), and traveler's checks. Combined, these three elements are called M1 and are a useful measure of the money supply.

$$M1 = Currency + Transaction\ Deposits + Traveler's\ Checks$$

Currency in the United States includes coins minted by the US Treasury and paper currency (technically called Federal Reserve notes) issued by the banks of the Federal Reserve. Virtually every country produces its own local currency, but many use US dollars as well. In fact, as much as two-thirds of the American currency in existence is actually spent outside its borders.

Transaction Deposits. Most people do not carry very much cash on them at any given time. Most large transactions, like paying your rent or buying a textbook, are carried out using checks or debit cards. When you use one of these avenues of payment, you are tapping into a transaction deposit or checking account. What you are actually doing when you write a check or swipe your debit card is transferring ownership of part of your deposits (checking account balance) to whomever you are buying from. Transaction deposits are the single largest component of the money supply.

Traveler's Checks. Traveler's checks are similar to traditional checks in that they transfer assets from your checking account to the seller. When you buy a traveler's check from a company and sign it, you authorize the issuing company to take that amount out of your checking account. When you sign it again and use it to purchase something, you are authorizing the person you are purchasing from to retrieve that same amount from the company that issued you the traveler's checks.

M2

While the transaction approach (M1) only takes into account assets that can be directly exchanged for goods, the liquidity approach includes other highly liquid assets—assets that can be converted into M1 assets without any loss of nominal value and with little cost. Any asset not already covered by M1 that fits this definition is called near money. The liquidity approach sees money as a store of value and thus includes M1 as well as some types of near money that we will now discuss.

$$M2 = M1 + Savings\ Deposits + Time\ Deposits + Money\ Market\ Mutual\ Fund\ Balances$$

Savings Accounts. All deposits in savings accounts are part of M2; they can easily be withdrawn or transferred to a checking account. This element also includes the newer money market deposit accounts that have higher rates of return, but also have minimum and maximum balances, as well as limits on the number of transactions (deposits and withdrawals) allowed per month.

Time Deposits. Some banks accounts (like checking accounts) called transaction deposits can be drawn from at any time as payment for goods and services. Other bank accounts, called time deposits, require the depositor to leave the funds in the bank for a set period of time in order to be paid interest. The classic example of this is a certificate of deposit (CD).

A time deposit is basically a bond, or a loan to the bank. You give the bank a deposit and they promise to give it back to you, plus some agreed upon interest, at a certain date (the maturity date). To be counted as M2, a time deposit must be less than $100,000; any amount larger and it is assumed that the deposit is more of a long-term investment than a form of money.

Money Market Mutual Funds. People also hold some of their assets in the form of shares of money market mutual funds. Unlike equity funds that invest in stocks, money market mutual funds invest in short-term credit instruments. Many of these funds even allow shareholders to write checks directly from their balances. While no one measure of the supply can be considered "correct," evidence shows that the business cycles for most countries are most closely tied to M2.

III. DEPOSIT CREATION

The Fractional Reserve System

The money supply can change in an instant because of fractional reserve banking. When you put your money in the bank, it does not lock the cash in the vault and wait for you to come back and withdraw it; the bank would never make any money that way. Bankers figured out a long time ago that the amount of money they held in deposits far exceeds the money people want to withdraw at any given time. Banks only keep the fraction they expect people to withdraw on hand and give the rest out as loans, charging interest in return. The reserves they do hold are either kept in their vault or at the regional bank of the Federal Reserve.

Legal Reserves. Reserves are kept in these two places because, by law, legal reserves (types of funds that can legally count toward fulfilling the reserve requirement) can consist only of deposits held in Federal Reserve banks and vault cash. Even though bank holdings of certain assets like government bonds can be easily turned into cash if its customers start withdrawing at a high rate, these holdings do not count as legal reserves.

Required Reserves. Required reserves are the minimum amount of legal reserves a bank must have to meet the needs of its customers (and government regulations). The reserve requirement is not a number, but a percentage of the bank's transaction deposits; every bank has the same reserve requirement ratio, but a bank with more transaction deposits will have higher total required reserves. The amount of reserves a bank is required to keep equals the value of its transaction deposits times the reserve requirement ratio.

$$Required\ Reserves = Transaction\ Deposits \times Reserve\ Requirement\ Ratio$$

Notice that the reserve requirement only applies to transaction deposits (checking account balances); there is no law governing what percentage of savings deposits or any other type of deposits banks must keep in reserves. The current reserve requirement ratio in the US is 10 percent (although it is only 3 percent for the first $50 million in deposits for any bank). For example, a bank with $1 billion in transaction deposits is required to hold no less than $100 million in legal reserves.

Excess Reserves. Any legal reserves the bank holds above the reserve requirement are called excess reserves. Excess reserves equal legal reserves minus required reserves.

$$Excess\ Reserves = Legal\ Reserves - Required\ Reserves$$

Excess reserves can be negative (the bank has not met the reserve requirement) for a short period, but the bank must quickly call in loans or sell some other type of asset to replenish its reserves.

In the analysis that follows we will see that the amount of reserves in the banking system has a profound influence on the size of the money supply. We will first show how the money supply grows in a world with only one bank, then extend the analysis to a more realistic multiple bank scenario.

Single Bank Case

Let's imagine that there is only one bank to cover all of the country's deposits and transactions. If you deposit $100 in cash into your checking account at the bank, what affect will that have on the money supply? Keep in mind that just because the reserves of the receiving bank increased by $100 due to the deposit, does not mean the money supply has increased. In fact, as figure 11.1 demonstrates, the $100 increase in total assets seen

Bank's Balance Sheet		Money Supply	
Assets	Liabilities	Change in Currency	−$100
$100 in cash	$100 in transaction deposits	Change in Transaction Account Balances	+$100
		Change in Money Supply	0

Figure 11.1 • **Initial Deposit in the Monopoly Bank**
When you deposit $100 in the bank, the money supply does not change since the increase in checking account balances is exactly offset by the decrease in cash in circulation.

Bank's Balance Sheet		Money Supply	
Assets	Liabilities	Change in Currency	No change
$100 in cash $100 in outstanding loans	$100 to depositor $100 to loan recipient	Change in Transaction Account Balances	+$100
		Change in Money Supply	+$100

Figure 11.2 • Additional Loans by the Monopoly Bank
When the bank gives a loan to someone, it essentially creates money by increasing the value of the loan recipient's account without decreasing anyone else's account.

by the bank is exactly offset by the $100 decline in cash holdings; M1 is still the same, M2 remains the same.

The Initial Loan. But since the reserves of the bank have increased, that means the bank can increase the amount of loans it gives. Exactly how much it can lend depends on the reserve requirement ratio, but let's assume for a moment that there is no reserve requirement so the bank can lend out 100 percent of its reserves as loans.

The company or individual who received this loan (assuming it is one recipient) will use the money on a purchase of some kind. The seller they bought from will likely want to put their money in the bank (still the only one around). Thus, as seen in figure 11.2, the bank has increased its reserves by $200 (both deposits) while only giving out $100. Thus, total bank reserves and the monetary base have increased.

IV. A MANY BANK WORLD

Changes in the Money Supply

Let us now turn the more complex case of a banking system with multiple banks and reserve requirements. If you were to deposit $100 in to your local bank (San Jac Savings and Loan) and the bank faced a reserve requirement ratio of 10 percent, $10 of that deposit would have to be held by the bank but the rest would be excess reserves. Since banks only make money when they loan out their excess reserves, the San Jac Savings and Loan will want to give out $90 in new loans. The recipient of the loan will then put the money in its bank (Last National Bank) until it is ready to spend it. The increase in transaction deposits at the bank created by a loan is not offset by a decrease in transaction deposits at any other bank. As figure 11.3 illustrates, total transaction deposits held by the public increase, and (since transaction deposits are part of M1 and M2) the money supply increases.

Taken alone, this process grants tremendous power to the banking system, but the money creation process does not stop here. Based on our earlier assumptions, no bank wants to hold excess reserves since they earn no interest. Instead, the bank will increase its loans in order to hold as little excess reserves as possible.

For simplicity, let's assume the recipient of the original loan spent the entirety of the loan buying a DVD player at Bob's Electronics. Bob will then deposit his earnings in his account at Last National Bank, as indicated in figure 11.4. Since the increase in Bob's account comes at the expense of a decrease in the loan recipient's account at Last National Bank, total transaction deposits and banking reserves remain unchanged. Since the re-

	San Jac S&L			Last National Bank			Money Supply	
Assets		Liabilities		Assets		Liabilities		
Required Reserves	$10	Your Account	$100	Required Reserves	$9	Loan Recipient's Account	$90	Change in Currency	−$100
Excess Reserves	$0			Excess Reserves	$81			Change in Transaction Accounts	+$190
Loans	$90							Change in Money Supply	+$90

Figure 11.3 • **Initial Loan in a Many Bank World**
The loan increased the checking account balance of the loan recipient without decreasing balances anywhere else, resulting in an increase in total banking system reserves.

serve requirement ratio is 10 percent, though, the bank only has to keep 10 percent of these new deposits and can loan out the rest. Instead of just sitting on these excess reserves, Last National Bank will increase its loans and continue the money creation process as indicated in the Round 3 section of figure 11.4.

More Deposit Creation

Let's assume that Last National Bank gives its $81 in excess reserves (remember its required reserves are $9) as a loan to one individual who banks at San Jac S&L. When the loan recipient deposits the loan into his transaction account, San Jac S&L's transaction deposits and reserves both increase by $81.

Since the reserve requirement ratio is only 10 percent, required reserves at San Jac S&L only increase by $8.10 (.1 × $81). San Jac S&L now has $72.90 ($81–$8.10) in excess reserves. The bank wants to loan these excess reserves out as soon as possible to earn more interest income and reduce its legal reserves to the minimum required amount.

You can see that this process would continue to Bank 4, 5, 6, and so on. Each successive bank will receive a smaller and smaller increase in transaction deposits and reserves since 10 percent of each increase must be withheld to satisfy the reserve requirement. Hence, each successive institution has fewer excess reserves from which it can make new loans.

The Money Multiplier

In the example just given—a loan of $100 with a reserve requirement of 10 percent—a $100 increase in reserves created by the initial loan will result in a $1,000 increase (ten times the original $100) in total deposits as banks continue to turn excess reserves into loans. Why ten times? Where does this factor come from? The final change in the money supply induced by an initial change in reserves can be determined by using a mathematical tool called the money multiplier.

Round 1: You place $100 in your checking account at San Jac S&L, San Jac S&L makes a loan and the recipient places the loan amount in his account at Last National Bank

San Jac S&L					Last National Bank					Money Supply	
Assets			Liabilities		Assets			Liabilities		
Required Reserves	$10		Your Account	$100	Required Reserves		$9	Loan Recipient's Account	$90	Change in Currency	−$100
Excess Reserves	$0				Excess Reserves		$81			Change in Transaction Accounts	+$190
Loans	$90									Change in Money Supply	+$90

Round 2: Loan recipient buys a DVD player from Bob's Electronics and Bob places the $90 in his account at Last National Bank

San Jac S&L					Last National Bank					Money Supply	
Assets			Liabilities		Assets			Liabilities		
Required Reserves	$10		Your Account	$100	Required Reserves		$9	Bob's Account	$90	Change in Currency	$0
Excess Reserves	$0				Excess Reserves		$81			Change in Transaction Accounts	$0
Loans	$90									Change in Money Supply	$0

Round 3: Last National Bank uses its $81 in excess reserves to make a loan to someone who puts the loan amount in his transaction account at San Jac S&L.

San Jac S&L					Last National Bank					Money Supply	
Assets			Liabilities		Assets			Liabilities		
Required Reserves	$18.10		Your Account	$100	Required Reserves		$9	Bob's Account	$90	Change in Currency	$0
Excess Reserves	$62.90		Loan Recipient's Account	$81	Excess Reserves		$0			Change in Transaction Accounts	+$81
Loans	$90				Loans		$81			Change in Money Supply	+$81

Round X: Some bank lends $1 in excess reserves. Transaction accounts and money supply increase by $1.

Figure 11.4 • **Continuing the Money Creation Process**
As the money creation process continues, increasingly smaller loan amounts are made as the reserve requirement eats away at the loan-creating potential of the banking system.

Since we assume that banks never want keep excess reserves and all earnings from purchases made from loaned funds are placed in a bank within the system, we can say that the potential (or theoretical) money multiplier is one divided by the reserve requirement ratio.

$$Money\ Multiplier = \frac{1}{Reserve\ Requirement\ Ratio}$$

This means the greatest possible amount that the money supply can increase from a change in reserves given the reserve requirement ratio is the potential money multiplier times the initial change in reserves.

$$Change\ in\ MS = Money\ Multiplier \times Original\ Change\ in\ Reserves$$

This is where the factor of ten comes from; the reserve requirement ratio in the United States is 10 percent or .1 so the potential money multiplier is ten.

In real world, however, the money multiplier is never as high as the potential money multiplier. Banks do not loan 100 percent of their excess reserves and loan recipients do not spend 100 percent of the loans they receive. Therefore, a more accurate description of the total change in money supply caused by a change in reserves is the actual money, which is closer to two or three in the United States multiplier times the initial change in reserves.

V. THE FEDERAL RESERVE

Structure of the Fed

The Federal Reserve is the central, or national, bank of the United States and is in charge of measuring and regulating the money supply. The Fed—as it is commonly referred to—was created in 1913 to help prevent the bank panics and financial crises that periodically occurred in the United States and other industrialized countries. The Fed's day-to-day operations include providing support services to commercial banks and acting as the personal bank to the US Treasury.

Regional Banks. The central bank system in most countries consists of a single bank where monetary authority is concentrated. The Federal Reserve, though, consists of twelve regional banks that meet the particular demands of their home regions while following the policies of the Board of Governors in Washington. The Federal Reserve System is broken up into twelve regional districts each with a regional bank and a total of twenty-four additional branches between them.

Board of Governors. A board of governors, appointed by the president for fourteen-year terms, manages the Fed and decides on its policy positions. The Chairman of the Board, currently Ben Bernanke, presents Fed policies and proposals to Congress and the president at regularly scheduled meetings.

While the Federal Reserve is part of the United States government it is actually privately owned. Each regional bank is technically owned by the commercial banks in its particular region. Whenever a new bank opens, it must buy shares in its respective regional bank. While these commercial banks hold the shares of the Fed, only the Board of Governors can determine its policies.

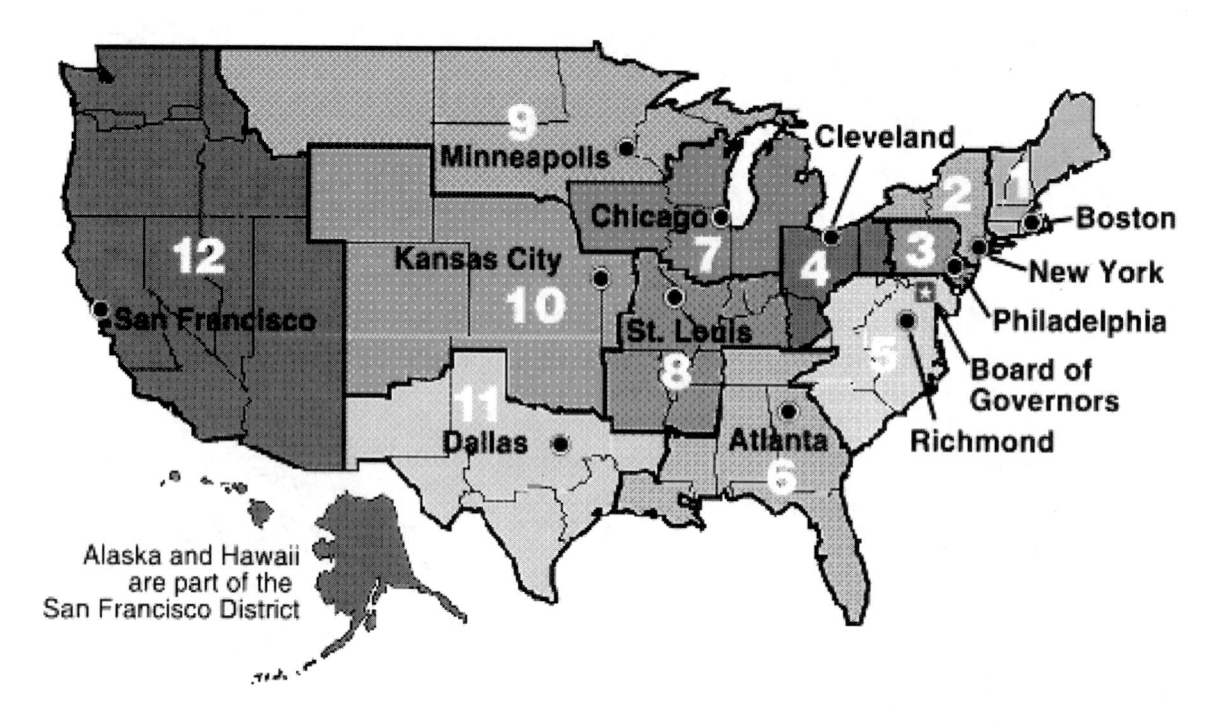

Figure 11.5 • **Federal Reserve System**
The regional banks of the Federal Reserve System serve the particular needs of the member banks in their region.

Unlike most federal agencies, the Fed actually earns a profit. But since the Board of Governors never see a dime of this profit the activities of the Fed are aimed at improving and strengthening the United States economy, not maximizing profits. The Fed rarely competes with private banks for customers.

The Federal Reserve was purposely set up to protect it from political pressure from Washington. While political pressures and special interests may sometimes influence the fiscal policy of the president and Congress, the Fed's independence allows it to control monetary policy without worrying about being popular: The board of governors never have election campaigns to worry about.

In fact, research shows that countries with independent national banks have lower inflation rates than those without. This makes sense, since it may be difficult for a government agency to increase interest rates to control inflation without a backlash from groups that would face a higher price for borrowing money. An independent monetary authority, on the other hand, can be the bad guy and make the hard choices necessary to maintain the health of the economy.

FOMC. It is actually the Federal Open Market Committee (FOMC), consisting of the board of governors as well as the president of the New York Fed and four other regional presidents that rotate in and out, which makes decisions about money supply. In particular, they decide when to buy government bonds from the public (increasing the money supply) and when to sell bonds to the public (decreasing the money supply).

Roles of the Fed

While you may not know it, the Federal Reserve plays a critical role in the functioning of our economy. Think of the Fed like an operating system; when you are using your computer to watch a video or type a paper, there is an operating system running in the background that allows those different applications to work. While the Federal Reserve is primarily known for its control of the money supply, it actually performs a variety of necessary tasks for the economy.

Check Clearing. The Fed offers check-clearing services to all depository institutions. It charges a fee for these services and competes with private companies like Telecheck; the Fed currently clears nearly one-third of all checks (in terms of dollar amount) in the United States. In addition, the Fed's electronic payment system, Fedwire, facilitates interbank payments. Banks make loans to each other and pay them back electronically using this system, lowering transaction costs. The average daily volume of all payments on Fedwire exceeds $1 trillion; and the Fed gets to keep a percentage of those payments as a fee.

Holding Reserves. For safety and convenience reasons, banks do not keep all of their reserves in their vaults. The regional banks of the Fed hold reserves for depository institutions. Banks are required by law to keep a certain percentage of their total deposits on reserve; funds held at the federal reserves count toward this requirement. In addition, some banks choose to keep excess reserves at their regional Federal Reserve Bank. As we have seen, these reserves are essential to the money creation process.

Providing Currency. The paper currency we use is called Federal Reserve notes; the Federal Reserve, not the Treasury, is responsible for supplying the economy with the cash it needs to make transactions. Whenever spending increases (like during the holiday season), banks have to dip into their vault reserves to meet the needs of consumers. These banks then turn to the Federal Reserve to replenish their reserves. The Fed must have sufficient funds on hand to meet these demands.

Banker's Bank. Instead of dealing directly with the public, the Fed generally takes deposits from and makes loans to other banks. As mentioned before, the Fed offers banks the opportunity to hold some of their legally required reserves at their institutions rather than in the banks' vaults, for convenience and security reasons. In addition, the Fed offers short-term loans to banks unable to meet withdrawal demands or those falling short of required reserves.

One of the original motivations for the creation of the Fed was the need for a place for banks to borrow when they ran low on cash and everyone wanted to take their money out at the same time. In the past, banks that faced an unexpected run on reserves were forced to close and consumers would lose their deposits as well as their confidence in the financial system. Now the Federal Reserve prevents these bank panics by standing as the lender of last resort.

The Federal Funds Rate

While the Federal Reserve can lend directly to banks in trouble, they would rather let the market handle it. The Fed limits its own lending by setting low borrowing maximums and establishing tight restrictions on its borrowers. As such, banks usually pursue borrowed funds on the federal funds market, an open market where banks borrow excess reserves from each other on a short-term (usually overnight) basis.

The rate at which banks borrow in the federal funds market, called the federal funds rate, offers a good measure of the price banks must pay to raise funds. As such, the federal funds rate is an important indicator of the health of the financial system and the future direction of monetary policy.

The federal funds rate provides a signal about the Federal Reserve's intention for the money supply. If the Fed injects reserves into the system through one of its policy tools, the desire for interbank loans will fall since there will be less need for these overnight loans. Hence, the federal funds rate falls when the Fed is trying to grow the money supply.

On the other hand, a reduction in the money supply by the Federal Reserve will be met by an increase in the federal funds rate as both policies aim at restraining the growth of the money supply. Remember that the Fed can only adjust the "target" federal funds rate; the actual rate is determined by the rate of loans between banks. The Fed uses its announcement of the target rate as a signal and then uses monetary policy tools to meet that target.

VI. TOOLS OF MONETARY POLICY

Increasing the Money Supply

Most believe the Fed's most important job is controlling the money supply. The Fed is charged with making sure that there is enough money in the economy to make spending match production, but not so much as to cause inflation. The money supply determines the interest rate which (at least in the short run) influences saving and expenditure. Increasing the reserves in the banking system can also help banks when people try to take too much money out at once. The Fed has a variety of tools at its disposal to speed up the money creation process.

Decrease the Reserve Requirement. Since the total change in money supply induced by a change in reserves is dependent upon the reserve requirement ratio (the money multiplier is the inverse of this factor), the Fed can speed up or slow down money creation by changing this ratio. The Fed is free to set the reserve requirement ratio within a broad limit set by Congress.

How might the Fed use the reserve requirement to adjust the money supply? If the Fed wants to increase the money supply by $50 billion, they will need to get banks to give $50 billion in additional loans. This "new" money will be deposited in some banks and increase total reserves.

But banks cannot give out more loans since they tend to hold zero excess reserves. The Fed can turn some of the banks' required reserves into excess reserves by reducing the reserve requirement. Let's assume that banks are holding $10 billion on hand because the reserve requirement ratio is 20 percent (that means total transaction deposits are $50 billion).

By reducing the reserve requirement to 10 percent, the Fed will reduce the level of required reserves to $5 billion, turning the other half of those $10 billion in reserves into excess reserves. The banking system now has $5 billion in additional funds to lend, increasing the money supply by that amount times the money multiplier, which is now ten. Assuming no leakages, the end result is a $50 billion increase in the money supply.

$$Increase\ in\ Money\ Supply = \frac{1}{.1} \times \$5\ Billion = \$50\ Billion$$

Decrease the Discount Rate. If a bank has an abundance of qualified candidates and wants to increase loans, but has no excess reserves, it can achieve its goal by borrowing reserves from some other source. One of the places the bank can go to borrow reserves is the Fed itself. The Fed loans reserves to depository institutions at an interest rate called the discount rate.

Banks borrow funds from the Fed in order to meet its reserve requirements and promise to pay the Fed back when some of its outstanding loans get paid back. This process is called discounting since the amount banks could borrow used to be based on the face value of their outstanding loans "discounted" by some fraction. While this is no longer the case, the name stuck.

The interest rate charged on these funds, the discount rate, provides the Federal Reserve with another policy tool. The higher the discount rate, the more expensive it is to borrow from the Fed. As a result, banks really do not want to find themselves in the position of needing to borrow and will keep more excess reserves as a cushion. These excess reserves represent a leakage in the money creation process and slow down the growth of the money supply.

The discount rate represents the opportunity cost of borrowing from the Fed. The lower this rate is the more willing banks are to create more loans since it increases the spread between this opportunity cost of borrowing and the profitability of lending (the interest rate the bank charges its loan customers).

We do not know for sure how much banks will change their borrowing and lending characteristics if the Fed changes the discount rate. As a result, we cannot calculate the exact rate we need to set to achieve a given monetary stimulus. Article 11.1 reports that low borrowing rates have eased tensions in a stingy loan market by lowering the cost of lending faced by banks.

Buy Bonds. The final policy tool, open market operations, directly changes the reserves in the banking system (and therefore the money supply) through the buying and selling of government bonds. When the Fed buys bonds from a bank or business it adds money to the economy, and when it sells bonds it takes money out of the economy.

In order for open market operations to work, the Fed needs to convince people to buy bonds when they want them to and sell them when that is required. Getting people to give up their cash to buy bonds will take money out of the banking system and getting people to accept Federal Reserve checks in exchange for bonds will add money to the banking system.

If the Fed wanted to increase the money supply, it would need to increase the amount of reserves in the banking system. Hence, it would have to convince people to put more money in the bank and less in bonds. How can it get people to sell their bonds? By offering to pay a higher than market price for bonds, the Fed will reduce the attractiveness of holding bonds by lowering their yield or rate of return on investment; you would be better off just selling them to the Fed. People will take the proceeds from their bond sales and place them in the banking system, increasing the money supply. You cannot buy anything with a check from the Fed; you have to put it in the bank first.

Buying bonds on the open market is the most direct and precise way to increase the money supply. Getting people to sell their US bonds and put their money into the banking system instead will certainly increase reserves and enhance the banking system's ability to create new money.

Given a reserve requirement of 10 percent, how many bonds would the Fed have to buy to achieve a monetary stimulus of $50 billion? Given what we know about the money multiplier, it would only take $5 billion of new reserves to increase the money supply by $50 billion if the reserve requirement ratio was 10 percent and there were no leakages.

After Fed hands over the $5 billion in checks to the bond sellers, they will deposits these checks into their personal banks. The banks will only need to keep $500 million of these funds as required reserves and will loan out the reminder. From that point the money multiplier takes over, ultimately creating $45 billion in new deposits to add to the original $5 billion injection by the open market purchase of the bonds.

Article 11.1:
Fed More Upbeat, but Keeps Lid on Rates
By Jon Hilsenrath

The Federal Reserve acknowledged the U.S. economy is picking up, but reaffirmed its plan to keep short-term interest rates near zero for at least several more months.

. . .

The Fed's unanimous decision Wednesday to give no indication of an imminent move to tighten credit sets the stage for tough decisions in 2010. Officials noted in a statement after the meeting that the economy has continued to "pick up," the deterioration in the job market is "abating" and financial conditions "have become more supportive of economic growth." Stock and bond markets dipped after the meeting, but mostly shrugged off the decision.

. . .

Because inflation was still low and unemployment still very high, the Fed said it would keep its key interest-rate target between 0 and 0.25% for an "extended period," a word it uses to signal several months.

. . .

If the recovery becomes entrenched as Fed officials generally expect, a tough debate could emerge there in 2010 about when to raise rates, and on other issues.

Some dovish members of the Fed's policy committee believe inflation is likely to remain so low that rate increases might not be needed until 2011. Others will want to move more quickly because interest rates are starting out from such a low point. Financial markets anticipate the Fed will boost rates to 0.5% after mid-2010.

"Though we have begun to see some improvement in economic activity, we still have some way to go before we can be assured that the recovery will be self-sustaining," Mr. Bernanke said last week.

. . .

The Fed could pull back other emergency measures long before pushing up its target for the federal funds rate—the rate at which banks lend to each other over night. It might, for instance lift the rate it charges on loans the Fed makes directly to banks, the "discount rate." Before the crisis, this rate was one percentage point higher than the fed funds rate. In August 2007, the Fed cut the discount rate to just a quarter of a percentage point above the fed funds rate to encourage banks to come to the central bank for emergency funds.

The central bank described the move at the time as a temporary measure. The discount rate is now at 0.5%. To restore the old relationship between the discount rate and the fed funds rate, officials could raise the discount rate without moving the fed funds target.

The Fed underscored in its postmeeting statement many of the emergency measures it has taken in the past two years were being unwound. . . .

Questions:
1. Why did the Federal Reserve choose to keep its target federal funds rate down at the meeting referred to in the article?
2. What is the danger of keeping this rate down for too long?
3. Why was the discount rate so much higher than the federal funds rate before the recession?

Reprinted by permission of *Wall Street Journal,* Copyright © 2009 Dow Jones & Company, Inc. All Rights Reserved Worldwide. License number 2561001064775.

Decreasing the Money Supply

While the Federal Reserve rarely aims to reduce the money supply as a major goal, it does typically make minor adjustments to money growth policies that require monetary restraint. All of the tools that Fed uses to increase the money supply can be reversed to limit or restrain it.

A growing economy with more and more workers and more and more spending every year needs a growing money supply. Rather than reduce the size of the money supply, the Fed typically uses these contractionary tools to simply slow the growth of the money supply and ultimately stave off inflation.

Increase the Reserve Requirement. Raising the reserve requirement decreases the amount of loans the banking system can give out for a given level of reserves. If the bank is already holding zero excess reserves, this will certainly slow down its rate of lending as it waits for loans to be paid back so it can fulfill its reserve requirement. Raising the reserve requirement also decreases the money multiplier, reducing the amount of money that can be created from any given increase in bank deposits.

Increase the Discount Rate. Raising the discount rate reduces the profitability of lending. Banks do not want to be overextended and have to borrow from the Fed when the discount rate rises, so they reduce the amount of loans they give out, slowing down the money creation process.

Sell Bonds. An open market sale of bonds creates the opposite effect from buying bonds, reducing bank reserves and decreasing the money supply. In order to get people to take their money out of the bank and buy more bonds, the Federal Reserve will sell the bonds at a lower than market price.

Bidding down the bond price increases its yield and makes it more attractive to the consumer. Unable to resist the deal, many savers will take their money out of the bank and buy bonds from the Fed. Reserves are eliminated from the banking system and the Fed locks the money away.

Selling bonds to people takes money directly out of the banking system. The checks that people write to buy these bonds, reduces the level of reserves in the banking system. Having fewer reserves reduces the amount of loans that banks can give out and therefore slows down the rate of money growth.

CHAPTER 11 SUMMARY

- Money today only has value because we expect that it will be **accepted** as a means of payment.
- Money must perform three functions: **medium of exchange, unit of account,** and **store of value.**
- M1 = *Currency + Transaction Deposits + Traveler's Checks*
- M2 = *M1 + Savings Deposits + Time Deposits + Money Market Mutual Fund Balances*
- Banks only have to keep a fraction, **the reserve requirement ratio**, of total deposits on hand at any time.
- Since banks only make money by giving loans and buying assets, they will **only keep a minimum amount of reserves.**
- **Every loan given out by banks increases the monetary base** since the loan recipient's account increases and no other account decreases.

- *Money Multiplier* = $\dfrac{1}{Reserve\ Requirement\ Ratio}$
- The total amount of money created by a single deposit is equal to the **money multiplier times the original deposit.**
- The **Federal Reserve** serves as the nation's central bank.
- The Federal Reserve can change the money supply by altering the **reserve requirement ratio, the discount rate,** or **open market operations.**

CHAPTER 11

Exercises

Name _____

1) When money is used to acquire goods and services it is functioning as a
   A) unit of account.
   B) store of value.
   C) medium of exchange.
   D) commodity.

   1) _____

2) Which of the following appears in M2 but *not* in M1?
   A) savings accounts
   B) currency
   C) traveler's checks
   D) transaction accounts

   2) _____

3) The banking system can lend more than the sum of its excess reserves because
   A) the money multiplier is less than one.
   B) of the fraction reserve system.
   C) assets exceed liabilities.
   D) there are no leakages.

   3) _____

4) If the banking system has a required reserve ratio of 10 percent, then the money multiplier is:
   A) .9
   B) 10
   C) .1
   D) 1.1

   4) _____

5) Members of the Federal Reserve Board of Governors are appointed for one fourteen-year term so that they
   A) have time to learn how the Fed operates.
   B) will make decisions that support the people that appointed them.
   C) have time to get to know all 12 districts.
   D) make their decisions based what is right for the economy, not their political careers.

   5) _____

6) Which of the following is true about an increase in the discount rate?
   A) It signals that the Fed wants to speed up money growth
   B) It signals that the Fed wants to restrain money growth
   C) It makes borrowing from the Fed less expensive
   D) It reduces the cost of lending for banks

   6) _____

7) Which of the following is the tool used most frequently by the Fed?
   A) The reserve requirement.
   B) The fed funds rate.
   C) Open market operations.
   D) The discount rate.

   7) _____

8) If the Fed wants to sell more bonds than people are willing to buy, then the Fed should
   A) decrease the price it charges for the bonds.
   B) switch to another type of monetary policy tool.
   C) encourage a government agency to buy the bonds.
   D) raise the price it charges for the bonds.

   8) _____

9) Suppose a bank has $200,000 in deposits and a required reserve ratio of 10 percent.
   A) How much does the bank have to keep on hand (required reserves)?

   B) How much can the bank lend out (excess reserves)?

   C) What is the money multiplier?

   D) If the banks lends out all of its excess reserves, how much can the money supply increase?

10) Assuming a reserve requirement of 20 percent, if the Fed buys $20 billion in bonds in the open market, how much could the money supply increase if there are no leakages?

Chapter 12

Monetary Policy

I. THE MONEY MARKET

The actual effect of Federal Reserve policies results from changes in the money market. Like any other commodity, there is a demand for money and a supply of money. The supply of money comes from monetary policy and the demand comes from the economic agents that need it for transactions. These two forces interact and achieve an equilibrium price for money, which we call the interest rate.

Money Balances

While it may seem clear that the interest rate is the price of borrowed money, it is not so obvious that the interest rate is the price of all money holdings, or money balances. But the truth is that there is an opportunity cost of holding money in your pocket, your piggy bank, or even in a bank account that earns little to no interest. That cost is the interest you could be earning by loaning your idle funds out instead of holding them.

Liquidity and the Price of Money. Money is a part of a person's wealth, an asset. People have assets because they can be exchanged for goods and services in the future. No asset can be more easily converted into goods and services than money; it is the most liquid asset. An asset's liquidity is the ease with which it can be exchanged for goods and services with low transaction costs and without loss of value.

A house or some other form of real estate is also an asset, but it is much less liquid than money. To convert a house into goods and services you must first sell the house. Doing so requires a lengthy and complicated process involving a realtor whom you must pay a commission. Likewise, the house will likely sell for more or less than what you paid for it. If it sells for less, you lose money, but if it sells for more you have to pay capital gains taxes. All of these problems make real estate less liquid than money.

So the question is: Why would anyone hold any asset other than money? The reason is that there is a cost related to the liquidity of money; money on hand does not gain any interest. Therefore, by holding money, you are forgoing the money you could have earned if you had purchased some interest-bearing asset like stocks, bonds, or certificates of deposits.

Regardless of where you hold your money, if it is not earning the market interest rate, you are foregoing some level of income. In other words, you are paying a real cost to hold money in the form of cash or non-interest bearing checking deposits. The exact cost is the difference between the market interest rate and the interest your funds are earning.

The Demand for Money

Portfolio Decision. Since money is a commodity and has a price, it is not unreasonable to believe that it follows the law of demand. The lower the price of money (the interest rate), the more money balances people will demand. But why would people hold money at all? The opportunity cost of holding money could be easily avoided by converting your portfolio into nothing but interest-bearing assets.

Transaction Demand. Money is by definition the most liquid asset. We need it to make our daily purchases without having to go to the bank over and over, or having to sell a less liquid asset. Since people make transactions on a daily basis, it would be impractical and costly to hold all of your wealth in stocks or real estate.

How would you pay for a cup of coffee? You would have to call your broker, have him make a sale, then have him wire the money to your checking account. All of these actions take time and money, and you may earn a loss on your stock sale. The basic transaction demand for money requires that people keep some money in the form of cash or checking account balances.

Precautionary Demand. In addition to everyday transactions, many people hold a little bit of extra cash on hand or in their bank account for a rainy day. In the event of an emergency, people want to know they will be able to make a necessary purchase even if the bank was closed or they did not have time to sell off a less liquid asset. Credit cards have somewhat reduced this precautionary demand, but it still exists.

Speculative Demand. Some people hold money because they do not like the current value of other forms of wealth. Perhaps stock prices are too high or the housing market is weak. They want to be ready to strike when the market is hot so they hold money for speculative purposes.

The Market Demand Curve. These three motivations all lead us to the same conclusion: the demand for money is downward sloping. In other words, as figure 12.1 illustrates people demand less money the higher the interest rate. But to what extent? People might be very responsive to changes in the interest rate or they may demand pretty much the some amount of money regardless of the interest rate.

People are, in fact, fairly responsive to changes in the interest rate. Despite the need for money for transactions as well as for precautionary concerns, evidence suggests that sometimes the opportunity cost of holding money is just too high. The high interest rates of the 1980s caused many people to move their money out of checking accounts, greatly reducing the amount of money available for transactions and leading to a decline in business activity.

Even corporations had to be careful about where they put their money in these high interest rate periods. The constant watching of interest rates and frequent trips back to manage one's portfolio resulted in lost resources for the economy, but the high opportunity cost of money at the time demanded it.

Equilibrium

Just like any market, equilibrium in the money market comes from the intersection of the supply and demand curves. We have seen that the demand curve is downward sloping, what about the supply curve? We will assume the supply curve is vertical at an arbitrary level determined by Fed policy and the willingness of banks to lend. This supply will not change in the short run regardless of what the interest rate does; the Federal Reserve has no incentive to reduce or increase the money supply as result of interest rate changes.

The intersection point in figure 12.2 tells us that there is only one interest rate where the amount of money demanded is exactly equal to the amount of money supplied. At an interest rate above this equilibrium, consumers would not be willing to

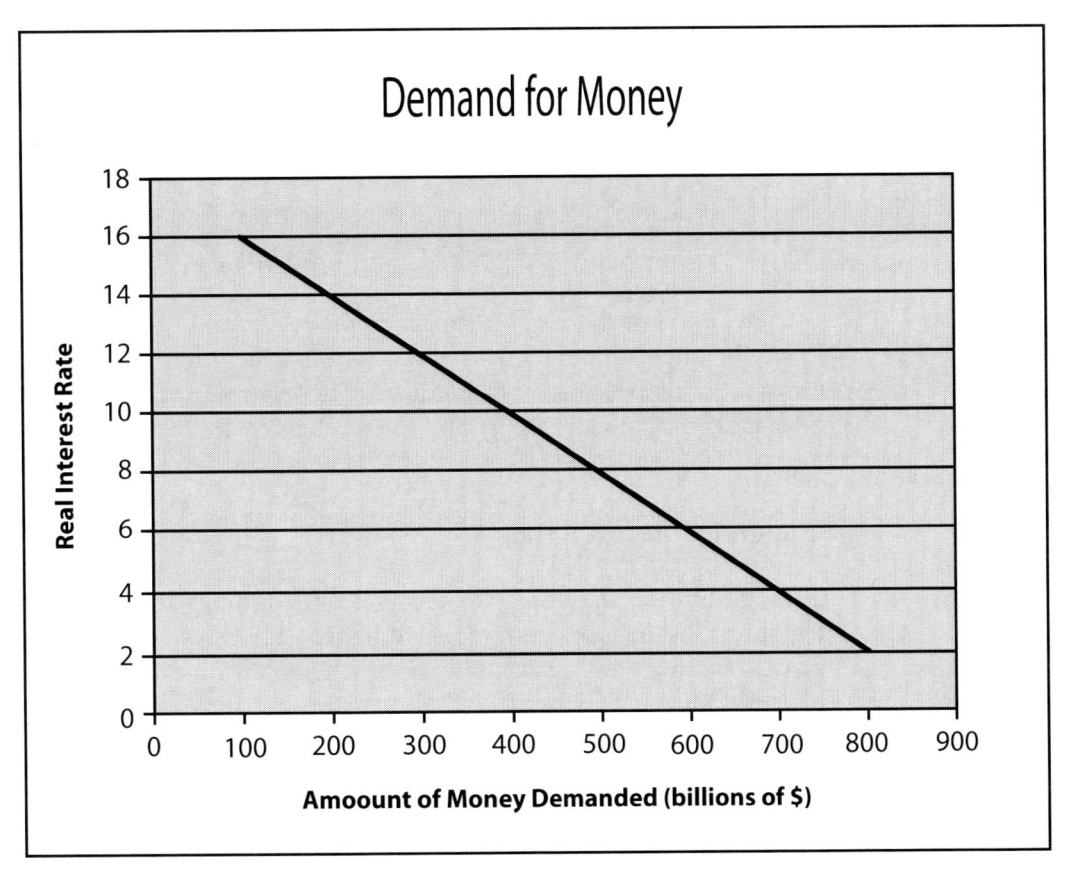

Figure 12.1 • Money Demand Curve
The demand for money slopes downward because as the interest rate rises, the opportunity cost of holding money rises.

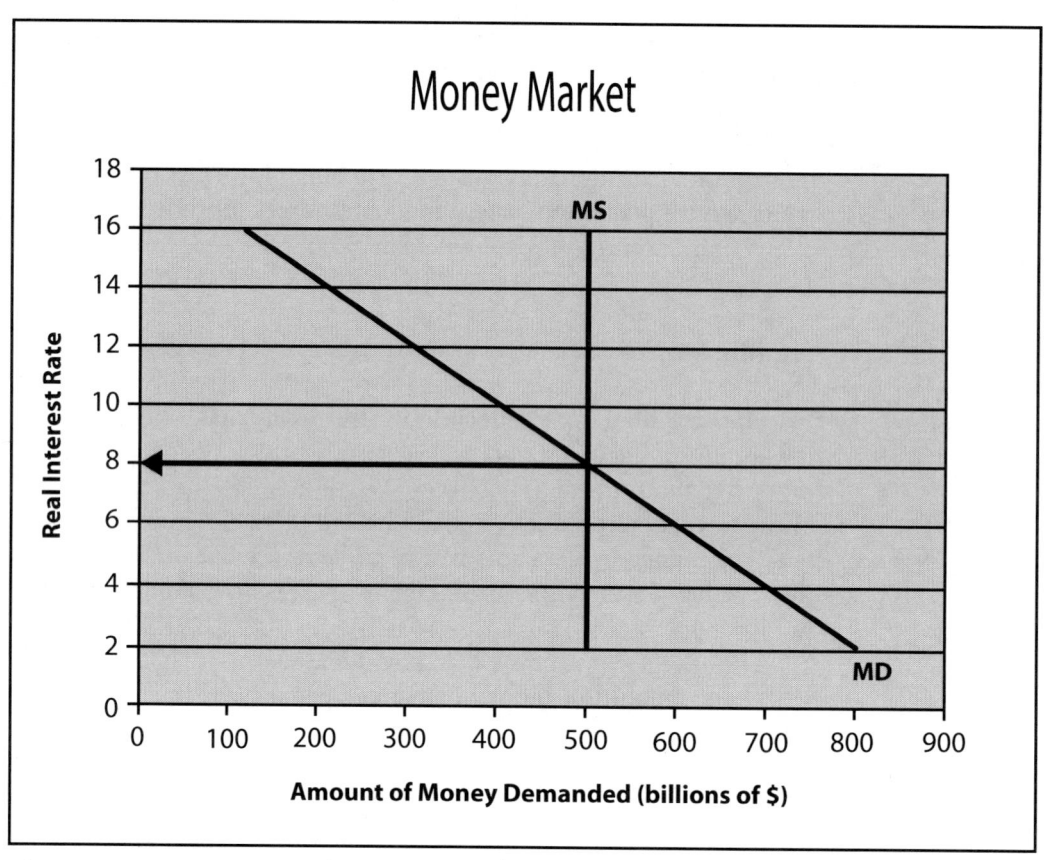

Figure 12.2 • **Money Market Equilibrium**
The intersection of the money supply curve and money demand curve determines the equilibrium real interest rate.

hold the amount money supplied by the banking system, and instead would buy up interest-bearing assets like stocks and bonds.

This flood of money into stocks and bonds would tend to inflate their prices and lower the interest rate. As market forces cause the interest rate to drop, consumers will move more money into cash holdings. These forces will stop once the market money demand equals money supply and the market reaches equilibrium.

Changing Interest Rates

This equilibrium shows us why changes in Fed policy alter the interest rate. When the Fed increases the money supply, as in figure 12.3, through reducing the reserve requirement, lowering the discount rate, or buying bonds on the open market the money supply curve shifts to the right.

Assuming no change in money demand, people will only be willing to hold this additional money if the interest rate falls. This feeling is reflected in the new equilibrium. A reversal of this policy, decreasing the money supply, would have the opposite effect. People would demand less money at a higher interest rate if the money supply curve shifted to the left.

Federal Funds Rate. As mentioned in Chapter 11, the federal funds rate (the interest rate on interbank loans) is the interest rate most affected by changes in Fed policy. Ex-

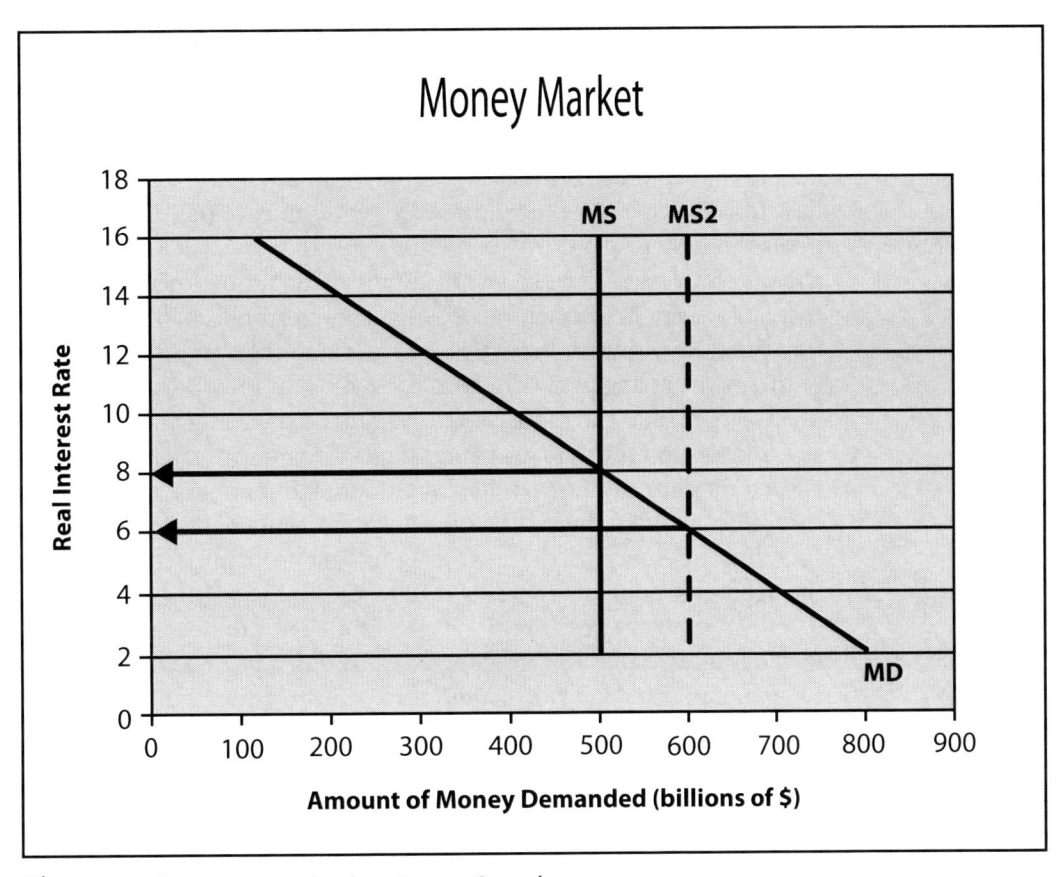

Figure 12.3 • Increase in the Money Supply
Federal Reserve policy that increases the money supply will reduce the equilibrium real interest rate.

pansionary policy decreases the federal funds rate while contractionary policy will cause it to increase. The more money is available, the less expensive borrowing from another bank will be. These rates in turn affect other market interest rates—loans, mortgages, credit cards, etc. A lower federal funds rate increases the profitability of lending at any interest rate, allowing banks to lower some of the interest rates they charge.

II. INTEREST RATES AND SPENDING

Monetary Stimulus

The goal of monetary policy is to alter the big macroeconomic outcomes—unemployment, GDP, and growth. What impact does changing the interest rate have on these outcomes? The goal of monetary stimulus is to get people to spend more money. Lowering the interest rate should help us achieve this.

Investment. First, we know from the investment demand curve in Chapter 9 that investment is inversely related to the interest rate: the lower the interest rate, the more businesses will spend on investment. Lowering the interest rate makes any potential investment more profitable by lowering the cost of borrowing. A lower interest rate will cause a movement along the current investment demand curve, encouraging more businesses to invest.

Aggregate Demand. Lower interest rates will induce more investment spending and that will certainly increase aggregate demand, but that isn't the end of the story. The people that sold the businesses the new capital, and the new workers they employ, will now have more money to spend. They will increase their spending, and so will the business where they spend this newfound wealth.

In a process known as the multiplier effect, one injection of new spending (in this case, increased investment spending) causes ripples across the economy by increasing the spending of multiple parties. At each step the amount of spending decreases a little, but the shift in aggregate demand caused by an increase in investment spending will be much larger than the increase in investment spending alone.

A lower interest rate also encourages consumption spending. As mortgage, car loan, and credit card interest payments fall, consumers have more money to spend on consumption goods. Lower interest rates may also encourage state and local government spending by lowering the cost of bond-financed projects. All of these increases cause the aggregate demand curve to shift to the right as shown in figure 12.4.

With so many possible effects, it can be hard to determine the impact of a reduction in the interest rate on aggregate demand. Former Fed chairman Alan Greenspan came up with a pretty good rule of thumb, however. He said that a .1 percentage point (or ten

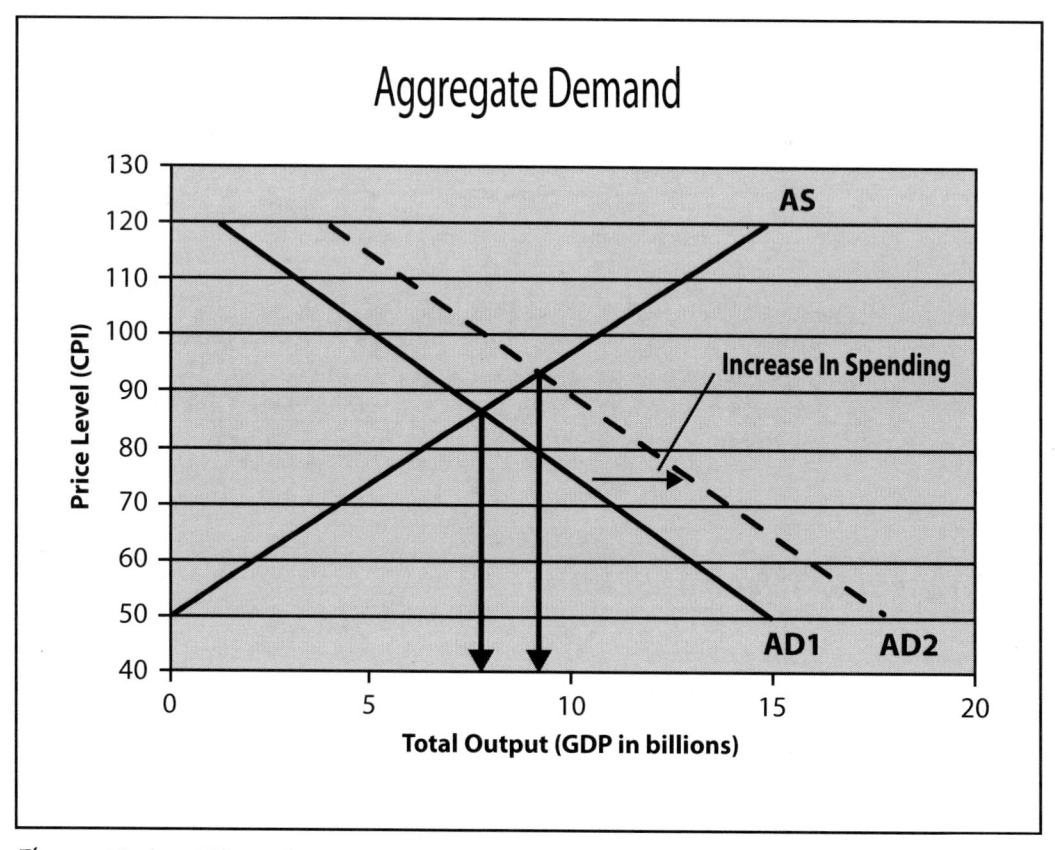

Figure 12.4 • Effect of Monetary Stimulus
A drop in interest rates will encourage more spending by households, businesses, and government. This increase will, in turn, shift the aggregate demand curve to the right and result in a higher equilibrium quantity of output.

basis points) decrease in the long-term interest rate would create about $10 billion in additional spending.

This explains why the Federal Reserve wanted to lower interest rate in the wake of the recession of 2007–2009. A full point reduction in interest rates could create a $100 billion stimulus, causing some serious shifting of the aggregate demand curve and hopefully saving or creating many jobs.

Monetary Restraint

As is the case with fiscal policy, sometimes we need monetary policy to reduce aggregate demand in order to stem inflationary pressures. If people increase spending faster than businesses can increase production, demand-pull inflation will result and people could lose faith in the dollar. In a case like this, we need a monetary policy that can reduce total spending.

Higher Interest Rates. The way contractionary monetary policy succeeds in reducing spending is by doing the opposite of what expansionary policy does, raising the interest rate. Open market sales of bonds, increasing the discount rate, and increasing the reserve requirement all make it more difficult for banks to make loans. As a result, the money supply falls and the interest rate rises.

Reduced Aggregate Demand. At higher interest rates, many investments that seemed profitable no longer look so good. Total investment falls and aggregate demand goes down with it, shifting to the left. Also, we expect consumers to postpone purchases of big-ticket items causing consumption spending to fall as well. Since dragging down the economy and slowing job growth is always a concern with monetary restraint, the Fed is very careful with its inflation-fighting policies.

III. POLICY CONSTRAINTS

Constraints on Monetary Stimulus

Short-Term vs. Long-Term Rates. While the effect of monetary policy can be easy to follow and measure in theory, the real-world ability of the Fed to affect the economy is limited by several constraints. One of the most evident limitations is the fact that the Fed only has direct control over very short-term rates (discount rate, federal funds rate), but economic stimulus comes from changes in long-term rates (mortgages, banks loans).

The ability of the Fed's policies to affect changes in these long-term rates has come into question in the two most recent recessions. During the 2001 recession, for example, the Fed lowered the target federal funds rate by three full percentage points to try to stimulate spending, but the market rate on mortgages fell only half of one percent.

The same problem occurs during monetary restraint as well, with big jumps in short-term rates only being partly reflected in longer-term rates. If the Fed cannot control long-term rates, its policies will not have as big an impact on macroeconomic outcomes as they desire.

Reluctant Lenders. Part of the reason that interest rates closer to the consumer do not change as quickly as Fed-controlled rates, is that during recessions banks are simply less

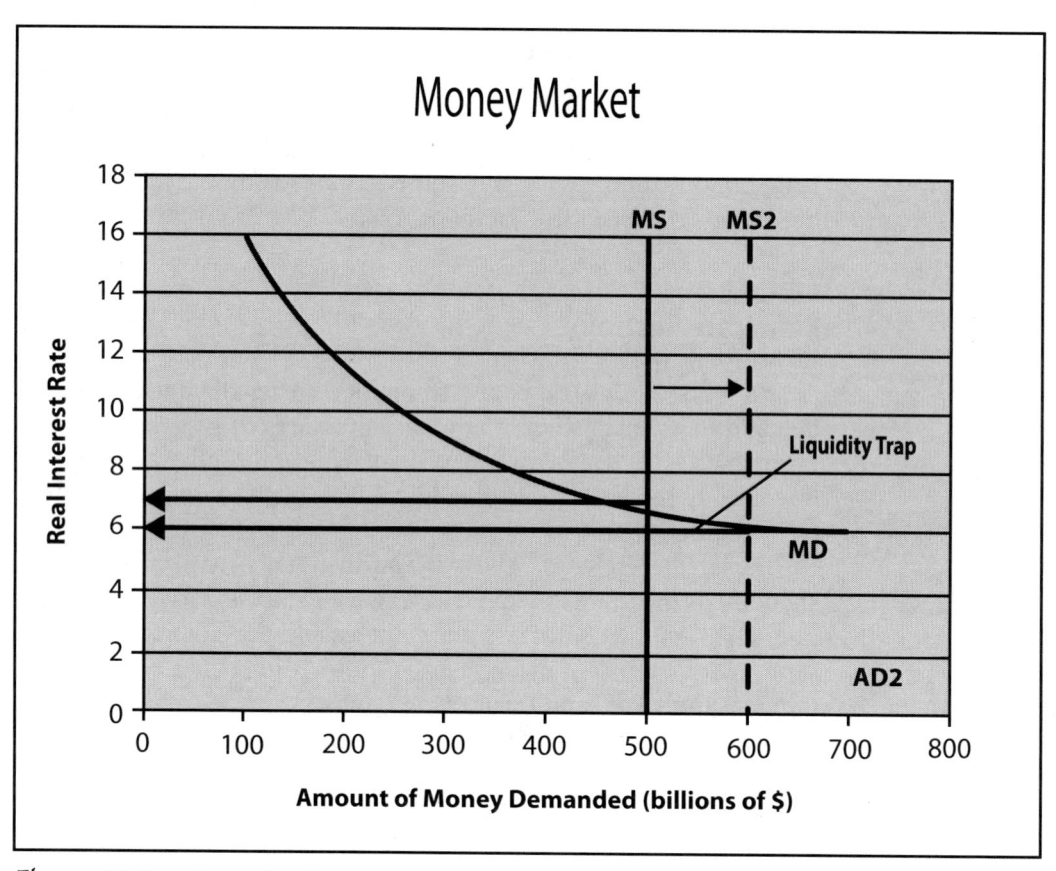

Figure 12.5 • Liquidity Trap
When the money demand curve experiences a liquidity trap, increasing money supply will have little effect on long-term interest rates.

willing to loan. The Fed can reduce the opportunity cost of loaning and even directly increase bank reserves, but they cannot force the banks to loan out these reserves if they do not want to.

In fact, in the depths of the most recent recession Congress debated whether or not to create legislation that would force banks to loan out excess reserves for just this problem. The reason is simple: If banks do not increase loans, the money supply will not increase. If the money supply does not increase, interest rates will remain high and no stimulus will occur.

Liquidity Trap. Another scenario where monetary stimulus may not be effective involves consumer behavior. If consumers are willing to hold any increase in the money supply as cash (precautionary and speculative demand for money are very high) than an increase in the money supply will not cause interest rates to fall.

Keynes called this problem the liquidity trap since increasing the money supply would have no impact on short-term spending and cause more long-term problems. Figure 12.5 illustrates that the liquidity trap appears as a flat or very elastic part of the money demand curve.

Low Expectations. Even if banks are willing to lend and people have faith in the banking system, monetary stimulus could have trouble getting off the ground if businesses are not willing to take out loans for new projects. During recessions, when monetary stimulus is most needed, businesses generally have a negative outlook of future

Investment Demand

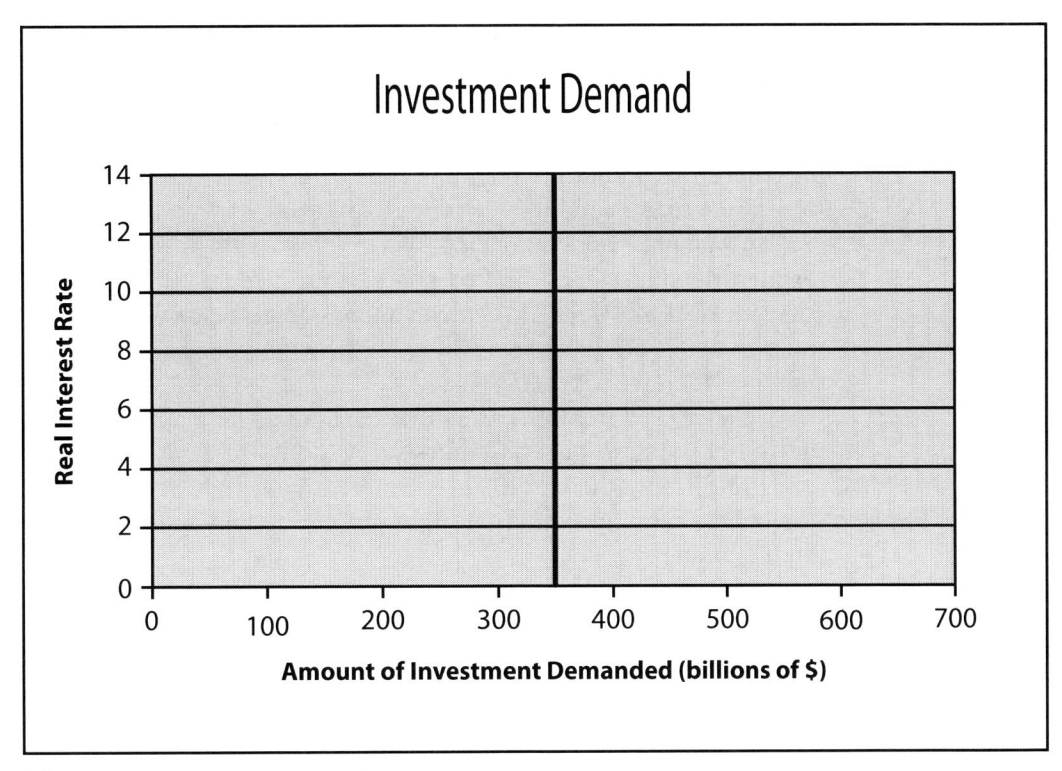

[Graph: Real Interest Rate (y-axis, 0 to 14) vs. Amount of Investment Demanded in billions of $ (x-axis, 0 to 700), showing a vertical line at approximately 350.]

Figure 12.6 • Low Expectations
If the investment demand curve is inelastic, lowering the interest rate through monetary policy will have no effect on how much businesses want to invest.

sales and profits. Hence, they may not increase investments even though the interest rate falls due to monetary stimulus.

Furthermore, a recession will probably cause expectations to worsen even more, shifting the investment demand curve to the left. When this happens, businesses may want fewer investments than before, even though the interest rate has fallen. If investment demand is not very responsive to changes in the interest rate, it is said to be inelastic. An inelastic demand curve takes the shape of a vertical line like the one in figure 12.6. Even if interest rates fall, investment demand will not change. Instead of increasing spending, businesses and consumers take the newly available "cheap" money and pay off debts. Businesses rarely want to expand production in such a poor economic climate, and not even historically low interest rates can convince them otherwise.

Time Lags. Finally, even if every step in the monetary stimulus process works, it takes time for lower interest rates to entice more spending and longer still for that increased spending to generate job growth. In other words, there is always some time lag between the implementation of monetary stimulus and any real change in macroeconomic outcomes.

It takes time for long-term rates to fall enough to attract new business investments or consumer spending on durable goods. It takes still more time for businesses to plan what type of investment they want to pursue or for consumers to determine whether it is the right time to refinance their house or buy a new a car. All of these lags mean that both the Fed and the country need to be patient with monetary stimulus, but by the time it takes effect economic conditions may have changed dramatically.

Limits on Monetary Restraints

The problems with monetary stimulus lead one to believe that it can be difficult to get people to spend more money when the economy is in trouble. It should not be surprising, then, that monetary restraint runs into similar problems trying to get people to slow down their spending when times are good.

Expectations. Good expectations could cause businesses to keep borrowing money for investments even if the Fed raises interest rates; the inelastic investment demand curve works both ways. If the investment demand curve is vertical, raising the interest rate will not be enough to slow down borrowing, especially if the curve is shifting to the right due to higher expectations.

We have seen in recent years that consumers may not reduce their spending even if the Fed is trying to put the brakes on. Despite the Fed continually raising the federal funds rate from 2002 to 2007, consumers kept reducing saving and increasing their spending. Their expectation of higher future income outweighed the increasing cost of holding money.

Global Money. The world does not have a single monetary policy. If credit markets become too tight in the United States due to monetary restraint, businesses and consumers that really want to increase their spending can often find cheaper sources of funds in other countries. The increased ease and availability of international financial intermediaries has further weakened the power of monetary restraint.

Effectiveness of Monetary Policy

With all of these barriers and constraints on effective monetary policy, it comes as no shock that many policymakers and economists no longer view it as a precise tool for changing economic outcomes. For example, Keynes thought that a combination of reluctant lenders, the liquidity trap, and inelastic investment demand would render monetary stimulus about as useful as pushing on a string. We have certainly seen some evidence in recent years that backs this up.

The constraints on monetary restraint are not as binding. Open market sales give the Fed the ability to take money directly out of the banking system. While the availability of foreign sources of funds can weaken the Fed's position, money growth (and therefore spending) will have to slow down when the Fed employs contractionary policy.

IV. MONETARIST PERSPECTIVE

The Keynesian view of monetary policy emphasizes the importance of the interest rate; the level of total spending changes as a direct result of changes in the interest rate. This three-step process—money supply change causes short-term rates to change, short-term rates affect long-term interest rates, long-term interest affect the level of aggregate demand—creates many opportunities for the whole process to unravel.

The monetarist school of economics argues that monetary policy should not be used as a tool for achieving a short-run stability. Changes in short-term interest rates can be unpredictable and therefore so are any changes in real output they create. They instead focus on the power of monetary policy to change the price level and therefore control the rate of inflation.

The Equation of Exchange

The monetarists base their theories on an idea called the equation of exchange. The equation of exchange states that the amount of total spending in the economy is equal to the amount of money in the economy times the amount of times that money is spent. Mathematically, the equation reads:

$$M \times V = P \times Q.$$

Where M represents the money supply, V represents the velocity of money, P is the price level, and Q represents output.

This equation is based on the idea of the circular flow; spending for one person represents income for somebody else. A single dollar can be used and reused in the same economy and end up creating much more than just one dollar of spending. The number of times money changes hands is called the velocity of money, the V in the equation of exchange. We can use this knowledge to determine the total spending (nominal GDP) of an economy. The amount of money in an economy times the number of times the money changes hands (velocity) has to be equal to the value of total output.

What makes this process so different from the Keynesian view is its simplification. There is no need to follow the effect of monetary policy from the federal funds rate to the banking system and so on; everything you need to know about the effect of a change in the money supply on output is right there in the equation of exchange. Simply put, if the money supply increases, price or quantity must rise or velocity must fall.

The equation of exchange, though, is not enough to tell us which of these variables will respond to an increase in the money supply. What we want is for quantity to rise; that means more sales and more jobs. It could be possible, however, for velocity to fall (leaving macro outcomes unchanged) or, even worse, for prices to rise while output remains stable. We will have to look at the evidence from history for our answer.

Stable Velocity

Which one of the variables will be most affected by a change in the money supply? Historical data tells us it won't be the velocity of money. In fact, monetary economists assume the velocity of money is fixed in the short-run. The velocity of money is mostly shaped by spending habits, which is set by people to meet long-term saving and consumption smoothing goals. These goals do not change quickly even during recessions.

If this is accurate, it gets us one step closer to understanding the macroeconomic impact of an increase in the money supply. If the velocity of money is stable, an increase of the money supply must be met by an increase in total spending. We still do not know, though, how much prices and output will be affected individually.

"Natural" Unemployment

Some monetarists take the extreme viewpoint that output is stable in the short run, as well. The result of this assumption is that any increase in the money supply should only cause an increase in prices. The rationale is simple, output in the short run is based on the production capacity and profit-maximizing hiring decisions of all the firms in the country and the money supply is unlikely to change this decision.

In other words, we are talking about the vertical aggregate supply curve from Chapter 8. Producers realize that as people begin to spend more money due to the monetary stimulus, both prices and costs of production will rise. As a result, any benefit they receive in terms of higher revenue will be immediately offset by having to pay more for workers and other inputs. There is no profit effect urging businesses to produce more or hire more workers.

According to this extreme view, the only thing that an increase in the money supply will do is drive up prices. Using the equation of exchange it is easy to see that if V and Q are constant (due to structural factors that do not change in the short run), then the result of any change in the money supply is an equal change in the average price level; in the short run, money growth equals inflation.

Emphasis on Money Supply

To monetarists, any impact caused by changes in interest rates is merely a secondary concern. Whether or not there are reluctant lenders, consumers unwilling to put money in financial markets, or businesses that do not respond to interest rate changes; if the velocity of money is stable, a rise in the money supply will cause total spending to increase. This is the primary effect of monetary policy.

From a policy standpoint, monetarists argue that the Fed should stop worrying about trying to manipulate interest rates. Any stimulus that comes through the lowering of the interest rate depends on both the supply of and the demand for money, and the Fed has no control over money demand. It should instead focus on the macroeconomic effect of the one thing it controls directly: the money supply.

Monetarist Policies

The monetarist view of the macroeconomic impact of monetary policy is certainly streamlined compared to that of Keynes. Instead of those moving parts and the steps required to get an economic stimulus from a drop in the interest rate we have one equation and a couple of assumptions to tell us everything we need.

These two schools of thought fundamentally differ on their views on both how the economy works and the effectiveness of monetary policy. These differences can best be seen by looking at the monetarist response to the two primary macroeconomic problems: inflation and unemployment.

Fighting Inflation. The Keynesian answer for fighting inflation was to raise interest rates to reduce the incentive to spend. Monetarists believe, though, that in periods of rapid inflation the interest rate will already be high since so many people are competing to borrow funds. Furthermore, if the monetary restraint is ineffective (and we know it can be) it may result in a lower price of money instead of a higher one.

Real vs. Nominal Interest. What causes this paradox? Monetary restraint will definitely lead to higher nominal interest rates—the actual percentages advertised on TV or in the window of a bank. What effects macroeconomic decision making, though, is the real interest rate—the actual return from a loan when subtract the purchasing lost from inflation.

You can simplify the relationship between these variables with the Fisher equation you were introduced to in Chapter 7: The real interest rate earned by the bank on a loan equals the nominal interest rate minus the rate of inflation.

Real Interest Rate = Nominal Interest Rate − Inflation Rate

Therefore, the higher the rate of inflation, the less the purchasing power of the bank will increase from a loan of any given nominal interest rate; the value of money paid back is less than that of money loaned out.

What will this do the profitability of lending? Banks and other financial intermediaries lend because they expect to have more purchasing power after the loan than before the loan. If inflation eats away at this gain, than they may be no better off or even worse off by giving out this loan.

As such, banks in countries with relatively stable inflation rates tack on an inflationary premium to the real rate of interest they want to earn.

Nominal Interest Rate = Real Interest Rate + Expected Inflation

If the expected rate of inflation increases, banks will just increase the nominal interest rate they charge so they can keep the real increase in purchasing power the same.

The belief that real interest rates (and therefore the profitability of lending) are constant in the short run is a key aspect of monetarist theory. If this is the case, then changes in nominal rates only come from changes in inflationary expectations; higher nominal rates are a symptom of rising inflation, not a cure. In fact, if inflationary expectations are rising faster than the Fed can push up nominal rates, then people may even continue to borrow at ridiculously high interest rates rendering monetary restraint ineffective.

We see a huge divide between the monetarist and Keynesian response to inflation. Keynesians believe that a decrease in the money supply will raise interest rates and slow the growth of consumption and investment. Monetarists, on the other hand, use the equation of exchange to show that a decrease in the money supply must reduce total spending over time. In fact, they believe that once market participants are aware of the contractionary policy, inflationary expectations will fall and so will nominal interest rates.

Short-Term vs. Long-Term Rates. The monetarist view helps us fill in the gaps left by the Keynesian view of monetary policy. Why aren't changes in short-term rates completely reflected by changes in long-term rates? Clearly, the long-term plans of consumers, businesses, and banks cannot be upended by changes in short-run policy.

According to the equation above, long-term rates will only rise (a necessary component for successful monetary restraint) if market participants expect higher rates of inflation. Absent of this expectation, the radical steps the Fed may need to take to stop rising prices (slow GDP growth, raise unemployment) may be worse than the disease itself. Instead, monetarists suggest predictable and steady changes in the money supply so that everyone is on the same page and the long-term growth rate is stabilized.

Fighting Unemployment. The link between inflationary expectations and nominal interest rates also limits the effectiveness of monetary stimulus. Keynesians believe that an increase in the money supply will lower interest rates and therefore increase the incentive for businesses and consumers to borrow and spend.

According to the equation of exchange, an increase in the money supply will lead to higher prices. Banks understand this, and as a result an unexpected injection of new money will raise inflationary expectations. Banks will charge higher nominal interest rates since they have reasonable expectation that the money they will be paid back will be worth less than the money they lend out. If nominal interest rates do not fall then aggregate demand will not increase. All we have done is added an inflation problem to our unemployment problem.

The monetarists do not believe there is much room for monetary policy in fixing the recessionary gap; they believe the only thing the money supply will change is prices. They do not see this ineffectiveness as much of a problem since they believe the economy will self-adjust in time as classical economists do. According to monetarists, the best thing you can do is not make any sudden adjustments to the money supply and let people adjust to the new reality without having to worry about changing prices or the value of the dollar.

CHAPTER 12 SUMMARY

- Money is **the most liquid asset**.
- The **quantity of money demanded** rises as the interest rate falls.
- The Federal Reserve can alter the **equilibrium interest rate** by increasing or decreasing the money supply.
- Lowering the interest rate should increase aggregate demand (**monetary stimulus**) and raising the interest rate should do the opposite (**monetary restraint**).
- Monetary stimulus might fail if **decreases in short-term interest rates** (discount rate, federal fund rates) **have little to no effect on long-term rates** (mortgages, credit cards).
- The effectiveness of monetary restraint is limited by **high expectations** of future income and profits and the availability of **foreign sources of funds.**
- Monetary economists believe that money supply changes **will have no effect on real output.**
- According to the equation of exchange, if velocity and output are constant, the **only effect of an increase in the money supply will be an increase in prices.**
- Monetary economists believe that the only monetary policy should be **a slow, predictable money growth rate** that does not change suddenly.

CHAPTER 12 Exercises

Name _____

1) *Ceteris paribus*, the quantity of money society is willing and able to hold
   A) decreases as precautionary demand increases.
   B) decreases as interest rates fall.
   C) increases as interest rates fall.
   D) decreases as the money supply increases.

   1) _____

2) Which of the following is true about the equilibrium rate of interest?
   A) The Fed can change this rate by changing the money supply.
   B) It is constant.
   C) Money demand exceeds money supply at this rate.
   D) Money supply exceeds money demand at this rate.

   2) _____

3) If the Fed's objective is to stimulate the economy, which of the following gives the correct sequence of events?
   A) The money supply decreases, interest rates increase, AD increases.
   B) The money supply increases, interest rates decrease, AS increases.
   C) The money supply decreases, interest rates increase, AD decreases.
   D) The money supply increases, interest rates decrease, AD increases.

   3) _____

4) Which of the following is NOT a reason why AD should increase when the interest rate falls?
   A) investments become more profitable
   B) buying consumption items becomes cheaper
   C) the incentive to save rises
   D) funding government projects through bonds becomes less costly

   4) _____

5) Monetary stimulus will fail if
   A) the investment demand curve is fairly elastic.
   B) banks are reluctant to lend money.
   C) the money demand curve is fairly steep.
   D) consumers increase spending.

   5) _____

6) Which of the following could cause monetary restraint policies to fail?
   A) Availability of credit from foreign sources
   B) consumers have low expectations for future income
   C) businesses have low expectations for future profits
   D) consumers decrease spending

   6) _____

7) To reduce the level of inflation monetarists advocate
   A) a sharp increase in short-term interest rates.
   B) steady and predictable changes in the money supply.
   C) a decrease in short-term interest rates.
   D) an increase in taxes.

   7) _____

209

8) If real output increases by 3 percent per year and velocity is stable, in order to keep the price level stable   8) _____
   A) the interest rate must increase by 3 percent per year.
   B) velocity must increase by 3 percent per year.
   C) the money supply must decrease by 3 percent per year.
   D) the money supply must increase by 3 percent per year.

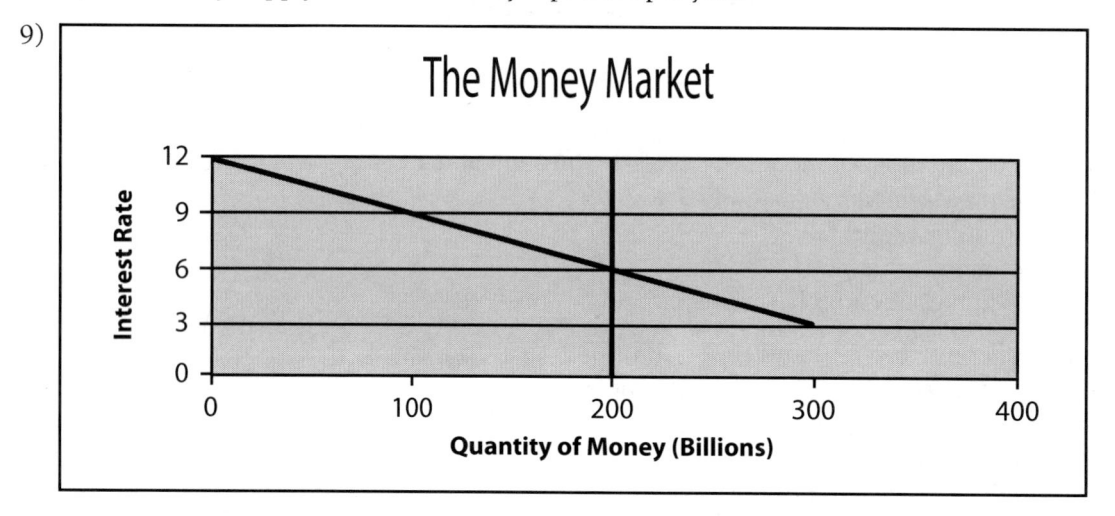

9)

The Money Market

Using the above figure, what would the equilibrium interest rate and quantity of money if the Federal Reserves increases the money supply to $300 billion?

_____
_____
_____
_____

10) What do monetarists believe will be the only effect of a sudden increase in the money supply? Why?

_____
_____
_____
_____
_____
_____

Article Review 3

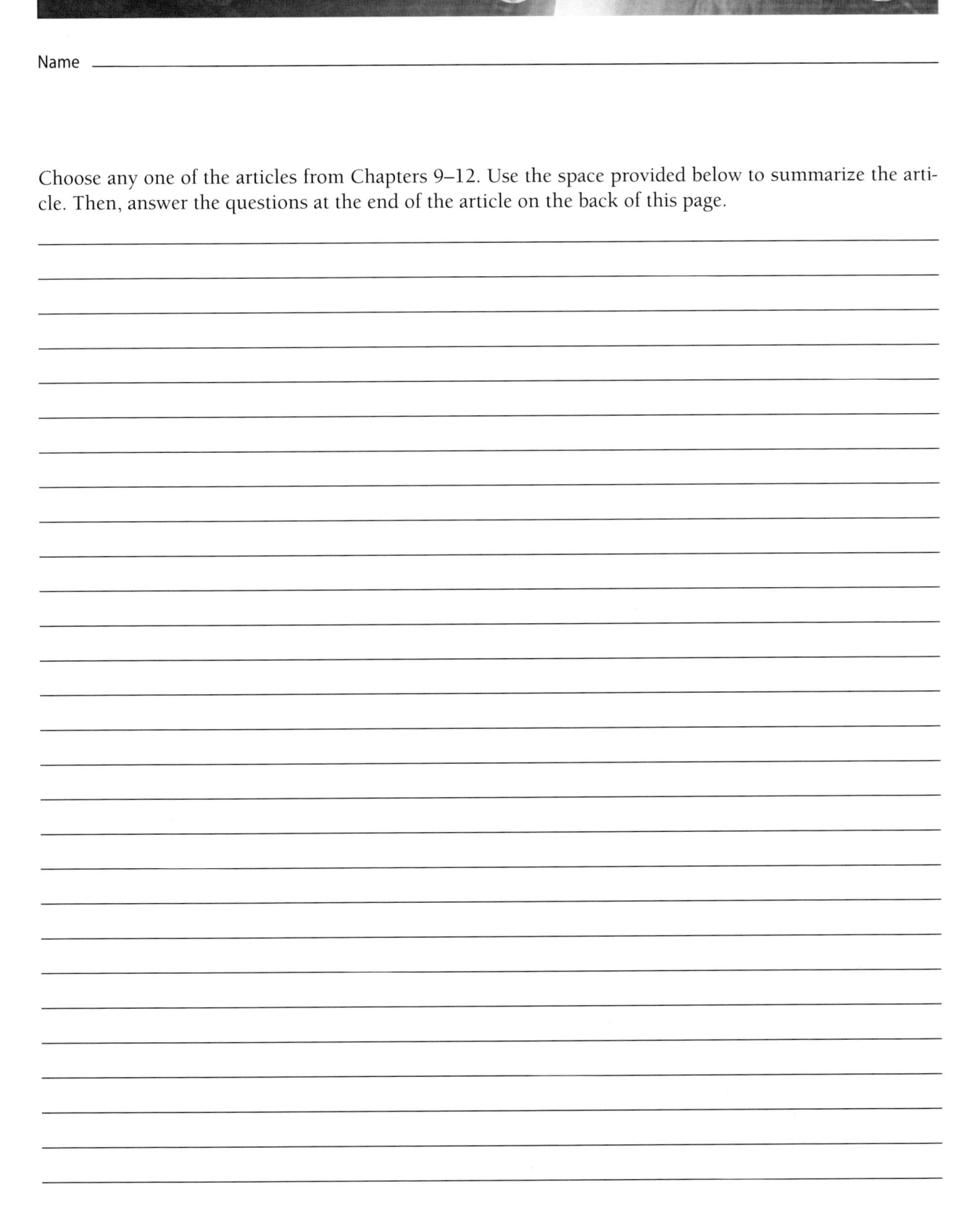

Name _____

Choose any one of the articles from Chapters 9–12. Use the space provided below to summarize the article. Then, answer the questions at the end of the article on the back of this page.

211

1.

2.

3.

Unit 3 Review

Name _____

Use this review to prepare for Exam 3. You can view the answers in the "unit review answers" section in the back of the text, but try to complete it on your own first.

1) An inflationary gap implies that
   A) the country is producing right at its production productions curve.
   B) aggregate demand exceeds aggregate supply at the full-employment price level.
   C) unemployment is at its natural rate.
   D) aggregate demand is less than aggregate supply at the full-employment price level.

   1) _____

2) The marginal propensity to save can be found by dividing
   A) total saving by the population.
   B) the change in total saving by the change in disposable income.
   C) total consumption by total saving.
   D) the change in disposable income by the change in saving.

   2) _____

3) If the MPC is 0.9 and the APC is 0.85, then the MPS equals:
   A) 1.75
   B) 0.15
   C) .1
   D) 0.05

   3) _____

4) Suppose the consumption function is C = $200 + 0.75YD. If disposable income is $500, consumption is:
   A) $575
   B) $500
   C) $650
   D) $200

   4) _____

5) Which of the following causes a movement along the investment demand curve?
   A) Business become more optimistic about future profits
   B) A new technology is discovered
   C) The stock market crashes
   D) The interest rate changes

   5) _____

6) The government is pursuing a policy of restraint if, regardless of the budget balance (surplus or deficit), it
   A) increases its spending and reduces taxes.
   B) increases its spending and increases taxes.
   C) reduces its spending and increases taxes.
   D) reduces its spending and reduces taxes.

   6) _____

7) Which of the following is an automatic stabilizer?
   A) Income taxes.
   B) Funding to NASA.
   C) Education.
   D) National security spending.

   7) _____

213

8) The concept of crowding out refers to the idea that
   A) increased borrowing from foreign countries will increase the current opportunity cost of borrowing.
   B) the Federal Reserve will refuse to lend if the government borrows too much.
   C) state and local governments cannot borrow when the federal government borrows too much.
   D) increased government borrowing will make private borrowing more expensive.

9) The opportunity cost of deficit financing is
   A) paid by future generations.
   B) forgone government goods.
   C) forgone foreign goods.
   D) forgone private-sector goods.

10) The primary burden of the external portion of the debt is incurred
    A) approximately one year after the debt is incurred.
    B) when the debt is refinanced.
    C) by future generations.
    D) when the government uses the borrowed funds.

11) When money is used to compare the value of different products it is functioning as a
    A) unit of account.
    B) commodity.
    C) medium of exchange.
    D) store of value.

12) Which of the following appears in M1 but NOT in M2?
    A) currency
    B) traveler's checks
    C) transaction accounts
    D) All of the above are in M2

13) If the banking system has a required reserve ratio of 20 percent, then the money multiplier is:
    A) .1
    B) 5
    C) 20
    D) .2

14) Which of the following is true about a reduction in the discount rate?
    A) It signals that the Fed wants to restrain money growth
    B) It signals that the Fed wants to speed up money growth
    C) It makes borrowing from the Fed more expensive
    D) It increases the cost of lending for banks

15) If the Fed wants to buy more bonds than people are willing to sell, then the Fed should
    A) raise the price it offers for the bonds.
    B) decrease the price it offers for the bonds.
    C) switch to another type of monetary policy tool.
    D) encourage a government agency to buy the bonds.

16) If the Fed's objective is to restrain the economy, which of the following gives the correct sequence of events?
    A) The money supply increases, interest rates increase, AD decreases.
    B) The money supply decreases, interest rates increase, AD decreases.
    C) The money supply increases, interest rates decrease, AS increases.
    D) The money supply decreases, interest rates increase, AD increases.

Name _____

17) Which of the following is **NOT** a reason why AD should decrease when the interest rate rises?
   A) investments become less profitable
   B) funding government projects through bonds becomes more costly
   C) the incentive to save falls
   D) buying consumption items becomes more expensive

17) _____

18) Which of the following is **NOT** an issue that could cause monetary stimulus to fail?
   A) Banks are reluctant to lend money.
   B) The money demand curve is fairly steep.
   C) The investment demand curve is fairly elastic.
   D) Consumers increase spending

18) _____

19) To reduce the level of unemployment monetarists advocate
   A) a decrease in short-term interest rates.
   B) a decrease in taxes
   C) steady and predictable changes in the money supply.
   D) a sharp increase in short-term interest rates.

19) _____

20) If real output decreases by 2 percent per year and velocity is stable, in order to keep the price level stable
   A) velocity must increase by 2 percent per year.
   B) the money supply must decrease by 2 percent per year.
   C) the money supply must increase by 2 percent per year.
   D) the interest rate must increase by 2 percent per year.

20) _____

21) What is the marginal propensity to consume and marginal propensity to save of a consumer whose income went up $2,000 and increased his consumption from $250 to $1,800?

_____
_____
_____
_____

22) Why do businesses want to invest more at lower interest rates?

_____
_____
_____
_____

23) What is the opportunity cost of deficit spending by the government and when must it be paid?

_____
_____
_____
_____

24) Assuming a reserve requirement of 10 percent, if the Fed buys $30 billion in bonds in the open market, how much could the money supply increase if there are no leakages?

25) Why do monetarists believe that monetary stimulus will not work?

Exam 3 Formula Sheet

Name _____

Chapter 9

$$APC = \frac{Total\ Consumption}{Total\ Disposable\ Income} \qquad APS = \frac{Total\ Savings}{Total\ Disposable\ Income}$$

$$MPC = \frac{Change\ in\ Consumption}{Change\ in\ Income} \qquad MPS = \frac{Change\ in\ Savings}{Change\ in\ Income}$$

$$Expected\ Rate\ of\ Return = \frac{Expected\ Net\ Profit}{Cost\ of\ Investment} \times 100$$

Consumption Function: $C = a + MPC \times DI$

a = autonomous consumption, DI = disposable income

Chapter 10

Total Deficit = Structural Deficit + Cyclical Deficit

Chapter 11

M1 = Currency + Transaction Deposits + Traveler's Checks

M2 = M1 + Savings Deposits + Time Deposits + Money Market Mutual Fund Balances

Required Reserves = Transaction Deposits × Reserve Requirement Ratio

Excess Reserves = Legal Reserves − Required Reserves

$$Money\ Multiplier = \frac{1}{Reserve\ Requirement\ Ratio}$$

Change in MS = Money Multiplier × Original Change in Reserves

Chapter 12

Equation of Exchange: $M \times V = P \times Q$

Nominal Interest Rate = Real Interest Rate + Expected Inflation

Chapter 13

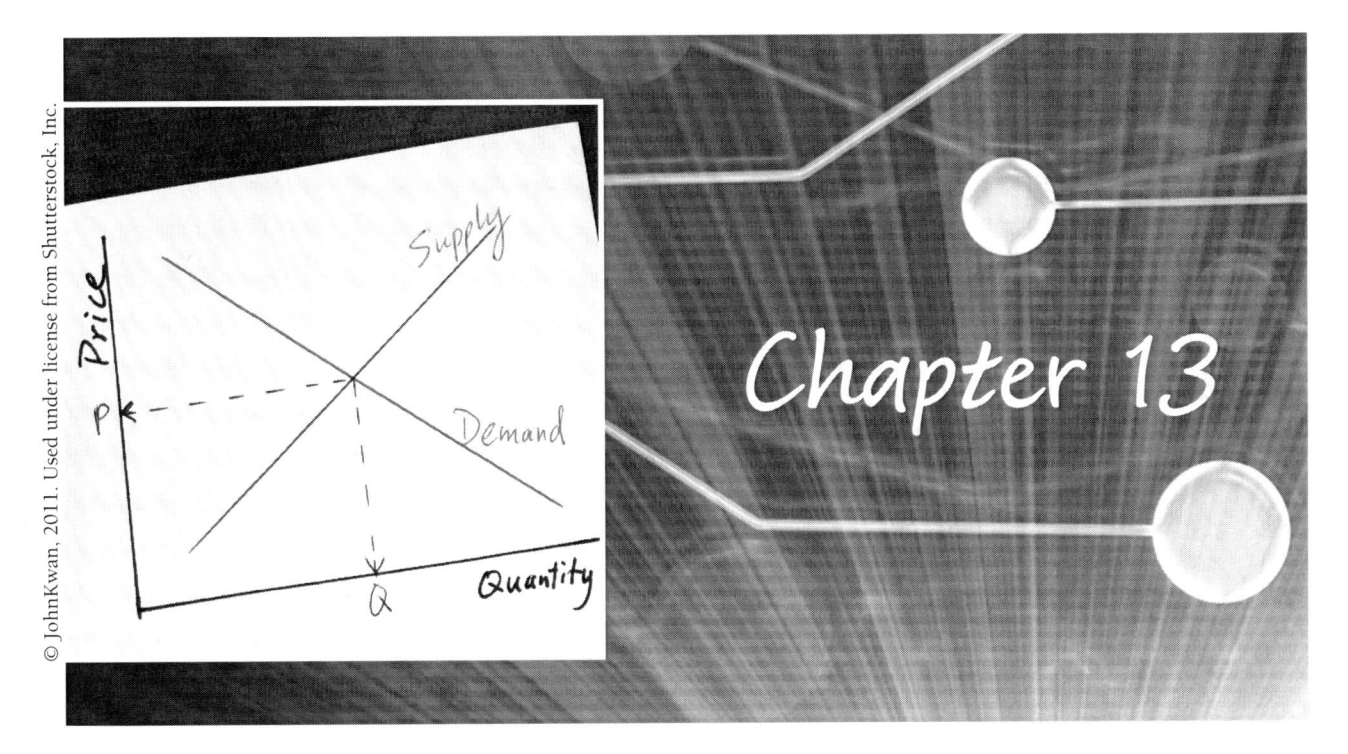

Review of Economic Foundations

Microeconomics is the study of individual economic decisions. If we want to fully explore these decisions, we need to understand the foundations that the economy is built upon. Chapters 1 through 4 of this text explain the theories, institutions, and interactions that define the market economy. The following chapter contains excerpts from the first four chapters, but only serves as a review of Unit 1. If you have not taken a course in macroeconomics, or it has been a while since you did, I recommend rereading Chapters 1 through 4 before continuing on to Chapter 14.

I. DECISION MAKING

Scarcity and Choice

Economics would not exist if we did not have to make choices. If we could have whatever we wanted whenever we wanted it, there would be no need to make the tough choices in life. Unfortunately, humans have unlimited wants and must attempt to satiate them through the proper allocation of limited resources. This is what it means to live under the condition of scarcity. Since we can't have everything we want, we must decide what to purchase and what to forgo. Economics is the study of how to do so.

Scarcity does not mean a shortage of something. A shortage is a specific condition in a market that can be corrected by a price change. Scarcity always exists since goods and resources cannot be had for a zero price. Scarcity is not only a problem for people with little money or resources. Even Bill Gates has to decide how to use his limited time and money. He cannot give infinite amounts of money to all of his business and charitable endeavors or spend more than 24 hours in day on any combination of activities. No amount of money can buy away scarcity.

Opportunity Costs

Since resources are scarce there is indeed no such thing as a free lunch, as the saying goes. Everything produced and purchased in the economy has a price, but that price is more than just monetary. Every time you choose to spend your time, money, or resources on one activity, you are implicitly choosing to not spend those resources on some other activity. The value of the next best alternative that could have been produced using the resources consumed by a choice is called the opportunity cost of that choice, since the opportunity to pursue that alternative activity has been lost.

The opportunity cost is the true cost of any decision. For example, suppose you chose to go to class from 8AM–9:30AM. What is the cost of that decision? You might be tempted to say the tuition and books required for the class. These, however, are sunk costs. Regardless of whether you go to class or not, you will never get the money you paid in tuition or books back (assuming we are past the refund date). As a result, sunk costs are irrelevant to the decision. So then, what is the true cost of attending class? It is simply the value of the time that you spend in class. Time, a resource, could be spent in a variety of ways—you could sleep in, chat with friends, do work for another class, or even go to work. It is important to note the opportunity cost of a choice is only the value of the *best* foregone alternative. You can only do one thing with a given amount of time, resources, or money so it does not make any sense to add up the value of every alternative since you could only do one thing at a time.

Rationality

Another key component of economics is the assumption that people do not make choices randomly or without thinking. Instead, economists propose that people behave in a way that maximizes their utility subject to their limited income. Utility here doesn't mean electricity or water, but happiness or satisfaction. The idea that economic agents act rationally does not mean that people are walking calculators that never make mistakes. All the rationality assumption means is that people make decisions based on some sort of analysis and choose the option that will benefit them the most.

You make rational decisions based on your own self-interest every day. For example, when you signed up for this class you had no idea who I was; you signed up for this class because it was the best option you had to further your own goals. Yet, the more people that sign up for my class, the better off I am, so without knowing it you helped me.

This is how capitalism works; people usually have to satisfy somebody else's wants in order to pursue their own self-interest. People who seem like they are "giving money away"—philanthropists who donate to charity, parents who send their children to the best schools they can afford, and businesses that forgo sales today in order to invest in new technology—are all actually behaving rationally based on their desires.

If people avoid decisions that leave them worse off, and by extension pursue decisions that leave them better off, it is safe to assume that people respond to incentives. People make choices either to attain rewards or avoid punishments. For example, as the gap between what people earn with a high school degree and what they can earn with a college degree grows, enrollment in college increases since the incentives related to education choice are changing. Incentives are the signals the market gives to help people make decisions.

On the Margin

People make rational economic decisions based on marginal analysis. This means that they analyze the effect of small changes in behavior on their utility. The reason for this is that most decisions focus on a small change from the normal routine, or "status quo." Should I buy two quarts of milk this week or just one? Should a company increase or decrease its advertising budget? Should the government lower taxes or keep them the same? In each of these cases there is a marginal benefit and a marginal cost associated with the proposed change.

The marginal cost of any choice is what you have to give up (in terms of opportunity cost) in order to obtain one more unit of something (study for one more hour, go to school for one more year, or buy one more pack of gum). Marginal also means additional, so the marginal cost is only the cost of adding one more unit, not the total cost.

It is important to note, though, that almost every activity experiences increasing marginal costs. That means, the more you do something, the more it costs each time. This may not make sense at first since no matter how many slices of pizza you eat, for example, the menu price never changes. But if you think of the opportunity cost of eating too much pizza as a queasy feeling in your stomach and an expanding waistline, you can see that eating two slices a week may not be so bad, but for each slice you eat your health suffers more and more.

The benefit from a choice to obtain one more unit of something is called the marginal benefit. In dollar terms, the marginal benefit is equal to the amount of money someone would have to give you for you to give up one more unit of a good. Just like marginal cost, the marginal benefit of an activity changes as you increase its frequency. The first trip on a roller coaster may be exhilarating, but if you've been riding roller coasters all day you may not be willing to stand in line again. The more you have of something, the less willing you are to give up anything to get more of it; that is, the marginal benefit falls as the amount of the good you have increases.

Factors of Production

Improving the economy requires finding the optimal allocation of its scarce resources: land, labor, capital, and entrepreneurship. With so many possible uses for our resources, how do we know which activity is best? Luckily, the market helps us with this problem. If resources are not being put to the most profitable use, someone will buy them and put them to better use.

Land. Improving the economy requires finding the optimal allocation of its scarce resources: land, labor, capital, and entrepreneurship. With so many possible uses for our resources, how do we know which activity is best? Luckily, the market helps us with this problem. If resources are not being put to the most profitable use, someone will buy them and put them to better use.

Labor. Labor consists of the physical and mental effort exerted by workers of all types. This factor is usually measured in hours or man-hours and is paid wages.

Capital. Capital goods are those that aid in the production of other goods and services like factories, tools, and machinery. Businesses pay interest to those that lend them capital. Be sure to note the difference between the capital we are talking about here, physical capital, and the financial capital you hear about on the news. Financial capital is not counted as a factor of production since it is just the money used to buy factors of production.

Entrepreneurship. Entrepreneurship was recently added as a factor of production. Entrepreneurs need to be involved in the productive process because they combine the other factors of production in strategic ways and bear the risk if the product fails. Entrepreneurs earn profits for their services.

Trade-offs

Just as individuals face opportunity costs when choosing between alternative uses of their time, society faces costs when choosing where and how to employ its scarce resources. The production possibilities model illustrates all of the possible combinations of two alternatives a society can choose from, assuming full employment and given that technology and the amounts of resources do not change.

One simple way of looking at the production possibilities of an economy is through a production possibilities table. The production possibilities table illustrates that society must give up some of one of the alternatives to get more of the other—there is always a trade-off. Take a look at the table in figure 13.1. What do you notice about the trade-off as you produce more tanks? The table tells us that as you produce more tanks the amount of trucks you have to give up in order to get the same amount of tanks rises.

The downside to this table is that you can only get so many alternatives onto a single table. In contrast, we can see all of the alternatives available to the society with a production possibilities curve. The production possibilities curve is the first of many graphs we will be using in this course. As you can see in figure 13.2, the production

Tanks	Trucks
0	60
5	57
10	52
15	45
20	37
25	28
30	16
35	0

Figure 13.1 • **Production Possibilities Table**
You only have to give up three trucks to produce the first five tanks. The next five tanks cost five trucks. As you produce more tanks, you are taking away resources that are better at truck production so the price of tanks in terms of the number of trucks given up rises.

possibilities curve uses a line on a graph (the production possibilities frontier, or PPF) to separate the possible combinations from the impossible ones.

Increasing Opportunity Costs

One special characteristic you may notice about the PPF is that it is not a straight line; in fact, it bows away from the origin. The reason for this is the law of increasing opportunity costs. At the society level, the opportunity cost related to the production of a certain good increases as the production of that good increases. As you can see the from the PPF in figure 13.2, the amount of trucks you have to give up in order to get one more tank increases as the amount of tanks increases. In economics terms, the relative price—the price of tanks in terms of trucks—increases as you go from left to right.

The economic rationale is much simpler. Imagine you start off producing only trucks. If you decided you wanted some tanks, you need to pull resources away from producing trucks. What resources would you start with? You would pull away the resources that are the most effective at producing tanks first. As a result, you would not have to pull very many resources away in order to get quite a bit of tanks. But as you produce more and more tanks (moving down the PPF) you are going to pull resources that are not as good as producing tanks into production. The resources used to produce the two goods are not interchangeable; some are better at producing one or the other. The rubber used to produce the truck tires, for example, is probably not very useful when trying to build a tank track. The law of increasing opportunity costs becomes especially important when trading off between two very different goods—like health care and military spending, for example.

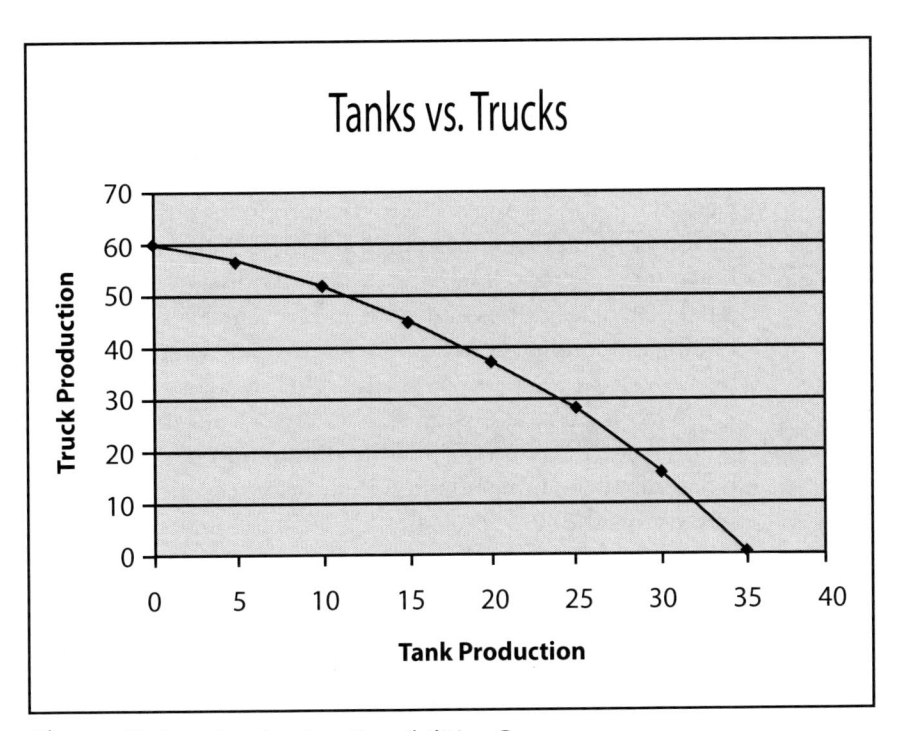

Figure 13.2 • Production Possibilities Curve
Like most production possibilities curves, Figure 13.2 bows away from the origin due to the law of increasing opportunity costs. The more different two products are, the greater this bowing will be.

224 ECONOMICS TODAY

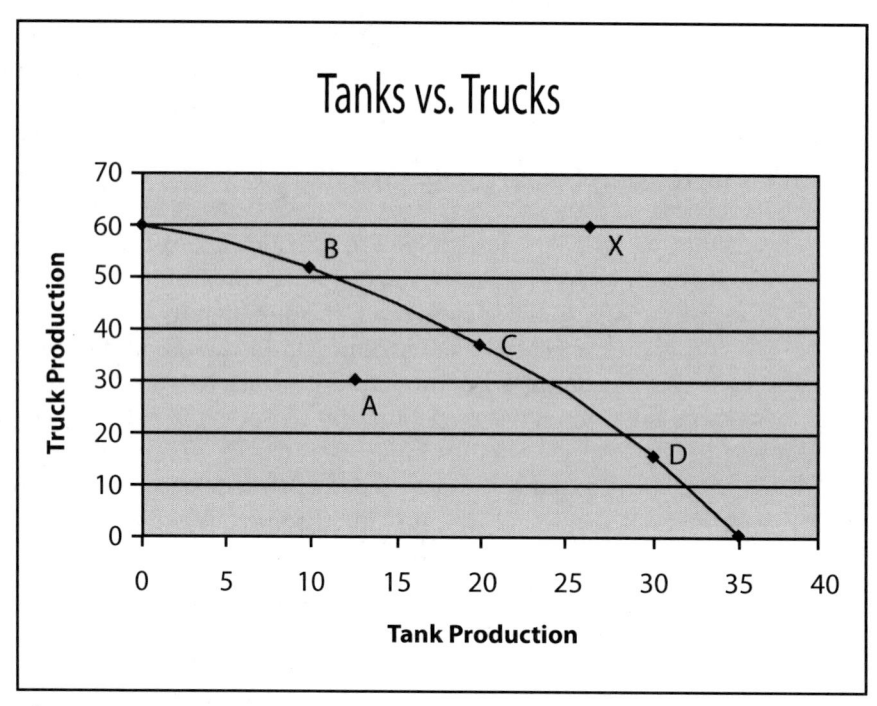

Figure 13.3 • **Efficient, Inefficient, and Unattainable Combinations**
In this production possibilities model, the government trades off tank production for truck production. If it wants to produce more military goods, it must produce fewer consumer goods. On this PPC, points B, C, and D are all productively efficient, but point A is inefficient. Point X is impossible to reach given current levels of resources or technology. What might the government do to reach Point X?

Efficiency and Inefficiency

Technically, any point along the production possibilities frontier is productively efficient since you cannot increase the production of one good without giving up some of the other. If there are many points at which a society can produce at full employment, how do they choose one? Just like individuals, societies weigh marginal cost and marginal benefit. Societies continue an economic activity (like trading off trucks for tanks) as long as marginal benefit exceeds marginal cost. In other words, optimal allocation of resources is at the point where marginal benefit equals marginal cost.

What is certain, however, is that every point on the PPF is more efficient than any point inside the curve. While the production possibilities curve shows the output combinations that can be attained if all resources are used efficiently, we know that this is not always the case. Bureaucracy, laziness, and other inefficiencies lead to output not being maximized. A point inside the production possibilities curve illustrates this type of inefficient production.

As figure 13.3 illustrates, having a point inside the curve means that you can produce more of one of the goods without giving up any of the other. This is the definition of inefficiency; you do not have to obtain more resources to produce more, just use the ones you have smarter or better. Another way to achieve inefficient allocation (a point inside the PPF) is through higher than usual unemployment. During economic downturns, like the Great Depression, or even the recession of 2007–2009, the economy may not be performing at full employment. Remember that full employment was one of the

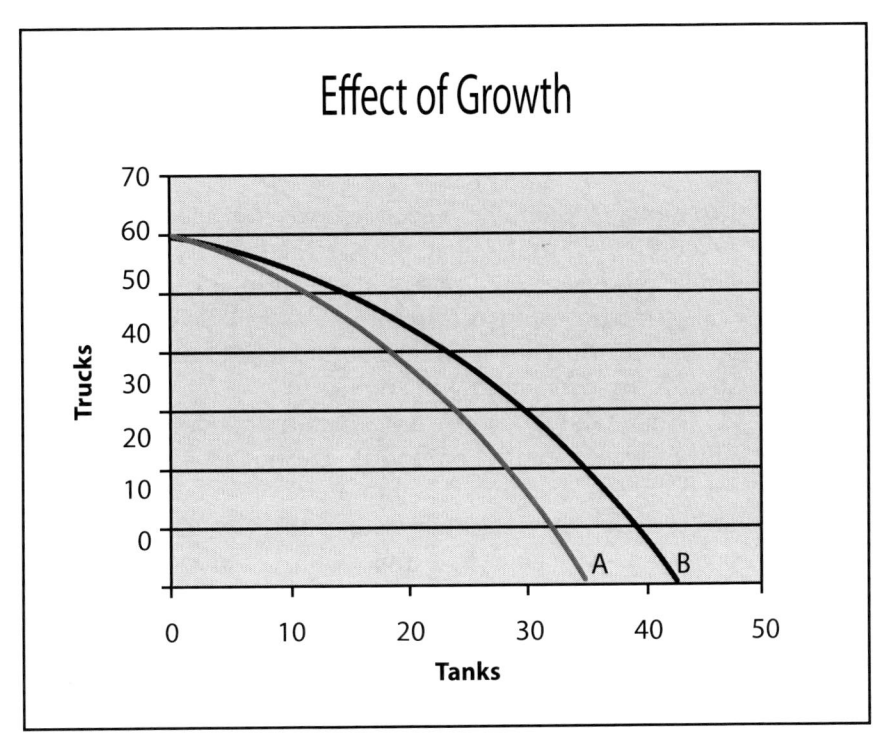

Figure 13.4 • Economic Growth

If a technological improvement made it possible to produce tanks using fewer resources, then we would be able produce more tanks given our current level of resources. The shift of the x-intercept of the PPF from thirty-five to forty-two illustrates this improvement. Further, each truck given up produces more tanks since more tanks can be produced within any given amount of resources.

assumptions that the production possibilities model was based on. If we relax this assumption, we see that the optimal choice allocation may lie within the PPF, not on it.

Economic Growth

Another way to shake the model up is to relax the assumption of fixed resources. Labor quantity (population), as well as quality, is improving over time; and new resource deposits and extraction techniques are constantly being discovered, so assuming fixed resources for any lengthy period of time is not very realistic. Such resource growth makes it possible for society to produce more of one or possibly both goods at each alternative, causing the PPF to shift to the right.

In a more realistic setting, technology is not fixed either. New production techniques and the proliferation of computer and telecommunications technology will continue to improve productive processes. By reducing costs and speeding up production, technology also leads to a rightward shift in productive capacity. Figure 13.4 illustrates the result of improvements in the technology used to produce tanks, for example.

A country does not have to wait for economic growth to kick in to live beyond its PPF. Through specialization and trade, a country can go beyond the limits of PPF by trading with another country. This is why the US is the highest volume trading nation on Earth; we want to exceed our PPF now, not in a few years. We will talk more about comparative advantage and mutual gains from trade later.

II. UNITED STATES ECONOMY

What to Produce?

In a capitalist economy, incentives are set in such a way that goods and services that are produced at a profit will continue to be produced, while those that do not sell well will not be produced. An industry in which total revenue exceeds total costs for producers will attract investment of resources as well as new firms, causing the industry to expand. Industries in which total costs exceed total revenue will contract as a result of resources and firms fleeing the industry.

When talking about what a country produces, we usually break production down into various categories or sectors. The percentage of production coming from each sector is known as a country's output mix. This output mix constantly changes over time. For example, the percentages of production coming from the farming and manufacturing sectors have fallen over time while the production coming from the health care and service sectors have risen.

One of the biggest changes to the output mix of the US economy has been the fall in the production of tangible goods and the rise of the service sector. You have no doubt heard the United States referred to as a service-oriented economy and that we don't make anything anymore. This transition is not necessarily a bad thing and certainly not unique to the US. This transition is consistent with development patterns we have seen throughout the world. The pattern of development is the idea that most countries start with most of their resources going toward producing food in the agriculture sector. As technologies advance, some people are able to move off the farm and engage in manufacturing. As technologies streamline manufacturing, incomes rise and people start demanding more services.

How to Produce?

In capitalist countries, the how to produce question is answered by the forces of competition. In fact, to achieve profitability in a competitive market, firms must produce at the minimum cost level given current technology and resource prices. Since different resources have different costs, firms must find the least costly mix of inputs. Changes in technology, the mix of resources needed to produce the amount of output, or resource prices can change the cost minimizing combination.

The reason the US produces so much more than most other countries in the world is not because we have more resources, but rather that our resources are much more productive. Labor, in particular, is much more productive in the US than in other countries. Labor is much more productive in advanced economies than it is in developing countries in general; it takes less man-hours to do the same amount of work. The reason for this is that the average worker in a developed country has much more human capital than that of developing countries. Not only is the population of advanced countries more educated and afforded better opportunities for training, they are generally healthier and better fed than workers in developing countries, and that helps them work harder and smarter.

But the major disparity that differentiates developed countries from developing countries is the level of capital available in each country. Remember businesses use capital because the most efficient method of producing something is often the least direct. For example, if you want to get a delivery across town you could walk it over item by item until you were done, or you could use a truck. Often, businesses in developing countries do not have access to capital like delivery trucks and have to make do with human or animal power, reducing the amount of business that can be done.

For Whom to Produce?

In the capitalist system, those who are willing and able to pay will receive the goods and services produced by society. Willingness comes from a consumer's preference ordering, and ability to pay comes from the consumer's income as well as the price of the good they want to purchase. A person's share of society's output is a function of two market values: the value of the property and human resources supplied to the market by the consumer, and the price of the goods that consumer wants to buy. At a given price level, a doctor can buy more goods and services than a janitor.

When households supply resources for economic activity they receive income. Although capitalism is sometimes thought of as a system that abuses and exploits workers, the vast majority, over 70 percent, of all income in society is paid to labor in the form of wages. This does not even include income paid to proprietors like small-business owners, farmers, and doctors and lawyers with their own practice, even though the money made, at least in part, comes from their labor.

You have no doubt heard that the distribution of income in the US economy is relatively unequal. In fact, the richest 20 percent of households in the US receive about 50 percent of the income in a given year. In addition, the personal distribution of income in the United States has become more and more unequal in recent years. Certainly, the rich are getting richer, but it is not necessarily the case that the poor are getting poorer. What is going on instead is that the income of people in the middle and lower parts of the income distribution is not growing as fast as that of the richest people. One of the prime reasons for this change is that the real wage at the middle and lower parts of the income distribution has been stagnant for the last thirty-five years. In other words, people who are not at the top of the income distribution have about the same buying power as people in similar occupations had in 1975. This stagnation can partially be explained by an increase in the labor force, particularly among women and minorities. New entrants into the work force tend to go into middle and low paying jobs, thus creating more competition and keeping the real wage from rising.

III. SUPPLY AND DEMAND

In capitalist countries, the market organizes economic activity. That is, no one has to tell people what to buy and sell; they simply buy what they want and sell what people want to buy. The market system works because everyone wants to get the most out of their limited resources. Since people do not have unlimited income, they will only purchase goods which they deem the most valuable. Likewise, businesses want to make the most profits possible so they will allocate resources to the products that people want to buy the most. Markets also exist because it is more efficient to specialize in one type of production than to try to make everything yourself. Specialization requires trade with others to get the most of the goods and services we use in our daily lives.

A shift in demand refers to the situation where the quantity demanded at every price increases or decreases at the same time. These shifts occur due to the relaxing of one or more of the *ceteris paribus* conditions, the factors that are held constant when drawing a demand curve. Figure 13.5 illustrates the effect of an increase in demand;

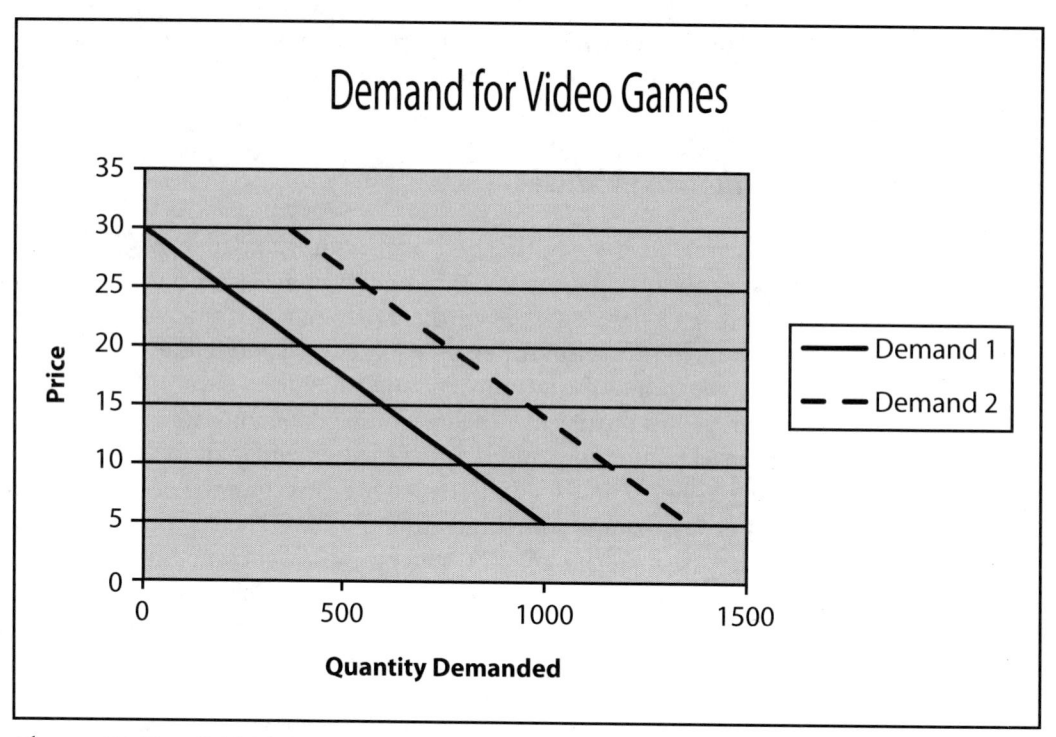

Figure 13.5 • **Shift in Demand**
When the demand for a product increases, the consumers in the market want to buy more at each price, causing the curve to shift to the right. A change in price will only move you from one point on the existing demand curve to another point on that same curve.

every point on the original demand curve shifts to the right, creating an entirely new demand curve. A decrease in demand would cause every point to shift to the left.

Income. There are many factors that can shift the demand curve. The most obvious factor that shifts the demand curve is consumer income; losing one's job or winning the lottery would certainly have an effect on how much we buy of a particular good. For most goods, an increase in income will lead to an increase in demand at every price, shifting the demand curve to the right. These goods are known as normal goods.

However, some goods work in the opposite fashion. People purchase fewer of these informal goods as their income rises. Lower quality foods such as beans and hamburger meat sometimes behave as inferior goods. The term inferior here contains no value judgments; it only conveys the way the demand curves shift with changes in income. In fact, some people enjoy products like secondhand clothes, canned meat, and bus travel and would buy more of these goods when their income rises, treating them like normal goods. As a result, no definite list of inferior goods exists; it is a purely individual distinction. However, when talking about market demand, an inferior good is one that is treated as inferior by most people.

Tastes and Preferences. Fashions, fads, and trends can shift demand curves. When consumer tastes turn in favor of a particular good or service the demand curve for that product shifts to the right. When the trend dies out, the demand curve shifts to the left. The demand for certain products also change with the season. Christmas trees fly off the lot in November and December, but cannot be sold at any price in July. The demand curve for this product is very sensitive to consumer tastes.

Prices of Related Goods. The price of related goods is an important factor to hold constant when drawing a demand curve, since related goods have interdependent demands. What would happen to the demand for generic drugs if the price of name brand drugs were to rise? It would increase or shift to the right. This occurs because name brand drugs and generic drugs are substitutes, goods that satisfy the same basic want. A change in the price of one good will cause the demands of its substitutes to move in the same direction. This does not mean no one will buy name brand drugs anymore, but some people will be convinced to switch.

Substitutes are not the only types of related goods; goods can also be complements. Complementary goods are goods that tend to be or need to be consumed together. What would happen to the demand of peanut butter if the price of jelly were to rise? Some people who were buying peanut butter only to pair it with jelly will now find the combination too expensive and cease buying either product. As a result, demand for peanut butter would decrease, or shift to the left. A change in the price of a good causes the demand of its complements to shift in the opposite direction.

Expectations. Expectations can affect demand curves in many ways. In economics, perception is reality, so the way consumers view the future can be just as important in determining demand as current conditions are. If consumers were to believe that the price of a certain good was going to rise or that it would be completely unavailable in the future, they would want to stock up on that good now, causing demand to increase. If consumers anticipated a future rise in incomes, they would have the power to spend more money today, again causing demand to shift to the right.

Number of Buyers. Holding income constant, an increase in the number of buyers in a market will increase demand in that market. Market demand is simply the sum of every individual demand. What would happen if we added another consumer to the market? As long as he or she will demand at least one unit of the product, adding another buyer will certainly increase the amount demanded at each price.

Supply

While a change in price moves the market from one point on the supply curve to another, any factor other than price that changes the willingness of firms to supply a good will shift the supply curve to the left or right. Just as with demand, an increase in supply is illustrated by a shift of the curve to the right and a shift to the left represents a decrease in supply. In general, any factor that reduces the cost of production will increase profits and convince firms to supply more at the market price, shifting the market supply to the right. Figure 13.6 illustrates the effect of a decrease in supply: every point on the original supply curve shifts to the left, creating an entirely new supply curve. An increase in supply would cause every point to shift to the right.

Price of Inputs. All firms need inputs—raw materials, workers, and equipment—to produce their goods. An increase in the cost of inputs causes the cost of production to rise and will lead firms to produce less at every price. The opposite will occur if input prices fall. This is similar to the idea of complements in our discussion of determinants of demand. Since your inputs and output are used together, like complementary goods, the price of one affects the other.

Technology and Productivity. Increases in technology can lead to falling production costs. New production techniques find more efficient methods of putting resources together and allow for more production at every price, shifting supply to the right. Natural disasters on the other hand can wipe out capital and decrease productivity. The tsunamis, hurricanes, and fires that constantly threaten human life also increase the cost of production and cause supply to shift to the left.

Price of Related Goods. Just like there are substitute and complement goods in demand, there are substitutes and complements in production. A substitute in production is something a firm can make instead of what it is currently making at very little or no additional cost. Cars might be a substitute in production for trucks, for example. What

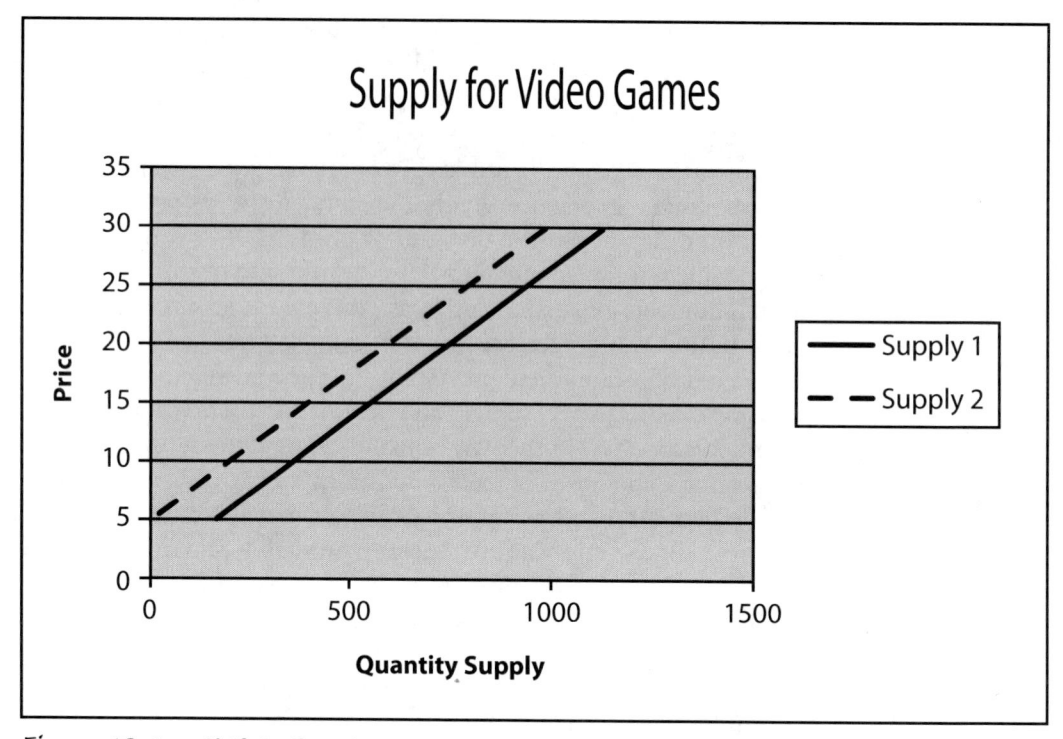

Figure 13.6 • **Shift in Supply**
If something occurred in the economy that increased the cost of production, businesses would want to produce less of the product at every price, causing the supply curve to shift back to the left.

happens when the market price of trucks rises? Firms want to put more resources toward building trucks and less toward building cars. In general, when the price of a good changes the supply of its substitutes in production change in the opposite direction.

Likewise, there are complements in production—goods that tend to be produced together. Beef and leather are complements in production. When beef prices rise, firms want more resources in cattle production to reap the large profits in the beef market. Doing so necessarily increases the supply of leather since there are more cows around, lowering the price of a major input for leather manufacturers. When the price of a good changes, the supply of its complements in production change in the same direction. Notice the difference between how supply responds to changes in the price of related goods and how demand responds to the same.

Expectations. Firm expectations can affect the market just like consumer expectations do. If firms anticipate a future rise in prices, they may hold back a portion of their output today, causing supply to shift to the left. If firms anticipate a fall in prices in the future, they will try to unload their output today causing supply to increase. Firms also respond to disasters such as hurricanes and oil spills by limiting supply so more of the product will be available in the aftermath.

Number of Sellers. The number of firms in a market can cause the market supply to change since the market supply is simply the sum of all individual supply schedules. An increase in the total number of sellers will cause market supply to rise.

Equilibrium

At most prices, combining the market supply schedule and the market demand schedule for a product will result in either excess quantity demanded (a shortage) or excess

Equilibrium in Video Game Market

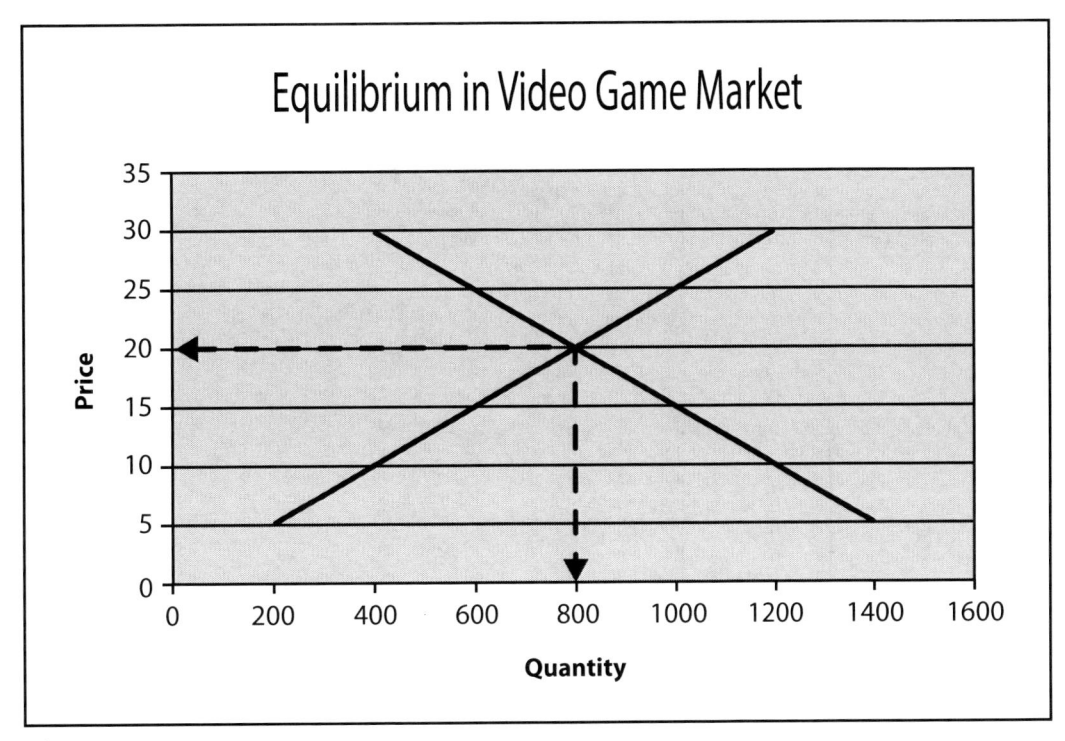

Figure 13.7 • Equilibrium
The supply and demand curves cross at one and only point. At a price of $20, consumers want to purchase 800 units and producers want to sell 800 units. The market clears at this price.

quantity supplied (a surplus). At one particular price, however, the quantity supplied and quantity demanded will be exactly equal. Since there is no excess quantity demanded or quantity supplied, the market is said to clear; every seller who is willing can sell as much as he wants at this price and every buyer who is willing can buy as much as he wants at this price. Hence, this special price is called the market-clearing price. We also call the market-clearing price an equilibrium price since it will not change unless the *ceteris paribus* conditions change. Any movement away from this point will be temporary, as market forces will force the market back into equilibrium; the equilibrium is stable. Producers and consumers can mutually do no better than the equilibrium point. Figure 13.7 shows that we can identify the market-clearing price as the point where the supply and demand curves intersect.

Surpluses and Shortages

Any price below the market-clearing price results in a shortage. Shortages occur because the quantity demanded exceeds the quantity supplied at any price below the equilibrium price, as shown in figure 13.8. At below-equilibrium, buyers demand more than firms are willing to sell. Luckily, market forces can help us adjust toward the equilibrium. Since quantity demanded exceeds quantity supplied, consumers will compete for the scarce output by bidding up the price, causing a movement up the demand curve. Firms will see this increase in price and increase production, causing a movement up the supply curve. These forces will continue to act until equilibrium is reached.

Any price above the market-clearing price results in a surplus. As figure 13.9 illustrates, surpluses occur because the quantity supplied exceeds the quantity demanded at any price above the equilibrium price; sellers offer more than consumers are willing to

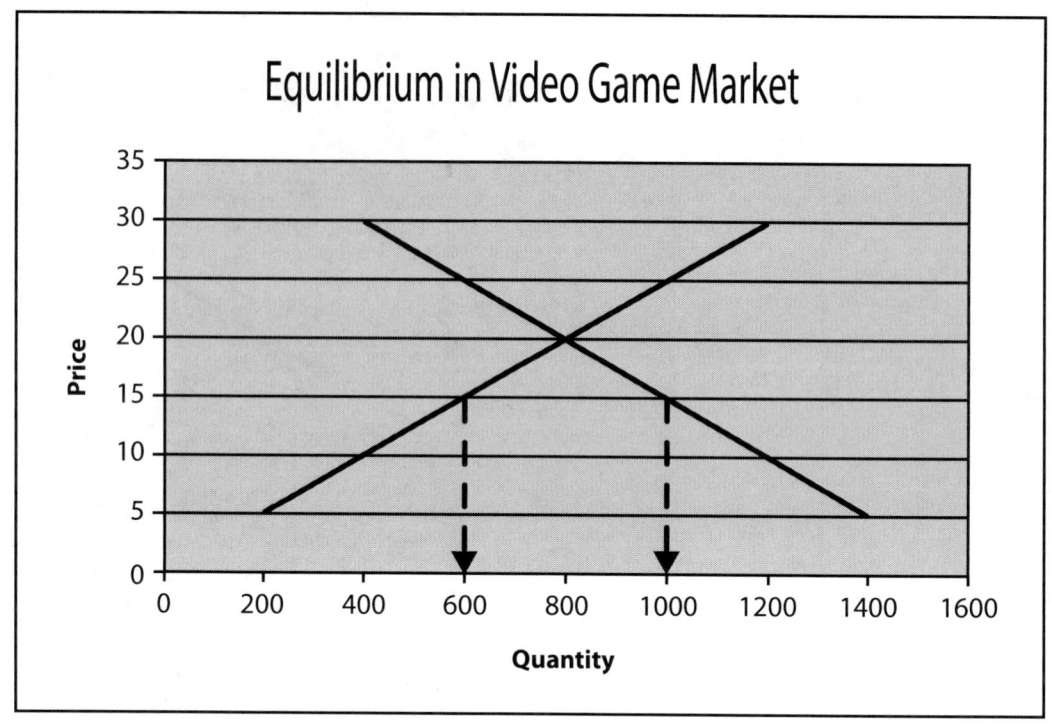

Figure 13.8 • Shortage
If a price of $15 was imposed on the market consumers would want to buy 1000 units, but producers would only want to sell 600. A shortage of 400 units would occur and consumers would bid up the price, pushing the market back toward equilibrium.

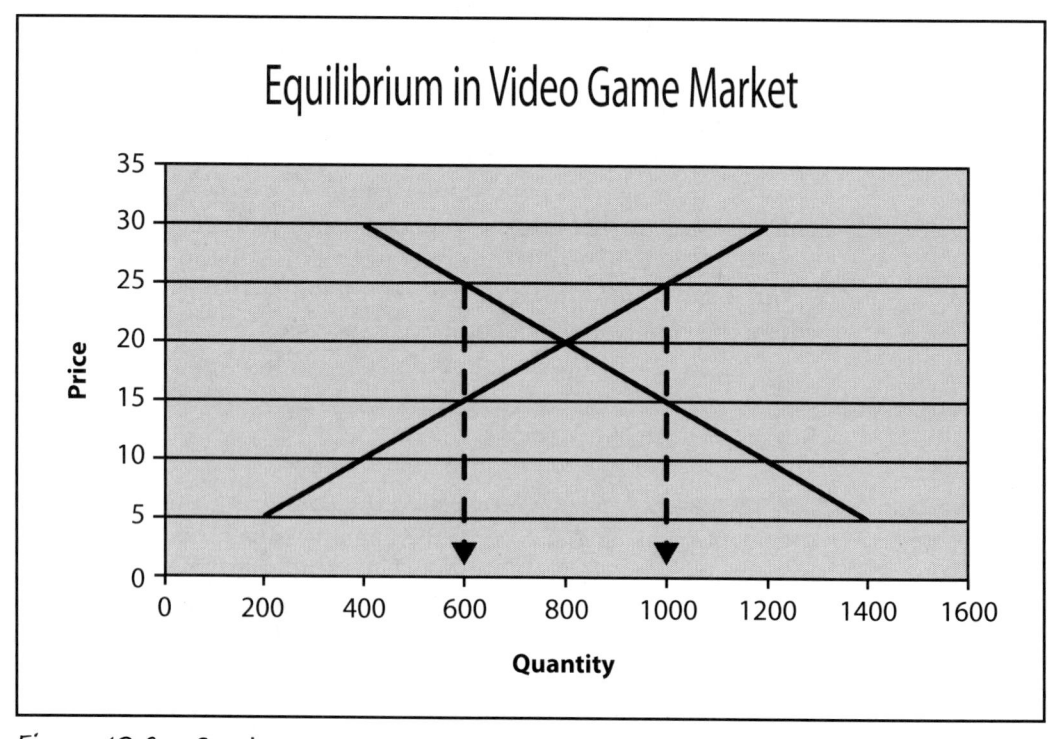

Figure 13.9 • Surplus
If a price of $25 was imposed on the market, producers would want to sell 1000 units but consumers would only want to buy 600 units. A surplus of 400 units would exist. Market forces would push the market back toward equilibrium.

purchase in the market at this price. In this situation, the market signals to firms to cut production and reduce prices. As prices fall, consumers are willing to buy more and move down along the demand curve. Again the economy will stabilize when the two parties meet at the equilibrium point.

IV. THE ROLE OF THE GOVERNMENT

Providing the Legal Framework

Although the market system is noted for its limited government involvement, the government still has a role to play in the United States economy. The government is also known as the public sector, since its intention is to focus on society's interests rather than any private interests. The primary role of government in the economy is to provide a legal framework. The government sets the rules of the game, encouraging policies that help the economy like ensuring property rights and competition, enforcing contracts, and punishing those who violate the rules.

The US government also sets up institutions that facilitate exchange and improve the allocation of resources. The government prints currency for use as a medium of exchange and increases the volume exchange by enforcing contracts and property rights. Of course, this leads to the question: How much should the government intervene in the economy? Just like any decision in the economy, the answer is based on marginal benefit and marginal cost. The government should increase regulation until the marginal benefit of regulation equals its marginal cost.

Protecting Consumers

The government also uses its authority to protect consumers from exploitation by businesses. Advocating for consumers can be helpful in getting a politician reelected, but most likely at the cost of shrinking the economic pie. Governments protect consumers by prosecuting companies that engage in anti-competitive practices and violate antitrust laws. These companies try to use monopoly power to extract additional profits out of consumers. Recent action against AT&T, Microsoft, and Intel show that the United States is serious about preventing monopolies.

The government further protects consumers by setting up consumer advocacy groups like the Better Business Bureau to enforce contracts and truth in advertising. One of the most visible ways the government intervenes on behalf of consumers is by fighting what it sees as "price gouging." In the aftermath of Hurricane Ike, for example, the government cracked down on gas stations charging what they saw as unreasonably high prices. But who decides when prices are too high? By not allowing prices to rise, the government created shortages and some people that really needed gasoline could not find any. In attempting to protect consumers, the government created even more problems for them.

Protecting Labor

The government also enacts policies to protect labor from being "exploited" by employers. Examples of such policies are child labor laws and the minimum wage. While it feels good to pass a law banning "exploitative" practices, the government must consider the true cost of these policies. For example, while child sweatshop labor is a horrible thing and in a better world it wouldn't exist, one must think about the alternative before condemning it. Children take these jobs because the alternative, either starving or getting involved in crime, gangs, or the sex trade, is so much worse. Should the government really be in the business of limiting the options of society's most vulnerable citizens? Most agree they should, but the answer is not so clear. Some argue that greater globalization and free trade are better ways to improve the lives of child workers than policies that prohibit child labor outright.

Fixing Market Failures

Another important role for the government is the solving of market failures. Market failures occur when the market either allocates a non-optimal amount of resources to the production of a good or service, or fails to produce the good at all. A misallocation of resources results from the costs or benefits of a product spilling over to a third party (not the buyer or the seller) and a lack of strong property rights.

I have mentioned before that the price system results in the efficient use of resources, but this assumes that all the benefits and costs of production are reflected in the supply and demand curves. For certain goods the benefits or costs may not be fully internalized by the buyer or seller. An externality exists when some the costs or benefits spill over to someone other than the immediate buyer or seller. They are called externalities because some party external to the market in question accrues some of the cost or benefits.

By dumping waste directly into a river untreated, for example, a firm forces an outside party to pay some of the cost of production. As a result the output of this product becomes too high and the price too low; the negative externality results in an overallocation of resources and leads to a market failure. It takes government intervention to fix a market failure. In the case of a negative externality the government needs to correct the overallocation by promoting policies that force producers to internalize the cost of production.

Government Failure

We know it is difficult to determine whether the government in general is too involved with the market or not. What we can say, however, is if we want the government to be more or less involved in a particular industry. If the benefit of increased government involvement in a particular economic activity exceeds the opportunity cost of that increase, then we should increase government involvement in that industry. If not, we should decrease it.

While cost-benefit analysis can help us determine whether or not increased government intervention is worth it, the problem becomes: How do we calculate the benefit of increased government intervention? How do we calculate the value of increased military spending, more police protection, or more teachers? It is not exactly straightforward. We can easily calculate the cost of a government project; it is the market value of the private sector goods that are given up to provide more resources to the government. On the other hand, most publicly provided goods and services do not have a reliable market value because they either create externalities or a free-rider problem. Therefore, the value of individual units of these goods must be estimated. As a result, cost-benefit analysis can only take us so far in determining the optimal amount of government involvement.

CHAPTER 13 SUMMARY

- People have to make choices because of **scarcity**. Since there are limited resources we search for ways to put those resources to their most productive uses.
- Every choice imposes an **opportunity cost**.
- People are **rational**. They do not make the correct decision every time, but they will never purposely make a decision that makes them worse off.
- The **production possibilities curve** illustrates the possible and impossible production combinations a society can choose between two goods.
- The government's primary role in the economy is to fix **market failures**, areas in the economy where the market system has failed to produce the socially optimal outcome.
- The **Law of Demand** states that as the price of a good rises, people will want to buy less of it.
- A change in price can only change **quantity demanded**; it cannot change demand. Only a change in one of the **determinants of demand** can shift the demand curve.
- The **Law of Supply** states that as the price of a good rises, businesses will want to sell more of it.
- A change in price can only change **quantity supplied**; it cannot change supply. Only a change in one of the **determinants of supply** can shift the supply curve.
- A market is at **equilibrium** at the price where quantity supplied and quantity demanded are exactly equal.
- At any price other than the equilibrium price, there will be **excess supply** or **excess demand**.
- The government attempts to keep the economy running smoothly by **providing the legal structure, promoting competition, redistributing income,** and **ensuring economic stability**.
- **Government failure** occurs when the cost of government action exceeds the benefit of the action.

CHAPTER 13

Exercises

Name _____

1) If you have a choice between doing your homework, watching a baseball game, and playing video games what is the opportunity cost of deciding to do your homework?
   A) the value of watching a baseball game
   B) the value of watching a baseball game and playing video games
   C) the value of playing video games
   D) only the value of the activity you like the most between watching a baseball game and playing video games

1) _____

2) Which of the following is NOT an example of capital?
   A) tools   C) factories
   B) machinery   D) money

2) _____

3) How is the 'how to produce' question answered in the United States?
   A) businesses produce the maximum amount with the least amount of resources
   B) unions tell businesses how to produce
   C) the government tells businesses how to produce
   D) businesses produce in the way that provides the most jobs for Americans

3) _____

4) Law of Demand states that as the price of a product rises
   A) demand rises.   C) quantity demanded falls.
   B) quantity demanded rises. D) demand falls.

4) _____

5) What would happen to the demand curve for cell phones if the price of cell phone service doubled due to government regulation?
   A) shift to the right   C) shift upward
   B) shift to the left   D) nothing

5) _____

6) In the 1970s, oil-producing nations of the Middle East refused to sell oil to the United States. What effect did this event have on the supply curve for gasoline in the United States?
   A) shifted to the left   C) shifted downward
   B) shifted to the right   D) nothing

6) _____

7) When a product is selling for a price above its equilibrium price, what kind of problem occurs?
   A) scarcity   C) surplus
   B) shortage   D) market failure

7) _____

8) Government failure occurs when
   A) the benefit of government action does not exceed the cost.
   B) the government does not act quickly enough.
   C) government action gets society closer to allocative efficiency.
   D) government action increases the national debt.

8) _____

9) Explain the concept of rationality and why focusing on the margin helps in rational decision making.

_____

_____

_____

_____

_____

_____

10) Draw what would happen to equilibrium if both supply and demand shifted to the right at the same time. What happens to equilibrium quantity and price?

_____

_____

_____

_____

_____

_____

Chapter 14

Consumer Demand

I. DETERMINANTS OF DEMAND

The Sociological Explanation

Understanding consumer behavior is the first half of understanding the dynamics of the market exchange. The question we will explore is a simple one, but one whose answer may be more complicated than you think: Why do people buy the things they buy? Many social scientists—psychologists, sociologists, and anthropologists—have their own explanations for what drives consumer behavior. From a biological perspective there are only a few things we need to buy to actually survive—food, water, and shelter, for example—but people clearly buy more than these bare essentials of life.

Socially speaking, one could argue that people are merely trying to "keep up with the Joneses" and maintain their social status by buying things others have bought. This helps explain why buying patterns are so different in different societies. Understanding the motivations behind consumer behavior can be a key factor in the success of a business.

The Economic Explanation

But why people desire certain goods and services is only half of the story. If you recall from Unit 1, production in a capitalist society is distributed according to the willingness and ability to pay. A person must not only desire a good; they must desire it enough to want to part with some of their limited income to get it, necessarily reducing their consumption of other goods.

So instead of focusing on desire or want, we will be focusing on trying to understand why consumers demand the goods they demand, since demand encompasses both desire and ability to pay. Remember from our discussion of demand curves that consumer tastes (desire) was only one of the many determinants of demand.

II. THE DEMAND CURVE

Utility Theory

Total vs. Marginal Utility. Unlike other social scientists, economists do not delve into why consumers prefer one good to another. Instead, they focus on the fact that the more pleasure or utility an individual receives from a good, the more he would be willing to pay to get it. Economists call this pleasure utility, and the central tenet of consumer behavior is that consumers make decisions to ensure they receive the greatest amount of utility possible.

When studying consumer demand it is crucial to make the distinction between total utility (the amount of pleasure derived from the consumption of the entire good), and marginal utility (the amount of pleasure obtained from the last unit of the good). Since economics is based on marginal decision-making, marginal utility is a much better indicator about how much a consumer would be willing to pay for a little more of the good in question. When trying to determine whether to ride a roller coaster one more time or not, for example, it's better to know how much you enjoyed the last ride than how much you fun you have had all day.

Diminishing Marginal Utility. Even people that love riding roller coasters do not do it endlessly. Why not? Certainly every time they ride the roller coaster their total utility increases (as long as it is enjoyable), but they still stop at some point. What is different about the first ride and each successive ride? The first ride is breathtaking; every turn is a surprise, and with all the anticipation you barely care about the long wait in line. Eventually your head or stomach may start to hurt, you start to memorize the ride so it doesn't thrill you like it did, or the line just becomes unbearable. Either way, the amount of pleasure derived from each successive ride decreases; the tenth or twentieth ride is never as fun as the first ride.

This phenomenon of the pleasure derived from an activity decreasing with every additional unit of it is called the Law of Diminishing Marginal Utility. The law states that even though a consumer enjoys a third slice of pizza, a tenth roller coaster ride, or a sixth beer, he will not enjoy it as much as the ones he consumed previously. This usually applies to consumption done in a single sitting; if your third slice of pizza comes three months after your second, you are probably going to like it just as much as the first. Diminishing marginal utility can also explain why a standout player may not be worth much to baseball team that is already loaded with talent. A new player will not have as big an impact on a team that already has three superstar players in the outfield as he would on a team bereft of talent.

We can understand this concept by graphing the utility gained from successive units of a product, as in figure 14.1. The marginal utility graph shows that first slice of pizza really hits the spot and gives a large amount of utility, but no successive slice can

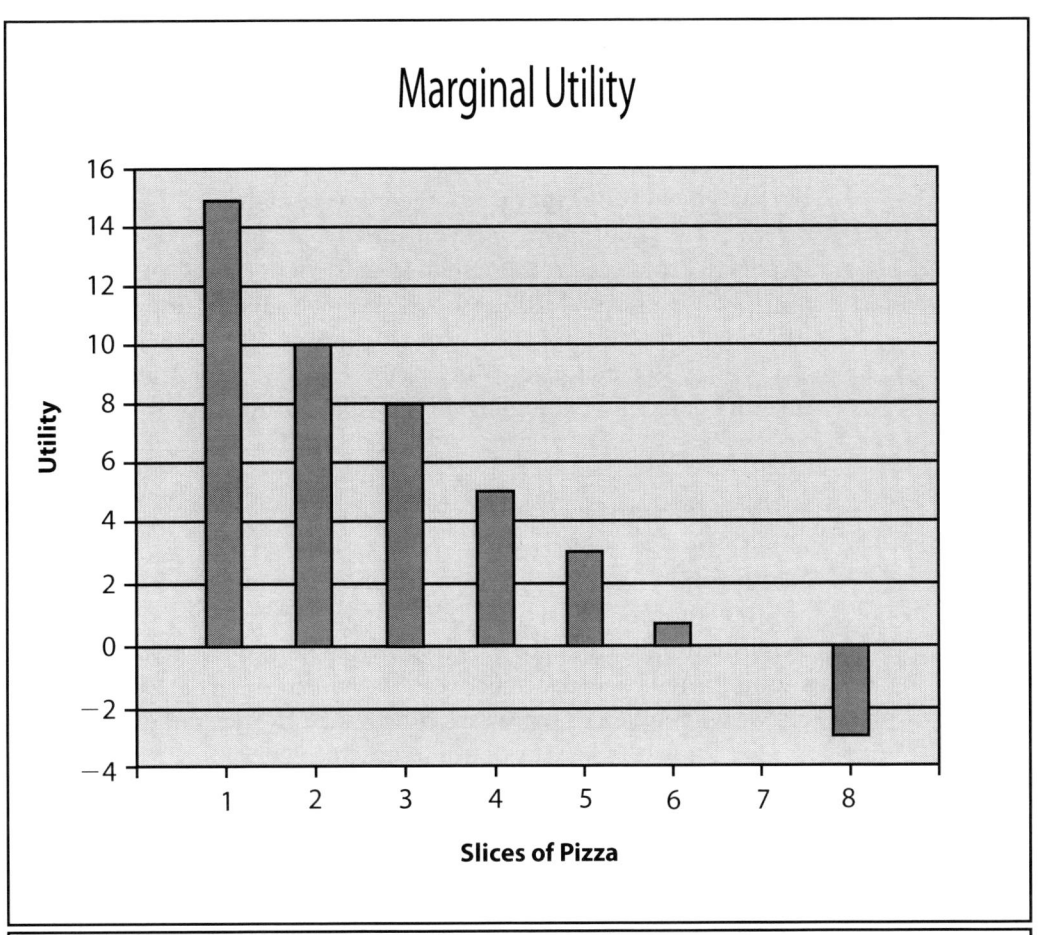

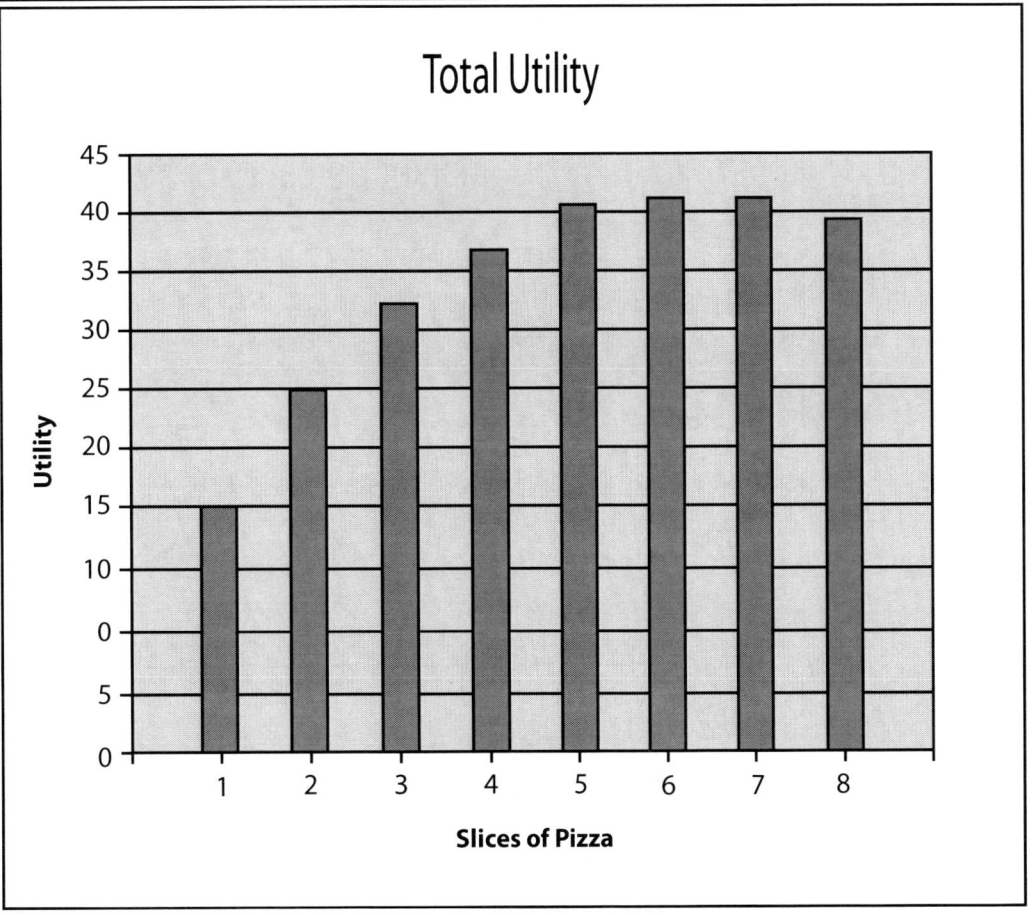

Figure 14.1 • Marginal Utility and Total Utility
Total utility rises whenever marginal utility is positive and falls when marginal utility is negative.

match that feeling and gives you less and less utility as you consume more and more. You do not dislike the pizza though, so total utility does increase as shown in the total utility graph, just by smaller and smaller amounts. Total utility increases with each unit, but marginal utility (the size of the increase) falls.

At some point, however, you may have consumed so much pizza that eating any more will actually hurt more than it feels good. Eating an additional slice of pizza at this point will cause total utility to fall. If consuming a unit of a product ever makes total utility fall, the marginal utility for that unit is actually negative. This makes sense, since the formula for marginal utility is the change in total utility divided by the change in quantity consumed; if total utility falls, the numerator is negative.

Price and Quantity

Clearly, utility is not the only factor that determines what we buy. If it were, we would only buy the products we like the most and never have to make compromises. Sometimes we buy a product that gives us less marginal utility than another because it is available at a lower price. The balance between desire and price determines how much of each product we will buy. Our choices are constrained by our limited income and resources.

We know the benefit of a purchase or economic activity is the marginal utility we will get from consuming it, but we must weigh this benefit against the cost. For most products, the cost is the price. Seeing purchases as a balance between benefit and cost gives us a new understanding of the demand curve from macroeconomics.

The demand curve slopes downward because the law of demand states that people want less of a good at higher prices. Take another look at the demand curve for pizza in figure 14.2. We know that the marginal utility for pizza falls the more pizza one con-

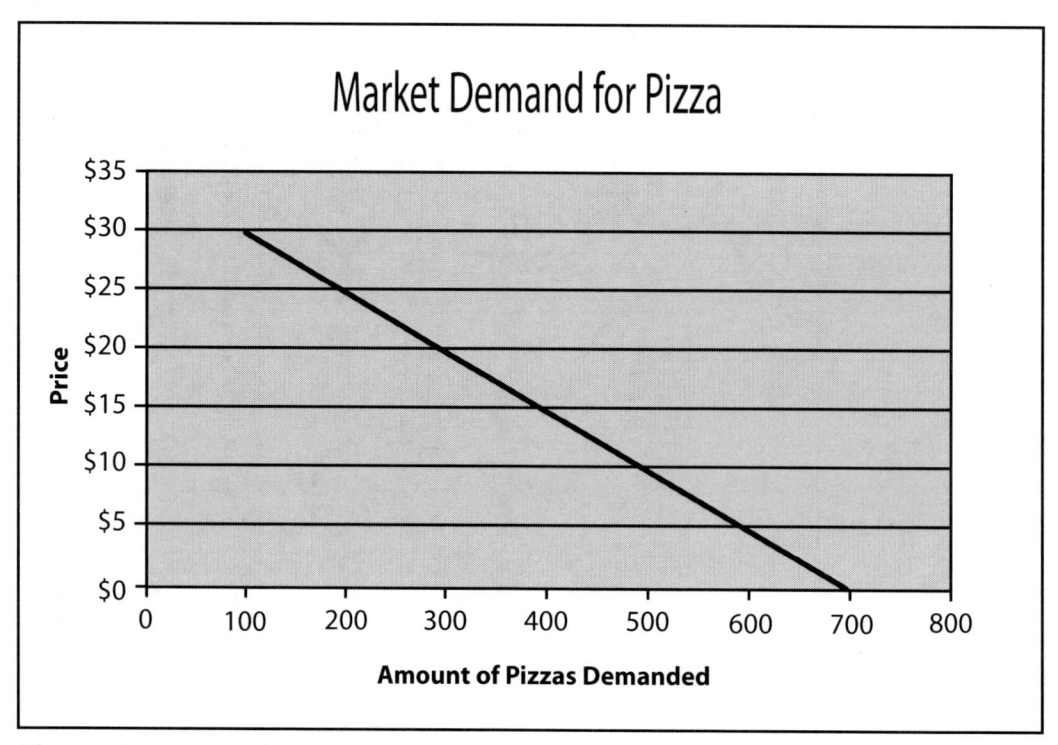

Figure 14.2 • **Demand Equals Marginal Utility**
Since marginal utility falls as the consumer eats more and more pizza, so does the amount of money he is willing to pay for more pizza.

sumes. We could therefore also say that the more of a good a consumer has, the less he is willing to pay for additional units of it. In a competitive environment, a consumer's demand curve and his marginal utility curve are the same thing, since it describes that people respond to diminishing marginal utility by putting a lower value on goods which they already have in large amounts.

III. PRICE ELASTICITY

We know that the amount of a good a consumer wants to buy decreases as the price increases. In other words, consumers respond to price changes. What a seller needs to know is exactly how responsive a consumer or group of consumers is to a price change in a particular product. A good business knows this responsiveness, which we call the price elasticity of demand.

The price elasticity of demand is very closely related to the slope of the demand curve and measures how much quantity demanded falls (rises) in response to a specific increase (decrease) in prices. The formula for elasticity is the percent change in quantity demanded divided by the percent change in price.

$$Price\ Elasticity\ of\ Demand = \frac{Percent\ Change\ in\ Quantity\ Demanded}{Percent\ Change\ in\ Price}$$

Since the law of demand states that price and quantity demanded always move in opposite directions, the number we get from this formula will always be a negative number. We generally convert it into absolute value for simplicity; that is, we just ignore the negative sign. That way we can simply say that the larger the price elasticity of demand, the greater the response to any price changes.

Computing Price Elasticity

Actually calculating elasticities without calculus requires a bit of a trick. We can easily read the change in quantity demanded and price from the demand curve or schedule, but what we need is the percent change in quantity demanded and the percent change in price. We can obtain these figures using a technique called the midpoint formula.

Consider the demand schedule facing a concession stand owner at a baseball stadium in figure 14.3. If the concession stand reduces the price of a hot dog from $3.50 to $3.00, the quantity demanded will increase from eighty to one hundred. To calculate the price elasticity of demand we first need to answer: What is the percent change in quantity demanded?

The absolute change is clearly twenty hot dogs, but to get the percent change we need to divide this by some base number. For the purpose of calculating elasticities, economists generally use the average of the beginning value and the end value (called the midpoint value).

$$Percent\ Change = \frac{New\ Value - Old\ Value}{Average\ Value}$$

Quantity Demanded	Price
0	$5.50
20	$5.00
40	$4.50
60	$4.00
80	$3.50
100	$3.00
120	$2.50
140	$2.00

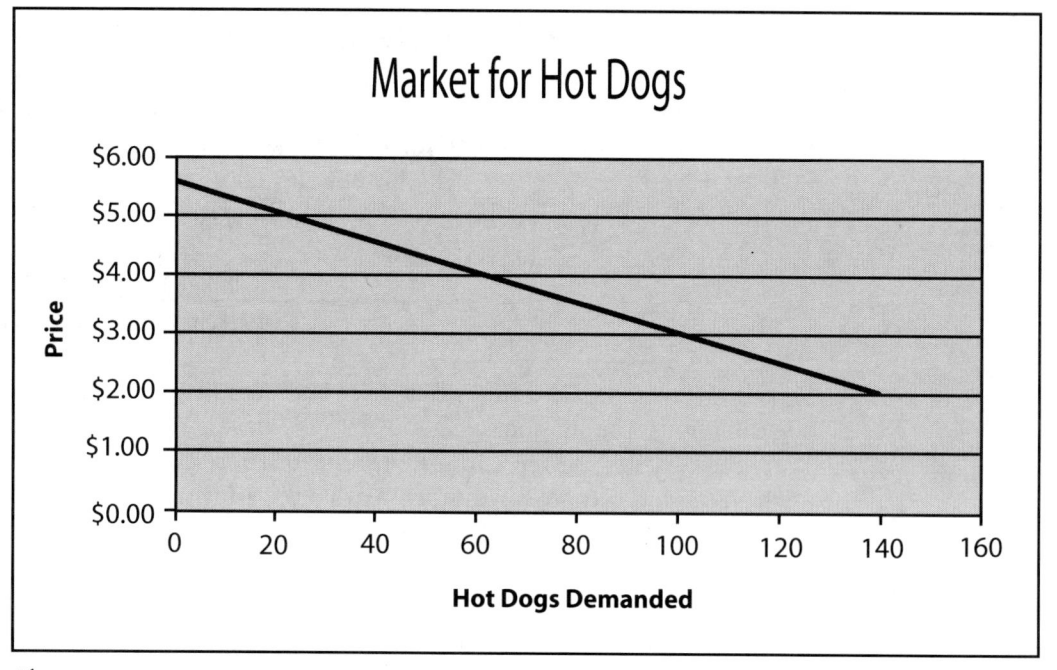

Figure 14.3 • A Market for Hot Dogs
Measuring the price of elasticity of demand informs the business how customers will respond to price changes.

In this case the midpoint value is ninety. Dividing the absolute change by the average value (twenty over ninety) we get a percent change in quantity demanded of .222. To calculate percent change in price we use the same procedure: absolute change divided by average value.

$$\text{Percent Change in Price} = \left| \frac{3.00 - 3.50}{3.25} \right| \approx .154$$

Remember that although the change in price is negative, we only care about the size of the change, not the direction.

Now we are ready to calculate the price elasticity of demand for hot dogs. Simply divide the percent change in quantity demanded by the percent change in price (.222

over .154). This leaves us with an elasticity of 1.44; the demand for hot dogs is fairly responsive to price at this level. The concession stand can lower prices 15 percent and increases sales by over 20 percent, good information to know.

Elastic vs. Inelastic Demand

Talking about whether price elasticity of demand for a product is high or low is all about relativity. Any elasticity higher than one, like the example above, is considered elastic; any change in price will be met by a more than proportional change in quantity demanded. If people will refuse to buy any of the good if you change the price at all, we say that the demand for the good is perfectly elastic.

When the elasticity of demand for a product is less than one, consumers are not very responsive to price changes; we say that the demand for such products is inelastic. In the rare case that people will buy the same amount of good no matter what the price is, we encounter perfectly inelastic demand. If the elasticity is exactly one, any change in price is met by an identical change in quantity demanded, resulting in unitary elastic demand.

Determinants of Elasticity

Necessities vs. Luxuries. Why is demand for some goods more elastic than it is for others? Many factors help determine how much consumers respond to a price change in a good. Some products, for example, are more necessary to our everyday lives than others. To varying degrees, people cannot imagine living without certain comforts like toothbrushes, salt, and electricity. Other products are considered luxury goods and would not make our lives miserable if we were to go without them. The more "necessary" a product is, the more likely it is to exhibit inelastic demand.

Availability of Substitutes. Even if a good is a necessity, people may still be responsive to price changes if close substitutes are available to take its place. For example, meat is a staple commodity in our lives and an important part in most of our diets, but since it has so many close substitutes—chicken, fish, or vegetarian proteins—meat producers cannot raise prices with impunity.

Coffee, on the other hand, has very few, if any, substitutes. For those people that rely on it to get their day started, it seems like nothing else will do. For that reason, coffee consumers are not very responsive to price changes in this product; regardless of price changes, they need their morning fix.

Price Relative to Income. Consumers are more responsive to price changes in big-ticket items than they are to changes in the price of cheaper items. Since it takes up such a large chunk of our income, a small percent of change in the price of a new car can have a much bigger effect on our ability to buy other items than a large percent of change in the price of coffee, for example.

The idea that elasticity changes with relative price tells us something about how elasticity changes along a demand curve. When we draw a demand curve we say income does not change (doing so will shift the demand curve since it is one of the determinants of demand). Therefore, as we move down the demand curve and the price of product decreases, its price relative to consumer income also decreases. As a result, it must be the case that the price elasticity of demand for a product decreases as you move down along the demand curve.

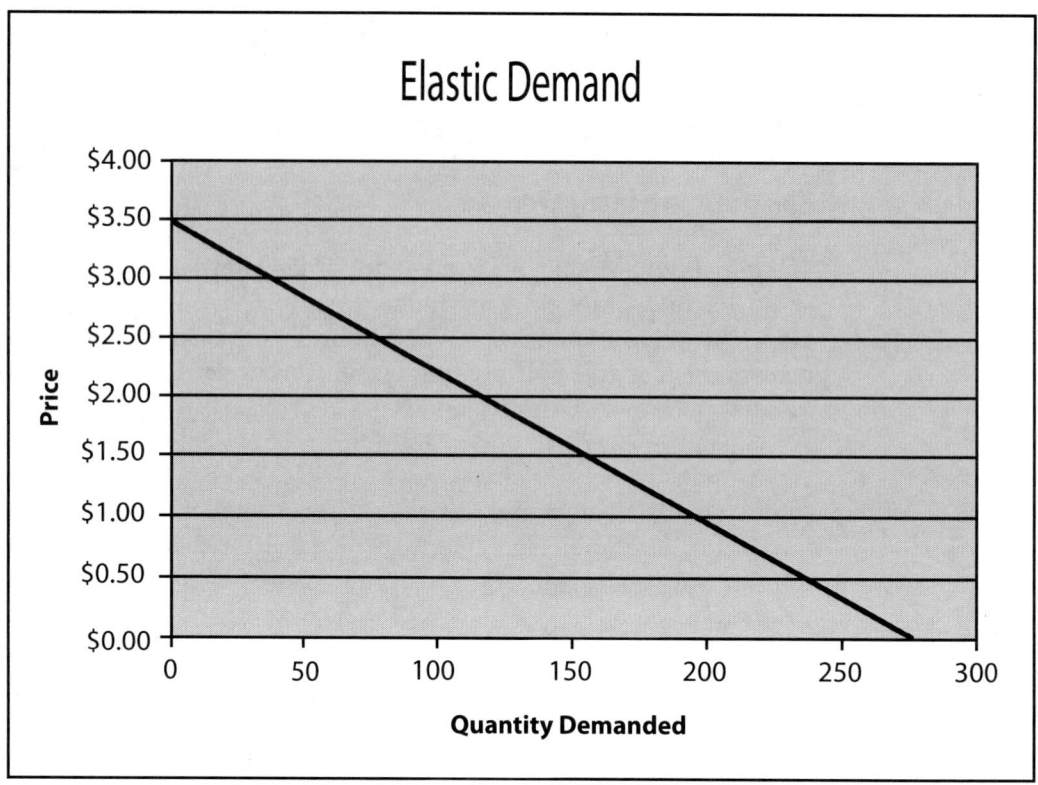

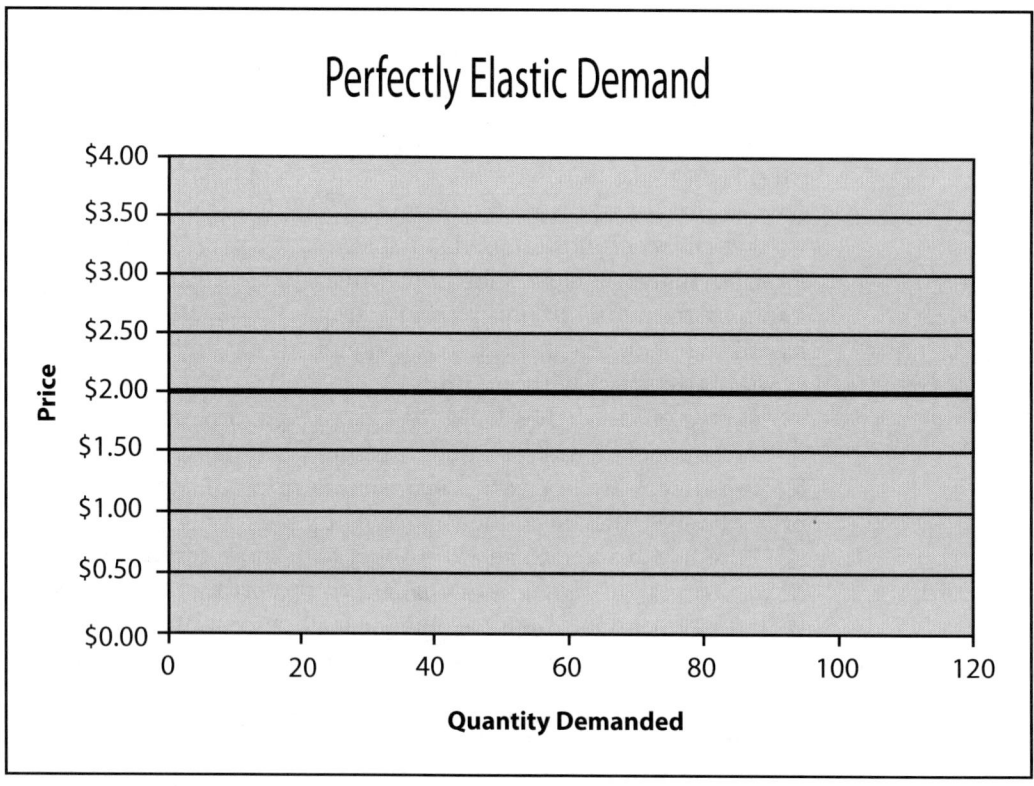

Figure 14.4 • **Different Levels of Elasticity**
The flatter the demand curve, the more price elastic the demand. Steeper demand curves illustrate price inelasticity.

Inlastic Demand

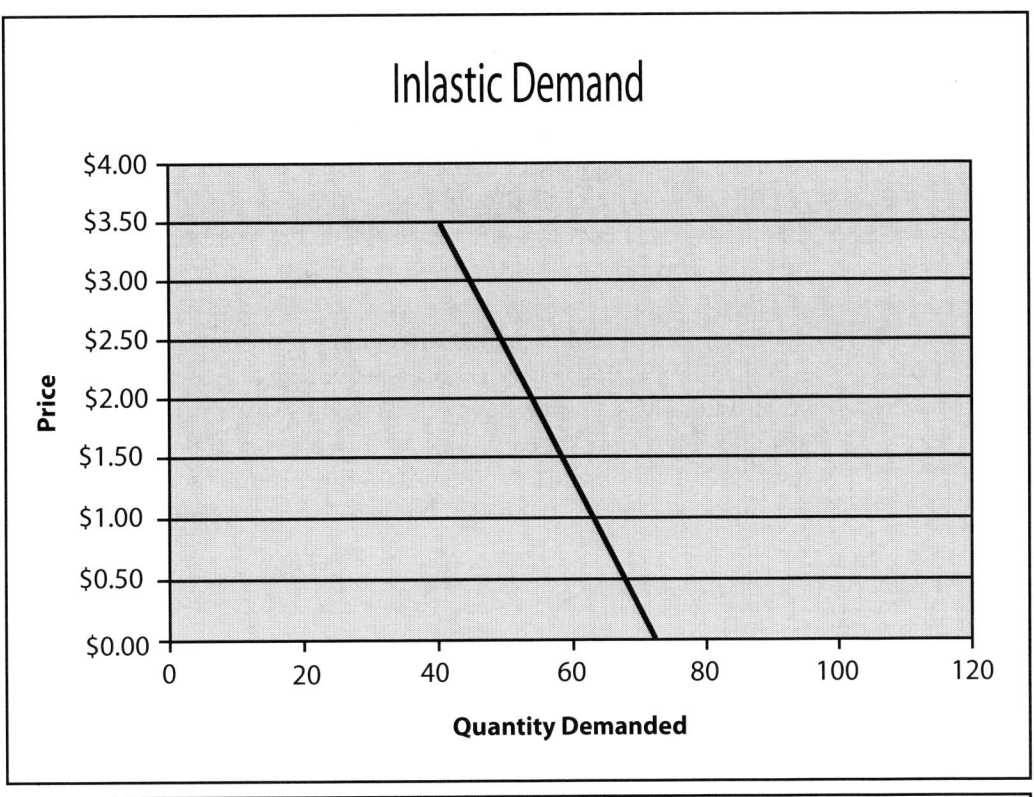

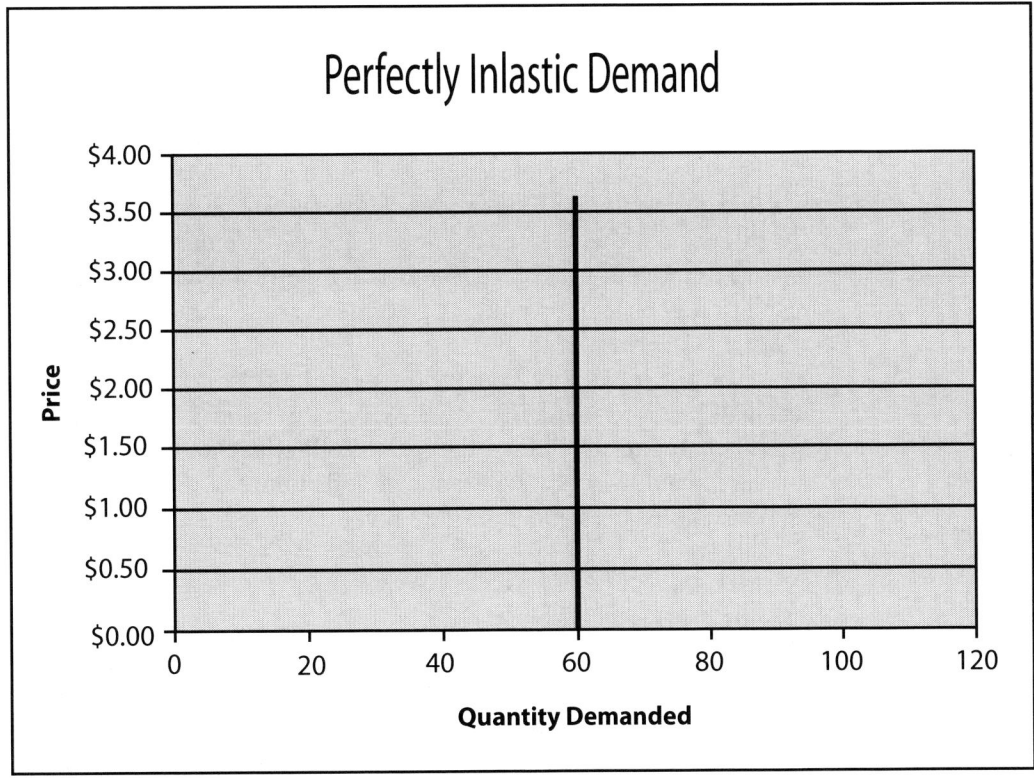

Perfectly Inlastic Demand

Figure 14.4 • Continued.

Think back to the demand for hot dogs in figure 14.3. The demand curve is a straight line, but that does not mean price elasticity is the same everywhere on the demand curve. We calculated price elasticity of 1.44 when the price was lowered from $3.50 to $3.00, but what about when the price is lowered from $2.50 to $2.00? The percent change in quantity demanded is $\frac{140 - 120}{130} \approx .154$ while the percent change in price is $\left|\frac{2.00 - 2.50}{2.25}\right| \approx .222$. It should not surprise us that the resulting price elasticity of demand (.694) is lower than the price elasticity of demand at higher prices since the same fifty-cent drop in price becomes less important to consumers as the product becomes cheaper.

Time. The final factor that affects price elasticity of demand is time. In the short-run, people cannot buy a hybrid or electric car every time gas prices go up; they are stuck with the car they have. In time, however, if they see that gas prices are consistently high, they may choose to buy an electric car when it comes time to buy a new car. In the long-run, consumers have more time to adjust to price changes and are more responsive to these changes, but in the short run elasticities are generally lower.

IV. PRICE ELASTICITY AND TOTAL REVENUE

Price elasticity helps explain why sellers, even those with a monopoly, do not charge the highest price possible for their products. The goal of business is not to get the highest price for a single unit of your product, but to get the most total revenue possible. Revenue is the product of sales and price, and if the elasticity of demand is high enough sales may fall so much that total revenue begins to fall.

Because of the law of demand, we know that quantity demanded (units sold) will fall every time the price increases. However, if the price elasticity of demand is small (less than one) the percent change in quantity demanded will be less than the percent change in price. If price rises faster than quantity demanded falls, the price increase will result in higher total revenue. A price decrease for a product with inelastic demand will result in a decrease in total revenue.

If, on the other hand, the product exhibits elastic demand, any increase in price per unit will be more than offset by the decrease in units sold. For a product with elasticity greater than one, any increase in price will reduce total revenue and a drop in price will increase revenue. A unitary-elastic good is unique in that a change in price in either direction will have no effect on total revenue since the two effects will exactly offset.

Changing the Value of *E*

Remember that elasticity is not always the same for a given product; it falls as you move along the demand curve. So even if a producer realizes the demand for his product is elastic and decides to lower price to increase revenue, this effect will not work forever. With each drop in price, the demand for the good becomes less elastic as the corresponding increase in quantity demanded begins to dwindle.

At some point the good begins to exhibit inelastic demand and the increase in quantity demanded cannot offset the decrease in price, and total revenue falls. As a result, there is exactly one price where the business cannot increase revenue by decreas-

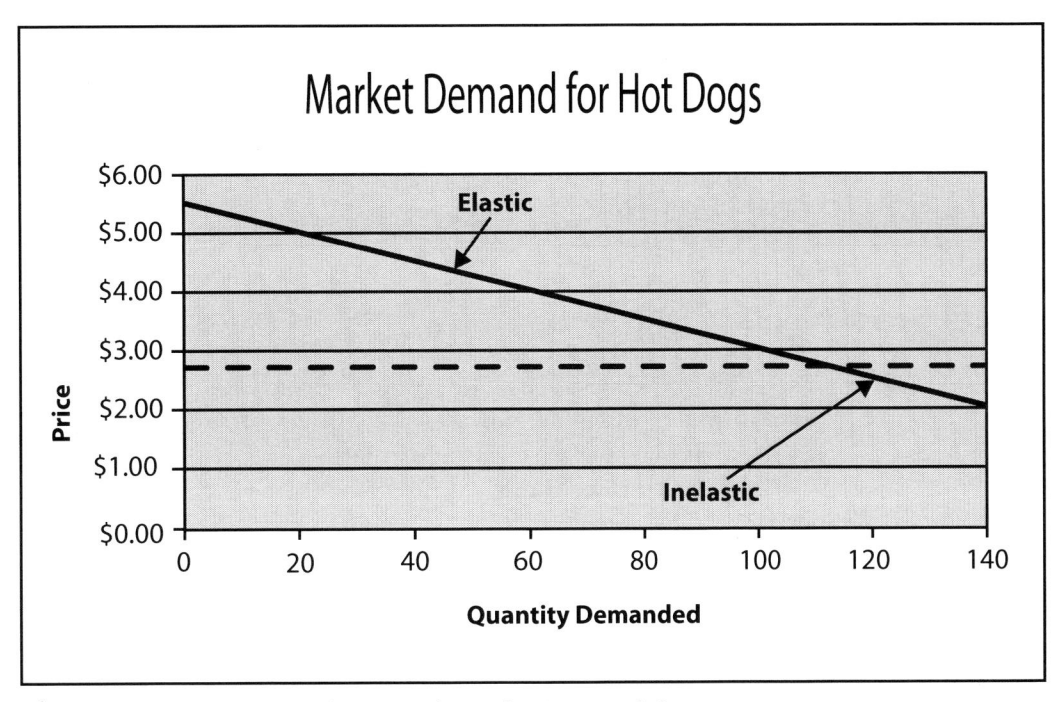

Figure 14.5 • Elasticity Changes along the Demand Curve
As the product becomes cheaper and cheaper it's price elasticity of demand falls. At one particular price, the price elasticity of demand is exactly one.

ing or increasing the price—namely, the price where the elasticity of demand equals one. This is where the firm maximizes its revenue.

V. OTHER ELASTICITIES

Shifts vs. Movements

The price elasticity of demand tells us how consumers will respond to price changes at different points in the demand curve. But remember that the demand curve is drawn with the *ceteris paribus* assumption in play. That is, if one of the determinants of demand changes, the demand curve will shift and our values for elasticity will be invalid.

Price elasticity demand measures the response to a price change (a movement along the demand curve) not a demand change (a shift of the demand curve to the left or right). We need different figures to calculate the response to a change in the determinants of demand.

Income Elasticity

Suppose, for example, income increases throughout the economy. It is likely that consumers will want to buy more hot dogs at every price as in figure 14.6. After a rightward shift in demand, quantity demanded increases at every price. This shift only gives us a general idea about how consumers respond to an increase in income. To get a full picture we need to calculate the income elasticity of demand.

The income elasticity of demand tells us how much quantity demanded changes relative to a change in income. It is calculated in a similar fashion to the price elasticity of demand, except with percent change in income in the denominator rather than percent change in price.

$$\text{Income Elasticity of Demand} = \frac{\text{Percent Change in Quantity Demanded}}{\text{Percent Change in Income}}$$

Just as with price elasticity of demand, percent changes are calculated using the midpoint formula. This time, however, we will need to keep track of any negative signs for reasons that will become clear momentarily.

Computing Income Elasticity. Suppose income increases from $110 a week to $120 per week. The percent change in income is $10 divided by $115 or 8.7 percent. We know from the graph that at the given price of $3.00 an ounce the quantity demanded increases by twenty from one hundred to 120 for a percent change of 18.2 percent.

The income elasticity equals the percent change in quantity demanded, divided by the percent change in income; 2.09 in this case. The demand for this product is quite responsive to income changes; we say it is income-elastic.

Normal vs. Inferior Goods. We know that it is not always the case that the demand for a good rises when income increases; this is only the case for normal goods. There is another category of goods, inferior goods, that consumers want less of when they have more money. Inferior goods are usually low quality products consumed out of necessity when income is low. The demand for these products rises when income falls and falls

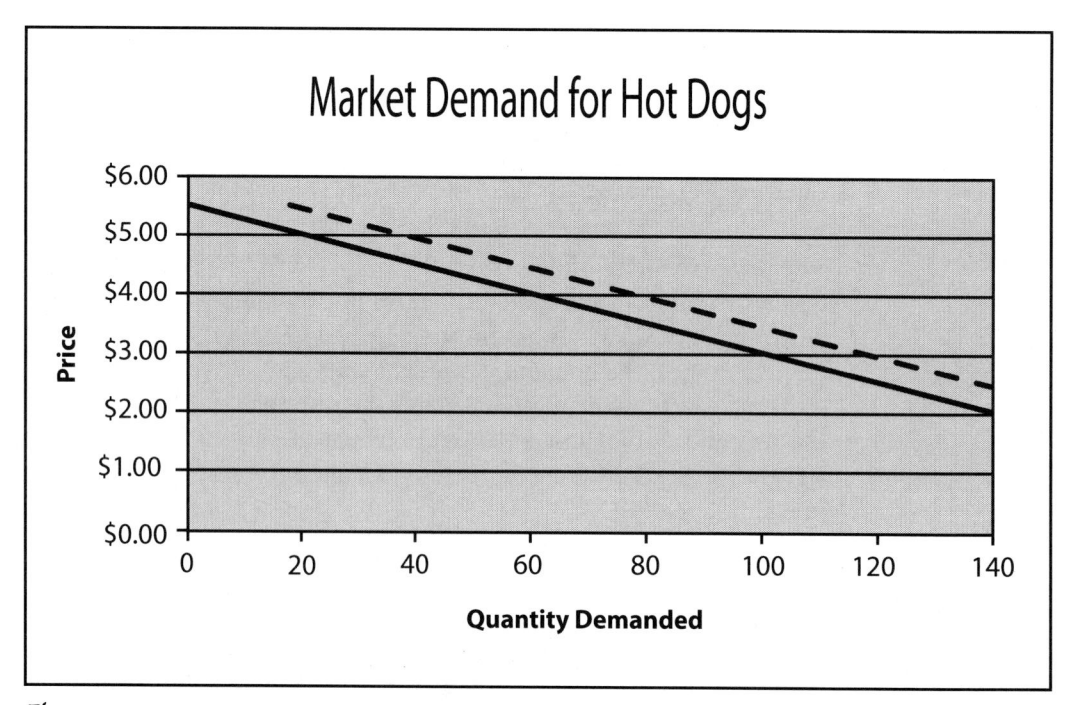

Figure 14.6 • An Increase in Income

As income increases, the amount demanded at every price increases. The income elasticity of demand tells us by how much.

when income rises. As a result, decreases in the sales of these products actually portend a positive turn for the economy.

Unlike the procedure with price elasticity of demand, we need to keep track of the negative sign when calculating income elasticity of demand so we can tell the difference between inferior goods and normal goods. Inferior goods always have a negative income elasticity of demand while normal goods will always have a positive income elasticity.

Cross-Price Elasticity

Income is only one of the shifters of demand we talked about before. Another one is the price of related goods—substitutes and complements. How does an increase in the price of Pepsi affect the demand for Coke? An increase in the price of Pepsi will cause Coke to seem relatively cheaper, resulting in an increase in demand for Coke because the two are substitutes. But exactly how much does it rise? We need to calculate another figure to determine this change.

Consider the concession stand once again. There are several substitutes for hot dogs people can choose from—candy, pickles, and nachos, among other things. How will a drop in nacho prices, for example, affect the demand for hot dogs? Since they are substitutes, you would expect a drop in the price of nachos to cause the demand for hot dogs to fall as more customers choose nachos over hot dogs. This decrease in demand would be experienced at every price, resulting in a leftward shift of the demand curve for hot dogs.

Not every good at the snack bar is a substitute for hot dogs. Some products, like sodas, tend to be purchased in conjunction with hot dogs. Hot dogs and sodas are complements in consumption and as such have a very different relationship than that of substitute goods. When the price of soda falls the quantity of hot dogs demanded at every price rises, which results in a rightward shift of the demand curve for hot dogs.

To sum up, with substitute goods the price of one good and demand for its substitute move in the same direction. On the other hand, the price of a good and demand for its complement move in opposite directions.

Calculating Cross-Price Elasticity. How can we relate these two facts to the idea of elasticities? The relationships between hot dogs and nachos and hot dogs and sodas clearly illustrate that demand is responsive to changes in the price of related goods. The two rules about substitutes and complements actually tell us the direction of this response: The demand for a product will always move in the same direction as the price change of its substitute (positive cross-price elasticity) and in the opposite direction of the price change of its complement (negative cross-price elasticity).

Computing this elasticity is almost identical to that of the price elasticity of demand, except instead of having the percent change in the price of the good in question we use the percent change in the price of a related good.

$$Cost\text{-}Price\ Elasticity\ of\ Demand = \frac{Percent\ Change\ in\ Quantity\ Demanded}{Percent\ Change\ in\ Price\ of\ Related\ Good}$$

Since we calculate this elasticity using the price of a good other than the good in question, we call this the cross-price elasticity.

The cross-price elasticity tells us the magnitude and direction of the demand curve resulting from the change in price of a related good. If the cross-price elasticity is negative (demand rises when the price of the related good falls) we are dealing with complements. If it is positive (demand falls when the price of the related good falls) we have substitute goods.

VI. CHOOSING AMONG PRODUCTS

Marginal Utility vs. Price

Consumer demand can be quite complicated when you think about all of the different factors that can affect how much of a product we want. But in reality, consumers have to choose which of the many goods available they want to purchase and how much of it they want to purchase, a daunting task indeed.

The motivation behind choosing the right mix of goods is the same as the motivation behind choosing how much of each good we want; we want to get the most utility possible from our limited income. We also know that each purchase means we have less income with which to make other purchases. In other words, each purchase entails an opportunity cost.

Suppose you have a gift card that you can use to purchase video games or books. How will you decide to use the card? You will use it to obtain the combination of video games and books that gives you the most utility possible. To do this you must consider not only the utility gained from each purchase, but the market price of each item. You might get twice as much utility from a video game as a book, but if it costs more than twice as much, it may not be worth it.

Rational decision-making requires comparing the expected utility of a purchase to the price. For example, let's assume you get twice as much utility from a video game as you do a book. In economics terms, this means the marginal utility from the first video game (the one you value the most) is twice the size of the marginal utility from the first book (the highest valued among all books). Before you know whether you want to spend the gift card on a video game, you need to know the relative prices.

If the video game were the same price as the book, it would make perfect sense to buy the video game instead of the book. That way, you get twice as much marginal utility per dollar than if you bought a book. If the video game costs more than twice as much as the book—say, three times as much—then a rational person would buy the book. You always want to choose the good that produces the maximum marginal utility per dollar.

Utility Maximization

Putting it in more concrete terms, imagine you are given a gift card that has $200 on it and you can buy only $20 books or $60 video games with it. What combination of books and video games will get you the most utility? The answer depends on the marginal utility of each unit of each of the products which figure 14.7 graciously provides. Figure 14.7 indicates that the marginal utility of the first video game is twice as high as the marginal utility of the first book—forty to twenty. With this information, it makes sense to purchase a book first since then you get more bang for your buck, or marginal utility per dollar in economics terms.

Remember the law of diminishing marginal utility; the second book or video game will not get you as much utility as the first. So the next choice is between the second

Video Game	MU	MU/$	Book	MU	MU/$
1	40	0.67	1	20	1
2	35	0.58	2	18	0.9
3	30	0.50	3	16	0.8
4	20	0.33	4	12	0.6
			5	10	0.5
			6	8	0.4
			7	6	0.3
			8	4	0.2
			9	2	0.1
			10	0	0

Video Games = $60, Books = $20, Total Available = $200

Figure 14.7 • **Choosing the Right Mix**
Using the utility-maximizing rule helps in choosing the combination that nets the most utility.

book and the first video game. We know the marginal utility of the second book will not be as high as the first—in fact, it drops to eighteen. Is it still better to buy the book than the video game? The book gets you 18 utils for $20 (.9 utils per dollar) while the video games gets you 40 utils for $60 (.667 utils per dollar).

You still choose the book; in fact, you will not choose the video game until buying a book gets you less than .667 utils per dollar. The third book gets you 16 utils for $20 (.8 utils per dollar) so you would still choose that over the first video game. With the fourth book, though, your marginal utility falls to twelve, resulting in only .6 utils per dollar. At this point, buying the first video game would be a better way to spend your money.

So now you have one video game, three books, and $80 remaining. Your next decision is between the fourth book (.6 utils per dollar) and the second video game (.58 utils per dollar). Again, you choose the book here. Finally, you choose between a fifth book (.5 utils per dollar) and a second video game (.58 utils per dollar). Now, the second video game is a better deal and you spend your remaining $60 credit on it.

You end up with four books, two video games and 141 units of total utility. This is higher than if you spent all of your money on books (96 utils) or bought the maximum amount of video games (115 utils). In fact, this combination is the optimal consumption mix because at each decision you maximized the marginal utility per dollar. Go ahead and try it for yourself, there is no combination you can buy for $200 that brings in more utility than the procedure we just employed.

Utility-Maximizing Rule

You could have found the utility-maximizing combination through trail and error; with only two items to choose from there aren't many possible combinations. In life, though, there are thousands upon thousands of goods and services we can buy. How can we be sure that the combination we choose gets us the most possible utility? Clearly, it is not just about which product gets us the most marginal utility because in our example we did not choose a video game until we already had three books.

Each of the first three books purchased added less to total utility than the first video game, but since they cost so much less, they gave us more bang for the buck. Technically speaking, the books had a higher marginal utility per dollar than the video games. When attempting to maximize your utility with a limited amount of income you want to confirm that each dollar you spend buys the most possible utility.

In other words, we purchased books as long as it gave us more utility per dollar than one video game. Once that stopped being true, we switched to buying video games instead. In general, utility-maximization requires buying more of good x as long as it yields more utility per dollar than any other good. Making this decision over and over, results in receiving the highest amount of utility possible from a given amount of income. Of course, doing so requires us knowing the marginal utility received from each unit of consumption as well as being able to calculate the marginal utility per dollar. In the end, a consumer's marginal utility per dollar from each good he or she buys should be equal. If it isn't, he or she could increase total utility by taking some spending away from a good with low marginal utility per dollar and spending more on a good with a higher marginal utility per dollar.

CHAPTER 14 SUMMARY

- Every product we buy gives us some amount of utility, or satisfaction.
- A consumer's goal is to maximize his **total utility** given a limited amount of income.
- The more you consume of a particular item, the less **marginal utility** each successive unit of that good will give you.
- Price Elasticity of Demand = $\dfrac{\text{Percent Change in Quantity Demanded}}{\text{Percent Change in Price}}$
- Consumers are more responsive to changes in prices of goods that are **necessities, have few substitutes, are relatively expensive,** or **are not purchased often.**
- The price elasticity of demand for a good **falls as you move down the demand curve.**
- The **income elasticity of demand** is how consumers will change their consumption of a particular item if their income changes.
- Inferior goods have a **negative** income elasticity of demand while normal have **positive** ones.
- The **cross-price elasticity of demand** is how consumers will change their consumption of a particular item if the price of a related good changes.
- Complementary goods have **negative** cross-price elasticities of demand while substitutes have **positive** ones.
- You should always consume good x if it gives you more **marginal utility per dollar** than any other good.

CHAPTER 14 Exercises

Name _____

1) If marginal utility is negative, then
   A) total utility will increase with additional consumption.
   B) total utility will decrease with additional consumption.
   C) the good or service being consumed is an inferior good.
   D) total utility is at its maximum.

1) _____

2) Which of the following would most likely have a price-elasticity coefficient less than 1?
   A) Cigarettes
   B) Televisions
   C) T-bone steak
   D) New car

2) _____

3) The higher you are on the demand curve for a good the
   A) more unitary elastic the demand for the good.
   B) smaller the income elasticity for the good.
   C) less elastic the demand for the good.
   D) more elastic the demand for the good.

3) _____

4) If the price elasticity of demand is 2.0, and a firm raises its price by 10 percent, the quantity sold by the firm will
   A) rise 10 percent.
   B) rise 20 percent.
   C) fall 20 percent.
   D) fall 10 percent.

4) _____

5) Assume the price elasticity of demand for Fred's Fabulous Flowers is 2.5. If he cuts the price of a bouquet of flowers, total revenue will
   A) increase because more bouquets will be sold.
   B) decrease because he will receive less revenue per unit sold.
   C) increase because the percentage increase in quantity demanded will be greater than the percentage decrease in price.
   D) Not enough information.

5) _____

6) If income rises 5 percent for a year and as a result the quantity of new cars demanded rises from 100,000 to 120,000 cars for the year, the value of the income elasticity of demand for cars is closest to
   A) 4
   B) 3.64
   C) .25
   D) 20

6) _____

7) MP3 players and MP3 files are complementary goods. The cross-price elasticity of demand between MP3 players and MP3 files is expected to be
   A) negative.
   B) positive.
   C) zero.
   D) Not enough information.

7) _____

8) Which one of the following is true when the consumer is maximizing his utility? 8) _____
    A) MU/$ from good x > MU/$ from good y
    B) MU/$ from good x = MU/$ from good y
    C) MU/$ from good x < MU/$ from good y
    D) None of the above

9) What is the difference between a good with a positive income elasticity and one with a negative income elasticity? How do they each affect the demand curve?

_____
_____
_____
_____
_____

10) Why do we sometimes have to choose products that give us less marginal utility than others? Why do we buy Fords when we really want to buy a Mercedes?

_____
_____
_____
_____
_____

Chapter 15

Costs of Production

I. THE PRODUCTION FUNCTION

Every economic activity requires the firm to purchase factors of production if it wants to produce anything. Resources spent on some economic activity are what we call the costs of production. Once resources are spent on one activity, they cannot be used on any other activity. The land that your school sits on, the desks and equipment in your classroom, as well as your teacher's efforts, make up the cost of production for an economics class, for example.

Remember that in order to be profitable and remain competitive, businesses need to produce their product with the least resources possible. Alternatively, you could say they need to produce the maximum level of output given a certain amount of resources at their disposal. This makes the business's problem analogous to the consumer's maximization problem, which was getting the maximum amount of utility out of a limited amount of income.

The production function is a mathematical description of how a producer turns different amounts of resources into output. For example, with one classroom, thirty desks, and one teacher, a school can teach 150 students per day. With two classrooms, sixty desks, two teachers, and an assistant, that same school might be able to teach 250 or 300 students. The amount of output changes when you change the number of inputs.

Varying Input Levels

While the production possibilities curve tells how a country can turn one good into another good at a given level of resources, the production function tells how a single firm can turn various amounts of resources into a single product given a certain technology. For simplicity, we assume that a firm cannot change its land input within a reasonable timeframe. Now we can consider how output changes when we vary the amount of capital and labor used in production.

The production function, like the one in figure 15.1, tells us how much output we get when we throw a certain amount of labor and a certain amount of capital into our current technology. With no labor and/or no capital employed, no output will be produced. A group of dedicated automobile workers cannot effectively produce cars without machinery and robots and a group of robots and machinery cannot produce cars without someone to turn them on and maintain them. In general the productivity of a resource depends on the amount of other resources available: The more capital you have, the more productive your labor will be and vice versa.

Figure 15.1 illustrates the production function for a certain car manufacturer. Adding a piece of capital to the labor force will add to the productivity of those workers and therefore increase the amount of output they produce. Each piece of capital will add more output as will each additional worker, up to a certain point. Does hiring a new worker always the produce the same amount of additional output? We will return to the discussion of additional output soon.

Efficiency

Like the production possibilities curve, the production function tells you the maximum output possible with a given level of inputs. It is most certainly possible for one company to produce less than another with the same amount of resources; a lazy worker may not work as hard as possible, a careless one may waste materials, or a manager might not put people in the right jobs to produce as efficiently as possible.

In other words, the production function shows the amount of output that will be produced if the firm produces at technical efficiency. When the firm is inefficient in some way they will produce less than the maximum output given their resource level.

Capital Inputs (Assembly Robots)	Labor Inputs (Work Teams per day)						
	0	1	2	3	4	5	6
	Output (cars per day)						
0	0	0	0	0	0	0	0
1	0	4	10	14	16	16	14
2	0	6	14	20	24	24	22
3	0	8	18	26	30	30	28

Figure 15.1 • Production Function
The level of output is determined by the combination of inputs employed.

At the society level, producing inefficiently means that we will be inside our production possibilities curve and our standard of living will suffer. A firm does not care about this, per se. To them, inefficiency means a waste of resources and therefore a waste of possible profits.

While we can always do worse than the output level implied by the production function, we cannot do better—at least, not with current production technology. The production function gives the upper limit of our ability to turn inputs into output. If we invent a new machine or production process that makes production easier or faster, the amount we could possibly produce with a given amount of resources will rise, illustrated by an outward shift in the production function.

Short-Run Constraints

For the moment, however, we are stuck with our current level of technology and each business aims to produce efficiently given that technology. Technology is not the only thing that limits the firm's choices, though. At a very real level the business is stuck with its current production facilities: its factory and large capital purchases.

A car manufacturer cannot instantly build a new factory or install a new robot every time it wants to increase production; these things take time to design and build. We say that the levels of land and most capital are fixed in the short run. The only things the car manufacturer can vary to produce more cars during the short run are the number of workers and the amount of small capital items like tools and materials. The long run is defined as the amount of time it would take the car manufacturer to design and build a new factory of its choosing.

Since the firm is stuck with its current factory and all the large equipment in it, its job in the short run is to maximize its profits given these fixed inputs. It does so by varying the amounts of variable inputs (labor and small capital) it hires. Let's assume that in the short run, the car manufacturer tries to maximize profits given a factory with one assembly robot. The production function for such a firm is given in figure 15.2. With the level of every other input fixed, the amount of output the car manufacturer produces will depend solely upon the amount of labor employed.

We can then draw the short-run production function for the firm with output on the y-axis and labor on the x-axis. As discussed, this production function shows the maximum amount of output possible at different levels of the variable input, labor. We already know that a firm with no workers produces no output, but we can now see how output grows with the addition of more workers.

II. MARGINAL PRODUCTIVITY

Marginal Physical Product

You may notice something else about the production function; its slope is not constant. It starts out fairly steep, then levels out and eventually starts to drop. The slope of the line tells us the marginal output produced by the last worker hired, his marginal physical product (MPP). MPP tells how much each additional worker adds to total output. Is this value the same for every worker? Of course not, the production function would be a straight line if this were the case.

(a)

Number of Work Teams	0	1	2	3	4	5	6
Total Output	0	4	10	14	16	16	14
Marginal Physical Product	N/A	4	6	4	2	0	−2

(b)

Production Function with 1 Assembly Robot

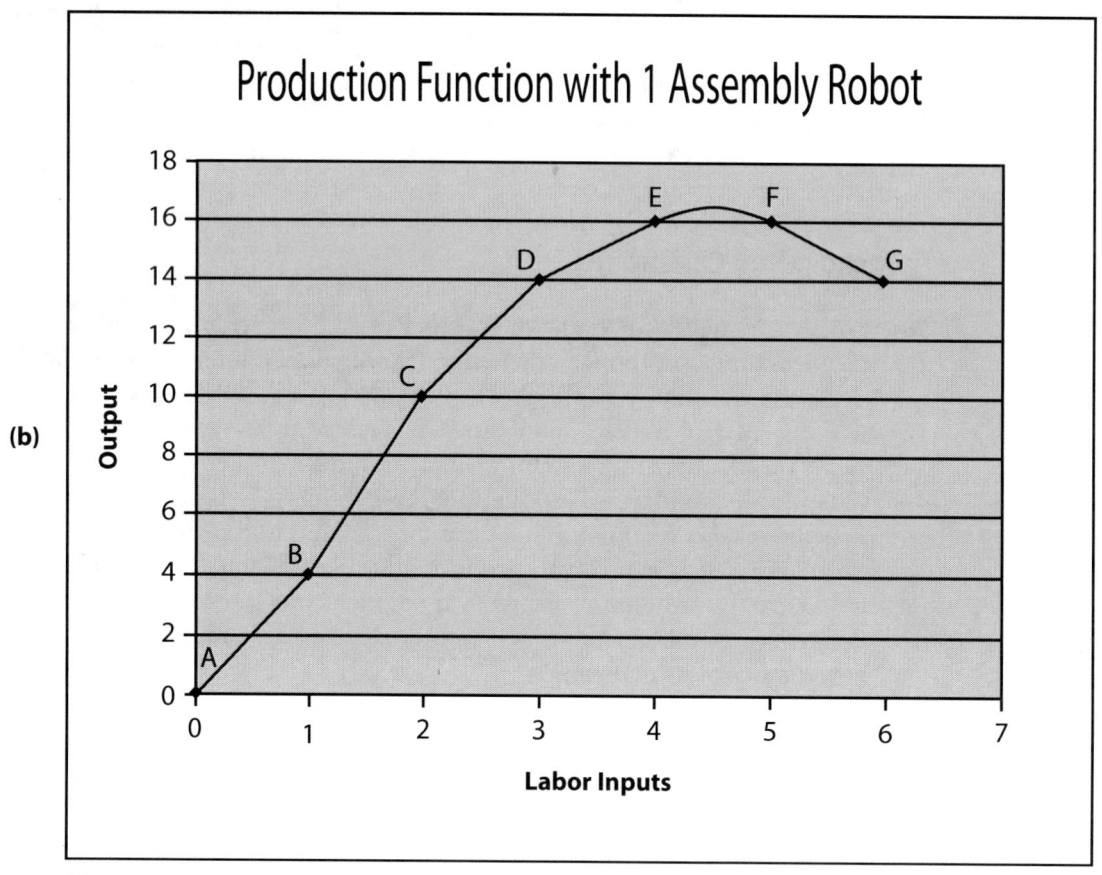

Figure 15.2 • Short-Run Production
At some point in short-run production an additional unit of labor will not increase production as much as the previous unit.

Why isn't marginal physical product the same for every worker? It isn't because of productivity; the labor we are talking about here is constant-quality, so that a worker that is twice as productive as the average worker would count as two workers. Then what is it? Think about the car-producing factory with one worker. He has to do everything himself and much of his time is spent moving between different workstations and getting equipped to do different tasks. All of this time is unproductive time.

Now imagine the firm hires a second worker. Now the workers can split up tasks so that the expensive equipment is never sitting idle, increasing productivity (output per hour). As a result the second worker adds more output than the first worker did. It isn't because he is a better worker; it is because they can do more as a team than they could alone.

Diminishing Marginal Returns

This increasing marginal physical product does not last forever, though. Remember that the size of the factory and the amount of machines are fixed. At a certain point the number of workers will overwhelm the productive capacity of the factory. Workers will get in each other's way and will sit idle waiting for a piece of equipment to open up. As the capital per worker ratio falls, each additional worker becomes less productive and marginal physical product falls; the factory cannot make as good a use of the third or fourth worker as they did the second.

There may even come a point that there are so many workers that adding more will hinder performance so much that total output will begin to fall. Whether or not it ends up causing a reduction in total output, the pinch of having to share a fixed amount of capital and land between a growing labor force affects just about every production process in the short run. The law of diminishing marginal returns states that at some point, the MPP of a resource will begin to fall as more of it is employed when the rest of the factors of production are fixed.

III. RESOURCE COSTS

Profit and Costs

All the production function tells us is how much a firm can produce with a certain amount of resources, not how much it wants to produce. A firm may choose to produce at its highest output level if demand is high enough, or choose to let its fixed inputs sit idle if revenue never covers costs. In every case, though, firms choose the amount of output that maximizes total profit, the difference between total revenue and total cost.

While increased production and sales increase revenue, they also increase costs. Firms need to weigh these costs against revenue to choose the optimum output level. From the law of diminishing marginal returns, we know that at some point each additional work team will add less and less to total car output for an automobile factory, for example. This also means that the cost of producing a single car (in terms of the resources needed to produce it) will begin to rise at some point.

Marginal Resource Costs

Since the first work team produces four cars in one day, the cost of producing one car (in terms of variable resource inputs) is one-fourth of a labor unit. Think of one-fourth of a labor input as three hours of a twelve-hour shift. In an entire twelve-hour shift, the workers can produce four cars, so producing one car should only take three hours. The second work team adds six cars per day, implying that the cost of these cars is only one-sixth of a work team's day. In the parts of the production function where MPP is rising, marginal resource cost (the amount of resource input it takes to produce one additional unit of output) is falling.

But what happens when we add the third, fourth, and fifth work teams? We already know that MPP falls for each additional unit of labor after the second. The third work team only adds four cars to total output, implying a marginal resource cost of one-fourth of a labor unit per car. The fourth work team adds only two cars for a marginal cost of one-half of a labor unit per car. As MPP falls, marginal cost rises.

This increasing marginal cost, just like diminishing marginal returns, is a direct result of the constraints inherent to the short-run environment. As you hire more workers, they tend to get into each other's way and have to sit idle while other workers are using the limited fixed inputs. As a result the firm cannot put them to as efficient a use as they can earlier hires, and the amount of them you need to produce any additional unit of output increases.

IV. DOLLAR COSTS

Total Cost

Most businesses do not concern themselves with whether or not the cost of production in terms of resources is rising. They mostly concern themselves with dollar costs. That's not to say that the two are unrelated. Clearly if the amount of labor you have to hire to produce one car rises, the amount of dollars it takes to produce that car rises as well. We can transform the production function so that it reflects dollar costs rather than resource costs, and get a better idea about how and why costs rise.

Remember that profit is the difference between total revenue and total cost. Total cost is simply the market value of all the resources used in production. The production of cars by the car manufacturer includes land, labor, and capital. Their total costs then can be calculated by adding the value of the land, labor, and capital inputs used to produce any level of output.

Let's assume the automobile factory chooses point B on figure 15.2b and operates with one work team to produce four cars per day. Figure 15.3 indicates the costs that the firm will face to produce this amount. They already have a factory (which costs them $2,000 per day to rent) equipped with one assembly robot ($500 per day), and since these are fixed inputs they will have these inputs and the costs associated with them at any output level. They also need to hire one work team at $2,000 per day. Let's also assume that the workers need some amount of materials (a box of car parts), which cost $100 per car produced. With these assumptions we see that cost of producing four cars per day is $4,900.

Total Cost of Point B (Four cars per day)		
Resource Input	Price per unit	Total Cost
Fixed Inputs:		
1 Factory	$2,000	$2,000
1 Assembly Robot	$500	$500
Variable Inputs:		
1 Work Team	$2,000	$1,000
4 Boxes of Car Parts	$100 per car	$400
Total Cost		$4,900

Figure 15.3 • Calculating Total Cost
Producing cars consists of both fixed inputs and variable inputs. Variable inputs change with the amount of output, but fixed costs do not.

Fixed Costs

Since we are talking about the short run, some of the costs of production will rise as the car manufacturer increases the amount of cars per day from four to six to eight and so on, and some will not. We know that the firm is stuck with a factory of a given size and capital stock that does not change whether they produce zero cars or at capacity. The costs associated with these fixed inputs are called fixed costs. These fixed costs will be the same no matter how much the factory decides to produce. For the example in figure 15.3, the fixed costs are $2,500—the sum of the value of the fixed inputs used in production.

Variable Costs

Variable inputs, like labor and material costs, do change as the level of output changes. Short-run decisions are based on how varying the levels of these inputs affect output. As a result, the costs associated with inputs whose levels change with the output level are called variable costs. If the firm produces no output, variable costs will be zero. As they produce more and more output, variable costs rise.

Total costs, then, are the sum of the fixed costs plus the variable costs. Since fixed costs do not change with output, any change in total costs is completely due to changes in variable costs. The total cost curve in figure 15.4 also shows us that there is an absolute limit to production. When the car manufacturer uses one assembly robot, the most the factory can produce is sixteen cars per day. The next hired work team will add to costs but give no additional output. You can keep hiring work teams and drive costs up indefinitely, but you can never produce more than sixteen cars.

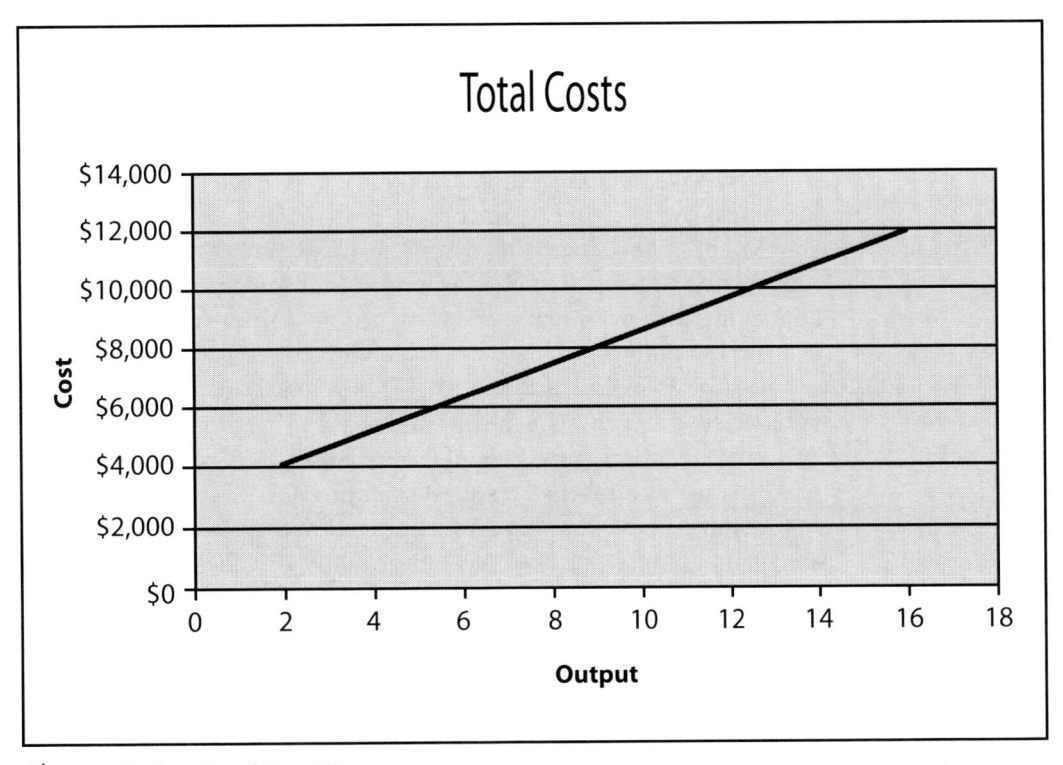

Figure 15.4 • **Total Cost Curve**
The total cost curve begins to get steeper as diminishing marginal returns kick in.

Average Costs

While total costs are important for understanding total profits, often businesses desire other measures of cost. One of the most common measures is the per-unit, or average cost. Calculating average costs is as simple as it sounds; you just divide total cost by total output.

$$\text{Average Total Costs} = \frac{\text{Total Costs}}{\text{Output}}$$

This figure tells you the average amount of money spent on the resources needed to produce a single unit of output produced to that point.

Just like total costs comes from the sum of fixed costs and variable costs at a certain output level, average total costs is the sum of average variable costs and average fixed costs at a given output level.

$$ATC = AVC + AFC$$

Both average fixed costs and average variable costs are derived the same way as average total costs: divide the total dollar cost by the output level.

$$AVC = \frac{\text{Variable Costs}}{\text{Output}}, AFC = \frac{\text{Fixed Costs}}{\text{Output}}$$

Average Fixed Costs Fall. Figure 15.5 contains the total and average cost information for the car manufacturer. Think about how average fixed costs are calculated: fixed costs divided by total output. Remember that fixed costs never change in the short run regardless of whether the output level is two cars per day or two hundred cars per day. As a result, what happens to average fixed costs as the output level rises? Just like any fraction when the numerator stays the same and the denominator gets bigger, average fixed cost falls as output rises.

Average Variable Costs Rise. Unlike AFC, AVC does not continue to decline as output increases. In fact, after a short drop, AVC begins to increase as output increases. This should not be too surprising since we already know that production exhibits diminishing marginal returns to increases in inputs at some point. As a result the amount of variable inputs you need to produce one unit of output (the per-unit cost) will begin to rise at the same point.

Average Total Cost Is U-Shaped. At low levels of production, fixed costs dominate variable costs. At these levels of output, AFC is falling (indeed, it is always falling) and AVC may be falling, too. Even if it isn't falling, AVC makes up a relatively smaller share of ATC at this point. As a result, ATC follows AFC and falls at low levels of production.

At some point, though, AVC begins to rise. As production increases, AVC makes up a bigger and bigger share of ATC. Eventually, ATC begins to follow AVC and rise as well. Combine this fact with the early drop in ATC and you get a typical U-shaped ATC curve as seen in figure 15.5a.

Minimizing Average Cost. The sheer amount of graphs and numbers in figure 15.5 seems intimidating, but some key landmarks can help us get our bearings. The bottom of the U-shaped ATC curve, the exact point where rising AVC takes over falling AFC, represents the lowest average cost possible. At this level of output the firm is paying the least per-unit production cost, given its possible choices.

(a)

Average Costs

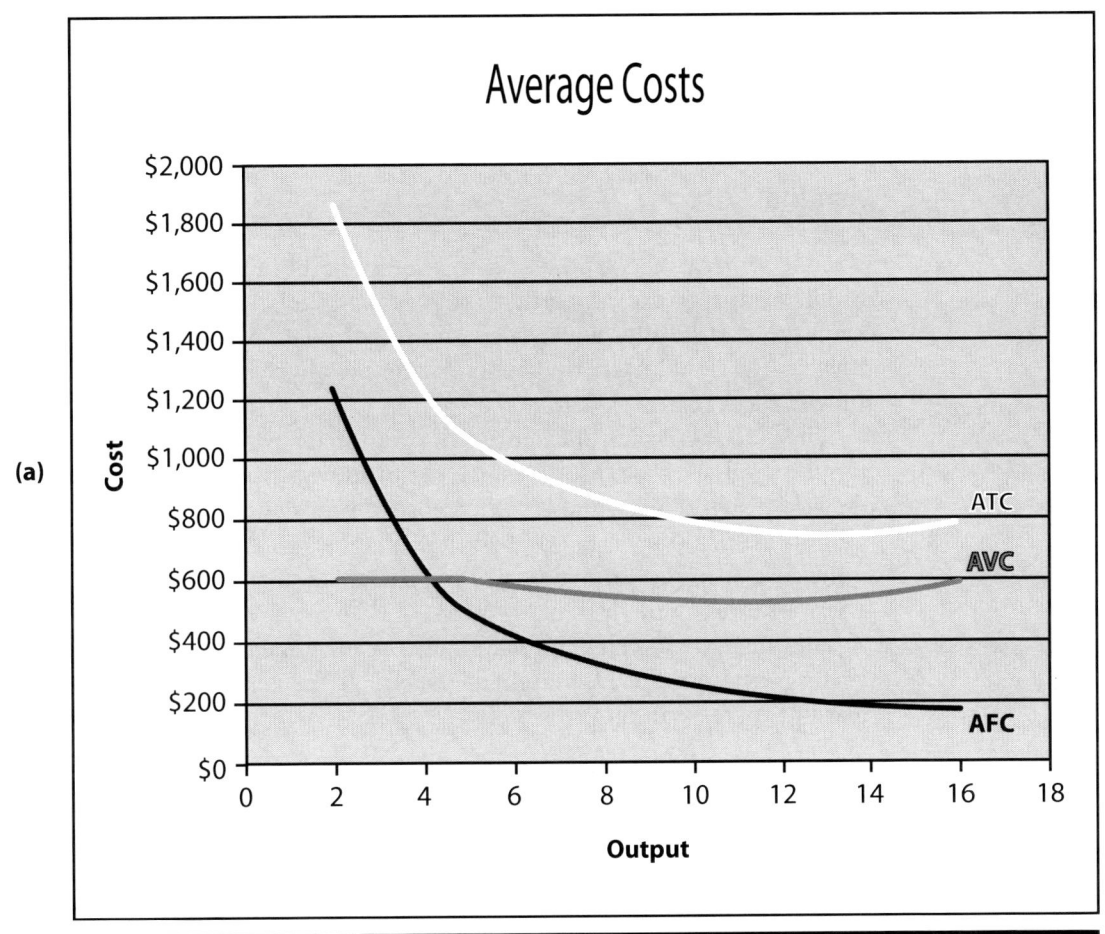

Output Level	Fixed Costs	Variable Costs	Total Cost	Average Fixed Cost	Average Variable Costs	Average Total Cost
0	$2,500	$0	$2,500	N/A	N/A	N/A
2	$2,500	$1,200	$3,700	$1,250	$600	$1,850
4	$2,500	$2,400	$4,900	$625	$600	$1,225
6	$2,500	$3,267	$5,767	$417	$544	$961
8	$2,500	$4,134	$6,634	$313	$517	$829
10	$2,500	$5,000	$7,500	$250	$500	$750
12	$2,500	$6,200	$8,700	$208	$517	$725
14	$2,500	$7,400	$9,900	$179	$529	$707
16	$2,500	$9,600	$12,100	$156	$600	$756

(b)

Figure 15.5 • **Average Costs**
Average total costs fall at low levels of output, but rise once average variable costs begin to dominate.

From the social standpoint, this is the output level at which we are getting cars for the lowest possible opportunity cost per car. There is no other output level at which you can produce a car for less resources (in terms of dollar value). But remember, firms are concerned about costs and revenues, so do not think that they will always produce at cost-minimizing level. This is no more accurate than assuming they always produce at

Marginal Cost

When it comes to the firm's decision about whether to produce one more unit of output or not, what they are concerned about is marginal cost—the cost of producing exactly one more unit. Earlier we learned about marginal cost in the context of resources and came to the conclusion that when marginal physical product is falling, marginal resource cost is rising.

There are two ways to calculate the marginal cost. First, we can simply calculate the monetary value of the resources used to produce one more unit of the good. For example, we know the marginal resource cost of producing the fifth car is one-sixth of a labor unit. At $2,000 per day, one-sixth of a labor unit costs approximately $333. Add this to the cost of the additional box of car parts you need ($100) and you see the marginal cost of producing the fifth car is $433.

Another way to calculate marginal cost is by measuring the change in total cost after the good is produced. Marginal cost equals the change in total cost associated with a one-unit increase in output.

$$\text{Marginal Cost} = \frac{\text{Change in Total Cost}}{\text{Change in Output}}$$

Instead of adding up the dollar value of the marginal resource cost, we could have just subtracted the total cost before the increase from the total cost after the increase. According to figure 15.6, the total cost at six cars is $5,767 and the total cost at four is $4,900. Dividing that difference by the change in output gives a marginal cost of $433, just as we calculated before. This type of calculation is typically easier for businesses,

Output Level	Total Cost	Marginal Cost
0	$2,500	N/A
2	$3,700	$600
4	$4,900	$600
6	$5,767	$433
8	$6,634	$433
10	$7,500	$433
12	$8,700	$600
14	$9,900	$600
16	$12,100	$1,100

Figure 15.6 • **Marginal Cost**
Marginal cost falls for every output level where MPP rises, and rises whenever MPP falls.

but it's important to understand that just like marginal resource cost, marginal cost increases when marginal physical product falls.

The Intersection of MC and ATC

An interesting thing happens when we graph MC (marginal cost) and ATC together as seen in figure 15.7. The MC curve always intersects the ATC curve at its lowest point, the minimum cost production level. The low point of the ATC curve is the exact point where ATC stops falling and starts rising. But why does it stop falling and start rising?

Whenever ATC is falling, the cost of producing the next unit is lower than the average per-unit cost. Think about what happens to the average height of individuals in a room when someone shorter than the average walks in—the average height falls. The same relationship exists between MC and ATC. But what does it mean for the cost of the last unit of output produced to be less than the average? That means MC is less than ATC.

We know that at some point MC rises and does not stop rising. At some point, then, MC will stop being less than ATC and be exactly equal to it. At any production level after this point, MC will be more than ATC and continue to drag the average up with it, causing ATC to rise. Therefore, ATC will never be lower than the point when the MC curve crossed it and started dragging it upwards.

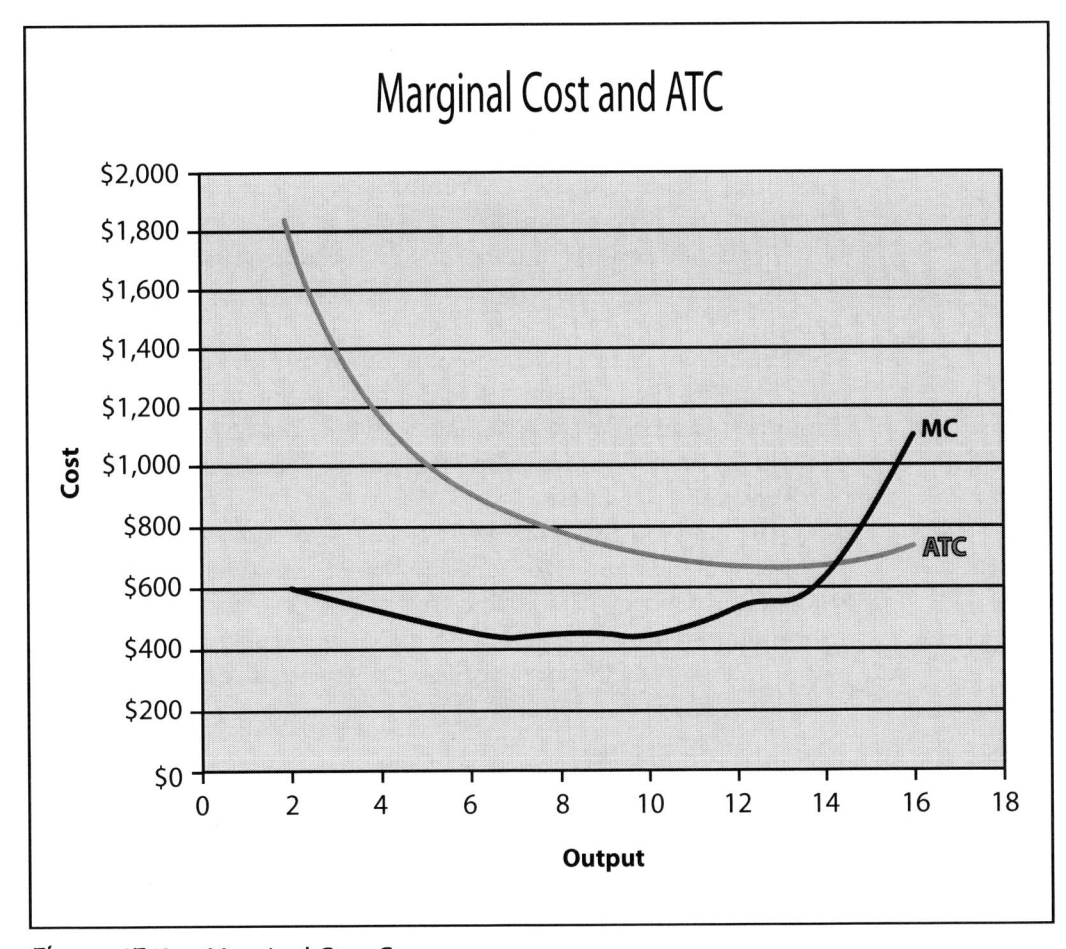

Figure 15.7 • Marginal Cost Curve
The MC curve always crosses the ATC curve at its minimum point.

V. ECONOMIC VS. ACCOUNTING COSTS

Explicit Cost

All the costs we have talked about so far assumed that the costs of production are related to the market value of the resources used in that production. For simplicity, we assumed that the car manufacturer rented the factory and equipment so that they actually paid something out to get those resources. The reason we did this is so dollar costs would equate with resource costs.

The actual amount of money spent on production, the explicit costs, does not necessarily have to equal the true cost of production. What if the car manufacturer owned the factory and didn't have to pay rent? What if the owner of the firm did not hire any workers and decided to put the cars together himself? Would producing a car be any cheaper? In terms of explicit costs, yes. Not having to pay rent on the factory saves the firm $2,000 in fixed costs at every output level. The cost of producing four cars per day, for example, falls from $4,900 to $2,900.

Economic Cost

Any company that could cut its production costs by over 40% would be hailed as geniuses. But we know there is more to the story. The true cost of production, the economic cost, is the value of the resources used in production. The fact that the company owns the factory and uses it to produce cars means that it cannot be used to produce anything else. Using it to produce cars foregoes the opportunity to rent it out to someone else and earn rent. Whether the firm owner writes a check or not, $4,900 worth of resources is still being used to produce those four cars. The only difference is that now the $2,000 factory is an implicit, or unseen, cost.

Economic cost, the total value of all resources used in production, is the sum of all explicit costs and implicit costs. While businesses and accountants only care about explicit costs (because they represent actual dollar outlays by the business), economists realize that implicit costs are important as well.

Think of the time you spend doing your homework, mowing the lawn, or washing your car. All of these are economic activities and have some value. You could pay someone to do these things for you and bear an explicit cost, but even if you don't you will still pay an implicit cost.

The time you give up to do these things could have been used in a variety of other activities, and the value of the next-best use of your time (your opportunity cost) is the economic cost you pay. The same is true for the car manufacturer. They could rent their factory out to someone else and earn $2,000 instead of using it to build cars. That $2,000 they don't receive when the they use the factory to produce cars is part of the cost of production.

VI. LONG-RUN COSTS

The Long Run

All of our discussions of costs so far have focused on the short run. Most business decisions are focused on making the best production decisions based on certain levels of fixed inputs—things like factory size and major capital investments that cannot be changed in a timely manner. The firm's job in the short run is to choose the best level of output given those fixed investments.

Not all business decisions are made in the short run, however. At some point, businesses get a chance to start all over with whatever production facilities they want; assuming they can afford it. In the long run, no inputs are fixed; businesses can change output by changing the level of any input, not just labor.

In the long run, the car manufacturer not only has to decide how many workers to hire, but also what size of factory it wants. Let's assume the firm has three choices: small, medium, and large. Obviously each of these choices has advantages and disadvantages. These advantages and disadvantages are related to the differences in the three ATC curves associated with the three factories.

Long-Run Average Costs

Figure 15.8 shows the short-run ATC curves associated with each of the choices. Since the small factory involves the lowest fixed costs, ATC starts off at a much lower level than the other two factories. The problem is, the factory is so small that it doesn't take long before peak capacity is reached and costs start to skyrocket. If you were planning on producing a lot of cars, you probably wouldn't want to choose this factory size. The large factory has the opposite problem. The ATC doesn't even begin to rise until way beyond

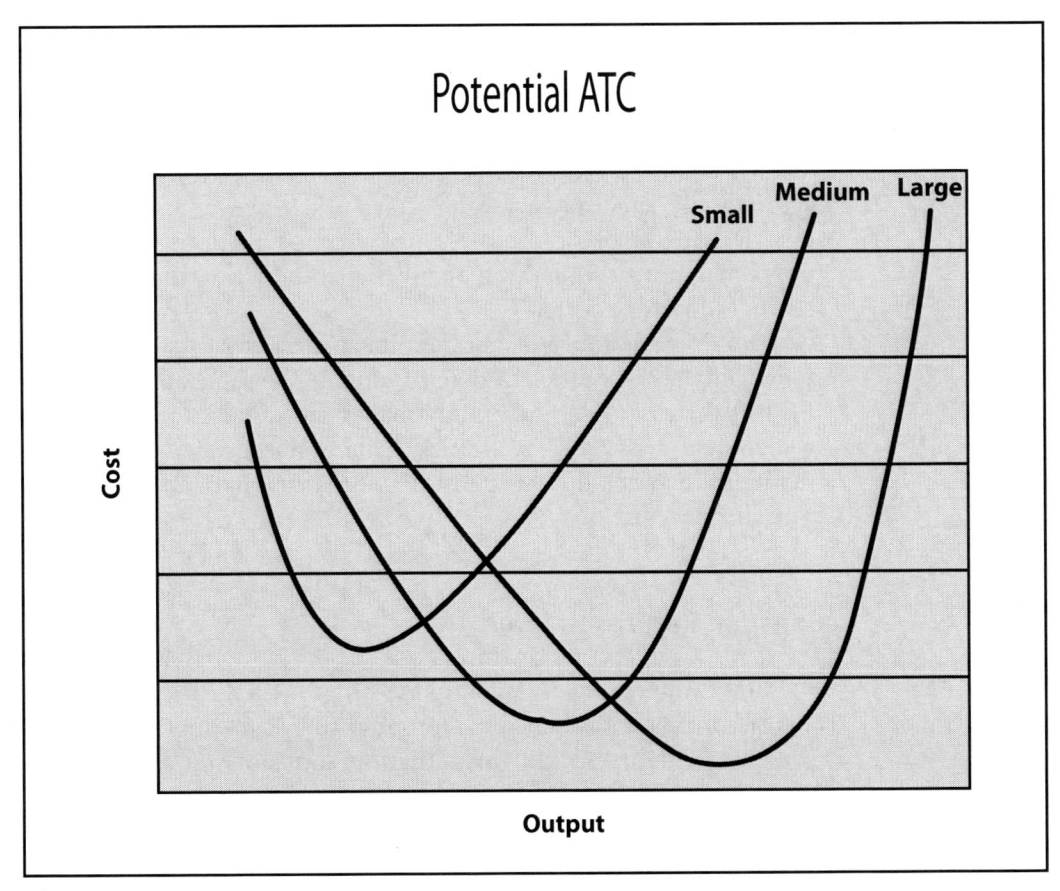

Figure 15.8 • Long Run ATC
Each potential factory the firm could choose has its own short-run ATC curve.

even the medium factory's capacity. On the other hand, the fixed costs for this factory are prohibitive if you only planned to build a few cars.

The medium curve lies in between these two extremes. The fixed costs associated with this factory size are certainly higher than the small factory's, but they are much lower than those of the large factory. This factory can also produce more before reaching peak capacity than the small factory can, but it falls short of the large factory's capacity. This factory is ideal for a large, but not too large, level of output.

How does the firm know which factory to choose? It should choose its desired output (the one that maximizes profit) and then choose whichever factory has the lowest ATC at that particular level. There will be a cutoff, call it a, where the production starts to overwhelm the small factory and it becomes cheaper to produce in the medium-sized factory. This cutoff occurs exactly where the small and medium factory ATC curves intersect. There will be another cutoff, b, where the medium and large factory ATC curves intersect and it will then be cheaper to use the larger factory.

In fact the firm's long-run ATC curve is constructed by connecting the three of these cutoff points. For the time when the small factory is the cheapest, the small factory's short-run ATC curve is the firm's long-run ATC curve, and so on. In reality, a firm does not only have three choices of factory size; it can choose a factory of any size. The long-run ATC curve is then simply a series a points; the minimum cost points of an infinite number of short-run ATC curves from an infinite number of potential factory size choices.

VII. ECONOMIES OF SCALE

When it comes to long-run production, sometimes the decision is not between a large factory and a small factory. Sometimes a firm has a certain output level in mind and must decide whether to produce it in one large factory or several smaller facilities. Businesses may notice something about their production that leads them to believe bigger may not always be better.

Many production processes exhibit economies of scale; producing in one centralized facility is more efficient than producing the same amount at several small facilities. If this is the case, then it certainly makes more sense for a firm to produce at one large factory than at several small ones. This is not always the case, however. In fact, figure 15.9 illustrates the three distinct scenarios that can occur when a firm chooses to centralize production.

Constant Returns to Scale

The first thing that can happen is nothing. If the firm can produce twenty cars in two factories for the same cost it can produce forty cars in one factory, there is no advantage to centralization. We call this situation constant returns to scale production. Figure 15.9a shows that in a constant returns to scale scenario, the short-run ATC curve for the small factory and the larger factory have the same minimum cost level, so there is no cost savings from centralizing production.

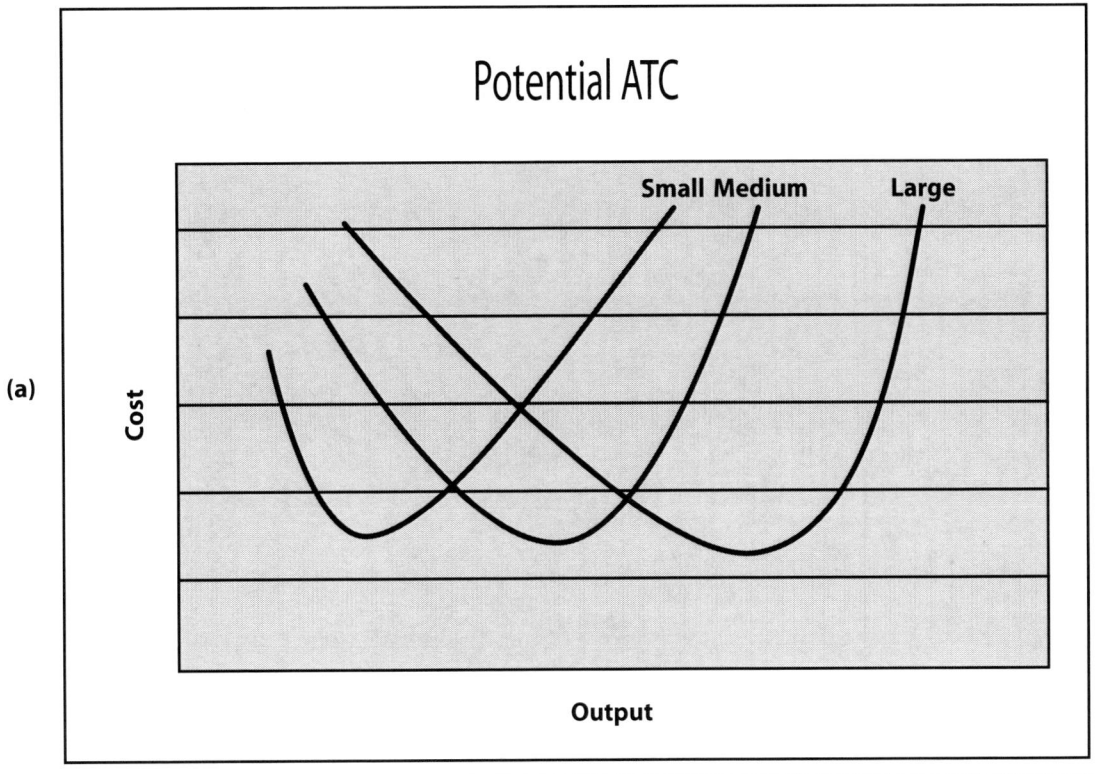

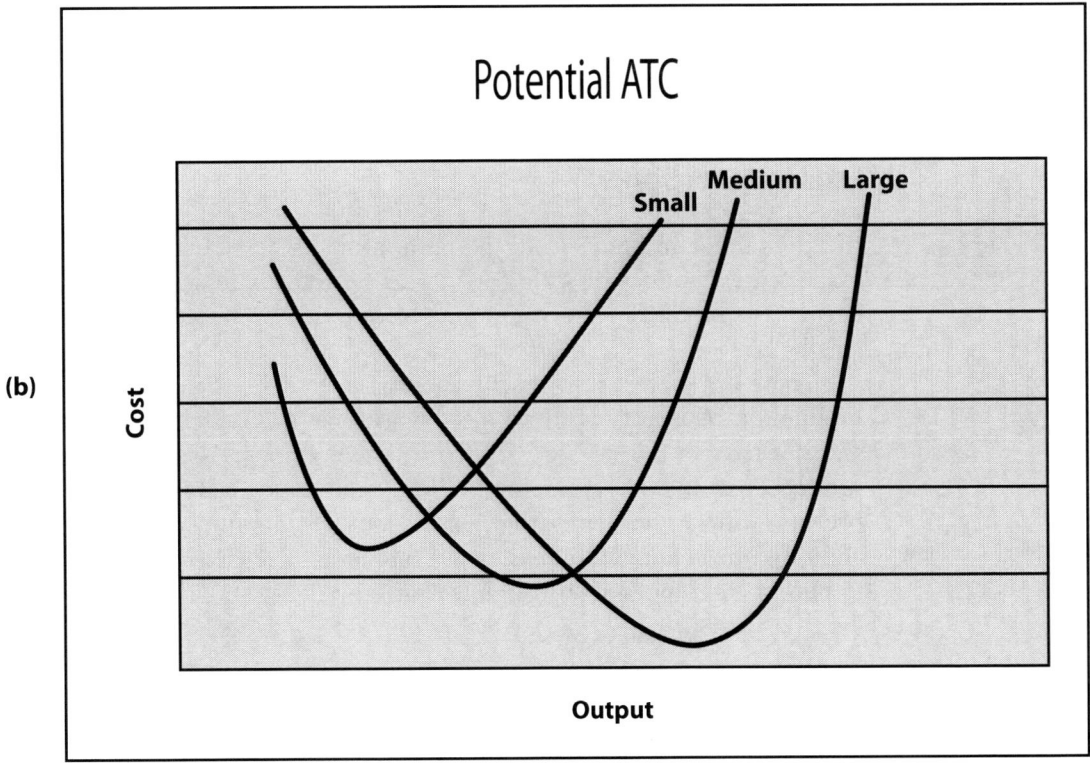

Figure 15.9 • **Returns to Scale**
A, Constant Returns to Scale. In constant returns to scale, the size of the factory has no bearing on the minimum ATC. **B, Increasing Returns to Scale.** Increasing returns to scale occurs when producing at a larger facility is cheaper than producing at a smaller one.

Continued.

(c)

Potential ATC

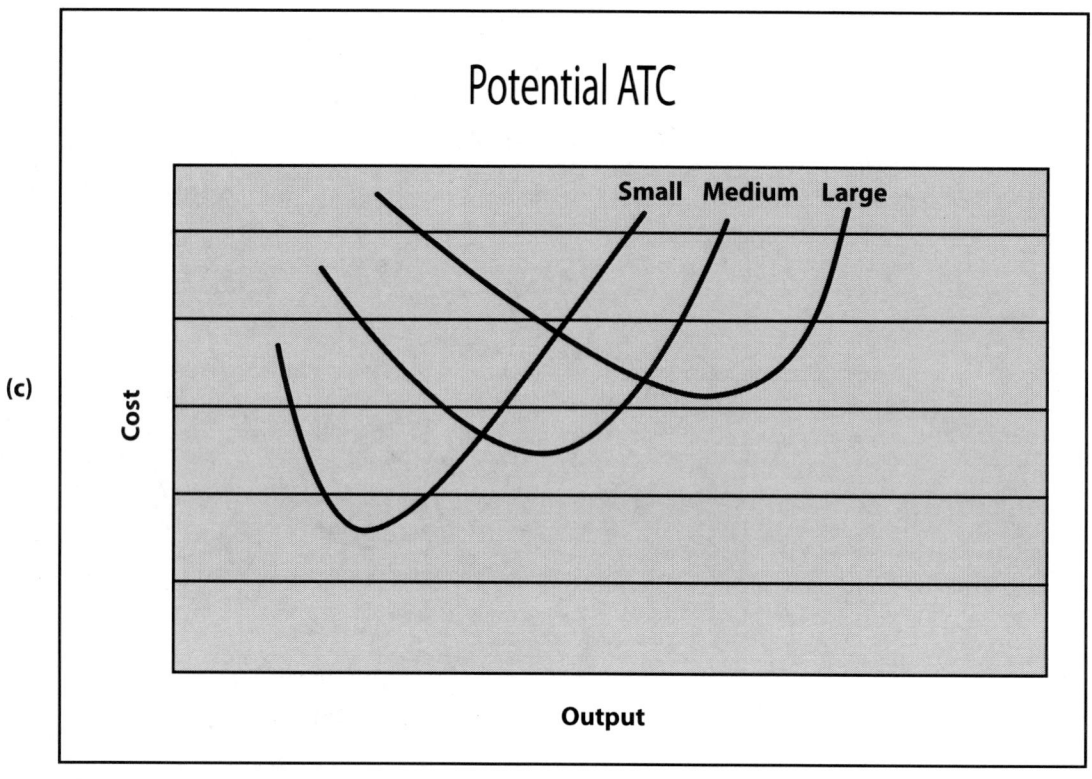

[Graph showing Cost vs Output with three U-shaped curves labeled Small, Medium, Large, with minimums rising from left to right]

Figure 15.9 • **Returns to Scale,** *continued.*
C, Decreasing Returns to Scale. Decreasing returns to scale occurs when producing at a larger facility is more expensive than producing at a smaller one.

Economies of Scale

In the example in figure 15.8, the minimum cost level fell as the factory size increased exhibited economies of scale (or increasing returns to scale). In this case it would be cheaper to produce a given amount of output at one large factory instead of several small ones.

There are many reasons why increasing returns to scale occurs in some forms of production. A factory with a bigger workforce has a greater opportunity to specialize and not have one person do several different things. Also the sheer volume of output produced at the larger factory allows it to take advantage of certain production processes and technologies that just are not feasible to use at lower levels of output. In addition, the greater volume they put out allows the factory workers ample opportunity to perfect their methods through learning-by-doing.

Diseconomies of Scale

As I said before though, bigger is not always better. In particular, a larger factory is not necessarily more efficient. Many firms today have gotten so large that workers can feel like a faceless cog in a machine. This lack of connection lowers morale and productivity. Larger firms also tend to exhibit a bureaucracy that stifles innovation. A smaller factory on the other hand might have more of a family atmosphere that fosters teamwork and growth. If the costs of production rise with the factory size, as in figure 15.9c, you have diseconomies of scale (or decreasing returns to scale).

CHAPTER 15 SUMMARY

- The **production function** describes how effectively a business turns factors of production into output.
- In the **short run**, we assume that the land and capital inputs are fixed—labor is the only input that can be changed.
- Since the other factors are fixed, the amount of additional output produced by an additional labor input—**marginal physical product**—falls at some point.
- When MPP falls, **marginal costs rise.**
- Total Costs = Fixed Costs + Variable Costs
- $Average\ Total\ Costs = \dfrac{Total\ Costs}{Output}$
- $AVC = \dfrac{Variable\ Costs}{Output}, AFC = \dfrac{Fixed\ Costs}{Output}$
- The ATC curve is **U-shaped.**
- $Marginal\ Cost = \dfrac{Change\ in\ Total\ Cost}{Change\ in\ Output}$
- Marginal cost crosses ATC at the **minimum level of ATC.**
- **Economic costs** include the value of all resources used in production.
- In the **long run**, no inputs are fixed.
- Centralizing all production in a single, large factory is only cost-minimizing if the industry exhibits **increasing returns to scale.**

CHAPTER 15 Exercises

Name _____

1) Which of the following statements is true about the production function?
   A) It represents the minimum amount firms can produce with current resources.
   B) It shows the dollar cost of different output levels.
   C) It expresses the maximum output attainable from various combinations of inputs.
   D) It always slopes in a straight line.

1) _____

2) The law of diminishing returns occurs with each additional unit of a variable input when
   A) total output begins to decline.
   B) total output reaches zero.
   C) marginal physical product becomes negative.
   D) marginal physical product begins to decline.

2) _____

3) In the short run, the law of diminishing returns
   A) can be overcome by hiring more inputs.
   B) only happens in poor countries.
   C) causes total output to become negative.
   D) will occur in every production process.

3) _____

4) Assuming each unit of variable inputs cost the same, marginal cost will increase as output increases if
   A) variable cost is rising.
   B) total cost is rising.
   C) marginal physical product is rising.
   D) marginal physical product is falling.

4) _____

5) In the short run, when a firm produces zero output, total cost equals
   A) fixed costs.
   B) variable costs.
   C) zero.
   D) average total cost.

5) _____

6) Economic cost includes
   A) only the value of resources used to produce a good for which a monetary payment is made.
   B) the value of all resources used to produce a good.
   C) only implicit costs.
   D) only explicit costs.

6) _____

7) If an industry exhibits economies of scale
   A) factory size makes no difference, lowest cost production will always be achieved.
   B) it would be better to produce at several small factories.
   C) it would be better to produce at one large factory.
   D) minimum ATC is higher at a large factory than at a small one.

7) _____

275

8) The best measure of the economic cost of any activity is 8) _____
   A) the amount you would have to pay to do it.
   B) the economics cost plus the accounting cost.
   C) the most valuable opportunity you give up to do it.
   D) only explicit costs.

9) Why does marginal cost always cross the ATC curve at its lowest point?

_____
_____
_____
_____

Chapter 16

Producer Theory: The Competitive Firm

I. THE PROFIT MOTIVE

Businesses produce goods and services with the expectation that they will receive profits. Businesses are not benevolent agencies that produce to make people happy; they produce to make money. Profits, the difference between revenues (money coming into the business) and costs (money leaving the business) can either flow to the sole owner of a private business or the shareholders of public corporations. Either way, the pursuit of profits is the incentive that makes the owner of a business continue to operate.

Other Motivations

Still, there are some non-monetary benefits of business ownership. Many small business owners are forgoing higher incomes, better benefits, and easier working conditions for the stress and long hours of ownership. The status and power afforded a business owner can be a powerful lure as well.

In public corporations, on the other hand, the shareholders, the actual owners of the firm, do not usually make production decisions. Instead the shareholders hire executives to manage the day-to-day business of the firm. These executives may not have any direct stake in the firm's profitability; instead they make production decisions that elevate their own status, possibly at the expense of the firm's profits.

We call this conflict of interest the principal-agent problem. Whenever a firm hires someone to manage its interests, it is difficult to tell if they are working toward their own goals or the firm's. Most modern corporations get around this problem by pegging much of the executives' compensation to profitability through bonuses and stock options. In the end, it is still the pursuit of profits that drives the business to produce.

Is the Profit Motive Bad?

Studies consistently show that the general public mistrusts the profit motive as the coordinator of economic activity. The problem is that without the profit motive very few people would supply goods and services. There would be a few people who would teach, make clothes, or fix cars for free, but not enough to satisfy the market demand for these products. Without the profit motive guiding economic activity we would turn inward; making our own clothes, growing our own food, and so on. Economic activity would grind to a halt to the point that supporting the sheer number of people on the planet would be infeasible. Article 16.1 describes some of the life-saving activities that would not be possible without the profit motive.

Article 16.1:
The Multi-nationals Save Lives
By Dr. Anthony Daniels

Published: 12:00AM BST 22 Apr 2001

WE like to divide everything neatly into good and evil. It assures us that life on earth has a moral meaning that it would otherwise lack. Moreover, we prove our virtue by denouncing vice and our generosity by hating greed.

For many years, the large pharmaceutical companies have been, for all right-thinking people, symbols of capitalist rapacity, second only in their wickedness to the tobacco companies. What could be more heartless than to make large profits from human suffering? The defeat of these companies in South Africa on the question of the sale of cheap generic drugs for the treatment of Aids has therefore been widely seen as a victory for decency, compassion and justice.

In the eternal struggle between good and evil, the expensive patented drugs manufactured by multi-national pharmaceutical companies have come to represent all that is evil, while the cheap (or cheaper) generic drugs manufactured by smaller drug companies have come to represent all that is good. The division could not be clearer.

The companies that manufacture generic drugs are driven by the profit motive as surely as the multi-nationals. They, too, make profits from human suffering. Their return on capital invested is much the same as that of the larger companies, though of course they deploy much smaller sums. Personally I doubt whether this represents a morally relevant difference.

The multi-nationals are portrayed as blood-sucking parasites, feeding off human misery. But if that is the case, then the companies that produce generic drugs are feeding off the pharmaceutical multi-nationals' expenditure on research. Is the parasite of your parasite really your friend?

The hatred of the multi-nationals is, at heart, an old-fashioned hatred of the profit motive, a protest at a world in which "it is not from the benevolence of the butcher, the brewer, or the baker, that we expect our dinner." It is a protest against the complexity of a world in which good results do not necessarily result from the best motives, or bad results from discreditable ones. The lesson is a perennially unpalatable one, an affront to our vanity.

Questions:
1. What motivates both patented drug and generic drug manufacturers?
2. How do generic drug manufacturers eat away at the expected profits of patented drug makers?
3. What effect would allowing generic drug manufacturers to consistently violate patents have on the development of new drugs?

© Telegraph Media Group Limited 2009

Without some kind of reward, people will not willingly use their scarce resources for the production of the goods and services we all desire. Doubtless, the profit motive creates an incentive for business to pollute, restrict competition, and mistreat their workers—and those forces need be kept in check. On the other hand, the profit motive also acts as the invisible hand of the market mechanism, encouraging businesses to produce the goods and services people want at prices they are willing to pay in order to make money. One can understand the motivation for wanting to overturn the profit motive as our allocation mechanism; but without some alternative, the cost of getting rid of the profit motive is just not worth the benefits.

II. ECONOMIC VS. ACCOUNTING PROFITS

While the common perception is that businesses are exploiting workers and consumers and making exorbitant profits, the reality is that the average person has no idea what kind of profits the average firm earns. Surveys show that people believe that 35 percent of every dollar earned by businesses through sales goes to profit. The actual average is closer to 5 cents per dollar of sales, seven times smaller. The major disparity comes from the fact that most people, including business owners and accountants, do not distinguish between economic profits and accounting profits.

Economic Profits

Miscalculation. The formula for profits is a simple one: total revenue minus total costs. So how can there be any confusion when it comes to calculating it? The problem comes with what we count as part of total cost. Recall the treatment of accounting costs and economic costs in Chapter 15. Since most people view total costs as being equivalent to accounting costs, perceptions about total costs tend to be understated.

In other words, they completely ignore the implicit costs related to resources used in production that might already be owned by the firm. Since these resources make up part of the economic cost of productions, businesses often understate the true cost of production by not including their cost as part of total cost.

Looking at the formula for profits (total revenue minus total cost) we see that any understating of costs will lead to an overstating of profits. Parts of these inflated accounting profits (profits based on explicit costs only) are actually compensation to the resources used in production that already belong to the firm owner and therefore were not explicitly paid for. Economic profit, then, equals accounting profit minus implicit cost where accounting profit equals total revenue minus explicit costs only.

$$Accounting\ Profit = Total\ Revenue - Explicit\ Costs$$
$$Economic\ Profit = Accounting\ Profit - Implicit\ Costs$$

As an example, let's think of a business owner running a flower shop. As the table of his costs in figure 16.1 indicates, he needs a store location, pots, flowers, a cashier, and someone in the back to put the arrangements together in order to make his business work. He also has to pay utilities and taxes on his building and sales. Which of these costs are explicit and which are implicit? The answer depends on which resources he owns, and which he has to hire.

Let's assume that he rents his building, hires a cashier, and buys his pots and plants from a wholesaler. Instead of hiring someone to work in the back, though, he decides to

Balance Sheet for Fred's Fabulous Flowers	
Revenue	$8,000
Explicit Costs:	
Rent on Store	$1,000
Pots and Flowers	$3,000
Taxes	$200
Cashier	$1,000
Total	$5,200
Implicit Costs:	
Foregone Wages	$1,500
Forgone Interest	$800
Total	$2,300
Economic Costs	$7,500

Accounting Profit	$8,000 − $5,200 = $2,800
Economic Profit	$8,000 − $7,500 = $500

Figure 16.1 • Accounting Profit vs. Economic Profit
While Fred does not have to write a check to anyone for the foregone wages and interest, that money is not in his pocket because he chooses to invest his labor and capital into his business and it therefore represents a real cost.

save on labor cost and make the arrangements himself. According to figure 16.1, he has to pay $1,000 a month for rent and utilities on the building, $1,000 a month on paying wages to his cashier, $3,000 a month on the merchandise for his shop, and $200 a month on taxes. In total, he has to pay $5,200 a month just to keep his business open. This $5,200 represents his explicit cost since he has to actually pay this money out to some factor owner.

How much profit is this business owner making if his monthly revenue from the shop is $8,000? If has to pay out $5,200 a month in expenses, he will have $2,800 left over every month. This figure represents his accounting profit, not his economic profit. The $2,800 does not take into account the implicit costs in figure 16.1.

The business owner is saving on explicit costs by making the arrangements himself and not hiring a worker to do it, but the work still needs to be done. By doing it himself, he is forgoing the additional income he could have had working as an arranger at someone else's flower shop. Assuming he could have made $1,500 a month working at another flower shop, we need to subtract this from accounting profits.

What about the thousands of dollars he pumps into this store every month to purchase pots and plants? He could have easily invested this money in another company or bank account and earned interest on it. We also need to subtract this lost interest from accounting profit as well. Let's assume this forgone interest income equals $800 per month as indicated in figure 16.1. Now we can subtract the implicit costs ($1,500 in foregone wages and $800 in foregone interest income) from accounting profit to find the flower shop owner's economic profit. In the end, the flower shop only comes out $500 ahead.

Normal Profits. To understand whether the flower shop is successful or not we need to know whether or not the profits earned from it are higher than the owner's next-best use of his resources (working and investing in another business). Economic profit will only be positive if operating the business earns more than its opportunity cost. Economic profits need to represent the value of operating the firm over and above the "normal profit" that can be earned simply by investing in an average business. In our example the business owner is earning $500 more (his economic profit) by running his business, than he could earn by simply working in another flower shop and investing his money into the stock market, a bank account, or another business.

Entrepreneurship and Risk

While every business owner wants his or her business to earn an economic profit, it just isn't possible. In fact, as we will see a little later, perfect competition requires the average level of economic profit to be zero. So, for every business earning positive economic profits, there has to be a business losing money.

In order to be one of the businesses earning positive profits, Fred the flower shop owner can't just be one of the pack. He needs to have something special to offer; a new product, a better production process, better customer service, or just something a little different. Those who innovate will be rewarded with economic profits. In fact, economic profits can be thought of as the payment to entrepreneurship.

In our flower shop example, the owner makes enough to cover his expenses, so clearly there is a demand for flower shop services in the area. But why would the owner take on the stress and responsibility of running a business when he can make $2,300 working and investing in another business? It is exactly the $500 in economic profit that lures him to business ownership.

If there were no potential for economic profit (income above what he would earned without the business) he would have no incentive to take on the risk of running his own business. Remember that there is risk involved; there is no guarantee of economic profits, only an opportunity for it. If sales revenue at the shop fell below $7,500, for example, economic profit would be negative and the owner would be better off without the business even though there would still be some accounting profit.

III. MARKET STRUCTURE

Imperfect Competition

The fact that there are many flower shops in town (that is, the owner is in a competitive market) makes it more difficult for the flower shop to earn an economic profit. The structure of the flower market is such that to earn an economic profit you need to differentiate yourself from your competitors. In less competitive market structures, however, earning an economic profit may be much simpler.

Monopoly. In a monopoly, for example, a single seller controls the entire market supply of the good; if consumers want the good they must buy it from the monopolist. As a result the monopolist can raise prices without the fear of losing customers to competitors, and rake in the profits.

As with most spectra in economics, few firms in the real world fit into the extreme categories of perfect competition or monopolies. Even when monopolies do exist, the government tends to act quickly to eliminate the firm's market power. Most firms operate in a market characterized by imperfect competition. Firms in an imperfectly competitive market hold some power to control prices, but only limited power.

Duopoly and Oligopoly. A duopoly is a market structure where two firms—not one as in a monopoly—control the market supply. The soda market, with Coke and Pepsi dominating, is an example. Many different scenarios can occur in a duopoly depending on whether the firms compete or work together. The amount that the firms sell will depend not only on how consumers will respond, but on how the other firm will respond as well.

An oligopoly is a slightly more competitive market structure than a duopoly. In an oligopoly, a small number of firms (but more than two) control the supply of the good. The financial services market is an example of an oligopoly, with large banks such as Chase, Bank of America, and Citibank controlling the market. Again, these firms will have to act strategically in order to gain profits without drawing the wrath of their competitors.

Monopolistic Competition. Most firms, though, operate in monopolistically competitive markets. In this type of market there are many firms, but their products are just different enough for them to be able to raise prices without worrying about losing all of their customers. The fast food industry, with its many different choices, is a classic example of monopolistic competition. We will discuss each of these market structures in depth in their own chapters, but for now let us focus on the perfectly competitive environment.

Features of Perfect Competition

Structure. Perfect competition has certain specific characteristics that distinguish it from the other market structures. First, a perfectly competitive market has many firms. Unlike a monopoly, duopoly, or oligopoly, a perfect competitive market consists of many firms that have little or no market power: no one firm can affect the price through independent action.

A perfectly competitive market also differs from the market structures with few firms in that there are little or no barriers to entry and exit. If a company has a monopoly they will set up many roadblocks to prevent competition from entering the market. In perfect competition, firms are so busy just trying to earn a profit that there are no resources to set up these barriers and it is relatively easy for a new firm to enter, or an old one to exit.

Perfect competition differs from monopolistic competition in that all the firms in a perfectly competitive market sell identical products. Because products in a monopolistically competitive market are slightly different, firms can control prices to a degree and customers will still keep coming back; this is not the case with perfect competition.

Price Taking. Because there are many firms selling the exact same product, no one firm can raise its price in order to rake in greater profits; people will just stop shopping there and go somewhere else. In this sense, all firms in a perfectly competitive market are price takers; they sell the product for whatever the market will bear. Any higher and they will lose all of their business to a competitor. In other words, firms in a perfectly competitive market have no market power.

Of course, the firm has the option of raising the price of its product above the market price, but no one will buy it and the market price (the average price the product actually sells for in the market) will remain unchanged. Imagine at the end of the semester you want to sell your textbooks back to the bookstore. With so many other students trying to sell books, you have no market power and have to accept the going price. You can ask the bookstore to pay full price for it, but they will refuse and you will get nothing.

One lone producer in a perfectly competitive market cannot change the market price by altering his production decisions either. No matter how much they reduce or increase their output, the impact on market supply will be so small that there will be no increase or decrease in market price.

Demand Curve Facing a Single Firm. Since the perfectly competitive firm will lose all of its customers if it raises its prices, it is safe to assume that the firm faces a perfectly elastic (horizontal) demand curve as in figure 16.2a. The firm can sell as much output as it wants at the competitive price, but will sell zero at any price above. Changes in the firm's output have no effect on market supply and therefore no effect on market price. Selling at a price below the market price is not a good idea either. If the firm becomes the price leader, every buyer in the market will come to them. Unfortunately, a single firm cannot handle that type of demand. Costs will skyrocket as the firm hires more and more workers trying to keep up with demand, causing profits to fall.

From the standpoint of the market, though, the demand curve is still downward sloping as figure 16.2b shows. If all the firms at once decide to increase production, supply will shift to the right causing a movement down along the market demand. Each individual firm is powerless to affect changes in market price, but the changes we do see are caused by collective response to external factors—the determinants of supply.

284 ECONOMICS TODAY

(a)

Market for Flowers

(b)

Market for a Single Firm

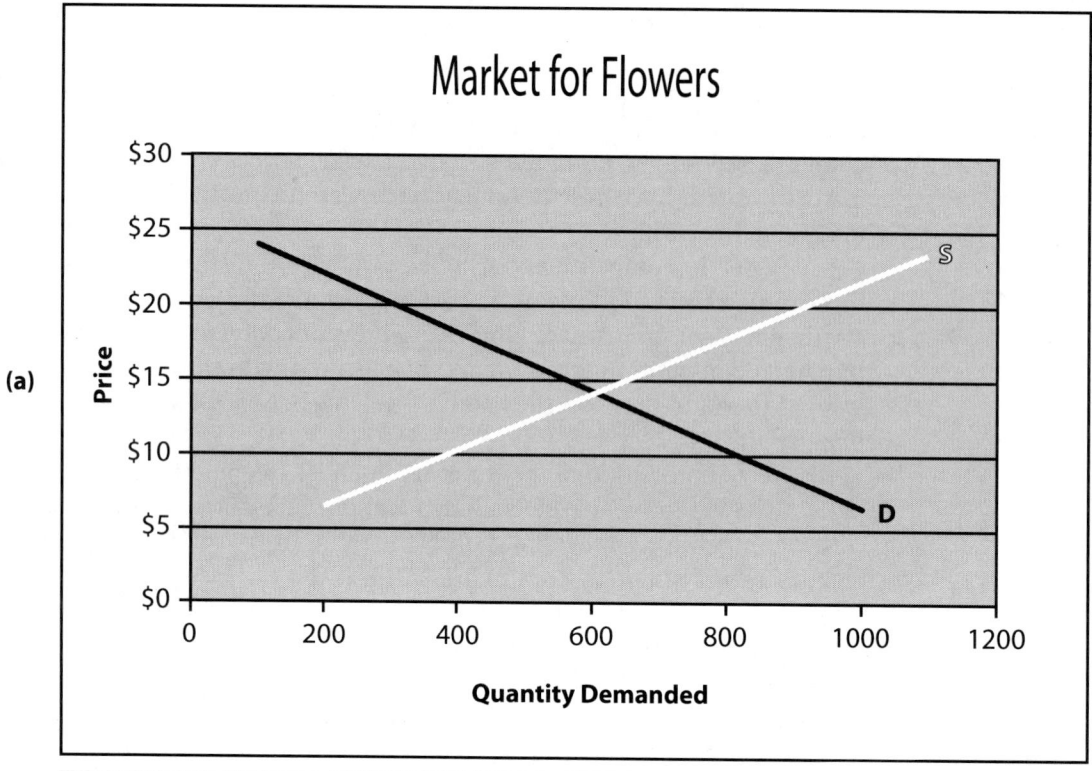

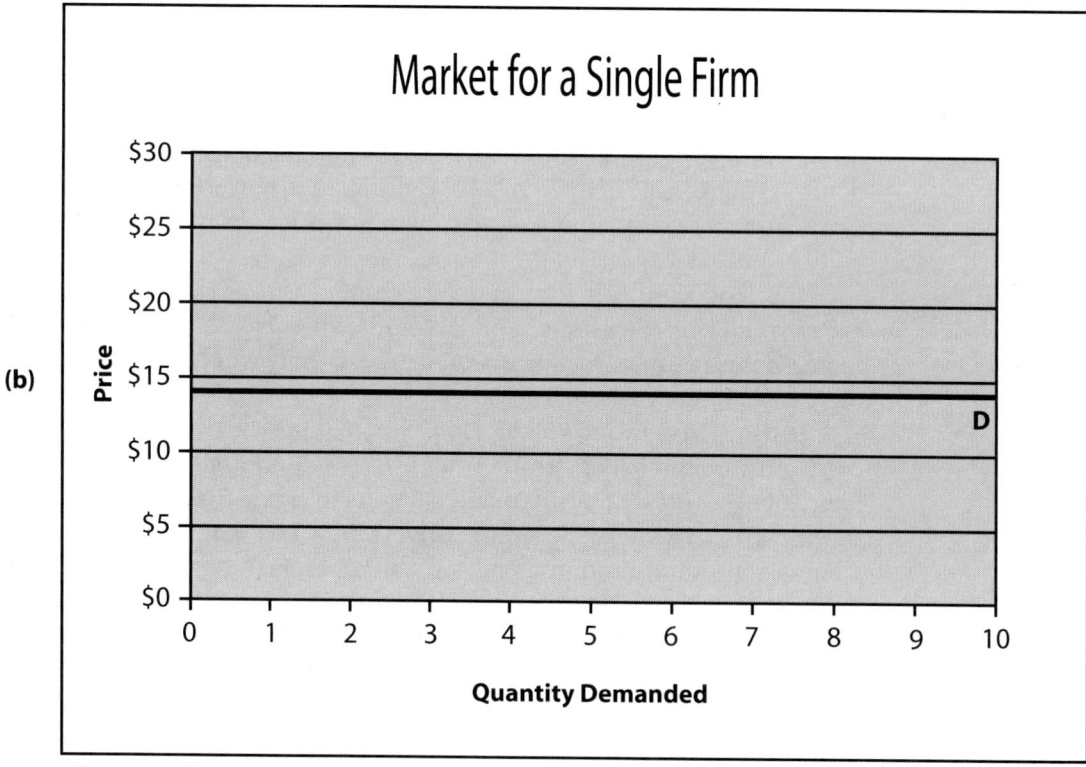

Figure 16.2 • **Market Demand and Firm Demand**
The perfectly competitive firm faces a perfectly elastic demand curve. They can sell as much as they want at the market price, but cannot sell any amount at any other price.

IV. THE PRODUCTION DECISION

Output and Revenues

Since the competitive firm cannot change prices, its only decision is how much to produce. Should the firm produce where cost is minimized? Should it produce as much as possible in order to maximize revenue? Or should it produce at some other point entirely? It may be tempting to think that the firm should produce at its factory's capacity, after all that is how the firm will bring in the most money. Remember, though, that the firm's goal is to maximize profit (the difference between revenue and cost) not just total revenue. The firm will maximize its profits when the total revenue and total costs curves are as far apart as possible.

Since we know exactly how much the firm will earn for every unit it sells, the market price, its total revenue will simply be this price times the amount of output it sells. In other words, the total revenue curve for a competitive firm will be a straight, upward-sloping curve with the slope equal to the market price for every output level as figure 16.3 illustrates.

Output and Costs

We also know that total costs vary with output, and these costs will influence the firm's production decision as well. In the short run, the business faces certain fixed costs that

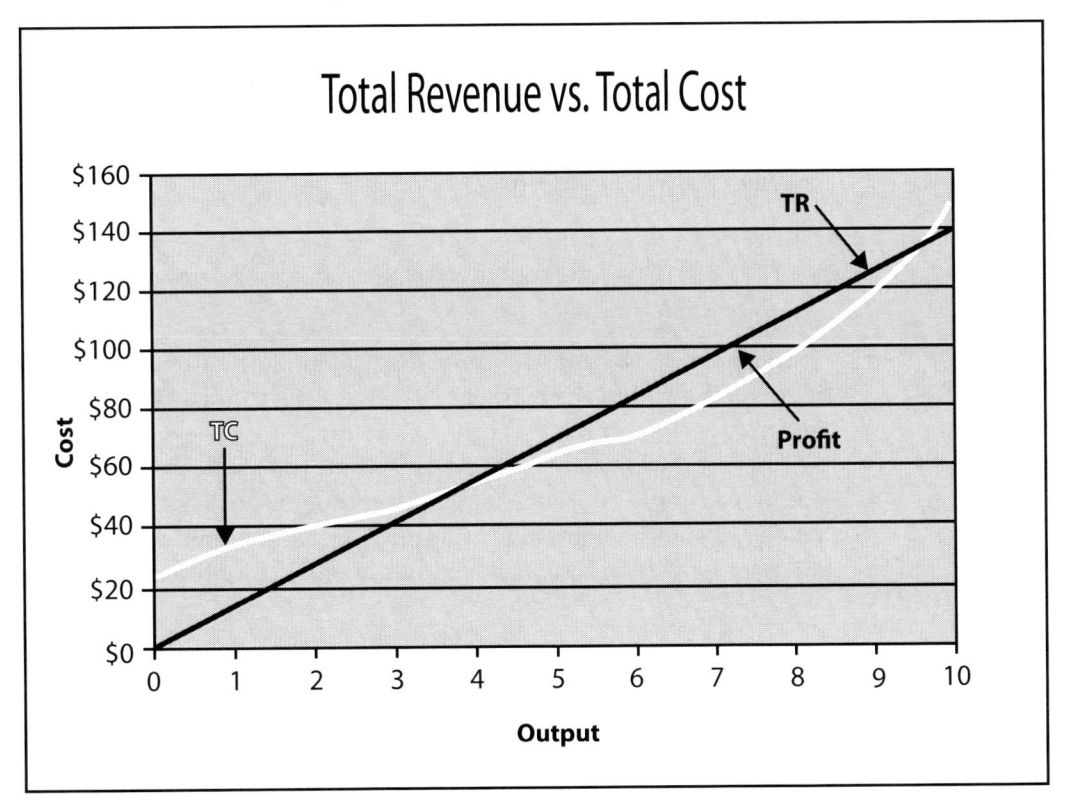

Figure 16.3 • Total Revenue and Total Costs
When total revenue is above total cost, the vertical distance between the two curves is the firm's total profit.

do not change with output, as well as variable costs that increase as output increases. Since variable costs change as output changes, the total cost curve will not be a straight line. This will cause it to have some interesting interactions with the total revenue curve.

Because of diminishing marginal returns the total cost will be steeper at high output levels and flatter at low output levels. Because of high average fixed costs, total costs often exceed total revenue at low output levels. Also, since costs tend to skyrocket near the maximum output level, total costs exceed total revenues at very high output levels as well.

In some range in the middle, total revenues might exceed total costs. This area is where the firm is profitable. So the key to maximizing profits is finding the output level in the profitable range where the vertical distance between the total revenue curve and the total cost is the largest. Of course, there may never be a range where total revenues exceed total costs. In this case, the best the firm owner can do is minimize firm losses by finding the output level where the distance between the curves is the smallest.

V. THE PROFIT-MAXIMIZING RULE

Marginal Revenue Equals Price

The best way for a firm to ensure it is making profit-maximizing decisions in the short run is quite easy: Never produce a unit of output that costs more than it brings in. This profit-maximizing rule incorporates marginal decision-making; only produce if the marginal revenue of the next unit of production exceeds the marginal cost.

As a result, in the short run the only things the business needs to know to maximize profits are marginal revenue and marginal cost. Marginal revenue is the amount of money brought in by the next unit of output produced; that is, how much the next unit of output will add to total revenue. Much like marginal cost, marginal revenue is calculated by subtracting total revenue before the last unit was produced from the total revenue after it was produced.

$$\text{Marginal Revenue} = \frac{\text{Change in Total Revenue}}{\text{Change in Output}}$$

For a competitive firm, we know that the amount of revenue brought in by every unit they sell is equal to the market price. Since the firm faces a horizontal demand curve, it will always sell its product at the market price regardless of whether it is the first, tenth, or hundredth unit they've sold. As a result the change in total revenue after selling an additional unit of output, marginal revenue, is always equal to the market price for a competitive firm. Note that this is only the case for perfectly competitive firms; firms in all other market structures have slightly more complicated marginal revenue curves.

$$\text{Marginal Revenue} = \text{Price}$$

Marginal Cost

Knowing how much each additional unit of output brings in to the firm is only half of the problem; we also need to know how much each unit costs to produce. Considering what we already know about diminishing marginal returns and the shape of the total cost curve, you can probably guess that it is going to be a little trickier than calculating marginal revenue.

Let's start off by assuming the flower shop's fixed costs (the building) are $25 per hour. The owner must pay these fixed costs regardless of how much he produces, but his variable costs change as the output changes. As a result, his total costs change as output changes. Due to diminishing marginal returns, we expect that as you hire more workers, the amount they add to total production will fall. As a result, it takes more labor time to produce additional output as output rises. And since labor time equals money, marginal costs rise as output increases. Figure 16.4, which summarizes the costs faced by the flower shop, bears this out.

Profit-Maximizing Level of Output

If we know that the market price, and therefore the marginal revenue, for a bouquet of flowers is $14 (from figure 16.2) we have the information we need to make a profit-maximizing decision. We know that the flower shop does not ever want to produce a unit of output that brings in less than it cost to produce. Using our information we can say that we will produce if and only if the price (marginal revenue) is greater than or equal to the marginal cost of producing it.

Produce more if Price ≥ MC

Let's take a look at the eighth unit of output. It costs $15 to produce this unit, but just like every other unit it only brings in $14 in additional revenue. Is it worth it to produce this unit? No, selling it will reduce total profits as figure 16.4 indicates. If marginal cost exceeds the price, the firm should reduce production.

Produce less if Price < MC

Output	Total Revenue	Total Cost	Price = MR	Marginal Cost	Total Profit
0	$0	$25	$14	—	−$25
1	$14	$35	$14	$10	−$21
2	$28	$41	$14	$6	−$13
3	$42	$48	$14	$7	−$6
4	$56	$55	$14	$7	$1
5	$70	$64	$14	$9	$5
6	$84	$75	$14	$11	$12
7	$98	$88	$14	$13	$13
8	$112	$103	$14	$15	$12
9	$126	$120	$14	$17	$6
10	$140	$150	$14	$30	−$10

Figure 16.4 • Maximizing Profits
Total profit is maximized where marginal cost is as close to price as possible without going over.

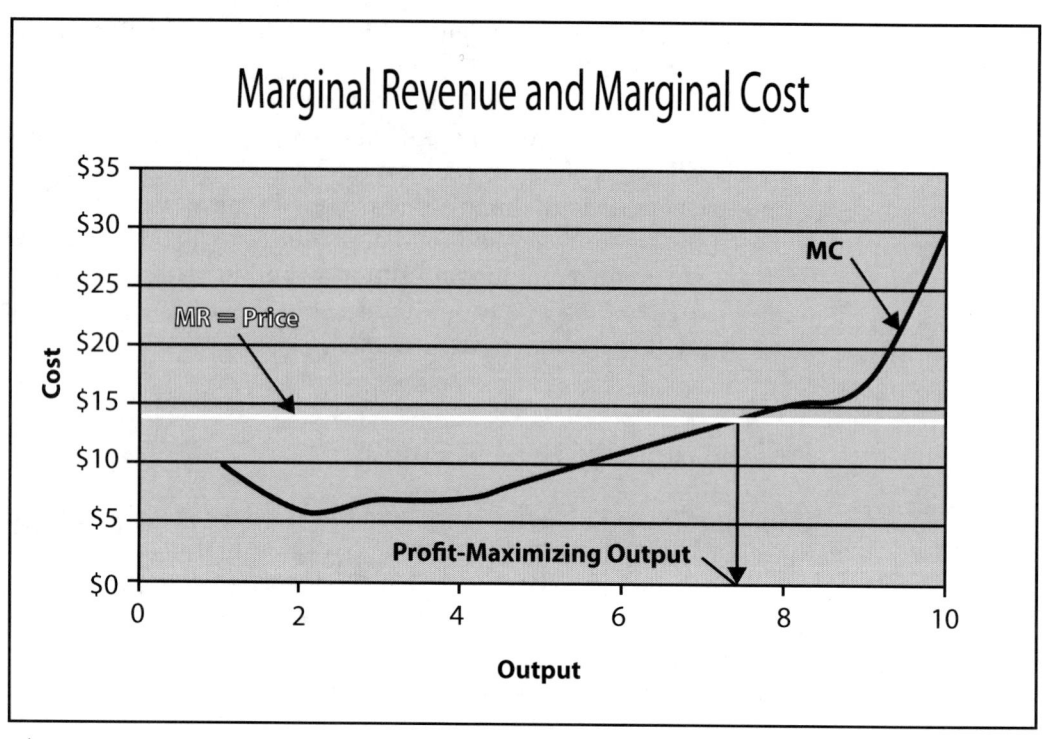

Figure 16.5 • **Profit-Maximizing Output Level**
The competitive firm maximizes profit at the output level where P = MC.

What about the first unit? The first unit only costs $10 and brings in $14. Selling this unit increases total profits. The same is true for the second through seventh units, since their marginal costs are below the market price. You should increase production if price exceeds marginal cost since there are additional profits to be made.

However, since marginal costs rise we know that price will not exceed marginal cost forever. Eventually, marginal cost will exceed the price and you will need to decrease production. Therefore, the optimal output level for the firm is the output level where marginal cost exactly equals price. Any attempt to increase or decrease output from this point cannot possibly increase profits. If there is no output level where price equals marginal cost (as in figure 16.4), they should produce at the last output level possible before marginal cost starts exceeding price.

Figure 16.5 illustrates that as long as price exceeds marginal costs, increasing production will increase total profits. When the firm reaches the seventh unit of production, marginal cost and price are nearly equal: This unit brings in one dollar more in revenue than it costs to produce. It adds exactly one dollar to total profits.

The eighth unit of production, on the other hand, does not bring in as much revenue as it cost to produce it. Producing this good will reduce total profits from $10 to $9, and that is not something the firm wants to do. As a result, seven units is the maximum amount the firm desires to produce.

Adding Up Profits

Even though we are maximizing total profit, we used marginal decision-making to find our solution. It may be useful to go back and look at what kind of total profits our decision earned us. We know that total profits are measured by the vertical distance be-

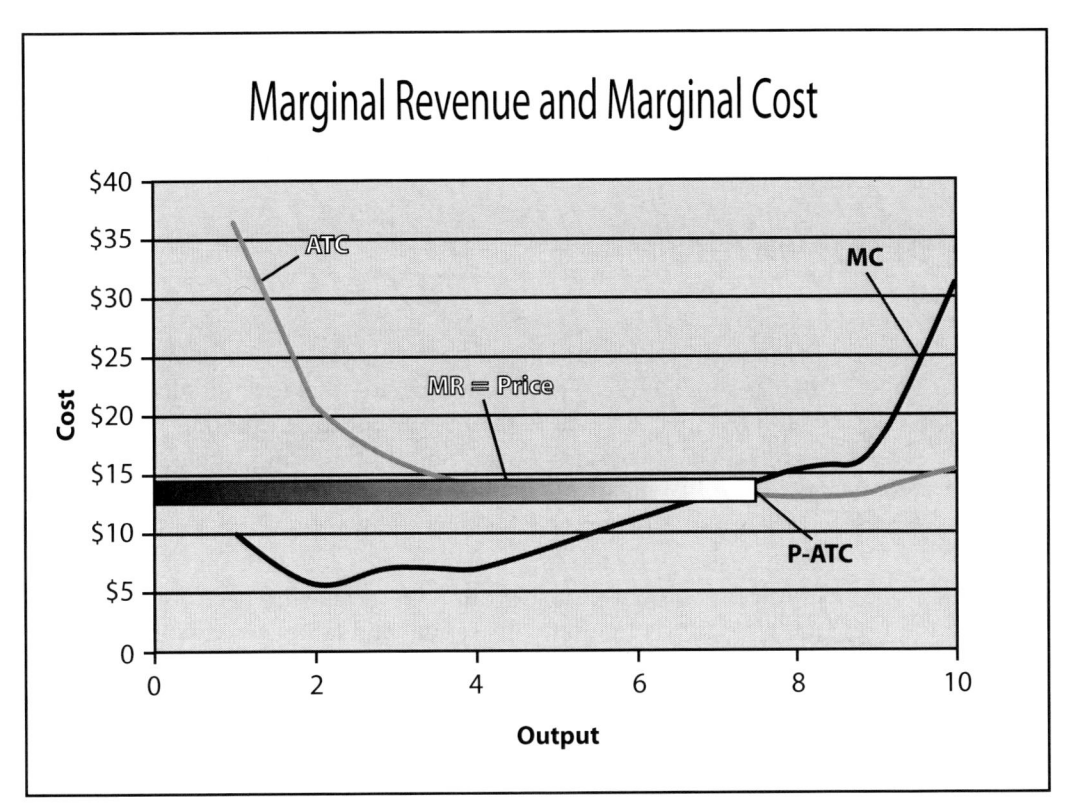

Figure 16.6 • Graphing Total Profit
Total profit can be found on a graph with price, marginal cost, and ATC as a rectangle with sides of P-ATC and the profit-maximizing output level.

tween the total revenue and total costs for the firm and that distance is maximized at seven bouquets an hour for the flower shop, but what is the magnitude of that distance?

We could also ask what the amount of profit earned on each of the seven bouquets sold is. In other words, what is the average level of profit? Since profit equals revenue minus cost, average (or per-unit) profit equals average revenue minus average cost.

$$Profit\ per\ unit = Price - ATC$$

Since the revenue is the same for every unit (it is simply the price) the average revenue is equal to the price as well. Average per-unit costs are equal to the ATC we learned about in Chapter 15 (total cost divided by output). One can also calculate average profit by looking at the vertical distance between the price (average revenue) and the ATC curve. Then we can get total profit for any output level by multiplying average profit times the level of output. This total profit can be seen as the rectangle in figure 16.6.

$$Profit = (Price - ATC) \times Output$$

While per-unit profits are important (they are the source of the idea of a markup), the businesses goal is not the maximization of per-unit profit. Would you rather sell one ice cream cone for a five-dollar profit or one hundred cones for fifty cents profit each? Of course you would rather sell one hundred at fifty cents profit each because that will get you more total profits.

We can also see when we graph marginal cost, price, and ATC together as in figure 16.6 that there is no reason for the business to want to produce at minimum cost.

The MC curve intersects the ATC curve at its minimum just like in Chapter 15, but since the MC curve is still below the price the business can earn more profits by increasing output according to the profit-maximization rule.

VI. THE SHUTDOWN DECISION

Throughout all of our calculations, tables, and graphs we have made the assumption there is some range of production where total revenues exceed total cost, but there is no guarantee that this will happen. What if the output at which marginal revenue equals marginal cost generates a loss? Should the firm produce at this level or shut down the factory and try his hand at something else?

Your first instinct may be to shut down the factory and cut your losses, but this may not necessarily be the smartest course of action in the short run. Remember that in the short run, you have to pay your fixed costs whether you shut down production or not. You have to pay rent on your capital and land even if you don't use them.

So now the question is about the lesser of two evils: Do I lose more money by shutting down the factory and eating my fixed costs, or by producing at the optimal output level? So you should only shut down if the loss from producing at the profit-maximizing output level (Q^*) exceeds loss from producing at zero output.

$$\text{Shutdown if } TR(0) - TC(0) > TR(Q^*) - TC(Q^*)$$
$$0 - FC > TR(Q^*) - FC - VC(Q^*)$$
$$0 > TR(Q^*) - VC(Q^*)$$
$$TR(Q^*) < VC(Q^*)$$
$$P < AVC(Q^*)$$

Remember that loss is just negative profit and still equals total revenue minus total cost. Total cost equals fixed cost plus variable costs. Since fixed costs are on both sides of the inequality we can cancel them out and we are left with the rule that says shut down if total revenue minus variable costs is less than zero. In other words, if the total revenue you bring in at the optimal level of production does not cover your variable cost, it is not worth it to produce at all and you should shut down.

Price vs. AVC

Now that we know the key to shutting down is actually the relationship between revenue and variable cost, we can the use the AVC curve and the price (average revenue) to determine the shutdown decision. At a price of $14, for example, Fred will produce seven bouquets of flowers per day and earn a profit of $10. Price exceeds ATC and the firm is profitable; no worrying about shutting down here.

A problem occurs when the price falls below $13, the firm's minimum average total cost. There is no output level where price exceeds ATC; the firm is never profitable. But should it shut down? At a price of $11, for example, the flower shop would produce only six bouquets per hour at a total loss of $12 per hour ($2 per bouquet) as figure 16.7a illustrates. Fred has to pay his $25 per hour fixed cost anyway so if he shut down he would be incurring a loss of $25 ($0 of revenue minus $25 of total cost).

(a)

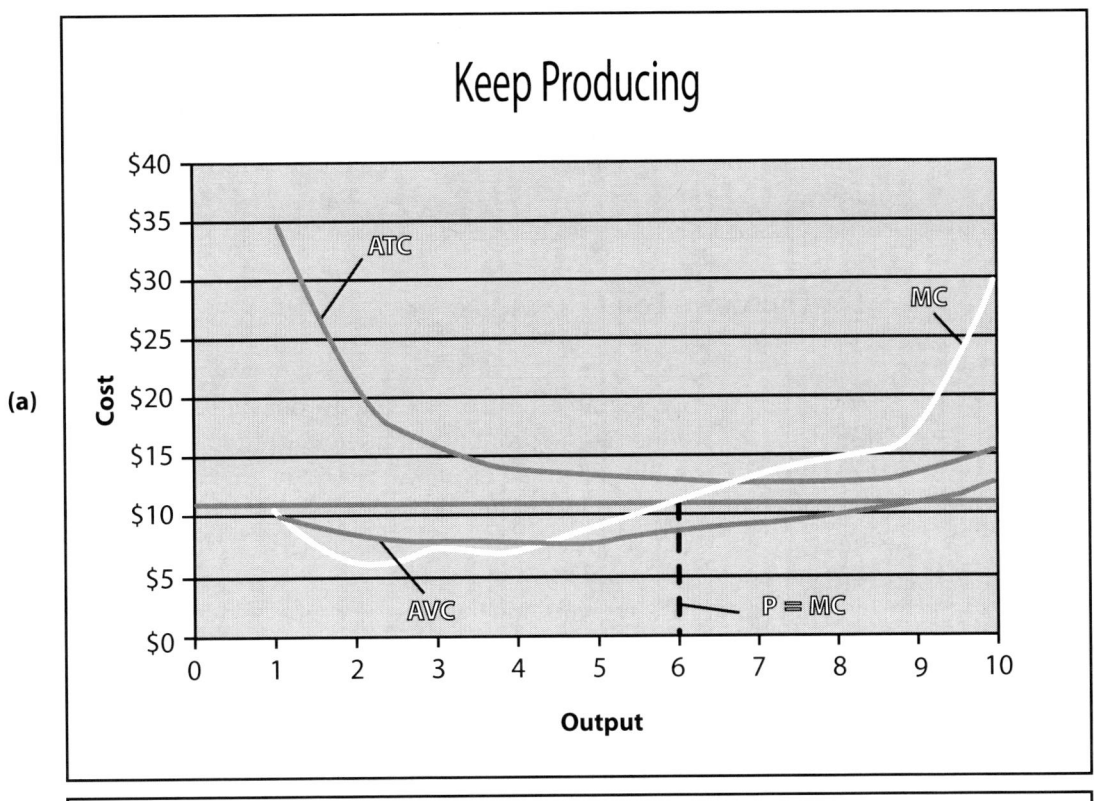

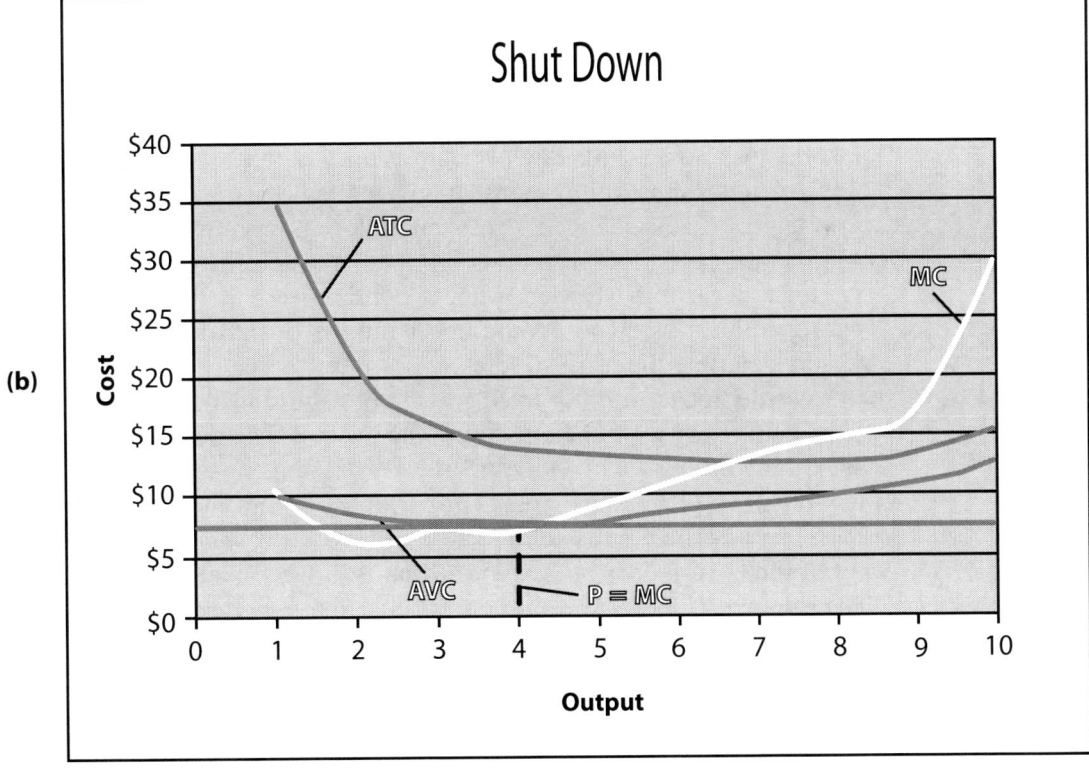

Keep Producing

(b)

Shut Down

Figure 16.7 • Shutdown Decision
The firm should only shut down if the price is never high enough to cover AVC. In figure b the AVC is always above price, meaning the firm is better off producing zero.

So even in this case, Fred should still produce. He minimizes his losses by producing at the optimal level rather than shutting down because the sales, even though they result in a loss, more than cover his variable costs. He has to pay the fixed costs either way, so they don't factor in. When stuck in the short run, businesses often make the decision to continue producing at a loss since they will never get back their fixed costs anyway.

The Shutdown Point

Suppose the price of a bouquet of flowers fell all the way to $7. This price does not even cover the average variable cost of producing one bouquet at its minimum ($7.50). Choosing to produce at the profit maximizing output level, four bouquets according to figure 16.7b, would result in a loss of $27 per hour. Higher levels of output would result in even worse average losses. In this case, loss incurred by shutting down ($25 per hour) is not as bad as loss incurred by producing so shutting down would be the smart thing to do.

You should always shut down if the price falls below the minimum point of the average variable cost curve and continue to produce at the optimal output level if the price rises above it. If price is above the minimum of the ATC curve you will be maximizing profits, and if it is below the curve you will be minimizing losses.

VII. THE INVESTMENT DECISION

Just because a firm shuts down a factory, does not mean it has to exit the market. Shutting down is a short run response to given fixed costs; when the long run comes up the firm might be able change its costs enough that production is profitable. The problem was the firm owner's expectations about what his profits would be when he made his investment decision—whether or not to build or lease the factory in the first place—were wrong; a business owner would never purposely start business where his best option would be letting the plant sit idle.

We did not account for fixed costs in our shutdown decision because they will have to be paid either way. The only thing the business can do is to try to pay off its debts by selling the product above its AVC. If it can do this, it can take that excess revenue and pay off some of the fixed cost. This is all assuming the factory already exists and we have to make the best use of it.

If the factory does not exist yet (that is, if we are talking about the long run) fixed costs do matter. No one would purposely enter a money-losing enterprise, so the business owner needs to make sure that his anticipated profits exceed all of his costs at his chosen rate of output (the profit-maximizing level of output).

Long-Run Costs

We know that in the long run the firm is not faced with one set of potential costs, or even three choices. It can choose from an infinite number of factory sizes and equipment levels, each with its own cost curve. From our discussion of long-run costs and returns to scale we know the firm will choose the factory that has its minimum average cost point exactly at the firm's desired output. This gives the firm the best shot at profitability and avoiding shutdown.

CHAPTER 16 SUMMARY

- Businesses are motivated to produce by the **lure of potential profits.**
- *Accounting Profit = Total Revenue − Explicit Costs*
- *Economic Profit = Accounting Profit − Implicit Costs*
- Economic profits are the **payment to entrepreneurship.**
- In **monopoly, oligopoly,** and **monopolistic competition** firms have the power to set prices to one degree or another.
- Under **perfect competition**, the firm is a price-taker and faces a **perfectly elastic demand curve.**
- For a competitive firm, the **total revenue curve** is upward-sloping, but the **total cost curve** is flatter at low levels of output and steeper at higher levels due to diminishing marginal returns.
- **Profit is maximized** at the output level where total revenue is as high above total cost as possible.
- For a competitive firm, marginal revenue equals price.
- A firm should **never sell a good that brings in less revenue than it cost to produce.**
- A competitive firm maximizes profit by producing at the output level where **P = MC.**
- In the short run, a **firm should shut down** if P < AVC at every output level.
- No one would ever invest a firm in the long run without an expectation of profits.

CHAPTER 16 Exercises

Name _____

1) Which of the following is true about the demand curve confronting a competitive firm?
   A) Downward-sloping, as is market demand
   B) Downward-sloping, while market demand is flat
   C) Horizontal, as is market demand
   D) Horizontal, while market demand is downward-sloping

1) _____

2) If the market price in a competitive market for sugar is $5 per pound, then an individual firm in this market can
   A) always sell an additional pound of sugar at $5.00.
   B) only sell an additional pound if they can raise prices.
   C) only sell an additional pound if they reduce prices.
   D) only sell an additional pound after a successful advertising campaign.

2) _____

3) At the profit-maximizing output for a perfectly competitive firm:
   A) price = marginal cost
   B) total cost = total revenue
   C) average cost = price
   D) marginal cost = AVC

3) _____

4) If a perfectly competitive firm is producing a rate of output for which MC exceeds price, then the firm
   A) is definitely earning a loss.
   B) can increase its profit by increasing output.
   C) can increase its profit by decreasing output.
   D) is maximizing profit.

4) _____

5) A firm experiencing economic losses will only shut down if
   A) price is below AVC.
   B) price is above AVC.
   C) price is below ATC.
   D) price is above ATC.

5) _____

6) When price exceeds average variable cost but not average total cost, the firm should, in the short run
   A) shut down.
   B) produce at the rate of output where P = MC.
   C) produce where ATC is minimized.
   D) produce where total cost is minimized.

6) _____

295

Use the following information to answer questions 7 and 8:
A perfectly competitive firms faces market where:
Market Price = $12
Total Cost = $30 + 3Q + .5Q^2$
Marginal Cost = $3 + Q$

7) What is the firm's profit-maximizing output level?   7) _____
   A) 0
   B) 12
   C) 9
   D) Not enough information.

8) What amount of profit does the firm earn at the profit-maximizing level?   8) _____
   A) $12
   B) $108
   C) $10.50
   D) $97.50

9) Why is the demand curve facing a single competitive firm perfectly elastic? What will happen if they try to charge any price other than the market price?

_____
_____
_____
_____
_____

10) What is the difference between the shut down decision and the investment decision? Why is it acceptable to produce at a loss in the short run and not the long run?

_____
_____
_____
_____
_____

Article Review 4

Name _____

Choose any one of the articles from Chapters 14–16. Use the space provided below to summarize the article. Then, answer the questions at the end of the article on the back of this page.

1.

2.

3.

Unit 4 Review

Name _____

Use this review to prepare for Exam 4. You can view the answers in the "unit review answers" section in the back of the text, but try to complete it on your own first.

1) Which of the following is a microeconomic issue? 1) _____
   A) the economic growth rate
   B) inflation
   C) the national unemployment rate
   D) one firm's decision about how many workers to hire

2) Which of the following is NOT a role of the government in the market system? 2) _____
   A) fixing market failures   C) breaking up monopolies
   B) owning the factors of production   D) redistributing income

3) Assuming milk is a normal good, what would happen to the demand curve for milk if everyone expected his income to rise in the near future? 3) _____
   A) shift upward   C) nothing
   B) shift to the right   D) shift to the left

4) When the government imposes a price floor, what kind of problem occurs? 4) _____
   A) surplus   C) shortage
   B) market failure   D) scarcity

5) What happens to equilibrium price when demand and supply both increase? 5) _____
   A) price rises   C) price remains unchanged
   B) price falls   D) price is indeterminate

6) Which of the following would most likely have a price elasticity greater than 1? 6) _____
   A) coffee   C) cigarettes
   B) gasoline in the short run   D) new car

7) If the price elasticity of demand is 0.5, and a firm raises its price by 10 percent, the quantity sold by the firm will 7) _____
   A) fall 10 percent.   C) rise 5 percent.
   B) fall 5 percent.   D) rise 10 percent.

8) Assume the price elasticity of demand for Fred's Fabulous Flowers is .75. If he cuts the price of a bouquet of flowers, total revenue will 8) _____
   A) decrease because the percentage increase in quantity demanded will be less than the percentage decrease in price.
   B) increase because more bouquets will be sold.
   C) decrease because he will receive less revenue per unit sold.
   D) Not enough information.

299

9) If income rises 5 percent for a year and as a result the quantity of cans of Spam demanded falls from 120,000 to 100,000 cars for the year, the value of the income elasticity of demand for cars is closest to:
A) −4
B) 4
C) −3.64
D) 3.64

9) _____

10) BlackBerries and iPhones are substitute goods. The cross-price elasticity of demand between BlackBerries and iPhones is expected to be
A) negative.
B) positive.
C) zero.
D) Not enough information.

10) _____

11) What causes diminishing marginal returns in the short run?
A) Workers have to share a fixed space and a fixed amount of capital.
B) Workers hired later do not work as hard as those hired earlier.
C) Workers hired later do not know how to work as part of the team.
D) Workers hired later are not as qualified as those hired earlier.

11) _____

12) Assuming each unit of variable inputs cost the same, marginal cost will decrease as output increases if
A) marginal physical product is rising.
B) variable cost is rising.
C) marginal physical product is falling.
D) total cost is rising.

12) _____

13) In the short run, when a firm produces zero output, total cost equals
A) variable costs.
B) average total cost.
C) zero.
D) fixed costs.

13) _____

14) Accounting cost includes
A) all economic costs.
B) only the value of resources used to produce a good for which a monetary payment is made.
C) the value of all resources used to produce a good.
D) only implicit costs.

14) _____

15) If an industry exhibits diseconomies of scale
A) it would be better to produce at several small factories.
B) it would be better to produce at one large factory.
C) factory size makes no difference, lowest cost production will always be achieved.
D) minimum ATC is lower at a large factory than at a small one.

15) _____

16) Which of the following is true about the demand curve for a competitive market?
A) Horizontal, while the demand for each firm is downward-sloping
B) Downward-sloping as is the demand for each firm
C) Horizontal, as is the demand for each firm
D) Downward-sloping, while the demand for each firm is flat

16) _____

17) If a perfectly competitive firm is producing a rate of output for which price exceeds marginal cost, then the firm
A) is maximizing profit.
B) can increase its profit by increasing output.
C) is definitely earning a loss.
D) can increase its profit by decreasing output.

17) _____

Name _____

18) When price fails to exceed average variable cost and average total cost, the firm should, in the short run:
    A) produce where ATC is minimized.
    B) produce where total cost is minimized.
    C) produce at the rate of output where P = MC.
    D) shut down.

18) _____

Use the following information to answer questions 7 and 8:
A perfectly competitive firms faces market where:
Market Price = $15
Total Cost = $30 + 5Q + .5Q^2$
Marginal Cost = $5 + Q$

19) What is the firm's profit-maximizing output level?
    A) 0
    B) 15
    C) 10
    D) Not enough information.

19) _____

20) What amount of profit does the firm earn at the profit-maximizing level?
    A) $15
    B) $150
    C) $130
    D) $20

20) _____

21) Draw what would happen to equilibrium if supply shifted to the right and demand shifted to the left. What happens to equilibrium quantity and price?

_____
_____
_____
_____

22) What is the difference between a pair goods with a positive cross-price elasticity and one with a negative cross-price elasticity? How does a change in price in one of the goods affect the demand curve for the other?

_____
_____
_____
_____

23) Describe the utility-maximizing rule for a consumer.

_____
_____
_____
_____

24) What is happening to the ATC curve when marginal cost is below it? What about when the marginal cost curve is above it?

_____
_____
_____
_____

25) What is the profit-maximizing rule for a competitive firm? What should always be true if the firm is produces at the level of output that maximizes profit?

Exam 4 Formula Sheet

Name _____

Chapter 13

Size of Surplus = $Q_s - Q_d$

Size of Shortage = $Q_d - Q_s$

Chapter 14

$$\text{Marginal Utility} = \frac{\text{Change in Total Utility}}{\text{Change in Consumption}}$$

$$\text{Price Elasticity of Demand} = \frac{\text{Percent Change in Quantity Demanded}}{\text{Percent Change in Price}}$$

$E > 1$ = Elastic Demand, $E < 1$ = Inelastic Demand, $E = 1$ = Unitary Elastic Demand

$$\text{Percent Change} = \frac{\text{New Value} - \text{Old Value}}{\text{Average Value}}$$

$$\text{Income Elasticity of Demand} = \frac{\text{Percent Change in Quantity Demanded}}{\text{Percent Change in Income}}$$

$$\text{Cost-Price Elasticity of Demand} = \frac{\text{Percent Change in Quantity Demanded}}{\text{Percent Change in Price of Related Good}}$$

Chapter 15

$$\text{Marginal Physical Product} = \frac{\text{Change in Output}}{\text{Change in Input}}$$

$$\text{Average Total Costs} = \frac{\text{Total Costs}}{\text{Output}}$$

$$AVC = \frac{\text{Variable Costs}}{\text{Output}}, \quad AFC = \frac{\text{Fixed Costs}}{\text{Output}}$$

$ATC = AVC + AFC$

$$\text{Marginal Cost} = \frac{\text{Change in Total Cost}}{\text{Change in Output}}$$

Economic Cost = Explicit Cost + Implicit Costs

Chapter 16

Accounting Profit = Total Revenue − Explicit Costs

Economic Profit = Accounting Profit − Implicit Costs

Produce more if Price ≥ MC

Produce less if Price < MC

Shutdown if TR(0) − TC(0) > TR(Q*) − TC(Q*)

Profit per unit = Price − ATC

Profit = (Price − ATC) × Output

Chapter 17

Perfect Competition

I. DETERMINANTS OF SUPPLY

In Chapter 16, we learned three decision rules based on the perfectly competitive firm's pursuit of profits. The firm will decide to invest in a production facility if they anticipate they can make an economic profit (revenue at the desired output rate exceeds total costs at that point). Once the factory is built (the short run), the firm will expand production if price exceeds marginal cost and decrease it if price falls short of marginal costs. If they are incurring a loss at the optimal output level, the firm will shutdown if the total revenue at this output level does not cover its total variable costs.

Unfortunately, most people who plan to go into business do not have complete information about future revenues, costs, or profits. Therefore, production requires considerably more risk in real life than in theory. Potential investors may not be able to determine these figures directly, but certain other factors send them signals about potential profits and will influence the amount they want to produce.

Short-Run Determinants

Since a competitive firm cannot change its price, its decision about how much to produce is dominated by its marginal cost: The more it costs to produce a good, the less profit you receive from it, assuming price stays the same. As a result, the firm's

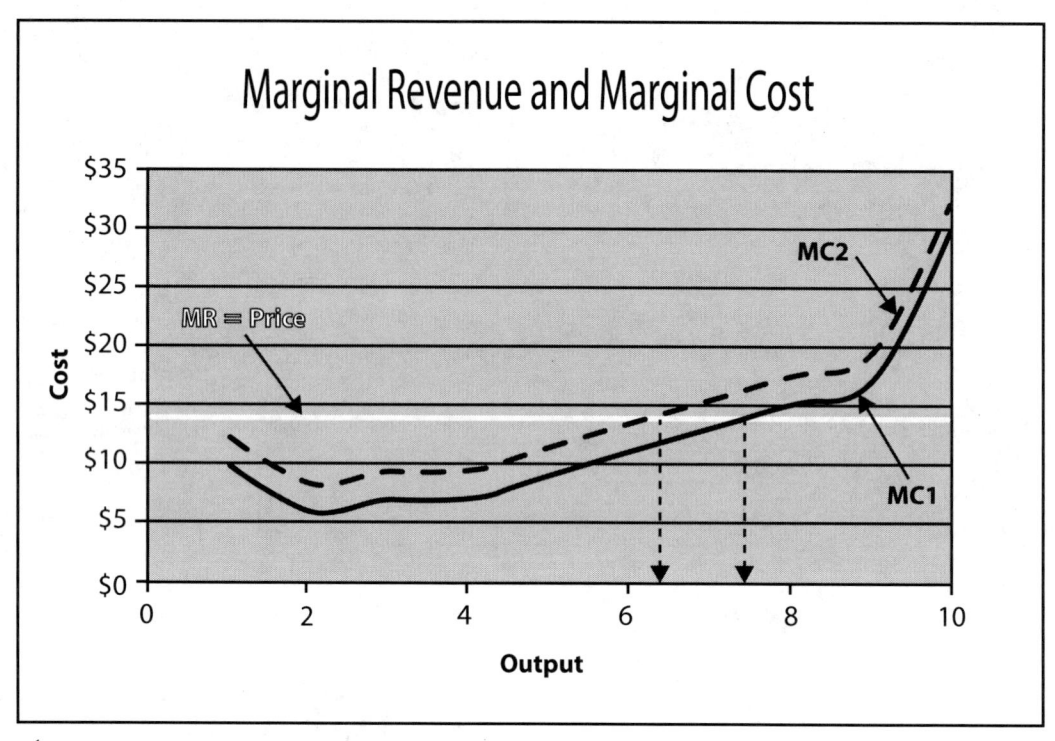

Figure 17.1 • **Changes in the Marginal Cost Curve**
As the marginal cost of producing a product increases from MC1 to MC2, each perfectly competitive firm will want to produce less of it.

production, or quantity supplied to market, will be influenced by all the factors that alter marginal costs.

Input price. An increase in the price of inputs will cause marginal cost to rise. If the minimum wage were to rise, for example, the marginal cost of producing additional hamburgers at a fast food restaurant would rise and the firm would alter its quantity supplied. Any factor that raises marginal cost will cause the marginal cost curve to shift upward and move the profit-maximizing output level down, as seen in figure 17.1.

Technology/Productivity. On the other hand, if minimum wage stayed the same and the firm was able to figure out a way to produce with less labor (that is, technology changed) marginal cost would fall and they would produce more at the profit-maximizing output level. If workers got discouraged by the low wages and did not produce as much per hour (productivity fell), marginal costs would rise.

Expectations. Expectations are hugely important in production decisions. Toys R Us ramps up production during the holiday season because they expect more people to buy toys and games. Since there is less risk involved at this time of year, marginal costs fall.

Taxes. Taxes and subsidies also affect the cost of producing a good. If the government increases the subsidy on sugar, for example, the cost of producing would fall (just like if the price of an input fell) and producers would supply more to the market.

The Short-Run Supply Curve

Since we know any of these factors will alter the amount the business wants to sell at any price—these are the same shifters of supply from Chapters 3 and 13—when we draw the short-run supply we hold of these factors constant (the *ceteris paribus* as-

Marginal Cost for Fred's Flower Shop

(a)

Supply Curve for Fred's Flower Shop

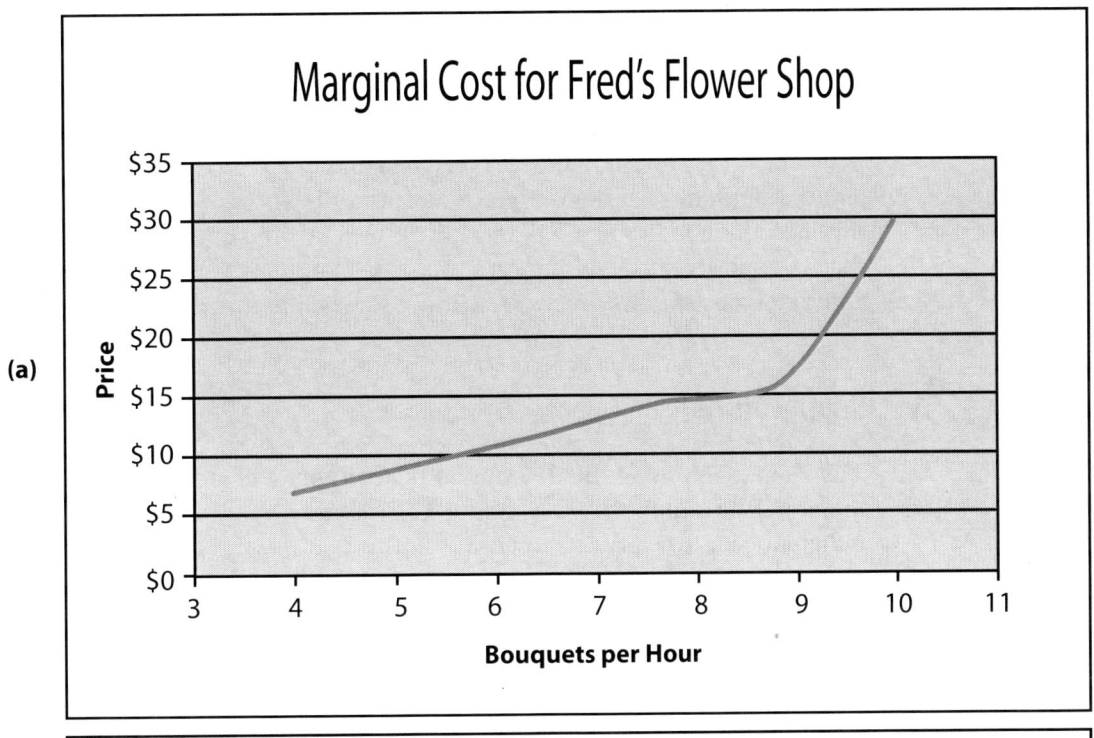

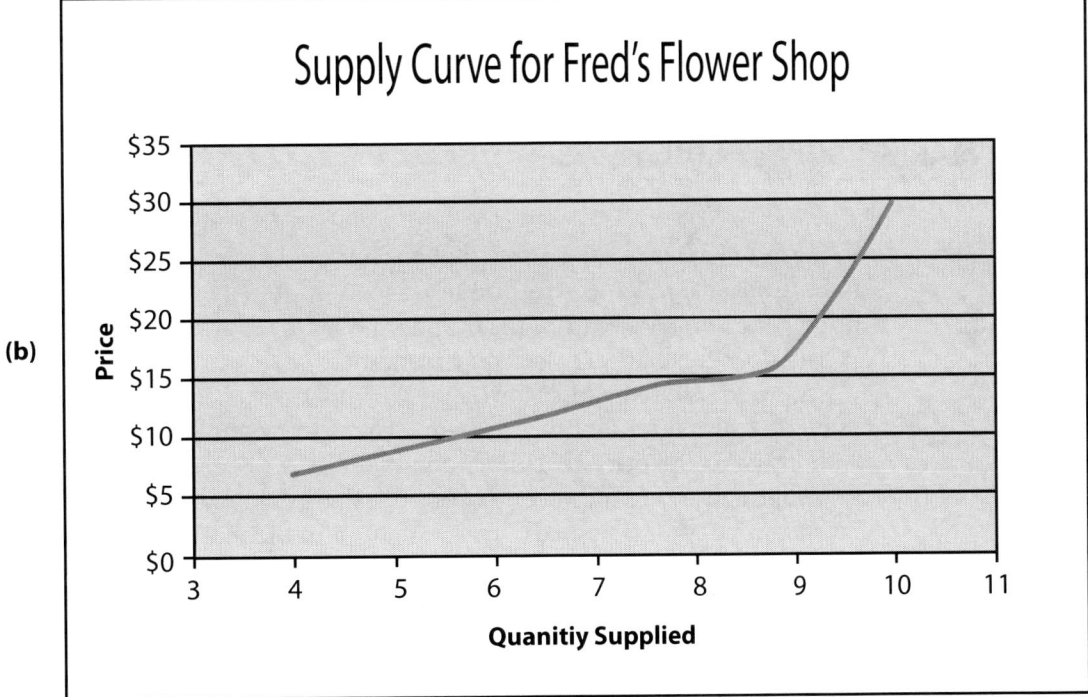

(b)

Figure 17.2 • Supply Curve for a Competitive Firm
The price at each quantity supplied represents the least amount of money the firm would accept to produce that unit, its marginal cost.

sumption). The only thing we allow to change is price, because we want to isolate the effect of a price change on quantity supplied.

Since the profit-maximization rule says that the firm should never produce when marginal cost exceeds price, marginal cost represents at minimum acceptable price for a good at any output level. The supply curve for the flower shop shown in figure 17.2

shows that at the output level of four bouquets an hour, Fred will not accept any price below $7 since he would be reducing total profits if he did. The same is true for $9 at five, $11 at six, $13 at seven, and $15 at eight. Marginal cost and output are directly related just like price and quantity supplied.

In fact, they are the same curve. The competitive firm will never produce a unit unless the amount of money it receives (price) is at least equal to the amount it cost to produce the good (marginal cost). The reason the supply curve is upward sloping is that as quantity supplied increases so does marginal cost. The firm will only bear these additional costs if customers are willing to pay a higher price.

Supply Shifts

Any change in one of the determinants of supply will shift the marginal cost curve and therefore the supply curve as figure 17.3 demonstrates. An increase in wages will shift marginal cost upward as shown in figure 17.3 (it will cost more to produce any given unit of output) and lower the amount business could profitably offer for sale at any price.

An improvement in technology or decrease in taxes (increase in subsidies) would have the opposite effect. The cost of producing any given unit of output would fall (shift the marginal cost curve to the right) and therefore allow the business to increase quantity supplied at every price.

II. THE MARKET SUPPLY CURVE

In the last chapter we discussed the behavior of an individual competitive firm. In order to be profit maximizing, this firm must set output to a level where marginal cost equals price. As a competitive firm, the firm has no market power and is therefore a price taker. Where does the market price come from then?

As we discussed earlier, prices in a competitive market come from the interaction of market supply and market demand. The price where these curves cross, the equilibrium price, is the price that the individual firm will base its productions decisions on. It would benefit us then to discuss how the market supply curve, and therefore the market price, is determined. The calculation of the market supply is one of simple addition; the quantity supplied by the market at any price is the sum of quantities supplied by every firm in the market. Add these quantities for each price and you have market supply.

Since we just discovered that the individual supply curve and the marginal cost curve are the same thing, the market supply is also the sum of all the marginal cost curves for the firms in the market. As such, the market supply will depend on the same factors that influence marginal costs: price of inputs, technology, taxes and subsidies, and expectations. To this we will add the number of sellers, since we know adding more sellers will add to quantity supplied at some prices.

Low Barriers to Entry

The idea that more firms can enter the industry easily is a key component of a perfectly competitive market. As more firms enter the market, the quantity supplied at any price

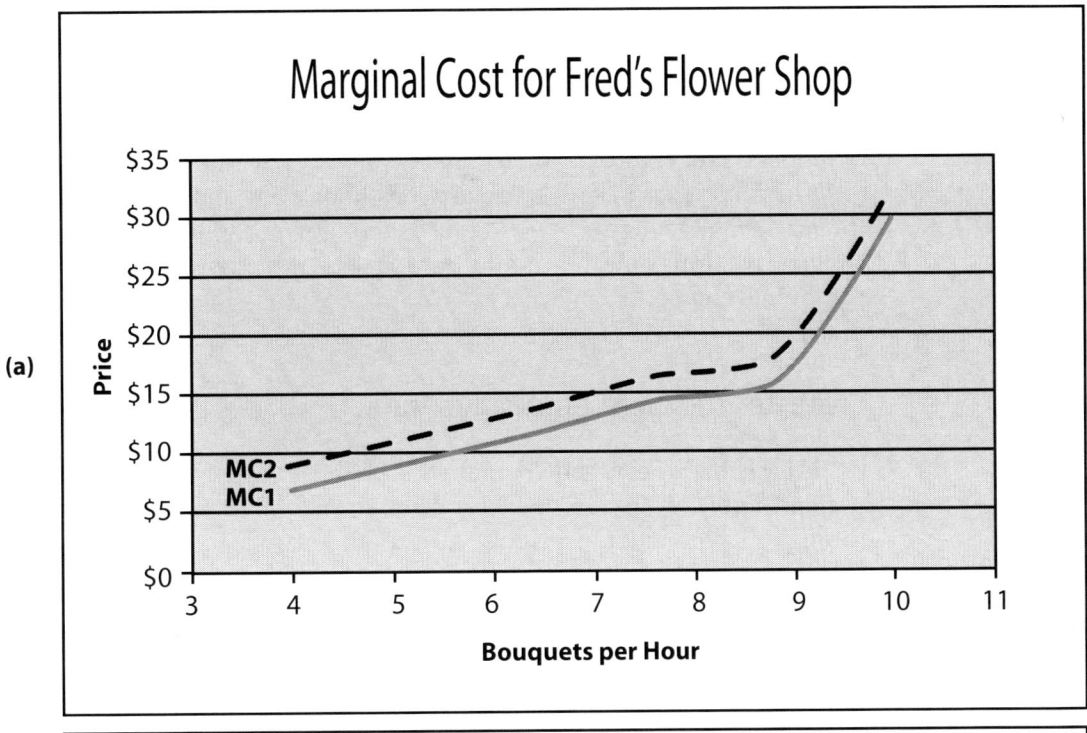

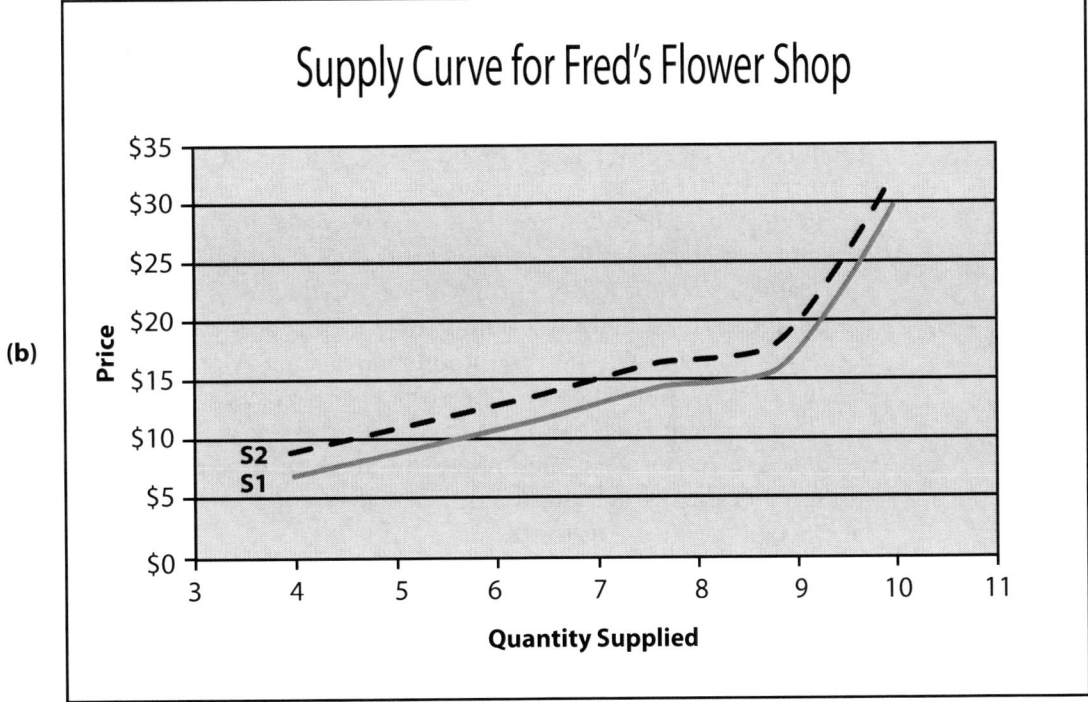

Figure 17.3 • How Marginal Costs Affect Supply
An increase in marginal cost means the firm will want to produce less at every price, resulting in the supply curve shifting to the left.

increases; there are simply more people selling. In an industry with low startup costs (the investment decision is an easy one) many new firms may enter a market very quickly. But what happens when supply shifts to the right and demand stays the same? The market price falls and profits fall with it. As this happens, some firms may leave the market, shifting supply back to the left.

Remember, this ability to enter the market easily is a trademark feature of perfect competition. Industries with more market power like monopolies and oligopolies may make it significantly more difficult for new firms to enter the market and ruin their high profits. These barriers include patents and copyrights that restrict competition, control of inputs (vertical integration), brand loyalty, or government regulation.

These barriers make it extremely costly or even impossible for new firms to enter the market, allowing the existing firms to enjoy economic profits much longer than a competitive firm could. Without these barriers, it is open season whenever investors see profits in a competitive market.

Characteristics of a Competitive Market

Many Firms. A competitive market is characterized by having many firms. More importantly, none of these firms has a large enough market share to affect market supply through its production decisions. As a result, every firm is a price taker with zero market power resulting in a perfectly elastic demand curve facing each firm, as seen in Chapter 16.

Identical Products. Firms operating in the same competitive market offer identical products for sale. If they were differentiated, firms would wield some control over pricing and we would be talking about monopolistic competition.

Perfect Information. Firms respond quickly to reports of high profits in a competitive market because of perfect information. Everybody (buyers, sellers, and potential new firms) have identical and complete information on supply, demand, prices, and profits. Furthermore, perfect information means consumers are fully aware that all products are identical making brand loyalty impossible.

Low Barriers. As we have discussed, competitive markets offer no significant barriers to entry or exit. When economic profits appear in the market, many new firms will enter to reap the benefits. As these profits dwindle, some firms will leave the industry.

Marginal Cost Pricing. No firm will ever produce a product that brings in less than it cost to produce it, and for a competitive firm that means price equals marginal cost. Competitive firms will increase production as long as price exceeds marginal cost, and decrease production when marginal cost exceeds price.

Zero Economic Profit. Markets in which firms are making large economic profits attract new firms to make the investment decision to join the industry. But as new entrants enter the market, the supply rises (the market is flooded) and price falls as businesses compete over customers.

As the price falls (and marginal costs rise because of higher equilibrium output), the economic profits earned in this market begin to fall. Some business owners who were earning a loss somewhere else might still want to invest in this industry, however. In fact, firms will keep entering the market until supply rises so much that economic profits are driven to zero.

Of course, the original members of this industry would have preferred it if the new entrants did not come in and ruin it for them, but what power do they have to stop it? The nature of competitive market means that there are little to no barriers to entry. In addition, each of their individual supplies is so small that they could not manipulate the market enough to force the newcomers to leave. They could do nothing but watch as their profits dwindled from increased competition.

This explains why businesses like fruit stands, farms, and t-shirt stores are not very profitable. Any time things look good (an increase in demand or decrease in cost raises profits) new entrants will rush to the market to cash in. As long as it is easy for new firms to enter the market, profits will not last long.

III. MOBILE PHONE MARKET

As mentioned previously, hardly any firms in the United States actually function in perfectly competitive markets; one or more of these characteristics are missing from just about every industry. Still, many markets experience a similar tendency toward zero profit due to extreme competition and easy entry.

Markets with nearly indistinguishable products and low startup costs (beauty salons, grocery stores, print shops, and furniture stores) cannot have excessive profits for very long because new firms will enter the market and drive down prices. The markets for certain financial and legal services have also become increasingly competitive with the advent of the Internet.

Another industry that has evolved through intense competition is the consumer electronics industry. As consumer prices have tripled since the 1970s, the prices of electronic devices like VCRs, calculators, and home computers have fallen sharply even while the quality of these prices have risen. Digital watches have fallen from over $2,000 to under $10, DVD players have dropped from $1,500 to under $100, and computers, which were once only available to government and university laboratories, can be seen in nearly every dorm room in the United States.

Clearly this drop in prices is not due to a lack of consumer demand. Instead, increased competition caused by wave after wave of new entrants has shifted the market supply to the right, lowering the equilibrium price. Would the price of these products be falling so dramatically if one company had been supplying them all along? Of course not, they would have had no incentive to improve technology and lower prices.

Market Evolution

As a concrete example of how competition can cause an industry to change and prices to fall, we will take a look at the history of the mobile phone market. This market is interesting since it is relatively young and we can trace its entire history. Because of the ease of entry in the early years, the mobile phone industry always had most of the elements of perfect competition.

When the mobile phone industry first started, a few companies were offering service to major cities, but the technology was still not ready for widespread use. After seeing the enormous profits that could be earned in this industry, hundreds and eventually thousands of firms jumped on the bandwagon. The increased competition forced firms to improve their product in order to stay profitable.

Some companies could not remain profitable in this transformed market and were forced to leave the industry, while others went bankrupt. Left in the wake of this crash was a new large-scale mobile phone industry with a vastly superior product, but lower profits. Let's take a closer at the evolution of the mobile phone market because it will inform about similar industries like Internet services, video games, and digital music players.

The Initial Condition

In the beginning, there was Motorola. Motorola had been making car phones for years, but the products were so inefficient and bulky they could only work while the car was running. When Ameritech, one of the pieces left after the government-imposed breakup of AT&T, brought the first cell phone network to the Chicago area in 1983,

Motorola stepped in with its infamous "brick" phone—the Motorola DynaTAC. Though it was far less than we would expect from even the cheapest mobile phone today, the DynaTAC was an immediate success.

Although Motorola pretty much invented the consumer mobile phone industry, they never had market power. They could not control the flow of inputs; the chips and other parts needed to build their phones were available to any company willing to join the industry. In other words, there were no barriers to entry.

As a result, when others saw the massive profits Motorola was making in this infant industry, the light bulb came on. The mobile phone industry swelled throughout the 1980s with a total market supply of one million mobile phones by 1990 selling at a market price of $2,500 each, already less than the DynaTAC's original price point of nearly $4,000.

The Production Decision

Each firm in the market at this point wants to maximize profit. Given that they are already invested in producing, that means they will make their short-run production decision based on the profit-maximizing rule; they will produce at the output level where price equals marginal cost.

The cost and revenue curves for this market look similar to those of other markets, as figure 17.4 shows: marginal revenue is equal to price which is constant at the equi-

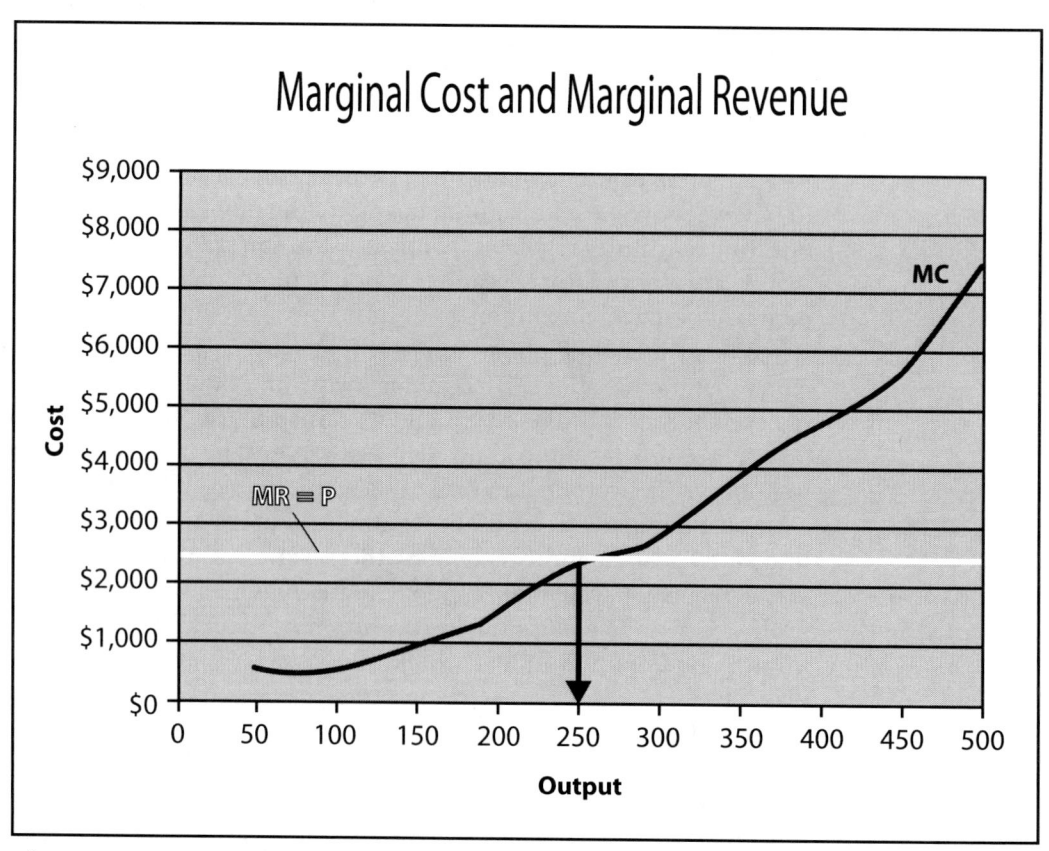

Figure 17.4 • Production Decision of a Single Mobile Phone Firm in 1990
Based on the market price of $2,500 and the marginal cost curve, the average mobile phone firm produced 2500 phones per month in 1990.

librium price at any given time, and marginal cost increases with output. In the short run, the production facility is of a fixed size, meaning any increase in output comes from shoving more workers into the factory. Eventually marginal product will fall and marginal costs will rise. Based on our information about the number of firms in the market and the total market supply, the upward-sloping marginal cost curve for Motorola in 1990 intersected the price line at an output level of 2500 mobile phones per month.

This average firm would maximize profits by producing exactly that many mobile phones each month. Every additional phone would cost more to produce than it would bring in. Reducing production would also decrease total profits by depriving the firm of potential profits from selling units that would bring in more than they cost to produce.

Adding up Profits. We can uncover what this maximum total profit actually was by writing out the total revenues and costs for the firm at different levels of output as seen in the table in figure 17.5. Total revenue increases by exactly $2,500 for each additional unit sold since that is the market price; marginal revenue equals price. Total cost increases by larger and larger amounts as output increases because of increasing marginal costs.

Just like any business, the cell phone firm needed to find the exact output level that maximized the difference between total revenues and total costs. By marginal and graphical analysis, we determine this output level to be 2500 phones per month. Looking at total profit in figure 17.5, we find that indeed there is no output level that offered greater total profits than producing 2500 phones did.

We could have also used our graph like figure 17.6 to find total profits. Average profit (profit per unit) is the vertical distance between the price line and the ATC curve at the profit-maximizing output level. Total profit equals the product of this average profit level and the output. For example, the average profit per unit at 2500 is $900. Multiplying this average profit by the total quantity sold (2500) gives us a total profit of $2,250,000 per month.

Output	Price	Total Revenue	Total Cost	Marginal Cost	Profit
0	$2,500	$0	$1,000,000	—	−$1,000,000
500	$2,500	$1,250,000	$1,250,000	$500	$0
1000	$2,500	$2,500,000	$1,500,000	$500	$1,000,000
1500	$2,500	$3,750,000	$2,000,000	$1,000	$1,750,000
2000	$2,500	$5,000,000	$2,750,000	$1,500	$2,250,000
2500	$2,500	$6,250,000	$4,000,000	$2,500	$2,250,000
3000	$2,500	$7,500,000	$5,500,000	$3,000	$2,000,000
3500	$2,500	$8,750,000	$7,500,000	$4,000	$1,250,000
4000	$2,500	$10,000,000	$10,000,000	$5,000	$0
4500	$2,500	$11,250,000	$13,000,000	$6,000	−$1,750,000
5000	$2,500	$12,500,000	$17,000,000	$8,000	−$4,500,000

Figure 17.5 • Profits for a Mobile Phone Firm in 1990
No output level provided the firm with more total profits than producing 2500 per month did in 1990.

Average Profit

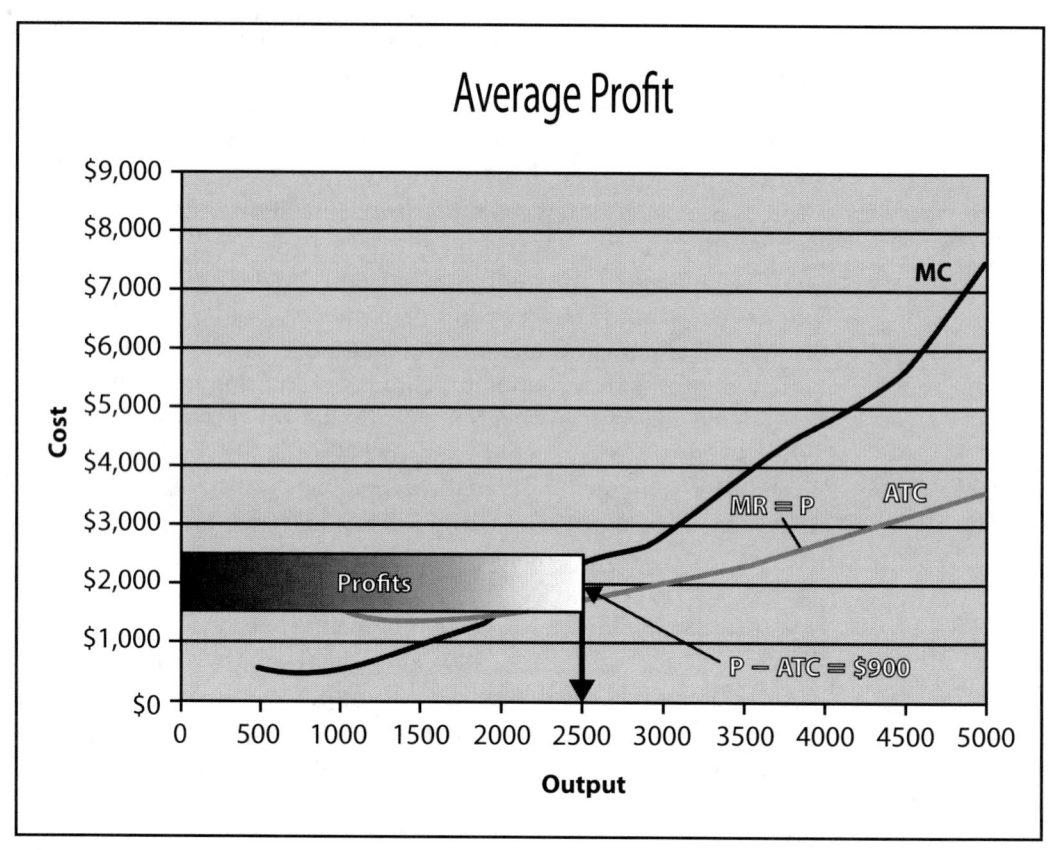

Figure 17.6 • **Finding Total Profits with a Graph**
The vertical distance between price and ATC at the profit-maximization is the average profit per unit. The rectangle created by this vertical distance and the output level ($900 × 2500) equals total profit.

Lure of Profits. Such huge profit levels would have made just as much noise then as it does now. Soon, entrepreneurs everywhere wanted to get into the action. The possibility of economic profits attracted many new entrants into the market. By the end of 1990, many new companies such as Nokia, NEC, and Samsung had made the investment decision to start producing in the mobile phone market.

Low Barriers to Entry. Why wouldn't the original members of the mobile phone industry want to keep their profits high by keeping new entrants out? Well of course they wanted to, but they lacked the ability. The inputs needed to produce a mobile phone and the expertise needed to do so were widely available during this time. The monetary investment to start a mobile phone company was miniscule compared to the profits that could be had.

Shift of Market Supply

With the signal of high profits going out and the lack of significant barriers to entry, many new companies came to the mobile phone industry. As they did, they increased the quantity supplied by the market at every price; they shifted the market supply curve to the right.

But some of these new entrants were in for a disappointment. As the new firms jockeyed for position in the market, they soon realized that they could only sell their new quantity if the price fell. Indeed, figure 17.7 illustrates that an increase in supply

Entry into the Market

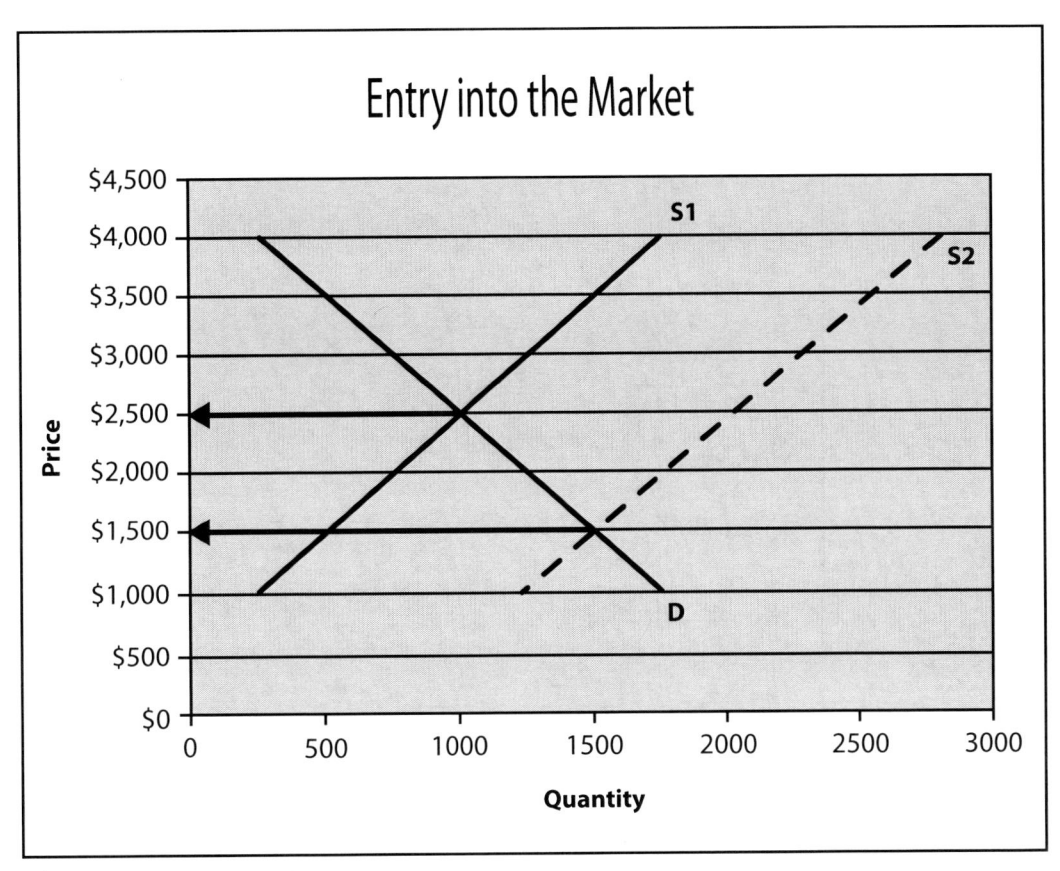

Figure 17.7 • Effect of New Entry
As more firms enter the market, supply rises. If demand remains the same, the market price will fall.

results in a decrease in equilibrium price if demand remains the same. The surplus created by the new wave of inventory resulted in a price drop from $2,500 in 1990 to $1,500 in 1992.

New Equilibrium. As the price fell, the intersection between price and marginal cost for each firm changed as well. Assuming all of the firm's costs remained the same, the firm's profit-maximizing output level fell to 2000 mobile phones per month as indicated by figure 17.8. Average profit per unit also tumbled, as the price line is much closer to the ATC curve. The reduction of both average profit and output resulted in much lower total profits for the average firm ($250,000).

While this seemed low compared to the previous level, it was certainly high enough to still attract more new entrants. In fact, as long as any positive economic profits are available in a perfectly competitive industry, new firms will continue to enter. And enter they did, reducing the price to $1,350 and profit-maximizing output to 1880 phones per month.

By this time the price line reached its limit: price equals average total costs. At this point price, marginal cost, and average total cost are all equal at the profit-maximizing output level and economic profit equals zero; the profit rectangle has been reduced to a single point as figure 17.9 illustrates. Firms will no longer have any incentive to enter the industry; they can do just as well by earning normal profits outside the market.

Since the lure to enter the industry has ceased, the supply curve is not going to shift any more. Assuming everything in the economy (demand and costs in particular) remain constant, this output level will persist and P = ATC will be the long-run equilibrium for the market.

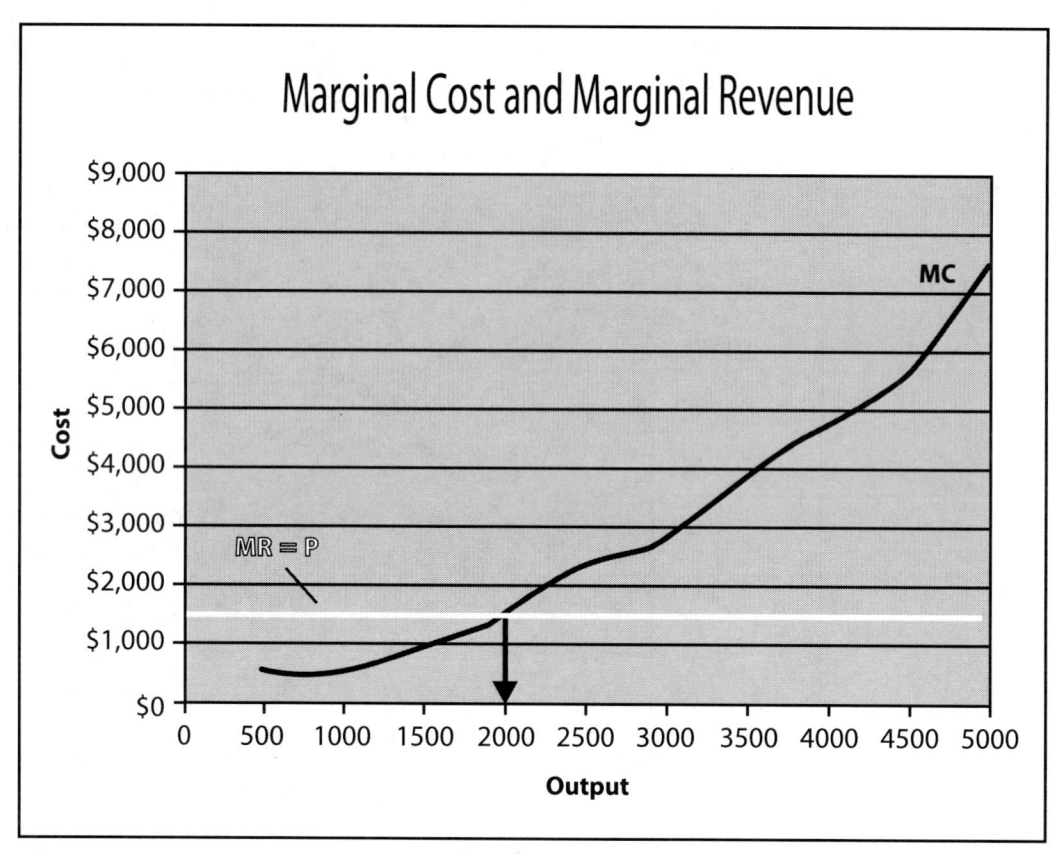

Figure 17.8 • New Equilibrium
When the market price fell from $2,500 to $1,500 the profit-maximizing output level for the average firm fell from 2500 to 2000.

If price ever rises above ATC (due to a drop in costs or an increase in demand) there will be excessive profits that will attract new entrants until the price falls back into equality with ATC. If price ever falls below ATC (due to an increase in costs or falling demand) losses will force firms out of the market until price rises back into equality with ATC.

Market Splits: Smart Phones

The firms in the zero-profit mobile phone industry realized that profits would only increase if they improve their product (increasing consumer demand) or affect a cost reduction. While both strategies would increase profit margins, reducing costs would be a safer strategy since the other option would have you putting money and effort into an improved product that the consumer might reject.

At this point the mobile phone market split as different firms took on the two different strategies. The market where firms improved the mobile phone with new features became known as the smart phone industry while other firms attempted to make the basic, utilitarian mobile phone at lower and lower cost in another market.

Nokia was one of the many companies that chose to improve its product and enter the smart phone market. The Nokia 9000 Communicator, released in 1993, integrated fax, email, and web browsing capabilities at a time when few home computers could accomplish as much. Soon hundreds of other companies, attracted by the profits earned by Nokia's new design, followed suit with their own sophisticated new models.

Long-Run Equilibrium

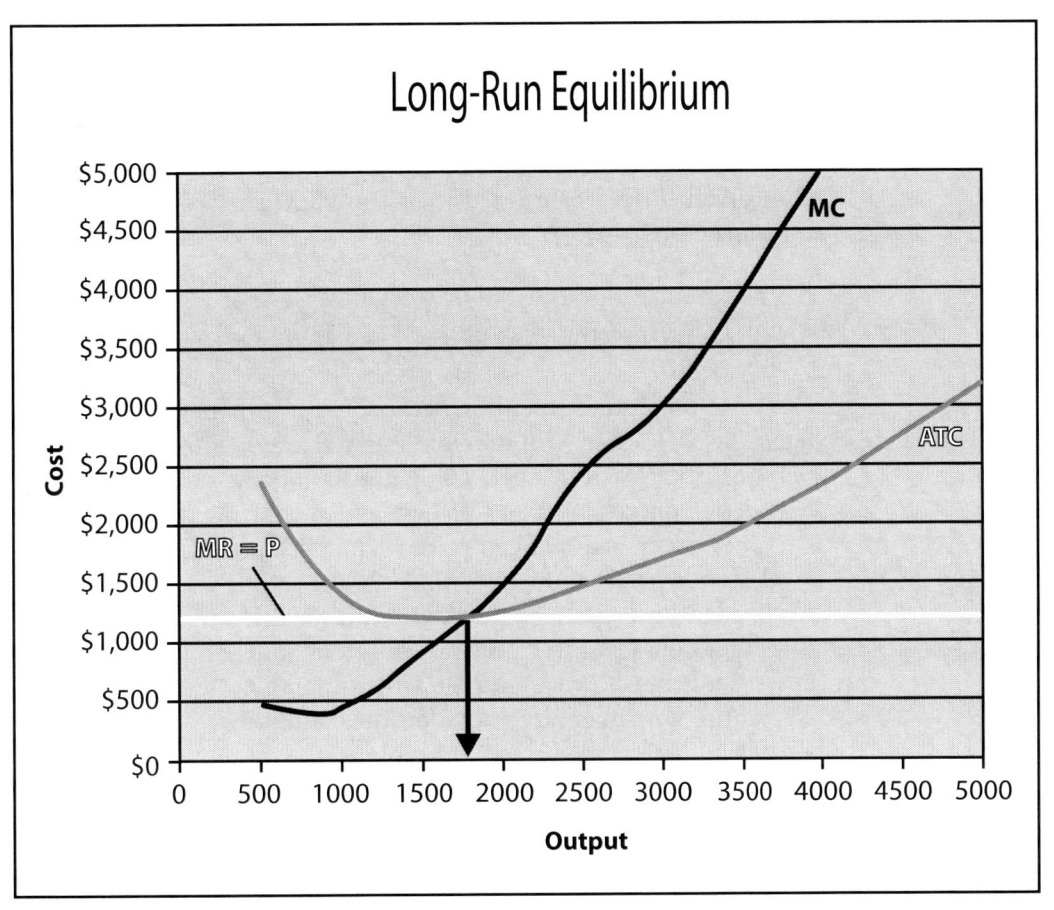

Figure 17.9 • Zero Profit Equilibrium
Firms will not stop entering the market until economic profits have completely disappeared. When price equals ATC at the profit-maximizing output level, there is no profit rectangle to be seen.

Other companies chose to tinker with the existing basic mobile phone and make it cheaper. Firms learned about the components of the mobile phones and the process of putting the phones together over time, leading to more efficient and cheaper production. This lower cost of production slowly caused the ATC curve to shift downward and profits to emerge in this market as well.

Price Competition. The primary means of lowering costs was reducing the level of technology in the phones. Not only were the internal components a major part of the material cost, installing them involved heavy labor cost as well. The explosion of the mobile phone industry provided technical components at much lower prices and allowed cell phone manufacturers to reduce cost and every firm in the market had to do so if they want to stay profitable.

Further Supply Shifts

In the beginning of this chapter we discussed that one of the ways to decrease the marginal cost curve was through technological improvement. The emergence of low-cost digital and technical components was just such an improvement. It allowed the firms to produce phones at a lower average and marginal cost at every output level. The result was a shift in the intersection of the price line and the marginal cost curve.

As average costs fell, profits reappeared. Once again, existing firms had incentives to increase production and new entrants had incentives to enter the market. This rush into the market caused the same supply curve shift as in figure 17.7 and a race toward zero profits as before; increased supply led to lower market prices and lower profit margins. Needless to the say, the profits generated by this technological improvement were short-lived. Prices continued to fall as old firms competed with new firms for customers' dollars.

Shutdown Decision and Exiting the Market

At a certain point, competition became so great that even some of the biggest firms were facing heavy losses. With the investment decision already made, however, they couldn't just turn their back on their company. As long as sales covered variable costs, the factory stayed open since that was better than shutting down and eating its fixed costs.

Once entry had reduced price so much that ATC lied above price at every output level, firms were earning loses in the short run. It was then up to these firms to decide whether to keep producing at the profit-maximizing output level or cease production until they could exit the industry. Motorola, for example, has already ceased production at its Hangzhou, China, and Singapore plants because the price it received no longer covers the cost of producing additional units there. Despite the success of its Droid smart phone, it is likely that Motorola will exit the mobile phone market once it is free of its fixed costs.

Market exit causes the opposite effect to market entry. As firms leave the market the market supply shifts to the right, causing the market price to rise. The surviving firms see their profits rise. Exit will continue until the average profit level in the industry returns to zero. Entrepreneurs will flee markets with negative profits just as quickly as they will rush toward industries with positive profits.

IV. THE COMPETITIVE PROCESS

Allocative Efficiency

While competition in the mobile phone market led to a dramatic decrease in profits over time, it also resulted in great benefits to the consumer. Modern mobile phones work better, faster, and longer than the original Motorola DynaTAC and cost much less in terms of real dollars.

The high profits that originally existed in the cell phone industry provided a signal that consumers were willing and able to pay high prices for mobile phones. New firms heeded this signal and entered the industry, increasing the allocation of resources. The market mechanism and the profit motive coordinated this reallocation. As long as consumers wanted more mobile phones (profits remained high) more resources moved into this industry, providing more of this highly desired good to society.

In fact, a competitive industry must provide us with the most efficient allocation of resources because of marginal cost pricing. Since the amount consumers are willing to pay for every good (the market price determined by supply and demand) equals the opportunity cost of producing that good (the marginal cost), society is getting the optimal amount of every good produced in a competitive market. Article 17.1 discusses how a lack of competition in the postal delivery has led to inefficiencies in the market.

Article 17.1:
Competition in Postal Delivery is the Solution

Customers must be offered an alternative to the service which has been constantly interrupted by unofficial action, and which now threatens them with a total stoppage, argues Madsen Pirie.

by Madsen Pirie

Published: 8:21AM BST 20 Oct 2009

The impending mail strike makes it clear how near-monopoly services seem to breed dinosaur unions. The ability to shut down a service ups the ante for the unions. In services where there is a competitive market, customers can turn to other suppliers. Lord Mandelson rightly points out that a mail strike now will turn customers to alternative communications technologies, customers who will probably not return.

Some will turn to other mail deliverers, rather than other technologies, but the problem here is that the Royal Mail does the end delivery, the so-called 'last mile.' Other firms such as the Dutch-owned TNT, use Royal Mail postmen and women for the final delivery through letterboxes. This means that the Communication Workers Union (CWU) has the power to shut down the service totally, giving it a massive industrial muscle it has shown itself quite prepared to use.

One reason why this state of affairs has continued is that the Post Office is uniquely exempt from paying VAT on its services, as its would-be competitors have to. This means that a rival has to be 15 percent (and soon 20 percent) more efficient to compete effectively. Most markets are won or lost on much smaller percentage margins than that. TNT has a case pending before the European Court protesting the unfairness and calling for a level playing field. Until then, though, it is effectively priced out.

The strike is about modernization, as postal services have to streamline to take on the challenge of electronic communication. The government and management know that more efficient and automated practices must come if mail delivery is to survive.

It would be a good move now for the VAT rule to be changed, putting a level playing field into place for postal services. This would give firms like TNT the chance to set up end delivery and keep the mail services running despite the CWU shutdown. This would give the customers an alternative to the service which has been constantly interrupted by unofficial action, and which now threatens them with a total stoppage.

Questions:
1. What market power does the Dutch post office have over its competitors?
2. Why does the Dutch government exempt the post office from paying VAT tax?
3. How would removing the tax exemption limit the postal union's ability to raise prices and lower service?

© Telegraph Media Group Limited 2009

Productive Efficiency

Since competitive markets also drive price down to the level of minimum average costs in the long run, they also achieve productive efficiency. In the long run, firms produce at an output level where price not only equals marginal cost, but minimum ATC as well. At this minimum ATC point, the market is producing the good with the least amount of resources possible leaving the maximum amount of resources available for other forms of production.

Zero Economic Profit

While competitive markets tend toward zero profits in the long run, this equilibrium is hardly ever reached; there is constant entry and exit into competitive industry, causing profits to fluctuate. But since it is a possibility, firms in competitive industries are constantly trying to improve their product or cut costs. Competition creates an incentive for innovation of new products and production processes. Increased competition in the market for legal services, realtors, and other services has led to price decreases for consumers in recent years.

CHAPTER 17 SUMMARY

- For a competitive firm, the **supply curve** and **marginal cost curve are identical.**
- The market supply curve of a perfectly competitive industry **will shift to the right** as new firms enter to take advantage of economic profits.
- As more firms enter the industry **the market price falls**, reducing firm profits.
- As long as **economic profits are positive**, firms will continue to enter a competitive industry.
- As long as **economic profits are negative**, firms will exit a competitive industry.
- In the long run, **perfectly competitive firms earn zero profits** because price equals minimum ATC.
- Competitive markets are **productively efficient** because all firms are forced to produce at the output level that minimizes ATC.
- Competitive markets are **allocatively efficient** because all firms produce where price equals marginal cost.

CHAPTER 17

Exercises

Name _____

1) Which of the following is **NOT** a shifter of the market supply curve?
   A) Number of sellers C) Price of inputs
   B) Demand D) Technology

   1) _____

2) Why do prices tend to drop over time in a competitive market?
   A) People get tired of the good and demand falls
   B) Deflation
   C) Firms use discounts to attract customers
   D) New entry causes the market supply curve to shift to the right

   2) _____

3) Entry in a competitive industry will stop when
   A) barriers to entry are used. C) profits become negative.
   B) profits drop to zero. D) P < AVC.

   3) _____

4) What is the relationship between price and ATC in the long run for a competitive market?
   A) P = min ATC C) P < min ATC
   B) P > min ATC D) Not enough information.

   4) _____

5) Refer to the figure below for questions 5 and 6

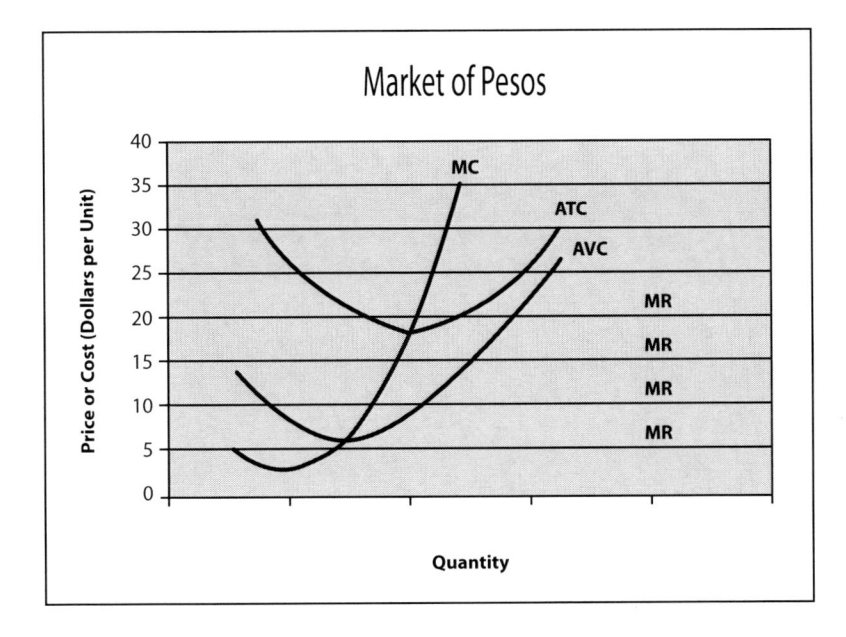

   Market of Pesos

   The firm in the figure should shutdown in the short run if the market price is below:
   A) $5 C) $15
   B) $10 D) $20

   5) _____

321

6) In the long run, this firm would stay in this market only if the market price was equal to or higher than:
   A) $5
   B) $10
   C) $15
   D) $20

   6) _____

7) In the long run, competitive firms earn
   A) zero economic profit.
   B) zero accounting profit.
   C) positive economic profits.
   D) negative economic profits.

   7) _____

8) What type of efficiency is achieved when the market produces the exact right mix of goods and services that society most desires?
   A) Productive efficiency
   B) Technical efficiency
   C) Allocative efficiency
   D) Social efficiency

   8) _____

9) Why are the profits in any competitive market only temporary?

   _____
   _____
   _____
   _____
   _____
   _____

10) Explain how a perfectly competitive market promotes productive efficiency (production at minimum ATC).

   _____
   _____
   _____
   _____
   _____
   _____

Chapter 18

Monopoly

I. MARKET POWER

The Downward-Sloping Demand Curve

Unlike the competitive firms we have discussed so far, monopoly firms have significant market power. Monopolies develop out of the ability to set up barriers to entry, but the essence of market power is the ability to set the price in your market.

Remember that competitive firms faced a horizontal demand curve; no matter how much they produced, the product they sold always brought in the same price. The market as a whole faced the typical downward-sloping curve, which is why the market price fell when more firms entered the market.

Although these two demand curves seem to contradict each other, they arise because each individual firm in the competitive market is so small relative to the total market, that its choice of output has no effect on market supply. Any one firm makes up so little of the industry that they have no market power and cannot change the price.

Monopoly

The market structure of a monopoly industry is quite different. Since the monopoly firm is the only firm selling in the market, the monopoly firm's supply decision and the

324 ECONOMICS TODAY

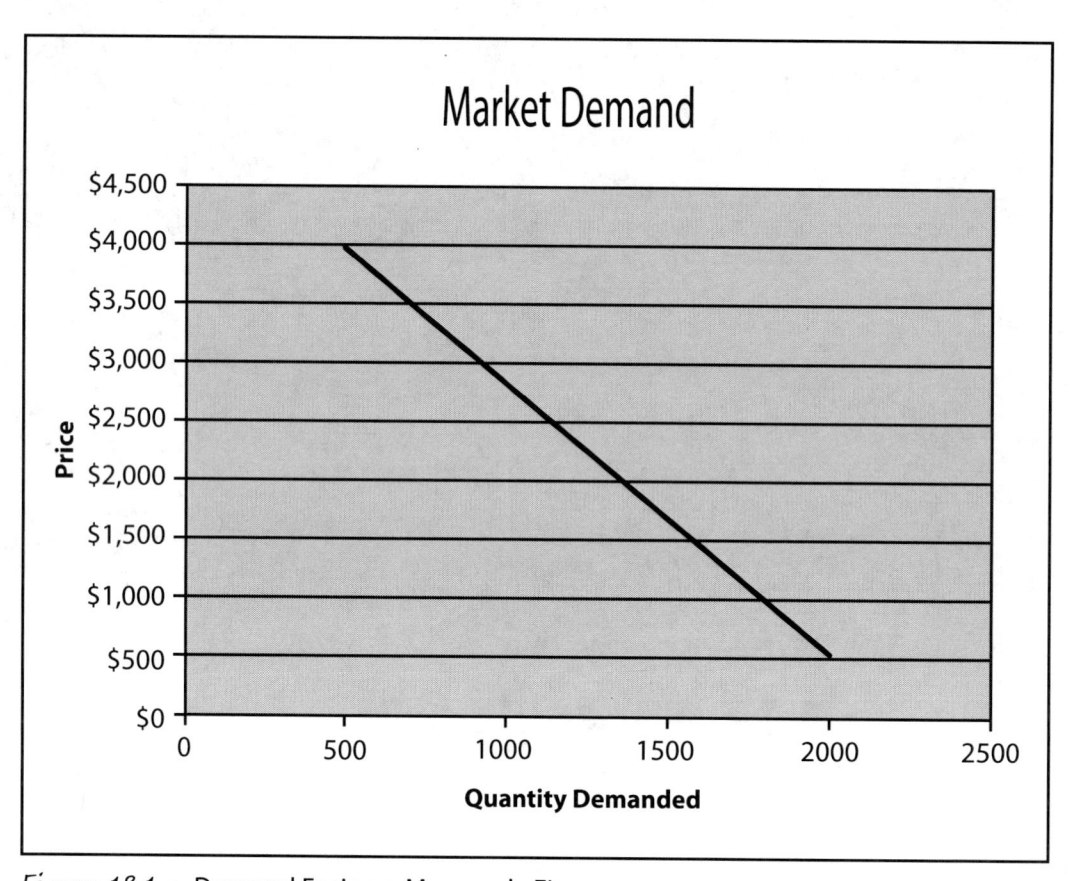

Figure 18.1 • Demand Facing a Monopoly Firm
Since a monopoly firm is the only firm in the market, its demand curve is the same as the market demand curve.

market supply are the same thing. As a result, the demand curve facing the monopoly firm is downward sloping just like the market demand curve, as figure 18.1 illustrates.

The monopoly firm faces a downward-sloping demand curve because its choice of output completely determines the market supply; it has complete market power. Whatever amount it decides to produce will be the amount available for purchase.

Price and Marginal Revenue

While it may seem like having only one firm instead of an infinite number of competitive firms might simplify things, the monopoly firm actually has a more complicated profit maximization problem. They still have the same basic profit maximization rule as the competitive firm: never produce a unit that brings in less money than it costs to produce. The profit-maximizing output level is still where marginal revenue equals marginal cost.

Since the competitive firm faces a horizontal demand curve, we know that the amount of money brought in by individual unit will always be equal to the market price. The monopoly firm, on the other hand, faces a downward-sloping demand curve. As a result, marginal revenue does not equal price for the monopolist.

In fact, figure 18.2 shows marginal revenue is always below price for the monopoly firm, where price is identified by the demand curve. In such a scenario, setting output to where price equals marginal cost will certainly not maximize profits for the monopoly firm since marginal revenue will be below marginal cost at this point.

Marginal Revenue

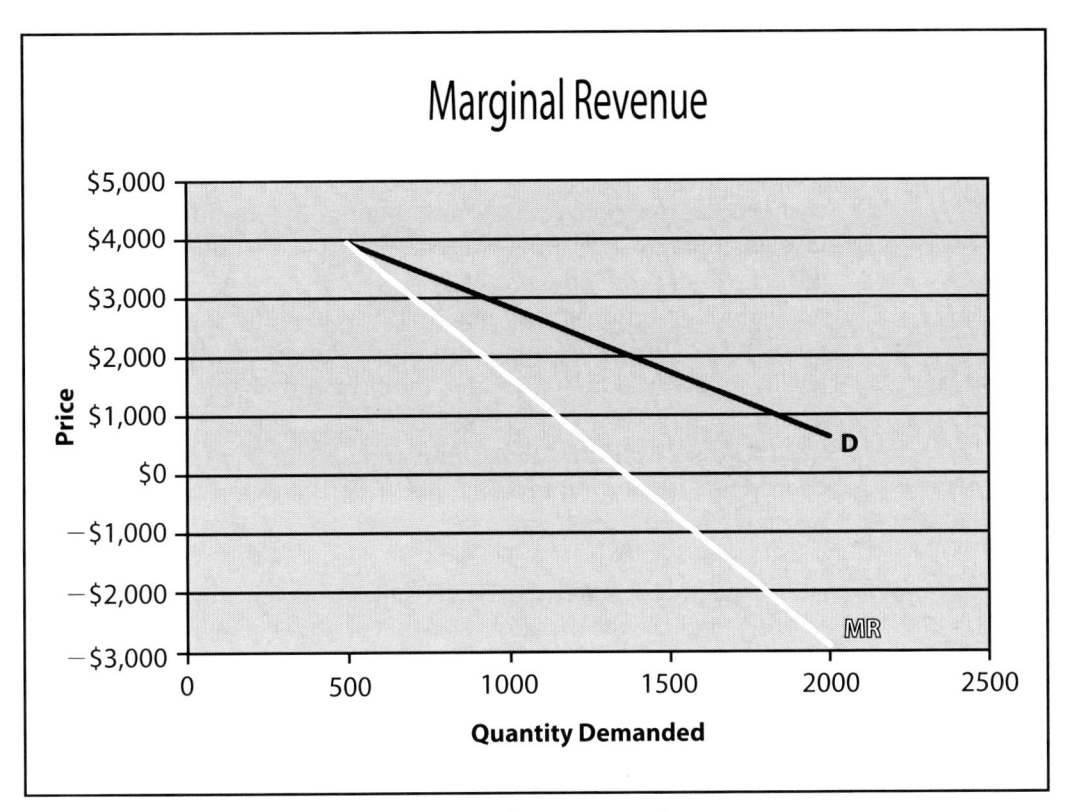

Figure 18.2 • Marginal Revenue Curve for a Monopoly Firm
If a monopoly firm wants to sell more units, it must lower the price of all units it plans to sell, resulting in marginal revenue being lower than price for every output level.

How can marginal revenue be less than price if it represents the amount of money generated by selling one more unit of the good? The issue here is that because of the downward-sloping demand curve, the firm must decrease its price if it wants to sell more; they can sell 250 phones for $4,000, but if they want to sell 500 phones they have to lower the price to $3,500, for example.

But it's not just the additional 250 phones that sell for $3,500; the first 250 units must also sell at that price. So the options are selling 250 phones at $4,000 or 500 for $3,500. We can use this information to calculate the marginal revenue of each of the 250 additional phones. Marginal revenue tells us how much additional total revenue the firm gets by selling the additional phones.

$$\text{Marginal Revenue} = \frac{\text{Change in Total Revenue}}{\text{Change in Output}}$$

$$\frac{\$1,750,000 - \$1,000,000}{500 - 250} = \$3,000$$

The second 250 phones brought in an additional $875,000 in revenue, but reduced the amount brought in by the first 250 units by $125,000, resulting in an increase in total revenue of $750,000. Dividing this increase by the increase in output tells us that each of the additional phones brings in $3,000 in marginal revenue. Each successive phone will bring in less and less, not just because of a lower selling price, but because it will reduce the price of the previous goods as well. As long as the demand curve is downward sloping, marginal revenue will be below price, resulting in the marginal revenue curve lying below the demand curve.

Profit Maximization

The addition of a downward-sloping marginal revenue adds a new wrinkle; the monopoly firm needs to find the intersection of the marginal cost curve and marginal revenue (not price) to determine profit maximization. At any output level above this, marginal cost exceeds marginal revenue and total profits would decrease. At any output level below this, marginal revenue exceeds marginal cost and the firm is sacrificing potential profits by not producing more.

The intersection of the marginal revenue and marginal cost curves in figure 18.3 gives the profit-maximizing output level, but to calculate the total profits at this output level we need to know the price the firm will charge. It might be tempting to say the firm will charge as much as it wants because people have no choice. But people are limited in how much they are willing and able to pay for something—they could always choose not to buy the product, and that limitation is completely summarized by the market demand curve.

The market demand curve tells the firm exactly how much it can charge and still sell all it wants to sell. If it determined its profit-maximizing output level is 1000 units, for example, it will use the demand curve to tell it how much people are willing and able to pay to 1000 phones—in this case, $2,500. Then we can use the same rectangle between price, ATC, and quantity we used in Chapters 16 and 17 to find the total profits for this firm.

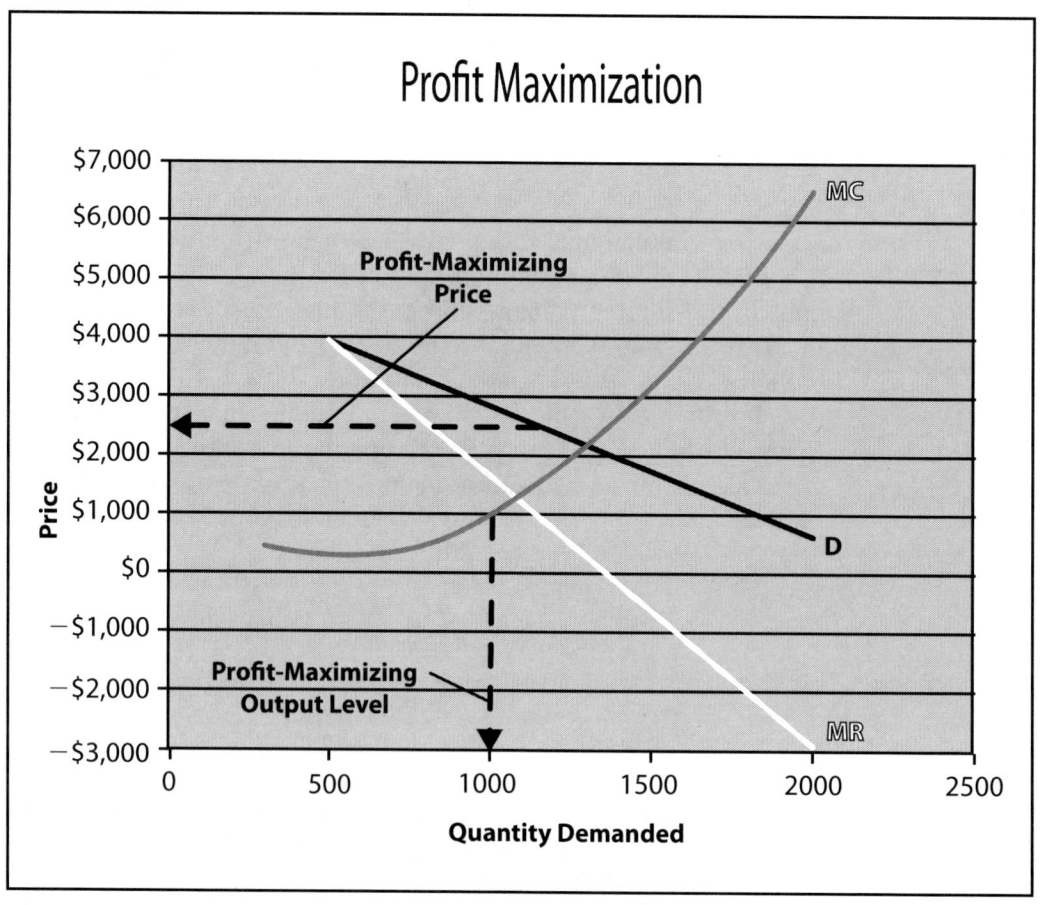

Figure 18.3 • Production Decision for a Monopoly Firm
The profit-maximizing output level for a monopoly firm is determined by the intersection of the marginal revenue and marginal cost curves. The maximum amount that consumers are willing to pay for that output level is given by the demand curve.

II. MARKET POWER AT WORK

Structure

Remember that when we went through the history of the mobile phone market we saw that competition and low barriers to entry led to a better product at a lower price. Would that same result have occurred if the mobile phone industry had started as a monopoly? Let's investigate how the mobile phone industry would have evolved if Motorola had been able to create and sustain a monopoly.

Let's suppose that Motorola was able to get a patent on the technology that makes a mobile phone work. With this legal right, Motorola could have effectively barred any new firms from producing mobile phones for sale: They would have erected a barrier to entry. Clearly, the market evolution we saw in Chapter 17 would not be possible in this case. We saw what happened when new firms entered the competitive cell phone industry—profits fell for all of the original firms. A monopoly will want to avoid this so restricting supply is going to be one of their key objectives.

To better compare monopoly structure with perfect competition, let's look at the production at one of the monopoly firm's many plants across the country and compare it to that of the average firm in the early competitive mobile phone market. Just to make the comparison easier, let's assume no economies of scale so that the single monopoly plant and the competitive firm face the same costs.

This way we can use the same marginal cost and ATC curves from the competitive mobile phone industry in Chapter 17. Likewise, market demand should remain unchanged. There is no reason to believe people would be more or less willing to buy mobile phones at any particular price whether they came from a competitive firm or a monopoly firm; market structure is not a demand shifter.

Production Decision

The difference here is going to be the production decision. Since the monopoly firm faces a downward-sloping demand curve, its marginal revenue curve is not going to be a horizontal line at the market price. Instead, its marginal revenue curve will be downward sloping and below the demand curve. As figure 18.4 indicates, its profit-maximizing output will therefore be lower than that of the competitive firm.

Unlike a competitive industry, a monopolist can coordinate the production of its plants so that they don't compete with each other and lower the price. Competitive firms realize they can sell as much as they want at the market price without affecting marginal revenue. The monopolist also realizes that any increase in production at any of the plants will cause a movement down the demand curve and a drop in the price.

Marginal Revenue. Since marginal revenue always lies below price for the monopoly firm, producing at the competitive equilibrium (Price = MC) is not profit maximizing. Any individual plant that acted this way would get a stern warning by the corporate headquarters.

The competitive mobile phone market reached this equilibrium due to the intersection of the market supply and market demand curves. At a price of $2,500, each firm could sell as much as they wanted in 1990. Each individual firm then chose to produce until marginal cost equaled that price, which occurred at 2500 units for the average competitive firm.

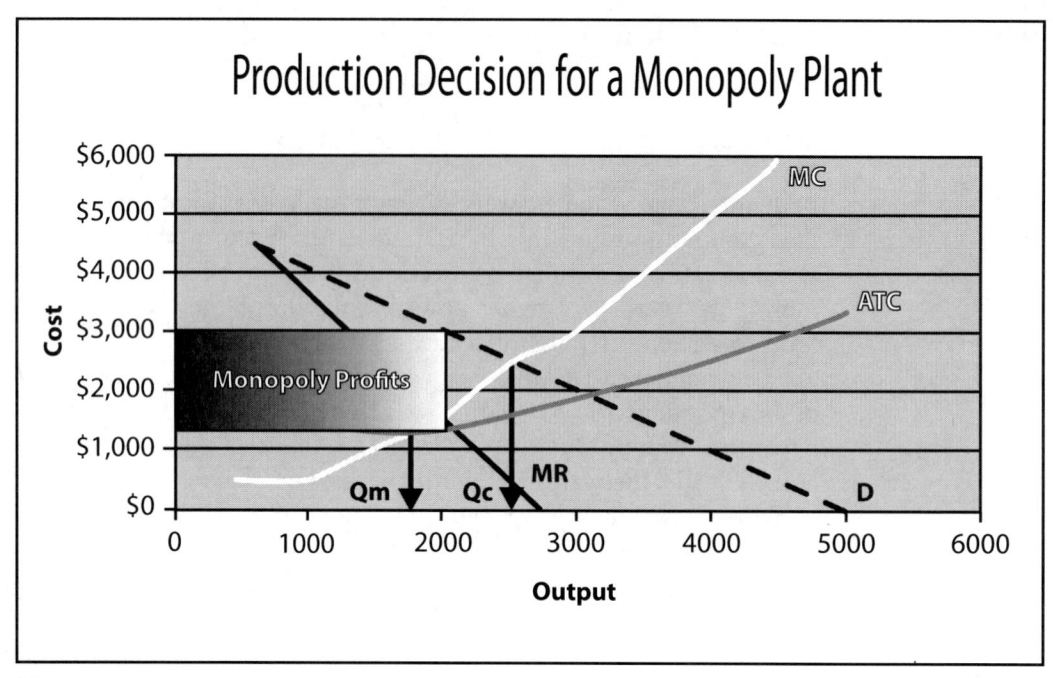

Figure 18.4 • Cell Phone Monopoly
Since the monopoly is able to coordinate production, it can earn higher profits than a competitive firm. This monopoly equilibrium occurs at a higher price and lower output level than the competitive equilibrium.

Reduced Output. Since all of the plants in a monopoly firm act in a coordinated fashion, any production decision happening at one plant is simultaneously occurring at all of the other plants; that is, the output decisions at an individual monopoly plant affects the market price and the marginal revenue.

This impact means the marginal revenue of the 2500th phone for the monopoly plant is only $500, instead of the $2,500 received by the competitive firm. Since the marginal cost of that unit is still $2,500, the monopoly plant clearly wouldn't choose the same output level of the competitive firm if it wanted to maximize profits.

In fact, since marginal revenue falls with output and marginal cost rises with it, the profit-maximizing output for each plant in the monopoly firm must be less than 2500 units. Just like any firm, this optimal output level is found by the intersection of the marginal revenue and marginal cost curves, at about 2000 mobile phones. The difference between the monopoly output and the output of the competitive market in the long run (where ATC is at its minimum) is called the monopoly's excess capacity. The monopoly's profit-maximizing output will always fall short of where ATC is minimized because of the firm's downward-sloping demand curve. Due to excess capacity, monopolies will not result in productive efficiency.

Monopoly Price

The reduction in output would cause a shortage at the market of price of $2,500. As consumers competed for this now scarcer quantity supplied, they would bid up the price. We can observe this in the fact that the monopoly equilibrium is further up the market demand curve than the competitive equilibrium. According to this demand curve, consumers are willing and able to pay $3,000 for each of the plant's 2000 phones. Monopolists purposely reduce output to raise the equilibrium price.

The difference between the monopoly price and marginal cost is called the markup. Markup exists not only in monopoly industries but in the imperfectly competitive market structures of oligopoly and monopolistic competition, as well. As a result of markup, monopoly firms will not achieve allocative efficiency since price exceeds marginal cost at the profit-maximizing output level for the monopoly.

Monopoly Profits

Now that we know the plant's production decision, we can calculate its total profits and see if keeping new entrants out of the industry paid off. We can use the profit rectangle from figure 18.4 to determine total profits.

Total profits equal average profits times the quantity at profit-maximizing output level. The price is $3,000 and the ATC at 2000 phones is $1,375 (same as the competitive firm from Chapter 17), for an average profit of $1,625. Multiply this by 2000 and you will get a total profit of $3,250,000, much higher than the $2,250,000 competitive firms were receiving at even the earliest stages of the mobile phone market.

The monopoly firm has squeezed additional profits out of the industry by coordinating its individual plants to reduce quantity supplied and push up prices. A monopoly will always have less output, a higher price, and larger profits than a competitive industry at equilibrium.

Barriers to Entry

Perhaps more importantly, the barriers to entry held by the monopoly firm mean that its profits aren't going anywhere. We saw that new firms flooded into the mobile phone industry, reducing the prices so far that many firms were convinced to exit for lack of profits. In fact, every competitive industry tends toward zero profits in the long run.

This monopoly doesn't have to worry about that, though. Since we assumed Motorola has control of a key input for its product, new firms cannot enter the industry without being sued out of existence. Without this surge of competition, that downward pressure on prices and profits is nowhere to be found. Without that pressure, the monopolist has no incentive to reduce costs, lower prices, or improve its product. Until someone comes out with a viable alternative, consumers will be forced to pay the monopolist's price, and many who would have bought a mobile phone in the competitive scenario will go without one.

III. COMPARISON WITH COMPETITION

Sequence of Events

In the competitive industry, high profits created an incentive for new firms to enter the market. Without any barriers to entry, new firms entered and increased the supply in the market. This increased supply lowered the price closer and closer to the minimum ATC, reducing the profit rectangle. At all times, each individual firm produced where price equaled marginal cost. If firms wanted to bring back profits they needed to reduce costs or improve the product.

In a monopoly market, even higher profits create an even greater incentive for new firms to enter. However, these firms are not able to enter because of the barriers to entry set up by the monopoly firm. Without any outside competition, the monopoly has no incentive to reduce prices and sets his output to maximize profits.

Since the monopolist faces a downward-sloping demand curve, price is always above marginal revenue and therefore above marginal cost at the profit-maximizing level. The monopoly firm also does not have to worry about improving its product or reducing costs because there is no downward pressure on prices or profits.

Incentive to Improve

Because competitive firms have to continuously improve their product and reduce costs if they want to remain profitable, competitive industries improve our production possibilities; more efficient production means more resources left for other types of production. Since there are no such incentives to improve in monopoly industries, monopolies tend to limit productivity and economic growth.

Mix of Output

Another area where the two market structures deviate is in marginal cost pricing. Since each individual competitive firm faces a horizontal demand curve, they will keep producing until marginal cost equals price. When every firm does this, we are assured that people are getting the right amount of the competitive good.

Monopoly firms coordinate the production of their individual plants. They will restrict supply if it increases profits, regardless of how many mobile phones the people want. This will lead to more resources going into less desired goods and ultimately a less efficient mix of output. The reallocation of resources caused by a monopoly has far-reaching impacts for the economy. Restricting output below the competitive equilibrium affects not only the price in the mobile phone market, but the employment level in that market, the amount of resources allocated to other markets, and the distribution of income.

Limits to Power

Even though the monopolist has control over the entire market supply of its product and consumers have no choice of where to purchase it, there is an unmistakable limit to the monopoly's power. They can decide the output for the entire market, q_m, but cannot set the price above the demand curve. They may want to sell 1000 phones—the profit-maximizing output for the monopoly—at $3,000 or $4,000 or $1 million, but they cannot; people will just refuse to buy the product.

In fact, the monopoly only has one power the competitive firm does not have: It can completely determine the quantity supplied for the market. This gives the monopolist the power to shift the supply curve so that equilibrium is at any point on the demand curve that it wants. Of course is it will choose the quantity consistent with MR = MC. What the monopoly cannot do is change the demand curve.

The limit on the monopoly's power lies in the demand curve itself. The more elastic the demand (the more responsive consumers are to price changes), the less the monopolist will be able to squeeze additional profits from the market. If consumers greatly re-

(a)

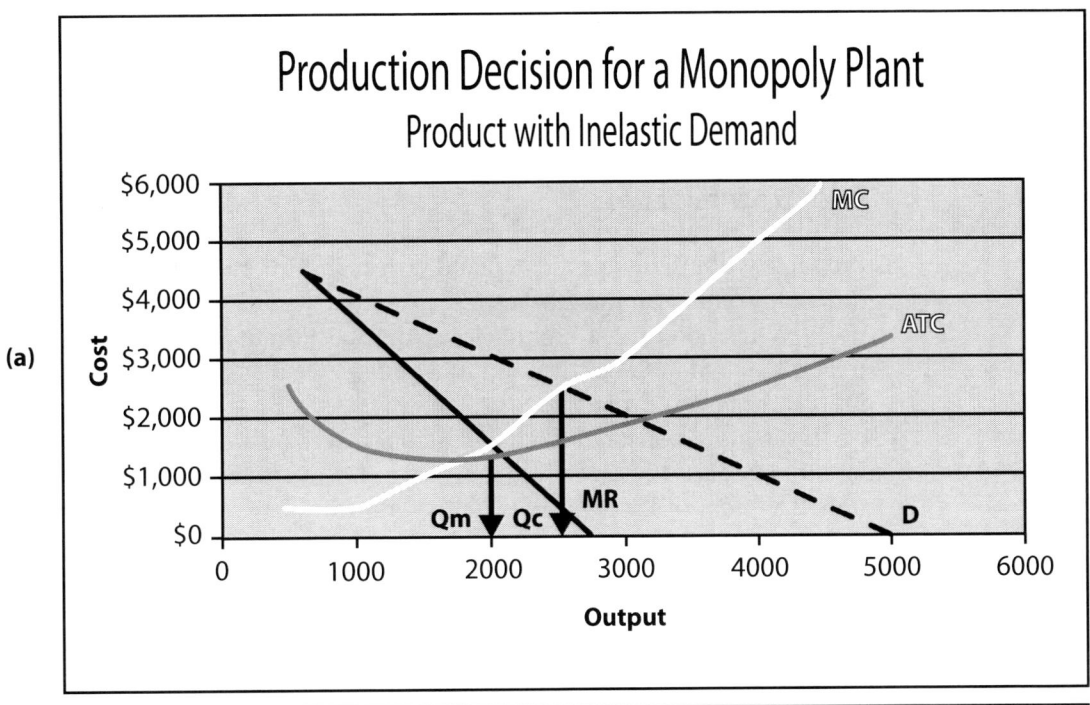

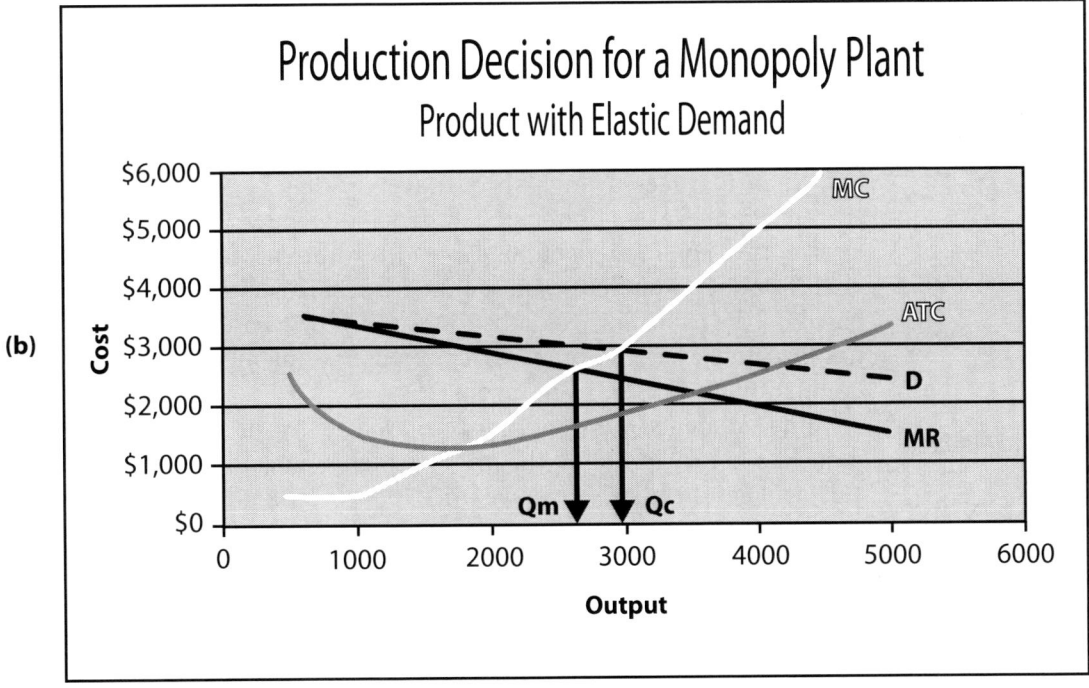

Production Decision for a Monopoly Plant
Product with Inelastic Demand

(b)

Production Decision for a Monopoly Plant
Product with Elastic Demand

Figure 18.5 • Monopoly Power
The difference between the monopoly outcome and the competitive outcome shrinks when the demand for the good is more elastic. The less elastic the demand for a good is, the greater the monopoly's power will be.

duce quantity demanded when price changes only a little bit, as in figure 18.5a, the monopolist cannot choose an output level very far from the competitive outcome without sacrificing a great amount of sales.

On the other hand, if consumers do not respond very much to a price increase, resulting in the very inelastic demand curve presented in figure 18.5b, the monopoly can increase price far above the competitive price without giving up much sales. Monopolies that sell products that are considered necessities or have few substitutes can reap huge profits by taking advantage of this fact.

Price Discrimination

Products with highly elastic demand curves limit the monopolist's ability to extract additional profits from the market. This is only true if the firm charges everyone the same price. When good has a highly elastic demand, there are usually some consumers who treat it like a more inelastic good; they might see it as more of a necessity, or the substitute might be too expensive for them.

If the monopolist could charge higher prices only to these consumers, he might not lose many sales. Charging different prices for the same good is called price discrimination. The goal of the firm is to sell every unit at the maximum price each individual consumer is willing and able to pay. Local businesses often force tourists to pay higher prices, since they do not have the time or language skills to haggle over prices as much as locals do.

A classic example of price discrimination is in the airline industry. Have you ever wondered why plane tickets are so much cheaper when you buy them in advance? It is because airlines have two prices: one for business travelers and one for nonbusiness travelers. Nonbusiness travelers usually plan trips in advance and have many alternative modes of transportation. Airlines have to compete with these different forms of travel for these customers. Business travelers often have to be somewhere on short notice and have no choice but to use air travel. Airlines do not have to compete with anyone when it comes to high-speed travel so they charge a higher price to those consumers who have less options; their demand is much less elastic.

Another common example comes from the movie theater. Movie theaters tend to give discounts to students and senior citizens. However, this price discrimination is not based on the availability of substitutes as in the airline industry; presumably everyone has the same access to other forms of entertainment. A more likely source of the discrimination is differences in income.

Since students and senior citizens are usually on a fixed income, movie tickets are more of a luxury for them; the price elasticity demand is higher. As a result, movie theaters will get the highest average price for each ticket by lowering the price for students and senior citizens and charging everyone else full price.

Barriers to Entry

Patents. Without the ability to keep potential competitors out of the market, monopoly power and the profits that come with it would not last very long. In order to keep other firms from producing identical or similar goods, monopolies impose a variety of barriers to entry to their industry.

One such barrier is a patent or other form of intellectual property rights. In the United States, a patent gives a company the exclusive right to produce a particular product for twenty years. Other forms of property rights, like copyrights and trademarks, operate in a similar fashion.

Monopoly Franchises. Even without patents, the government can bestow the exclusive right to produce a good or service in a particular area. The teams in the four major professional sports leagues are examples of monopoly franchises; they are protected from having another team in that league being established without their approval. In addition, local TV affiliates are given exclusive rights to broadcast network TV shows in a particular region.

Control of Inputs. While a monopoly may not hold a patent on the product it produces, it can still create a barrier to entry by controlling inputs necessary to the production of its product. For example, an entrepreneur can have all the airplanes, pilots, and flight attendants he wants, but without landing rights and terminal gates at an airport, you cannot compete in the airline industry. Microsoft and Intel were both found guilty of exerting monopoly power by not sharing the features of its operating system to competing vendors and making their products incompatible with competing products.

Litigation. If a new firm tried to challenge and overcome existing barriers to entry it might find itself sued by the monopoly firm. The monopoly's lawyers would tie up the case in court so long that the new firm would run out of time and money well before the case was settled. Often, just the threat of facing an established monopoly firm in the courts is enough to scare away potential competition.

Merger and Acquisition. Another way a monopoly could deal with a potential rival firm would be to just buy it out. If a new firm ever did come up with an idea good enough to challenge the monopoly, the monopolyfirm might find it in its interest just to pay the innovator to go away. This process, called horizontal integration, often results in higher consumer prices and may not result in a higher quality product if the monopoly firm just represses the new technologies.

Economies of Scale. Finally, many production processes exhibit increasing returns to scale; the bigger the company, the cheaper it is to produce. In other words, it is more efficient to produce in a large factory than a small one. In such a market, the entrenched monopoly can also produce at a lower cost than the start-up company and may price them out of the market before they even get started.

IV. PROS AND CONS OF MARKET POWER

Society usually has a negative view of monopolies. People do not like companies to have the ability to manipulate prices and markets. Still, it is possible that a monopoly structure might be benign or even beneficial to society.

First, the additional profits earned by monopolies means it has more funds to use for research and development. These high profits also encourage other people to innovate in other industries so that they might have their own monopoly some day. Increasing returns to scale might mean that a monopoly produces at a lower average cost than a competitive industry. Finally, it is thought that the potential for competition might limit the power of monopolies as much as actual competition would.

Research and Development

Since monopolies are sheltered from competition and have plenty of funds from monopoly profits, it might make sense that they are in a better position to undertake research and development than a competitive firm would be. A competitive firm might be so worried about staying in business on a day-to-day basis that it might not take such a long-term view.

While a monopoly has the means to undertake R&D, they do not really have an incentive. As we saw in Chapter 17, competitive firms must improve their products or reduce costs just to maintain profits. Since monopolies have barriers to entry, a monopolist does not have to do anything to keep making high profits. In fact, the monopolist might suppress any improvement that makes current technology obsolete.

A perfectly competitive firm has to keep innovating to stay ahead of the competition. This pressure to keep profits positive draws them toward research and development. Without this pressure, monopolies will not want to waste resources improving a product that is still bringing in significant profits.

Incentives to Produce

The second argument for monopolies does use incentives as its basis. The existence of monopolies and the high profits they earn, encourages entrepreneurs to develop new products in the hopes of one day having their own monopoly. Since monopoly profits are higher than competitive profits—especially in the long run—allowing monopolies to operate will create a greater incentive for entrepreneurship.

While the incentive argument has merit, it is not entirely accurate. The innovator of a new product would still make large profits in a competitive market, if only at first. The continued innovation in the United States economy throughout history illustrates that the profits in competitive markets are not insignificant when it comes to attracting entrepreneurs.

Further, the existence of monopolies might limit improvements since monopolies might buy out companies with promising ideas or discourage innovation within their own companies. Barriers to entry might deter enterprising young minds from pursuing the production of a revolutionary new product, limiting the country's economic growth.

Economies of Scale

The third argument for monopolies is the most convincing: in markets with economies of scale, having one large firm produce the good is cheaper than having many competitive firms do so. In our hypothetical discussion of a monopoly in the mobile phone industry earlier in this chapter we assumed that the monopoly faced the same costs as the competitive firms. But what if this wasn't the case?

It is certainly reasonable to think that a single, centralized producer of cell phones could do the job better (cheaper) than hundreds of independent firms working in cramped production facilities. If the monopoly can produce its supply of phones at a lower average cost than the competitive industry can in its many firms, those resource savings would translate to an outward shift in the production possibilities curve.

Of course, there is no guarantee that increased size relates to increased efficiency. It may be the case that centralizing production offers no cost saving to the monopoly or may even increase cost (diseconomies of scale). In addition, just because a monopoly does offer cost savings over a competitive market does not mean it is good for the people.

For example, the merger between Sirius and XM Satellite Radio effectively created a monopoly in the satellite radio industry. The two companies argued that the merger would be a good thing since the money they saved by eliminating duplicate stations, sharing transmission systems, and reducing marketing expenses would be transferred to the consumer in the form of lower prices. However, the lack of competition after the merger has led to an increase in prices for the consumer and with no outside pressure from new entry that trend does not seem likely to change in the near future.

Natural Monopolies

Sometimes there are industries where it is always more efficient to have one company produce the good instead of a whole competitive market. As the company that produced the good increases in size, its costs fall so low that would-be rivals have no chance to compete with it. The company's significant economies of scale act as a natural barrier to entry, creating a natural monopoly.

Common examples of natural monopolies are local telephone and utility companies. Since any potential rival would have to set up its own delivery system with cables and grids connected to every house and business, the costs would be so high that there is no way it would be able to compete with the entrenched company in the short run. While natural monopolies may be desirable since they reduce average costs, they may still be abused just like any other monopoly. The government watches natural monopolies carefully to ensure that consumers are getting a higher output for a lower price.

Contestable Markets

There is a fourth argument which states that monopolists' behavior is limited and somewhat controlled by the understanding that there are a significant number of potential competitors just waiting for the monopoly to slip up. If the barriers to entry are insurmountable then this potential competition does not matter, but some monopolies have imperfect barriers and operate in contestable markets.

The idea of contestable markets redirects the discussion of monopolies; it is not the monopoly structure that creates an outcome below the competitive equilibrium, it is the monopoly behavior. If potential competitors scare the monopoly enough, it can be forced into behaving more like a competitive firm, reducing or even eliminating the cost the monopoly imposes on society. In reality, though, a monopoly will not change its behavior until a competitor actually forces its way into the market, shifting the market supply curve to the right and lowering prices and profits.

CHAPTER 18 SUMMARY

- The demand curve facing a monopoly firm is **downward-sloping** because the firm faces the entire market demand.
- Marginal revenue for a monopoly firm **is always below price** because the firm must reduce the price on all units if it wants to increase sales.
- A monopoly firm **maximizes profits where MR = MC**, not Price = MC.
- The monopoly outcome has a **higher price and lower output level** than the competitive equilibrium.
- Monopoly profits are higher than competitive profits in the short run, and are maintained because of **barriers to entry**.
- Monopolies can extract greater profits from the market by charging higher prices to those with a **low price elasticity of demand** for the product.
- **Natural monopolies** may be more efficient than competition in industries with high fixed costs and economies of scale.

CHAPTER 18 Exercises

Name _____

1) The demand curve facing a monopoly is
   A) flat, as is the market demand curve.
   B) flat, while the market demand curve is downward-sloping.
   C) downward-sloping, while the market demand curve is flat.
   D) downward-sloping, as is the market demand curve.

1) _____

2) The marginal revenue curve for a monopolist
   A) is equal to price.
   B) is above price because the firm is a price setter.
   C) is below price because to sell more units the firm must reduce the price of all units.
   D) is below price because the firm is a price taker.

2) _____

3) Which of the following rules is satisfied when a monopoly maximizes profits?
   A) P = MC
   B) MC = ATC
   C) MR = MC
   D) P = MR

3) _____

Use the following information to answer questions 3 and 4.
   A monopoly firm has its profit-maximizing output level at thirty units.
   Its monopoly price is $50 and its ATC at thirty units is $30.

4) What is the firm's average profit per unit?
   A) $20
   B) $50
   C) $25
   D) $30

4) _____

5) What is the firm's total profit?
   A) $600
   B) $1,500
   C) $20
   D) $900

5) _____

6) Price-discriminating firms charge higher prices to those who
   A) have lower price elasticities of demand.
   B) have few substitutes available to them.
   C) have very small incomes relative to the price of the good.
   D) want the product less.

6) _____

7) Which of the following is not a barrier to entry used by monopolies?
   A) Patents
   B) Merger
   C) Diseconomies of scale
   D) Litigation

7) _____

337

8) The argument that monopolies enhance research and development efforts may be weak because 8) _____
   A) monopolies cannot afford research.
   B) a monopoly has no incentive to improve its product or reduce costs.
   C) no current monopoly has a research and development program.
   D) monopolies have to worry about competition.

9) How is the outcome (price and quantity) of the monopoly market different from that of the perfectly competitive market?

10) Why does a monopoly result in both productive and allocative inefficiency?

Chapter 19

Oligopoly

I. MARKET STRUCTURE

We have discussed the differences between the competitive industry and the monopoly, but these two structures are only the two extremes on a broad spectrum of market structures in our economy. Sometimes businesses have some control over price, but not complete control like a monopoly does.

Degrees of Power

The four types of market structures are distinguished by the level of market power held by the firms in it. While a monopoly faces no competition and the competitive firm faces perfect competition, the firms in the other market structures face some level of imperfect competition.

One such type of imperfect competition is the oligopoly market structure. In an oligopoly—a Greek word meaning "few sellers"—only a few firms have market power (the ability to change the market price). This may occur because the few firms erect barriers to prevent entry or they control such a large portion of the market relative to the other firms that they can manipulate market price and quantity.

Determinants of Market Power

There are several factors that result in a firm gaining market power. First, if there are only a few firms in the market to begin with (or only one firm in the case of the monopoly), those firms are going to have significant control over the market. In addition, even if there are many firms a few of them could have market power if they have a large share of the market. Both the number of firms and the relative size of those firms matter for the development of market power.

Next, any successful oligopoly needs to create barriers to entry to defend its profits. Without barriers to entry new firms will want to enter, increasing the number of firms in the market and pushing the market towards the competitive outcome. Finally, the availability of close substitutes makes exercising market power difficult. Consumers will not be pushed around by monopolies or oligopolies it they can get a cheaper substitute elsewhere. Just as in a monopoly, the power of oligopoly firms is limited by the consumers' demand curve; the more inelastic (steeper) the demand curve, the more power firms have in setting quantity and price.

Measuring Market Power

Concentration Ratio. Economists combine these determinants into a single number to describe the market power in an industry: the concentration ratio. The concentration ratio reports the market share (the percentage of total output or market supply) accounted for by the four largest firms in the industry.

Firm Size. While we mentioned before that it is not necessarily firm size but the size relative to other firms in the industry that matters, almost all oligopoly firms are large and fairly wealthy. It is certainly possible that a firm could be a big fish in a small pond and exhibit market power, but most oligopoly firms enjoy huge sales and revenue figures.

Herfindahl-Hirschman Index. While the concentration ratio is an effective tool for measuring market share, it gives an incomplete view of the competitiveness of an industry. Take the case of the following two markets, each with nine total firms, for example.

Market One: Firm one (40 percent), Firm two (25 percent), Firm three (15 percent), Firm four (10 percent), remaining five firms (4 percent each)
Market Two: Firm one (84 percent), remaining eight firms (2 percent each)

Both these markets have a four-firm concentration ratio of 90 percent, but would you say they are equally competitive? Clearly, the first market is more competitive and we need a different measure to adequately reflect this fact. The Herfindahl-Hischman Index (HHI) uses the square of the market share of each of the top fifty firms—unless there are less than fifty total firms, in which case it uses all of the firms—in a market to give a measure of competitiveness.

$$HHI = (S_1)^2 + (S_2)^2 + (S_3)^2 + (S_4)^2 + \ldots$$
Where S_1 = Market Share of Firm 1, etc.

The main advantage of the HHI over the concentration ratio is that it gives more weight to firms with a larger market share since these firms are the biggest threat to competitiveness.

The maximum HHI of one represents a pure monopoly; only one firm has 100 percent market share. The minimum HHI depends on the size of market, but is always 1/N where N is the number of firms in the market. In the example above, the two markets have identical concentration ratios but vastly different HHIs. The HHI of Market One equals $(.4^2) + (.25^2) + (.15^2) + (.1^2) + 5(.04^2)$ or .2625 and the HHI of Market Two equals $(.8^2) + 5(.02^2)$ or .6432, meaning Market Two is far less competitive. In the United States, any market with an HHI over .18 is considered to be concentrated and the government will closely scrutinize any potential mergers in such an industry.

Calculation Problems. The concentration ratio and Herfindahl-Hirschman Index are good indicators for which markets contain firms with market power, but if they are our only measuring sticks, we may miss some industries with market power. For example, coordination by thousands of individual producers could result in changing the price and quantity in the market without any of the producers having a very big market share.

While it may seem unrealistic for thousands of competitive firms to coordinate like this, think about doctors. The cost of doctor visits and medical treatment is fairly uniform no matter what office or hospital you go to. Shouldn't the doctors be competing with each other and lowering the price like we saw in the mobile phone industry in Chapter 17?

Years ago, the American Medical Association, a professional association for doctors and medical students, set a uniform fee schedule of what every doctor should charge. This pricing schedule prevented doctors from competing with each other on price and kept profits high, despite no one doctor or hospital having significant market power. Even though the courts have ruled this practice illegal, most doctors still follow these guidelines due to pressure from the AMA.

II. OLIGOPOLY BEHAVIOR

Structure

Just like with a monopoly, an oligopoly structure will have a different outcome than the competitive market. With so much market power in the hands of a few firms, it is unlikely that these firms will act as if they face the horizontal demand curve of the competitive firm.

Since we are already familiar with it, let's return to the mobile phone industry. Instead of observing hundreds of competitive firms or a single dominant monopoly firm, let's imagine three companies hold the patent rights to produce cell phones while all other potential competitors are shut out. Since these three firms have a 100 percent concentration ratio, it's safe to say that this is an oligopoly.

The Initial Equilibrium

To start, we will assume that firms are all competing with each other for customers so they end up at the competitive equilibrium of one million phones at $2,500. Instead of producing 2500 phones each, though, the amount of the total output they produce will be based on the firm's market share. A firm with 40 percent of the market share, for example, will sell 400,000 phones.

The Battle for Market Shares

While each company is making profits, indeed more profits than the individual competitive firms were making in Chapter 17, they always want more. They know that if they can increase their market share by reducing the market share of their competitors, they can have an even bigger chunk of the industry's total profits.

How can an oligopolist obtain a larger market share? In a competitive market, a firm can just increase production at will without affecting the market price. In an oligopoly where the entire market is made up of only three large firms, any increase in sales, whether at the prevailing market price or at some lower price, would be noticed by the other firms and may cause retaliation.

Increased Sales at Prevailing Market Prices. Suppose a firm with 40 percent market share increases its sales at the prevailing market price. What effect will this have on the other two firms? The market equilibrium of one million phones at $2,500 is based on the consumers' demand curve; at $2,500 consumers are only willing and able to buy a total of one million phones from the three oligopoly firms.

If Firm One increased its sales to 450,000, the other two firms can sell only 550,000 phones, less than the 600,000 they sold previously. These two firms would immediately notice a reduction in sales and market share and would not be happy about it.

Increased Sales at Reduced Prices. In reality, increasing your sales and market share at the prevailing market price can be difficult. You may need to spend a lot of time and money advertising your product or improving it over your competitors' product in some way. One time-tested way to increase sales easily, though, is by selling your product at a lower price.

What effect will this strategy have on the other two firms? That depends on whether the firms produce in a pure or differentiated oligopoly. In a pure oligopoly, each firm produces the exact same product. In this type of market structure people will buy from all of the firms when the prices are the same, but as soon as one of them drops its price all the customers will flock to that firm and the others will lose all of their business.

Just as with perfect competition, a pure oligopoly is a rare thing in economics. More likely, consumers perceive some differences in the products sold by the oligopolists even if they aren't really there. As a result, a firm can capture some of its competitors' market share by reducing its price, but not all of it; some consumers will still remain loyal to the more expensive firms. Again, the other firms would notice this reduced market share and not want let Firm One get away with it.

Retaliation

Oligopoly firms do not have to sit back and take it when they see one of their competitors increasing its market share at their expense. The action taken, or retaliation strategy, depends on what strategy the first firm used to increase its market share.

If Firm One increased its market share by selling more at the prevailing price (probably by marketing or product differentiation) the other firms can retaliate by stepping up their own marketing efforts. They can attempt to attract a market or demographic Firm One is ignoring through advertising, packaging, and grass roots efforts.

If they do not want to do that, a surefire way to stop customers from flocking to Firm One is to lower their own price. Just like Firm One could grab a great deal of the market share by lowering its price, so can the other firms. Some customers will stay loyal to Firm One, but many will stop buying there, reducing its share of the market.

If Firm One increased its market share by lowering its prices in the first place, the other firms really have no other choice but to retaliate by lowering their own prices, such as in the video game console market described in Article 19.1. All of the advertising in the world

Article 19.1:
Sony Sparks Price War with PlayStation 3 Cuts

Japanese giant reduces price of PS3 by $100 to $500 in the US and is poised for similar move in UK

Sony has sparked a video games console price war by slashing the cost of the PlayStation 3 in the United States by $100 (£48) or 17 per cent after fierce competition from Microsoft and the Nintendo Wii.

The PlayStation 3, which comes complete with a 60-gigabyte hard drive and Blu-ray high-definition DVD player, will now cost $500 in the US.

This is only $20 more than Microsoft Xbox 360 but still double the cost of the top-selling Nintendo Wii.

. . .

Jack Tretton, the chief executive of Sony Computer Entertainment America, said that he expected the price cut to double sales "at a minimum."

. . .

Analysts believe that it is more likely that the cut will push sales up by about 50 per cent to 120,000 units a month.

Sony is also introducing a new more expensive version of the PS3 featuring an 80-gigabyte hard-drive, priced at $600. It is being aimed at gamers who download material from Sony's fast-growing online network.

Microsoft is predicted to respond with price cuts of its own this week. It has ruled out a move in Japan.

. . .

Questions:
1. What effect does Sony expect its price cut to have? Do outside observers agree with this assessment?
2. What would happen if Nintendo and Microsoft refuse to match Sony's price cut?
3. Who benefits from a price war between video game console manufacturers?

From *The Times*, July 9, 2007. Copyright © 2007. Reprinted by permission of NI Syndication.

is not going to keep price-conscious consumers from flocking to Firm One, so price cuts are the only way to stop Firm One from stealing market share. Therefore, any price cut by an oligopolist will lead to price cuts by its competitors and a reduction in the market price.

This kind of activity where firms continually undercut each other is called a price war. A prolonged price war will keep pushing the market price just like the entry of new firms did in the competitive industry. Since oligopolists want to keep their profits high and avoid the competitive outcome they tend to pursue product differentiation as a means of increasing market share, rather than price competition.

III. THE KINKED DEMAND CURVE

The key to understanding the production decision of an oligopolist is the same as it was for the competitive firm and the monopoly firm: What type of demand curve does the firm face? An oligopoly firm does not face the entire market demand curve like the monopoly firm, but it doesn't face a horizontal demand curve either. In fact, the market response to a change in price by one oligopoly firm (its demand curve) will depend on how the other firms respond. A monopoly firm's output choice does not affect any other firms since it is the only firm in the market. Perfectly competitive firms are so small relative to the market that their production decisions do not impact any of the other firms. Oligopolies are unique in that the production decisions of one firm affect the decisions of the other firms in the market.

Response to Price Cuts

The oligopolist's competitors may react differently depending on whether the firm is raising or lowering its prices. When the first firm lowers its price to $2,000 per phone there are two possible responses by the other firms: Match the price cut or do nothing. If the other firms choose not to match, the first firm will eat into their market shares and increase its quantity supplied at $2,000.

It is highly unlikely, though, that the other firms will just sit back and let one firm take away their market share. Instead, they will probably match the price cut. When this happens, the market price falls to $2,000 and the quantity demanded for the whole industry rises. This additional quantity will be sold by each firm according to their market share and the increase in sales will be a lot smaller for the firm that moved first.

Response to Price Increases

The first-moving firm could also choose to raise its prices and receive a higher price for each cell phone sold. The other firms might match this price increase resulting in a mar-

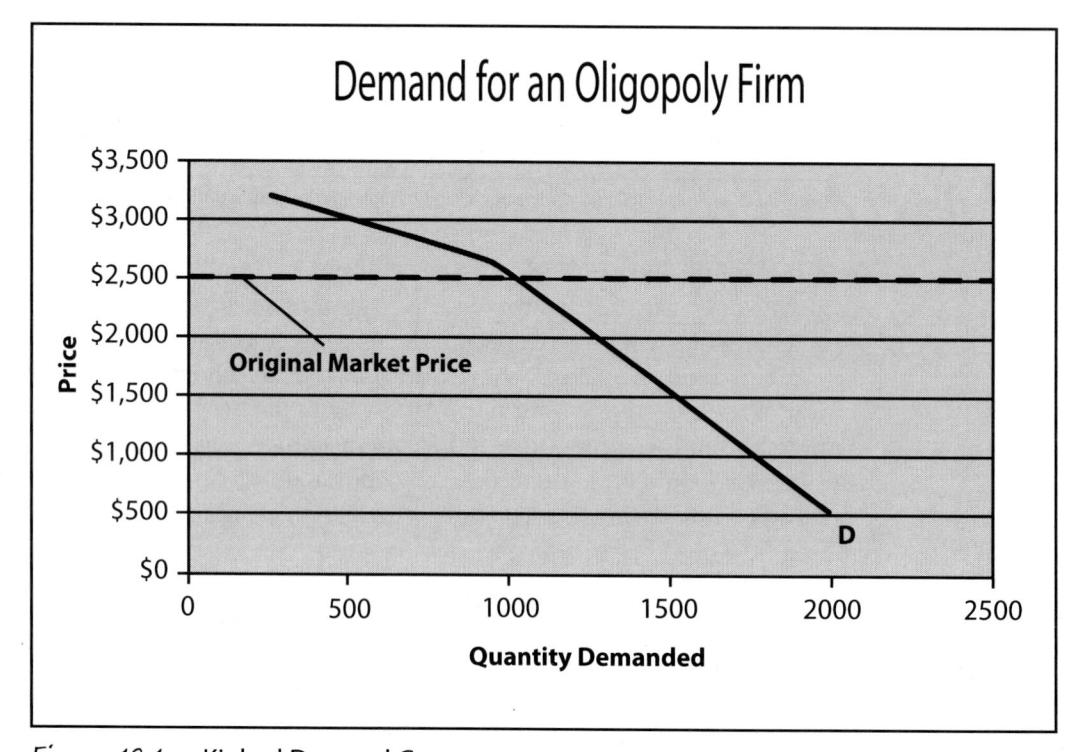

Figure 19.1 • Kinked Demand Curve
An oligopoly faces a kinked demand curve since its competitors will likely match price cuts, but not price increases.

ket price of $2,700 and a lower equilibrium quantity for the market. Each firm would sell a little a bit less, maintaining the same market shares they started with.

But since one of its competitors raising its price leads to a greater market share for the other firms, each remaining firm is unlikely to match a price increase. Instead, they will let the price-raising firm hang itself and lose most of its market share to the firms that did not raise their prices. If the market is a differentiated oligopoly, some customers will remain with the higher-priced firm out of loyalty or convenience but most will move to the other firms.

We predict, then, that oligopoly firms will match price decreases, but not price increases as illustrated in figure 19.1. The result of these two most likely scenarios is a kinked demand curve since the firm will lose a great deal of sales (flat demand curve) when it raises prices, but not gain many sales (steep demand curve) when it lowers prices. In all cases, the result of any move by an oligopoly firm depends on the responses of its competitors.

IV. GAME THEORY

Uncertainty and Risk

The monopolist does not have to worry about potential responses to its output decisions because it faces no competition. Likewise, competitive firms have no effect on market outcomes so their competitors would not even notice if they make changes. Oligopolies are special because the results of price and output decisions are not known until the other firms respond.

Oligopolies are defined by this strategic interaction, the study of which is called game theory. Deciding whether or not to increase market share by cutting prices requires that an oligopolist undertake some risk; they do not know for sure how the other firms will react. If there is some chance the other firms will not match its price cuts, the first firm might be willing to take the risk.

The Payoff Matrix

The possible results of any strategic interaction, or game, are summarized in the payoff matrix such as the one in figure 19.2. The payoff matrix tells us how much each player gains (or loses) from each possible result. It becomes abundantly clear that we need to know how the other firms will respond to determine the effect of first firm's decision to

		Player 1's Strategy	
		Do not Cut Prices (D)	Cut Prices (C)
Player 2's Strategy	Do not Cut Prices (D)	No Change, No Change	Big Gain, Big Loss
	Cut Price (C)	Big Loss, Big Gain	Small Loss, Small Loss

Figure 19.2 • The Oligopoly Payoff Matrix
The point that maximizes total utility (D, D) is unlikely to occur since each player can benefit from deviating. As one does deviate, the other firm will retaliate and force the market into the suboptimal equilibrium (C, C)—a price war.

cut prices on its own profits. According to the payoff matrix, the only way that first firm's profits increase after it cuts its price is if the other firms do not match.

Every other move by the first firm will either result in no change in profits or a reduction in profits. The firm cannot raise profits by keeping its price the same; it must take a risk to increase profits. In fact, if the other firms reduce their prices while it stands pat, it may end up losing big time.

So the firm faces a dilemma. The other firms are very likely to respond to a price drop, resulting in a movement down the market demand curve and lower profits for everyone. On other hand, if it maintains its price while the others cut theirs, it could end up losing a significant piece of its market share.

Expected Gain

In order to determine what to do the firm needs to know what the expected (or average) value of each choice is. The first step toward that is ascertaining what the actual chances of its competitors not responding to a price change are. Let's assume that based on the firm's knowledge of its competitors and the history of the market, it figures there is a 5 percent chance of them not matching a price cut.

That also means there is a 95 percent chance that they will match any price cut. Then, if the firm chooses to cut its price, there is a 95 percent probability that they will all end up with a small loss (say $10,000) and a 5 percent chance that the price-cutting firm ends up with a big gain (say $100,000). So the firm can expect an average gain (loss) of .95*(−10,000) + .05(100,000) = −$4,500 if attempts a price cut.

Therefore, being the first one to cut prices usually isn't a winning proposition. This especially comes into play when you consider that this will most likely be a repeated game; that is, any benefit the firm gets from cutting its price while the others do not will only be temporary. The oligopolists all understand that the best thing for them to do is to all agree to not change prices. If one of them gets greedy and decides to cut prices, the other firms will quickly retaliate, resulting in a small loss for everyone.

This idea of retaliation and mutually assured destruction is what keeps oligopolies in check. Price wars certainly help the consumer by increasing output and lowering prices, but it lowers profits for every firm in the long run. Oligopoly firms constantly struggle between their dual interests of wanting to increase market share while keeping industry profits high.

V. COMPARISON TO COMPETITION

Price and Output

Using price competition to battle for market share ends up deteriorating oligopoly profits. In a repeated game scenario like this, oligopoly firms might end up trying to maximize industry profits instead of firm profits. When we first studied the oligopoly's kinked demand curve, all we wanted to know was what happened when an oligopolist changed its price from the prevailing market price, but we just assumed it started at the competitive market price ($2,500). This is probably not a good assumption since an oligopoly exhibits fairly imperfect competition.

Like a monopoly, an oligopoly controls market output and therefore market price; this power is just shared among a few firms instead of being concentrated in one monopoly firm. Like a monopoly, an oligopoly will attempt to maximize industry profits by producing where marginal revenue equals marginal cost and charging the price that will get consumers to buy exactly that amount. The problem, then, is for the oligopolists to replicate the monopoly outcome by finding the monopoly price and maintaining it. This involves some delicate coordination as the oligopoly firms try not to undercut each other's prices and settle on market shares on which each firm can agree.

VI. COORDINATION PROBLEMS

To successfully replicate the monopoly outcome, the oligopolists need to restrict output. This will be difficult because the payoff matrix tells us each firm wants to increase output and grab a larger share of the market. The threat of retaliation and reduced profits for the industry keeps this desire in check, however. The oligopoly outcome will be stable as long as the oligopolists coordinate production so that the monopoly outcome is reached and each firm is happy with its market share.

Price-Fixing

An explicit agreement among firms to charge a uniform price for the maximization of industry profits is called price-fixing. Once the firms determine the output level that maximizes industry profits, the must all charge the same price for that output to be sold. Once that is decided, they just need to worry about how that output is shared among them.

Many oligopolies have been found guilty of price-fixing, a competition-restricting activity. The United States Justice Department and the Federal Trade Commission have been very active in recent years at finding and punishing price fixers. Industries as diverse as colleges, milk producers, auction houses, and elevator manufacturers have all been caught trying to replicate a monopoly instead of competing with each other.

Price Leadership

Since the chance and price of getting caught fixing prices is so high, many industries have found subtler ways to achieve uniform pricing. Instead of signing their names to explicit agreements to change prices together, firms can simply follow the lead of a particular firm in changing prices. While price-fixing is illegal, deciding to change the price of your product after your competitor has is perfectly legitimate.

This can lead to some gray area problems. For example, airlines began using their shared reservation systems to announce planned price changes. However, only after it was known that all airlines would match this price change would the price change actually occur. The Justice Department ruled that this electronic dialogue amounted to price-fixing and put a stop to it.

Allocation of Market Shares

An oligopolist realizes that increasing its price will lead to a decrease in sales; the kinked demand curve still follows the law of demand. The extent of this drop will depend on the elasticity of the demand curve and whether or not the other firms match its price increase. Since no single firm wants to take the hit of a price increase, the oligopoly must find a fair way to share this hit among all the firms if they want to raise the market price closer to the monopoly price.

One way to accomplish this is through an explicit agreement defining both the price and the output share allotted to each firm. An oligopoly with an open arrangement like this is called a cartel. OPEC, the group of oil-exporting countries, is an example of a cartel. Since cartel activity is illegal under United States law, oligopolies in the United States again must be clever in splitting up and maintaining market shares.

One way to achieve this split is by alternating which firm has the lowest price at periodic intervals. Since the lowest price firm will get a large share of the market, each firm will have a turn selling a great deal of output at the agreed-upon monopoly price. The other firms will charge an even higher price, sacrificing market share for a brief period, and have to wait their turn.

In reality though, oligopolists mainly let consumer demand naturally determine which firms gain or lose market share after a price change, only intervening when these market shares are thrown wildly out of whack. If one firm is losing too much market share or a new competitor is trying to gain market share, the firms might engage in predatory pricing—purposely setting below-market prices to manipulate market share—to steal some market share back.

Barriers to Entry

Patents. Since the oligopolists are replicating the monopoly outcome they attract potential new entrants due to their large profits just as monopolies do. Without significant barriers to entry, these new entrants will thin out profits and turn the industry into a competitive one.

Like a monopoly, an oligopoly can be protected from potential competition by patents. You cannot produce a patented good without developing an alternative method of producing it or buying the right to produce it from the patent holder. Either of these alternatives can be very costly and will turn away most competitors before they even start.

Distribution Control. Another way that oligopolies restrict entry is by controlling the distribution network. By signing long-term exclusive agreements with retailers, oligopolists can prevent new firms from finding shelf space at retailers. Even without these contracts, retailers are sometimes afraid to sell products from new companies because they do not want to upset the dominant firms in a market from which a majority of their business comes.

Mergers and Acquisitions. Just as mergers and acquisitions help monopolies get rid of potential competition, oligopolies can control output by buying out or integrating with upstart firms. Sometimes the oligopoly firms use the new technology and markets offered by the new firm, but sometimes they just blow the potential rival up and sell it off piece by piece to get rid of the potential competition.

Examples of using mergers and acquisitions to maintain market power abound in economic history. General Motors and General Electric are so-named by because they developed after the merger of dozens of independent firms. Other companies like US Steel, US Rubber, Kraft, Nabisco, and Frito-Lay also came to be dominant in their industries through merger and acquisition.

Government Regulation. While the government has a role in encouraging competition, it is sometimes government involvement that creates or sustains market power.

Patents, franchising, and international trade restrictions all limit competition and increase the market power of oligopoly firms in the United States.

An example of government regulation that limits competition is the taxi license system in New York City. As difficult as it can be to hail a cab in New York, it seems like someone could make some money by providing more cabs for New York's travelers, but there is a government-imposed barrier to entry in this industry. You cannot drive a cab without a medallion and buying this right can cost over $400,000. That high cost to enter the industry clearly indicates that the good is being underproduced and the few firms lucky enough to have medallions are reaping big profits.

Nonprice Competition. A successful marketing campaign can also provide a significant barrier to entry. Once a firm has achieved brand loyalty, a new entrant must not only produce a product as good as the entrenched firm's product, but it must also convince the public that it is just as good through its own advertising.

To this end, oligopoly firms usually produce several different brands of its own products to circumvent any new firms coming in and taking over an underserved corner of the market. Coca-Cola, for example, sells not only its signature product but diet sodas, energy drinks, water, root beer, and dozens of local beverages to prevent any new company from penetrating the soft drink market.

Training. Being first can also create its own barrier to entry. In today's world of technology and electronic communication, retraining your entire staff on new software or hardware can be extremely costly. As a result these training costs provide a barrier to entry for anyone wanting to enter these types of market, even if their product is better or cheaper.

For example, have you ever thought about why a keyboard looks the way it does? When it was introduced, typewriters functioned in such a way that you needed to keep the most common letter pairs apart so the machine would not jam up. That's right, the QWERTY keyboard was invented to actually make typing slower. While technology has evolved far beyond worrying about typebar clashes, the QWERTY keyboard still endures because that is the system on which everyone learned. While an alphabetic keyboard would undoubtedly result in faster typing once everyone got used to it, no one wants to manufacture it because no computer company would buy it. This massive coordination failure discourages entry into the keyboard market.

Network Economies. This coordination issue also extends to consumers. Once an application or product spreads or has many users, it becomes more difficult for a new product to break into that market. No one wants to have a Zune when everybody else has an iPod. Video game developers won't spend a lot of resources making games for consoles other than the Wii, Xbox 360, or PS3 since they don't expect anyone to buy a console that no one else has. In a world that has increasingly come to be defined by interconnectivity, being out of the loop is just not an option.

Efficiency

Oligopolies have the ability to cooperate and produce the same high-price, low-output outcome as a monopoly would. Just as with a monopoly, this market would be inefficient since the firms would be producing at a level where price was well above marginal cost representing an underproduction of the good relative to society's demand. In addition, the firms all have excess capacity at the monopoly output level meaning the market is not productively efficient either.

While oligopoly firms want to reproduce the monopoly outcome, this may not be possible if they do not cooperate and instead engage in a price war. But even if they do compete with price cuts, it is unlikely they will ever reach the point where price equals marginal cost; the firms will just exit the market before this happens. Likewise, although this price war may help consumers in this market, the advertising and research costs of an oligopoly firm result in higher average total cost than competitive firms experience, leaving fewer resources available for other productive activities.

CHAPTER 19 SUMMARY

- Some of the factors that determine market power include **the number of sellers in the market, the relative size of each firm,** and **the availability of substitutes.**
- Market power is measured by the **four-firm concentration ratio** and the Herfinadahl-Hisrchman Index (HHI).
- $HHI = (S_1)^2 + (S_2)^2 + (S_3)^2 + (S_4)^2 + \ldots$
- Oligopoly firms can increase their market share through **nonprice competition** (advertising) or **price cutting.**
- Since rival firms will likely match price cuts, but not price increases, the **demand curve facing an oligopoly firm is kinked.**
- Since the result will not be known until the rival firms react, oligopoly firms base their output decision on the expected gain.
- *Expected Gain = Probability of Move 1 × Gain from Move 1 + Probability of Move 2 × Gain from Move 2*
- The best possible scenario for the oligopoly would be to cooperate and try to **replicate the monopoly outcome.**
- Explicitly coordinating production through **price-fixing and cartels** is illegal in the United States.
- Oligopolies result in **neither productive nor allocative efficiency.**

CHAPTER 19 Exercises

Name _____

1) Which of the following is **NOT** a determinant of market power?
   A) Number of sellers
   B) Availability of substitutes
   C) Barriers to entry
   D) The country the market operates in

1) _____

2) Suppose there are only three firms in a market. The largest firm has sales of $500 million, the second-largest has sales of $300 million, and the smallest has sales of $200 million. The market share of the largest firm is:
   A) 100%
   B) 20%
   C) 30%
   D) 50%

2) _____

3) What is the HHI of the market in question 2?
   A) .5
   B) .38
   C) 1
   D) Not enough information.

3) _____

4) If oligopolists start a price war, the end result will be
   A) identical to the monopoly outcome.
   B) lower total industry profits.
   C) decreased output.
   D) higher total industry profits.

4) _____

5) The demand curve facing an oligopolists will be kinked if its rivals
   A) never match price changes.
   B) match both price cuts and price increases.
   C) ignore the actions of other firms.
   D) match price cuts but not price increases.

5) _____

6) Oligopolists will maximize industry profits if they produce at the rate of output where
   A) MR = MC for the market.
   B) MR = MC for each firm.
   C) P = MC for the market.
   D) TR = TC for the market.

6) _____

7) Price-fixing occurs when
   A) oligopolists charge lower than market prices to change market share.
   B) oligopolists agree not to price compete in order to maintain industry profits.
   C) oligopolists follow the price changes of an industry leader.
   D) a price war returns price to the competitive level.

7) _____

8) Which of the following is **NOT** a reason oligopolies will always produce inefficiently? 8) _____
   A) Their advertising costs push price above min ATC
   B) Their downward-sloping (kinked demand) means price is above MC at the profit-maximizing level
   C) They will always mirror the monopoly outcome
   D) There is an incentive to collude and price-fix

9) Fill out the following table regarding the oligopoly for dog walking services. What is the HHI of this industry?

Firm	Output	Market Share
Puppy Pals	200 dogs/day	
Canine Carriers	100 dogs/day	
Fido's Feet	60 dogs/day	
Roving Rovers	20 dogs/day	
Walk n' Wag	20 dogs/day	

_____

_____

10) Why can training costs and network economies be considered barriers to entry?

_____

_____

_____

_____

Chapter 20

Monopolistic Competition

I. STRUCTURE

Low Concentration

Monopolistic competition lies farther down the market power scale from oligopoly. In it, there are many firms each with a small amount of market power. The term "many firms" is not an exact specification, but we do know it is more than the number firms in an oligopoly, but fewer than that of a perfectly competitive firm.

The easiest way to distinguish monopolistic competition from oligopoly is that a monopolistically competitive industry has a much lower concentration ratio. While a few firms usually do stand out in monopolistic competition, the concentration ratio of the top four firms is usually between 20 and 40 percent, not over 60 percent like with an oligopoly. Using the Herfindahl-Hirschman Index, any market with an HHI between .1 and .18 is considered moderately concentrated and more than likely exhibits monopolistic competition.

While Starbucks may seem like a behemoth in the coffee market, for example, it only possesses 15 percent of coffee bar sales. In fact, the top four coffee bars only account for 28 percent of all output in this industry, while small local coffee shops make up a significant portion of the industry. Further, some businesses might be members of an oligopoly in one market but be a monopolistic competitor in another. McDonald's, for example, shares a hamburger oligopoly with Burger King and Wendy's, but is merely another monopolistic competitor in the much larger fast food market.

Market Power

Although industries with monopolistic competition have relatively low concentration ratios, the firms are not powerless: It is called monopolistic competition for a reason. Firms in monopolistic competition do not face a horizontal demand curve like perfectly competitive firms do. When monopolistically competitive firms raise their prices, they lose some of their customers but not all of them; the demand curve is not perfectly elastic. That is, firms in monopolistic competition face a downward-sloping demand for their product, just like monopolies do.

Independent Production Decisions

Oligopolies also risk losing some of their customers when they raise their prices, but the exact level of this drop depends on how the other firms respond. However, in monopolistic competition there are so many firms that no one else will notice a reasonable change in price or sales by a single company.

That is, monopolistically competitive companies can make output decisions independent of the rest of firms in the market; there is no strategic interaction or game theory. In this way, they are more like competitive firms. Since the other firms will not match any price change, firms in monopolistic competition will face a smooth demand curve, not a kinked one.

Low Barriers to Entry

Low barriers to entry also help characterize monopolistic competition. There would not be so many firms if it were difficult to enter the industry. Since it is easy to enter monopolistically competitive markets, it is difficult for firms in these markets to maintain positive economic profits. Just like perfect competition, profits in this type of market will be pushed toward zero by the appearance of new entrants.

II. BEHAVIOR

Product Differentiation

The key difference between perfect competition and monopolistic competition is product differentiation. In perfect competition we assumed homogenous products; every firm produced the exact same product. More importantly, consumers could not perceive any differences between the products at any two firms.

Since consumers saw the products at any two companies in a perfectly competitive market as interchangeable, there was no reason to pay more than the market price for it. This is why perfectly competitive firms face a horizontal (perfectly elastic) demand curve; consumers will respond to any price increase by simply buying from another firm. Since monopolistic competition entails products that are slightly different, these firms can raise their price slightly without customers running for the exit.

The crucial element to this market power is developing a brand image, a perception that your product is different from the others. Nowhere is the importance of brand image more evident than the bottled water industry. While Pepsi and Coke sell nothing more than filtered tap water—under the brand names Aquafina and Dasani, respectively—they are able to raise prices over their competitors and still maintain high sales due to successful advertising and brand management.

Advertising

While creating subtle differences between one firm's product and those of its competitors can develop a strong brand image, creating a belief in the minds of consumers that the product is different can be just as effective. In fact, monopolistically competitive firms spend billions of dollars annually on advertising and packaging their products to set them apart from the pack. As a result, a large fraction of a good's selling price in a monopolistically competitive market comes from the cost of selling the good, not actually manufacturing it. High advertising costs in the pharmaceutical industry, for example, have helped in the skyrocketing of prescription drug costs in recent years.

Selling Costs. Direct expenditures on advertising are only one component of the cost of selling a good. Selling costs also include the wages of salespeople, distributors, and administrators as well as the construction and upkeep of retail centers like shopping malls. Because of advertising costs, firms in a monopolistically competitive market face higher average total costs than perfectly competitive firms as represented in the upward shift in the ATC curve in figure 20.1.

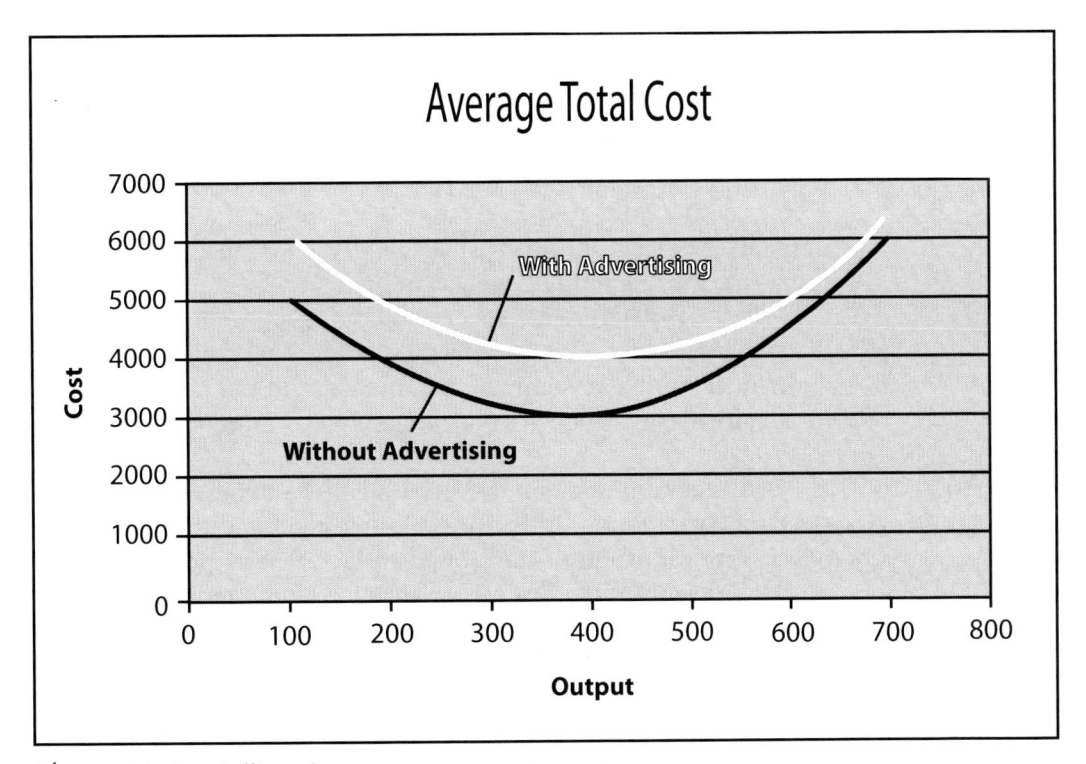

Figure 20.1 • Selling Costs
Since advertising costs are fixed, the gap between ATC with and without advertising falls as output increases.

Average Total Cost

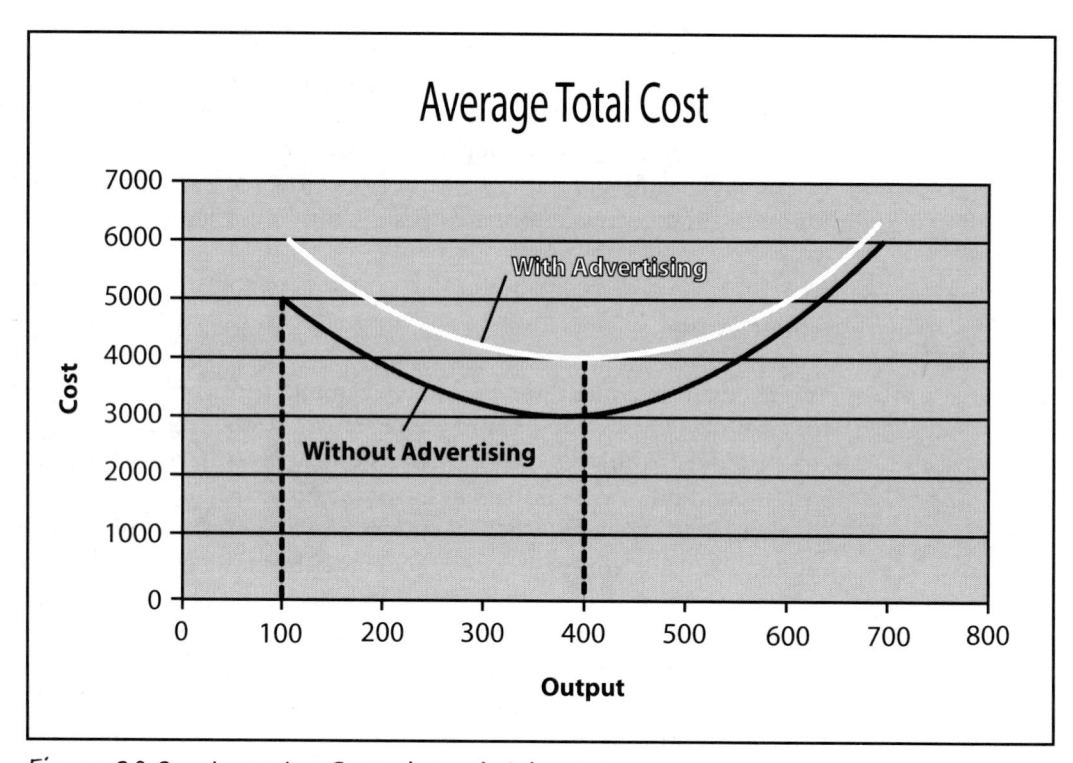

Figure 20.2 • Lowering Costs through Advertising
If advertising increased the firm's sales from 100 units to 400 units, its average cost of production per unit would fall even though it is now on a higher ATC curve.

Much like the cost of renting a factory or a piece of capital, advertising costs are fixed—they do not change as you increase output. When a firm hires an advertising firm to design a campaign, the contract usually does not specify that the advertising firm be paid more if the firm sells a lot and less if the firm sells very little. As a result, average advertising costs fall as output increases. Advertising can increase sales enough to get to a point on the new ATC curve that is lower than the firm's ATC without advertising. This may result in advertising actually lowering average total cost for the firm at its profit-maximizing output level, as in figure 20.2.

Selling Costs and Profits. Firms would not engage in advertising if it had no effect on demand. Without an increase in sales, additional advertising would simply raise costs and reduce profits. Assuming everything else in the market stays the same, an increase in advertising will inform consumers about a product's unique features and increase sales.

Is this assumption about everything else staying the same legitimate? When firms see their rival touting the features of their new product they will often retaliate with an advertising campaign of their own. In fact, just as perfectly competitive firms had to produce cheaply and efficiently to survive, all monopolistically competitive firms have to advertise to survive. As they survive and maintain profits, they attract new entry—which they cannot stop because they lack barriers to entry. This new entry makes the demand curve for each firm less elastic, reducing markup. While advertising increases sales, it decreases markup—making the resulting effect on profits unclear.

Advertising as a Signal. While advertising seems to be an effective way to communicate the best qualities of a firm's product to consumers, many advertisements are absurd, confusing, or offer little information about the product at all. In reality, multimillion dollar ad campaigns are often little more than a signal of the firm's faith in the overall quality of its product.

By hiring a well-known actor or athlete to endorse its product, a firm knows it is taking on a huge advertising cost. If the increased sales brought on by this advertisement do not outweigh its costs, then the marketing campaign is a failure. The firm would not put itself in this situation if it did not believe it had a quality product, because if consumers try the product once and hate it the firm could be in big trouble. Since consumers recognize this faith when they see the firm's flashy and expensive advertisement, they might decide to give the product a try regardless of whether the ad had anything to with the product's qualities or not.

Brand Loyalty

At first glance, the demand curve facing a firm in monopolistic competition, as seen in figure 20.3a, seems identical to the downward-sloping demand curve facing the monopoly, but they are actually quite different. The monopoly faces a downward-sloping curve because it is the entire market and change in its output decision changes the market outcome.

A monopolistically competitive firm, on the other hand, is a competitive firm that has a monopoly only over its brand image. The key to brand loyalty is convincing the consumer that the firm's product has no true substitutes, reducing the price elasticity of demand for the good. Without this brand image the monopolistically competitive firm would face a horizontal, or perfectly elastic, demand curve like any other competitive firm. It is the power of the brand image that makes the demand curve less elastic and turns it into a downward-sloping demand curve. Brand loyalty exists even for products that are virtually identical. For a given octane rating, gasoline at every gas station should legally be the same, yet people seem to stick to one brand even if the price is slightly lower somewhere else. Surveys show that people will stick with their favorite brands even after a massive price cut in a virtually indistinguishable substitute.

Effective brand management, therefore, reduces cross-price elasticity. That is, the producer can increase its price (or its competitors can reduce their prices) without fear of massive changes in the quantity demanded for its product. All of this results in a downward-sloping demand curve rather than the horizontal demand curve facing a perfectly competitive firm. In addition, effective brand management might lead to consumers maintaining their demand for a product despite changes in income, keeping consumers from substituting toward lower-priced substitutes even during a recession.

Repurchase Rates

One way to measure brand loyalty is through repurchase or consumer loyalty rates. Even though most computers use identical parts and offer similar performance, nearly 90 percent of Mac users will buy an Apple product for their next computer; PC companies have similar rates of return customers.

Just like oligopoly firms, firms in monopolistic competition often find it cost-effective to reach into new markets to make it difficult for new firms to enter. Since Starbucks knows it is cheap and easy for anyone to enter the coffee business, they have begun to expand their menu to keep their customers from going to McDonald's, Dunkin' Donuts, or even local coffee shops.

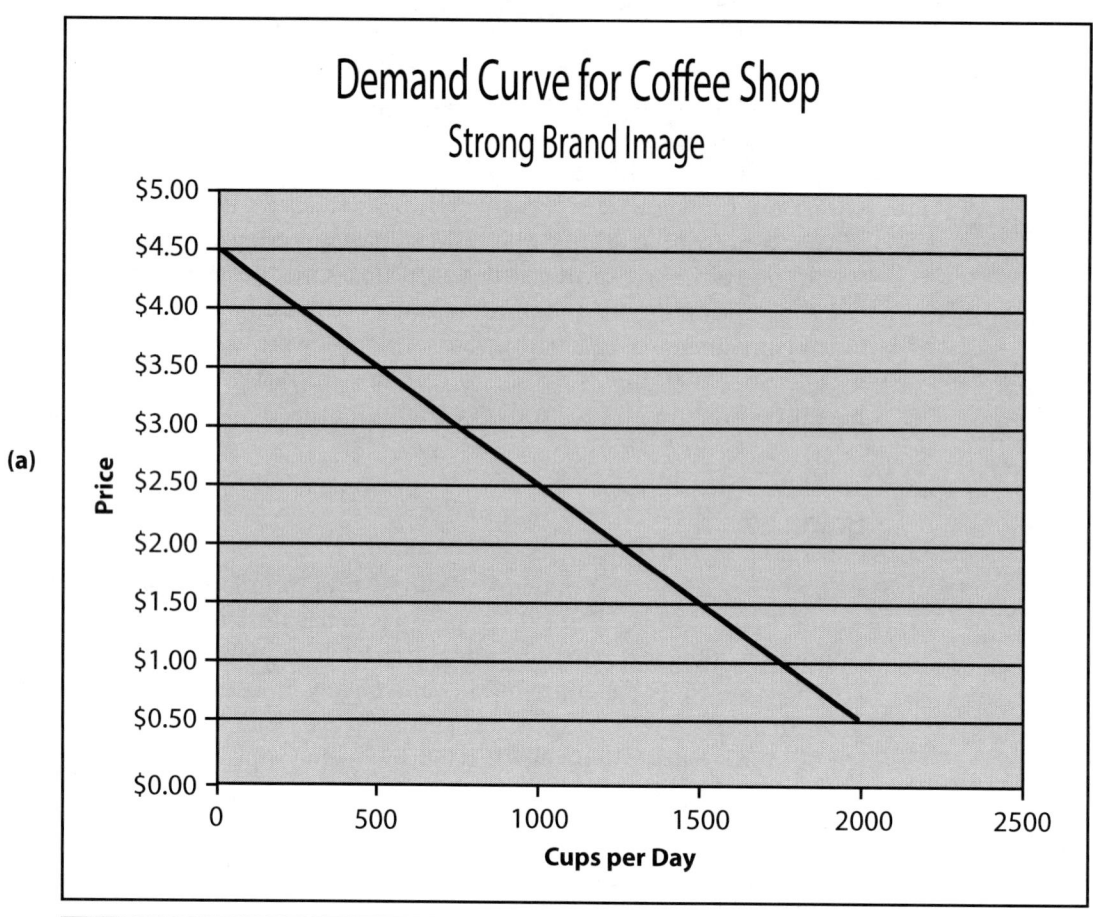

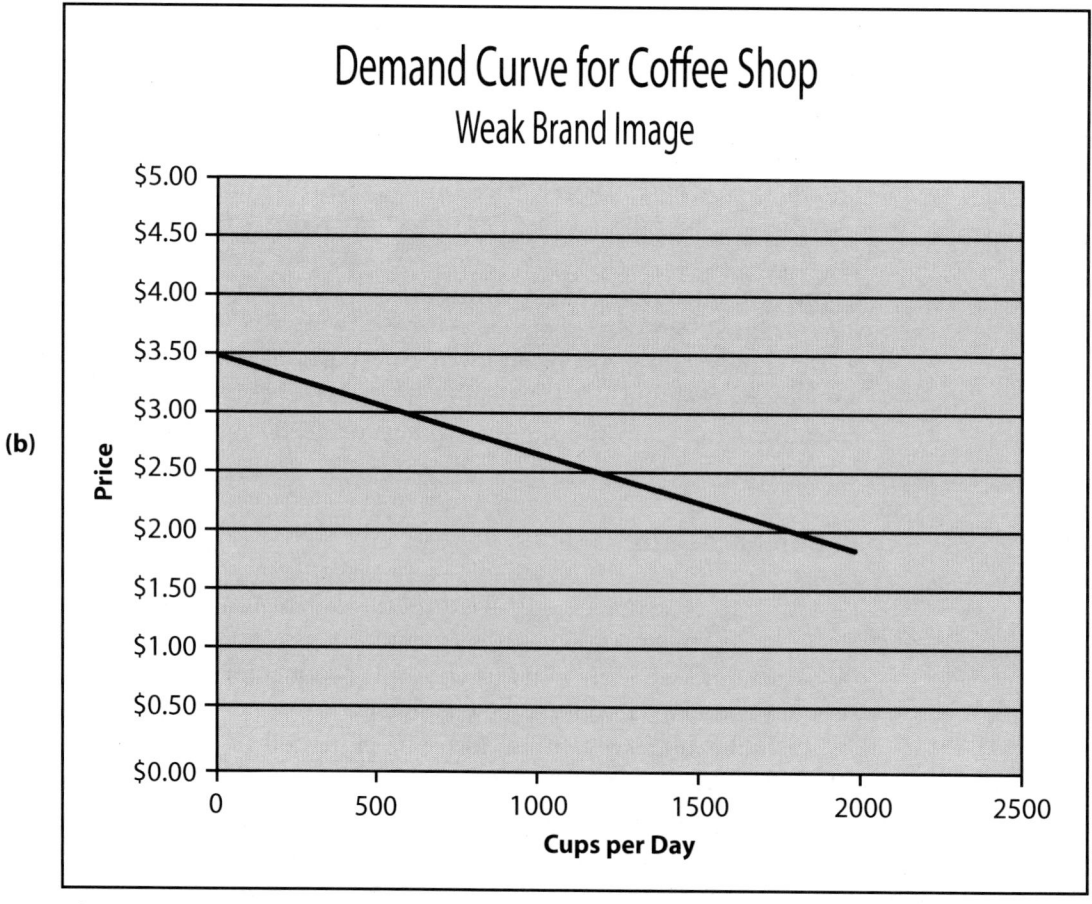

Figure 20.3 • **Demand Curve Facing a Monopolistically Competitive Firm**
A strong brand image allows the monopolistically competitive firm to reduce the elasticity of its demand curve.

III. OUTCOME

Short-Run Price and Output

Since the monopolistically competitive firm faces a downward-sloping demand curve, its production decisions will be similar to the monopolist's. It, too, will seek to produce at the output level where marginal revenue equals marginal cost, as seen in figure 20.4. There is only one price (indicated by the demand curve) that will convince customers to buy exactly that amount and the firm to charge exactly that much, resulting in profits identical to that of a monopoly.

Entry and Exit

What about the long run? When we studied a monopoly, we stopped here. Though the monopoly made enormous profits at its chosen output level, no new firms could enter the market because of substantial barriers to entry. Low barriers to entry, though, characterize monopolistic competition. It is highly unlikely that savvy entrepreneurs will sit back and let Starbucks, or any monopolistically competitive firm, rake in these huge profits.

As this new entry occurs, figure 20.5 demonstrates that the supply curve and marginal cost curve for the industry shift to the right, leading to a higher desired output level for the firm. At this higher output level, the firm cannot charge as high a price, forcing it to move down the demand curve toward the perfectly competitive outcome.

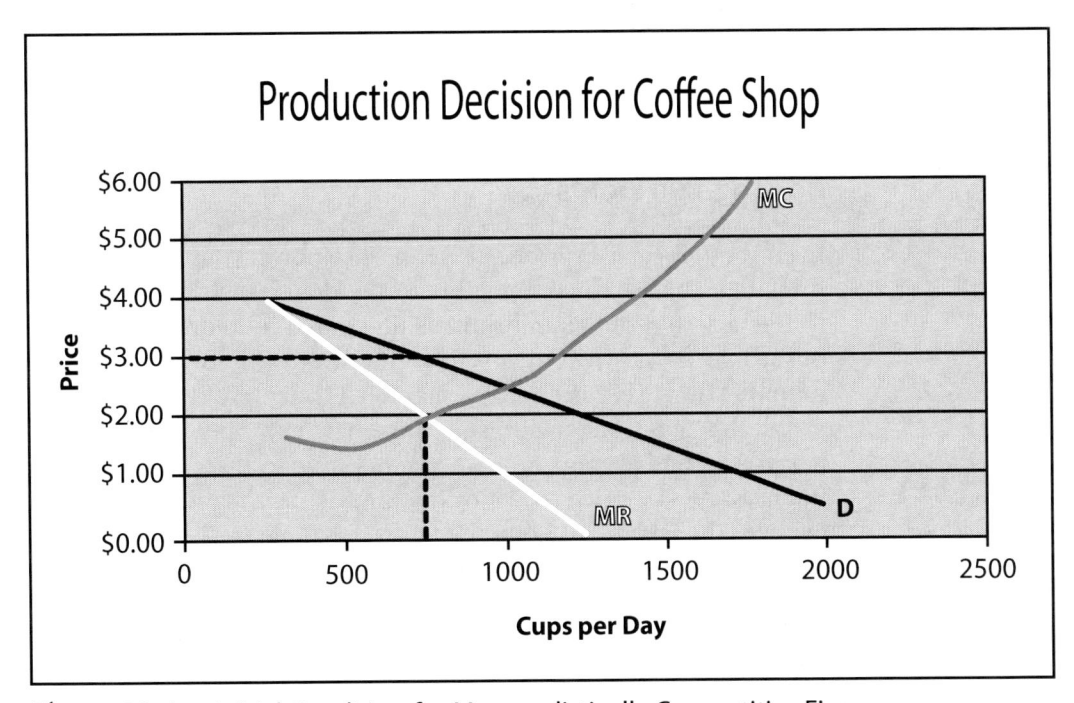

Figure 20.4 • **Initial Condition for Monopolistically Competitive Firm**
Initially the production decision for the monopolistically competitive firm is identical to that of the monopoly, since it controls the entire market for its particular version of the good.

Production Decision for Coffee Shop

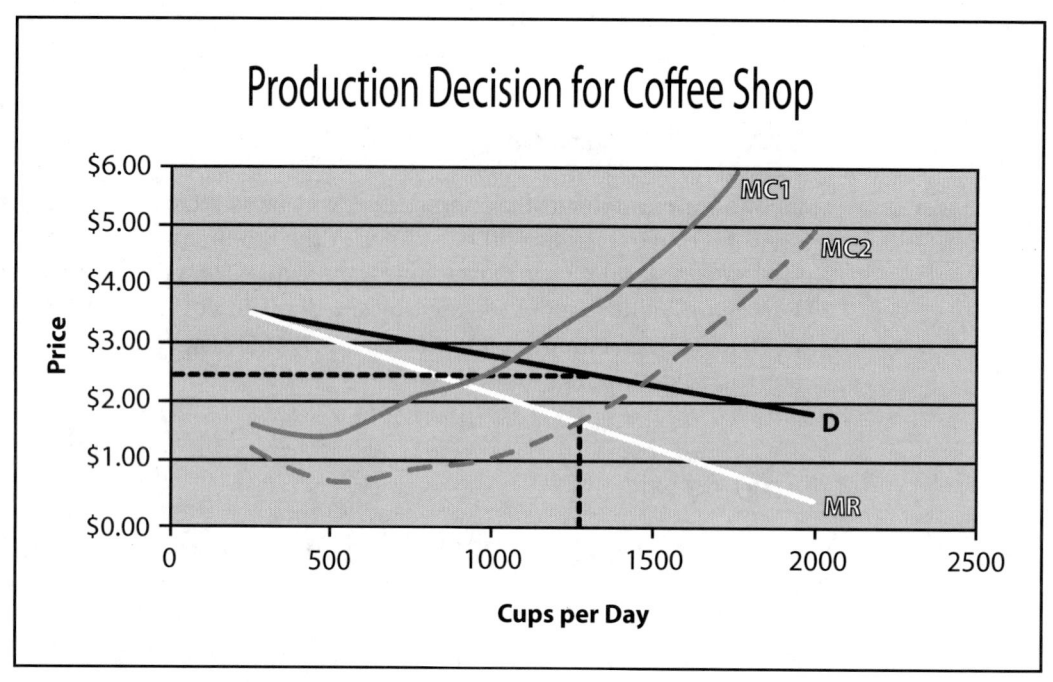

Figure 20.5 • **New Equilibrium**
Entry into the monopolistically competitive industry causes the firm to produce more, but on a new, flatter demand curve. This results in a lower price and a higher output equilibrium, but the profits of the established firm suffer.

This is not the only effect of new entry on the firm. Figure 20.5 also shows that as new firms enter the industry, they also take away some customers from the firm; its demand curve becomes more elastic as more substitutes become available. As the demand curve becomes flatter so does the marginal revenue curve, forcing the firm to make a new production decision.

No Long-Run Profits

Even though each firm has some market power, the continually leftward shift of the firm's demand curve combined with the downward pressure on prices will eventually lead to a zero profit equilibrium as illustrated in figure 20.6. Eventually the demand is pushed so far down for each firm that the price corresponding to profit-maximizing output (MR = MC) is exactly equal to ATC; the profit rectangle is gone.

At this point there will be no more new entry because that would cause price to be below ATC and average profits to be negative so there is no more incentive to enter the industry. At any price with positive profits new firms will enter, pushing the demand curve to the left and causing the profit rectangle to shrink until it reaches zero.

Inefficiency

Just because monopolistic competition and perfect competition result in a zero-profit equilibrium does not mean they both result in efficient production. Remember that at the long-run equilibrium for a competitive market (where profits equaled zero) the demand

Production Decision for Coffee Shop

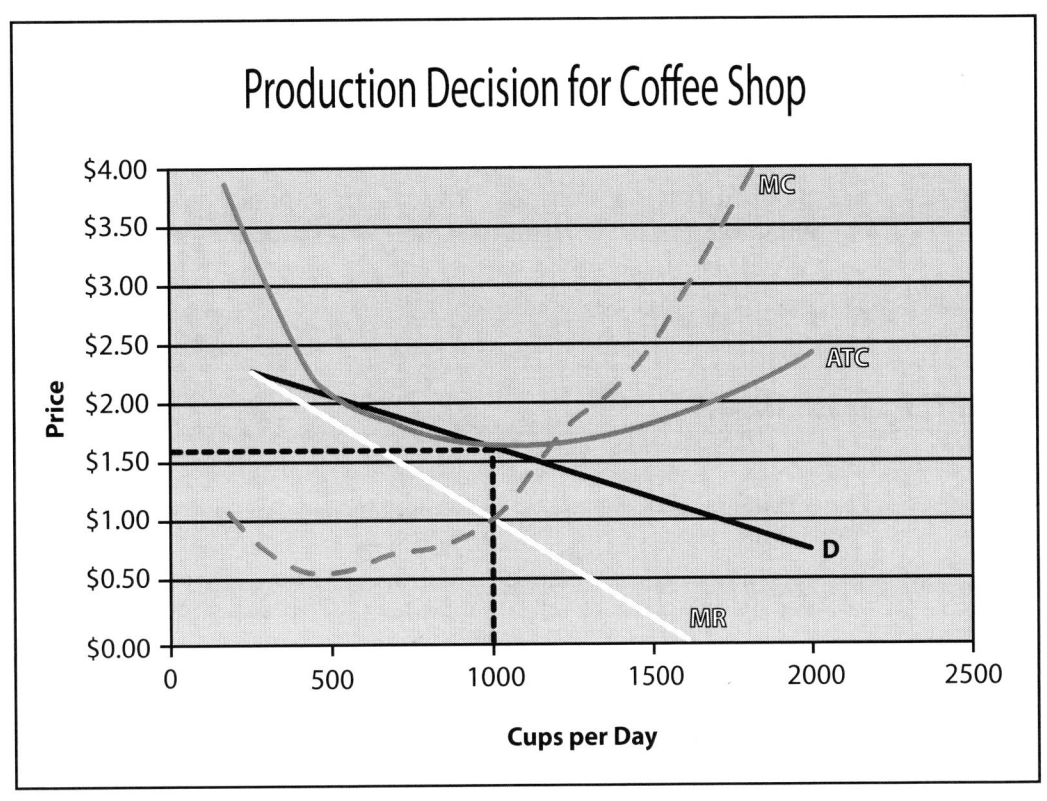

Figure 20.6 • Zero Profit Equilibrium
As new entry continues to flatten and push the demand curve downward, eventually the gap between price and ATC (average profit per unit) at the profit-maximizing output level disappears, resulting in zero profits.

curve intersected the ATC at its minimum. Perfect competition implied productive efficiency, producing every product with the least amount of resources on a per-unit basis.

Since the demand curve for monopolistic competition is downward sloping and not horizontal, there is no way it can intersect the ATC at its minimum point—where MC crosses it. As a result, at the long-run equilibrium of a monopolistically competitive market, goods are not being produced at their lowest possible cost and we are missing out on some potential output.

In addition, since monopolistically competitive firms face a downward-sloping demand curve they will produce a level of output where price is greater than marginal cost rather than equal to it. Just like a monopoly, then, they will underproduce their goods relative to consumer demand. As a result, monopolistic competition leads to both productive and allocative inefficiency.

Benefits of Product Variety

Just like with perfect competition, though, it is unlikely for the zero profit equilibrium to actually occur in a monopolistically competitive market—the market will merely tend toward this equilibrium. Instead, firms will attempt to maintain profits by constantly improving their goods and their advertising campaigns. In fact, since price competition will only depress profits further, nonprice competition is the firm's only chance at regaining profits.

Since the basis of a monopolistically competitive firm's profit is product differentiation, the entry of new firms creates a drive toward constantly improving product quality and variation. This improved product variety—which does not exist in perfect competition since all products are identical—may actually make up for the inefficiencies inherent to monopolistic competition. Indeed, monopolistic competition presents a trade-off between consumer choice and productive efficiency. Greater specialization and product variety result in greater excess capacity and less efficient production, but provide consumers with a wider array of products from which to choose.

CHAPTER 20 SUMMARY

- Monopolistically competitive markets have **many firms and low barriers to entry** like perfectly competitive markets, but each firm can **set its own price** as in monopolies.
- Monopolistically competitive firms face **downward-sloping demand curves.**
- Each monopolistically competitive firm sells a **slightly different product.**
- Monopolistically competitive firms must **advertise** to either inform the public about the **quality** of its product or at least **send a signal** that they believe in their product.
- Product differentiation creates the **brand loyalty** that gives monopolistically competitive firms their market power.
- Brand loyalty makes the demand curve steeper; it **reduces the price elasticity of demand.**
- Since monopolistically competitive markets have little to no barriers to entry, each firm will earn **zero profits in the long run.**
- Monopolistically competitive markets are **less efficient** than perfectly competitive markets, but the greater **product variety** they offer might be worth it.

CHAPTER 20 Exercises

Name _____

1) Which of the following characterizes monopolistic competition?
   A) Many firms, each producing a particular version of a product.
   B) Many firms selling an identical product.
   C) A few firms, each producing a particular version of a product.
   D) A few firms controlling the entire market.

1) _____

2) The demand curve faced by a monopolistically competitive firm is
   A) flat.
   B) kinked.
   C) upward-sloping.
   D) downward-sloping.

2) _____

3) Brand loyalty usually makes the demand curve for a product
   A) unitary elastic.
   B) more price elastic.
   C) less price elastic.
   D) more income elastic.

3) _____

4) Without a brand image, the demand curve for a monopolistically competitive firm would look like that of
   A) a monopoly firm.
   B) a perfectly competitive firm.
   C) an oligopoly firm.
   D) a duopoly firm.

4) _____

5) Advertising costs
   A) rise as output rises.
   B) fall as output rises.
   C) first fall, then rise as output increases.
   D) do not change as output rises.

5) _____

6) Advertising may result in reducing average costs if
   A) sales increase enough to offset the rise in total costs.
   B) sales increase by any amount.
   C) advertising results in cheaper production.
   D) costs only increase at higher levels of output.

6) _____

7) In the short run, a monopolistically competitive firm
   A) makes profits just as it does in the long run because of barriers to entry.
   B) may make economic profits, but those profits disappear in the long run because of the entry of new firms.
   C) may make profits just as it does in the long run, because firms can enter easily.
   D) produces where P = MC.

7) _____

8) Monopolistically competitive firms are productively inefficient because long-run equilibrium occurs at an output rate where
   A) ATC > minimum ATC.
   B) MR > MC.
   C) MC > MR.
   D) P > MC.

8) _____

363

9) Why do some advertisements have very little to do with the qualities of a particular product, but are still be effective?

10) Why don't monopolistically competitive firms engage in marginal cost pricing (allocative efficiency) as perfectly competitive firms do?

Article Review 5

Name _____

Choose any one of the articles from Chapters 17–20. Use the space provided below to summarize the article. Then, answer the questions at the end of the article on the back of this page.

1.

2.

3.

Unit 5 Review

Name _____

Use this review to prepare for Exam 5. You can view the answers in the "unit review answers" section in the back of the text, but try to complete it on your own first.

1) Which of the following is a **NOT** shifter of the market supply curve?   1) _____
   A) Taxes
   B) Consumer income
   C) Productivity
   D) Number of Sellers

2) Why do profits tend to drop over time in a competitive market?   2) _____
   A) People get tired of the good and demand falls
   B) New entry causes marginal costs to fall
   C) New entry causes the market price to fall until it hits min ATC
   D) Taxes

3) What is the relationship between price and ATC in the long run for a competitive market?   3) _____
   A) Not enough information.
   B) P < min ATC
   C) P = min ATC
   D) P > min ATC

4) Refer to the figure below for questions 4 and 5

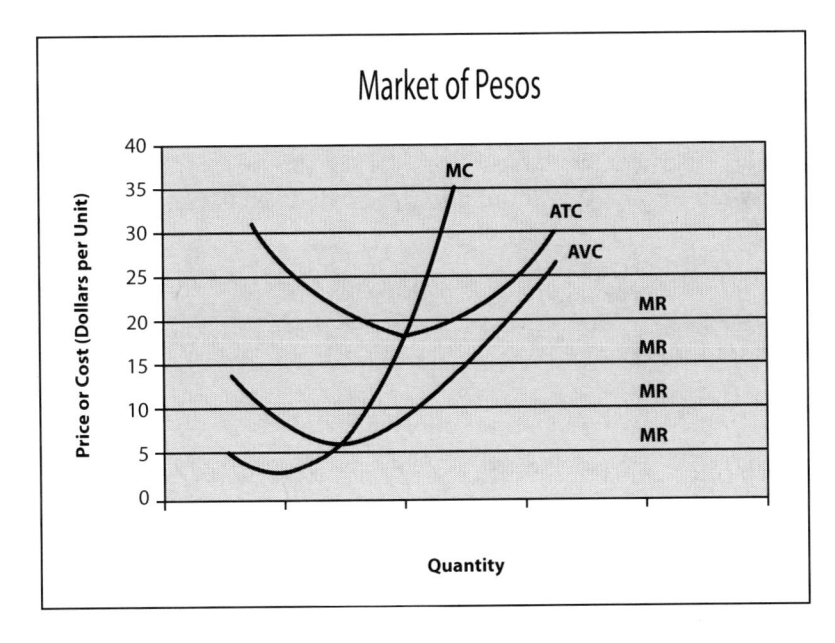

Market of Pesos

   New firms will stop entering the market when the price falls below   4) _____
   A) $5
   B) $10
   C) $15
   D) $20

5) In the short run, firms will keep producing as long as the price is above   5) _____
   A) $5
   B) $10
   C) $15
   D) $20

6) Which of the following rules is satisfied when a monopoly maximizes profits?
   A) MR = MC
   B) MC = ATC
   C) TR = TC
   D) P = MC

Use the following information to answer questions 7 and 8.
   A monopoly firm has its profit-maximizing output level at 40 units.
   Its monopoly price is $30 and its ATC at 40 units is $20

7) What is the firm's average profit per unit?
   A) $20
   B) $30
   C) $10
   D) $400

8) What is the firm's total profit?
   A) $1,200
   B) $400
   C) $800
   D) $10

9) Price-discriminating firms charge lower prices to those who
   A) consider the product a necessity.
   B) have higher price elasticities of demand.
   C) have very large incomes relative to the price of the good.
   D) have many substitutes available to them.

10) All of the following are reasons that monopolies discourage innovation EXCEPT
    A) The existence of monopoly might discourage an entrepreneur from even trying to improve an industry or product.
    B) Monopolies prevent the entry of new products into the market through barriers to entry.
    C) The existence might encourage someone to invent a new product in order to secure a patent and earn monopoly profits.
    D) Monopolies might buy out innovate new companies and repress their discoveries.

11) Suppose there are only three firms in a market. The largest firm has sales of $900 million, the second-largest has sales of $600 million, and the smallest has sales of $500 million. The market share of the largest firm is
    A) 30%
    B) 90%
    C) 45%
    D) 25%

12) What is the HHI of the market in question 11?
    A) 1
    B) .36
    C) .45
    D) Not enough information.

13) If an oligopolist's competitors match price cuts but not price increases, its demand curve will be
    A) flatter at high prices and steeper at lower prices.
    B) steeper at high prices and flatter at lower prices.
    C) horizontal at every price.
    D) identical to the monopoly demand curve.

14) Oligopolists will maximize industry profits if they produce at the rate of output where
    A) P = ATC for the market.
    B) MR = MC for the market.
    C) P = MC for each firm.
    D) MR = MC for each firm

Name _____

15) Price-fixing occurs when 15) _____
   A) oligopolists charge lower than market prices to change market share.
   B) oligopolists agree not to price compete in order to maintain industry profits.
   C) a price war returns price to the competitive level.
   D) oligopolists follow the price changes of an industry leader.

16) The demand curve faced by a monopolistically competitive firm is 16) _____
   A) upward-sloping.   C) flat.
   B) downward-sloping.   D) kinked.

17) Brand loyalty usually makes the demand curve for a product 17) _____
   A) more income elastic.   C) more price elastic.
   B) less cross-price elastic. D) unitary elastic.

18) Average advertising costs 18) _____
   A) rise as output rises.
   B) do not change as output rises.
   C) fall as output rises.
   D) first fall, then rise as output increases.

19) In the long run, a monopolistically competitive firm 19) _____
   A) sees any economic profits disappear because of the entry of new firms.
   B) makes profits because of barriers to entry.
   C) produces where P=MC.
   D) may make profits because firms can enter easily.

20) Monopolistically competitive firms are allocatively inefficient because long-run 20) _____
   equilibrium occurs at an output rate where
   A) MR > MC.   C) P > MC.
   B) P > minimum ATC.   D) MC > MR.

21) Explain how a perfectly competitive market promotes allocative efficiency (the production of the best mix of goods and services).

_____
_____
_____
_____
_____

22) What limits the power of a monopoly to charge whatever price it wants?

_____
_____
_____
_____
_____

23) Name three barriers to entry used by monopolies and oligopolies and give examples of how each would restrict competition.

24) Why do oligopolies prefer to determine market share by nonprice competition rather than through price wars?

25) Although it is less efficient, how might monopolistic competition represent an improvement over perfect competition?

Exam 5 Formula Sheet

Name _____

Chapter 17

$Profits = Total\ Revenue - Total\ Costs$

$Shutdown\ if\ TR(0) - TC(0) > TR(Q^*) - TC(Q^*)$

$Profit\ per\ unit = Price - ATC$

$Profit = (Price - ATC) \times Output$

Chapter 18

$Marginal\ Revenue = \dfrac{Change\ in\ Total\ Revenue}{Change\ in\ Output}$

$Excess\ Capacity = Output\ where\ price\ equals\ min\ ATC - Monopoly\ output$

$Markup = Monopoly\ Price - MC$

Chapter 19

$Concentration\ Ratio = S_1 + S_2 + S_3 + S_4 \ldots$
Where S_1 = Market Share of Firm 1

$HHI = (S_1)^2 + (S_2)^2 + (S_3)^2 + (S_4)^2 + \ldots$
Where S_1 = Market Share of Firm 1

$Expected\ Gain = Probability\ of\ Move\ 1 \times Gain\ from\ Move\ 1 +$
$\qquad Probability\ of\ Move\ 2 \times Gain\ from\ Move\ 2$

Chapter 20

$Price\ Elasticity\ of\ Demand = \dfrac{Percent\ Change\ in\ Quantity\ Demanded}{Percent\ Change\ in\ Price}$

$Income\ Elasticity\ of\ Demand = \dfrac{Percent\ Change\ in\ Quantity\ Demanded}{Percent\ Change\ in\ Income}$

$Cost\text{-}Price\ Elasticity\ of\ Demand = \dfrac{Percent\ Change\ in\ Quantity\ Demanded}{Percent\ Change\ in\ Price\ of\ Related\ Good}$

Government Regulation

I. ANTITRUST VS. REGULATION

Market Failure

As we have seen throughout the previous chapters, the only market structure that provides productive and allocative efficiency is perfect competition. Any market structure with any amount of market power will lead to society not getting the maximum use out of its resources, a situation we call market failure.

The domination of markets by large producers can reduce output, raise prices, restrict competition, and stifle innovation. This is a big problem in the United States as almost every market has some level of market power. The use of this market power will lead to suboptimal market outcomes: higher prices and lower output than the competitive outcome.

Structure vs. Behavior

The government, in its role to promote economic growth through competition, can look at the problem in two ways. Anti-trust laws attack the market structures that cause market failure. When companies try to merge into an entity so large that competition will be threatened, the government may step in and prevent the merger.

Anti-trust laws also cover the second focus of government intervention: anti-competitive behavior. Anti-trust legislation can prevent firms that already have significant market power from using it to harm customers. For example, the United States government stepped in and stopped Microsoft when it found it was stifling competition in the operating system industry, and forced it to split into two companies.

Governments have another tool in preventing monopoly behavior by firms with market power: regulation. The government can modify the firm's behavior so that it does not threaten overall macro outcomes with market power by putting limits on the prices the firm can charge, the amount of output it can produce, and how much it must invest.

II. NATURAL MONOPOLY

In general, government will first have to choose whether anti-trust or regulation would be preferable in dealing with a particular market, but let's start with one where regulation would clearly be the choice. Natural monopolies are so named because the pervasive economies of scale in the market make it impossible for any competitive firm to produce the product as efficiently as a single large producer could. The economies of scale create a natural barrier to entry.

A natural monopoly, then, is actually preferable to having competition as society will get the good at the lowest possible cost in terms of resources. The government, therefore, may not want to break-up this monopoly through anti-trust action. Should they regulate industry instead? If the natural monopoly can produce the good at the lowest possible cost, should we even bother it with regulation or just let it do its thing?

As we learned in the Chapter 18, economies of scale are no guarantee of lower prices. Just because there is a point on the natural monopoly's ATC curve where they could produce cheaper than any competitive firm could, does not mean they will actually produce there or not charge a price above the competitive price. The government will need to regulate the firm's behavior if it wants to see those cost savings passed on to consumers.

Declining ATC Curves

High Fixed Costs. Because costs keep falling the bigger the firm gets in an industry with economies of scale, a natural monopoly has a downward sloping long-run ATC curve. As a result, it can undercut any smaller firm trying to enter the industry and price it out of existence. Without government intervention, the large company will come to naturally dominate the industry.

Natural monopolies generally arise in industries where total costs are dominated by fixed costs. For example, electric companies typically have a natural monopoly in an area because to break into the industry you need to build a power plant and set of power lines to deliver the electricity—very expensive operations. These high fixed costs mean the ATC curve for any electric company will start off very high.

Low Marginal Costs. The other half of the story is low variable costs and low marginal costs. While costs to get started in the electricity game are exorbitant, providing one more house with power usually involves nothing more than flipping a switch.

As a result, the marginal cost of additional production is so low that although it does rise (diminishing marginal returns) it never crosses the ATC curve, as figure 21.1 illustrates. Without this crossing, the ATC will not have its traditional U-shape and instead will be downward sloping throughout the entire range of possible output level.

Since a natural monopoly would enjoy this downward sloping ATC curve and a competitive firm would face the typical U-shaped one, the cost per unit at the desired output level would definitely be lower under natural monopoly. The problem remains, though, without regulation would the natural monopoly produce the desired amount?

Unregulated Outcome

Although the particular case of the natural monopoly makes it preferable to perfect competition in the same industry, its behavior may leave society worse off. The barriers to entry constructed by economies of scale end up giving natural monopolies significant market power, as with Google's domination of online advertising. Natural monopolies will use this market power to maximize profits and restrict competition, forcing consumers to pay higher prices then they would have if the market were competitive.

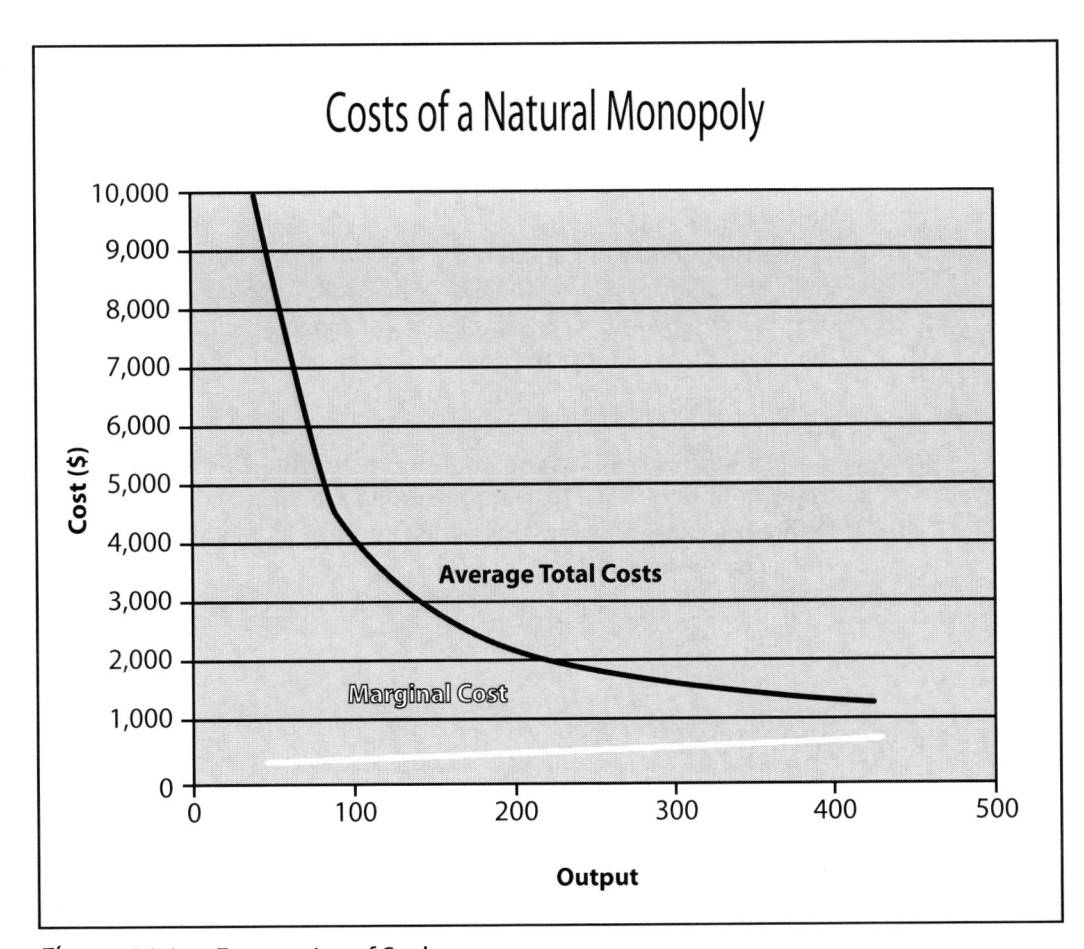

Figure 21.1 • Economies of Scale
Since marginal cost never crosses average total cost, ATC is declining over the entire relevant range for a natural monopoly.

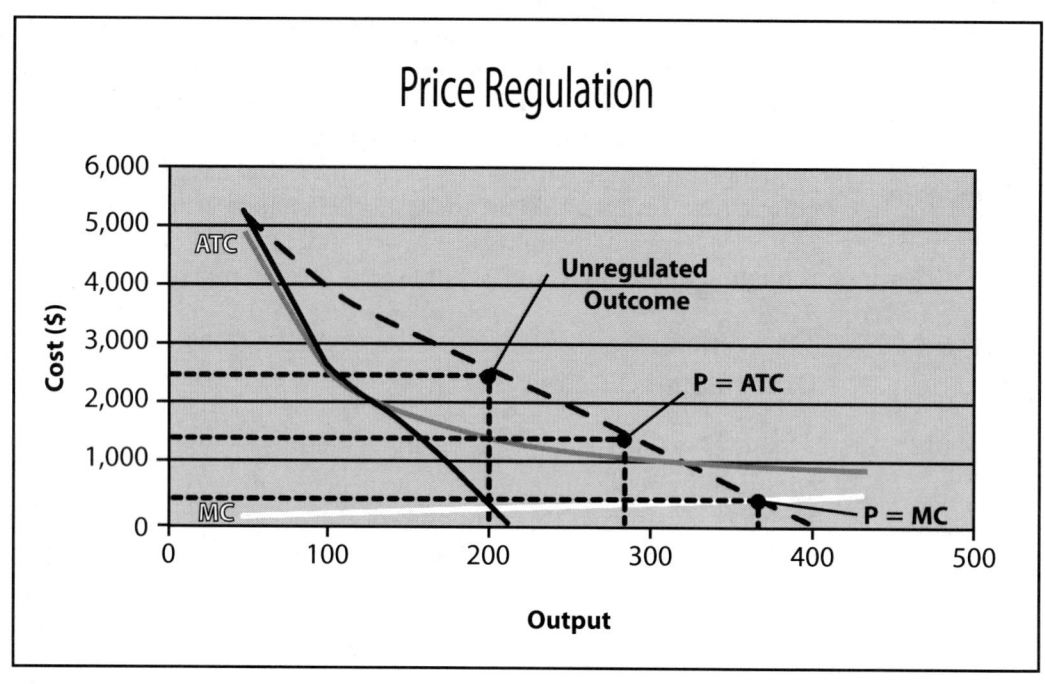

Figure 21.2 • Price Regulation
While the government wants to reduce the price from the unregulated monopoly outcome, each of the pricing regulation options creates more problems.

In short, a natural monopoly will seek to produce where marginal revenue equals marginal cost. Since they face a downward sloping curve, the outcome will be less output at a higher price compared to the competitive outcome as we saw in the monopoly outcome in Chapter 18.

As mentioned in Chapter 18, the monopoly outcome is both productively inefficient and allocatively inefficient. Since price exceeds marginal cost at the monopoly output level, people receive an incorrect signal about the opportunity cost of the good; they think it costs more to produce than it actually does. As a result, the monopoly will underproduce this good relative to society's desires and allocative efficiency will not be achieved.

In addition, without competition, there will be no downward pressure forcing price to the minimum ATC. Instead, the monopoly firm chooses a restricted output level at a higher price, as in figure 21.2. Since the firm faces a downward sloping demand curve and a downward sloping (not U-shaped) ATC curve, producing at minimum cost is impossible. As a result, we are not getting the good at lowest possible cost per unit.

III. REGULATORY OPTIONS

The massive profits earned by natural monopolies prompt consumers to demand government action. Assume the government does not want to break up the monopoly and instead wants to take advantage of its economies of scale. How exactly does the government regulate the monopoly? Figure 21.2 shows that if left unregulated the natural monopoly will want a high-price, low-output equilibrium that will certainly result in inefficiency. How can the government force the equilibrium in the market closer to the efficient solution?

Price Regulation

One common solution is price regulation. After all, the monopoly's ability to set price with impunity is a key cause of market failure. Governments across the country have set prices for utility and telephone monopolies throughout history with varying results. Clearly the government wants the price to be lower than the monopoly price, but where exactly should it set the price?

Price Efficiency. One possible option is to set price equal to marginal cost. This result, common to any competitive equilibrium, ensures allocative efficiency—the socially optimal amount of output. The rightmost dot in figure 21.2 illustrates the problem inherent with marginal cost pricing. Since marginal cost is always below ATC for a natural monopoly, forcing the monopoly into marginal cost-pricing means price will be below cost per unit; the firm will earn an average loss on every unit it produces.

Remember that the downward sloping ATC curve means that the marginal cost curve is always below the ATC curve. If the government forces the natural monopoly to sell at a price equal to marginal cost, it is forcing it into bankruptcy. There is no way the government can convince a firm to stay open under these conditions. It will simply close up shop and society will be left without any firm providing the good.

Subsidy. Therefore, if we want the firm to stay open and produce where price equals marginal cost, we will have to subsidize the firm; that is, pay them to produce an amount greater than profit-maximizing output level. Optimally, we would want that subsidy to be exactly equal to the loss caused by the lower price; the loss per unit times the quantity.

The problem with actually putting this strategy into practice is mainly a political one. It is hard to get people to vote for a subsidy to the same firms they thought were ripping them off a little while ago, even though they would be getting the product at a lower price. As a result, achieving marginal cost pricing in a natural monopoly remains a rare occurrence.

Productive Efficiency. In addition, marginal cost pricing would only provide allocative efficiency, not productive efficiency; we still would not be producing at minimum ATC. Figure 21.1 shows that ATC falls for the natural monopoly as they increase output, meaning the only way we would achieve minimum cost would be to have the firm produce at peak capacity—somewhere way beyond the right edge of figure 21.2. Since that would cause the firm to take on even bigger per unit losses than marginal cost pricing, an even bigger subsidy would be needed to induce them to do so, and we end up at the same problem as we did in marginal cost pricing.

Profit Regulation

Another way to ensure the natural monopoly isn't taking advantage of customers is to regulate its profits instead of its price. By regulating that the firm cannot charge a price higher than its ATC, we ensure the same outcome as with competition zero economic profit. We won't need a subsidy to achieve this outcome because the firm would be covering all of its costs and still taking home normal profits.

This strategy may also be preferable because of the ease of implementation. In theory, we wouldn't need to know anything about the demand and cost curves facing the firm; all we need to do is check its balance sheet at the end of the year to see if the firm is bringing home excessive profits. If they were, the government would just reduce the regulated price. For example, Article 21.1 reports that the Netherlands has proposed regulating stamp prices so that the postal services can only receive a "reasonable return" over costs.

Article 21.1:
Dutch Watchdog—TNT Stamp Price Regulation Workable

Wed May 9, 2007 10:41am EDT
By Niclas Mika

THE HAGUE, May 9 (Reuters)—A proposal before the Dutch parliament to regulate mail company TNT's ... (TNT.AS) stamp prices as part of market liberalisation is workable, the Dutch post and telecoms regulator OPTA said on Wednesday.

Analysts have said the proposal by the Christian Democrats and the Labour party, both part of the ruling Dutch coalition, could knock up to 10 percent off TNT's TNT.N valuation.

TNT shares were down 2.1 percent at 31.49 euros by 1440 GMT.

The proposal would set stamp prices for part of TNT's mail business based on costs and a "reasonable return" initially, followed by increases in line with inflation in the following years.

"The proposal as it is on the table now ... the benchmarking based on costs and a possible mark-up is something that we have plenty of experience with in the telecoms market," OPTA Chairman Chris Fonteijn said at the regulator's annual press conference.

"It's nothing that we think will saddle us with enormous problems ... Cost allocation is always an issue, but we think that it is a workable system in itself," he said.

The proposed amendment to the country's new postal law would affect the "universal service", which includes delivery of letters and parcels and represents a significant portion of TNT's mail revenue.

. . .

TNT still has a monopoly on letters weighing up to 50 grams, representing about half of the 2 billion euro ($2.7 billion) Dutch mail market. The government wants to open the market from January 2008.

Christian Democrats and Labour are at odds over whether the law should set minimum work regulations for the industry.

Labour has threatened to block the law unless it specifies that post companies can use only carriers with employment contracts.

TNT is one of the biggest employers in the Netherlands with about 59,000 people. Its two main local competitors, privately held Sandd and Deutsche Post's ... Selekt Mail, employ few permanent staff and pay carriers by the items delivered. . . .

Questions:
1. How will the proposed legislation limit the postal company's monopoly power?
2. What are the possible side effects of limiting the monopoly's profits to a "reasonable return" over costs?
3. What are the possible side effects of forcing the industry to hire full-time workers instead of paying workers per item delivered?

All rights reserved. Republication or redistribution of Thomson Reuters content, including by framing or similar means, is expressly prohibited without the prior written consent of Thomson Reuters. Thomson Reuters and its logo are registered trademarks or trademarks of the Thomson Reuters group of companies around the world. ©Thomas Reuters 2009. Thomson Reuters journalists are subject to an Editorial Handbook which requires fair presentation and disclosure of relevant interests.

Bloated Costs. A savvy firm can abuse the principle of profit regulation, however. As article 21.1 suggests, profit regulation does not impose a maximum dollar amount of allowable profits, but rather a rate of return over its costs. As a result, a firm under price regulation has every incentive to increase costs. By raising costs through inefficiency and wasteful spending, the firm can increase the total amount of profit it can legally take home.

For example, if a regulated railroad monopoly could only have profits equal to 10 percent over its cost, should it offer rides for $5 or $10? At $10 per ride the firm would earn a profit of $1 per customer while it would earn only $0.50 per customer if they charged $5. While a higher average profit does not guarantee higher total profits, you can see how a system of profit regulation could result in wasted resources and higher prices. A firm could further manipulate the system by buying products and equipment from an unregulated subsidiary at inflated prices. This would be doubly effective since it would pad the costs of the regulated firm (thus increasing its profit cap) and simultaneously drive up profits at the unregulated subsidiary.

Output Regulation

Another way to protect consumers from being exploited by monopolies is to require a minimum amount of output. Monopolies extract additional profits out of the market by restricting output below the competitive outcome. This restriction causes the consumers to pay a higher price for an artificially scarce product. The idea behind output regulation is that forcing the business to provide more of the product would reduce the price and allow more people to enjoy the product, as seen in figure 21.3.

Quality Deterioration. But again we have a problem. Forcing businesses to reduce their profits by forcing them to produce more than their profit-maximizing output level,

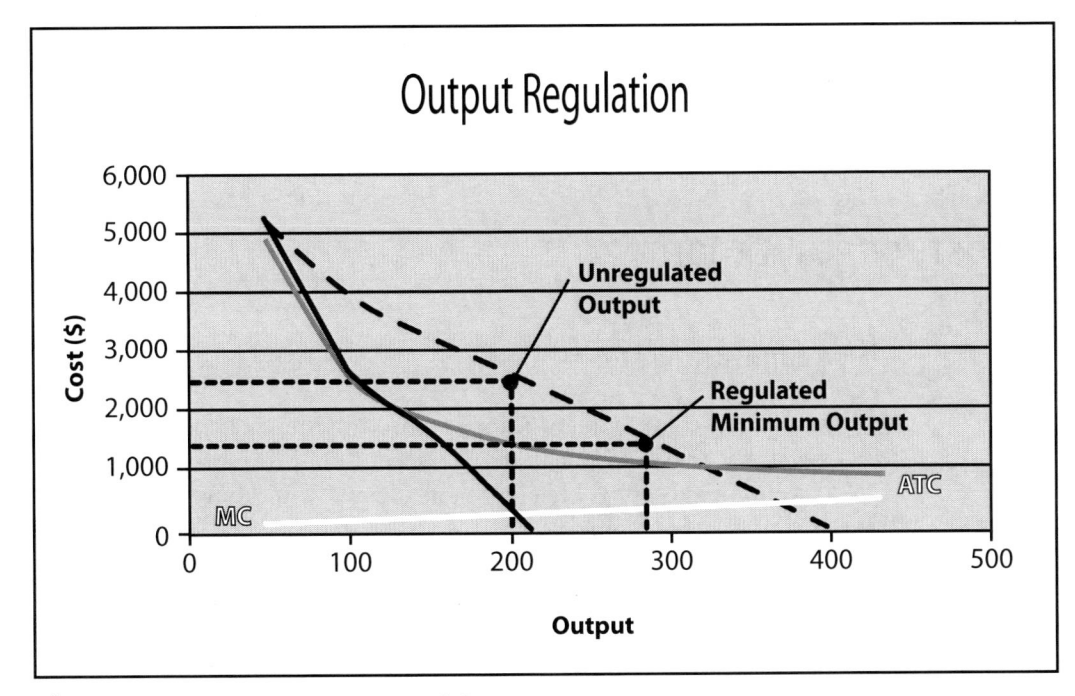

Figure 21.3 • Minimum Required Output
While output regulation forces monopolies to produce an amount greater than their profit-maximizing level, it does not guarantee that the firm will maintain a high quality of service.

basically gives them an open door to cut corners. Firms under minimum service regulations will put off capital improvements, reduce quality control, and let the overall quality of the product slip.

Since the monopoly has no competition, consumers will have to accept whatever the monopoly offers, no matter the quality. This may explain why people have so many complaints about the service at the local cable or telephone monopoly. Why would these companies spend money or resources on good customer service when their customers have no viable alternative?

Imperfect Answers

Even without quality deterioration, output regulation will not solve the market failure associated with a natural monopoly. Since we need the monopoly to produce the regulated output without a subsidy, there must be some positive profits at this output level as indicated by the gap between P and ATC. In addition, price is still above marginal cost and we are not producing efficiently. In fact, the previous sections indicate that any regulation goal requires sacrificing other goals. The call for regulation in a monopoly situation stems from the fact that the unregulated monopoly will produce too little at too high a price relative to the social optimum.

Each regulatory strategy, however, has its drawbacks. Regulating price to achieve marginal cost pricing or least-cost production forces taxpayers to pay the firm a subsidy in order to keep it in business. Regulating profits creates incentives to inflate costs. Forcing the firm to produce a certain level of output will induce them to cut corners and offer a lower quality product.

In reality, no amount of government intervention will not turn a market failure caused by a monopoly into a perfect market outcome. In fact, the goal of any regulation should only be to improve the market outcome, not perfect it. However, sometimes the price, cost, and output outcomes produced by government intervention are worse than those produced by the original market failure. If the government failure is in fact worse than the unregulated market outcome, it may be the case that deregulation would improve total social utility.

IV. COSTS OF REGULATION

Administrative Costs

Just because government intervention provides the consumer more of the product at a lower price does not mean it was successful. If the costs imposed by the government intervention exceed its benefits, then society would have been better off with the unregulated market outcome.

Determining the regulation strategy of the United States government requires the collection and analysis of a wide range of data about costs, prices, and output. The accountants, economists, and mathematicians that do this analysis could have been employed elsewhere in the private sector. The production lost by having them study the possibility of regulation is part of the administrative cost of that regulation.

The federal government alone employs nearly 200,000 people in different regulatory agencies. That does not even include workers with regulatory responsibilities in other agencies or departments, or regulators employed by state and local governments. The forgone production of these workers represents a significant cost of regulation.

Compliance Costs

Even beyond the lost profits caused by regulation, additional resources are lost by regulated industries having to comply with regulations. Entire departments are hired to learn about regulations, how best to comply with them, and to send reports on compliance to government regulators. Without regulation, these workers could have been employed in productive activities instead of dealing with issues of compliance. The productive resources spent on these activities comprise the compliance cost of regulation.

Efficiency Costs

While part of the goal of any regulation is to improve the mix of output, it is not uncommon for a combination of politics, incomplete information, and poor implementation to result in government intervention actually worsening the mix of output (getting farther away from the mix of output society desires the most). Social utility falls when less desired output is produced instead of more desired goods, imposing an efficiency cost.

As the demand curve changes, regulatory goals and mechanisms need to change, too. If not, regulations that were once helpful may end up being counterproductive and costly. Even more, regulations limit innovation because of questions about how new technologies fit in with regulation. These lost innovations further increase efficiency costs.

Balancing Benefits and Costs

Hopefully the previous pages have convinced you that achieving a perfect outcome through regulation is virtually impossible. Even if it were, the cost of imposing that regulation may outweigh the benefits. The government must constantly weigh the marginal benefit of regulation (improved market outcomes) with the marginal cost of that regulation (resources lost in developing, implementing, and complying with the regulation). If the marginal cost of the regulation exceeds the marginal benefit, the government should start deregulating until the two are equal.

V. DEREGULATION IN PRACTICE

The push for deregulation in modern times has come from two distinct factors. First, the efficiency costs of regulation caused regulated industries to stagnate and not keep up with new technologies. Second, the appearance of new products and processes broke down the barriers held by natural monopolies and made competition possible in an unregulated market. A brief overview of two deregulated industries will help illustrate the circumstances and consequences of removing regulations from monopolized industries.

Telephone Service

Telephone service is an industry that throughout its history has been dominated by natural monopolies. Once a company has established telephone lines and service, the marginal cost of one more phone call is almost nothing. As a result, introducing competition would create a maze of competing wires and cables at a high cost.

For these reasons, AT&T was allowed a monopoly on both long distance and local service in many areas, heavily regulated by the Federal Communications Commission. The introduction of satellite and cellular technology introduced the possibility of low-cost competition, however, and the profits allowed AT&T by regulation were so high that both consumers and potential competitors demanded a change.

Long Distance. The government ended AT&T's monopoly on long distance service through anti-trust action in 1982, breaking the company up and creating a more competitive industry. While several large firms still dominate, over eight hundred firms are in the market today, and prices have dropped sharply since the days of monopoly.

In addition, service has improved through the use of new technologies like fiber optic cable and the offering of new services through the phone line such as fax and Internet access. It is unlikely that these improvements would have been made by a monopoly firm protected by regulation.

Local Service. The effect of monopoly control over local service became painfully apparent as the long distance monopoly was being dismantled. As competition lowered long distance prices throughout the 1980s, local service rates increased. People wondered whether eliminating the monopoly in local services might cause a similar turnaround in price trends.

The former AT&T companies that dominated local phone service defended their high prices on the basis of the high cost of building and maintaining their distribution network. Unlike with long distance, no new breakthrough, such as satellite service, offered low-cost competition.

The government disagreed, forcing the companies to give new wireless phone companies access to their networks so they could compete without having to build their own. The monopoly companies have responded by putting up barrier after barrier to companies wishing to enter the local phone service industry—high access fees, purchase of excessive capital equipment, and the implementation of complicated access codes. The struggle to deregulate the local telephone industry continues today.

Airlines

Price Regulation. Airline industry also began as a government-regulated industry. The government created the Civil Aeronautics Board to control prices for air travel in order to ensure that both large and small communities would have access to air travel at a reasonable price. The key to this regulation was maintaining a profit level that will encourage airlines to provide a minimum amount of service to routes they normally would not bother with if left unregulated.

Originally, regulated prices were set along the same lines as train fares in the regulated railroad monopoly: the longer the ride, the higher the price. Over time, it became apparent that the government needed to make more intensive cost studies to better understand the actual costs faced by airlines on different routes. Once these costs were determined, the government regulated a price that would ensure an acceptable profit level (profit regulation).

The CAB aimed not only at maintaining a fair average profit level, but ensuring that airlines would keep servicing small communities. Since the marginal cost of an additional mile in the air is very low, a short flight has a higher average cost than a long one. The CAB then allowed the airlines to charge a little more on long flights in order to keep the prices on these shorter flights down, a process called cross-subsidization.

No Entry, No Price Competition. In order to maintain their regulated profit level and keep these short, unprofitable routes open, the CAB had to prevent competition among the airlines and from potential new entrants. If competition existed, airlines would immediately drop unprofitable routes and focus only on the long flights to big cities that make the most money. As a result, airlines were not allowed to change prices very much without asking the CAB for approval.

In addition, any firm that wanted to enter the airline industry had to apply for a route with the CAB and give proof of why their service was needed. The existing firms would then be given an opportunity to refute the claim or promise that they would offer the same service. With the existing firms having more experience offering airline service, the new entrants never had a chance. In fact, the CAB awarded zero major routes to new entrants from 1930 to 1977.

Bloated Costs. Without the ability to compete over price, though, firms were left only the ability to use nonprice competition to get people to choose their airline over another. Airlines tried to increase sales by increasing the frequency of flights, offering free meals and drinks, and giving other benefits. All of these attempts raised average costs and lowered profits, resulting in airlines reducing service on less profitable routes anyway. Profit regulation had failed.

New Entrants. The government finally ended strict CAB control over the airline industry in 1978, causing entry into the industry to skyrocket. Between 1978 and 1985 alone, the number of domestic airlines increased from thirty-seven to 174. As competition increased, prices reduced sharply, especially on longer flights that no longer had to cross-subsidize shorter ones.

Increasing Concentration. However, there were some tradeoffs when deregulation occurred in the airline industry. As prices dropped, many airlines realized they could not stay profitable and exited the industry. The remaining companies therefore were left with a greater market share, increasing the concentration ratio on many routes.

Some carriers even have a monopoly on certain routes. Today, 10 percent of all routes are completely controlled by one airline. Customers of monopolized air travel routes pay a much higher price than they would if the market was competitive; upwards of 45 to 85 percent more in some cases.

Entry Barriers. The fact remains, however, that entry is now much easier than it was under regulation. While some carriers are able to keep rivals out of certain markets, it is in general much easier to start a new airline now. Although barriers to entry still exist, the market is at least now contestable; the legitimate possibility of new entry forces airlines to be at least a little less exploitative.

While many routes are still monopolized and the concentration of the industry in the hands of the biggest three carriers (American, United, and Delta) is higher than ever, the percentage of monopolized routes has decreased greatly since deregulation.

Future of Deregulation

While deregulation has proven beneficial in both the telephone and airline industry that does not necessarily mean that all regulation is bad. In a scenario where a natural monopoly has no significant competition, completely leaving that monopoly unregulated would likely result in a negative outcome for consumers.

In addition, there are some industries (such as food and drug production) that the government believes simply cannot be trusted to the judgment of individual consumers and businesses. The safety of food and drug is so important, the Food and Drug Administration imposes myriad regulations and guidelines before a new product is launched. While this regulation certainly limits the growth of the industry and imposes some costs, the government believes the benefit of FDA regulation easily outweighs these costs.

The key to the future of regulation relies on continually checking regulated industries to distinguish which ones have outdated regulations or no longer need regulations because of significant competition. Failing to deregulate industries that no longer need such protection discourages innovation and can be just as disastrous as an unregulated monopoly itself.

CHAPTER 21 SUMMARY

- Governments can fix monopoly outcomes either by **breaking up** the monopoly or by **regulation**.
- Natural monopolies might be preferable to competition in markets with **economies of scale**.
- Natural monopolies have **declining ATC curves** since increasing the output decreasing minimum ATC.
- If left unregulated a natural monopoly will pursue a **high-price, low-output equilibrium** relative to the competitive outcome.
- **Price regulation** will result in having to **subsidize the monopoly** in order to convince it to produce the efficient amount.
- **Profit regulation** will result in inflated costs.
- **Output regulation** will result in the monopoly producing a lower-quality product to cut costs.
- If the cost of regulation **outweighs the benefits**, the government is better off leaving the market unregulated.

CHAPTER 21 Exercises

Name _____

1) Why would the government allow a monopoly to exist?
   A) It always charges a lower price than a competitive firm.
   B) It always more efficient than a competitive firm.
   C) It may have economies of scale that allow it to produce at a lower cost than a smaller firm.
   D) It always improves total social utility.

1) _____

2) The ATC curve for a natural monopoly
   A) falls as output increases.
   B) rises as output increases.
   C) stays the same as output increases.
   D) is u-shaped.

2) _____

3) At what point would the government need to subsidize a price-regulated monopoly in order to keep it from exiting the market in the long run?
   A) Price < ATC   C) MR < MC
   B) Price < MC   D) ATC > MC

3) _____

4) If profit regulation is used to regulate a natural monopolist, then the monopolist is likely to
   A) cease production unless the government provides a subsidy.
   B) reduce costs through improved efficiency.
   C) reduce costs through improved efficiency.
   D) inflate costs to increase maximum allowable profits.

4) _____

5) Forcing a natural monopoly to provide a minimum amount of a good or service would likely cause the firm to
   A) cease production unless the government provides a subsidy.
   B) reduce costs through improved efficiency.
   C) reduce costs through improved efficiency.
   D) inflate costs to increase maximum allowable profits.

5) _____

6) Regulation is appropriate if
   A) market failure exists.
   B) market failure exists and the benefit of regulation outweighs the cost.
   C) the regulation improves total utility.
   D) regulation is costless.

6) _____

7) Before the deregulation in the airline industry, airlines charged higher rates on long flights in order to make short flights cheaper. Such a practice is an example of
   A) cross-subsidization.
   B) price discrimination.
   C) public goods.
   D) externalities.

7) _____

385

8) A case can be made for deregulating industries because 8) _____
   A) market outcomes maximize equity.
   B) sometimes regulation results in a worse outcome than it was designed to fix.
   C) competitive markets enjoy greater economies of scale than monopolies.
   D) government regulation increases efficiency.

9) Describe where the government should set a monopolist's price to insure allocative (price) efficiency. What is the problem with setting the price at this level?

10) Has deregulation improved the airline industry? Why or why not?

Labor Markets

I. LABOR SUPPLY

There isn't an economic indicator watched more closely than employment and the unemployment rate; not even GDP. Employment tells us not only about the view of the future held by businesses, but also about how much people are willing to work at the prevailing wage rate in the economy.

The amounts of labor that people are willing and able to supply to businesses at various wage rates comprise the supply of labor. Much like the supply for a consumer good, people will supply more labor at higher wage rates (the price of labor) than at lower rates. In general, the greater the rewards for working, the more people want to work; leading to upward-sloping labor supply, such as in figure 22.1.

Income vs. Leisure

The payoff from employment actually takes two forms—the feeling of satisfaction one gets from working and one's paycheck. Since people want to buy the goods that come with labor income, clearly people will supply labor to a free market if the rewards are high enough.

Labor supply is a little different from most markets because not working has a reward, too. We call this reward leisure. We know that leisure has some positive value or else everyone would be working three jobs and trying to make the most money possible each day. Instead, people spend at least some time each day resting, shopping, and enjoying consumption goods. Labor supply, therefore, implies a tradeoff between working

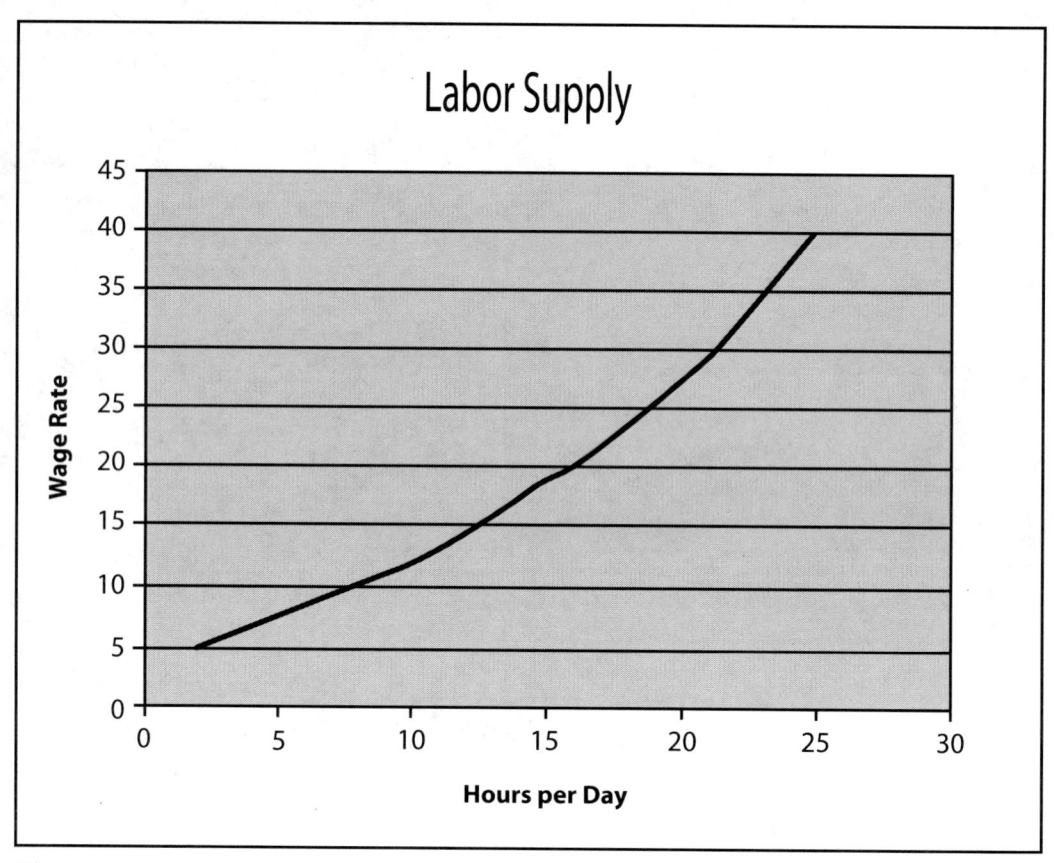

Figure 22.1 • Supply of Labor
People will only be willing to work additional hours if the return to labor (the wage rate) rises.

and leisure; every hour spent on one activity imposes the opportunity cost of an hour of the other activity lost.

The tradeoff between labor and leisure implies that people, and societies as a whole, will not work longer and longer hours for the same wage rate. Every additional hour a person works, takes away another hour of leisure. As leisure becomes scarcer, the marginal utility of leisure rises and with it, the opportunity cost of working. People must be compensated for this increasing opportunity cost and thus will only increase work hours if the wage rate rises.

At the same time, as people work more and earn more wages, the marginal utility of one more dollar falls. The worker has already met his basic needs and any additional income will go towards less necessary consumption. As a result, it will take a higher wage to induce more working since they worker does not need the money as much.

Backward-Bending Supply Curve

The reason people work more when the wage rate rises is that it essentially becomes too expensive not to work; the opportunity cost of leisure rises. Every increase in the wage rate represents an increase in the opportunity cost of leisure since a person must pay for leisure by forgoing wages. In other words the substitution effect dictates that a person substitutes away from leisure (and toward work) when leisure becomes more expensive (the wage rate rises).

But wherever there is a substitution effect there must be an income effect. For labor supply, the income effect dictates that as the wage rate rises workers must consume a little more of everything—including leisure. Therefore, the substitution effect and income effect work in opposite directions.

Labor Supply

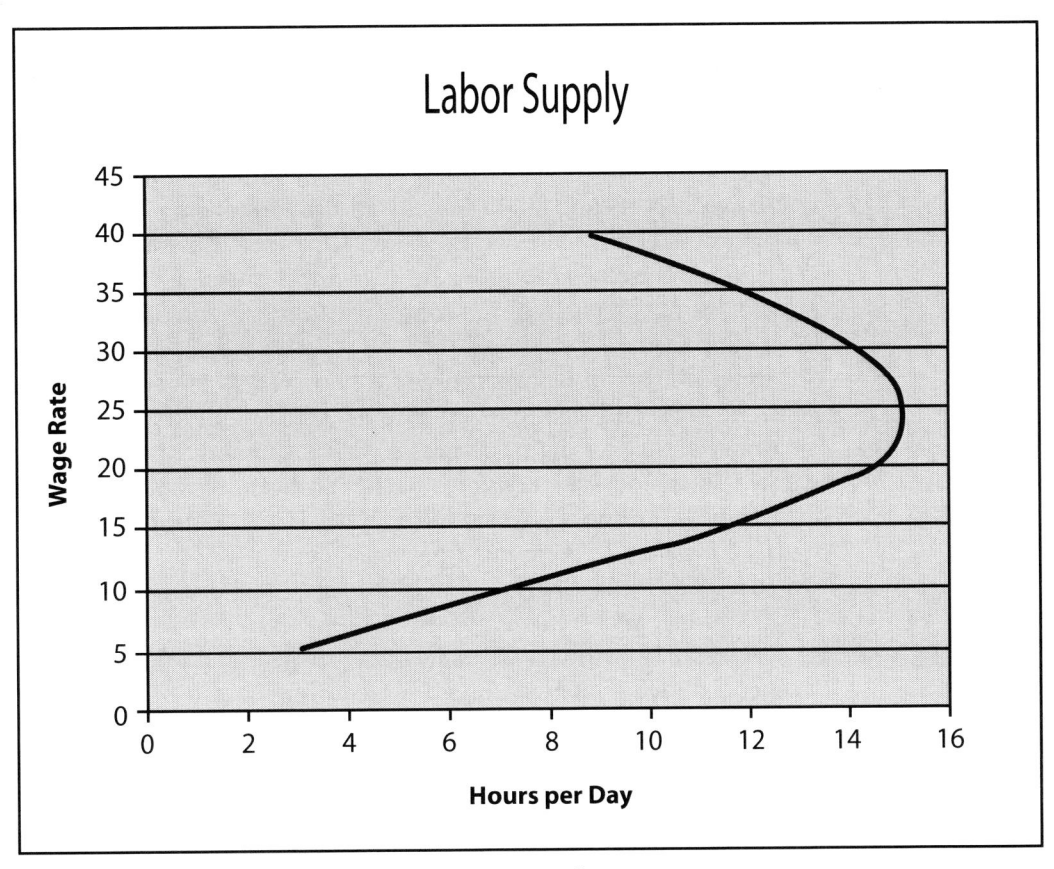

Figure 22.2 • Backward-Bending Labor Supply
For some workers, their wage rate becomes so high that the income effect dominates the substitution effect and they end up "buying" more leisure time as their wage rises instead of working more.

For most people, and society at large, the substitution effect dominates and we have the typical upward-sloping labor supply curve. For some extremely rich workers with high-paying jobs, though, the income effect dominates. That means there is a wage rate so high that they will actually work less if they get a raise. Think about boxers: journeyman boxers fight as often as once a month in order to get the most money they can before their careers end, but big-time prize fighters only fight once or twice a year because the prize money and appearance fees they receive are so much larger.

Why might they behave this way? When wages rise above a certain level, the benefit of working another hour becomes so small relative to total income that the worker would rather just enjoy the income he has and work fewer hours; the marginal utility of leisure has overcome the marginal utility of additional wage income. Figure 22.2 illustrates that the result is a labor supply curve that becomes vertical and then bends backward at the point where the income effect begins to dominate.

II. MARKET SUPPLY

Determinants

Just as with the supply for a single product in Chapters 3 and 13, adding up all of the labor supply curves for all of the members of the labor force, employed and unemployed, gives us the market supply. The market supply of labor provides us an aggregate view of how the United States labor force will respond to wage changes. While a small fraction of workers will be in the backward-bending part of their supply curves, nearly everyone will have a positive response to a wage increase. Therefore, the market supply curve of labor is upward sloping.

The market supply only represents the labor decisions of a particular point in time, *ceteris paribus*. If the United States had the same labor supply curve forever, the only way workers could have achieved the wage increases they have experienced over the years would have been to move up the supply curve by working longer hours. As time goes on, however, changes in economy lead to changes in the position and slope of the labor supply curve.

Determinants of labor supply that may lead to shifts in the curve include: worker tastes, income and wealth, expectations, prices, and taxes. We know the labor supply curve has shifted in the past because in 1890 the average worker in the United States worked sixty hours a week for 20 cents an hour. By 2007 those numbers became less than thirty-four hours a week and $18 per hour. While much of this change has to do with labor demand, there must have also been a serious leftward shift in the labor supply curve. Figure 22.3 shows that a decrease in labor supply will lead to fewer hours of labor supplied at any wage rate.

Increases in income and wealth have decreased marginal utility of income for most workers, allowing them to choose more leisure over work. At the same time, the implementation and growth of unemployment benefits and income security programs has encouraged people to find the perfect job and decreased the bargaining power of the firm. Finally, leisure itself has become more diversified. Article 22.1 discusses some of the

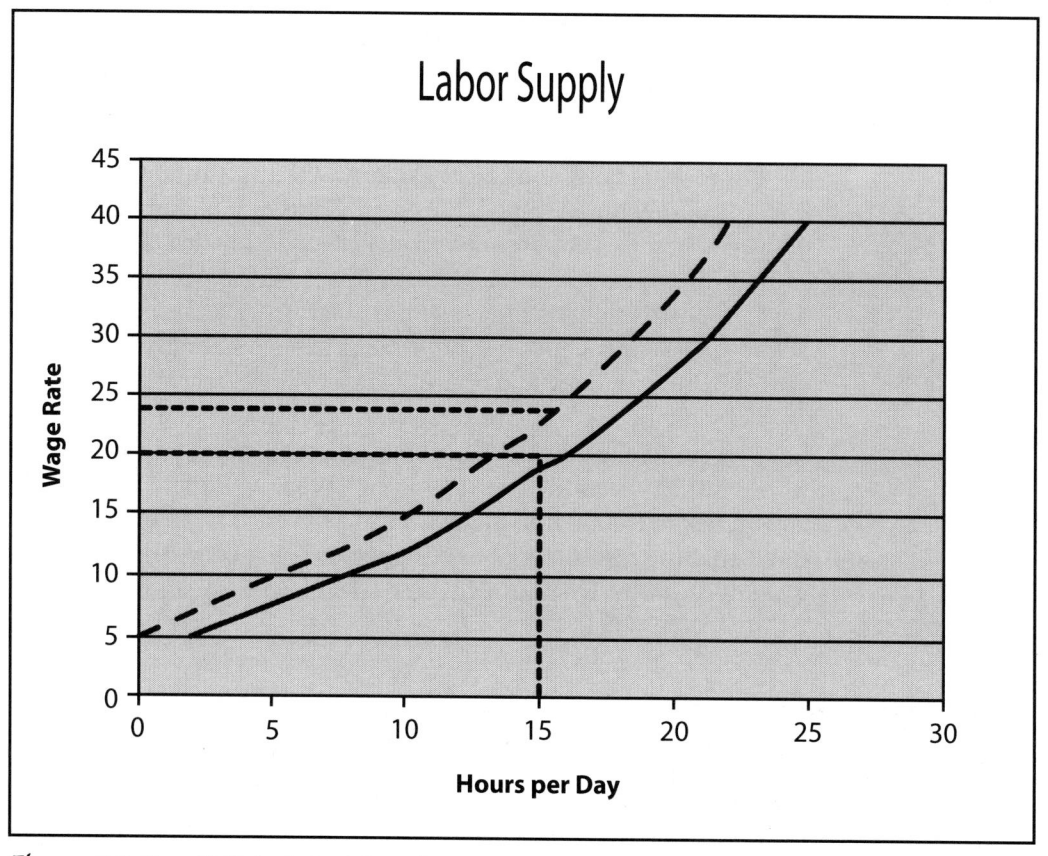

Figure 22.3 • **Shift in Labor Supply**
When the labor supply curve shifts back, businesses will have to offer higher wages to get workers to work the same amount of hours.

Article 22.1:
Labor supply debated as slower output looms

Wed Jun 20, 2007 2:00pm EDT

By Tamawa Kadoya

CHATHAM, Mass., June 20 (Reuters)—A steady decline in the U.S. working-age population as baby boomers retire may significantly reduce potential economic output, requiring new rules of thumb to guide the Federal Reserve as it seeks to keep inflation at bay. . . .

The outlook may be dire. A paper presented by Bruce Fallick of the Federal Reserve Board and Jonathan Pingle at Brevan Howard Asset Management showed the projected population aging will lower the aggregate labor force participation rate by 6 full percentage points over the next 35 years.

The participation rate, the proportion of the working-age population in the labor force, peaked in the late 1990s after about a half-century of gains. It stood at 66 percent in May and many analysts expect it to gradually trend lower.

"The implication of this for monetary policy is that potential output would be much less, holding everything else constant," said Lisa Lynch, economics professor at Tufts University, who is also chair of directors at the Boston Fed.

. . .

STRUCTURAL SHIFTS IN SUPPLY

A number of cross currents make judging the outlook for labor supply complicated: retiring baby boomers; an increase of older workers, especially men; changing work patterns for women; and difficulties in measuring immigrant labor.

Older Americans may have to work longer for financial reasons as benefits and pensions are contracting, according to one paper presented at the conference.

Eugene Steuerle of The Urban Institute, who specializes in Social Security, said that underutilized older workers will likely play the role women did in the recent past. The participation rate for women aged 25–54 began a steady rise in 1977 until leveling off earlier this decade.

. . .Many policy-makers are hopeful this is a temporary shift reflecting recent economic weakness and not a more disturbing shift in trend. However, it gives them one more factor to worry about as they seek to gauge how fast to let the economy grow.

Questions:
1. Why would a drop in the labor force participation rate cause potential total output to fall?
2. According to the article, why has the labor supply curve shifted back over recent years?
3. What has happened to the labor supply of older workers in recent years? Why has this happened?

All rights reserved. Republication or redistribution of Thomson Reuters content, including by framing or similar means, is expressly prohibited without the prior written consent of Thomson Reuters. Thomson Reuters and its logo are registered trademarks or trademarks of the Thomson Reuters group of companies around the world. ©Thomas Reuters 2009. Thomson Reuters journalists are subject to an Editorial Handbook which requires fair presentation and disclosure of relevant interests.

factors affecting the labor supply curve today. All of these changes mean that labor supply has constantly shifted to the left, and firms have had to increase wages to attract workers over time.

Elasticity

While all of these factors are important for understanding the long-run behavior of the labor supply curve, in the short run the curve is fixed. As a result, short-run movements in labor supply will be dependent upon the shape of the curve at that point in time—its elasticity. The elasticity of the curve tells us how much people will change the amount of labor they supply when the wage rate changes.

$$\text{Elasticity of Labor Supply} = \frac{\text{Percent Change in Quantity of Labor Supplied}}{\text{Percent Change in Wage Rate}}$$

A labor supply elasticity of .5 means workers will reduce labor by 5 percent when the wage rate falls by 10 percent. At different points in history, workers have been more or less responsive to wage rate changes and that responsiveness is reflected in the elasticity of labor supply.

Institutional Constraints

One problem with the labor supply curve and the elasticity of labor supply is that they imply perfect flexibility in the labor market. While it may be true that an entertainer or athlete may be able to dictate exactly how many hours he or she is going to work, most workers have very limited choices when it comes to quantity of labor supplied.

Rather than choosing between thirty-four and thirty-five hours, people usually have very discrete choices such as taking a "9 to 5" job or staying unemployed, working overtime or not, or picking up a second job or not. While it may not accurately reflect the actual choices faced by workers, the labor supply curve is still effective at representing how many hours people would be willing to work if the labor market were completely flexible.

III. LABOR DEMAND

Derived Demand

The number of hours people are willing to work is only half of the labor market equation. There also need to be businesses willing and able to hire these workers at mutually acceptable wage rates in order for the labor market to work. Labor demand describes the willingness and ability of businesses to hire workers at various wage rates.

Labor demand, like the demand for any other factor of production, is a derived demand. That means that the driving force behind why businesses want to hire workers and how much they are willing and able to pay them, is how well the product they produce is selling.

Businesses want to produce at an output level that maximizes their profit. The firm will therefore hire the amount of workers it needs to produce this amount as cheaply as

Labor Demand

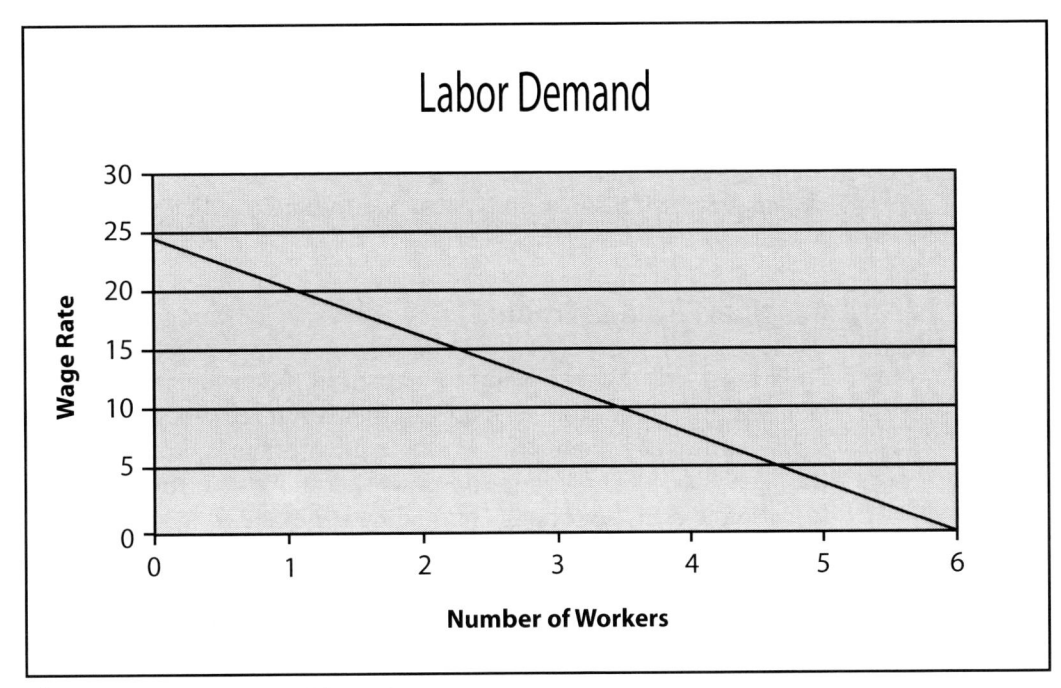

Figure 22.4 • Demand for Labor
As the wage rate rises, firms are less willing to hire as many workers.

possible given its fixed inputs. The low wages earned by farm workers, for example, have little to do with the greed of their employers and more to do with the market for agricultural products.

Computer programmers and information technology workers, on the other hand earn relatively high wages. Computer companies do not pay higher wages than agricultural companies out of the goodness of their hearts. These higher wages come partially because IT workers are relatively scarce (low labor supply), but also because the services they produce are more highly valued (high labor demand). In other words, if you are concerned about the living standards of a particular group of workers, don't boycott the company—as so many people are wont to do—buy more of their products!

The Labor Demand Curve

The demand curve for labor services will look much like the demand for any other product. While the demand curve will shift right or left with the demand for the product they are producing, all else being equal, firms will want to hire more workers when the wage rate is lower (profit effect). Hence, we get our typical downward-sloping demand curve as seen in figure 22.4.

Marginal Physical Product

Just as the determinants of labor supply influence the shape and position of that curve, several factors control the placement of the labor demand curve at any point in time. For example, a business owner would be crazy to hire a worker that did not produce enough output to justify the cost of paying him or her. In other words, a worker's marginal physical product must be high enough to justify his or her continued employment.

Remember that worker's marginal physical product is the additional output he or she brings to the firm. For example, a skilled auto worker can produce ten cars per day or a high school dropout can sell three sets of encyclopedias per day. The marginal physical product sets the upper limit on the firm's willingness to pay for labor; there is no way a car manufacturer will pay more than the value of ten cars per day to hire the skilled worker if his marginal physical product is only ten cars per day.

Marginal Revenue Product

Since most auto workers want to be paid in money and not in cars, firms need to convert this upper limit for wage into a dollar value. In other words, we need to know how much additional revenue the worker generates instead of how much additional output they generate; a firm will not pay a worker more than the additional total revenue they bring to the firm. The change in total revenue caused by the hiring of the new worker is called the worker's marginal revenue product.

In a perfectly competitive market where the firm can sell as much as it wants at the market price (horizontal demand curve), the marginal revenue product is simply equal to the marginal physical product multiplied by the price.

$$Marginal\ Revenue\ Product = Marginal\ Physical\ Product \times Price$$

If a grape picker can pick four bushels in an hour of work, for example, and those bushels bring in $3 each, the worker brings in $12 in additional revenue with an additional hour of work—his marginal revenue product.

Since firms are in the business of maximizing profit, we know they will never hire an input that brings in less revenue than it cost to hire. As a result, the marginal revenue product represents an upper limit on the wage rate a firm will pay a particular worker. The lower limit is set by the worker's labor supply curve. If the worker will supply an hour of work for less than his marginal revenue product, the firm will be eager to hire him. But as the firm hires additional labor in the short run, what happens to marginal physical product and marginal revenue product?

The Law of Diminishing Marginal Returns

Diminishing MPP. Since the labor demand curve is drawn in the short run, there are limitations to how many workers the firm can shove into the factory, field, or classroom before marginal returns begin to diminish. Eventually, the workers will be crammed so tight together they will start getting in each other's way.

As we saw in Chapter 15, as the number of workers rises, the additional output produced by additional workers will fall; marginal physical product diminishes. At very low levels of output, it may be possible for laborers to work together and maintain or even increase marginal productivity, but at some point it will begin to fall.

As more and more workers are hired, they will have to share the same amount of fixed capital and land leading to waste and idle time. This leads to the reality that the third worker hired will not bring as much additional output as the second, while the fourth will bring in even less, and so on. At some point it may even be the case that an additional worker will reduce total output (negative marginal productivity).

Diminishing MRP. Since marginal revenue is constant at the market price for a perfectly competitive firm, marginal revenue product will fall when marginal physical product does—the two numbers are proportional. Even if the demand curve of the firm were downward sloping (a monopoly, for example), the price of product would fall as output increased leading to marginal revenue product falling even faster than marginal physical product. This diminishing value of additional workers explains the downward-sloping labor demand curve. Since the marginal productivity of additional workers falls, firms will only hire more workers if they can get them at a lower wage rate.

IV. FIRM'S DECISION

Firm's Labor Supply

Just like a competitive firm experienced a horizontal demand curve, a competitive firm will face a horizontal labor supply curve as pictured in figure 22.5. At the market level, people will work more hours in the grape-picking industry (or any competitive industry) only if the wage is higher, but any one firm can hire more hours of labor at the prevailing wage rate. Any lower and the workers will go to a different firm, any higher and the firm would get too many qualified applicants and short-run costs would skyrocket.

Therefore, a perfectly competitive firm can hire as many workers as it wants at the prevailing market wage rate. Perfect competition in the industry implies that the firm is so small that changes in its hiring decision have no effect on the market supply or market wage. From the standpoint of the small, independent firm, there is an endless supply of workers available at the market wage and the firm just has to choose how many it wants to employ.

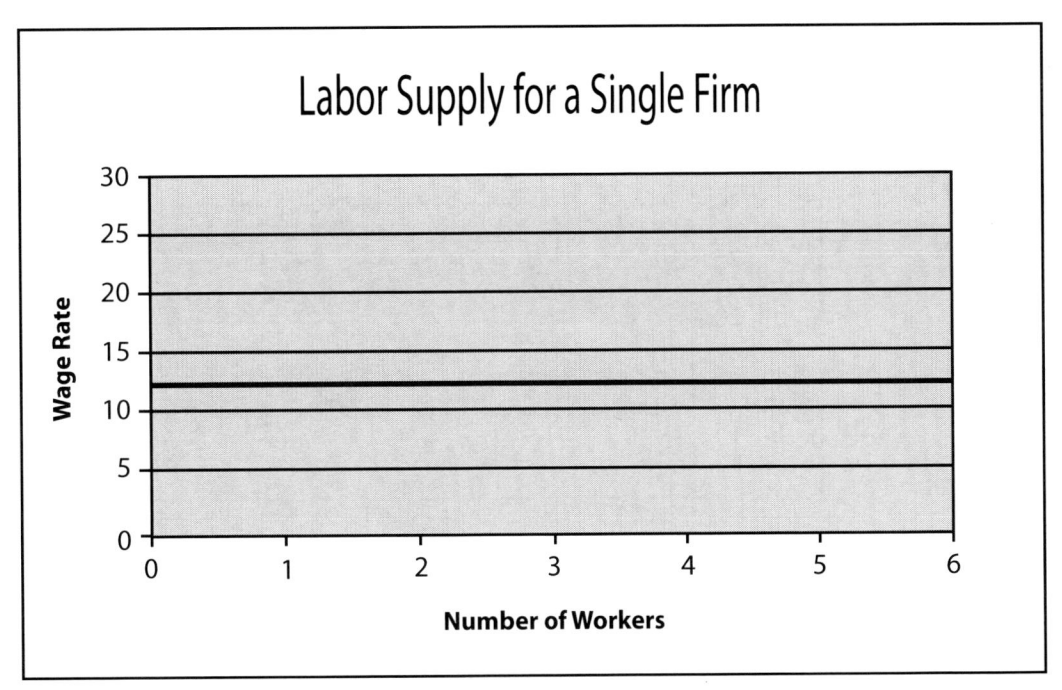

Figure 22.5 • Horizontal Labor Supply Curve
Since a single perfectly competitive firm is so small relative to the rest of market, its hiring decision has no impact on the market supply of labor. As a result, they can hire as many workers as they want at the market wage rate.

Firm's Labor Demand = MRP

The firm will hire more and more workers at the market wage rate as long as the marginal revenue product of the last worker equals or exceeds the market wage rate. Looking at figure 22.6, the firm will clearly want to hire the first worker since that worker's marginal revenue product exceeds the wage rate. That decision may change as the number of workers increases, however, since the marginal revenue product falls as the firm hires more workers.

At some point, the additional revenue brought in by hiring one worker will be exactly equal to the wage rate—three workers in figure 22.6. Hiring another worker at this point will mean paying more for that worker than the worker brings in additional revenue, and a profit-maximizing firm will never do that. Instead it chooses to hire just enough labor so that the marginal revenue product of the last worker hired is equal to the wage rate.

All the workers will be paid the same wage since the law of diminishing returns would have occurred regardless of what order they were hired in. It isn't fair to pay the fifth worker a lower wage than the first worker just because he has a lower marginal revenue product; all the workers become less productive as the factory gets more crowded and the capital-to-labor ratio falls, not just the newest worker.

Changes in Wage Rates

Many workers do not believe they are being paid a high enough wage and see this low pay as exploitation. Forcing firms to raise the wage rate (assuming the demand for labor stays the same) will certainly shift the labor supply curve and result in a new equilib-

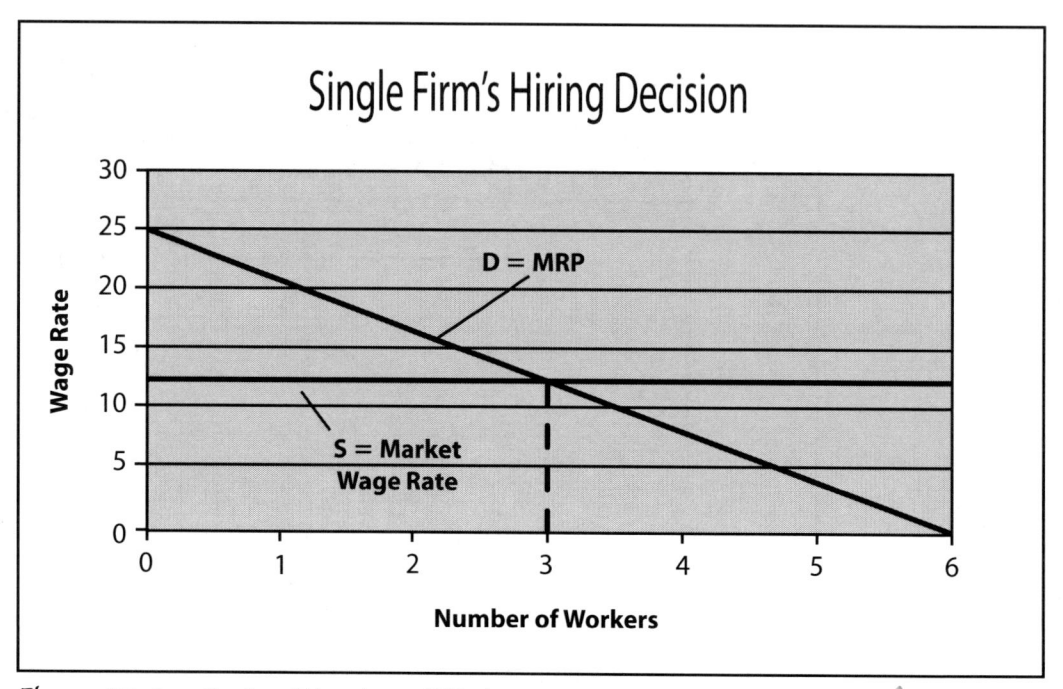

Figure 22.6 • Optimal Number of Workers
A single competitive firm will hire workers until the next worker's marginal revenue product falls below the market wage.

rium as in figure 22.7. While all the workers at this new equilibrium will earn a higher wage, what happens to the number of workers hired in this scenario?

When wage rates are forced up (due to union activity or minimum wage laws, for instance) the number of workers demanded by firms falls. When the wage rate rises, the firm now has workers employed that cost more than their marginal revenue product and they must let them go if the firm is to be profit maximizing. Wage floors—artificially high wages set by some force outside of the market—create unemployment.

Changes in Productivity

As noted by the history of our economy, it is possible for wages to rise without people losing their jobs, but it must come from an increase in labor demand. Since the labor demand curve for a firm is really its MRP curve, then the firm will be willing and able to pay workers more if marginal physical product rises or the demand for its products rise.

Workers need to accumulate more human capital and can increase their marginal productivity through training and education. With a given price, a more productive worker will produce more value and therefore increase his marginal revenue product, shifting the labor demand curve to the right as in figure 22.8. Now the firm can still employ the same amount of workers at a higher wage, or maybe hire more workers at the prevailing wage rate.

Changes in Price

The other factor that influences marginal revenue product is the price of the product the firm produces. Any increase in the demand of grapes, for example, will increase the value

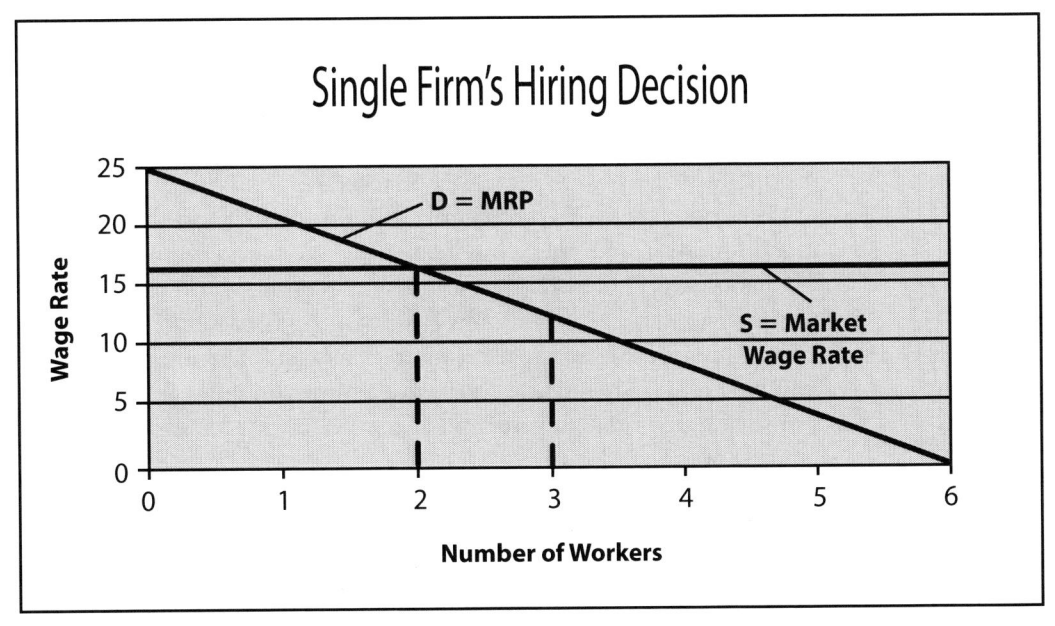

Figure 22.7 • A Rise in Wages
While the workers remaining employed will earn a higher wage when the wage rate rises from $12 to $16, the number of workers hired falls from three to two.

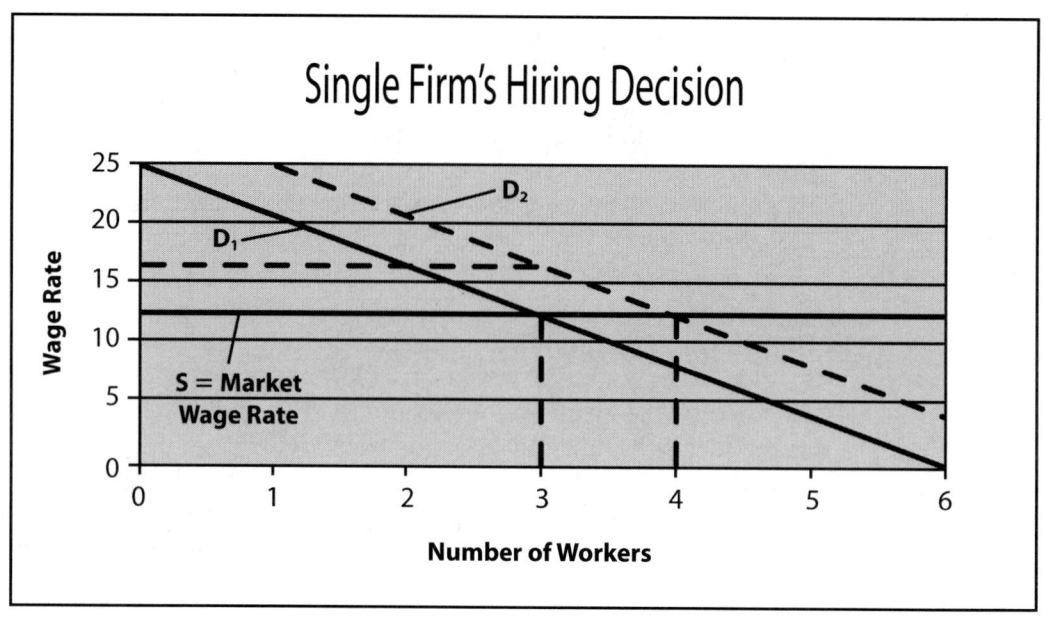

Figure 22.8 • Increase in Labor Demand
When labor demand increases—either because of rise in productivity or rise in the demand for the firm's products—the firm can either hire more workers or pays its current workforce higher wages.

of grape pickers to their employer by raising the market price. The same result occurs as if they increase their productivity: the labor demand curve shifts to the right and firms can hire more workers at the same wage rate or pay the original workforce a higher wage rate.

V. EQUILIBRIUM

Overview

The concepts that govern labor demand for a single firm can be extended to that of the entire market. The market demand for labor will increase when the marginal revenue product of the workers increases; that is, if the productivity of the workers or the price of the product rises. In addition, adding more firms to the market will increase the demand for labor, and removing firms from the market will do the reverse.

Labor supply, on other hand, depends on the worker's willingness to work. We have already seen that tastes, income, taxes, expectations, and prices all contribute to this decision. In addition, the market matters as well. The more people available to do a certain type of job, the greater the market supply of labor. Jobs that require strict qualifications (like doctors, lawyers, and star athletes, for example) will have a relatively small labor supply.

Equilibrium Wage

When discussing the firm's hiring decision, we treated both the firm and the potential workers as if they take the market wage as given, and they do. Neither party has enough power to alter the wage rate through independent action alone.

Labor Market

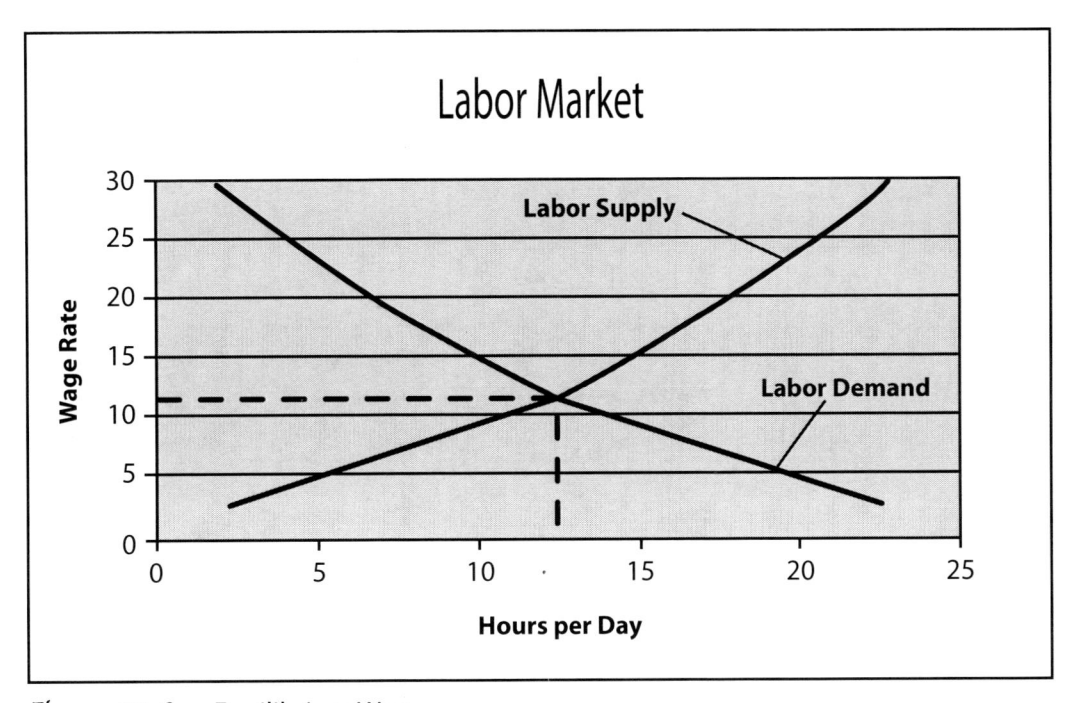

Figure 22.9 • Equilibrium Wage
The market wage rate is determined by the intersection of the market supply and market demand curves for labor.

In a competitive industry, the wage rate (labor supply curve) faced by the individual firm is determined by the intersection of the market demand and supply curves for labor ($12 in figure 22.9), just like the market price taken as given by a competitive firm is determined by the market supply and demand for that product. Hence, the firm faces a horizontal labor supply curve while the market supply curve is upward sloping.

Minimum Wage

Of course, hardly anybody is ever happy with the equilibrium wage; firms wish it was lower and workers want it to be higher. When this outcry for higher wages is strong enough, it may force the government to intervene in the labor market and change the market wage rate. Minimum wage laws are designed to increase the wage rate of a particular industry, state, or country.

Like many government interventions into the economy, the minimum wage began during the Great Depression (1938, to be exact). In terms or real purchasing power, the minimum wage actually hit its peak in 1964, but it has stayed consistently between 40 and 50 percent of the average manufacturing wage throughout its history.

We all know the purpose of the minimum wage is to ensure a better standard of living for the lowest-skilled workers than the market would provide (assuming the minimum wage is above the equilibrium wage); no one can argue with that. But as you should know by now, this increase in standard of living is not free; someone has to pay the price.

The minimum wage is simply a price floor, setting a minimum price that employers can pay for workers in the labor market and resulting in a surplus of workers as evidenced by figure 22.10. These surplus workers must move to another industry (which will result in a decrease in their utility or else they would have been in that industry to

Labor Market

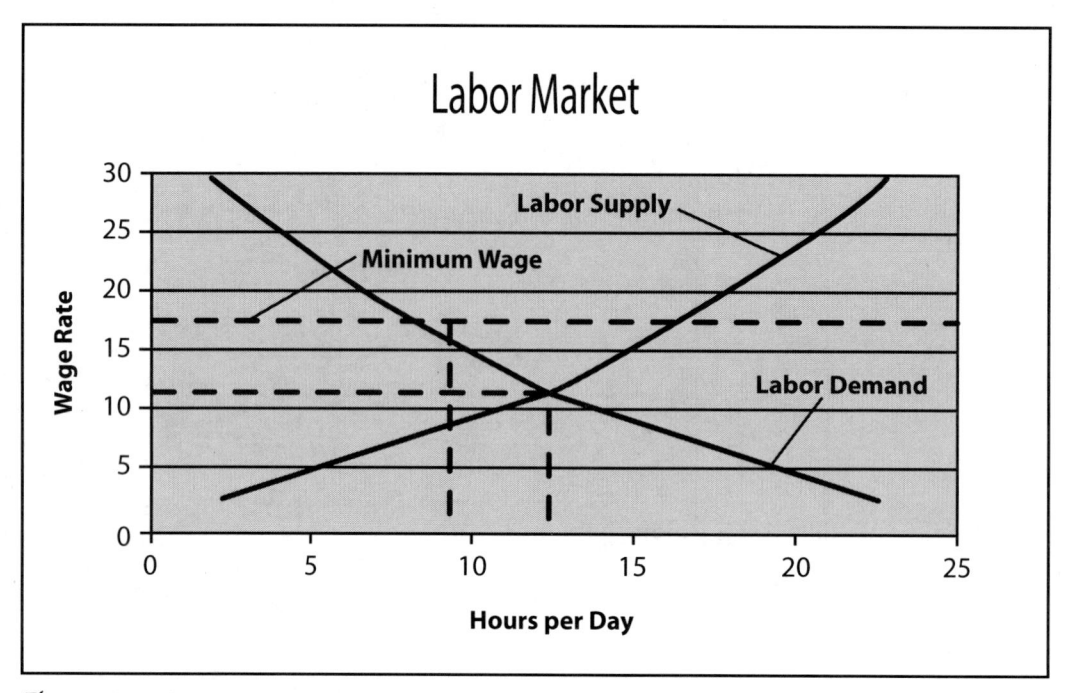

Figure 22.10 • Minimum Wage
At a minimum wage of $17 per hour, firms do not want to hire as much labor as they did at $12, resulting in unemployment.

begin with) or face unemployment. In time, some firms will not be able to keep up with the rising costs of labor and are forced out of the market altogether.

The benefits of minimum wage laws are not free, but come at the expense of others. The exact size of these costs is still a matter of debate, but these costs likely outweigh the potential benefits of a higher minimum wage. In question here is the elasticity of the labor demand curve: Exactly how much do firms reduce employment when the wage rate rises? If the labor demand is relatively steep, then a minimum wage increase will not cause very much unemployment, but raising the wage rate in an industry with a relatively flat labor demand curve will leave many workers without jobs.

VI. CHOOSING AMONG INPUTS

When wage rates rise, employers might choose to decrease labor and output to maintain profit maximization. Another option is to substitute capital for labor. Most production processes allow at least some interchangeability between the two types of inputs. At what point does a firm decide to make this substitution?

Cost Efficiency

Let's imagine there is a donut-making machine that can make twice as many donuts as any laborer at the donut factory. That is, the marginal physical product of this machine is twice as high as that of a laborer. Should the donut factory always choose to hire the machine over a worker? That answer depends on the relative cost of the two inputs.

Just like an individual divides up his spending to get the most utility per dollar, a business will divide up its cost of production to get the most output per dollar. The firm therefore needs to compare not only the price of the inputs, but also the cost efficiency of the various inputs. Cost efficiency is the ratio of an input's marginal physical product to its cost, or how much additional output per dollar you are getting by hiring the input.

$$\text{Cost Efficiency} = \frac{\text{Marginal Physical Product}}{\text{Price of Input}}$$

Let's assume, the first worker in the donut factory can produce ten boxes of donuts and the going wage rate is $8 per hour. That gives him a cost efficiency of 1.25 boxes per dollar invested. The machine can produce twenty boxes, but costs $25 per hour to operate, a cost efficiency of only .8 boxes per dollar.

As such, the donut factory will maximize its profits by going with the laborer over the capital since it produces the most output per dollar. Firms do not always choose the cheapest or most productive input; going with the most cost efficient is the only way to ensure profit maximization.

This helps explains why all jobs have not been outsourced to India, China, or Bangladesh. Cheap labor is not always the most cost-efficient input. American workers produce so much more output per hour that most jobs stay here in spite of the obvious cost disadvantages. Yet, that productivity advantage is not enough to save all jobs; it is the ratio of productivity to cost that attracts firms.

Alternative Production Processes

In reality, firms do not necessarily choose between hiring one more labor input or one more capital input. The choice is more often between a relatively labor-intensive production process and a relatively capital-intensive production process. While a large company does not compare the marginal physical product of each individual input to its cost, it employs the principles of cost efficiency to choose between several potential production processes.

CHAPTER 22 SUMMARY

- The labor supply curve is **upward sloping** because the benefit of working (wage income) falls as the number of hours worked rises.
- Some workers might experience a **backward-bending** labor supply curve if they get paid enough.
- *Elasticity of Labor Supply* $= \dfrac{\text{Percent Change in Quantity of Labor Supplied}}{\text{Percent Change in Wage Rate}}$
- The demand for labor is a **derived demand**. Firms only want to hire workers because the products they produce can make profits for the firm.
- *Marginal Revenue Product = Marginal Physical Product × Price*
- A firm will never pay a worker more than his **marginal revenue product**.
- The labor demand curve is **downward-sloping** because of **diminishing marginal returns to labor**.

- An increase in **productivity** or **the price of the product the firm sells** will shift the labor demand curve to the right.
- A **minimum wage** above the equilibrium wage rate will **increase unemployment**.
- Firms want to produce using the inputs that are the most **cost efficient**.
- $Cost\ Efficiency = \dfrac{Marginal\ Physical\ Product}{Price\ of\ Input}$

CHAPTER 22 Exercises

Name _____

1) The opportunity cost of working is the
   A) wage rate.
   B) value of foregone leisure.
   C) output that can be purchased with wage income.
   D) wage rate at the next-best alternative job.

1) _____

2) Which of the following explains why firms need to pay higher wages to induce people to work more hours?
   A) Law of Demand
   B) Law of diminishing marginal returns
   C) the opportunity cost of working rises as the number of hour worked rises
   D) the elasticity of the labor demand curve

2) _____

3) If consumer tastes shift toward leisure activities and away from work, there will be a
   A) movement up the labor supply curve.
   B) movement down the labor supply curve.
   C) leftward shift of the labor supply curve.
   D) rightward shift of the labor supply curve.

3) _____

4) Marginal physical product falls as additional workers are hired because
   A) each worker now has fewer inputs to work with.
   B) each worker now has more inputs to work with.
   C) each additional worker is less skilled than previous hires.
   D) each additional worker is lazier than previous hires.

4) _____

5) At the current market wage rate, the firm will only hire an additional worker if
   A) the worker is willing to accept less than the market wage rate.
   B) the firm will make a profit after hiring the worker.
   C) the worker's marginal physical product equals or exceeds the wage rate.
   D) the worker's marginal revenue product equals or exceeds the wage rate.

5) _____

6) If the marginal revenue product of labor decreases, which of the following shifts in the labor market should occur?
   A) Labor supply curve shifts to the left
   B) Labor supply curve shifts to the right
   C) Labor demand curve shifts to the left
   D) Labor demand curve shifts to the right

6) _____

7) When the government increases the minimum wage
   A) some workers are worse off well others are better off.
   B) all workers are better off.
   C) all workers are worse off.
   D) all firms are worse off.

7) _____

8) What is the cost efficiency of a labor input that adds twenty units of output and costs $30?   8) _____
   A) 1.5   C) 30
   B) .67   D) 20

9) What makes an individual's labor supply curve backward-bending?

10) What are the two reasons why the labor demand curve for an individual firm would shift to the right?

Financial Markets

I. THE ROLE OF FINANCIAL MARKETS

Financial Intermediaries

Financial resources are not valuable in and of themselves. Yet, the saying goes "it takes money to make money." While you cannot produce anything with money, you need funds to buy the scarce productive resources—land, labor, capital, and entrepreneurship—that any business needs to produce output.

Most entrepreneurs do not have the money necessary to start a business just lying around. To get started they need to obtain financial capital from one of two sources: borrowing or inviting others to invest in their business. The process of direct fund-raising can be costly, though, so most businesses rely on borrowing from financial intermediaries.

Financial intermediaries are institutions that exist to connect savers and borrowers. Savers could finance business directly, but the process would be haphazard at best. Trying to pick which businesses to invest in on your own would be costly and time-consuming; not to mention incredibly risky. Financial intermediation is the primary function of all banks and financial institutions; they want to bring savers and borrowers together more efficiently.

Financial intermediation is critical because of the existence of asymmetric information; lenders do not know exactly what borrowers intend to do with the money. Individuals do not have the time or expertise to check the credit-worthiness of each potential borrower, but banks specialize in testing whether a business or individual is a good credit risk. They employ highly paid professionals and sophisticated statistical tools every day to accomplish this.

Since fewer total resources are spent researching potential borrowers, financial intermediation increases efficiency. Still, it is not possible for all entrepreneurs to receive the start-up funds they need. The actual amount of borrowed funds and which businesses get them depends on the willingness of savers to loan money (supply of loanable funds) and how much borrowers are willing and able to pay for those funds (demand for loanable funds).

The Supply of Loanable Funds

Time Preferences. One of the factors that influence the supply of loanable funds is the time preference of savers. People will save more money (supply more loanable funds) if they have a greater preference for future consumption. Saving is essentially trading off current consumption for more future consumption—assuming the interest rate is high enough to offset inflation. This helps explain why young people tend to save more than older people; they have a greater preference for future consumption.

Interest Rates. Figure 23.1 shows that the supply curve for loanable funds describes the relationship between the amount of money available to borrow and the real interest rate. The real interest rate is the price of money; therefore, the higher the real interest rate, the greater the opportunity cost of not saving (consumption). The interest rate also represents the rate of return on saving: the higher the return, the more people will want to save.

Risk. Even if the interest rate is extremely high, savers may still not want to put their money in the loanable funds market if there is a high level of risk involved. For ex-

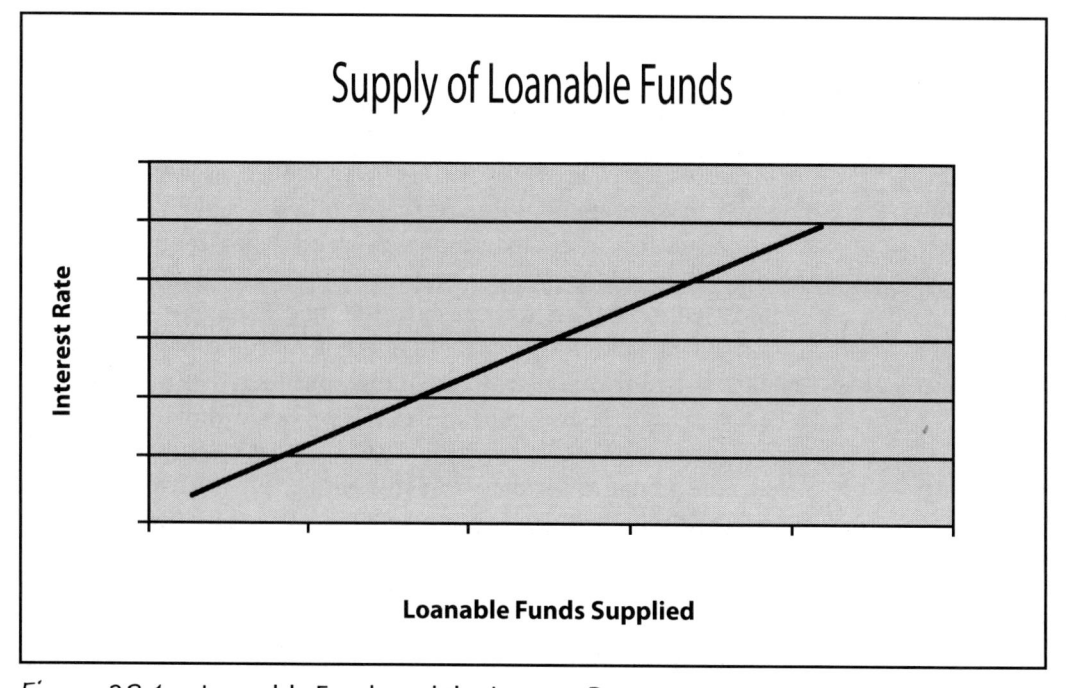

Figure 23.1 • Loanable Funds and the Interest Rate
Savers will supply more loanable funds to the market only if they are compensated with higher interest rates.

ample, people put their money in savings accounts and government bonds even though the average rate of return on stocks is much higher. People are just not willing to take on the additional risk. In other words, higher levels of risk shift the supply of loanable funds to the left.

Risk Premiums. For a given level of risk, savers will flock to the loan or financial market that will give them the highest interest rate for their funds. But if savers are to invest in a project with an above-average level of risk, they will need to be compensated with a higher interest rate. The difference between this higher interest rate and the return on a "safe" investment (like a government bond) is called the risk premium.

Banks will give lower-interest loans to big corporations (in the form of corporate bonds) than they will to the average consumer. The reason for this disparity is that the average consumer is much more likely to default; they are a riskier bet. The difference between the two rates, the risk premium, compensates the bank for taking on the additional risk of default.

Risk Management. Risk explains why financial intermediation is so important. No one wants to take on the risk of being the only investor in a company or project; if the project fails, you lose everything. Instead, people would rather diversify their portfolios, putting some funds in many projects. That way, if any one project fails, the loss is shared among all of the investors. Reducing the average risk of portfolio through diversification is called risk management. In fact, article 23.1 points out that poor risk management was one of the causal factors of the most recent recession.

Article 23.1
Risk Management Failures Major Cause of Crisis—IMF
Reporting by Lesley Wroughton; editing by Leslie Adler

Thu Apr 10, 2008 6:50pm EDT

WASHINGTON, April 10 (Reuters)—Risk management at large Western banks was deficient and "a major cause" of the current financial crisis, the International Monetary Fund said on Thursday.

The shortcomings showed a lack of "judgment and governance" by the banks, the IMF said in a document prepared for finance ministers and central bank chiefs before weekend IMF and World Bank meetings in Washington. . . .

"Both managers and supervisors need to play a more active role in scrutinizing these practices, especially with regard to liquidity management, off-balance-sheet entities and structured products, and to pursue more active stress testing," the IMF said.

The IMF said credit-rating agencies also failed to capture risks posed by structured investment vehicles.

It said investors relied too heavily on the ratings. Looking ahead, it said there may be merit in a broader approach to revamp the role and use of credit rating agencies.

"This suggests the need to improve methodologies and to adopt a differential rating system for structured instruments, taking better account of their different risk profile, and to review how prudential norms would then need to be modified," it said.

. . .

The challenge will be for national authorities and international institutions to coordinate better on cross-border accounting and regulatory standards and disclosure practices, the IMF said.

The fund said the crisis revealed a need to adapt tools and practices to manage liquidity and cross-country differences in emergency liquidity frameworks.

Continued.

"Central banks may need to broaden the range of collateral and counterparties that they can deal with and, given the level of cross-border finance, work to avoid significant differences in practice," it said.

More supervision and better crisis management was needed, especially when it came to new financial instruments, the IMF said.

Questions:
1. How does risk affect the level of investment?
2. What are some of the proposals the article gives to improve the accuracy of risk ratings?
3. How could inaccurate risk rates be responsible for the recent "financial crisis"?

All rights reserved. Republication or redistribution of Thomson Reuters content, including by framing or similar means, is expressly prohibited without the prior written consent of Thomson Reuters. Thomson Reuters and its logo are registered trademarks or trademarks of the Thomson Reuters group of companies around the world. ©Thomas Reuters 2009. Thomson Reuters journalists are subject to an Editorial Handbook which requires fair presentation and disclosure of relevant interests.

II. PRESENT VALUE OF FUTURE PROFITS

For the financial intermediary or any investor, lending involves weighing the risk of an investment against its potential rewards. These rewards, however, will not come until some point in the future. Sometimes businesses will have to operate for two years or more until they start making profits. Since the investor must bear the cost of lending today, he must be able to accurately compare the cost of lending today with the return on his investment in the future.

Time Value of Money

Even without inflation, a dollar received today is more valuable than a dollar received in two years time. If you put a dollar into the bank or some other interest-bearing security today, it will be worth much more than a dollar in the future. Because of interest-bearing opportunities, people will always value current dollars more than future dollars.

In other words, people discount the value of future dollars. How much so depends on the interest rate. The present discounted value of a future payment equals the amount of that payment divided by one plus the interest rate to the power of the number of years in the future you will receive this payment.

$$Present\ Discounted\ Value = \frac{Future\ Payment}{(1 + r)^n}$$

Where r = real interest rate, n = number of years you must wait for future payment

While this formula may seem complicated, it is really just a calculation of interest in reverse. The present discounted value of a $2,000 payment in five years, for example, equals how much money you would have to put into an interest-bearing account today to have exactly $2,000 in that account five years from now. That is exactly how much that future payment is worth to you today and exactly how much you would pay to buy an investment that promised a $2,000 return five years from now.

Since the number of years is the exponent of the denominator, the denominator gets bigger as the payment gets pushed further and further into the future. As a result, the longer one has to wait for a future payment, the lower the present value for any given amount and interest rate.

Lottery winners often have a choice between a single lump sum payment and an annuity. Why is it that the total value of the annuity is usually much higher than the lump sum payment? Many of the annuity payments are very far (up to thirty years) in the future and thus have a small present discounted value. If the two payments were the same, the winner could put the lump sum payment in a money market account or in the stock market and end up with a much greater amount of money at the end of thirty years.

Interest Rate Effects

Since the interest rate, too, is in the denominator of the formula, the higher the prevailing interest rate, the lower the present discounted value of any future payment is. As a result, lump sum lottery payouts will be even lower when interest rates rise. On a broader scale any future payment becomes less attractive the higher the interest rate is, resulting in fewer loanable funds supplied and a much slower growth rate for the economy.

Uncertainty

As important as the time horizon and the interest rate are to the potential return on any loan, the risk of nonpayment adjusts the lender's valuation of any future payment just as much. Since state governments have never been known to default on lottery payments, a winner is just as well off choosing an annuity or a lump sum payment equivalent to the present discounted value.

Not all debts are so sure a thing, however. When Columbus or any of the New World explorers took investor funds to sail across the ocean, no one was sure they would come back alive let alone bring back enough treasure to pay back their debts. What effect does this uncertainty have on the willingness to lend?

Expected Values

Thus far, we have assumed that all investments will pay off in the future. Whenever a future payment is not guaranteed, lenders will value this payment a little less than its true present discounted value. This additional discount factor adjusts for the possibility of nonpayment. The expected value of an uncertain future payment equals the probability of repayment (or one minus the probability of default) times the present discounted value.

$$\text{Expected Value} = (1 - P) \times \frac{\text{Future Payment}}{(1 + r)^n}$$

Where P = probability of default

Expected values help explain why people buy more lottery tickets when the jackpot is higher. The potential payoff from an investment is simply a product of the likelihood of payoff and the size of the payment. As the value of the jackpot rises, the likelihood of

Demand of Loanable Funds

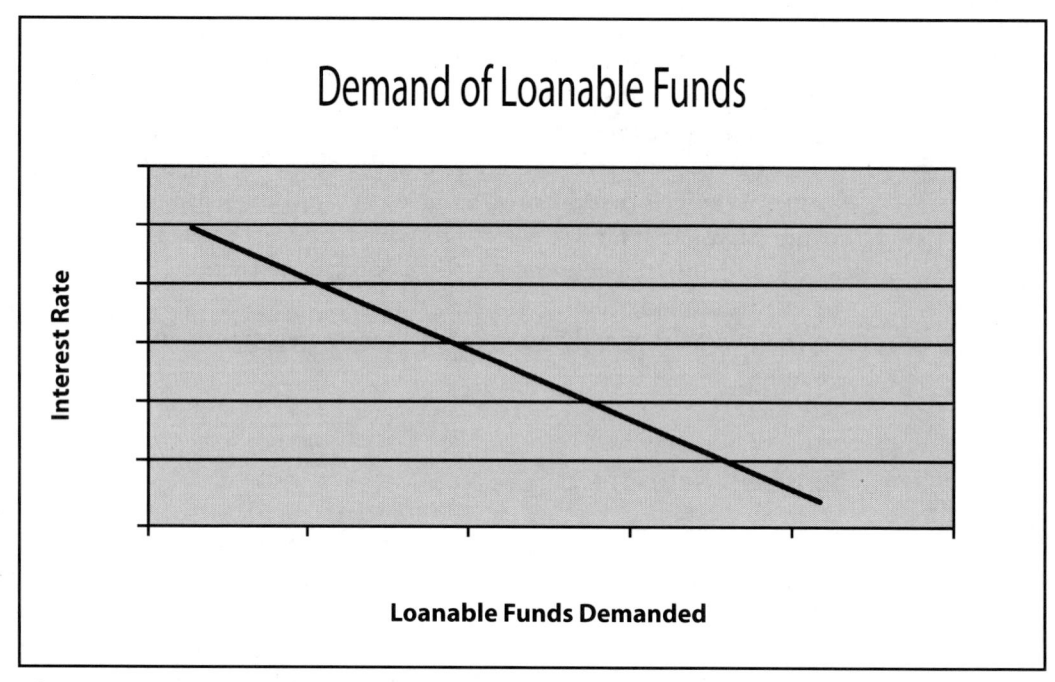

Figure 23.2 • Demand for Loanable Funds
As the interest rate rises, the loanable funds become more expensive. As a result, firms will demand fewer loanable funds at higher interest rates.

any one ticket being the winner remains the same—causing the expected value of every ticket to rise and the demand for tickets to soar.

The Demand for Loanable Funds

Businesses do not often invest in lottery tickets, but they do invest in other projects. Many times they need to borrow to finance these projects. As a result, their willingness and ability to borrow changes with the interest rate (the cost of borrowing) and the expected rate of return (the benefit of borrowing).

Just like the demand for a commodity, businesses will demand more loanable funds at lower prices (interest rates) than at higher prices (interest rates). This gives us the typical downward-sloping demand curve such as the one in figure 23.2. Combining this with the upward-sloping supply curve, figure 23.3 shows that the market interest rate will be determined by the intersection of the supply and demand curves.

III. THE STOCK MARKET

One of the most recognizable financial markets is the stock market. In a stock market, people buy shares of ownership in public corporations in hopes of earning dividends or making capital gains by selling the stock at a higher price later. While the New York Stock Exchange is the most visible one, stock markets exist in many cities like London, Tokyo, and Hong Kong.

Market for Loanable Funds

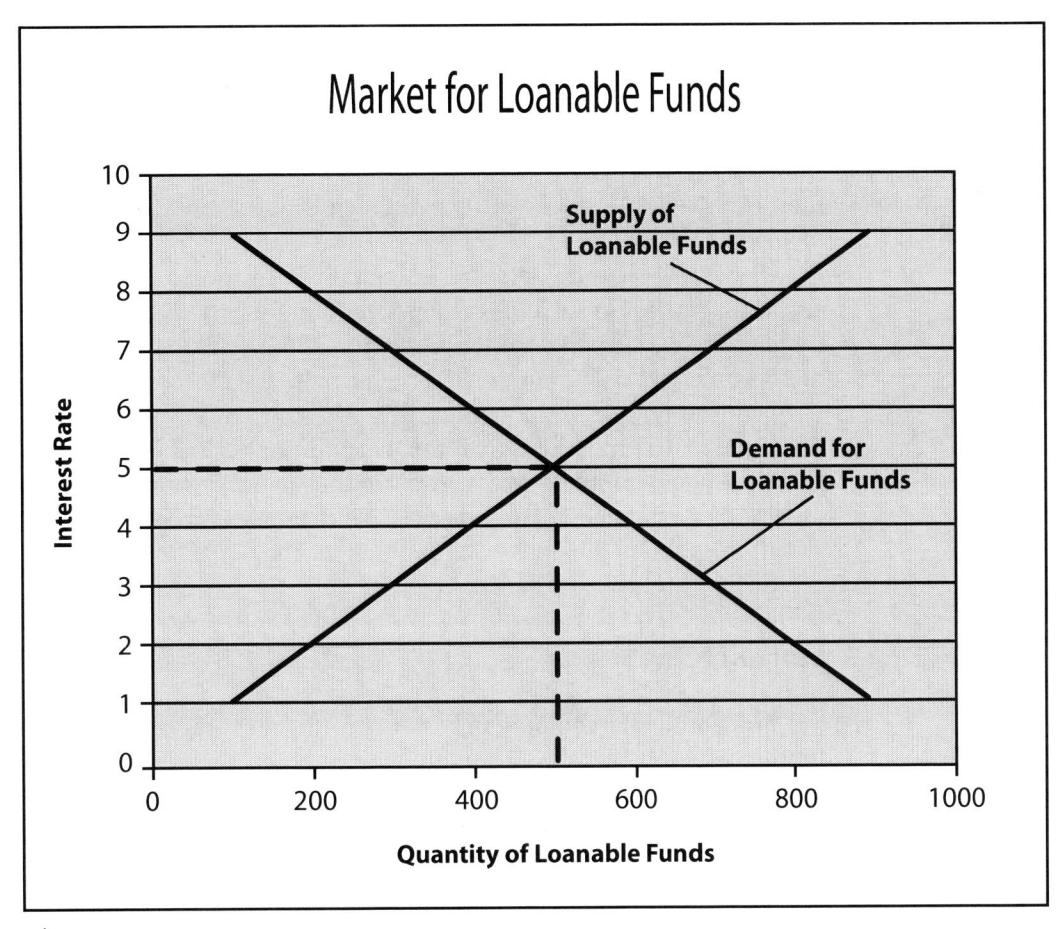

Figure 23.3 • Equilibrium Interest Rate
The market interest rate is the only interest rate where the amount of loanable funds that savers want to invest equals the amount of loanable funds firms that debtors want to borrow.

Since the stockholder is not guaranteed a particular return, buying stocks is generally thought of as being more risky than other forms of portfolio investment. Bonds and bank deposits, for example, have guaranteed rates of return. However, stocks offer a higher average rate of return than bonds in order to compensate for this additional risk.

Corporate Stock

Limited Liability. While any type of business organization (proprietorship, partnership, or corporation) can sell stock, corporations have certain advantages over the other forms of businesses that have led them to become the dominant sales leader in the United States. The primary advantages that corporations have over the other forms of businesses are the benefits of limited liability and shared ownership.

If you own a small business and it fails, you may have to declare bankruptcy or face default. In a corporation, shareholders risk only what they paid for their stock; their personal assets are never in jeopardy. Creditors can sue corporations since they are legal entities, but they cannot sue individual shareholders. The corporation itself, not the shareholder, is responsible for the corporation's debt. This relationship is known as limited liability.

Shared Ownership. Corporations also have a much easier time of raising funds through equity financing, the selling of stock. Stocks represent a share in the ownership of a corporation; owners of stock are entitled to a share of the dividends reported by the corporation and votes at the corporation's annual meeting equal to the share of stock they hold. If someone owns 1,000,000 of Microsoft's 10,000,000 shares, for example, they are owed 10 percent of their dividends and 10 percent of the votes at the annual meeting.

Of course, shareholders do not actually run the corporation; they hire executives and managers to do so. This creates a problem where the goals of the shareholders and those of the executives do not necessarily match. This situation is an example of a common problem in economics called the principal-agent problem.

Managers (agents) may only care about the power, prestige, and pay that the position gives them regardless of the corporation's stock price. You can see how the principal-agent problem leads to a conflict of interest with managers pursuing their own goals (wasting company money and resources on expensive perks and unwise but attention-grabbing business transactions) at the expense of profitability.

Stock Returns

Dividends. Shareholders may not run the corporation, but they receive the profits. Profits earned by a corporation are split in three ways: 35 percent goes to the government in the form of corporate taxes, some are kept in the corporation as retained earnings for new investments or a "rainy day" fund, and the remainder is returned to the shareholders as dividends.

Capital Gains. Investors who hold onto stocks long term usually count on dividends for most of their rate of return, but some stockholders are in for more of a short-term gain. These are the types of people that buy stocks with the intention of selling them at a higher price. The difference between what a stock was worth when you bought and what it is worth when you sell it is called the capital gain. Capital gains represent another possible reward from stockholding.

Total Return. Adding these payoffs together gives you the total return on any stock investment. People choose to put their money into stocks rather than other forms of wealth because of possible dividends and capital gains. Of course, none of this return is guaranteed; people can only rely on the expected rate of return to help in their portfolio decision.

IPO

The market for blue-chip stocks for companies that have been around forever is easy enough to understand. The sellers in the market are betting that the total return on the stock will fall (or not rise as fast as other investments) and the buyers are betting that the total return will exceed other's expectations.

A brand-new company trying to sell stock for the first time has no shareholders. The seller in this case is the company itself, offering potential dividends and capital gains in order to get the funds it needs to get started or to embark on an investment project. Hence, this process is called the initial public offering (IPO). At least some of the ownership of the company is turned over to the shareholders in exchange for their financial capital.

Visa, for example, had been supported by a variety of banks throughout the second half of the last century. Knowing they needed to raise more funds to survive in a struggling financial services industry, Visa decided to issue stock to the public for the first time in 2008. They raised $17.9 billion that first sale: the single most lucrative IPO in history. Even if they could have found enough banks to loan them that amount of money, they would have had to pay interest on the loans from here to eternity. Instead, the original owners gave up much of their control to the public in exchange for much needed funds.

Secondary Trading

P/E Ratio. Since the expected rate of return on a stock can be a very difficult thing to calculate, traders rely on other figures to decide which stocks are "good buys." One such tool is the price to earnings, or P/E, ratio. The P/E ratio gives the rate of return of a stock in terms of price per dollar of profits.

$$P/E\ Ratio = \frac{Price\ of\ Stock}{Annual\ Earnings\ per\ Share}$$

The P/E ratio therefore takes into account not only total dividends, but also what you had to pay to get them.

The stock of new company will generally have a poor P/E ratio. It usually takes five years or more for a company to start seeing high profits because of high ratio of fixed costs to variable costs and also slow adoption rates. With a low profit per share and high price, Google had a very high (and therefore, unattractive) P/E ratio when it was first offered in 2004, as did many computer and Internet companies. So why did people buy it?

Profit Expectations. Dividends, or a share of a firm's profits, are just one reason why people buy stocks. They also buy because they expect the company to grow and the stock to go up in value. In other words, for longer-term investors, the future P/E ratio matters just as much, if not more, than the current one. Google shares rose to as high as $450 each only two years after IPO and those investors who gambled on Google's IPO could make a killing in capital gains if they sold today.

Another interesting point is the fact that Google's share price has gone up by nearly a factor of seven since its IPO just five years ago which does not help the company one bit. The company received $1.7 billion in funds from the initial sale and that's it. All of the capital gains and dividends earned through stock trades on stock exchanges take place between individual investors and have no bearing on Google's balance sheet.

Market Fluctuations

Just like any commodity, corporate stocks have a supply and a demand. Almost anybody would like to buy a piece of Google or Visa, just not at the current price. If someone offered me those stocks at $5 or $10 apiece I couldn't say yes fast enough.

Figure 23.4 shows that the demand for stocks follows the laws of supply and demand; the lower the price the more people want to buy while people will only sell more stocks if you offer them a higher price. Imagine an investor has 1,000 shares of Visa stock. Since stocks, like any good, have a diminishing marginal utility, he does not value his 1000th share as much as his first. As a result you will have to give him more money to part with his final share than you did to buy the first share.

Changing Expectations. What happens to the supply and demand for a stock when expectations about the company's future profitability change? When traders perceive that a company may not be as profitable in the future as they once thought (a new government regulation increases its production costs, a new product fails, etc.) demand for the stock falls and supply rises. Both of these shifts result in a lower equilibrium price for the stock as seen in figure 23.5.

Demand falls because traders see a lower expected rate of return and will only buy it at a lower price. Supply falls because shareholders want to dump the stock for something with a better expected return. As a result, the busiest trading days, the ones with the most buying and selling, usually end up with the stock falling in price as the market adjusts to a new equilibrium.

Asymmetric Information. All of this trading occurs because of fluctuations in the expected rate of return. No one knows what the future profitability of a company will be; we all take the information available and make educated guesses.

Sometimes, though, people have an unfair advantage because of access to certain types of information that will affect stock prices before everyone else does. If they use this to make money, they may be guilty of insider trading. The value of this inside information is undeniable. People often risk huge fines and jail time in insider trading schemes. Others spend thousands of dollars a year on brokerage services and newsletters from supposed Wall Street insiders in hopes they will be one step ahead of the competition.

Booms and Busts. Other than the problem of imperfect information, stock markets are actually some of the most efficient markets in the economy. Everybody knows what a stock's price is and can make purchases accordingly. Yet we still see huge variations in

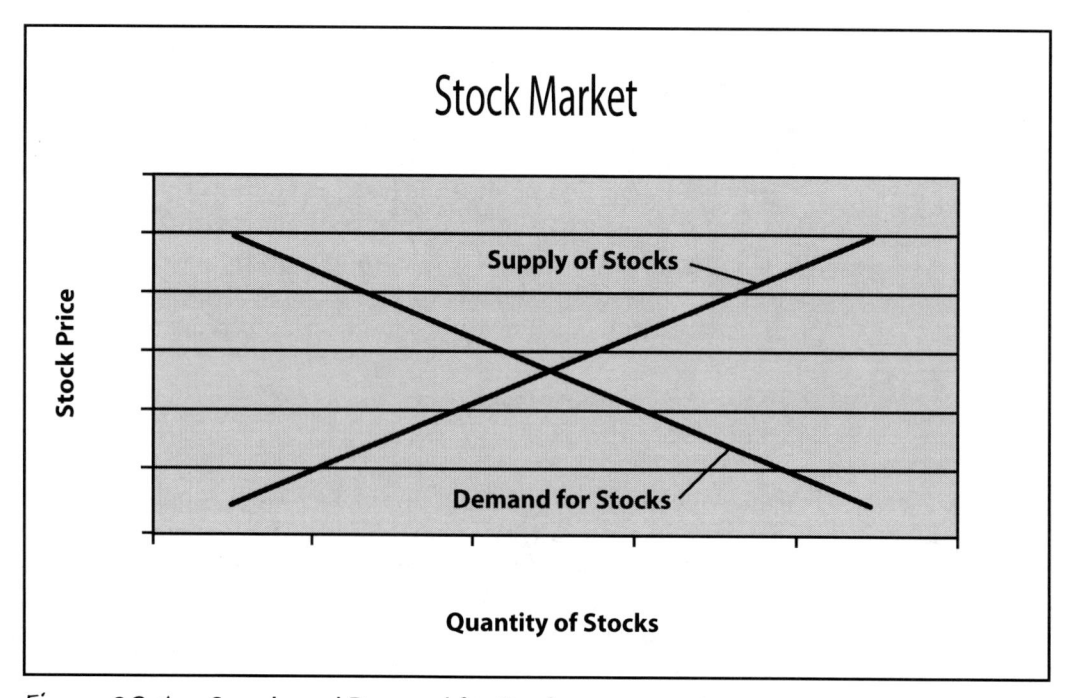

Figure 23.4 • Supply and Demand for Stocks
Stocks follow the laws of supply and demand like any other commodity.

both the price of individual stocks and the stock market as a whole. What might be responsible for these abrupt changes?

Changes in macroeconomic variables, like the money supply or interest rates, might have some effect on stock prices. The higher the interest rate, the lower the present discounted value of any future dividend or capital gain from a stock is. In other words, higher interest rates reduce the demand for stocks and, assuming the supply doesn't change, the price of stocks.

It isn't just the interest rate that affects the demand for stocks; many macroeconomic policies and actions can disrupt the stock market. Increasing budget deficits, reduced consumer confidence, and the opening up of free trade all reduce the outlook for future sales and profits for businesses in the United States, lowering stock prices across the board.

These broad changes, however, often occur slowly and predictably over a period of several years. The stock market, on the other hand, tends to change much faster than the general economy does. These radical movements are believed to be the result of changing expectations rather than changing economic conditions. Remember that the demand for stocks relies on expectations of future dividends and capital gains, and small changes today can cause a big change in the expectations of the future. Even a small change in interest rates, for example, could signal a policy of fiscal or monetary restraint, dampening expectations and driving the stock market downward.

Shocks. Stock markets are also more responsive to shocks than the general economy is. For example, while the attacks on September 11th were undoubtedly devastating from a human life standpoint, productive capacity, unemployment, and most other economic indicators were able to recover quickly. The stock market, on the other hand, took it much harder.

At the current level of return, investors were not willing to take the risk that consumers and businesses would want to keep spending at pre-9/11 levels and withdrew

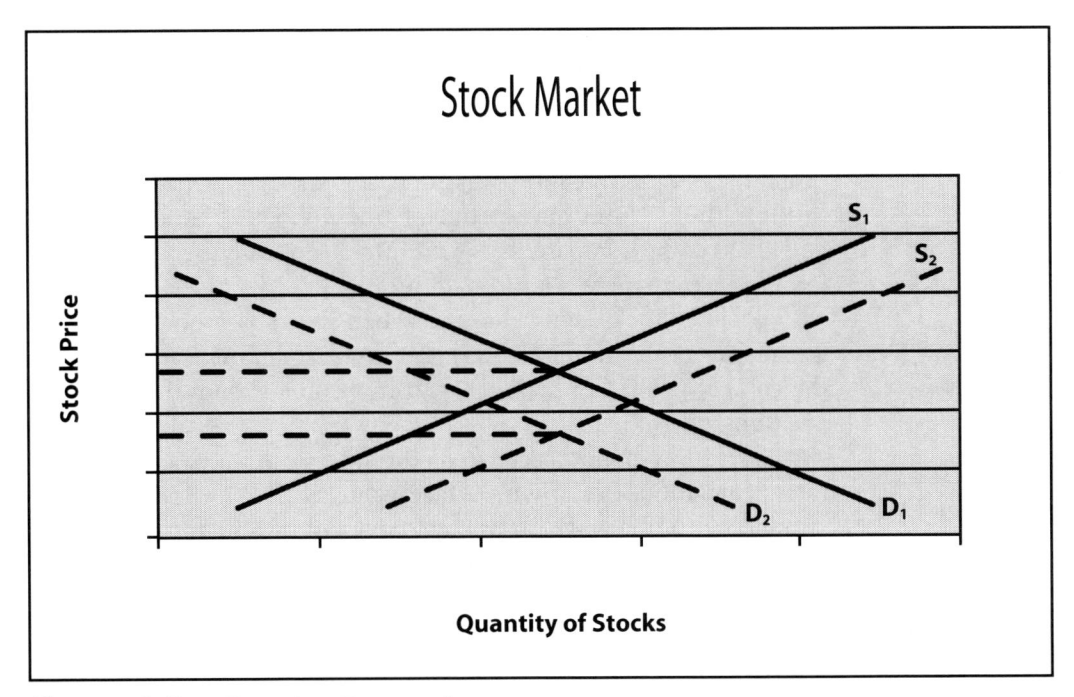

Figure 23.5 • Changing Expectations
When the outlook for a particular firm declines, more people want to sell the stock and less people want to buy, resulting in a drop in the price of the stock.

their funds from the market. The result was the single biggest one-day drop in the history of the Dow Jones Industrial Average, the primary tool for measuring the value of the NYSE. In just a month's time, once investors were satisfied that things were back to normal, prices picked up again.

Resource Allocation

While secondary trading tells us much about people's expectations about particular firms, industries, and the economy in general, it doesn't really help any businesses build up productive capacity. But the stock market still performs a valuable financial intermediary function for our economy in the form of the IPO. Stock markets, and in particular IPOs, are a mechanism for allocating resources to new and growing businesses.

Without the stock market, Visa would have been hard-pressed to find another source to procure the funds they needed to grow. Given the massive success of Visa's IPO, whatever goods would have been produced with the resources allocated to Visa in this process would not have been as valuable to society as the financial service giant's services. Stock markets, and financial markets in general, facilitate the movement of resources to their highest-valued use.

IV. THE BOND MARKET

Another way for financial capital to flow from individuals to businesses is the bond market. A bond does not provide the buyer with a share of ownership like a stock does, but instead functions like an IOU: It promises to pay a specified amount at a specified date. Both businesses and governments offer bonds.

Issuing Bonds

Much like stocks, businesses issue bonds to raise funds. The benefit is they can raise funds without losing ownership of the company; bondholders are not owners. The downside is the company is forced into a repayment schedule that can be undesirable for a new company without much profit.

Just like stocks, only the initial bond purchase goes to the company. Any subsequent sales of the bonds on secondary trading markets accrue to the bondholder, not to the company. The key aspect is getting people to buy the initial bonds for the highest price possible.

People buy bonds because of the interest they pay. A 5 percent interest (coupon rate) bond from Exxon with a face value of $1,000, for example, guarantees that the bondholder will receive an interest payment of $50 annually (5 percent of $1,000) for the life of the loan. At the maturity date, Exxon will pay the bondholder back the original $1,000.

A riskier company, like start-up Google, would have to pay a higher coupon rate to attract funds than a stable company like Exxon would. Since Google may or may not have caught on, there was a serious chance of default—bondholders not being paid back their principal. As a result, investors would demand higher yearly payments as a risk premium.

Bond Market

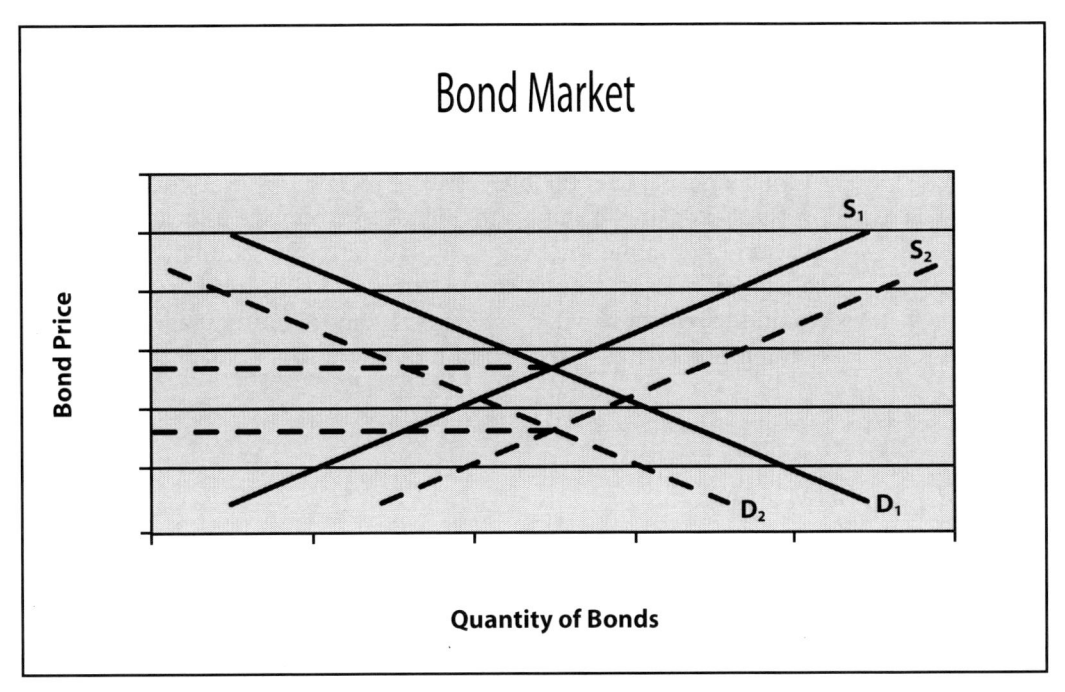

Figure 23.6 • Current Yields
The current yield of a bond falls as the market price of a bond rises, meaning the firm can offer to sell bonds at a lower interest rate the next time they issue them.

Trading Bonds

Often times, bondholders do not want to wait until the maturity date to get their principal back. They cannot give the bond back to the company and demand their money, but they can sell the bond to someone else. Secondary trading not only helps bondholders, it helps bond issuers since initial buyers know they won't be trapped into holding the bond until the maturity date since they will probably be able to find someone to buy the bond from them if they want cash now instead of waiting.

The same factors that affect the supply and demand for stocks affect those of bonds. Changes in the opportunity costs of bondholding (the returns on other interest-bearing securities) or expectations of the business's future, will shift the supply and demand curves for bonds to the left or right.

Current Yields

As it becomes clear that an upstart company is going to succeed, investor expectations of the company rise and its perceived risk plummets. This reevaluation makes consumers more willing to supply funds to the company, shifting the demand for this company's bonds to the right as figure 23.6 illustrates. Since the company had already issued its bonds, though, it could not start paying its bondholders a lower interest rate.

In the end, it is the bondholders that benefit in the short run. As the demand for the company's now-safer bonds rose, so did their price in the market. Many bondholders resold their bonds in the secondary market and earned a hefty profit. People willing to pay higher prices and accept lower yields for a bond indicate a consensus that the company is doing well. The current yield for a bond equals the annual interest payment divided by the purchase price.

$$\text{Current Yield} = \frac{\text{Annual Interest}}{\text{Price of Bond}}$$

Since the annual interest payment is fixed once the bond is issued, higher bond prices in the market means the buyers were receiving lower current yields. These rising bond prices also create an important signal for resource allocation. While the company does not save any money in terms of loan repayment today, rising bond prices signal that consumers will be willing to buy their bonds at lower coupon rates in the future. As a result, the company will be able to raise more funds at a lower rate in the future and buy even more resources for expanding production.

CHAPTER 23 SUMMARY

- **Financial intermediaries** help **reduce the risk** involved in borrowing and investing.
- A greater **preference for future consumption**, a higher **interest rate**, or a lower level of **risk** will cause people to want to lend more money.
- People do not value a future payment as much as an **equal amount of money today**.
- $\text{Present Discounted Value} = \dfrac{\text{Future Payment}}{(1 + r)^n}$

    Where r = **real interest rate**, n = **number of years you must wait for future payment**
- When a future payment is not guaranteed, investors make decisions based on **expected value**.
- $\text{Expected Value} = (1 - P) \times \dfrac{\text{Future Payment}}{(1 + r)^n}$

    Where P = **probability of default**
- The value of holding stocks comes from the potential **dividends** and **capital gains**.
- $\text{P/E Ratio} = \dfrac{\text{Price of Stock}}{\text{Annual Earnings per Share}}$
- A drop in the expectations for the future profits of a company will cause the **demand for its stock to fall** and the **supply of its stock to rise**.
- The **IPO** is the only time the firm receives any payment from the sale of its stock.
- An **increase in the market price** of a bond causes its **current yield to fall**.
- $\text{Current Yield} = \dfrac{\text{Annual Interest}}{\text{Price of Bond}}$

CHAPTER 23 Exercises

Name _____

1) Financial intermediaries
   A) reduce the risk of investing.
   B) increase the cost of investing.
   C) allocate resources to the least productive uses.
   D) benefit savers, but not borrowers.

   1) _____

2) Which of the following does NOT affect how much people want to save?
   A) time preferences
   B) interest rate
   C) occupation
   D) risk

   2) _____

3) The present discounted value of a future payment will increase when the
   A) the date of repayment is pushed further into the future.
   B) the value of the future payment falls.
   C) the opportunity cost of holding money rises.
   D) interest rate falls.

   3) _____

4) What is the difference between present discounted value and expected value?
   A) Present discounted value takes into account the possibility of default.
   B) Expected value takes into account the possibility of default.
   C) They use different interest rates.
   D) Expected value does not use a specific date of repayment.

   4) _____

5) The only time a firm receives money for the sale of its stocks is
   A) during its IPO.
   B) when the stock sells for higher than its original price.
   C) when the stock sells for less than its original price.
   D) when more than 10% of total stock changes hand in one sale.

   5) _____

6) The most important determinant of the demand for a stock is
   A) how much the CEO gets paid.
   B) the expectation of future profit.
   C) how old the firm is.
   D) whether the firm has a monopoly.

   6) _____

7) All of the following are reasons for buying bonds EXCEPT
   A) bonds provide a guaranteed source of income.
   B) bonds can by sold on a secondary market.
   C) bonds confer a share of ownership in a firm.
   D) bonds are safer than stocks.

   7) _____

419

8) If the market price of a bond rises
   A) its current yield falls.
   B) it current yield rises.
   C) the issuer can reduce its payments to the bondholder.
   D) the bond is earning dividends.

8) _____

9) Calculate the present discounted value of $2,000 payment to be received five years from today if the interest rate is 5 percent.

10) Explain limited liability and why it makes buying stocks so attractive.

Chapter 24

International Trade

I. THE UNITED STATES AND WORLD TRADE

International Linkages

The US economy is an open economy; that is, it is connected to other economies throughout the world. It is well known that the United States trades goods and services with other countries. These imports and exports are called trade flows. The United States is the largest importer and the third-largest exporter in the world. Imports and exports are not the only things that connect international economies, though.

Less recognized, but still important flows also occur in international resource markets. American firms move capital to foreign countries and those foreign countries move capital to the United States. These capital flows may be in the form of investment in established firms, such as buying stocks or bonds from a foreign company, or building new production facilities. As we know, labor also moves from country to country in the form of immigration. Since labor is a resource, this movement counts as a resource flow as well.

Money also flows between countries. This money goes towards paying for imports, investing in foreign assets, and providing aid to foreign countries. Since only money is changing hands here, these movements are called financial flows. The United States also transmits information about the economy to other countries to facilitate exchange. This flow of information helps both the United States and foreign countries meet the needs of society more efficiently.

Volume and Pattern

Volume. Virtually every nation that employs the market system depends on trade to some degree. While the United States has been blessed with a large and diverse resource base and can produce nearly every type of good and service, some countries are not so lucky. Countries with sparse resources have to depend heavily upon trade to meet the demands of its citizens. While they may not necessarily have the volume of trade the United States does, it will certainly take up a larger share of its national output.

For both the United States and the world, the volume of trade has been increasing over the last thirty years. Doubtless you have heard that the United States is currently running a trade deficit; that is, it imports more than it exports. This has not always been the case. If you refer to figure 24.1, you can see that the primary reason for this shift is that, beginning in the late 1990s, imports rapidly increased while exports grew very little relative to the total economy. This rapid growth of imports results from the emergence of new players on the international economic scene, especially China.

Dependence. While the United States produces many different types of goods within its borders, it is almost completely dependent on the rest of the world for its supply of many products such as cocoa, coffee, spices, tea, silk, and diamonds. This is just a short list of key imports to the United States. There are also some industries in which domestic producers compete with goods imported from abroad.

Likewise, there are many goods produced in the United States that rely on demand from foreign markets to stay profitable. These industries get the bulk of their revenue from exports. Key United States exports include computers, chemicals, aircraft and automobiles, as well as agricultural products such as rice, wheat, cotton, and tobacco.

Trade Patterns. Countries can adopt many different trade strategies. Observing these trade strategies over time can allow us to see patterns in trade. One trade strategy that the United States employs is running a trade deficit or allowing imports to exceed exports. The other primary strategy is running a trade surplus; having exports exceed imports. While the United States runs a trade deficit, it does export more services than it imports so the country is said to have a trade surplus in services.

Despite what you may hear and read about the control that China or Japan has over the United States economy, the US's largest trading partner is one of our closest allies: Canada. Nearly a quarter of our exports go there and over one-sixth of our imports originate there. The fact remains, though, that the United States has sizable trade deficits with both China and Japan, and this fact alone engenders much worry.

Financial Linkages. How is it possible, for example, for the United States to import more from a country than it exports to it? How do they pay for those additional imports? Luckily, our system of international trade has many complex financial linkages built into it to facilitate trade even when exports and imports are not exactly equal.

The United States can maintain its large trade deficits by borrowing foreign funds or selling its real assets. The United States is the world's largest debtor nation; it borrows more money from other countries than any other country. Countries are quite willing to loan these funds since it increases production in the form of more exports to the United States. Foreign countries also help make up the difference by buying real assets in the United States (factories, firms, and real estate) in the place of imports.

Rapid Trade Growth

Transportation Technology. Several factors have led to an explosion in international trade that has come to be called economic globalization. One of the more obvious ad-

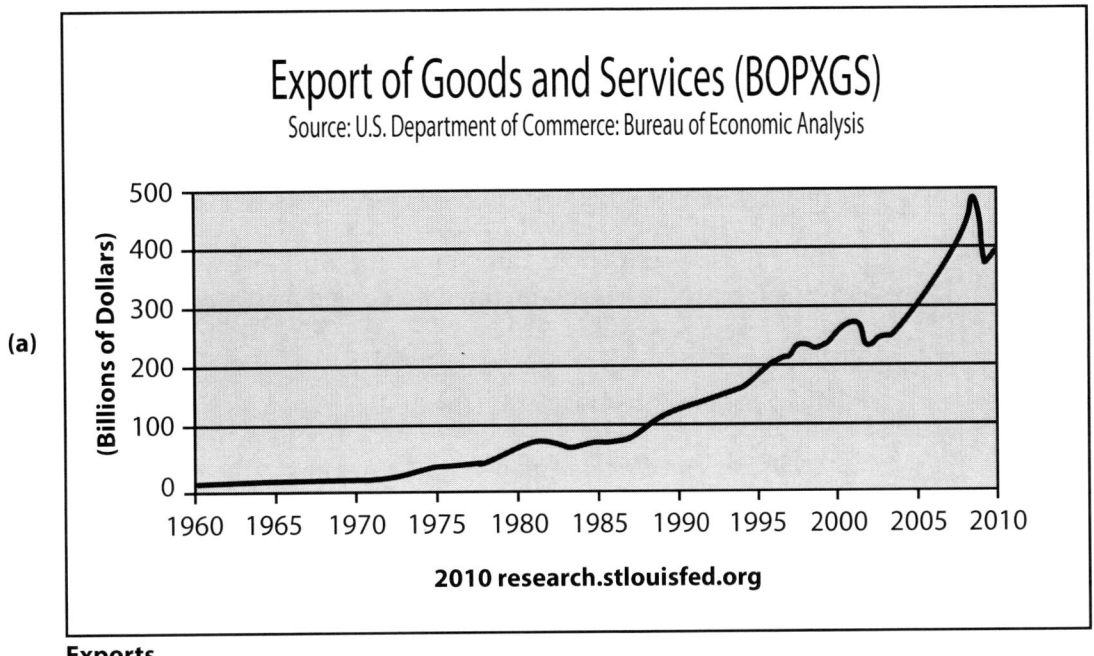

Export of Goods and Services (BOPXGS)
Source: U.S. Department of Commerce: Bureau of Economic Analysis

(a)

Exports

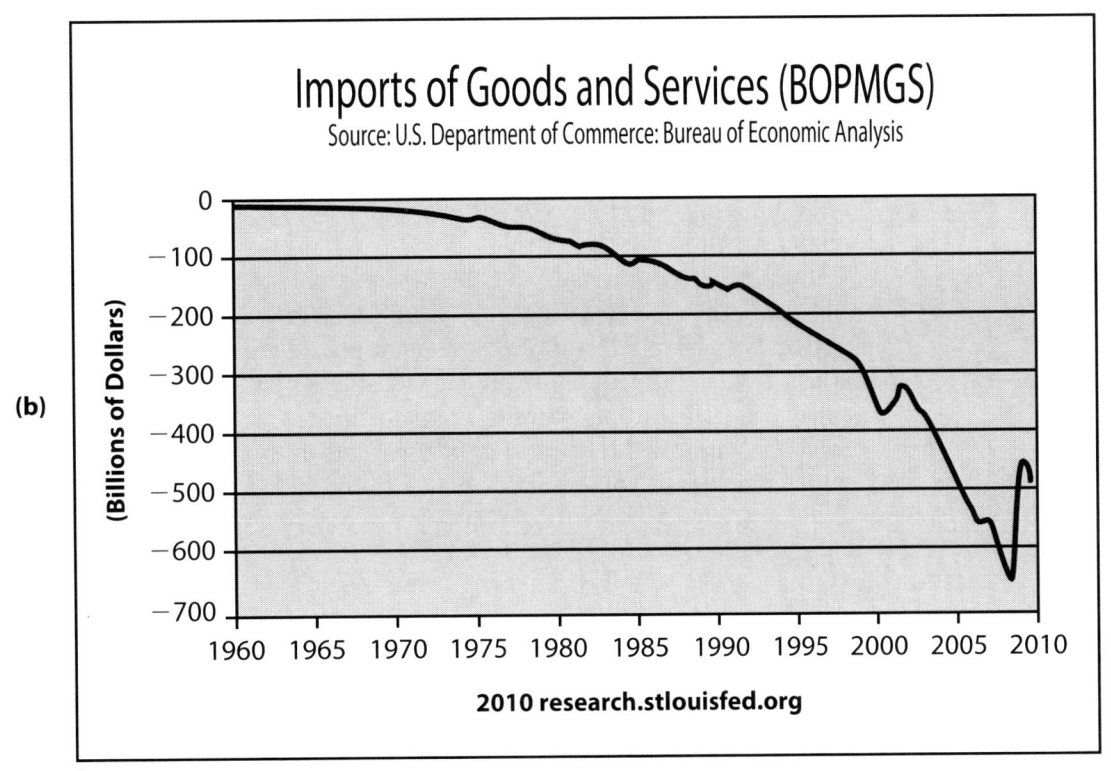

Imports of Goods and Services (BOPMGS)
Source: U.S. Department of Commerce: Bureau of Economic Analysis

(b)

Imports

Figure 24.1 • Balance of Trade
In the late 1990s, export growth flattened out while imports continued expanding, causing the trade deficit to rise.

vancements that have led to increased trade has been the reduction in costs of transportation. Continued improvements in airplane and shipping technology allow countries to move both delicate and massive products cheaper and more safely. Pipelines allow the movement of oil and natural gas from one part of a continent to another. These improvements have effectively caused the world to become smaller.

Communications Technology. You should also not discount the importance of improvements in communications technology in increasing the volume of trade in recent years. The proliferation of the Internet, email, and mobile phones has allowed greater connectivity between buyers and sellers around the world. Distance has now become no deterrent in the exchange of information and money.

General Decline in Tariffs. Through a series of international agreements following World War II (which we will discuss in detail later), the level of tariffs (taxes on imports) and trade restrictions throughout the world has decreased greatly. A decrease in tariffs decreases the cost of imported goods and increases the volume of trade.

Participants in International Trade

US, Japan, and Western Europe. Not surprisingly, the countries of the industrialized West (the United States, Canada, and Western Europe) and Japan dominate the volume of international trade. In addition, the United States, Western Europe, and Japan also provide the headquarters for many of the multinational corporations that dominate world markets. These are corporations that have significant production and distribution facilitates in foreign countries.

New Participants. While the industrialized West and Japan have been involved in international trade since the end of World War II, what caused the major changes in trade patterns recently has been the emergence of new participants in the international economy. China, in particular, has grown incredibly fast since it turned away from Communism and with that growth has come an increase in international trade. China's exports in 2005 totaled $762 billion with one-fifth of those exports going to the United States. As a result of its rapid growth, China has also become the number one destination of foreign investment in the world.

Many other countries of East Asia (Singapore, South Korea, and Taiwan), collectively known as the Asian Tigers, have become increasingly important as exporters in the past twenty years as a result of government policies to encourage production for foreign markets. The fall of Communism has led to new markets in formerly Soviet-controlled areas of Eastern Europe opening them to trade with Western Europe and the United States. The continued transition to free markets in Russia will allow this large country to become an increasingly important player in the global economy of the future.

II. SPECIALIZATION AND COMPARATIVE ADVANTAGE

Since the United States is not a closed economy, it can produce more of some goods (exports) and fewer of others (imports) than it would if it was forced to be self-sufficient in all areas of production. The question is then: Why does the United States choose to move resources away from automobiles and clothing (products it imports) and toward aircrafts and wheat (products it exports)? Are there economic benefits from these decisions?

The answer, of course, is yes. Specializing and trading allow for both parties to gain and produce beyond their production possibilities curves. Adam Smith wrote about mutual gains from trade in 1776; it does not make sense to make at home what you can buy in the market at a lower cost. The shoemaker does not bake his own bread and the baker does not try to make his own shoes; people specialize and trade. Smith asserted that what is true for individuals must be true for nations as a whole.

Assumptions and Comparative Costs

Specialization occurs because people incur different costs from the same activities; that is, they experience different opportunity costs. Someone who can perform a task at a lower opportunity cost than someone else is said to have a comparative advantage in that activity.

Someone who can produce more than someone else in the same amount of time in every activity they perform is said to have an absolute advantage in production. For example, if an economy can produce either soybeans or avocados and the United States can produce more of either than Mexico with the same amount of resources, then the US is said to have an absolute advantage over Mexico in the production of both.

This does not mean there can be no mutually beneficial gains from trade, however. Since the United States is more productive in both types of goods, it faces substantial opportunity costs when it reallocates resources from one type of production to another. Each trading partner can produce one good at a lower opportunity cost than the other partner, so they can both gain by specializing in the one good in which they have a comparative advantage and trading with each other.

Terms of Trade

The actual rate at which countries trade one good for another is called the terms of trade. It is important to note that a country will only accept terms of trade that are lower than the trade-offs it faces in domestic production. For example, if the United States has to give up one ton of soybean production to produce three tons of avocados, it will only trade one ton of soybeans if can get more than three tons of avocados in return. By finding terms of trade both countries can agree on, the trading partners can both overcome their resource constraints and produce beyond their production possibilities curves.

Gains from Specialization and Trade

If both countries are producing beyond their production possibilities curves, then both populations are enjoying more avocados and/or soybeans without giving up any of the other good. It seems like we have performed economic magic here; we have achieved greater world output with the same amount of world resources. The increased efficiency provided by comparative advantage and trade allows the trading partners to overcome their domestic production constraints and consume beyond their production possibilities curves.

III. THE FOREIGN EXCHANGE MARKET

Overview

Since sellers denominate the price of their goods in terms of their own domestic currency, buying foreign goods first requires the purchase of foreign currency. Foreign currency is bought and sold in the foreign exchange market at a rate known as the exchange rate. The exchange rate between two currencies is the equilibrium price of one currency on the foreign exchange market in terms of another.

With this knowledge we can now determine the price of any good in terms of US dollars; simply multiply the local price by the exchange rate.

$$\text{Price in Dollars} = \text{Price in Local Currency} \times \text{Exchange Rate}$$

For example, if the dollar-peso exchange rate is $.10 (ten cent US) per peso and a barrel of oil from Mexico cost 500 pesos, then it costs 50 US dollars. Any increase in the exchange rate (that is, any time it costs more to buy one peso) would cause the price of all Mexican products to rise for American consumers.

The Dollar-Peso Market

To learn about how foreign exchange markets work in general, let us focus more closely on the market for dollars and pesos. When American firms export goods to Mexico they want payment in dollars not Mexican currency so anyone who wants to buy these imports must first exchange their pesos for dollars in the foreign exchange markets.

Where do the dollars they obtain come from? There are also many consumers in the United States who wish to buy Mexican imports and need pesos to pay for them. This demand for pesos combines with the supply from Mexico to create an equilibrium price (exchange rate) for pesos in the foreign exchange market as illustrated in figure 24.2.

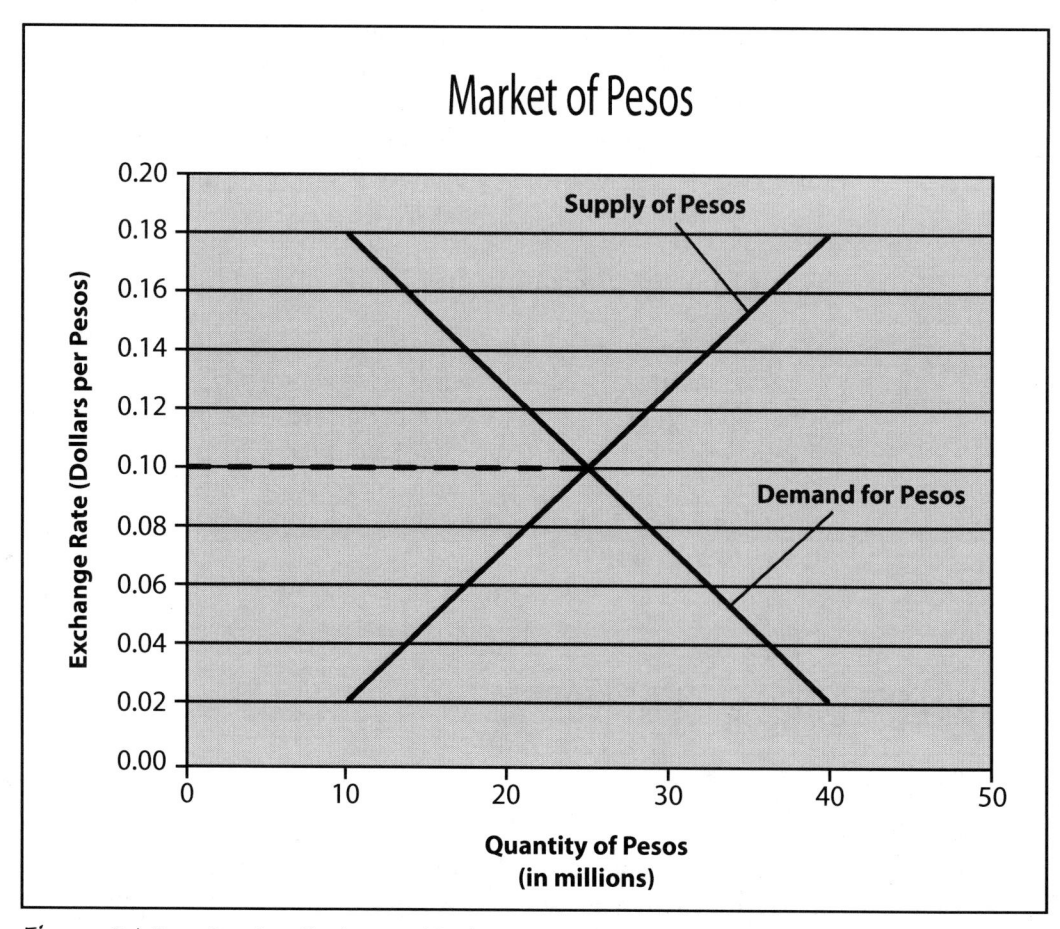

Figure 24.2 • **Foreign Exchange Market**
The market exchange rate is determined by the intersection of the supply and demand for that currency in the foreign exchange market.

Depreciation and Appreciation

In most cases, especially in the case of two industrialized trading partners, exchange rates are floating; that is, they are free to move and change as supply and demand changes. Similar to the demand and supply of goods and services, many factors can cause the demand and supply of foreign currency to shift.

An increase in the income for American consumers or a change in people's taste in favor of Mexican products, for example, will lead to increases in the demand for pesos. All other things being equal, an increase in demand results in an increase in price as seen in figure 24.3; in this case the price in question is the dollar price of a peso, the exchange rate.

Such an increase in the dollar price of any currency is referred to as a depreciation of dollar relative to that currency. When the dollar depreciates relative to another currency it takes more dollars to buy a single unit of that currency, causing all goods from the country that uses that currency to become more expensive to American consumers.

If, on the other hand, the demand for American products in Mexico increases, the supply of pesos in the foreign exchange market would have to increase. This increase in supply leads to a fall in equilibrium price as in figure 24.4; the exchange rate has fallen. Since the dollar price of the peso has fallen, we say that the dollar has appreciated relative to the peso. It now takes fewer dollars to buy any amount of pesos and therefore

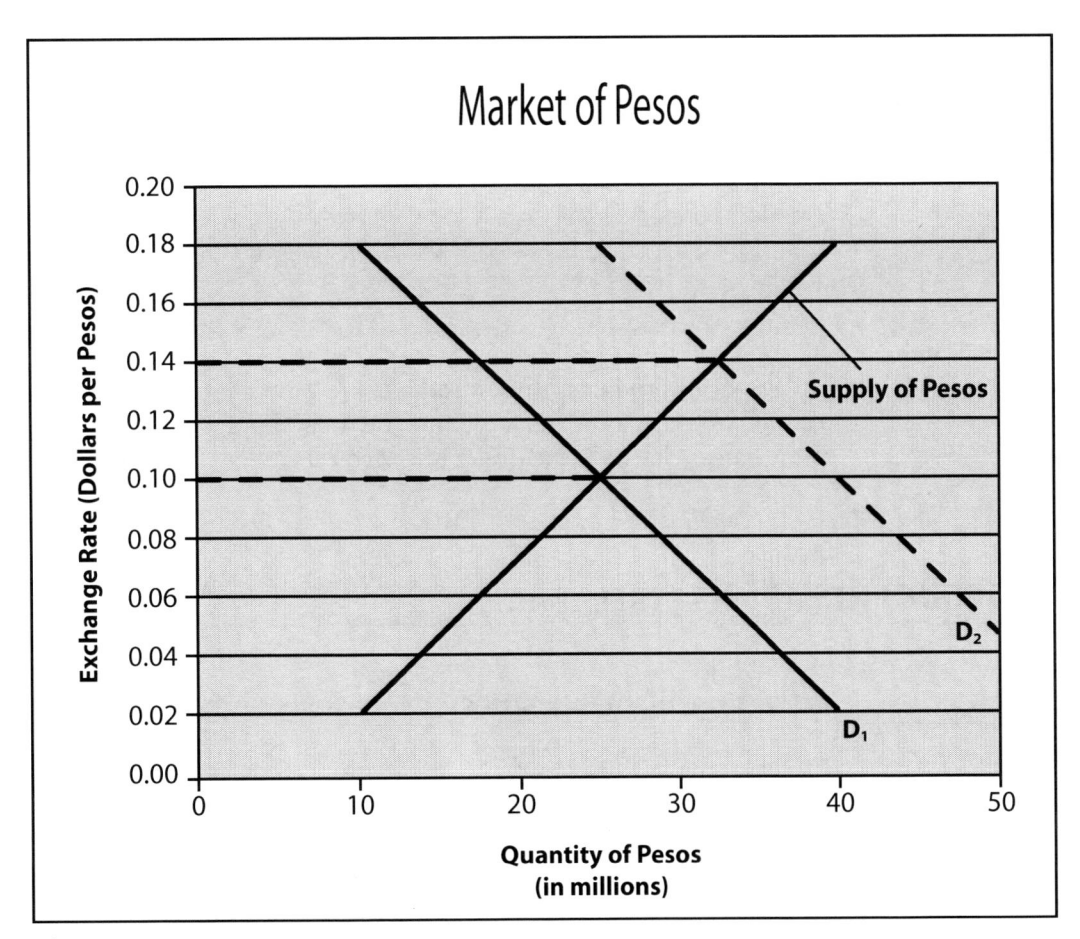

Figure 24.3 • Dollar Depreciation
As the demand for Mexican products rises, so does the demand for its currency. As a result, the dollar depreciates relative to the peso.

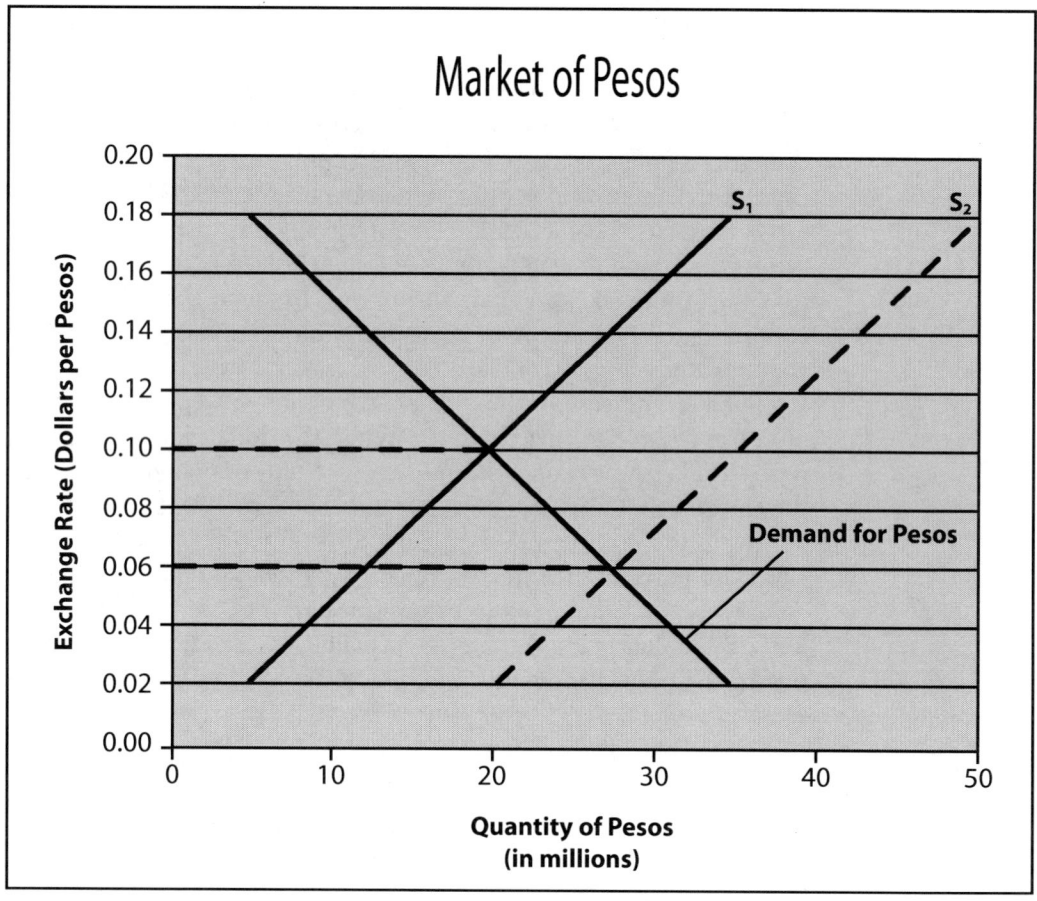

Figure 24.4 • Dollar Appreciation
If Mexican consumers want to buy more American products, they would need to buy more dollars by increasing the supply of pesos to the foreign exchange market. This increase in supply causes the dollar to appreciate relative to the peso.

any Mexican products; these products are now cheaper to American consumers. It is also important to note that any time the dollar appreciates relative to the peso, the peso depreciates relative to the dollar and vice versa.

IV. ARGUMENTS AGAINST FREE TRADE

Protecting Infant Industries

People argue against free trade for a variety of reasons, though often they ignore the benefits of trade to the economy as a whole and focus only on the costs free trade imposes on a small fraction of the population. One of the most common arguments against free trade—in fact, it has been used by most of the wealthiest nations in the world at one point or another—is the infant industries argument.

The infant industries argument centers on an industry that is important to the country, but it cannot compete on the world market yet. By allowing the industry to operate without global competition for some period, it is expected that the industry will increase in efficiency such that the market supply will shift to the right enough for the firm to be profitable at the world price. At this point the industry can thrive without trade restrictions.

Unfortunately, this argument is often abused. Governments have no way of knowing beforehand which industries will become productive enough to compete in the global market, so they often just extend protection to industries controlled by their friends and supporters. In addition, protection may continue long after the industry has been given every chance to mature, forcing consumers to pay higher prices than they would have without trade restrictions. These restrictions are basically a redistribution of money from the consumers and taxpayers to the shareholders of the firm and its resource suppliers.

Competing Against Subsidized Industries

Another reason countries often use to justify their use of trade restrictions is the fact that they are just retaliating against subsidies and trade restrictions imposed by their foreign competitors. When governments subsidize production in one of their industries (like the United States does for many types of agricultural production) they encourage overproduction and lower the world price. Other countries can then claim that their restrictions on exports from the United States are only an effort to keep prices high enough for their workers to make a living, the same argument the United States uses to defend its agricultural subsidies.

Protecting Jobs

The most common argument against free trade is that encouraging people to buy goods produced abroad is somehow stealing jobs away from United States citizens. While it is true that specializing in soybeans and allowing your trade partners to specialize in avocados would be disastrous for the people that used to be employed in the avocado industry, the question should be: Does trade create more jobs than it destroys?

Many people argue that importing shoes from Korea hurts shoe factories in Oregon. If this is the case, then shouldn't the opening of a new shoe factory in Arizona hurt them just as much? In fact, the existence of any other shoe factory "hurts" the original by creating competition and reducing profits, but that does not mean we should encourage monopolies.

Increased competition lowers prices and increases aggregate demand, which in turn increases employment and domestic output. In addition, studies have consistently shown that consumers in the United States would save money by allowing free trade and compensating the people that lose their jobs. That is, each job "saved" by trade restrictions costs more in terms of higher prices than it saves in terms of wages.

New Arguments

Recently, objections to international trade have arisen based on environmental and national defense arguments. In particular, many believe the increased use of genetically modified food may lead to unintended consequences and that reliance on oil from the Middle East and Venezuela may be funding terrorist activities. While these objections cannot be answered on economic grounds and will require serious deliberation, it is unequivocal that countries that impose broad trade restrictions and espouse isolationism are only hurting their consumers and their potential future growth.

V. GOVERNMENT AND TRADE

Trade Barriers and Subsidies

Protective Tariffs. Despite the mutual gains from trade, governments often impede free trade and they have many policies to employ if they wish to do so. One of the oldest barriers to trade is the protective tariff; an excise tax placed on imported goods. These taxes raise the price of imported goods relative to domestic goods, thereby protecting domestic producers from competition with lower-priced foreign goods.

Import Quotas. Another common way government interferes with trade is through the establishment of import quotas, limits on the total value or amount of a certain good that can be imported over a set time period. An import quota is a more direct means of restricting imports since after the cap is met, the good cannot be imported at any price.

Nontariff Barriers. In addition to tariffs and quotas, governments use nontariff barriers to restrict imports. Nontariff barriers are policies that restrict trade without directly affecting the price of an import or setting a quota. These policies often involve elaborate licensing and quality assurance requirements that impede imports.

Export Subsidies. Subsidies to domestic industries that export their products lower the cost of production and increase supply. This increased supply lowers the (world) equilibrium price and affects producers around the globe. For example, subsidies to United States agribusiness cause devastation by lowering the price received by farmers in third world countries, limiting their ability to compete in the global market.

Why Does the Government Intervene in Trade?

Misunderstanding of Gains from Trade. If all of these problems arise from governments interfering with trade, why do it at all? The first and possibly more innocuous reason for interfering with trade is a fundamental misunderstanding of how countries gain from trade.

Many policymakers still believe that the only way to "win" from trade is to have high exports and low imports. In this view, exports are "good" because they are produced at home while imports are "bad" because they deprive citizens of jobs. This type of thinking went out of favor with economists somewhere during the 1600s.

What the politicians that espouse this view are forgetting is that the reason countries trade in the first place is to increase total output. The United States could produce almost all of the things it imports at home but at a higher opportunity cost, resulting in lower productivity and lower average well-being. It is only through trade that the country can consume beyond our production possibilities curve.

Political Considerations. A misunderstanding of the gains from trade is a relatively inoffensive problem since presumably you can teach anyone to understand why favoring an exports-only strategy is wrong. Intervening in trade for political considerations, on the other hand, is more dangerous since it involves people knowingly going against the interest of society in favor of the interests of a few individuals.

When economies specialize and trade, the industries that we choose not to put resources into—the ones our trading partners are producing for us—suffer. The workers and owners in these industries have huge incentives to convince the government to protect them from imports via one or more of the methods we discussed earlier.

While the benefits of protectionism are received by a very small group of producers, the costs are hidden in small increases in prices that are spread over an entire nation of consumers. Therefore, the voice of those asking for trade restrictions is going to be much louder and more desperate than those asking for free trade. The "Buy American" marketing campaign combined with political deals in Washington where senators back trade restrictions for industries in each other's states, lead to a series of interventions that benefit the few at the expense of the many.

Costs to Society

The implementation of trade restrictions hurt consumers in the United States in many ways. First and foremost, it forces consumers to pay a price higher than the world market price for the protected goods. In addition, firms that use protected goods as inputs must pay a higher price causing them to lower supply and increasing the equilibrium price of their goods. Also, the lack of competition depresses the incentive to innovate in the protected industries. In addition, the damage of protectionism peaks during recessions, the times when countries are even more likely to "take care of home" first.

VI. TRADE AGREEMENTS AND FREE TRADE ZONES

When a country enacts trade restrictions to protect domestic industries, the affected country that now has fewer exports can retaliate with restrictions of its own, precipitating a trade war. In the wake of the stock market crash of 1929, the United States enacted high tariffs to encourage the purchase of American products. This action set off a chain reaction of trade restrictions and protectionism across the world that experts agree exacerbated the Great Depression. Since the Great Depression, and particularly after World War II, most industrialized countries have continued to work together to reduce tariffs to facilitate international trade and avoid another global economic collapse.

Reciprocal Trade Agreements Act

The first legislation aimed at bringing tariffs down in both the United States and abroad was the Reciprocal Trade Agreements Act of 1934. It focused on two specific goals to reduce tariffs. First, it authorized the president to negotiate with foreign governments on behalf the United States on agreements that would reduce tariffs by up to 50 percent. Such agreements, of course, required potential trading partners to reduce tariffs on United States exports to their countries.

Secondly, the establishment of most-favored nation clauses simplified the generalization of new reductions in tariffs to existing trading partners. For example, if the United States agreed on a new agreement that reduced a tariff on imports from one country, that reduction automatically applied to the imports from other countries that had signed most-favored nation agreements with the United States.

GATT

While the Reciprocal Trade Agreements Act only applied to deals between two countries, the General Agreement on Tariffs and Trade (GATT) was a multilateral agreement signed by twenty-three nations, including the United States, in 1947. GATT aimed to promote equal trade treatment for all member nations (similar to most-favored nation clauses), reducing tariffs through multilateral negotiation and eliminating import quotas.

GATT members held regular meetings where officials from each member country had a say in whether the groups provisions were approved or not. Throughout its existence it succeeded in reducing tariffs by 33 percent, allowing for the global marketing of services, reducing agricultural subsidies, protecting intellectual property rights, and eliminating quotas for textiles and clothing.

WTO

The final round of GATT meetings established its replacement, the World Trade Organization (WTO). Much like GATT, the WTO oversees trade agreements among member nations and attempts to settle disputes between them. Its also continues to hold meetings (called rounds) where all member nations come together to negotiate the reduction and elimination of tariffs, quotas, and agricultural subsidies.

The free trade principles espoused by the WTO provide a necessary counterpoint for the protectionist cries of special interest groups. This liberal attitude toward world trade, however, has its opponents. Many believe that the increased globalization will allow firms to circumvent laws protecting workers and the environment by shifting production to countries that have weaker protections and continuing to sell their products in the United States. Free trade proponents argue that it is not the WTO's fault that some countries have different laws and that is a problem for a political organization not a trade organization. Further, free trade will allow developing countries to raise productivity in such a way that makes better standards for workers and environmental protection possible.

The European Union

The EU Trade Bloc. Trade agreements do not only occur in one-on-one meetings or global sessions like those of the WTO. Sometimes countries choose to reduce tariffs and liberalized trade by establishing free-trade zones like the European Union (EU) and the North American Free Trade Agreement (NAFTA) region. Europe has been working on liberalizing trade among its countries since the 1950s with the development of the European Common Market. The EU has not only abolished virtually all tariffs and quotas between its member nations, but it has liberalized the movement of labor and capital within its borders. It has become a cohesive trade bloc, a group of countries with common policies on economic issues.

The EU has effectively transformed Europe from a continent composed of many independent countries to a single economic entity comparable to a United States of Europe. Increased specialization, use of economies of scale, and greater productivity has allowed the EU to grow much faster as a group then it ever could have as a group of small, competing markets.

The Euro. A significant achievement of the EU was the establishment of the Euro. Many members of the EU decided to phase out their traditional currencies in favor of a single common one, the Euro. Economists believe that the Euro will improve the standard of living in the member countries by further facilitating the free flow of goods and reducing the price of inputs and outputs.

NAFTA

NAFTA is a free trade agreement among Canada, Mexico, and the United States. The NAFTA region produces about the same output as the EU while encompassing a much larger geographic area. NAFTA has significantly reduced trade barriers between the member countries and has targeted to eliminate them completely in the near future.

Not everyone was happy when NAFTA was signed, however. Some predicted that many American firms would quickly move to Mexico to take advantage of cheaper labor and that Japanese and Korean firms would move there as well to avoid paying tariffs. On the contrary, the unemployment rate in the United States dropped drastically in the ten years following the signing of NAFTA and every statistical measure of well-being has increased in the three member nations.

VII. GLOBAL COMPETITION

Globalization has become a defining characteristic of the modern economy. Yes, the benefits of economic growth are spread farther than ever, but at what costs to the environment and to those being left out? One of the most controversial elements of globalization is competition from foreign companies. Competition may force some inefficient and unproductive firms out of business, but it will provide higher quality and lower cost goods for the entire population.

This increased prosperity will flow back into the economy, particularly into industries that are performing well in the international economy. These industries will increase production and hire some of the workers that lost their jobs due to international competition. While international competition may cause some painful adjustments in the beginning, the end result will be greater productivity and well-being for society as a whole.

CHAPTER 24 SUMMARY

- The United States is the **largest importer** and **third-largest exporter** in the world.
- The United States currently **imports more than it exports.**
- The number one trading partner of the United States is **Canada.**
- **Improvements in technology**, a **reduction in trade restrictions**, and the **emergence of new countries** in the international market have all led to a rapid increase in trade over the last thirty years.
- In a trade between two parties, each producing two goods, each party has a **comparative advantage in producing one of the goods.**
- **Specialization** and trade increase total production.
- *Price in Dollars = Price in Local Currency × Exchange Rate*

- **Depreciation** is an increase in the amount of dollars it takes to buy a certain amount of foreign currency or products.
- **Appreciation** is a decrease in the amount of dollars it takes to buy a certain amount of foreign currency or products.
- Some of the reasons governments restrict trade are to **protect infant industries**, to **retaliate** against the trade restrictions of other countries, and to **protect domestic jobs**.
- There has been a sizable international **movement toward free trade** since World War II.
- **Free trade zones** like the EU and NAFTA give a hint at the prosperity that true free trade can provide.

CHAPTER 24 Exercises

Name _____

1) The United States currently
   A) imports exactly as much as it exports.
   B) exports more than it imports.
   C) imports more than in exports.
   D) does not engage in international trade.

1) _____

2) Which of the following is **NOT** a reason for the rapid increase in trade over the past thirty years?
   A) improvements in technology.
   B) subsidies to agricultural firms in the United States.
   C) emergence of new countries in international trade.
   D) reductions in trade restrictions.

2) _____

3) If the United States has to give up 3 apples to produce 1 banana and Honduras only has to give up 2 apples to produce 1 banana, then
   A) Honduras has a comparative advantage in both goods.
   B) the United States has a comparative advantage in both goods.
   C) Honduras has a comparative advantage in banana production.
   D) the United States has a comparative advantage in banana production.

3) _____

4) If a German car cost 20,000 Euro and the dollar-Euro exchange rate is 1.25 dollars per Euro, what is the cost of the car in dollars?
   A) $25,000   C) $20,000
   B) $16,000   D) $12,500

4) _____

5) Which of the following would occur in the foreign exchange market if foreign consumers want to buy more American products?
   A) The demand for US dollars will fall
   B) The supply of foreign currency will fall.
   C) The dollar will appreciate.
   D) The dollar will depreciate.

5) _____

6) Which of the following is **NOT** an argument used to defend trade restrictions?
   A) They protect infant industries.
   B) They allow domestic producers to compete against products that other countries subsidize.
   C) They protect domestic jobs.
   D) They increase total production.

6) _____

7) All of the following are reasons the government imposes trade restrictions EXCEPT:
   A) They want to protect domestic jobs.
   B) Trade restrictions provide consumers with lower-priced, higher-quality goods.
   C) They do not understand the costs and benefits of trade.
   D) They make deals with other politicians to protect important industries in their districts.

7) _____

8) What was the original cause of the modern movement toward free trade?
   A) Trade protectionism made the Great Depression worse.
   B) The Cold War.
   C) The development of the Internet.
   D) The success of the European Union.

8) _____

9) How might free trade actually increase the number of available jobs in the long run?

10) Has NAFTA improved the economy United States? Give reasons why or why not?

Article Review 6

Name _____

Choose any one of the articles from Chapters 21–24. Use the space provided below to summarize the article. Then, answer the questions at the end of the article on the back of this page.

1.

2.

3.

Unit 6 Review

Name _____

Use this review to prepare for Exam 6. You can view the answers in the "unit review answers" section in the back of the text, but try to complete it on your own first.

1) What the two ways the government can deal with a monopoly? 1) _____
   A) Anti-trust action and taxation
   B) Taxation and regulation.
   C) Anti-trust action and regulation.
   D) Taxation and economies of scale.

2) The marginal cost curve for a natural monopoly 2) _____
   A) is always below the ATC curve.
   B) is always above the ATC curve.
   C) crosses the ATC curve at its minimum.
   D) is downward-sloping.

3) At what point would the government force the monopoly to produce if it wanted 6) _____
   to achieve allocatively efficient pricing?
   A) MR = MC
   B) P = ATC
   C) ATC = MC
   D) P = MC

4) Profit regulation allows the monopoly 4) _____
   A) to earn only a certain dollar amount of profits.
   B) to earn only a certain percentage above costs as profits.
   C) to be subsidize if it does not earn a profit.
   D) reduce costs through improved efficiency.

5) Regulation is appropriate if 5) _____
   A) regulation is costless.
   B) the regulation improves total utility.
   C) market failure exists.
   D) market failure exists and the benefit of regulation outweighs the cost.

6) The opportunity cost of leisure is the 6) _____
   A) wage rate at your current job.
   B) wage rate at the next-best alternative job.
   C) wage rate at all of the jobs you could be working at added together.
   D) time given up to enjoy leisure.

7) If consumer tastes shift away from leisure activities and toward work, there will 7) _____
   be a
   A) movement up the labor supply curve.
   B) movement down the labor supply curve.
   C) rightward shift of the labor supply curve.
   D) leftward shift of the labor supply curve.

439

8) At the current market wage rate, the firm will only hire an additional worker if 8) _____
   A) the worker is willing to accept less than the market wage rate.
   B) the worker's marginal revenue product equals or exceeds the wage rate.
   C) the firm will make a profit after hiring the worker.
   D) the worker's marginal physical product equals or exceeds the wage rate.

9) If the marginal revenue product of labor increases, which of the following shifts in the labor market should occur? 9) _____
   A) Labor supply curve shifts to the left
   B) Labor supply curve shifts to the right
   C) Labor demand curve shifts to the right
   D) Labor demand curve shifts to the left

10) What is the cost efficiency of a labor input that adds 10 units of output and costs $20? 10) _____
    A) 2
    B) .5
    C) 10
    D) 20

11) Financial intermediaries reduce the risk of investing by 11) _____
    A) increasing the cost of investing.
    B) creating asymmetric information.
    C) allocating resources to the least productive uses.
    D) spreading the risk over many investors.

12) Which of the following affects how much people want to save? 12) _____
    A) occupation
    B) risk
    C) political affiliation
    D) gender

13) The present discounted value of a future payment will decrease when the 13) _____
    A) the value of the future payment rises.
    B) the date of repayment is pushed further into the future.
    C) interest rate falls.
    D) the opportunity cost of holding money falls.

14) All of the following are reasons for buying stocks EXCEPT: 14) _____
    A) stocks confer a share of ownership in a firm.
    B) stocks provide dividends.
    C) stocks can by sold on a secondary market.
    D) stocks provide a guaranteed source of income.

15) If the market price of a bond falls 15) _____
    A) the issuer can reduce its payments to the bondholder.
    B) the bond is earning dividends.
    C) it current yield rises.
    D) its current yield falls.

16) Which of the following is a reason for the rapid increase in trade over the past thirty years? 16) _____
    A) improvements in transportation and communication technology.
    B) increases in tariffs.
    C) increases in import quotas.
    D) subsidies to agricultural firms in the United States.

Name _____

17) If the United States has to give up 1 computer to produce 10 cell phones and Korea has to give up 2 computers to produce 10 cell phones, then
   A) Korea has a comparative advantage in both goods.
   B) the United States has a comparative advantage in both goods.
   C) Korea has a comparative advantage in cell phone production.
   D) the United States has a comparative advantage in cell phone production.

17) _____

18) If a Sony television cost 50,000 yen and the dollar-yen exchange rate is .01 dollars per yen, what is the cost of the TV in dollars?
   A) $500
   B) $5,000,000
   C) $50,000
   D) $5,000

18) _____

19) Which of the following would occur in the foreign exchange market if American consumers want to buy more foreign products?
   A) The demand of foreign currency will fall.
   B) The supply of US dollars will fall.
   C) The dollar will depreciate.
   D) The dollar will appreciate.

19) _____

20) Which of the following is **NOT** an argument used to defend trade restrictions?
   A) They protect infant industries.
   B) They allow domestic producers to compete against products that other countries subsidize.
   C) They increase total production.
   D) They protect domestic jobs.

20) _____

21) Describe where the government should set a monopolist's price to insure productive efficiency. What is the problem with setting the price at this level?

_____
_____
_____
_____
_____

22) What has caused the market labor supply curve in the United States to shift back over the years?

_____
_____
_____
_____
_____

23) Why does a minimum wage above the equilibrium wage create unemployment?

_____
_____
_____
_____
_____

24) Calculate the expected value of $1,000 payment to be received five years from today with a 10% chance of default if the interest rate is 4 percent.

25) Why do governments impose trade restrictions despite the evidence that they reduce total output?

Exam 6 Formula Sheet

Name _____

Chapter 21

$Profits = Total\ Revenue - Total\ Costs$

$Profit = (Price - ATC) \times Output$

Chapter 22

$Elasticity\ of\ Labor\ Supply = \dfrac{Percent\ Change\ in\ Quantity\ of\ Labor\ Supplied}{Percent\ Change\ in\ Wage\ Rate}$

$Marginal\ Revenue\ Product = Marginal\ Physical\ Product \times Price$

$Cost\ Efficiency = \dfrac{Marginal\ Physical\ Product}{Price\ of\ Input}$

Chapter 23

$Present\ Discounted\ Value = \dfrac{Future\ Payment}{(1 + r)^n}$

Where r = real interest rate, n = number of years you must wait for future payment

$Expected\ Value = (1 - P) \times \dfrac{Future\ Payment}{(1 + r)^n}$

Where P = probability of default

$P/E\ Ratio = \dfrac{Price\ of\ Stock}{Annual\ Earnings\ per\ Share}$

$Current\ Yield = \dfrac{Annual\ Interest}{Price\ of\ Bond}$

Chapter 24

$Price\ in\ Dollars = Price\ in\ Local\ Currency \times Exchange\ Rate$

Unit Review Answers

UNIT 1

1) D
2) B
3) A
4) B
5) B
6) C
7) D
8) C
9) A
10) A
11) A
12) D
13) D
14) C
15) C
16) B
17) D
18) B
19) B
20) D
21) A country maximizing efficiency wants to produce the greatest amount of output possible given society's limited resources. They also want to produce the combination of goods and services that society desires the most. In essence, they want the economic pie to be as large as possible. Pursuing equity means trying to make the slices of the economic pie as equal as possible.
22) Without property rights, people would have to spend resources protecting their property instead of producing. As a result, economic activity would slow down.
23) There would be a surplus of 105,000 units.
24) Equilibrium quantity falls, but equilibrium price depends on the relative size of the shifts. If the demand curve shifts more, then price falls; and if the supply curve shifts more, price rises. If both curves shift the exact same amount, equilibrium price is unchanged.
25) When the marginal benefit of increased government involvement benefit exceeds the value of the private sector production sacrificed to increase government involvement.

UNIT 2

1) D
2) D

446 ECONOMICS TODAY

3) B
4) A
5) D
6) B
7) A
8) D
9) D
10) D
11) D
12) B
13) B
14) C
15) A
16) C
17) A
18) D
19) B
20) D
21) Real GDP is a better measure of standard of living across time because it only measures changes in output. Nominal GDP can increase simply because prices rise, even though higher prices to do not result in a higher standard of living.
22) First of all, trying to drive unemployment below the natural rate of unemployment can cause inflation as firms bid over increasingly scarce workers. In addition, getting unemployment to zero means eliminating frictional and structural unemployment, which would not be possible unless you never allow people to change jobs or businesses to improve production methods or develop new products.
23) The only way to drive inflation down to zero would be down reduce prices through contractionary policy. However, taking money out of people's hands would reduce business activity and create unemployment. Since the government isn't willing to take that risk, they pursue a policy of mild (3 percent) inflation.
24) Promoting education, allowing free trade, reduced regulation of business, encouraging saving
25) Classical: Long-run, individual decisions, economy is self-stabilizing
    Keynesian: Short-run, aggregates, economy is inherently unstable

UNIT 3

1) B
2) B
3) C
4) A
5) D
6) C
7) A
8) D
9) D
10) C
11) A
12) D
13) B
14) B

15) A
16) B
17) C
18) D
19) C
20) B
21) MPC = (1800 − 250)/2000 = .775
MPS = 1 − MPC = .225
22) Businesses will only invest if the expected rate of return is greater than the real interest rate. The lower the real interest, the easier it is to find an investment that satisfies this condition. As a result, businesses will spend more money on investment when the interest rate falls.
23) The opportunity cost of deficit spending is the private sector production that is given up when the government increases its spending. Since the private sector production is lost today, the opportunity cost of deficit spending is paid today.
24) Increase in MS = $30 billion X (1/.1) = $300 billion
25) While Keynesians believe that an increase in the money supply will decrease interest rates, monetarists realize that an increase in expected inflation caused by monetary stimulus will actually raise interest rates. Without a fall in consumer interest rates, monetary stimulus cannot work.

UNIT 4

1) D
2) B
3) B
4) A
5) D
6) D
7) B
8) A
9) C
10) B
11) A
12) A
13) D
14) B
15) A
16) D
17) B
18) D
19) C
20) D
21) Equilibrium price falls, but equilibrium quantity depends on the relative size of the shifts. If the demand curve shifts more, then quantity falls; and if the supply curve shifts more, quantity rises. If both curves shift by the exact same amount equilibrium quantity is unchanged.
22) Two goods with positive cross-price elasticity are substitutes; a rise in the price of one will cause an increase in the demand for the other. Two goods with negative cross-price elasticity are complements; a rise in the price of one will cause a decrease in the demand for the other.
23) A consumer will continue purchasing a good as long as the good provides the consumer with more marginal utility per dollar than any other good.

24) ATC is falling whenever the marginal cost curve is below it and rising whenever the marginal cost curve is above it. It reaches its minimum where it crosses the marginal cost curve.
25) Never produce a unit of output that brings in less revenue than it cost to produce. P = MC.

UNIT 5

1) B
2) C
3) C
4) C
5) A
6) A
7) C
8) B
9) C
10) C
11) C
12) B
13) A
14) B
15) B
16) B
17) B
18) C
19) A
20) C
21) Allocative efficiency means that the market is producing the correct mix of output. Producing the correct mix of output requires that the value of the good to society (price) equals what it cost to produce the good (its marginal cost). Since P = MC at any equilibrium in a competitive market, allocative efficiency will be achieved.
22) The market demand curve limits the monopoly's power. It must charge the price at which consumers will demand precisely its profit-maximizing output. The more elastic (flatter) the demand curve is, the less power the monopoly has to extract additional profits out of the market.
23) Patents: Gives the firm an exclusive legal right to a produce a product.
Control of inputs: Prevents other firms from getting the components necessary to produce a good.
Distribution control: Keeping other firms from selling their goods at prime retailers.
Mergers and acquisitions: Consolidates power and buys out smaller firms.
Nonprice competition: Creates a brand consumers trust.
Economies of scale: Large firms can produce more cheaply than smaller firms.
24) Price wars just erode profits, moving the industry closer to the competitive outcome. Oligopolies can keep prices up by only engaging in nonprice competition.
25) Monopolistic competition provides greater product variety while perfect competition provides a single, identical product.

UNIT 6

1) C
2) A
3) D
4) B
5) D
6) A
7) C
8) B
9) C
10) B
11) D
12) B
13) B
14) D
15) C
16) A
17) D
18) B
21) C
22) C

21) To insure productive efficiency the government needs the monopoly to produce where ATC is at its minimum. Since ATC falls as output increases for a natural monopoly that means producing at capacity—the maximum amount the firm can possibly produce. This output level is so high, though, that the firm would be earning a loss, forcing the government to subsidize the monopoly in order to keep it from exiting the industry.

22) Over time, workers in the United States have developed a greater taste for leisure, leisure has become more diversified, and average wages have risen above the minimum required for survival. All these reasons have led to the labor supply curve for US workers shifting to the left.

23) A minimum wage sets the minimum price that firms must pay for labor. Since a competitive firm will never hire a worker whose marginal revenue product does not meet or exceed the wage rate, moving the wage rate without any change in labor demand will lead the firm to reduce its quantity of labor demanded. In other words, the intersection of labor demand and labor supply for each firm has moved up and to the left on the graph, leading to fewer workers being hired.

24) $EV = .9 \times [\$1,000/(1.04)^5] = \$739.73$

25) Governments impose trade restrictions for a variety of reasons. First, there is a general misunderstanding about how to "win" from trade. Many politicians believe winning at trade means having high exports and low imports. In addition, politics play a large role. While they are smaller in number, the people that would be helped by trade restrictions have a great deal more at stake than those that would be hurt by trade restrictions. As a result, they work much harder to get the government to act in their favor. Finally, trade restrictions may result from backroom deals where senators agree to back policies that protect industries in a particular state at the expense of the national economy.

Southwest Tennessee Community Col
Gill Center Library
3833 Mountain Terrace
Memphis, TN 38127